BUSINESS, GOVERNMENT, SOCIETY

The Global Political Economy

Arthur A. Goldsmith
University of Massachusetts at Boston

IRWIN

Chicago • Bogotá • Buenos Aires • Caracas
London • Madrid • Mexico City • Sydney • Toronto

Cover illustration: William Conger: "Lakeview Suite #47," Oil on wood, 12" x 12", 1990. Courtesy of Roy Boyd Gallery, Chicago.

© Richard D. Irwin, a Times Mirror Higher Education Group, Inc. company, 1996

Irwin Book Team

Sponsoring editor:	*John E. Biernat*
Editorial assistant:	*Kim Kanakes*
Marketing manager:	*Michael Campbell*
Project editor:	*Paula M. Buschman*
Production supervisor:	*Dina L. Treadaway*
Assistant manager, desktop services:	*Jon Christopher*
Designer:	*Matthew Baldwin*
Cover designer:	*Ellen Pettengell*
Compositor:	*ElectraGraphics, Inc.*
Typeface:	*10/12 Times Roman*
Printer:	*R. R. Donnelley & Sons Company*

Times Mirror
Higher Education Group

Library of Congress Cataloging-in-Pubilication Data

Goldsmith, Arthur A. (Arthur Austin), 1949–
    Business, government, society : the global political economy /
    Arthur A. Goldsmith.
        p.   cm.
    Includes index.
    ISBN 0-256-12833-2
    1. Business.   2. Economic policy.   3. International economic
    relations.   4. Business—United States.   I. Title.
    HF1008.G64   1996
    337—dc20   95–13447

Printed in the United States of America
1 2 3 4 5 6 7 8 9 0 DO 2 1 0 9 8 7 6 5

This book is dedicated to my parents, Carol and Art Goldsmith.

The world has become a new place in the last decade. Familiar political and economic arrangements have changed forever, yet what will replace them is not clear. Tomorrow's managers—today's management students—are going to be called on to be more creative than earlier generations of managers had to be in understanding and mastering the global, outside forces that confront business and other formal organizations.

Facing unprecedented external change, most firms now recognize that coping with their environment calls for more than outmaneuvering rival companies while keeping customers and shareholders happy. In the 1990s, firms also have to deal with worldwide social, political, legal, ethical, cultural, and technological forces whose combined impact is far stronger than before. The typical large company now has a public affairs unit, explicitly charged with monitoring and trying to influence these nonmarket forces. Since many environmental forces are generated beyond U.S. borders, the job of the public affairs unit is even more complex than it appears. General managers and nonspecialists also have been forced to spend an increasing amount of their time on business environment problems.

The Environment of Business

Because of these pressures, today's employers demand personnel who are equipped to understand the socioeconomic context for business. Management schools have responded with courses on business and environment, variously entitled Business and Society; Business, Government, and Society; the Legal Environment of Business; Business, Government, and the International Economy; or sometimes, with a somewhat different emphasis, Social Issues in Management or Business Ethics. This book is designed for such a course. Political science, public administration, or economics courses on public policy and economic strategy also can use the book.

The aim is to furnish students with the tools for fathoming the business environment. I go beyond the day's headlines, with its sensational tales of business scandal, ludicrous government regulation, and economic crisis, to try to grasp the forces that drive the business environment. My attention is on two fundamental concerns of managers: to what social trends and public policies must firms conform today and in the likely future? How do firms try to manage these trends and policies for greatest advantage?

Business, Government, Society: The Global

Political Economy shows how lobbying, legal action, subsidies, and many other government economic activities work in the United States and, to a lesser degree, other political systems. It is not a handbook with directions about how to set up a political action committee, bring a lawsuit, or apply for a government subsidy. More fittingly, it aims to inform readers about the reasons firms turn to government as part of the struggle for competitive advantage and how that interplay can affect a company's welfare and the welfare of society. After reading the book, students will have rich knowledge of today's major public policies toward business, how those policies limit and enhance management freedom, and how managers try to change, defend, or adapt to the rules that surround them.

This Book's Approach

Business and environment is an evolving, unformed field that borrows from many disciplines. Sometimes it is taught by licensed attorneys, other times by people trained in political science, economics, or philosophy. The result is four or five different approaches to the subject, oriented toward law, politics, economics, moral philosophy, or strategic planning. Thus, there is no generally accepted paradigm for studying the outside influences on business, no standard set of recipes for dealing with these forces.

This book approaches the business environment by way of public policy—government laws, rules, edicts, and statutes to attain common goals. I stress public policy because it is the medium through which society—or, more accurately, the groups and factions that compose society—attempts to alter the conditions for business. Public policy also is a vehicle business uses to defend and promote its interests. As the bridge between business and society, public policy is an excellent entry point for exploring the broad context of management decisions.

Many fine textbooks are available for business and environment courses, but most are apt to treat the business environment as a residual category—everything that is left over after ordinary business considerations have been made. They usually miss the extent to which private enterprise and markets have public characteristics, and they tend to have a limited view of the international aspects of the business environment. These books also often lack a systematic theoretical framework. Topics are liable to be presented in a descriptive way that makes it difficult to generalize about them. Having taught from such books myself, I always thought they could be strengthened by using economic and political theory to weave together the disparate elements that make up the business environment.

Business, Government, Society: The Global Political Economy is my effort to produce the theoretically coherent, comparative text that I wish had been on the market years ago. As someone with an interdisciplinary background in management, comparative politics, public policy, and economic development, I bring a fresh point of view to business environment studies. The text is written with the latest American Assembly of Collegiate Schools of Business Accreditation guidelines (1991) specifically in view. According to those guidelines, students need to be exposed to ethical and global issues; the influence of political, social, regulatory, environmental, and technological issues; and the impact of demographic diversity on organizations. I explore these AACSB-mandated topics. Specifically:

• The book stresses national competitiveness. I show how government action and inaction affects the capability of domestic firms to win in global markets, often without intending to do so.
• It is explicitly comparative. The book contrasts the U.S. business environment with that of other countries, especially advanced nations like Germany and Japan, and newly industrialized countries like Taiwan and South Korea. It also makes comparisons over time, to put modern events into a proper historical context. How the

past shapes the present is stressed. The goal of these comparisons is to understand the strengths and weaknesses of the current U.S. policy-making system, and to learn how it helps and handicaps American firms vis-à-vis foreign companies working within different systems.

• The book pays attention to the whole public policy process: political inputs (voting, lobbying), policy making (how legislatures and public bureaucracies work), and policy outputs (government programs and projects that affect business). I analyze how business uses the policy process as an element of corporate strategy. The aim is to see how the U.S. system works, and how it might work better.

• The book puts the business environment and public policy on an equal footing with other, more conventional management concerns. I highlight how pervasive is public policy in the new global economy, and I show the surprising ways government action touches almost every decision, both routine and strategic, taken by managers. When looked at closely, firms and states turn out to be integrated and mutually dependent, not largely autonomous, as some people think.

• The book features social accountability as an important concern of managers. Firms are being held to account by a wider range of groups and interests than in the past. Managers cannot focus on maximizing profits without regard to the likely reaction of the media, public interest organizations, regulatory agencies, the courts, and other constituencies. Moral considerations, especially claims for rights, often decide how these groups do react to a company's activities. A subtext in the book is the way ethics are used—and sometimes misused—in public policy debates.

• The book uses political economy (the idea that politics and economics are linked) as a lens through which to observe the business environment. Political economy is fruitful because it employs the same assumptions about human behavior to account for both political and economic conduct—namely that in a given situation people usually try to do what they think is best for themselves. I rely heavily on ideas from leading thinkers in this tradition, including giants of the past like Smith, Marx, and Weber. The result is a clean and systematic cut at the material. Few business and environment textbooks use the political economy model, despite its analytical power and its growing acceptance in schools of management.[1]

Political scientists and economists will find my approach particularly congenial. So will instructors with knowledge of or interest in international business affairs. The book is intended, however, for general use and does not presume any specialized training. It is pitched toward college juniors and seniors. It also can be used as the main reading for an MBA course on business, society, and the international economy or on business and government relations.

Organization

There are 18 chapters. They cover much the same ground established in other texts, though often from a novel perspective. The first chapter sets the book's subject matter in the context of other management studies. The next three chapters lay down the theoretical framework for the book. The subsequent section concentrates on the basics of the business–government relationship in practice. There follows a group of three chapters on the public policy process. The next two parts of the book look at the social policy and the economic policy outputs of government decision making. I conclude with observations on the status of the United States in the global economy.

Cutting across each chapter are international comparisons. The goal is to give students a better chance than they have with other texts to see American practices from a worldwide standpoint. We will try to step back from the popular debate

---

[1] See Barry R. Weingast, ed., *Political Economy and the Business School Curriculum* (St. Louis: John M. Olin School of Business, Washington University, 1987).

over the globalization of business, a debate that is apt to polarize into alarmist and complacent points of view, to find the middle ground. By the end of the course, students should have a realistic understanding of current economic and technological trends, and how public policy can (and cannot) help the nation's ability to compete in the international economy.

Linking the chapters is the political economy framework and its twin themes of market failure (collectively suboptimal results of "rational" individual choices) and government failure (unintended, damaging consequences of public policy making and implementation). The logic of political economy is that markets do some things well and other things poorly. The same is true of government: it is good at some things, bad at others. We will not join the sterile debate over which is inherently superior, the "free" market and individual choice, or socialism and government intervention in business affairs. Rather, this book tries to identify in a nonideological way the most productive mixes of specific public and private activity obtained in different political and economic systems. Markets and states are viewed as complementary, not as alternative policy instruments. My quest is to identify ways the public sector can enable the private sector to operate more productively.

Following the chapters is a collection of management cases. The purpose of these cases is to give students the opportunity to apply material from the text to management problems.

The book is written as simply as possible, though technical terms cannot be avoided. They are needed as a shorthand way to discuss complex ideas. The level of argument is as demanding as the editorial pages of, say, *The Wall Street Journal* or *The Economist.* In fact, one secondary goal of this book is to equip students to read the business press with greater insight and skepticism. To help students master the more challenging vocabulary, key terms are highlighted in bold letters. All the key terms are defined in the text and again in the glossary at the end of the book.

The material is rich and subtle. Students ought not to get bogged down in the detailed data and examples presented. They are there to illustrate points, not to be memorized. As with any textbook, observant readers should look for the main themes and trends.

After students have finished reading (and rereading) this text, they should have a good grasp of political and economic theory. More important, they should see how these systems of ideas can illuminate the business environment problems that managers come across every day. Students also should get a basic understanding of important domestic and international public institutions, how these institutions work, and how their policies affect private companies.

Arthur A. Goldsmith

A C K N O W L E D G M E N T S

Many people have helped me in this project in one way or another. I would like to thank my colleagues at the *University of Massachusetts* at Boston, Lawrence Franco, Jane Ives, Erwin Jaffe, and Vivien Schmidt, for their suggestions. Others who were generous in reading drafts of particular chapters were Gardner Clark of *Cornell University,* Aline Kuntz of the *University of New Hampshire,* and Mark Silverstein of *Boston University.* As part of the review process the following persons provided input: Candace Hetzner, *Rutgers University;* Kenneth E. Hoffman, *Emporia State University;* Harvey Nesbaum, *Wayne State University;* Kathleen Rehbein, *Marquette University;* Douglas N. Ross, *Towson State University;* and Robert W. Weight, *University of Phoenix.*

My students have been using portions of early drafts of this book for several semesters. Their reactions and critical comments have helped me to fine-tune the presentation, clarifying obscure points and eliminating some peripheral material. I would like to thank them collectively for their input; it has helped me to craft a more accessible manuscript. My graduate assistant, Xiaolin Chen, helped with the yeoman's task of checking references and updating tabular data. She made that tedious task surprisingly easy.

Elizabeth Goldsmith was always an inspiration. Her analysis of the early chapters made me rethink my approach. I am particularly grateful for her understanding and encouragement while I wrestled with this material over the past several years.

I trust readers will find my cut at this material illuminating. I have tried to write a book that is evenhanded yet that challenges conventional thinking. Many topics covered are ambiguous and impossible to resolve in a way that satisfies everyone, in which case competing views are presented. Some business and economics students may be uncomfortable with the lack of right answers to some problems posed. They will have to stretch themselves to choose sides and to connect the results to the everyday job of working in organizations. I believe the effort is worth the results.

Without doubt, and despite my best efforts and the input from my colleagues, errors of fact and interpretation remain. I would greatly appreciate further comments and observations from readers so I can improve later editions of this book. Feel free to contact me at the Management Department, University of Massachusetts at Boston.

T A B L E   O F   C O N T E N T S

12   Public Policy and Workers' Rights   253

13   Public Policy and Safety   285

14   Public Policy, Pollution, and Resource Conservation   308

AFL-CIO	American Federation of Labor-Congress of Industrial Organizations
ARPA	Advanced Research Projects Agency
ATP	Advanced Technology Program
CERES	Coalition for Environmentally Responsible Economies
CPSC	Consumer Product Safety Commission
EEOC	Equal Employment Opportunity Commission
EPA	Environmental Protection Agency
ERISA	Employee Retirement Income Security Act
E.U.	European Union (formerly the E.C. or European Community)
Ex-Im Bank	Export-Import Bank
FAA	Federal Aviation Administration
FCPA	Foreign Corrupt Practices Act
FDA	Food and Drug Administration
FSIS	Food Safety and Inspection Service
FTC	Federal Trade Commission
G-7	Group of Seven (the seven largest industrial countries)
GATT	General Agreement on Tariffs and Trade
HDTV	High-definition television
HUD	Department of Housing and Urban Development
IMF	International Monetary Fund
IRCA	Immigration Reform and Control Act
ITA	International Trade Agency (U.S. Department of Commerce)
ITC	International Trade Commission
IWC	International Whaling Commission

MCC	Microelectronics and Computer Technology Corporation
MITI	Ministry of International Trade and Industry (Japan)
NAFTA	North American Free Trade Agreement
NAM	National Association of Manufacturers
NASA	National Aeronautics and Space Administration
NHTSA	National Highway Traffic Safety Administration
NIH	National Institutes of Health
NIST	National Institute of Standards and Technology
NLRA	National Labor Relations Act
NLRB	National Labor Relations Board
NRC	Nuclear Regulatory Commission
NSF	National Science Foundation
NTSB	National Transportation Safety Board
NUMMI	New United Motor Manufacturing, Inc.
OECD	Organization for Economic Cooperation and Development
OFCCP	Office of Federal Contract Compliance Programs
OMB	Office of Management and Budget
OPEC	Organization of Petroleum Exporting Countries
OSHA	Occupational Safety and Health Administration
S&L	Savings and loan institution
SEC	Securities and Exchange Commission
Sematech	Semiconductor Manufacturing Technology Institute
USCAR	United States Consortium for Automotive Research
USDA	United States Department of Agriculture
USTR	United States Trade Representative
WARN	Worker Adjustment and Retraining Notification Act
WTO	World Trade Organization

I BUSINESS AND ITS ENVIRONMENT

1 POLITICAL ECONOMY, PUBLIC POLICY, AND THE MARKET

Total government laissez-faire *is of course a contradiction in terms. No modern government can* not *influence economic life, because the mere existence of government must do so . . .*
E. J. Hobsbawm[1]

The field of management has traditionally looked inward, at how to administer efficiently operations, budgets, human resources, and other variables inside the firm. In recent decades, the field has put more emphasis on looking outward, to the **business environment,** to the external conditions and influences that affect a firm's performance. Environmental factors are harder to oversee than internal ones because they are not as directly subject to managers' control. Yet, they are critical for business and other kinds of organizations to thrive and endure.

The American business environment is no longer what it was. Managers used to face a fairly stable set of circumstances, under what Labor Secretary Robert Reich (formerly of Harvard University's Kennedy School) calls the "national bargain." According to Reich, society in the recent past expected little more from business than steady employment and a flow of new products and services. Government treated business managers with a light hand, allowing them significant freedom of movement. Companies coordinated their activities with each other to assure profitability and growth. There was little competition from overseas to threaten industry's well-being or impinge on managers' decisions. When called upon to do more for society, such as meeting new legal and regulatory requirements, their preeminent position allowed big companies to pass on the cost through price increases.[2]

The national bargain collapsed sometime in the 1970s. The environment of U.S. companies grew much less secure. Although the American economy is largely self-contained, global rivalry put established companies under intense pressure. They found it far harder than before to guarantee good jobs, strong

3

profits, and competitive products.[3] At the same time, society continued to expect more and more from the corporate sector—expectations often enforced through new laws and regulations.

Similar upheavals are shaking other industrial nations. Under the threat of global competition, business everywhere has been forced to become more efficient, to get more from its resources. The result is often fewer workers, including managers, and diluted pay and benefits for those who stay. Companies may become more profitable in the end, but they will not easily play the same social role demanded of them in the recent past.

Public Policy and the Business Environment

To explore the business environment, this book centers on **public policy** toward business. Public policy in the business arena is an action (or inaction) by government to encourage companies to do something. As defined here, public policy includes explicit steps by governments to reward or penalize the conduct of business organizations (and not-for-profit organizations, too). It also includes things governments do not do, for refraining from action can have as profound an effect on business as action does. In either case, public policy is a government effort to change private decisions.

Public policy is critical for managers to understand because it is the filter between companies and their environment. That environment is often conceived as two distinct spheres: one market-based, the other made of nonmarket considerations. The former sphere, the more familiar one to business students, embraces competitors and consumers and is about buying, making, and selling products. The other sphere is social and political, and involves demand for things such as cleaner production methods, safer products, or more social equality.

These two categories were always fuzzy, for all "market" acts are conditioned by laws, culture, tradition, and the like, and all "nonmarket" decisions affect company earnings. In the real world, most things blend and overlap. Increasingly, economics and politics are merging, making it harder than ever to separate the economic and the sociopolitical contexts of business.

Rather than splitting the business environment into two realms in the conventional manner, this book will develop a holistic image—one where society tries mainly through public policy to influence business and, vice versa, where business uses public policy to improve its environment. As depicted visually in Figure 1–1, companies must work through, and adapt to, government to reach their ends. Public policy is the buffer between business and society.

Figure 1–1 highlights three important external forces affecting business. One is **globalization,** or the increased integration of world markets and the rise of global competition. Public policy affects **national competitiveness**—a nation's ability to make goods that meet the test of the international marketplace. National competitiveness is an issue that has been abused by politicians and writ-

FIGURE 1–1

Business and its environment

ers looking for scapegoats for domestic economic ills. Most of the country's difficulties begin at home.[4] Yet, while *national* competitiveness has been embellished as an issue, an individual company's ability to vie for markets, domestic and foreign, is a point of concern for managers.

A major theme of this book is that public policy abounds with national and international ramifications for companies. We will see how almost everything the U.S. government does has some effect, whether for good or ill, on how well given American firms weather foreign competition—and, more generally, on how profitable they are.

The second external force featured in Figure 1–1 is technological change. Rapid improvements in production methods and products are wiping out older industries, while creating new ones. Again, companies try to use public policy to master these changes, or at least to cope with them.

The third external force is social and political change. Society is quickly evolving. People have new tastes, different skills and attitudes, shifting perceptions of their problems. These social changes prompt new demands on government, which in turn may lead to public policy that can bind business decision making. Simultaneously, businesspeople try to use public policy to alter society in ways favorable to business or, barring that, to protect themselves from unwanted social and political demands.

Of course, these three forces—globalization, technological change, and sociopolitical change—are part of a whole. They are connected, and they interact with each other. World economic integration is driven by new technology, and new technology is a key to success in international competition. Globalization and technological innovation, in turn, are shaping society and politics, just as social attitudes and political action affect the pace of change in world markets and the rate of adoption of new technology. It is not easy to separate these forces in practice.

Business–Government Relations Are Critical

The importance of business–government relations is revealed in recent research by Michael Porter of Harvard Business School. He tried to identify what factors allow a nation to have international success in a particular industry. Porter found the answer in four attributes that shape the environment of local firms:

> *Factor conditions*—the country's labor, natural resources, technology, and infrastructure (**factors of production** in the language of economics) needed to compete in a given industry.
>
> *Demand conditions*—domestic demand for the industry's output.
>
> *Related and supporting industries*—the presence or absence of local suppliers, and of related industries with which the industry can share activities such as research and development.
>
> *Firm strategy, structure, and rivalry*—the country's rules for creating, organizing, and managing companies, and for governing domestic market competition.

Government obviously influences, and can be influenced by, each of these four determinants of national competitiveness. Public policies toward education, capital markets, the environment, and the like affect factor conditions. Public policies toward product standards and regulation affect demand conditions. Related and supporting industries are moved in countless ways by government activity, as are firm strategy, structure, and rivalry. Government is not the sole factor that determines national competitive advantage, but it can significantly raise or lower the odds of a country's businesses succeeding in the global market.[5] Managers need to know how public policy can help or hurt their companies, both at home and abroad.

Porter is not making a simplistic call for *more* public policies to improve national business conditions. His point is to find the *right* policies, to get government to do things that add value and to stop doing things that take away value. Additional public activity may be called for in some areas, and less in other areas.

Though distinctive national styles of policy making remain, many policy outcomes are converging among the United States and its main competitors.[6] Worries over competitiveness are pushing U.S. policy makers to look overseas for guidance—and are leading foreign policy makers to look similarly to the United States. These facts do not mean there are public policy panaceas for the travails of modern business. There are not. The lack of easy solutions has not stopped political and business leaders from looking for them. Readers will become skeptical about predictions for simple policy reform.

The force of government action cannot be stressed too much. In Boston University professor Robert A. Leone's words:

> For some businesses, profits increase when government acts; for others, profits fall . . . [E]very act of government, no matter what its broader merits or demerits for society at large, creates winners and losers within the competitive sector of the economy. These gains and losses, which accrue to both individuals and corporations,

become the object of intense political attention at the same time they help shape the nation's international competitiveness ... This outcome is so predictable that it constitutes virtually an Iron Law of Public Policy.[7]

This Book's Design

Business, Government, Society is not a typical how-to book. The business environment is too dynamic, and too different among countries, to lend itself to easy prescriptions. Even if we know a country's sociopolitical landscape well, there is less agreement compared to other management disciplines about what actions to prescribe for firms working there. Public policy matters greatly to business, yet the problems posed by the business environment and public policy are over-complicated to resolve with rules of thumb.

The text's intention is more basic—to give students knowledge about why the social and political conditions of business change, about what drives these conditions and where they are heading. This knowledge is necessary for understanding the public and government affairs functions of today's companies, functions that are of growing importance. It is important to see how social and economic forces and public policy affect managers and their firms, and vice versa. It is particularly important to understand the business climate in other countries, to know what it would be like to manage there, and to appreciate the support and encumbrances foreign rivals get at home.

The facts and theories explained in the chapters that follow are designed to assist students in comprehending the business conditions and influences they will meet in the real world. They should be a base for quicker on-the-job learning about how to deal with those external forces. By sharpening readers' awareness of political and economic clichés, the hope is they will become more sophisticated managers, adept at working in the world arena.

While *Business, Government, Society* will try to be impartial and nondoctrinaire, it does not claim to be value-free. To the contrary, it invites readers to reflect on their values, on their basic social principles and standards of behavior. Values are needed to evaluate any facet of public policy. Without values, one cannot judge a policy to be good or bad, effective or ineffective. An important intention of this book, thus, is to make business students more aware of where their values lead—to help them square the way they view how business, government, and society ought to interact.

A Changing World Environment

Four trends stand out in the business environment for U.S. companies today. All create demand for new public policies. First is the shrinking world of commercial activities. The revolution in communication has knit the world into a web of instant financial transactions. Cheap and quick transportation moves a growing volume of people and goods quickly from country to country. Information about fashions and lifestyles travels even faster.

Globalization is eroding national governments' power.[8] The assets of the capital, bond, and currency markets go wherever it is profitable to do so, and government can do little to affect these flows. Likewise, many jobs are moving to countries with the lowest cost, regardless of whether government likes it. Governments can no longer easily insulate their businesses from events overseas. In fact, many governments are *encouraging* globalization by supporting policies to free international trade and to decontrol their home economies. They are voluntarily trying to reduce the scale and scope of government activities with the belief that to do otherwise is to invite economic stagnation.

The second trend in the business environment is the growth of business–government partnerships. This trend is most visible in societies such as Japan, South Korea, and, to a lesser extent, Germany that are marked by close ties between business and government to gain world markets. Professor George Lodge of Harvard Business School dubs these practices "communitarian capitalism."[9] American competitive capitalism is supposed to be very different, based on individualism and mutual suspicion between the public and private sectors. Still, business–government partnerships are becoming more common in the United States, though it is seldom noted.

Unlike the first trend, this one tilts the balance toward more government intervention in the economy. Public/private cooperation is not an all-powerful combination anywhere. There have been outright failures and unwitting successes even in Japan.[10] But the example of foreign countries is likely to bring U.S. business and government closer together anyway.

The third trend is a set of connected problems that threaten the entire planet—air and water pollution, climate change, soaring populations, and mass migration.[11] These problems, the byproduct of ordinary business activity, reach over national frontiers. They are beyond the capability of any single government or company to resolve. Supranational institutions may supplant national governments in some domains to settle these global problems, though probably not all of them. In either scenario, the potential impact on the way Americans do business is profound.

The fourth trend is the spread of democratic capitalism to new corners of the world. According to *Business Week*, roughly 3 billion people now live in capitalist economies, three times the level just 10 years ago.[12] The Soviet Union and its allies have collapsed and are fragmenting into smaller social units. That event, and less publicized but parallel political and economic reforms in the developing countries, are creating novel opportunities for business. There may be 400 million new members of a global middle class, providing a vast opening market for Western goods and know-how.[13] To boost their economic prospects, nations such as India, Vietnam, and Cuba also are unlocking their economies to foreign investment. That creates more business opportunities.

With these opportunities, however, come more economic competition. According to World Bank forecasts, output in rich industrial countries will grow by 2.7 percent a year from 1994 to 2003. The rest of the world is expected to grow nearly twice as quickly.[14] Some of that growth will be at the expense of established U.S. companies. American managers are going to have to deal with new generations of business rivals.

Each trend—the globalization of business, the spread of business–government partnerships, the ecological threat to the earth, and the spread of democratic capitalism—pulls in a different direction. Yet two things are clear. First, the trends mean the environment of U.S. companies is changing radically, and in ways that are less easily controlled than earlier. Second, the trends are clashing with the public policy status quo. There is political pressure on government to find new policies to prepare for the economic future.

Types of Public Policy

It is useful to have a typology of public policies. One revealing way to organize them is by who wins and who loses. While the lines among policies are seldom sharp, three policy types stand out: distributive, redistributive, and regulatory policies.[15]

Distributive policies are the most common form of government action. They use general revenues to provide benefits directly to individuals. The distributive category includes so-called **pork barrel** projects—funds for roads, bridges, dams, scientific research projects, and so forth. These projects are called *pork barrel* because they can be broken into small pieces and shared just like salt pork from a curing barrel. There are no obvious losers from such a policy, since every group can get a bit of the benefit.

Redistributive policy making means taxing or otherwise harming one group of people to provide benefits for a different group. A redistribution of income results from the government action. Redistributive policies are associated with any kind of zero-sum action, where one group's gains are roughly equal to another group's losses. An example is a proposal to lower tariffs, which will help some commercial interests (anyone who sells imported goods, for example) and hurt others (anyone who makes goods that compete with imports, to continue the illustration).

Regulatory policies are government limits on behavior. They include legal restrictions on criminal activity, monitoring of business to assure that its practices are fair, and forcing companies to protect public health and safety. What these specific policies have in common is that they all try to control what people and organizations do. We often assume that regulatory policy is not favored by those it regulates; "obviously" everyone prefers the freedom of an unregulated environment. Yet, sometimes business and other organizations do embrace regulation because it makes their environment safer or more predictable.

The Trap of Ideology and Political Labels

To raise issues about public policy and business is to risk triggering an ideological response over Big Government. As business students know, a **conserva-**

tive's reflex is usually that government needs to be cut back and business unleashed. The best policy is to leave managers and consumers alone to make economic decisions, without government intrusion. A **liberal's** automatic rebuttal often is no, more public investment and regulation are needed. The best policy is for an activist government to back and guide the economy.

U.S. students should be aware that the tag "liberal" means something different in the rest of the world. Elsewhere, a liberal on economic issues is an advocate of minimal, not activist, government—what Americans call the conservative position. People who support state intervention in the economy are usually called **social democrats** instead of liberals. To make matters more confusing, so-called conservatives in other countries have often backed state intervention as a way to assert national political power in the world—not what one normally associates with conservatism.

It pays to be careful when using loaded, ideological labels like liberal and conservative. Many political leaders act differently than would be predicted based on their overall view of government and the economy. President Richard Nixon, a conservative, for example, instituted wage/price controls, nationalized several railroads, expanded affirmative action programs, and proposed a universal health-care program. President Jimmy Carter, a liberal, deregulated the airline industry and the trucking industry. The need to act and to keep different interests happy makes governing a more pragmatic activity than is often imagined.

Whatever name one chooses for the pro- and anti-government positions, an arid debate follows that gives future managers little practical guidance about what kind of public policies they should seek. The issues get framed too superficially. The meaningful choices are not the universal ones of big versus limited government, of free versus regulated markets, of socialism versus capitalism. The meaningful choices are much more restricted: What public policies work best for what particular ends? The answers can only be made case by case.

Peter Drucker, a prolific observer of business and society, notes the fashion to be antigovernment. "But," he concludes, "this won't work. We need strong, effective government. In fact we can expect more rather than less government in the next decades . . . But [the new tasks] will require a *different form of government* [stress in original]."[16] He is correct; simpleminded slogans about active government or free markets just cloud matters. Continued economic development does not require small government, but it does require a capable one.

Private Organizations: A Kaleidoscope of Forms

The central player in Figure 1–1 is the private organization, which comes in many forms. It is helpful to go over the chief varieties before we proceed in later chapters to analyze the business environment.

Most businesses are uncomplicated, owner-operated operations, what are known formally as sole proprietorships. The owner/manager is personally responsible for liabilities incurred by the organization and has control over its action. No special government approval is needed to set up a sole proprietorship, unless the firm is engaged in a trade that needs licensing or zoning approval. Otherwise, the owner simply opens up shop. Because sole proprietorships rely on one person to raise capital and to provide management and labor, they have to be small. Only mom-and-pop corner stores, dry cleaning establishments, cobblers, restaurants, and the like can survive as sole proprietorships.

Partnerships avoid some shortcomings of sole proprietorships. Partnerships are businesses owned by two or more people who share responsibilities. The extra people make it easier to find funds and to do the work of the firm. No written agreement is needed to set up a partnership, though often the partners do write an agreement tailored to their particular needs.

In the United States, partnerships are the most common business form in professions such as accounting, law, and medicine. One reason for professional partnerships is to reassure clients: To show good faith, lawyers and doctors sometimes do *not* want to have the protection of limited liability that goes with incorporation. They see an economic advantage in being held personally accountable. But more complex businesses that need lots of capital and expect to continue unabated after the founders have left find partnerships unwieldy.

A larger type of business organization is the **cooperative** or mutual firm. Examples include mutual life insurance companies, mutual savings banks, credit unions, and agricultural marketing and supply cooperatives. In these firms, the role of owner and customer are theoretically combined. The motive for forming a cooperative is not to seek a return on invested capital, but to get goods or services at reduced cost. Any surplus is returned to customers in proportion to their purchases from the cooperative. This type of organization gets preferential tax treatment in the United States, but outside insurance and agriculture, where they are very important, cooperatives are not a significant feature of the American economy. By contrast, cooperatives are more important elsewhere in the West, particularly in Scandinavia.

Another type of entity that engages in economic production is **nonprofit organizations.** They, too, can grow large, as lots of universities, museums, and hospitals attest. The term *nonprofit* is misleading, for most such institutions sell goods and generate a surplus. That they do not call this surplus a profit is a semantic detail. What separates them from for-profit firms is that nonprofit firms cannot pay any excess revenue to people associated with the organization but must plow it back into their operations. Nonprofit firms thus lie somewhere between the private and public sectors, as conventionally defined, and are sometimes called, collectively, the third or independent sector.

More than ever, nonprofit organizations compete head-on with for-profit business today. Competition is especially prevalent in health, education, culture, and entertainment. For example, Harvard University, the Boston Symphony Orchestra, the Boston Museum of Fine Arts, and similar nonprofit institutions run gift shops and restaurants that look like any other gift shops and restaurants.

Since nonprofit organizations get special tax exemptions, and often qualify for charitable donations, some businesspeople are crying foul.[17] Information is fragmentary, but, in the United States, nonprofit entities (there are nearly 900,000 of them) account for perhaps 4–5 percent of GNP. And the figure is growing.[18]

Corporations

Still, by far the most important form of business organization is the moneymaking corporation. Even in the professions, incorporated entities are gradually replacing partnerships as the preferred mode of organization. A corporation is a firm created by government charter. The charter licenses the corporation to exist and lays down the basic rules of its existence. In the United States, the 50 states and the District of Columbia each has its own corporate code, and companies are chartered, or incorporated, under the laws of a single state. Corporations need not have a physical presence in the state to get a charter. The United States is unusual in this regard, for other countries usually have a uniform system of national charters.

Delaware is the most popular state in which large U.S. companies incorporate, having long had the most easygoing standards. It is home to more than half the 500 largest U.S. corporations. Most other states have followed Delaware and avoided strict chartering rules for fear of losing corporations to other states. California is a notable exception. Its rules favor shareholders, and many large companies have left California to reincorporate in Delaware. Ralph Nader, the consumer activist, has proposed federal chartering of U.S. corporations to avoid the competitive laxness of state chartering. The likelihood of such a reform is slim.[19]

U.S. Business–Government Relations: A Summary

How can one generalize about U.S. business–government relations? It is widely believed that business and government have clashing interests and pull against each other. Many people characterize business–government relations in the United States as adversarial.[20] This characterization is a half-truth.

Business and government are probably more openly at odds here than in many other countries, particularly those like Japan or Germany that lean toward a more collaborative mode of economic policy making. Distrust between the private and public sectors is deeply embedded in our history, and regulatory policies often irritate owners and managers, for they reduce profit and interfere with companies' freedom to maneuver.

Yet conflict is only half the business–government relationship, even in the United States. There is another side, one of mutual support, and its historical roots are just as deep. Cooperation between business and government gets less attention than the adversarial side because it goes against the grain of U.S. ideology, which holds that government is supposed to stay out of the way of business, not work with it.

Though largely hidden from view, the cooperative side of the business–government relationship may be dominant. Charles Lindblom holds that business always has a privileged position in capitalist or mixed economies like the United States. Lindblom's idea is that democratic states are too dependent on business to defy it on major issues. Delegated major economic decisions by the state, private companies can count on government help, or at least on noninterference, when they need it.[21] Lindblom's thesis has been criticized for being oversimplistic, but the core point is certain. Public policy helps determine how well, or how poorly, the private sector works, though often in ways so mundane people do not notice them.

The relationship between business and government is reciprocal, of course. Companies play critical parts in supporting the public sector. Among other inputs, they provide tax revenues, election funds, new products and technology, and advice on policy. Most fundamentally, in any capitalist society, companies brace the state by providing the lion's share of the jobs to the people living under it. If jobs become scant, the government's popular favor and even its legitimacy will be challenged.

The two sides of the business–government relationship are shown graphically in Figure 1–2. One side (portrayed in the bottom half of Figure 1–2) is government supports *for* business. These are public policies that are apt to increase companies' profits. Support policies include direct subsidies, indirect subsidies (like tax expenditures and loan guarantees), regulatory relief, and government sales and contracts (including privatized activities).

The other side of the business–government relationship (the top half of Figure 1–2) is government restraints *on* business. This type of public policy usually reduces profits. Profit-reducing policies are mainly taxes and regulations. Remember, however, that regulations do not always mean problems for business. Regulations sometimes become a mechanism by which one group takes advantage of another. Resourceful companies use the government rule book in creative ways against present or potential competitors—for example, to block access to their markets.

Together, these two sets of policies—supports and restraints—have an enormous impact on every company's earnings. To the extent business managers are

FIGURE 1–2

The relationship between business and government has two sides

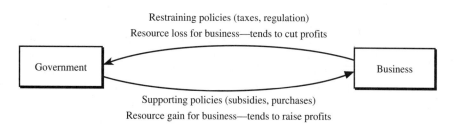

Restraining policies (taxes, regulation)
Resource loss for business—tends to cut profits

Government

Business

Supporting policies (subsidies, purchases)
Resource gain for business—tends to raise profits

economically rational and want to maximize profits, they usually like the government supports and dislike the government restraints. Because public policy is so important for profitability in the modern mixed economy, managers have been compelled to get more and more involved in policy making. Their goal: to get government to create a policy atmosphere in which *their* firm can flourish.

Figure 1–2 is generic. It applies to all countries. The specifics will differ, with each country favoring a different mix of policies. But everywhere government helps and restrains the private sector, and everywhere the private sector resists and supports government.

It is important to remember that the business–government relationship is symbiotic. The resource flow depicted in Figure 1–2 is circular: what is an output for business is an input for government, and vice versa. Government uses the resources it gets from business to help do its job, which partly entails spending on things to aid business. Sitting in a different place than business leaders, government officials may want a different mix of policies, one that enhances their influence. But this separate point of view does not mean that business and government are foes. They are partners in the political economy and need each other to survive.

Figure 1–2 also does not represent a closed system. Other groups in society—workers, consumers, community residents—give and get resources. They, too, favor different public policies. Even the business community is not a monolithic interest. Exporters and importers, big companies and small companies, mature industry and emerging industry—each has separate needs that can bring them into conflict with each other.

Conclusion

This chapter has introduced the idea that the business environment—the range of external forces that surround and limit managers' decisions—is critical for any private sector organization's success. The environment is made of market forces, narrowly understood, and so-called nonmarket forces—everything else that affects business. More than ever, the external stresses on business push and pull in different directions. As the title of one recent book has it, today's managers must learn to thrive on chaos.[22]

The business environment was not frozen in the 1950s and 1960s. But the pace of change was far slower than now. A major reason was the lower level of international competition. As competition heats up and the business environment grows more uncertain, government is being called on to play new roles. Public policy is in many ways the shock absorber between firms and the outside forces that impinge on them.

Government intervention in markets has profound effects—both positive and negative—on firms. Thus, the ability to analyze the roots, the implications, and the dynamics of public policy is an important skill for managers. They want two main things from government. First, they want to influence public policy so it does not harm them—and sometimes so they can gain at the expense of other groups or organizations. Second, they want to adjust quickly to the policies that are put into effect, to avoid being penalized.

To be objective about public policy, we proposed the method of international and historical comparisons. There is no reason to assume that all systems for making policies are equally suited to helping remedy the problems posed by the business environment. Lessons can be learned from other countries. By taking a comparative and historical perspective, the pluses and minuses of the American system become clearer, as do the convergences and divergences with other countries.

Questions

1. Describe the business environment. How is it changing?

2. What are the major forms of private sector organization? How do they differ? How are they similar?

3. Describe how the economy is becoming globalized. Discuss the implications for business. For government.

4. What is public policy? How may public policies be categorized? Why are they important for business?

5. Define the terms liberal and conservative. What ambiguities do you see in them?

End Notes

1. E. J. Hobsbawm, *Industry and Empire* (Harmondsworth, England: Penguin, 1968), p. 226.

2. Robert Reich, *The Work of Nations* (New York: Vintage, 1991), p. 67. Also see John Kenneth Galbraith's *The New Industrial State* (Boston: Houghton, Mifflin, 1967) for an overly confident projection into the future of the stable business environment of the 1950s and 1960s.

3. Michael Dertouzos, Richard Lester, and Robert Solow, *Made in America: Regaining the Productive Edge* (Cambridge, MA: MIT Press, 1989).

4. Paul Krugman, *Peddling Prosperity* (New York: Norton, 1994).

5. Michael E. Porter, *The Competitive Advantage of Nations* (New York: Free Press, 1990), pp. 71, 127–28.

6. See, for example, Peter Gourevitch, *Politics in Hard Times* (Ithaca, NY: Cornell University Press, 1986).

7. Robert A. Leone, *Who Profits: Winners, Losers, and Government Regulation* (New York: Basic Books, 1986), p. 3.

8. See Reich, *Work of Nations*; and Kenichi Ohmae, *The Borderless World: Power and Strategy in the Interlinked Economy* (New York: Harper Business, 1990).

9. George C. Lodge, *Perestroika for America* (Boston: Harvard Business School Press, 1990), p. 13.

10. Russell Hancock, "A Farewell to Japanese Industrial Policy," *Stanford Journal of International Affairs* 2, no. 1 (1993), pp. 11–28.

11. Paul Kennedy, *Preparing for the Twenty-First Century* (New York: Random House, 1993).

12. "Financing World Growth," *Business Week,* October 3, 1994.

13. "Selling to the New Global Middle Class," *Business Week,* October 25, 1993, p. 152.

14. "A Survey of the Global Economy," *The Economist,* October 1, 1994.

15. This typology, with minor modifications, is common in the public policy literature. See, for example, Kenneth J. Meier, *Politics and the Bureaucracy,* 2nd ed. (Belmont, CA: Brooks/Cole, 1987), chapter 4.

16. Peter Drucker, *Post-Capitalist Society* (New York: Harper Business, 1993), p. 159. For discussion of the major views of how economies work see Benjamin Ward, *The Ideal World of Economics: Liberal, Radical, and Conservative* (New York: Basic Books, 1979).

17. James T. Bennett and Thomas J. DiLorenzo, *Unfair Competition: The Profits of Nonprofits* (Lanham, MD: Hamilton Press, 1989).

18. Burton A. Weisbrod, *The Nonprofit Economy* (Cambridge, MA: Harvard University Press, 1988), pp. 169 and 172.

19. Archie B. Carroll, *Business and Society: Ethics and Stakeholder Management* (Cincinnati: South-Western Publishing, 1989), p. 443.

20. Typical is Rogene A. Buchholz, *Business Environment and Public Policy,* 4th ed. (Englewood Cliffs, NJ: Prentice Hall, 1992), pp. 151–53.

21. Charles E. Lindblom, *Politics and Markets* (New York: Basic Books, 1977).

22. Thomas J. Peters, *Thriving on Chaos* (New York: Knopf, 1987).

II MARKETS AND POLITICS

2   HOW MARKETS WORK

[Planned interventions] disturb nature in the course of her operations on human affairs, and it requires no more than to leave her alone and give her fair play in the pursuit of her ends. . . Little else is required to carry a state to the highest degree of affluence from the lowest barbarism, but peace, easy taxes, and a tolerable administration of justice; all the rest being brought about by the natural course of things.

Adam Smith[1]

Managers have to work with and through many markets—markets for labor, raw materials, capital, and other inputs, as well as markets for their output. Most core courses in the management functions, for example, finance, personnel, or marketing, teach students how to deal with one or more of these specific markets.

Often missing in specialized management courses is any overarching analysis of how public policy influences the varied markets that businesspeople confront. Government intervention in, say, the capital, labor, or consumer markets has important effects on a firm's strategic options and performance. *Business, Government, Society* tries to fill that gap to explore systematically how and why public policy constrains private management decision making.

Before we can examine the place of public policy in the business environment, we need to anchor ourselves with a good understanding of how markets work. That is the purpose of this chapter. Thus we begin with a discussion of political economy and the idea that there are both economic and political markets. The rest of the chapter reviews elementary ideas about economic competition. Advanced students can scan this material as background for subsequent chapters. Students who are not well-grounded in introductory microeconomic theory will need to read the next sections more carefully, for the ideas presented here are the base on which this book's analysis rests.

The Market

Anyone with an interest in improving a country's material well-being must understand workings of the **market.** The market (singular not plural) is a system of social coordination. It is a network of institutions within which people buy, sell, and rent. Whenever the term *the market* appears by itself in this book, the reference will be to this network.

The market is made of individual markets (plural)—figurative places where people gather to exchange particular commodities. Markets exist for cars, for houses, for stocks and bonds, and potentially for anything else that people can buy and sell. As most Americans are taught, markets do remarkably well in bringing together the efforts of hosts of self-serving individuals.

More than ever, governments are trying to extend the scope of markets in their economies. Around the world, programs are under way to allow firms and consumers greater freedom to make economic decisions. Yet, paradoxically, governments are trying simultaneously to correct more perceived defects in the market system. Today's managers must have a good grasp of what markets can and cannot do, or they will not be able to understand the role public policy plays in helping or harming private enterprise.

Political Economy

To make sense of business's changing environment of markets and public policy, it helps to have a consistent way of thinking, a lens to bring the issues into focus. We will rely throughout this book on **political economy,** a theory for understanding the links between economics and politics. Political economy can be useful in clarifying public policy and the business environment.

Americans have learned to think that the private sector and the public sector are opposites. In the popular culture, business represents mostly positive values—efficiency, productivity, innovation, and so forth. Government is usually portrayed in a more negative light, embodying incompetence, waste, and well-meaning but futile efforts to interfere with business to promote social goals. These polar descriptions of business and government are useful mainly as debating points, not as accurate depictions of reality. By typecasting the two sectors, they probably confuse more than they enlighten. The truth is: Business and government are more alike than most people realize.

As Lester Thurow, former dean of management at the Massachusetts Institute of Technology, observes, one reason for black-and-white thinking about business and government is the Cold War.[2] The Soviet Union exemplified all that was wrong with having too little private business, too much government. Communism's failures were seen as proving the view that politics and economics do not mix.

Another reason for seeing business and government as antithetical is the way universities have divided up the social world for study. Different specialties have evolved to ask how business, on the one hand, and government, on the other, operate. Economics and business management focus on the private sector; political science and public administration concentrate on the public sector.

This division of intellectual labor evolved over the last 100 years and would have been surprising to scholars writing at the start of the industrial era. They practiced a more universal science they called political economy,[3] which centered on the ties between civil society and the state (the private and public sectors in today's terms). The goal of political economists through the nineteenth century was to uncover policies that would best augment the community's wealth—roughly equivalent to what we now know as the gross national product or **GNP.** Adam Smith, author of the classic treatise *An Inquiry into the Nature and Causes of the Wealth of Nations* (1776), was typical of this focus on economic development through good government. We will return throughout this book to Smith's keen insights, many of which retain their validity today. Later in history, political economy became associated with Marxism and riveted on the deeper structure of society and how the distribution of property affected power.

This comprehensive way of looking at business and government largely died out and was replaced by the more specialized fields of study familiar today. Critics of political economy came to believe that values tainted that discipline, rendering it unscientific. Yet in recent years political economy has made a comeback. After all, people undertake economic and political actions for much the same reason—to get things they want. Because material goods are always limited compared to potential demand, people have to make hard choices about how to expend their energy. But their motive is constant in both the political and economic realms. As the title of Harold Lasswell's famous government text put it, politics is about who gets what, when, how.[4] The same title could easily be used for an economics text.

Feeling confined by the limits to the usual disciplines, many social scientists and some practitioners have started to take a fresh look at political economy, especially as practiced by the pre-Marxist or classical political economists. The result is a renaissance in studying political and economic events as more of a whole. The so-called new political economy seeks broad knowledge about socioeconomic facts and tries to put back together what social science has pulled apart. This approach lends well to a complicated subject like business and its environment, a subject that draws many variables—social, economic, cultural, technological, and legal, to name a few—into its orbit.

Modern political economy is diverse. As mentioned above, there are Marxist and conservative wings, for example.[5] We will borrow freely from all branches of the discipline. What unifies them is the idea that economics and politics, or business and government, cannot be understood in isolation. The two realms are seen to be intimately linked.

Not everyone agrees that commercial and public life can be fused so easily. Jane Jacobs, for example, argues that society has evolved two radically different systems of values. One system (the commercial orientation) stresses qualities such as work, honesty, and thrift. The other morality (the more political one) shuns trading and exalts ostentation and gift-giving, among other things, to be esteemed.[6] People, in other words, are motivated and guided by conflicting values. This is an old and obvious truth.

Political economists are prone to play down the inconsistencies in human motivation. They like to think that people respond predictably to rewards and punishment. Scratch a businessperson or a civil servant, the political economist argues, and you will find that both are competing for resources. Only the rules for competition are not the same. Business and government are arranged differently, and these different arrangements create different incentives for action. To explain human behavior, the place to start is with organizational structures and the inducements they spawn.

The result is a unified approach to behavior that can help managers interpret and even forecast events across the spectrum of their organizations' environments. Political economy cannot answer all questions about public policy satisfactorily. Like all schools of thought, it can mislead if pushed too far. Yet, if used prudently, political economy is a fertile source of wisdom about the environment of modern business.

Three Working Assumptions

Let us look at the new political economy's assumptions. Following mainstream economics, most political economists take for granted three important points—familiar to anyone who has taken a first-year economics course.

- Individual people should be the first unit of analysis. To explain the action of big social units—say a company or a public agency—political economy starts at the bottom, with the people working there. It builds up from each person's motives and way of acting, to understand the larger groups they form. This assumption is known formally as **methodological individualism.**

- People are strongly marked by **self-interest.** They are driven by what Smith called "the desire for betterment." What this assumption means is that people usually look out for themselves. They prefer to do things they like and avoid things they dislike.

- People are **rational.** In trying to further their welfare, they look to the future. They consistently choose to do things they think will give them the greatest benefit at the least cost. In the somewhat abstract language of political economy, people are utility maximizers.

This trio of assumptions—individualism, self-interest, and rationality—are the building blocks for political economy. Writers often speak of **economic man** as a shorthand way to denote the view that in the marketplace people are purposeful agents, the defenders of personal gain. The novelty of political economy is to extend the logic of economic man to political and social affairs. Whether one looks at the profit-making, the voluntary, or the government sectors, people are presumed to be similar in thought and deed.

Economic man is a metaphor. Like any metaphor, it is not to be taken literally. Critics (including many political economists themselves) point out how one-sided, even degrading it is as a model for human behavior. People are moved by purposes other than egoism; their actions are not always deliberate and directed toward particular goals. Coercion and ideology, culture and morality, can be as important stimulants as self-interest.[7]

Consider, for example, the person who leaves a tip in a roadside restaurant to a stranger who he or she will never see again. Others routinely give away their blood. Such acts of generosity cannot be explained through individual economic calculation and must be driven by ethical considerations. As Smith himself observed, "How selfish sovever [sic] man may be supposed, there are evidently some principles in his nature, which interest him in the fortune of others. . ."[8] People are guided by, and sometimes live up to, standards of benevolence and self-sacrifice. They do not always have ulterior motives for acts of seeming generosity.

Other pragmatic and philosophical objections to the rational actor model have been offered. To fix on individuals can be to mislead, for instance, since the whole (society) is more than the sum of its parts (people). Logicians call this mistake the fallacy of composition. "No man is an island," the saying goes, and one person's well-being usually is influenced by his perception of people around him and whether they are suffering or content.

Also, self-interest and utility are very elastic notions that can be used to explain almost every behavior. Does Mother Theresa work with Calcutta's homeless from self-interest, as she defines it? Is she maximizing her utility through personal denial? One could argue yes, but that is stretching self-interest and utility so far they lose much meaning. Rationality also has limits, for people can hold contradictory preferences. Consider a cigarette smoker who buys a cigarette pack every day but who also pays to join a program to quit smoking. What is his or her real preference—to smoke or to quit?

As these examples suggest, the economic model is not meant to give a plausible account of *all* human behavior, just a lucid one. Much gets left out. Of course, humans can be generous and self-destructive, impulsive and erratic. It is fortunate for business and society that human motivation is complex. Were we not able to mix selfish and selfless behavior, for instance, economic teamwork and group loyalty would not occur the way they do—making it much harder to organize for economic activities.[9]

Reducing flesh-and-blood beings to economic man is being simplistic on purpose. The object is to gain in clarity what is lost in accuracy. Rich insights come from supposing that, much of the time, humans try to promote their well-being, as they see it. In particular, the rational actor model of human behavior gives a coherent picture of how markets and governments work, and why they sometimes falter.

Ethical Concerns

Due to the flaws in the economic man model, only modest claims will be made for it in this book. Economic rationality is not a prototype for everything people do. It is a convenient fiction for explaining and predicting many business and society relations. We will use the economic model of behavior with proper caution. Still, it is a safe bet that in commerce and politics, people do tend to seek advantage for themselves.

Students also should keep in mind that political economy, as used here, does not recommend how people should behave. In the language of philosophy, political economy is a positive theory (based mainly on observation), not a normative one (having more to do with values). The rational actor framework tries to predict behavior rather than to prescribe it. In depicting what people in industry and government tend to do, it does not necessarily make a judgment about what those people *ought* to do. While the framework does presume that managers, public servants, consumers, and other economic actors are likely to put self-interest first, this presumption is not intended as advice. There are many other values, such as altruism, self-sacrifice, fairness, and respect for rights, that have a legitimate claim to take precedence over self-interest.

Some political economists, it is true, do make a strong ethical argument for self-interest as a supreme value.[10] Unregulated pursuit of individual ambition, in their view, is likely to help society as a whole. As the tycoon Gordon Gekko said in the film *Wall Street*: "Greed is good." Smith, who held a chair in moral philosophy, would have found such claims self-serving and overstated. He asserted in his largely forgotten tract, *The Theory of Moral Sentiments* (1767), that ambition can have hurtful consequences for others. Untamed by scruple or by law, greed is not good.[11]

The need to step beyond economic man, to take a broader and more morally satisfying view of human behavior, has given birth to the field of **business ethics.** Business ethics call for managers and organizations to heed carefully thought-out rules of moral philosophy. Ethical behavior in business goes beyond making a profit or obeying the law, and requires conformity to higher standards of professional duty and obligation to others. We will return to the important and controversial subject of business ethics in Chapter 4.

How the Market Is Supposed to Work

The critical feature that allows markets to meet people's needs is that, when they are working right, markets are voluntary. Everybody is a willing participant. Individual buyers and sellers come together and trade resources because they want to. The stress must be on voluntary exchanges. As we will see shortly, when markets involve people without consent, they break down.

By interacting in a market, buyers and sellers combine inputs or factors of production (land, labor, capital) to make outputs—useful goods and services that can be consumed or used for further production. Individual rewards and penalties, primarily financial gains and losses, determine what gets produced and how. Political economists have long noticed the unintended social benefit of these individual incentives. Each person's quest for his or her profit, when taken altogether, leads to goods and services that improve everyone's position. A private vice (greed) transforms into a public benefit (consumer choice). This positive result comes about without anybody's conscious intent.

Smith was among the first to point out how the market channels human energy toward socially useful ends. In a celebrated passage at the beginning of *The Wealth of Nations,* he asserts that: "It is not from the benevolence of the butcher, the brewer or the baker, that we expect our dinner, but from their regard to their own interest." Smith develops the argument more fully later:

> He [any participant in the economy] generally, indeed, neither intends to promote the public interest . . . he intends only his own gain, and he is in this, as in many other cases, led by an *invisible hand* to promote an end which has no part of his intention . . . By pursuing his own interest he frequently promotes that of society more effectually than when he really intends to promote it [stress added].[12]

The **invisible hand** was a powerful metaphor for a striking observation: the market can spontaneously serve the society's interests. Through commercial activities people unknowingly promote social welfare.

Smith's insight has led many people to advocate **laissez-faire** government policies toward business. Taken from the French term for "leave alone," laissez-faire doctrine holds that an economic system works better the less government intrudes. The natural economic order, that is, one left undisturbed by man-made restraints or support, is seen to meet the needs of both individuals and society.

We will see throughout this book that Smith never pushed this doctrine to its logical extreme to make a blanket rejection of government. A sophisticated thinker, he was no libertarian or anarchist, and he credited public policy with a critical role for supporting commerce. Unlike some economic fundamentalists today, Smith did not hold that the best economic policy is, in effect, always to have no policy at all.

Historically, laissez-faire was a reaction against mercantilism, a system where states tried to control industry and foreign trade to make their countries rich. These well-intended actions could backfire and hold down living standards. Laissez-faire became the dominant theory (less the reality) of public policy in the United States after the Civil War (1861–65). It was also prominent in Britain then.

Later, laissez-faire fell from fashion for being a simplistic doctrine.[13] Hands-off policies work best for exchanges that lack major implications for third parties. Frequently, third parties *are* implicated, a point to which we will return in Chapter 3. By the 1930s and into the post–World War II period, government activism and interventionism became the conventional wisdom in the West—a loose, geographically inaccurate term that covers Western Europe, North America, Australia, New Zealand, and, often, Japan.

Since about 1980, laissez-faire has reappeared as a serious guide to public policy, particularly in Anglo-Saxon countries. Ronald Reagan in the United States and Margaret Thatcher in Britain are among the many leaders who came to power in the last two decades praising the benefit of unregulated economic competition. Let us look more carefully at the case for leaving the market alone.

Arguments for Laissez-Faire

The case rests on three claims. Unregulated markets are said to be efficient, innovative, and liberating (see Table 2–1).

Efficiency

By saying the market is **efficient,** political economists are usually thinking mostly about the best mix of goods (sometimes called *allocative* efficiency). Their meaning is not the everyday notion of efficiency, which refers to producing goods at low cost (also known as *productive* efficiency). Markets do encourage companies to be businesslike and productive, too, for reasons we will explore in the next section on innovation. First, we discuss efficiency in the allocative sense.

By this term political economists mean the market theoretically can produce a desirable social outcome by serving out the economic pie in a way that suits everyone, *given their income.* The distribution of income is, of course, uneven, since people have uneven skills, ideas, strengths, and inherited wealth they can offer for exchange. People may be unhappy with the initial hand they are dealt. Still, within that constraint, the market parcels out goods and services so that everyone gains and no one loses.

How does this efficient pattern of exchange happen? If people are economically rational, *and if nothing impedes their actions,* efficient results are certain. People will trade until a balance is reached where no one could be made better off without someone else being made worse off. (It should be clear immediately that many things can hamper an exchange, leading to inefficient results.) When people share the slices of the economic pie the way they want, given their income, they obviously will stop trading with each other.[14]

Should an imbalance occur, where someone thinks he can improve his well-being through a voluntary exchange with someone else, the resulting transaction automatically removes the imbalance. In this sense the market is said to be self-correcting. It adjusts for any source of instability, such as a change in someone's tastes or needs. Using the language of political economics, the market tends toward equilibrium, a resting point.

Proponents of the efficiency argument acknowledge that no society ever reaches an equilibrium at which everyone's welfare is as great as possible with-

TABLE 2–1   **Decentralized Decision Making and Individual Choice by Consumers Have Many Advantages in Organizing an Economy, at Least in Theory.**

Efficiency: Markets allow mutually satisfactory exchanges among consenting individuals, and thus promote social welfare.
Innovation: Markets force companies to innovate.
Liberty: Markets are desirable because they permit voluntary cooperation and are not binding.

out hurting anyone else. To get to that happy point requires so-called perfect competition. The following ideal conditions must be in place:

- All firms are small and there are lots of them, so no buyer or seller can influence prices through independent action.
- Entering or leaving the market is easy.
- Consumers act to maximize utility, and firms act to maximize profits.
- Production technology has constant or decreasing returns to scale (the rate of output stays the same or falls as inputs are added).
- Buyers and sellers have full knowledge, available at no cost, about the performance and quality of items being traded.
- The offerings of sellers are identical in all respects.
- Prices of goods and services are not sticky and move up or down quickly, and they reflect full costs.
- Finally, the cost to penalize cheating by either party, and to protect their property, is zero.

Why think about such unrealistic market conditions? Nowhere do we see hordes of small competitors, unrestricted entry, perfectly informed buyers, and homogeneous products. The answer is that perfect competition is not meant to describe actual markets (though some agricultural and financial markets may come close). Instead, these conditions are put forward as a model against which real markets can be tested. The nearer real markets come to the ideal, the better.

Admirers of markets find many rough analogues to perfect competition in the real world. They argue that partly competitive markets are usually better than the alternative—allowing government to allocate resources. A case in point is the former Soviet Union. Government planners created a warped economy, with an overdeveloped military sector and an underdeveloped civilian sector. Had producers and consumers been given more range to choose, the economy would have made more butter and fewer guns. With greater freedom of choice, soviet society would have come much closer to meeting society's wants than it ever did under the commissars.

Market competition, it must be stressed, never produces the best possible *distribution* of resources—just the best distribution given the pattern of wealth and income. Thus, market competition can have dreadful results in unequal societies. Many famines, for example, take place when there is enough food to go around. People starve to death, not because of absolute shortages, but because the food that is available is unevenly distributed. Hoarding, high prices, and poverty make it impossible for some people to buy the nourishment they need to live.[15] The play of supply and demand produces this outcome, but it is only something a sadist or masochist would freely choose.

Innovation

Competition figures in the second argument for laissez-faire, too. This argument holds that free markets are unparalleled for promoting innovation. By making firms compete, markets not only squeeze out waste (what we called productive efficiency above); they stimulate new techniques and new products. Whereas allocative efficiency refers to the best way to hand out the slices of a given economic pie, the innovation argument is based on the idea that people are made happier by baking a bigger and tastier economic pie—that is, by creating more and improved goods.

To create more and improved goods, companies must innovate. Laissez-faire advocates think the best spur for innovation is competition. In a market economy, companies are forced to reduce production cost or risk being replaced by rivals who can develop and use less costly methods. They have to try new methods of organizing, motivating, and training. Should they not, someone else will. Companies are made to respond to their customers' needs on penalty of being driven out of business. The result is a flow of improved, low-priced merchandise.

Lack of competition has the opposite effect. It allows firms to turn lazy and insensitive. If they have captive customers, they are apt to give up the quest for new and better ways to produce value. Refusals to change or listen to customers are charges frequently made against **monopolies**—not by large companies that dominate their market and do not have to compete.

For proof, defenders of laissez-faire again point to the old Soviet Union. Soviet enterprises were monopolies, undisciplined by the need to compete. They were notorious for being lax and unwilling to change. They made shoddy goods that people often did not want. In a market economy, these dinosaurs would have become extinct quickly.

Because capitalism is decentralized, it is good at conducting experiments. They can be conducted on a small scale and be repeated. The cost of failure is not great to society. Successful experiments can produce large rewards and are a signal for others to follow.

That a decentralized economic arrangement works is sometimes surprising. Emile Durkheim (1858–1917), the famous French sociologist, is reported to have been motivated to study society by his wonderment that he could open the back door of his apartment every morning and find a bottle of milk waiting, and he did not even know the milkman.[16] This remarkable degree of coordination happens with no central blueprint along soviet lines.

Liberty

Competition is also part of the third rationale for markets—that they encourage human freedom. A most powerful appeal of a market exchange is that it is based on compromise and agreement. Neither party is forced to enter the deal; the parties get together because each sees a gain. Haggling may result, but the outcome is, by definition, mutually acceptable since the parties have alternatives. People are freed by having other buyers and sellers to whom they can turn, and by having money-making opportunities they can choose to exploit.

The old Soviet Union is the paradigm for how lack of markets restricts freedom. There, government tried to ration many goods in roughly equal amounts. It also refused to give consumers many products they wanted, and tried to get them to accept products government thought they should have. By cutting down on people's economic choices, the soviet system exercised economic tyranny.

Milton Friedman, the 1976 Nobel-laureate economist, is among the writers who extends the freedom argument from the economy to the political realm. He asserts that the liberties of capitalism and democracy are strongly linked.[17] The links are easy to see. There is a natural parallel between choice in the marketplace and choice in elections, and both business and government leaders depend on freedom of information to know what customers/citizens want. In each realm, the economic and the political, competition checks power from amassing.

On the other hand, the free market can create economic inequality that subverts the political equality on which democracy is based. The biggest inequality is often the gap between the owners of capital and wage earners. From this viewpoint, capitalism and democracy are contradictory. Also, the freedom of the market is but one of several types of freedom that philosophers have identified. We will look at these issues more closely in Chapter 4.

A further shortcoming of markets is that voluntary exchanges will not do for every social task. Even if the market does tend toward an equilibrium from which no possible movement would make everyone better off, there are times when it is preferable to impose a loss on some people. The United States is better off today for having forcibly freed slaves, whose owners were not paid for the property they lost. Similarly, Japan and South Korea are richer because 50 years ago U.S. occupiers took land from unwilling landlords and gave it to peasants. None of these events happened voluntarily. As Charles E. Lindblom, former president of the American Political Science Association, points out, "Insofar as markets can organize only voluntary, mutually advantageous acts of coordination, it will be necessary to find nonmarket alternatives."[18] Society sometimes needs coercion.

The Price Mechanism

Thus far we have reviewed three good things the market can do—it can promote efficiency, innovation, and freedom. For the market to do these good things, its participants need knowledge. Prices provide that knowledge. In Lindblom's words, prices "are a device for declaring in standardized form the terms on which exchange is offered or consummated."[19] The total of all prices is a kind of intelligence network for the market.

Prices thus play a central part in the laissez-faire argument. They reveal what the best use of resources is—where workers can get the best wage, where investors can get the highest returns, where consumers can get the lowest price, and so on. They also warn which goods and services are scarce (high priced) and which are plentiful (low priced). Prices convey an enormous amount of information in very compact form, and swiftly. Absent that information, the market's ability to correct itself is impaired.

When a price is right—that is, when it reflects an item's true value to people—it clears the market. Demand meets supply; buyers and sellers both get the best deal they can from their noncompulsory exchange. Alternatively, when a price is too high, an unwanted surplus results. In a smooth running market, buyers and sellers will bid the price down until the surplus goes away. Something similar happens if a price is too low. A shortage develops, and market forces will drive the price up until the shortage (or the waiting line of customers) disappears.

Scarcity Pricing

Market-clearing prices are sometimes called **scarcity prices** because they match the assessment of both parties—buyers and sellers—of an item's scarcity or abundance. They also are known as efficiency prices because they aid efficient or mutually agreeable exchanges. When the amount of money charged for something is not based on mutual agreement, that is, it does not reflect the interplay of supply and demand, it is called an arbitrary price. One reason laissez-faire advocates do not like government to intervene in the economy is that arbitrary prices often result.

An illustration of how scarcity pricing allows markets to self-regulate is the energy crisis of the 1970s. An oil shortage arose then, largely because oil-producing countries got together to restrict production. The price of oil went up to reflect this (artificial) shortage. Expensive oil, in turn, got American consumers to buy smaller cars, to insulate their homes, to install wood-burning stoves, and to take a thousand other steps to cut down their use of oil products and save money. Expensive oil also got oil producers to explore for more oil, to open new oil reserves, and to find other energy sources. Here, lower demand and greater supply eventually drove the price of oil back down. When adjusted for inflation, the cost per barrel was about the same in the early 1990s that it had been 20 years earlier.

Price Controls

If government starts to set prices, it ends by distorting them. Economic planners can never keep up with shifting supply and demand. In the Soviet Union, planners had to track *24 million* separate prices.[20] Inevitably, the wrong signals about surplus and shortage, value and waste, are given. Resources do not get pulled to their best use. Innovation slows.

We can use the 1970s oil crisis again to illustrate. To protect consumers, the U.S. government put a ceiling on gasoline prices. These prices were too low; they did not reflect the true scarcity of oil. Motorists saw the bargain and rushed out to fill their tanks. Car lines began to form around the pumps. Forced to give away gasoline at discount prices, service stations soon began to run out. Since they could not charge motorists more, service stations started limiting the volume of sales to preserve their dwindling stocks. Each driver was allowed only a few gallons at a time. The lines got longer. Motorists ended up paying with time and aggravation for gasoline's artificially low price. During more recent oil shocks, such as that triggered by Iraq's invasion of Kuwait, gasoline prices have been allowed to rise and fall freely, and no lines formed at the pumps.

To sum up, a working price mechanism both signals scarcity and allocates resources. As a resource gets used up, its price rises. The higher price, in turn, motivates buyers to conserve the resource and find cheaper substitutes, and it encourages suppliers to figure out less expensive ways to provide the resource. One advantage of organizing an economy around scarcity prices is that the supply and demand for goods and services tend to balance themselves automatically. The result is an agreeable compromise for the participants, for it meets their needs as much as possible given the availability of resources and the way they are allocated from the start.

Conclusion

We have introduced the theory of political economy and its core insight that, despite appearances, business and government are closely integrated. Political economy lets us understand how markets work and, more importantly for public policy, how they sometimes fail. It also gives us a basis for interpreting how public policy is made—through a kind of market for political influence (see Chapters 8, 9, and 10). The juncture of the private and public sectors, of market and nonmarket forces, is the unifying thread for the rest of this volume.

We also have probed the basis of free market or capitalist economies and identified several scenarios where the invisible hand of competition produces desired outcomes. Under the right conditions, laissez-faire policies work the best for all. They create a process akin to natural selection in biology, through which only the fittest firms, making things people want, survive. There is much to the point, often made by former U.S. President Ronald Reagan, that the market is miraculous. It is a wonder that self-interested beings can work together, without conscious knowledge, in the complex and large-scale job of producing, distributing, and consuming wealth. The linking of individual and social benefit, through the invisible hand, makes laissez-faire a hardy and appealing doctrine.

Yet conditions are not always so favorable for the competitive market. The invisible hand cannot be counted on to move resources to their best use all the time. In these cases, what might be called government's visible hand is needed. We probe deeper into government intervention in the next chapter.

Questions

1. What is the invisible hand? In your view, does it work? Why?

2. Do you think that people are mainly self-interested? Rational?

3. Describe perfect economic competition. How does reality differ from the theory?

4. What are scarcity prices? How do they allocate economic resources in an efficient way?

5. What are the pros and cons of laissez-faire public policies?

End Notes

1. Quoted by Jacob Viner, "Adam Smith and Laissez Faire" (1927), reprinted in *Essays on the Intellectual History of Economics,* ed. Douglas Irwin (Princeton, N.J.: Princeton University Press, 1991), p. 87.

2. Lester C. Thurow, *Head to Head: The Coming Economic Battle Among Japan, Europe, and America* (New York: Morrow, 1992).

3. The first known English use of this term was in 1767, with the publication of Sir James Steuart's *Inquiry into the Principles of Political Economy.* The term had appeared the previous century in France. Political economy fell out of fashion in the late 1800s and was replaced by the modern label, economics. For a history of the origins of political economy, see Terence Hutchinson, *Before Adam Smith: A History of Political Economy* (Oxford: Basil Blackwell, 1988).

4. Harold D. Lasswell, *Politics: Who Gets What, When, How* (New York: P. Smith, 1936).

5. For attempts to untangle the definitions, see Martin Staniland, *What Is Political Economy?* (New Haven, CT: Yale University Press, 1985), and Barry Clark, *Political Economy: A Comparative Approach* (New York: Praeger, 1991).

6. Jane Jacobs, *Systems of Survival: A Dialogue on the Moral Foundations of Commerce and Politics* (New York: Random House, 1992).

7. See, for example, Amitai Etzioni, *The Moral Dimension: Toward a New Economics* (New York: Free Press, 1988).

8. Adam Smith, *The Theory of Moral Sentiments* (1790; reprint, Oxford: Clarendon, 1976), p. 9. Also see Steven Homes, "The Secret History of Self-Interest," in *Beyond Self-Interest,* ed. Jane J. Mansbridge (Chicago: University of Chicago Press, 1990), pp. 267–86.

9. Amartya Sen, *On Ethics and Economics* (Oxford: Basil Blackwell, 1987), pp. 20–21.

10. For a cogent argument, see Milton Friedman, *Capitalism and Freedom* (Chicago: University of Chicago Press, 1982).

11. For revisionist commentaries that stress the altruistic side of Adam Smith's thinking, see Patricia Werhane, *Adam Smith and His Legacy for Modern Capitalism* (New York: Oxford University Press, 1991), and Jerry Z. Muller, *Adam Smith in His Time and Ours* (New York: Free Press, 1993).

12. Adam Smith, *An Inquiry into the Nature and Causes of the Wealth of Nations* (1776; reprint, New York: Modern Library, 1937), pp. 14 and 423.

13. See Andrew Shonfield, *Modern Capitalism* (London: Oxford University Press, 1965).

14. The technical term for this balance point, where all possible mutually beneficial exchanges have occurred, is the Pareto optimum, named after the Italian economist and sociologist Vilfredo Pareto (1848–1923) who discovered it.

15. Amartya Sen, *Poverty and Famine* (Oxford: Clarendon Press, 1982).

16. Cited in Adam Przeworski, *Democracy and the Market* (Cambridge: Cambridge University Press, 1991), p. 105.

17. See Friedman, *Capitalism and Freedom.*

18. Charles E. Lindblom, *Politics and Markets: The World's Political-Economic Systems* (New York: Basic Books, 1977), p. 81.

19. Ibid., p. 31.

20. Nikolai Shmelev and Vladimir Popov, *The Turning Point* (New York: Doubleday, 1989), p. 170.

3 MARKET FAILURE AND GOVERNMENT FAILURE

The important thing for government is not to do things which individuals are doing already, and to do them a little better or worse; but to do those things which at present are not done at all.

John Maynard Keynes[1]

The market under ideal conditions does a good job of allocating resources to their best use. Yet there is a catch. We noted in Chapter 2 that economic exchange works best where everyone involved is a willing participant, but, of course, many exchanges do not work that way. They involve people without their consent or knowledge. Often faulty prices are to blame—they mislead people into inefficient exchanges. When exchanges are involuntary or ill-informed, the invisible hand falters. Rather than automatically lead individuals to help the group, self-serving behavior leads them to outcomes that harm the group (see Box 3–1).

If the invisible hand can falter, it follows that unfettered markets cannot solve all economic problems. In the real world, buying and selling can fall well short of what would happen in the utopian world of perfect competition. Prices do not reflect all available information, and unregulated individual activity produces effects nobody wants. These **market failures,** as they are known formally, are built into the way many markets actually work. Because of market failure, Adam Smith himself never took laissez-faire literally, to mean that *all* intervention in the market is bad. Smith urged some intervention as imperative and desirable.

Correcting Market Failure

Hierarchies, bureaucracies, and other consciously directed institutions have evolved to coordinate people when the market does not. In the United States, as

---

Box 3.1

Prisoner's Dilemma

Political economists explain market failure without changing their assumptions about how people act. Recall that political economists see people as rational actors. Unsatisfactory exchanges happen not because people are irrational, but because incentives get distorted and lead otherwise clearheaded people astray. When incentives are wrong, utility-maximizing behavior creates social harm instead of social good.

The metaphor for this eventuality is the **prisoner's dilemma** rather than the invisible hand. The dilemma is as follows. Think of two people arrested for a crime. They are both guilty, but the evidence against them is only circumstantial. Each prisoner is questioned separately and offered a reduced sentence in return for a confession. Each has to decide what to do. Should they confess or keep quiet? The best solution would be for neither prisoner to admit anything. Without one or the other's testimony, no case can be made against them. Neither will go to jail. Obviously, both prisoners ought to keep silent. Saying nothing creates the best collective outcome—the dropping of all charges.

The dilemma occurs because the individual incentive pulls the other way. Neither prisoner can afford to keep quiet due to the risk of being sold out by the other. Better to confess now in exchange for a reduced sentence. The logic of plea bargaining is ironclad. In isolation, both prisoners admit guilt and both go to jail. It is a result they would have rejected had they negotiated with the police together. To use the jargon of political economy, individual rational choice failed to maximize their collective utility (which would be for both to be set free for lack of evidence). The uncomfortable implication of the prisoner's dilemma is that reasonable people, acting in their own interest, cannot be counted on to create efficient social outcomes. Rational men and women compose a society that often acts irrationally.

Fortunately, in social life we have more chances to communicate than the hapless prisoners in the illustration. And, unlike those culprits, we get to play the game repeatedly. Society, in other words, has chances to learn from past mistakes to make better decisions now. Still, the prisoner's dilemma is perhaps as prevalent as the invisible hand. Individual incentives—especially price signals—often get distorted. Uncertainty is endemic.

---

in all capitalist countries, public decision making routinely replaces the market through (1) subsidies such as tax breaks and loan guarantees (which *encourage* business and consumers to make certain expenditures) and (2) a variety of regulations (which *require* business and consumers to make certain expenditures). These represent the carrot and the stick of public policy toward business.

Because human beings have figured ways around the market's failures, to accent the positive it has been suggested these failures might better be called "organizational successes."[2] We shall stick with the traditional term, remembering that market failure is not something about which anyone should be disappointed. It just means that under certain conditions, unregulated economic exchange is not efficient for society. These deficiencies are built into the way we interact in markets.

The fact that government has intervened in economic life does not prove it is a good idea. Conservatives (classical liberals) are doubtful. The case for state intervention in business affairs often rests on the idea that the state is a benevolent force. The state, acting for society, supposedly does what is best for all. But such an account of public policy making looks as improbable as perfect competition in the market. Is there not a gap between the theoretical rationale for state intervention and what happens in practice? The 1993 Nobel laureate, Douglass North, asserts: "Throughout most of history the State has not provided a framework conducive to economic growth. Indeed the Mafia would be a more accurate characterization of the State in the past than an organization concerned with 'the public good.'"[3]

Political economists point out that the political system has defects that are the analogy to defects in the market. Categorizing the economic shortcomings of states will occupy us at the end of this chapter. We will see how individual self-interest pursued in the political arena can result in public policies that are collectively wasteful. Well-intended attempts to fix the market can boomerang as people try to use the state to create or sustain market failures that will help them.

Some economic fundamentalists push the fact of state or government failure to its logical end. They see the state as parasitic, as a nonproductive sector that makes little or no positive contribution to society. As is usually true with strongly stated positions, this one is wrong. Government does add value to commercial and economic affairs, just not always. There are some things that are easier to do collectively, other things that are not. Managers need to understand how interventionism sometimes succeeds, and how it often falters, so they can plan and justify their political strategies.

Roles of the State

Market failure signifies that other means, not solely the market, need to be found to allocate resources and make related decisions. A method to make collective choice is required, and that generally means getting the **state** or the government involved.

States are organizations that embody legal order within geographic territories. They are the central element of the domestic political structure. Since they cannot support themselves with voluntary contributions, or by selling their services, states use authority to get the resources they need. Max Weber (1864–1920), the eminent sociologist, made the most widely accepted definition of the state:

> It possesses an administrative and legal order subject to change by legislation, to which the organized corporate activity of the administrative staff, which is also regulated by legislation, is oriented. This system of order claims binding authority, not only over the members of states, the citizens, most of whom have obtained membership by birth, but also to a very large extent, over all action taking place in the area of its jurisdiction. It is thus a compulsory association with a territorial basis.[4]

The term *state* is often used as a synonym for **nation,** but that is an imprecise application of the word. A nation is a people who share a common language and culture. They often have their own state (a nation state), but there are many nationalities (the Kurds in Iran, Iraq, and Turkey, for instance) who lack a separate state. Similarly, some states are multinational and incorporate different national groups. An example is Canada, made of English-speakers, French-speakers, and indigenous people. States' defining characteristic is having sovereign control of territory, and thus ultimate authority to make and enforce laws, including contracts and property rights.

Because, in Weber's terms, states possess a monopoly of legitimate force, business has no choice but to work with them. One challenge for managers operating in today's global environment is to determine how to handle different kinds of states, each of which has different characteristics and may pursue different economic strategies. Another challenge is to understand how rival firms sometimes work in partnership with states for competitive advantage.

Clouding matters is that the American state is not unitary. It is a federation of 51 smaller states, including the District of Columbia. Other federal systems include India, Australia, Canada, Germany, and Switzerland, but these are the exceptions. Most countries have a single, central state. Though the subnational units in a federal system like the United States lack sovereignty in international law, they have authority to enact public policy affecting business. New Hampshire, for example, deliberately tries to promote commercial activity by being the only state with neither an income tax nor a sales tax. California even has its own foreign policy, with trade offices all over the world.[5] Whenever misunderstanding is likely, we will employ the more precise term *state government* to refer to American state-level public institutions.

The state has taken on many roles that are important to business. These roles are rule maker, umpire, producer, buyer, promoter, guarantor, broker, regulator, and economic manager (see Table 3–1). The state makes the rules for the market and is the umpire that guarantees the rules are followed. It produces goods and services, and it buys much of the product of private companies. The state promotes the private sector with aid of various kinds. It guarantees investors, lenders, bank depositors, and other economic actors against risk, and it brokers new investments. The state regulates business activities to make sure they conform to rules prescribed, at least outwardly, in the public interest. The state tries to manage the economy to keep it running at full capacity without price inflation. We will be looking at these roles throughout this book.

Not all the state's roles in the economy are equally important, nor does the state perform them equally well. But their effects can be felt everywhere. Joseph Stiglitz (a member of President Clinton's Council of Economic Advisors) capsulizes the point: "Market failures are pervasive; it is only under exceptional circumstances that markets are efficient. The issue for the appropriate role of government is to identify the large market failures where there is scope for beneficial government intervention."[6]

TABLE 3–1   The State Plays Lots of Roles that Affect Business.

Rule maker: Government makes the rules of the game of economic competition. *Example:* The Commodities Futures Trading Commission issues new guidelines on the sale of derivatives (securities whose performance is based on other, underlying securities).

Umpire: Government resolves disputes over those rules. *Example:* The National Labor Relations Board decides that professors at Boston University are management and thus may not organize for collective bargaining.

Buyer: Government is a major market for private companies. *Example:* The U.S. Agency for International Development awards a contract to a consulting firm to run a rural development project in Africa.

Producer: Government produces public goods that help business, such as infrastructure and human capital, and also many privately sold, individually consumed goods and services, sometimes in competition with the private sector. *Example:* The Tennessee Valley Authority produces and sells electricity at cheap rates.

Promoter: Government promotes business through direct and indirect subsidies, on either a planned or ad hoc basis. *Example:* Cities and states subsidize professional sports teams by building municipal stadiums with public bonds.

Guarantor: Government insures business and individuals against many types of risks. *Example:* The Overseas Private Investment Corporation reimburses U.S. companies for lost property suffered as a result of the Iranian revolution.

Broker: Government is a middleman that brings companies and communities (including foreign countries) together. *Example:* The Massachusetts Film Office helps a Hollywood producer find in-state locations for a prospective film.

Regulator: Government regulates many facets of business, such as safety standards, pollution standards, and employment practices. *Example:* The Interstate Commerce Commission gives truckers the right to drive longer and heavier rigs on most public highways.

Economic manager: Government uses macroeconomic policy to try to maintain full employment and stable prices. *Example:* The Federal Reserve Bank raised interest rates several times in 1994 to dampen potential inflationary trends and defend the dollar.

The Major Market Failures

Political economists have found several sources of market failure.[7] The more important market failures relevant for managers are listed in Table 3–2. They are discussed in the sections that follow.

Public Goods

Adam Smith understood the need for government to intervene in economic life. He proposed three "duties of the sovereign," three jobs for government on which almost everyone agrees. Because of market failure, none of these items is provided by the market in the right amount. They are "first, the duty of protecting the society from the violence and invasion of other independent societies; secondly, the duty of protecting, as far as possible, every member of the society from the injustice or oppression of every other member of it, or the duty of establishing an exact administration of justice; and thirdly, the duty of erecting and maintaining certain public works and certain public institutions. . ."[8]

Smith's three duties of government—to defend against foreign invasion, to protect life and property, and to maintain public works and institutions—all share aspects of what political economists call **public goods.** These are items (both tangible and intangible) that people use together. Public goods have value that

---

TABLE 3–2   Markets Can Fail to Work in Many Ways.

Public goods: Markets do not provide education, infrastructure, and other public goods in ample quantity due to the problem of free riding. *Example:* Private companies may choose not to train their workers for fear they will lose any trained workers to competitors.

Externalities: Markets do not protect people from the actions of others. *Example:* Secondhand smoke inflicts costs on nonsmokers who had nothing to do with the purchase or sale of cigarettes.

Monopoly: Due to obstacles to free entry, economies of scale, and other factors, markets may be dominated by one or a few companies that may try to take advantage of consumers. *Example:* Airlines charge very high fares to out-of-the-way communities where they face little competition.

Information asymmetry: Markets cannot work well when consumers are ignorant. *Example:* Lacking scientific knowledge, consumers can be enticed to buy dangerous patent medicines.

Agent misdirection: Agents need not act in their principals' best interest in a market. *Example:* Brokers sometimes mislead elderly clients into making high-risk investments that are not appropriate for their investment goals.

Social goals: Markets may not promote social goals, such as providing merit goods. *Example:* Real estate developers do not build homes for the indigent.

Inequality: Markets may be inequitable. *Example:* People with inherited wealth get to live extravagantly without working, while many hardworking people live in poverty.

Economic instability: Markets may not provide full employment, stable prices, or economic growth. *Example:* The transition to a market economy in Russia is accompanied by a loss of jobs and a collapsing currency.

---

spills over onto people without their assent or awareness. Decentralized, competitive markets do not produce as many public goods as people want. Why not? Because, in Smith's words, they are things that "can never be for the interest of any individual, or small number of individuals, to erect and maintain; because the profit could never repay the expense to any individual or small number of individuals, though it may frequently do much more than repay it to a great society."[9]

Since they are a major rationale for government involvement in economic life, let us look at public goods more closely. How do they differ from **private goods**? Political economists identify two attributes of goods to judge how they should be provided, through the market or through government. These attributes are **excludability** and **subtractability**.[10]

Excludability refers to the degree to which a potential user of a good can be excluded from its use by a potential supplier. While many items are easy to exclude people from using, public goods are not that way. They are products that are hard to render inaccessible; to provide them for one person is to provide them for all.

Take national defense and the legal system, both public goods singled out by Smith in *The Wealth of Nations*. Each is low on excludability: they cover everyone living in a territory, whoever they are. Nobody can be blocked from that coverage—not even people who object on principle to military spending or the legal system can escape! Some public works—lighthouses are a classic example—are similar in affecting many people's lives, with or without permission. A lighthouse owner has no say over the use of his service; every ship that passes by benefits.

Subtractability, also called rivalness, refers to the extent to which one person's consuming a good subtracts from another's ability to use the good without raising production cost. Like excludability, subtractability is relative. Goods have greater and lesser degrees of rivalness of consumption.

When an item is high on subtractability, two or more consumers cannot use the item at the same time. Many consumer goods are this way. By contrast, when something is low on subtractability, many people can use it without depleting it or lessening each other's use of it. Again, national defense and the legal system are good examples: after an immigrant moves to a new country, his or her being there does not mean less national defense or justice to go around for everyone else. Communication facilities can be similar. Take the lighthouse again, or a television transmitter. Extra users do not detract from others' enjoyment of the good. The lighthouse beam or the television signal does not get used up by more consumption.

The two types, of course, blend into each other. At the extremes, few pure public or pure private goods exist. Many private goods have a public side or **externality** to them. (Externalities are the nonpriced element in a transaction. We shall discuss them shortly.) The types refer to central tendencies, not mutually exclusive categories.

Political economy sees little reason for government to produce private goods, which business will provide itself. But government must take steps to assure the supply of public goods because the market will not. This does not mean that government has to take on the role of producer and supply all such items itself; but it does need to act as a buyer, promoter, guarantor, or regulator to encourage private sector suppliers—and to prevent abuses by companies delegated these responsibilities.

Problems of Collective Action

Public goods are valuable, even indispensable for civilized life. Why is the market unable to produce enough of these useful items? A major reason is **free riding.** The impracticality to exclude means people have access without paying. Few investors will want to go into the venture of making or selling something for which people have no reason to pay. Most profit will be captured by would-be consumers who can share the good for free—for example the lighthouse mentioned earlier. The inability to divide collectively consumed goods into units for individual use also deters investors, by making it difficult to sell the goods and recover cost. Consumers may need the good, but they have too little pecuniary incentive to get together themselves to provide it. The paradox of collective inertia may result, where no one seems able to cooperate despite widespread agreement that group action is needed to get to a common goal.[11]

The free-rider problem is illustrated by public television broadcasting in the United States. It is a nearly pure public good—anybody can watch for free at no harm to anyone else. People who watch agree that the news and entertainment on PBS are excellent, and viewers like that they are not subjected to the tedium of advertising breaks. Yet, most viewers do not donate money to public broadcasting, despite regular appeals to the audience's conscience during fund-raising drives. During these drives, the stations even offer private goods (coffee mugs, T-shirts, program guides) as an incentive to contribute. The government sweetens the offer by making it tax-deductible. Still, too much free riding or shirking takes place for the stations to support themselves, and public broadcasting has to rely on government for much of its funding. (The British solve the problem by charging people an annual fee for the right to have a television antenna, the proceeds of which help support the BBC.)

Free riding is related to the issue of **transaction cost,** the cost of specifying and enforcing contracts. A transaction cost does not directly benefit either party to an exchange; it makes the exchange more laborious and less attractive. It is the parallel to friction in mechanical systems. Perfect competition takes place in an imagined world of frictionless exchange, but transaction cost is not trivial in the real world.[12] According to one effort to measure its size in the United States, 45 percent of national income goes to pay for transacting (banking, insurance, legal services, accounting services, and the like).[13]

High transaction cost can encourage free riding. People might agree in principle that they need something to use collectively. Yet if they are a large group, organizing to provide the public good carries a high price. All parties need to invest time and effort to make the deal happen. The negotiations are apt to collapse before everyone can reach agreement on their individual contribution and compensation; many groups do not get off the ground to provide public goods.

The failure of private action to supply public goods is strong ground for having the government supply them. Coercion is imperative—for the benefit of all, all are forced to buy public goods with taxes levied on the community. With private goods, where private incentives do function and free riding does not happen, a presumptive case exists for letting the market do the job.

A major difficulty with government providing any goods is too little feedback from consumers. There may be a bias toward overproduction, as opposed to the underproduction that distinguishes the free market situation. We will return to the problem of providing the right amount of government services repeatedly in later chapters. The appropriate policy may be a mix of public and private enterprise, for instance, charging user fees for the good or licensing a private company to supply it.

Public goods should not be confused with *publicly provided* goods or services. The two need not be the same, for governments often provide private (individually consumed) goods to people. Examples include food stamps, social security payments, and health care benefits. From the political economist's vantage point, these examples are mainly private goods because they can be divided up and restricted to certain individuals. Alternatively, private foundations and charities may supply public goods, such as new technology or knowledge everyone can share. The defining trait of economic goods is not where the items come from—the public or the private sector—but how they are consumed.

Externalities or Neighborhood Effects

For many transactions, the cost or benefit spills over onto third parties who are not directly involved in the transaction. Alfred Marshall in 1890 began to call these spillovers *externalities* because they are external to market exchanges, and thus do not figure in producers' and consumers' internal accounting. They also are called neighborhood effects. Externalities lead to prices that do not reflect a good's full social cost or benefit. The market misfires. Without accurate price signals, private producers will make too many goods with external costs, and too few goods with external benefits.

A classic example of an external cost is pollution. If a power plant produces soot as a byproduct of making electricity, that soot imposes a cost on people in the neighborhood. They have to spend money to clean their windows more often, repaint their houses, and so forth. The neighbors of the power plant do not normally get compensated by the utility company for these costs. Because the company does not need to consider its neighbors' cleaning and painting costs, it charges a lower price for electricity than it would otherwise. This lower price, in turn, invites users of electricity to use more than they would if they also had to pay for damages to the utility's neighbors.

In a world of perfect competition, the victim of an externality could bargain with its perpetrators.[14] In such a world, for instance, the utility company's neighbors would simply go to court to recover the damages caused by pollution. These civil suits also would encourage the utility company to cut back its harmful emissions by raising the tangible cost of dirtying the environment. Alas, bargaining this way is not feasible in the real world. The transaction cost is too high. Most people do not have the time and patience to pursue legal action against polluting companies. Instead, we call on government to play the part of regulator and stop pollution at its source.

External benefit (also known as positive externality) is similar. Smith gives an excellent example. He singled out education as a critical duty of government. At first glance, education seems a typical private good—it is individually consumed, markets exist for it, and so forth. Yet, a large social gain also is associated with the solitary act of getting educated. The higher the average level of education in society, the more apt society is to be productive, to be adaptable, to be capable of governing itself. Smith recognized that education had too many public side effects to be left a private, voluntary affair. So compelling is the community's stake in education, government everywhere supplies it routinely. Most countries, consistent with Smith's logic, give consumers little choice and make education compulsory.

Careful readers will see a link here with the definition of public goods made earlier. In fact, another way to define public goods is they are items with large positive externalities. The internal cost of producing public goods is too high for individuals to bear, because it is impossible to charge third parties for their full gain from the public goods.

In sum, external effects are a deficiency in the market that often attract government action.[15] The solution is for government to tax or regulate activities creating negative externalities and subsidize activities creating positive ones. Officials, for instance, may order the power company to cut emissions or offer tax breaks to educators to open private schools.

Monopoly and Imperfect Competition

Not all real markets are competitive. Often, one seller (or a few sellers plotting together) is large enough to dictate terms to buyers, to try actively to influence prices rather than take them as given. A single seller is called a monopoly. Because it is unchallenged in the market, a monopoly can restrict its production or sales in an arbitrary way. To make the most profit, a producer in this position is tempted to make artificial shortages of things buyers want and sell them at inflated prices. Consumers have no other choice, and the resulting consumption pattern is far from optimum.

Sometimes monopolies are simply the winners in the market. One firm drives its rivals out of business by being the best. Other times, monopolies get their position by unfair means. One firm conspires with others to stop competing and combine forces. In either case, government often intervenes to make sure large companies play by the rules and do not use their market power to crush potential rivals and cheat consumers.

Situations exist when having one supplier is just the obvious way to provide a service at least cost. Monopoly, in other words, can be the best way to organize some industries. So-called natural monopoly situations are created when the fixed cost is very high. Public utilities (gas, electricity, local telephones, cable television) and mass transit (trains, trolleys) fall into this last category of monopoly. All face large fixed costs—constructing and maintaining sewer lines, utility poles, rights-of-way, and so forth. Think of the extra expense of having two competing gas companies, each with its own network of tanks and gas mains, or two subways, each maintaining a separate tunnel system.

Under these conditions, competition may raise, not lower, the cost to provide a service. Having a solo company allows fixed costs to be spread out. Governments either own these natural monopolies outright (the preferred public policy in most of the world) or they set up public service commissions to make them provide good service and stop them from charging too much for doing so (common in the United States).

Limited or Lopsided Information

Efficient exchange presumes a rich base of information. Yet, information about the quality of goods is neither free nor easy to get. With so many different items for sale in a modern economy, and so many sales taking place infrequently, buyers cannot be well-informed across the range of purchases. Ignorance is not bliss when one is dealing with complex, potentially dangerous items (machines, medicine, and so on), and when consumers for one reason or another have difficulty making informed choices (as happens to minors, illiterates, and so on).

To compensate for this obstacle to efficient exchange, people have mobilized to get public officials to help. Government may order that commodities be tested for safety and effectiveness. It may set standards for labeling. It may restrict sales to trained people. It may force manufacturers to recall products that prove hazardous. In the unreal world of perfect competition, such actions would be redundant; in the real world of poorly informed, harried consumers, they are a way to screen people from making dangerous or costly mistakes.

A related problem is that information about goods is never shared evenly. Producers or sellers are apt to know more about the things they sell than do their customers. They make the product and deal with it everyday. Customers, especially in consumer markets, rarely have as deep contact with the product and are less familiar with it. To the extent that producers are self-interested, they also may be tempted to conceal some information, to act in an opportunistic manner. Political economists label the result **adverse selection.**

An interesting illustration is the market for used cars. Harvard professor Thomas Schelling describes the situation as follows:

> [T]he seller of a used car knows whether or not it is a lemon; the buyer has to play the averages, knowing only that some cars are lemons but not whether the particular car he's buying is. Buyers will pay only a price that reflects the average frequency of lemons in the used-car crop. That average is a high price for a lemon but understates the worth of the better cars offered on the market. The owners of the better cars are reluctant to sell at a price that makes allowances for the lemons other people are selling . . . In the end, the market may disappear.[16]

Whenever information is skewed the way it is in the used car market, informed choice is difficult. The private transactions that follow get thrown off kilter. Again, government often enters the picture to try to level the field of play between buyers and sellers. Some jurisdictions even have "lemon laws" specifically covering defective automobiles, to try to improve that market.

Agency Problems

Adverse selection touches on another market failure: the **principal–agent problem.**[17] In complex societies we often have to rely on someone (an agent) to act on our behalf. We (the principals in these transactions) delegate decision-making authority to the agent. Agency relations pervade economics and politics. The link between client and attorney, shareholder and manager, and citizen and bureaucrat are illustrations.

No real-life agent is completely impartial, of course. Their interests and those of their principals may diverge. Being economically rational, they are not going to surrender their welfare to someone else, and this is a source of market failure.

If agents have some hidden information, they may use it to mislead the person they are supposed to oblige. A stockbroker, for instance, stands to make commissions by churning a client's (the principal's) portfolio, though a buy-and-hold strategy might better serve the client. There are subtle pressures on the bro-

TABLE 3–3   **Economic Agents May Try to Take Advantage of Their Principals.**

Agent	Principal	Result	Example
Hides information	Cannot evaluate agent's action	Adverse choice	Person taking out health insurance conceals health problems
Hides action	Cannot observe agent's action	Moral hazard	Person taking out health insurance engages in unhealthy behavior

Source: Adapted from Barry Mitnick, "Fiduciary Rationality and Public Policy: The Theory of Agency and Some Consequences," paper presented at the 1972 Annual Meeting of the American Political Science Association, New Orleans.

ker to misrepresent the facts. To put it differently, the principal can see what the agent is doing but is too ignorant to judge whether it really is advantageous. There is a monitoring problem that leads to adverse selection (see Table 3–3).

Principal–agent relations can create another related market failure—what political economists call **moral hazard.** This problem entails a lack of effort by an agent. Moral hazard arises when the agent's actions are unseen. In contrast to adverse selection, where the agent's deeds can be observed though not evaluated due to hidden information, here the obstacle is observation rather than evaluation. The principal could assess the agent if he or she could see better what the agent is doing. Unfortunately, the principal's view is blocked.

A routine instance of moral hazard is slack effort from workers, who employers cannot easily watch. Workers usually have an interest in working below peak energy and can shield their level of exertion from outside scrutiny. Despite modern supervisory systems, workers themselves often know best who among their number does his or her share and who does not.

Government tries to offset agent misdirection by introducing rules to punish agents for acting against principals' interests. There are public policies that penalize lawyers, brokers, accountants, and other professionals who make undue gains from their privileged position. These professionals often are compelled to take extra care to divulge information to their clients, to give them extra time to reconsider decisions, and to do other things to ensure impartiality and fairness. Public policies to curb agency abuses are not flawless, but they do inhibit the worst misconduct.

To illustrate, the Securities and Exchange Commission (SEC) enforces rules against insider trading of stocks and bonds. **Insider trading** is the practice of obtaining information from inside a company and using it for personal financial gain. Managers and consultants are in the best position to take advantage of such information, especially during corporate mergers, though it hurts small investors. During the takeover flurry of the 1980s, many prominent financiers, such as Dennis Levine, Ivan Boesky, and Michael Milkin, were prosecuted for not living up to their fiduciary duty by taking advantage of inside information. The bad publicity and law enforcement activity by the SEC dampened insider trading but could not eliminate it completely (see Box 3–2).

Social Goals

The market can be deficient by generating unpopular results. Some products of unregulated exchanges are going to be viewed, at certain times and in certain places, as immoral. Gambling, alcohol, narcotics, prostitution, pornography, abortion, and birth control are all examples of goods that sometimes have been condemned. While no one denies these products meet a real demand, society (that is, a politically dominant group or coalition) may not want them sold under any circumstance. Thus, governments are called on to license or regulate the trade in goods and services that offend customary ethical standards. Public policies run the gamut from sin taxes on tobacco products to the death penalty for so-called drug kingpins.

Alternatively, markets may not produce and distribute enough merit goods—basic needs such as water, food, clothing, shelter, and health care. These items are the reverse of the morally suspect items just mentioned. Conventional morality decrees that people, as a matter of right, ought to be able to eat, put a roof over their heads, and so forth. Not everyone in society can afford, or even wants, merit goods. Yet these goods are considered so important that government (acting for society) often steps in to provide them to citizens irrespective of ability to pay.

This market deficiency is the rationale behind the modern **welfare state**—the social insurance system of food stamps, public housing, family assistance, and free medical care for the poor. Not only does the government secure these

---

Box 3.2

Insider Trading Laws Are Unusually Strict in the United States

Insider trading refers to unlawful buying or selling of securities by persons who have material, non-public information about a company. Material information is information that could have a substantial impact on the price of particular stocks or bonds. In the United States, people who have inside knowledge that could affect security prices may not profit from it. They also have a duty to refrain from divulging confidential information to someone else. Anyone receiving a tip about, say, a proposed merger or acquisition is barred from using it, too.

These legal demands are covered by the Securities and Exchange Act of 1934. They are part of the larger effort to improve the market for stocks and bonds that followed the financial bust of 1929. The penalties and classes of securities that can be considered in legal action have been expanded in the Insider Trading Sanctions Act of 1984 and the Insider Trading and Securities Fraud Enforcement Act of 1988. Violators risk heavy fines and jail time.

The United States has unusually strict insider trading rules. Several famous Wall Street figures went to prison for insider trading associated with the merger boom in the 1980s. Many other nations have no such public policies against trading securities based on privileged information, or they are less vigorous in enforcing the policies that are on the books.

goods for people; it may even force people to consume them. For instance, there are people who, for some reason, prefer to sleep on the street rather than in shelters for the homeless provided at public expense. Legal powers exist to declare some of these people mentally incompetent and to compel them to enter institutions.

A national welfare state in America dates from the New Deal. Food aid using surplus commodities and subsidized public housing were both started in 1933. Two years later, unemployment insurance, Social Security, and aid to children started. The welfare state surged again under the Great Society proposed by President Lyndon Johnson (1963–69). That period saw the start of the food stamp program (vouchers for basic items) and limited public health insurance for the elderly (Medicare) and the poor (Medicaid).

The bargain among workers, managers, and civil servants that was implicit in the welfare state had pluses for business. By guaranteeing people's income, the welfare state made it easier for companies to reduce their labor force to adjust to changing market conditions. The welfare state also relieved companies of pressure to provide fringe benefits to their employees, since the government was already doing it. Finally, making workers feel more secure helped nullify any radical menace to the private enterprise system.

Despite these advantages for business, during the 1970s most rich countries started having second thoughts about their welfare states. Having government play this guarantor role is expensive. With the surge of world economic competition, many wondered whether rich countries could afford to be so generous. Companies and factories in the less developed countries did not have the same costs. Did not social programs tie up too many resources and handicap welfare states on world markets? The answer seems a partial yes.[18]

The major negative economic effects of the welfare state are said to be:

It hurts investment. The welfare state diverts resources from production to consumption, making it harder for business to update its facilities and compete.

It creates inefficiency. The welfare state stops or slows resources, especially labor, from moving to industry that earns the highest reward on the international market.

It saps motivation. The welfare state weakens the incentive for employees to work, innovate, and cooperate with management.

Many countries, notably the United States and Great Britain, tried to hold down or cut back social spending in the 1980s. These efforts may have kept the welfare cost in the United States and Britain below the costs of their European competitors, but social spending continued to creep upward everywhere.[19]

Inequality and Unfairness

Related to the problem of merit goods, individuals' share of income in the market mirror to a degree the assets they hold before they enter the market. Wealthy people have the edge, one that is often thought unfair. People born in poverty have fewer chances to get ahead. Limited education, lack of personal contacts, and isolated neighborhoods rig the odds against them. Governments can take the rough edges off the income distribution through transfer payments (the social welfare programs just mentioned) and progressive taxes (high rates for richer people).

Several specific arguments can be made favoring economic equality. Sharing between the haves and the have-nots has been interpreted as a kind of public good. It enhances the utility of the rich by satisfying their sense of fair play. Leveling the economic pyramid also may add to collective efficiency, given that the economic principle of diminishing returns implies that a poor person gets more benefit from an extra dollar than does a rich person. Equality may reduce the threat to social stability—a main cause of riots and revolution is people's sense that they are deprived compared to others.[20] Equality may enhance productivity by reducing the stress and resentment felt by people at the bottom. More equal societies, like Germany and Japan, tend to have the fastest productivity and income growth.

All governments intervene to change income distribution. Controversial is how far they ought to go. Conflicts arise because different people put forth conflicting claims on the economy's benefits and burdens. In the 1800s, for instance, influential Social Darwinists said no even to minimal help from government. Let the fit survive, they argued, and allow others to perish. Under no circumstances should anyone interfere with the market's process of natural selection. Most Americans disagree with such a severe position and feel that justice dictates a safety net be created to save people from cold and hunger. Few Americans go to the opposite extreme and say justice demands complete equality. Most of us think work ought to be rewarded more highly than idleness.

Other developed countries usually seek more level income distributions than we do. Consider the share of income earned by the richest 20 percent of the population compared to the poorest 20 percent. In 1992 the top 20 percent of American households received 11 times as much income (including all forms of income such as welfare benefits) as the bottom 20 percent. The ratios are far lower overseas. Germany and Japan have ratios of just 4 and 5.5, respectively.[21] About one American family in six lives below the official poverty line in the United States (set at $13,924 for a family of four in 1991). That is two to four times the rate in Europe.[22]

The gap between rich and poor is widening in the United States. Real incomes of America's poor have been sinking for two decades, driven by changes in technology and competition from developing countries that have made demand for unskilled workers drop. U.S. public policy has abetted these trends by encouraging a flexible labor market (see Chapter 12). Inequality is widening in other developed countries, too, but not as fast. They have done more to offset economic forces with powerful labor unions, centralized wage bargaining, and high minimum wages (see Chapter 6).

Economic Instability

The market is prone to boom and bust. Part of the business cycle, the market's downside serves the useful purpose of clearing out inefficient firms. But it also imposes pain on people who lose their investments or their jobs. While idle resources can and should move to better uses, they do so with friction. Some individual people never recover from economic downturns.

Worse, the Great Depression of the 1930s hinted that the market could get stuck at the bottom of the business cycle. The self-regulating mechanism did not seem to work as expected. In the United States, GNP went into a free fall between 1929 and 1933, dropping 30 percent. It barely budged for several following years. Economies need not rebound on their own, or at least not fast enough to avoid social unrest.

John Maynard (later Lord) Keynes (1883–1946), the most famous economist of the 20th century, identified the problem as the "paradox of thrift." This paradox is another example of rational individual behavior leading to bad social outcomes. When people think their jobs are at risk, it makes sense for them to cut back expenditures and put more money aside. Unfortunately, when everyone spends less, people really do lose their jobs. It is a self-fulfilling prophecy. The answer, Keynes showed, is public borrowing and spending **(fiscal policy)** to get the economy going again.

According to the precepts of **Keynesian economics,** in a weak economy with idle workers the government should spend to put them back to work. The military buildup for World War II, for example, was what finally pulled the United States out of the Great Depression. To be a stimulus, such spending must be financed by borrowing. One factor in the Great Depression was that the government did not borrow. Faced with falling tax receipts, the consequence of rising unemployment, federal and state authorities cut spending rather than go into debt. Keynesian theory holds that the government's response was backward from what needed to be done and that it prolonged the 1930s crisis needlessly.

Since the 1940s, American and other national governments have taken seriously the role of managing the economy. They self-consciously try to keep people working—hopefully without allowing the general level of prices to rise. Following Keynes's ideas, they often resort to deficit public spending to fight economic slowdowns. Governments are not always good in this role of economic manager. The early 1980s were a period of stagflation in many countries, marked by rising unemployment and inflation.

Today's governments are prone to run deficits even in good times. The last U.S. budget surplus was in 1969. When President Reagan took office in 1981, the government owed $26 for every $100 of GNP; when President Bush left office in 1993, the level was twice as high—$53 for every $100 of GNP.[23] No nation can indefinitely increase its debt faster than its ability to produce income. As the government goes deeper into the red, it needs more receipts to pay back earlier loans. The result is that our elected officials have less leeway than before to use Keynesian techniques to revive a stalled economy.

Business leaders have long professed that deficit spending has gone too far in the United States.[24]   Public borrowing absorbs private saving, saving that financial markets would otherwise make available to business.   Thus, U.S. companies may have a hard time raising the funds they need to buy new factories and machines.   The gravity of the crowding-out effect of public borrowing is controversial, but it may raise the cost of borrowing.[25]   More clearly, deficit spending has led to borrowing from foreigners who do have extra savings, which has added to the country's international trading woes (see Chapter 17).[26]

Ironically, business leaders are partly responsible for the fiscal problem. Public indebtedness has not stopped them from lobbying for policies to help their particular companies, policies that add to the debt burden.   (We explore that subject in Chapter 8.)

How States Fail

State intervention is central to the functioning of today's market economies. Markets can exist in the absence of government support and cooperation—witness Russia where the central state is fragmented and powerless, yet a private sector is busily establishing itself anyway.   But markets that exist outside government purview invite criminals to take them over, which is just what is happening in Russia.   Effective government is needed to block cheating and guarantee fairness in the world of trade.

This truth does not mean state intervention in business affairs always works well, however.   Far from it.   Public action may even move society further from a utopian balance point than private competition does.   While sometimes described in textbooks as impartial guardians of society's welfare, states err often and repeatedly, making society worse off even as they help favored groups and individuals.

Conservative or so-called neoliberal political economists do not think these errors, called government failures (also nonmarket failures), happen at random.   A **government failure** is a miscarriage of public policy that has a net social cost.   It is the political analogue of a market failure, which is a private transaction that has net social cost.   Government failures occur when a public transaction goes awry so the advantage for one group is less than the loss imposed on other groups.[27]

A branch of political economy known as **public choice** gives insight into government failures.   Though not a full explanation of politics, public choice provides a convincing portrayal of how government sometimes goes wrong.   The theory uses the same assumptions about individuals that we have been using—self-interest and rationality.   Like market failures, these defects in the political process are the logical consequence of individual efforts to increase personal utility.[28]

Rent-Seeking Behavior

A common denominator in many government failures is what political economists call **rent seeking**—attempts to exploit the state for private gain.   In the language of political economy, **economic rent** is income accruing to a factor of production above what that factor could earn in its next best use in a competitive market. It is a payment to a resource owner above his or her **opportunity cost**—the cost of forgone opportunities. Economic rent arises when the supply of something is fixed, so a higher price does not spark an increase in the quantity supplied.

Economic rent is usually associated with the use of land. Land is in fixed supply; the quantity of land does not change no matter how high a price is offered for using it. But economic rent is a broader concept that goes beyond land use. It applies to any situation where people can make more than normal profits (the minimum return to inputs that is necessary to keep them in a given activity). Monopolies, for example, are apt to earn extraordinarily large profits due to the economic rent they can capture from their market-dominating position.

Government action often spawns economic rent. Take, for instance, **licensing.** Licensing is a privilege awarded by government to do something that is otherwise unlawful.[29] States license many jobs, from health care to taxicab driving to barbering (see Table 3–4). You may not practice medicine, drive a cab, or cut hair without official permission.

By restricting the supply of doctors, taxi drivers, and barbers, states create economic rent. These jobs pay more than they would otherwise, due solely to the state intervention. Licensing may serve socially useful purposes, such as protecting public safety by keeping out unqualified persons, but it also rewards some jobs unevenly. The holders of these licenses naturally want to keep standards high to limit the ranks of potential competitors.

Other examples of public policies that create economic rent include franchises, permits, tax breaks, subsidies, and tariffs. All generate value for those

---

TABLE 3–4   Do These Occupations Need to Be Licensed in the Public Interest?

Licensed occupation	Number of states that regulate through licensing	Licensed occupation	Number of states that regulate through licensing
Auctioneer	24	Massage therapist	15
Boiler inspector	26	Nursing home administrator	49
Chauffeur	34	Pest control applicator	23
Collection agent	22	Private detective	35
Driving instructor	40	Shorthand reporter	13
Elevator inspector	12	Social worker	20
Guide	24	Surveyor	49
Hearing aid dealer	41	Tree surgeon	11
Landscape architect	35	Watchmaker	10
Librarian	23	Watchman/guard	9
Marriage counselor	6	Well driller	31

Source: Theodore J. Lowi and Benjamin Ginsberg, *American Government,* 2nd ed. (New York: Norton, 1992), p. 648.

groups or individuals favored by the policy. But the policy also may lead to a misallocation of resources and other inefficiencies that impose sacrifices on other groups and individuals. Public choice theory holds that people, being rational, devote themselves to getting the state to adopt public policies that will benefit them while shifting the cost onto everyone else. Humans are rent seekers, just as they are profit seekers. People naturally spend some of their resources on winning government handouts and transfers of various kinds, and they are not overly concerned with who pays for their gain.

According to the theory of public choice, rent seeking by itself adds nothing to social product and has an opportunity cost in lost production. It does not entail new productive activity, just an effort to capture the potential income generated by government intervention in the economy. Resources spent pursuing economic rent are wasted for society. Human energy gets redirected from creating wealth to fighting over its distribution. Instead of concentrating on satisfying their patients, doctors are tempted, say, to work on government to limit the number of foreign-trained physicians who may practice medicine. Instead of modernizing their cab fleets, cab medallion owners use their time and money to keep more taxi medallions from being granted to potential competitors. On average, the people at large lose.

How big is the cost to society? The estimates vary. For the United States, about the lowest figure is 3 percent of the GNP per year lost to rent seeking. Other estimates are in the range of 5 percent to 12 percent of GNP, though some go as high as 25 percent.[30] In other words, by pursuing government benefits and subsidies, Americans make themselves at least 3 percent poorer than they otherwise would be—and perhaps much more.

Not all rent seeking is a waste for society, however. In a political system, as opposed to the marketplace, decision makers have to be pleaded with, tempted, even badgered by constituents. How else are they to learn what constituents want? Nobel prize–winning economist Gary Becker observes that rent seeking sometimes serves other useful purposes. When groups try for government handouts or favors, they may accidently prevent policies that would cause social harm or promote policies that serve a social good. For instance, the soviet economy would have performed worse than it did had corruption not greased the wheels of decision making and overcome many central controls of the economy.[31] So rent seeking need not be socially inefficient, though often it is.

Rent seeking is featured in five aspects of the neoliberal critique of the state—the self-serving behavior of interest groups, politicians, and voters; the lack of feedback from consumers and dominance of agencies by bureaucrats; plus the near certainty that policies will not play out as expected. These government failures are summarized in Table 3–5.

Interest Groups and Lobbying

Lobbying is the classic example of rent-seeking behavior. Special interests exist in all political systems, and they proliferate in democracies. As James Q. Wil-

---

TABLE 3–5   Like Markets, the State Can Fail to Meet the Public Interest for Several Reasons.

Lobbying: Organized pressure groups work to take advantage of the unorganized. *Example:* Agricultural interests obtain government price supports for their crops, paid for by taxpayers.

Inadequate feedback: Public employees are not given clear signals from their clients about how they are doing and have little incentive to satisfy clients' needs. Example: Mediocre service from the U.S. Postal Service.

Office seeking: Professional politicians are tempted to mislead or buy off constituents to win elections. *Example:* Republican congressional candidates run on a "Contract with America" that calls for tax cuts, increased military spending, and a balanced budget—without saying how they would do these things.

Voting: Voters are poorly informed and apathetic. *Example:* Less than half the American electorate turns out on election day, meaning majority opinion may not be reflected when ballots are counted.

Unintended consequences: No one can accurately foresee the outcome of public policy. *Example:* Efforts to curb illegal immigration by getting employers to check employees' records fail due to a brisk trade in forged documents and too little staffing by the Immigration and Naturalization Service.

---

son, former president of the American Political Science Association and now professor of management at the University of California at Los Angeles, points out, the benefit of any government program is often concentrated on a small segment of the population, while the cost is dispersed among taxpayers. The narrowly affected group has a strong incentive to organize and lobby to approve or keep that particular program. The taxpayers are less motivated to resist, since the cost to the individual of any single program is usually small.[32] Government failure results.

A good example is the import quota on sugar. It benefits a handful of domestic sugar producers while costing consumers $1 billion a year. This quota survives because the $5 average cost per person is so small few notice it.[33] The beneficiaries are well aware of the sugar quota and maintain pressure to keep it. Foreign sugar producers, who do have a direct interest in changing this policy, have too little influence on U.S. internal politics to make a difference.

Another negative consequence of interest group lobbying is thought to be a deficit in the public budget (see Box 3–3). Once won, a government benefit will be defended against other claimants for resources, which tends to push up government spending without corresponding tax increases.

Too Little Feedback

As we saw earlier in Chapter 2, a competitive market constantly gives feedback. Firms that supply products that are not wanted learn about it quickly because their products go unsold. There is a link between revenue and cost. The funds necessary to sustain a firm are ready only while the firm is successful in the marketplace.[34]

Box 3.3

Why the Public Sector Grows

Many explanations have been given for the seemingly interminable rise of public spending: surging demand for government services, the tendency of programs, once started, to continue even after they have outlasted their usefulness, the increased complexity of modern problems.

At the heart of the public spending problem may, however, be another factor, what William Baumol calls the "cost disease of personal services." Baumol shows how **productivity** in personal services grows more slowly over time than productivity in manufacturing or primary production.[1] Productivity is the ratio between economic output and input. Today's factory workers, farmers, and miners are vastly more productive than those of 100 years ago. New machines and methods of organization empower them to turn out many more products per unit of effort.

Service workers have not made similar gains. Their work is less subject to mechanization so their output does not rise the same way. Consider a teacher. While audiovisual equipment, computers, and the like may make teaching easier, the underlying technology has changed little since Plato's Academy. No substitute exists for one-on-one interaction between teacher and student. Thus, the average teacher's productivity is roughly the same now as it ever was.

The problem for government is that it specializes in services with a high level of personal input. Teaching, social services, health care, police, and fire fighting are all labor-intensive handicrafts. In such jobs it is hard to change the ratio of input to output. Productivity in government thus lags behind other sectors for reasons that have little to do with bad management or bureaucracy.

The inevitable result is that the cost of government rises faster than average. For people working in the public sector to have a modern standard of living, the relative cost of their services must be greater than it used to be. Why? Because productivity in other sectors has not stood still, and neither have wages. This differential pushes up public sector wages even while public sector productivity is stagnant.

---

[1] The first place these ideas appeared in print was William Baumol, "Macroeconomics and Unbalanced Growth," *American Economic Reviews* 57 (1967), pp. 415–26.

This feedback loop does not exist in the same way in the public sector. Government agencies usually do not sell their services or have to turn a profit, so their output is not evaluated by the price mechanism. Nor is there a direct connection between demand and the funds used by the agency. Funding comes out of the general budget, and the level is set by political debate. The division between those who use the output of public agencies, and those who pay for it, reduces accountability. Citizens/voters are far removed from the process since they only get to vote every few years for a representative, who in turn stands for a bundle of policies that may not have been made clear to the electorate. Since profitability is not a consideration, it is difficult for a public manager to assess the performance of an agency. There may be little incentive to innovate, respond to consumer/citizen needs, maintain quality, or hold down cost.

Instead the civil servant has incentives to be an empire builder.[35] A larger agency means more opportunities for promotion, more funding, more influence.

Public agencies rarely go out of business, even when they have outlived their usefulness. Like any rational actor, bureaucrats are apt to resist change that threatens to reduce their prestige and power. By reaching a critical mass in size, most government agencies can perpetuate themselves by creating a constituency of employees and clients. The result may not be what the public really wants. Public agencies thus are said to tend to grow fat and indifferent to their clients' needs.

Politicians

In democratic states, elected officials are supposed to represent their constituents' views. This is a typical principal–agent relation—a type of link between people that pervades economics and politics. Always, it is *expected* that the agent serves the interest of his or her principals, but this expectation is naive. Rarely are the interests of agents and principals 100 percent congruent. As we discussed earlier, an agent can perhaps advance his or her interest more fully by acting contrary to the principal's interest rather than by promoting it. Politicians are no different; their needs and concerns need not be identical with those of the citizens whom they are supposed to represent.

Candidates are seen as unprincipled by public choice theorists. Their main goal is to stay in office, not to serve the public interest. Being rational in the pursuit of office, candidates tend to weigh the well-being of pressure groups more than the well-being of the average voter. To raise money for campaigns, they trade their votes on key issues for contributions from special interest groups. They also push for policies that benefit their home constituency, not that help other districts. When provided with "pork" to distribute, for instance, a public works project, politicians seek to maximize their chance of reelection by allocating it to preferred clients at home. Democratic competition thus pushes legislatures to think parochially, to disregard the larger view. When public policy is the aggregate of innumerable private deals, the majority's interest gets lost.

Candidates also are encouraged to take a short-term view of things, whatever will get them through the next election. They are biased toward the quick fix and against public policies that will pay off in the future, which will likely benefit their successors more than themselves.

Several negative results may follow. One can be to generate excessive rules and restriction on business or, what is at least as likely, unwarranted breaks and assistance for certain industries. Like hardening of the arteries on the body politic, too much regulation can block the flow of goods and services that people want. Special favors for companies simply reward the most effective lobbyist, not the most efficient producer. The result may be a lower average standard of living.[36]

Voters and Elections

Elections are supposed to provide control and review of public agencies, but they may not do it right. Since politicians are political entrepreneurs, they need to avoid controversy, which may jeopardize reelection. Thus, they duck difficult matters such as raising taxes or cutting social programs. During campaigns, they try not to offend any important constituency and compete based on images more than issues. Voters are left in the dark and cannot hold politicians to account for their actions in office.

In addition, voting takes time and effort, and rational individuals realize their single vote probably will have no impact on any election's outcome. After comparing the cost and benefit of a trip to the polls, few citizens will choose to vote. For the same reason, most citizens will not try to become informed about political issues (rational ignorance). Since the benefit of learning about these issues is small, citizens have no reason to go to the trouble of getting knowledge to vote wisely. It is no wonder, in this view, that participation in U.S. elections is low.

Special interests do have an incentive to vote, for by voting as a bloc, members can increase the value of each individual vote. Single-issue voting can account for a few percentage points of votes cast and can mean the difference between victory and defeat in close contests. Thus, elections may reinforce the power of interest groups at the public's expense.

Consider the example of rice farmers in Japan. Members of this bloc are strongly against allowing imported rice into their country that would undercut their product. Foreign rice is much cheaper. Most Japanese probably want greater choice; though prejudiced against foreign rice, when given the option to use it, they do not notice much difference. But for three decades the rice farmers frustrated the will of the majority. They imposed their preference by threatening to withhold votes from any politician who advocated opening the rice market. Wary representatives could ill afford to alienate the rice lobby. Only in 1993, when rice farmers had dwindled to less than 5 percent of the population, did the Japanese government find the backbone to permit limited rice imports.[37]

The Law of Unintended Consequences

Foresight is imperfect in the real world, and government activities usually have unintended consequences. Good intentions need not lead to good results. The main reason is that people, being opportunistic, discover ways to exploit policies for their advantage. This outcome is usually inadvertent, the accidental byproduct of government action.

Unintended consequences abound in regulatory policy. Regulations are passed ostensibly to control industry in the public interest. Yet, often, regulation becomes the mechanism by which one group takes advantage of another. Industries that are regulated sometimes, in effect, capture the public agencies doing the regulating and twist the regulations to their own end.

The U.S. air carriers, for instance, liked being regulated by the Civil Aeronautics Board (CAB) for the years it existed (1938–85). The idea of CAB regulation was to allow orderly competition so that carriers would make enough money to assure safety. No new entrants were allowed into the national airline industry to challenge the existing competitors, and ticket prices were kept high. Most carriers naturally wanted to keep the CAB in place, and they fought deregulation of the airline business in Congress in the 1970s. Similarly, the trucking industry for decades worked with the Interstate Commerce Commission to protect itself from new entrants and price competition—none of which was the main objective of the original regulation.

Another type of unintended consequence is government's creation of transaction cost. Public policy breeds red tape, rules that push up the cost of doing business. Armies of lawyers, civil servants, consultants, and others come to depend on these transaction costs for their livelihood. These groups are apt to fight to add more rules to keep themselves working. While companies do protest, rules and regulations tend to accumulate over time, even when they no longer serve their original use.

Finally, public policy may turn out to be contradictory, to work at cross-purposes with itself. Because government decisions are made through piecemeal bargaining, it is not rare for one unit of government to undermine what another is doing. No one takes the larger view. An illustration is the public stance toward tobacco farming. On the one hand, the government provides an allotment to farmers to grow this crop. On the other hand, it subverts that effort by banning smoking in public places, paying for antismoking publicity, and taxing tobacco products to discourage their use. These policies are hampering one another in ways that no one probably intended.

A Tempered View of Government Failure

Government failures are unsettling because they can be explained without having to assume ignorance, stupidity, or malice of citizens, managers, or policy makers. Individual self-interest itself is the culprit, dooming efforts by the state to intervene in economic life to backfire. Still, such blunders are not reason to reject all forms of government interventionism. The gloomy, neoliberal view of the political process is mellowed by several observations.

First, government failure is not as rampant as often supposed. We have seen individual and management ethics can cut the other way, against narrow self-interest. People are not 100 percent Machiavellian. Most of us, some of the time, can put aside our immediate self-interest. As Adam Smith once wrote, "The wise and virtuous man is at all times willing that his own private interest should be sacrificed to the public interest . . ."[38]

Voters, for instance, do not *always* vote to keep their pay. Upper-income people have been known to support a candidate who promises to raise their taxes, and lower-income people sometimes back a candidate whose policies benefit mostly the rich. Empirical research backs up this point. It finds the public seldom vote their pocketbooks and that parties do not feel free to adopt any position they believe the majority of the public favors. Nor do bureaucrats seek always to be budget maximizers.[39] Public policy sometimes can work efficiently.

Second, competition reduces the incidence of opportunism among politicians. Opposition candidates have the incentive to expose voting records and questionable activities, which raises the level of honesty. They use party brand name and their reputation to lower the cost to voters of informing themselves. Voters, who may not be as ignorant as sometimes assumed, can discount biased information and make reasoned choices among candidates.[40]

Third, the neoliberal view can be simplistic. The airline, trucking, and other regulated industries, for instance, have not blocked deregulation as public choice theory expects. They have only managed to slow it. Similarly, budget crunches are not just a result of organized interests clamoring for more services from government, and of officials caving in to stay elected (see Box 3–4). And budgets do not continue to balloon out of balance indefinitely as the theory seems to predict; eventually, political forces tend to correct the problem by some combination of taxes and spending cuts. Obviously, political change is driven by several factors, and rent seeking is not always the most important.

Fourth, some government shortcomings have to be accepted as a cost of social life. People will use their talents to extract economic rent from the public sector. A certain degree of waste, fraud, and abuse is inevitable in government activities. Narrow interests will frequently get their way at the public's expense. But it is rash to make a blanket rejection of the state because of the abuses that happen. The alternative of a shrunken, indecisive state can be worse for the business environment.

Finally, just as good intentions go awry, the obviously bad things about government and public policy can have positive (though not intended) consequences. The sociologist Robert Merton of Columbia University cites the example of political machines. They violate many moral codes. Political machines select personnel based on party loyalty, not qualification. They support policies out of personal loyalty, not on merit. They wink at bribery and graft.

But there is another side to political machines, what Merton calls their "latent functions." Political machines provide personalized assistance to people—food baskets, jobs, legal advice. They protect business from excessive government scrutiny and control. They provide channels of upward mobility for deprived groups. It is this hidden, salutary dimension of political machines that explains their persistence, despite widespread disapproval.[41] We have seen another example of latent, yet helpful, functions—Smith's invisible hand, which leads self-interested individuals unwittingly to promote society's welfare.

The inference of Merton's argument is not that harmful or socially useless behavior must be tolerated. Rent seeking can and should be curtailed, though probably never eliminated. How? Reformers urge making rules that cut the chance for private interests to take advantage of the public. Proposals include sunset legislation that forces review of specific public programs, term limits to assure fresh air in legislatures, campaign spending ceilings to reduce the influence of lobbying, and tax caps to cut off government income. The point is we do not have to reject government out of hand as a way to solve collective economic problems.

Box 3.4

A Public Choice Explanation for Budget Deficits

Budget gaps have been getting bigger in several industrial countries. As Table 3–6 shows, every government has trouble balancing its income and expenditures. Japan is the major country to deviate from the norm. For all the controversy over U.S. deficit spending, the magnitude is comparable to that of the major European powers.

A government budget deficit may be good for the business climate in the short run, especially if the economy is in recession, because it pumps up demand for business products. Permanent, large deficits are different, as we read in the text, because private investors have to compete with government for funds. When an economy is running at full capacity, the expansionary impact of the deficit may trigger inflation—or encourage the central bank to raise interest rates. Neither scenario is helpful for most businesses.

Public choice offers the following explanation for chronic deficits: When some groups gain economic rent from the government, their example encourages others to follow the same path, leading to a steady rise in demand for government programs. Nobody wants to get left out. At the same time, resistance to taxes becomes pervasive as citizens try to protect themselves from what they see as the state's power to exploit them to help special interests. Too much government spending, too little revenue, ensues.

Solving a fiscal crisis requires fewer programs, more taxes, or both, but no interest group wants to be the first to break the impasse out of concern that other groups will not share the burden. Ross Perot included, politicians are reluctant to advocate specific ways to reduce the government's red ink out of fear of driving off supporters.

As former Senator Warren Rudman explains: "When the American people say they are against big government, they are generally excluding Social Security, Medicare, Medicaid, federal civil service, military retirement, agricultural subsidies, student loans, and veterans benefits. They're against big government—except for the program that might be helping them."[1]

---

[1] Quoted in Michael Rezendes, "Unhappy with Government," *The Boston Sunday Globe,* November 13, 1994, p. A2.

TABLE 3–6   GOVERNMENT DEFICITS HAVE BEEN RISING AROUND THE WORLD, WITH THE NOTABLE EXCEPTION OF JAPAN.

	General Government Financial Balance (surplus or deficit) as Percent of GDP				
	1975	*1980*	*1985*	*1990*	*1992*
France	−2.4%	0	−2.9%	−1.5%	−3.9%
Germany	−5.6	−2.9%	−1.2	−2.0	−2.8
Japan	−2.8	−4.4	−0.8	2.9	1.8
United Kingdom	−4.5	−3.4	−2.9	−1.3	−6.7
United States	**−4.1**	**−1.3**	**−3.1**	**−2.5**	**−4.7**

Source: *OECD Economic Outlook* (Paris: Organization for Economic Cooperation and Development, June 1993).

Conclusion

Charles Lindblom once wrote, "A market is like a tool: designed to do certain jobs but unsuitable for others."[42] In this chapter, we have reviewed the conditions under which this tool does *not* work well. These market failures are caused by the same self-interest that, under different conditions, makes markets a fitting means for producing and distributing goods. The core problem is that there are many cases where cheating is advantageous to the individual. Other people will see the logic of the situation and will cheat too.

One factor that mitigates some market failures is business ethics. Businesspeople subscribe to moral codes that make them pay at least passing attention to the interests of others. Their sense of fair play and obligation tempers the inclination of businesspeople (and of consumers, employees, and so on) to act unscrupulously.

Important though moral philosophies are in channeling human action toward socially desirable ends, political economists know they are not enough to fix all the market's failures. Adam Smith points out that individual conscience is an incomplete check on behavior due to mankind's natural partiality. We are biased, often unconsciously, to take the side that helps us personally. Thus, external mechanisms also must be created to make people get along. Like many other Enlightenment thinkers, Smith thought humans thus agreed for their good to be coerced by government.

We also have seen that, just as unregulated markets can fail to perform as hoped, governments can fail to produce the results they promise. Instead governments may distort the economy in ways that are bad for the majority in society. There are many sides to government failure, but all grow out of people's using the state to promote their self-interest. This so-called rent-seeking activity leads individuals and organizations to pursue artificially high income and profits through public policy intervention.

Government failure should not push us to favor a minimalist state across the board, however. Economic exchange depends on state power, and, sometimes, for markets to thrive, the state must be reinforced, not dismantled. An effective, able government was key to the rise of modern market society in the first place and is important to preserving high standards of living. This does not mean, though, that government needs to do everything itself; the most effective government intervention is to create an enabling environment for private activity. These are the main subjects in Part III.

Questions

1. What are government's roles in the U.S. economy? Which are the most important?

2. What are market failures? Government failures? Think of some concrete examples.

3. Describe the notion of free riding. Again, think of some concrete examples.

4. What is rent seeking? What problems does it create?

5. What irreducible functions are there for government with respect to business?

End Notes

1. John Maynard Keynes, *The End of Laissez Faire,* cited in *World Development Report* (Washington, D.C.: World Bank, 1991), p. 128.

2. William Lazonick, *Business Organization and the Myth of the Market Economy* (Cambridge: Cambridge University Press, 1991).

3. Douglass C. North, "Comments 2," in *The Economic Role of the State,* ed. Arnold Heertje (Oxford: Basil Blackwell, 1989), p. 108.

4. Max Weber, *The Theory of Social and Economic Organization,* trans. Talcott Parsons (New York: Free Press, 1964), p. 156.

5. James O. Goldsborough, "California's Foreign Policy," *Foreign Affairs* 72, no. 2 (Spring 1993), pp. 88–96.

6. Joseph Stiglitz, "On the Economic Role of the State," in *The Economic Role of the State,* ed. Arnold Heertje (Oxford: Basil Blackwell, 1989), p. 38.

7. Similar lists are standard in any welfare economics text. An early framework is Francis M. Bator, "The Anatomy of Market Failure," *Quarterly Journal of Economics* 72, no. 1 (1958), pp. 351–79.

8. Adam Smith, *An Inquiry into the Nature and Causes of the Wealth of Nations* (1776; reprint, New York: Modern Library, 1937), p. 651.

9. Ibid.

10. The pioneering analytical thinking on public goods was by Paul Samuelson, "The Pure Theory of Public Expenditure," *Review of Economics and Statistics* 36, no. 1 (1954), pp. 387–89.

11. On the difficulty of organizing to provide public goods, see Mancur Olson, Jr., *The Logic of Collective Action* (Cambridge, MA: Harvard University Press, 1965).

12. On the problem of transaction cost, see Oliver E. Williamson, *Markets and Hierarchies* (New York: Free Press, 1975).

13. Douglass C. North, *Institutions, Institutional Change, and Economic Performance* (New York: Cambridge University Press, 1990), p. 28.

14. This is the point of the Coase theorem, proposed by Ronald Coase, the 1991 Nobel prize winner in economics.

15. An early attempt to use externalities as the basis for a theory of the state is William Baumol, *Welfare Economics and the Theory of the State* (Cambridge, MA: Harvard University Press, 1952).

16. Thomas C. Schelling, *Micromotives and Macrobehavior* (New York: W. W. Norton, 1978), pp. 99–100, citing an idea of George A. Akerlof.

17. For a review of the literature, see Barry M. Mitnick, "The Theory of Agency and Organizational Analysis," in *Ethics and Agency Theory,* ed. Norman E. Bowie and R. Edward Freeman (New York: Oxford University Press, 1992).

18. See, for example, Alfred Pfaller, Ian Gough, and Goran Therborn, eds., *Can the Welfare State Compete?* (Houndsmill, U.K.: Macmillan, 1991).

19. Margaret S. Gordon, *Social Security Policy in Industrial Countries* (Cambridge: Cambridge University Press, 1988), p. 15.

20. See, for example, Ted R. Gurr, *Why Men Rebel* (Princeton, NJ: Princeton University Press, 1970).

21. "For Richer, for Poorer," *The Economist,* November 5, 1994, pp. 19–21.

22. See Timothy M. Smeeding, "Why the U.S. Anti-Poverty System Doesn't Work Very Well," *Challenge* 35, no. 1 (January/February 1992), pp. 30–35.

23. Benjamin M. Friedman, "The Clinton Budget: Will It Do?" *New York Review of Books,* July 15, 1993, p. 38.

24. On the recurring controversy over public borrowing in the United States, see James D. Savage, *Balanced Budgets and American Budgets and American Politics* (Ithaca: Cornell University Press, 1988).

25. A reassuring view of the national debt is Robert Eisner, *The Misunderstood Economy* (Boston: Harvard Business School Press, 1994).

26. For a discussion of the international ramifications of public indebtedness, see David P. Calleo, *The Bankruptcy of America* (New York: William Morrow, 1992).

27. See Charles Wolf, Jr., *Markets and Governments,* 2nd ed. (Cambridge, MA: MIT Press, 1993).

28. These arguments were developed by several prominent economists, including the Nobel Prize–winner James Buchanan. For an elementary presentation of their critique of government, see David B. Johnson, *Public Choice: An Introduction to the New Political Economy* (Mountain View, CA: Bristlecone Books, 1991).

29. Theodore J. Lowi and Benjamin Ginsberg, *American Government,* 2nd ed. (New York: Norton, 1992), p. 640.

30. Jonathan Rauch, *Demosclerosis: The Silent Killer of American Government* (New York: Times Books, 1994), p. 117.

1 line long

31. Gary C. Becker, "To Root Out Corruption, Boot Out Big Government," *Business Week,* January 31, 1994, p. 18.

32. See James Q. Wilson, *Political Organizations* (New York: Basic Books, 1973).

33. Paul Krugman, *The Age of Diminished Expectations* (Cambridge, MA: MIT Press, 1990), p. 102.

34. H. Craig Petersen, *Business and Government,* 4th ed. (New York: HarperCollins, 1993), p. 18.

35. The classic statement of this view is Anthony Downs, *Inside Bureaucracy* (Boston: Little, Brown, 1967). Also see William Niskanen, *Bureaucracy and Representative Government* (Chicago: Aldine, 1971).

36. See Mancur Olson, Jr., *The Rise and Decline of Nations* (New Haven: Yale University Press, 1982).

37. T. R. Reid, "Japan to End Ban on Rice Imports," *Boston Globe,* December 14, 1993, p. 49.

38. Adam Smith, *The Theory of Moral Sentiments* (1790; reprint, Oxford: Clarendon, 1976), p. 235.

39. See Leif Lewin, S*elf-Interest and Public Interest in Western Politics* (New York: Oxford University Press, 1991).

40. See Samuel Popkin, *The Rational Voter* (New York: Basic Books, 1992).

41. Robert K. Merton, *Social Theory and Social Structure* (New York: Free Press, 1968), pp. 125–36.

42. Charles E. Lindblom, *Politics and Markets* (New York: Basic Books, 1977), p. 6.

4   Corporate Social Responsibility and Stakeholders

[T]he large corporation is a tool and organ of society. Hence society must demand of the corporation that it be able to discharge the specific economic functions which are its raison d'être. *This is an absolute, a supreme demand— as absolute and supreme as the demand that the corporation meet the necessities of its own functioning and survival.*

Peter Drucker[1]

The market and government failures classified in Chapter 3 may seem disheartening. People's inclination to take advantage of others, their reluctance always to share burdens—these traits complicate the task of organizing a business, not to mention organizing a larger commercial society. Yet, the inability of individuals to act in the larger group's economic interest is not as deep or as inevitable as it may seem. Humankind has created generally accepted rules of behavior that temper our self-interest. We can therefore cooperate more than the self-interest model of humankind seems to predict. Friendship, honor, and loyalty are present in every successful company.[2]

In fact, markets could not flourish if people did not believe, at least partly, in unselfish values. Honesty and trust are vital to business transactions because they reduce uncertainty and cut the cost of getting information. These virtues are the moral bedrock for commerce and good government. Without them, the transaction cost of enforcing contracts and protecting property would be far higher, making it impossible for a market economy to work efficiently.

Adam Smith himself devoted much of his writing to developing a theory of moral behavior. He believed that people, in his words, have an ethical sense called sympathy that is based on feelings for their fellow humans—we can stand as an objective spectator and identify with other people. In particular, according to Smith, people want to be praised *and*, more important, to be praiseworthy.[3] In his view, our principles and our conscience serve as a voice of self-control and are a reason people do not *always* cheat or pollute or otherwise seek unfair advantage when they can get away with it. Values such as these, he believed, underlie and reinforce our economic and political institutions.

Most professions have developed codes of conduct that are supposed to govern their members' behavior, to encourage charity and honesty. The doctors' Hippocratic Oath is the most famous. It is to their benefit for professionals to stick to these codes and protect their group's standing in society. Training, habit, and peer pressure encourage them to take the rules seriously. Thus, codes of conduct put up barriers, however imperfect, against acts that professionals collectively deem wrong. Like many public policies, but without the threat of government-imposed punishment, they blunt the excesses created by ambition and greed.

Management does not yet have a universal or comprehensive professional code. Most large American companies have particular codes, though, as do many British firms.[4] Some observers think that corporate codes of ethics restrain managers from making more moral lapses than they do. We will discuss corporate codes at the end of this chapter. First, we review business ethics and the notion of corporate social responsibility, focusing on how rights have been regarded over time. We also discuss the idea of organization stakeholders, or groups whose rights managers often must respect because of law and convention.

Business Ethics and Corporate Social Responsibility

Ethics are the standards or values on which a particular group or community acts (or is supposed to act). Business ethics are the beliefs about proper practices that pertain to the business community.[5] Capitalists have pondered ethics since at least the 18th century, as they looked for a moral basis to justify—and to guide—their profit-making activities. The quest for moral guidance grew more earnest in the 20th century as companies increasingly found they were having to defend themselves against accusations of bad conduct.[6]

What is the relationship between the law and business ethics? Commercial legal responsibilities are codified business ethics. Public policy sets down the basic standards on which business is expected to run. Managers are obligated to comply with the law under threat of civil or criminal penalties. While the public is cynical about corporate crime, legal compliance occurs because most business professionals believe in abiding by the law not because they fear punishment.[7]

The written law may specify merely the minimum acceptable behavior in commercial affairs. Social convention may hold the firm to a higher standard. Some management experts are advocates of **corporate social responsibility** and argue that companies need to go beyond their legal obligations to maintain legitimacy.[8] The idea of corporate social responsibility is that a narrow focus on short-term earnings is not usually in a corporation's long-term best interest. Good management requires acting in anticipation of social pressures, to maintain public trust—and perhaps to avert damaging public policy in the future.

From this point of view, there is no conflict between discharging duties to society and making a profit. By investing in social programs that fill the needs of their constituencies, they should, in the long run, see their companies prosper. As John Shad, former Securities and Exchange Commission chairman, sums it up: "Ethics pays: It's smart to be ethical."[9]

Smith would have been skeptical about any link between "doing good" and "doing well." As he once said, "I have never known much good done by those who affected to trade for the public good."[10] Hard evidence is scarce that efforts to be socially responsible do correlate with profits. And if profits and ethics were fully compatible, social responsibility would not even be a topic of debate. Ethics can pay, but sometimes they can be costly.

Still, the effort to be socially responsible leads many successful companies, such as Vermont's Ben & Jerry's Homemade Inc., to be more "green" or environmentally conscious than they have to. Other successful companies devote resources to social causes. An illustration is Stride Rite Corporation of Cambridge, Massachusetts, which gives 5 percent of its pretax earnings to a foundation and has pioneered on-site day care for employees. When such companies come under financial pressure, as Ben & Jerry's and Stride Rite have, they find it harder to stay so far ahead of legally mandated minimum acceptable behavior. Ben & Jerry's, for example, has abandoned its pledge to limit the salaries of top executives to seven times that earned by the lowest-paid worker.

Modes of Analysis in Business Ethics

Even written laws are often ambiguous, with no bright line to separate legal from illegal activities. Managers are often tempted to bend or push the law to its limits, exploiting every loophole, especially if competitors and colleagues in the industry are doing the same. It is hard to know sometimes where to stop. People wink at padding of expense accounts, using company supplies for personal purposes, or underreporting taxable income deductions, suggesting lawful restrictions often exceed personal morality. By conventional agreement the written law is not taken literally in these cases.

How is a manager to navigate through the grey areas? Moral philosophers have developed two modes of normative thinking that can help managers make ethical decisions. These two approaches are discussed below. Unfortunately, moral philosophers have not fine-tuned the two views enough to guide managers through the grey areas that pose the greatest difficulty.[11] But the modes of ethical reasoning are useful in thinking systematically through ethical problems.

Utilitarianism

One important ethical view is **utilitarianism.** This theory, first developed by Jeremy Bentham (1748–1832), advocates selecting action that maximizes social utility or benefit and minimizes social disutility or harm. The practice of cost–benefit analysis, which is widely used in business planning, is an example of a practical application of Bentham's utilitarian principles. The socially responsible direction for a business is, in the words of the utilitarian slogan, to produce "the greatest good for the greatest number."

When faced with choice, according to utilitarians, managers should tally the winners and the losers from each alternative they are considering. They ought to include both immediate and future consequences. After making the necessary calculations, they should add the benefit and cost, and pick the action that produces the most happiness. Note that utilitarian ethics do *not* mean the right action is the one that returns the highest utility for the person or firm doing the action. The precept is to maximize expected utility for society. Morality dictates that everyone's interest be taken equally into account. Thus, managers have a moral obligation to turn down actions that are profitable for their company, or that advance their careers, if they do not also advance society's well-being (see Table 4–1).

Utilitarianism looks like a simple moral code, but there are practical difficulties in applying it. How does one measure utility or happiness? Money is often used as the yardstick, but not all costs and benefits are easily expressed in monetary value. It is hard to be impartial in estimating other people's happiness, and perhaps even harder to make a comprehensive accounting of all who are affected by an action. There is also the problem of "the tyranny of the majority." Is it fair to impose cost on a few people without their consent to help the rest of society?[12]

Rights-Based Views

The major alternative to utilitarian ethics is the rights- or duty-based approach.[13] **Rights** are moral claims—things to which people are entitled. Rights-based ethics grant individuals the power to veto some decisions that hurt them for the benefit of others. Whereas utilitarianism holds an action morally right or wrong because of its effect on total human welfare, the rights-based approach maintains that actions can be right or wrong intrinsically. The moral test is whether it is fair to the individuals affected irrespective of the net gain or loss to society. Someone's rights should not be disregarded to help third parties.

According to duty-based theory, managers weighing their options ought to pick the one that treats people justly and respects their rights. The criterion for a decision is whether it is fair.[14] The most famous duty-based maxim is the Golden Rule: "Do unto others as you would have them do unto you." It implies

TABLE 4.1   There Are Two Main Modes of Ethical Reasoning in Management.

Mode	Focus	Decision Rule
Utilitarianism	Outcomes	Try to maximize social benefit
Rights-based	Actions	Try to respect rights and be fair

that managers ought to stop and ask themselves how they would feel if they were on the other end of a decision.

The two ethical systems, the utilitarian and the rights-based approaches, can overlap. Human rights themselves can be justified on the utilitarian grounds that they are needed to maintain a working society. Sometimes, applying the two approaches separately to a specific administrative problem can produce the same decision. More often, perhaps, rights-based arguments run directly counter to utilitarian arguments on subjects such as consumer rights, employee rights, and the fair treatment of suppliers.

The greatest difficulty in using rights and fairness as decision criteria is that these principles are themselves the object of dispute. Rights change over time and geography, and people do not agree about the priority one moral claim should take over another. Most actions taken by managers affect multiple rights; to treat them all the same is impractical. To avoid being paralyzed by moral indecision, principled managers need to have some means of ranking diverse rights. There are no universal standards. Different societies, and different people within those societies, uphold different rights.

But in Western countries, at least, rights fall into basic categories. The British social scientist, T. H. Marshall, in a famous paper, calls them **civil liberties**, **political rights**, and **economic rights**.[15] These rights are at the heart of government's rule-making and umpiring roles, and they have important implications for private behavior, too.

Civil Liberties.   Civil liberties were the first rights to be established (by the 18th century in Britain and the United States). Civil liberties are associated historically with liberalism, the philosophy that the individual should be allowed to develop, unbound by government, and thus are critical for the free play of business. Liberalism emerged against **absolutism,** the theory that government should define the scope of its powers. Liberals argued for constitutions to protect civil liberties, such as free speech and free assembly. Property is a particularly important right supported by liberal thought.

Civil liberties have been tagged *negative* rights, because they represent freedom *from* interference.[16] People should be allowed to think, believe, read, and write what they want, as long as they do not impose their thoughts, beliefs, and writings on other people. The major negative rights are enshrined, among other places, in the U.S. Bill of Rights. For employers, the most important negative rights include the freedoms to hire and fire (the employment-at-will doctrine), to make investment decisions on their own, and to earn and keep profits. Some philosophers have tried to show that negative rights are consistent only with the market mechanism as a means for allocating resources.[17]

Political Rights.   Marshall's second kind of rights became established later in the West, mainly in the 1800s. These are the democratic freedoms—the freedom to run for office, to vote for candidates (and to recall them), to vote directly on public questions (referenda), and to **lobby** or try to influence public officials. The thrust of political rights, except lobbying, is toward equality—in a democracy, all citizens should have the same say in setting public policy. Each person's vote weighs the same, and the majority rules. Lobbying points the other way, toward inequality, because wealthy persons and institutions are likely to have more than equal access and influence. The rich do not always get their way, but they do have an advantage in pushing their plans on policy makers.

Even open political systems such as those found in the United States and Britain restricted political rights to a minority until the 20th century. When the United States ratified its Constitution, only adult, white, Christian, male property owners could vote. Grudgingly, the limits to citizenship were lifted. Business generally resisted expansion of citizenship, which was feared to give too much influence to the poor and workers and to threaten the capitalist system.

These fears proved exaggerated. One reason is that companies (foreign-owned ones included) enjoy several rights of citizenship themselves: not only may they lobby for policies helpful to them, they may back candidates for office and speak out publicly on policy issues. They thus can curb much antibusiness pressure. We will look at corporate political activities fully in Chapter 8.

In contrast to civil rights, political rights are a *positive* freedom; they permit people, including businesspeople, to get involved in public life. While civil rights shield individuals from the whims of the majority, political rights empower individuals to join or influence the majority. So appealing are both sets of rights, the negative and the positive, the United Nations adopted them, without a dissenting vote, in the Universal Declaration of Human Rights (1948).

Still, negative and positive rights can collide. Eighteenth century civil liberties are a check on 19th century political rights. They keep elected officials from stamping out unpopular ideas and causes. Property and other civil rights are considered immutable and above the political fray, though in truth such rights do get adjusted by policy makers. For business, liberal rules have been important in helping to blunt efforts by democratic regimes to meddle with companies' decisions to invest or disinvest. Big Business has been deeply disliked at times in U.S. history, but it could usually shield itself behind the Constitution.

Another contradiction is that the economic inequality protected by liberal rights may overwhelm the political equality promised by democratic rights of citizenship. How is it possible to maintain a government of the people when some people (not to mention business organizations) are much richer and more powerful than others? Many political economic conflicts are about which set of rights, negative or positive, should take precedence. Consider, for example, the controversy over American campaign financing, which gives monied interests undue influence on politicians.

Economic Rights.   In the 20th century, a third set of rights has come to the fore. These are so-called social or economic rights—the right to a job, to health care, to a pension. Citizens claim these benefits not as charity but as their due by citizenship. It is revealing that another word for a social program in the United States is an entitlement. Though the U.S. Constitution does not refer to social programs, Americans have come to consider them their right, as something to which they are entitled.

Box 4.1

An Organization's Stakeholders Are Important to an Organization's Success

The term *stakeholder* refers to any group with a potential stake or claim in a company. Harvard Business School's Rosabeth Moss Kanter defines stakeholders as "those groups on which an organization depends—the people who can help it achieve its goals or stop it dead in its tracks."[1] They are constituencies who stand to gain or lose by an organization's performance and who can affect its actions in significant ways.

Many parties have a legitimate interest in what companies do. There are resource providers (owners, creditors, workers, and suppliers) and resource users (clients and customers). There are insiders (top and middle management, unskilled and skilled operators, and unskilled and skilled support staff) and outsiders (partners, competitors, and govern-

ment).[2] There are groups in the immediate environment (neighbors and local media) and in the distant environment (activist groups and national media).

Over the last several decades, the number of active stakeholders has mushroomed. New constituencies—consumer advocates, community organizations, environmentalists, and church groups, to name some—have started pressing claims on Big Business. These stakeholders confront companies in many, often novel ways, most importantly by trying to change law and public policy to turn companies in new directions. Successful managers have to develop skill in organizational politics and learn how to exercise leadership, negotiate, bargain, and form alliances among stakeholders.

---

[1] Rosabeth Moss Kanter, *When Giants Learn to Dance* (New York: Simon and Schuster, 1989), p. 127.

---

[2] Henry Mintzberg, *Power In and Around Organizations* (Englewood Cliffs, NJ: Prentice Hall, 1983).

Economic rights are embodied in the modern welfare state. As we discussed in Chapter 3, government throughout the West (including Japan) tries to modify the play of market forces to provide a social safety net and a degree of equality in incomes. Government does so by (1) guaranteeing everyone a minimum income, not just in cash but also in access to housing, food, and social services; and (2) helping people overcome economic problems caused by loss of a job, sickness, or old age.

Compared to the older civil and political rights, economic rights are more controversial with business, because business has to take a large role in assuring them. Employers are compelled by law to pay for the welfare state and to abide by its often restrictive rules. The calculus of political economy says business will work to slow the expansion of economic rights, and this has been the pattern.

Stakeholders and Business Obligations

Wherever they operate, managers are bound by the state to respect the formal rights of all groups with which they deal: shareholders, employees, customers, suppliers, community neighbors, and so on. These groups also can assert informal rights not recognized by law. Because they can claim a legitimate stake in what the organization does, they have been dubbed the organization's **stake-holders.**[18] (See Box 4–1.)

A map of stakeholders is shown in Figure 4–1. All these constituencies may have to be accommodated, but the primary stakeholders (owners, employees, creditors, customers, suppliers, and competitors) are the most important, since they have the greatest leverage over the company.

Stakeholders can claim legal rights through the courts and can lobby through legislatures to change laws. The option exists for them to try to influence management corporate governance procedures or to take more direct action—boycotts, demonstrations, publicity campaigns, and the like. Many business leaders resent the intrusion of new groups into company affairs; but they ignore these groups at their own peril.[19]

International Stakeholder Issues

Stakeholders' legal rights differ from country to country and are always evolving within countries, and thus need to be monitored carefully. Safety and environ-

FIGURE 4–1

Primary and secondary stakeholders

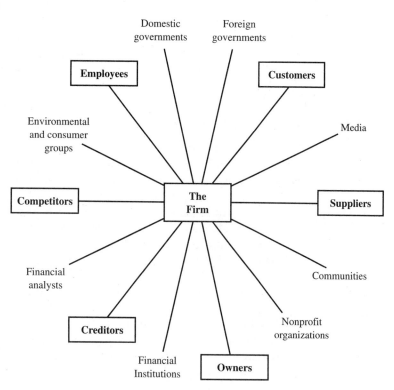

mental standards in India, for example, are much looser than in the United States. Lax regulation and pressure from the Indian government for local control contributed to the Bhopal disaster in 1984, when a gas leak from an American-owned Union Carbide plant killed or injured thousands of residents in nearby shanty towns. Had the company followed stricter safety guidelines, as it would have had to in the United States, the disaster might not have occurred. In the aftermath, Union Carbide could not shift blame to India and agreed to pay damages of $470 million in 1989, less than half of which was covered by insurance. The company paid legal fees estimated at another $100 million defending itself and suffered undetermined harm to its reputation that contributed to a vast corporate restructuring in the late 1980s.[20]

As the Union Carbide case shows, the law only specifies the least common denominator of rights. Today, managers are often called on to go beyond the legally mandated minimum, to promote and protect stakeholders' rights that are embodied in custom or professional codes of conduct, not law. Nestlé, for example, has been bitterly criticized since the 1970s for promoting infant formula in developing countries, where living conditions often render the product unsafe. Nestlé has broken no law, but it has transgressed what many people consider are basic standards of decency in safeguarding its customers. The results have been boycotts and much bad publicity for the company.

On the other hand, companies doing business in foreign lands may find they have to violate conventional morality (and sometimes the written law) to keep some stakeholders at bay. American managers in Russia, for example, are caught in unending ethical dilemmas as they try to work around Russian bureaucrats and mobsters. Bribes seem to be a cost of doing business. If they fail to make the right payoffs, hapless managers may even wind up as the target of hitmen.[21]

Competing Stakeholder Demands

The most difficult choices confront managers when they have to choose among competing claims to rights being put forward by different stakeholders. Who should come first—shareholders, customers, employees, or another group?

Stakeholders are not created equal. Traditionally, managers profess (not always truthfully) to put the interest of one stakeholder group—their stock owners—ahead of all others. The overriding *stated* goal of corporate America usually is to give owners a high return on their investment. Justifying the goal of high returns is the idea that companies are mainly a form of property, so stakeholders have a secondary interest to the owners.

All managers need to do is maintain earnings. Besides keeping owners happy, the quest for profit forces companies to assuage the secondary stakeholder groups with a legitimate interest in what the company does. As Milton Friedman expressed in the title of a well-known article: "The social responsibility of business is to increase its profits."[22] By making money, companies will naturally discharge their obligations to other groups in society. But any manager whose paramount concern is not to use corporate assets to increase shareholders' wealth is guilty of misappropriation.[23]

Political economic analysis of business firms finds Friedman's view naive. For one thing, it is not an accurate description of what really guides management decisions. American managers' main stated goal often is profit maximization, but that does not mean they do not have other objectives, too. More striking, managers in other cultures are apt to voice different priorities. (See Table 4–2.) As we observed in Chapter 2, human motivation is rich and complex.

More to the point, companies are not just property; they are a coalition of interests. Managing a company is a political activity of building support among these constituencies. Like any coalition, the stakeholders in a company can have a falling out with each other. Talcott Parsons, the late sociologist, once correctly observed that because organizations use resources that can have other applications, the appropriateness of their activities and the usefulness of their output are constantly being reassessed.[24] If companies offend too many important stakeholders, they lose legitimacy and can face a public policy crisis (or a private financial emergency) that will change the way they do business.

Stakeholders join the coalition represented by a company to get something of value. In exchange, they give resources to the organization that it uses to maintain itself or expand. Stakeholders may share a common interest in a firm's survival and prosperity, but their backing cannot be taken for granted and must be renewed continually. Not only do stakeholders assert a rightful claim to influence what a company does, sometimes they may have the leverage to destroy or severely harm it by withdrawing their support to a company that fails to deliver value *as they define it*. So it is not easy to separate owners' long-term interests from what other stakeholders want.

TABLE 4–2   Executives in Japan Are Less Preoccupied with Earnings, Dividends, and Share Prices than American Managers.

	U.S. and Japanese Ranking of Corporate Objectives* (10 = most important, 1 = least important)	
	Japan	*U.S.*
Market share	4.8	2.4
Return on investment	4.1	8.1
Ratio of new products	3.5	0.7
Rationalize production and distribution	2.4	1.5
Improve product portfolio	2.3	1.7
Improve company's image	0.7	0.2
Share price increase	0.1	3.8

* Based on a survey of 291 Japanese companies and 227 U.S. companies.
Source: J. C. Abegglen and G. Stalk, Jr., *Kaisha: The Japanese Corporation* (New York: Basic Books, 1985), p. 177.

Customers

Take customers. One axiom of business is that successful companies keep close to their customers.[25] This stakeholder group exchanges money for goods and services and is the final arbiter of the company's worth. Should customers drop their support, the company will suffer and the product may die, as happened to Dow Corning in 1991 after users of silicone breast implants decided the implants were a health threat.

A counterexample is Johnson & Johnson, which went to great lengths to reassure the users of Tylenol that the product was safe after several consumers were poisoned by tampered pills in 1982. Johnson & Johnson was under no legal obligation, but the company immediately withdrew the product and developed foolproof packaging to keep its customers in the fold. The strategy worked and, before long, Tylenol sales were higher than ever.[26] (Johnson & Johnson also paid millions to victims' families in out-of-court settlements. See Chapter 13 for more on product liability issues.)

Workers

Employees and their unions are also central stakeholders. They swap labor for wages, good working conditions, job security, and other benefits. To get what they want employees sometimes withhold labor from companies (by striking). Employees' claim for their share of company resources often bring them into conflict with owners and managers. Enmity from its labor constituency was what finally forced Eastern Airlines to be liquidated. Goodwill from workers, on the other hand, allowed Chrysler Corporation to cut wages and helped it survive its crisis in the early 1980s.

Creditors

Another critical group of stakeholders is creditors who lend cash to companies, expecting to be repaid with interest. Creditors' claims on the company often conflict with those of owners and workers—they often could not care less about the fate of the firm as long as enough of its assets can be resold to repay them. Creditors must be kept allied with the company, or lack of credit will force it to cease operations or severely cut them back. Such was the fate of Olympia and York, which had to file for bankruptcy in 1992 when its creditors decided to cut off loans to that company.

Local Communities and Government

The town or city in which the company operates is a set of important stakeholders. The groups that comprise the local community want the company to be a good neighbor. Neighborliness means preventive steps such as not allowing local facilities to become unsanitary or unsafe, and it means positive action such as donating funds for civic clubs and humanitarian activities. Most large companies have a community relations office that handles liaisons with the local community.

A last bloc of crucial stakeholders is government agencies charged with enforcing the law and regulating management practices. These bodies are unique because they can act both independently, based on their mandate, and on the behalf of other stakeholders. Thus, as we will see in later chapters, dealing with government stakeholders is tricky.

Balancing Stakeholders

Not only must a company keep its core constituencies happy or else endanger its survival, it also has to resolve disputes among stakeholder groups, each of which sometimes pushes the company in different directions. Whose views and whose interests should take precedence? There are no formulas to answer this question, which is one reason management is more art than science.

Stakeholders can affect organizations directly through private encounters or indirectly through public policy. This last course perhaps holds the greatest hazards for business. When they become irritated, stakeholders often turn to the government to change the ground rules for an entire industry or even the whole economy. After the savings and loan scandal of the late 1980s, for example, bank regulators put all financial institutions under closer scrutiny. Events such as this are why managers need to consider stakeholders' needs in developing company policy.

Laura Nash of Boston University argues that to resolve ethical dilemmas in business, executives ought to think of commercial affairs in terms of covenants with their stakeholders. According to these covenants, all parties should prosper from a voluntary exchange of resources. The principle should be to minimize the harm to stakeholders. Not only does such a stand make good ethics, it also can make good business sense in the long run.[27]

To remind themselves that all stakeholders are important, many companies enumerate their responsibility to different interests in their code of conduct. Several examples are presented in Table 4–3. These usually name duty to groups such as customers, workers, communities, and share owners. The point is to keep managers attuned to the needs and rights of every group in the corporate coalition.

Many anecdotes suggest that codes are helpful. Johnson & Johnson's management, for example, credits its corporate credo with the company's rapid response to the Tylenol tragedy mentioned earlier. The credo, which says the company's first responsibility is to those who use its products, is hammered into employees through frequent reviews. Right after the poisoning took place, before responsibility could be established, Johnson & Johnson took immediate drastic action to protect Tylenol users from possible harm. No one in the company questioned the huge expense.

TABLE 4–3   Many Companies Make Statements of Principles that Identify Responsibility to Stakeholders.

Borg Warner: Any business is a member of a social system, entitled to the rights and bound by the responsibilities of that membership . . . We impose upon ourselves an obligation to reach beyond the minimal . . . by making a larger contribution to the society that sustains us, we best assure not only its future vitality but our own.

IBM: [W]e expect every IBM employee to live up to the highest standards of conduct, in every business relationship—with each other, with the company, with our customers, business partners, and competitors.

Levi-Strauss: Our company, like any citizen of the community, has a basic obligation to that community.

Marks and Spencer (U.K.): We believe that a business cannot progress in isolation from the community in which it works and trades; helping whenever possible to restore a healthy and prosperous environment is a responsibility which is not only good citizenship but is good for business.

San Diego Gas and Electric: We believe that by fulfilling our obligations to our many constituencies we will best serve the needs of our shareholders: preservation of their capital and an attractive return on their investment . . . Employees are the Company's most important resource . . . As an integral member of the communities in our service territory, we have a corporate responsibility to support and be active in them.

Thomas Cook (U.K.): Our strategy is to substantially increase the profitability and value of the Thomas Cook Group by doing everything that is necessary to earn and retain the trust of our customers, our business partners, our people, and our stakeholders.

Sources: Walter W. Manley II, *Executive's Handbook of Model Business Conduct Codes* (Englewood Cliffs, NJ: Prentice Hall, 1991), pp. 27, 60, 65, and 186; Walter W. Manley, *The Handbook of Good Business Practice* (London: Routledge, 1992), p. 246; Francis P. McHugh, *Business Ethics* (London: Mansell Publishing, 1988).

Unfortunately, more empirical research finds that the relationship between company codes and company conduct is minimal.[28] Even the Johnson & Johnson credo turns out to hold less sway the further one gets from the U.S. headquarters, according to researchers.[29] The usefulness of these statements of intent as management tools is thus questionable, reflecting again the importance of public policy to reinforce good corporate citizenship.

Conclusion

This chapter has reviewed the question of corporate social responsibility, of society's expectation that companies do more than simply maximize profit. We also investigated the idea of organization stakeholders—influential groups and individuals, both inside and outside an organization, that can affect its actions in significant ways. Companies that are bad citizens may rouse stakeholders' ire and face damaging fallout down the way.

To provide some guideposts to managers, we briefly reviewed two modes of ethical reasoning. One is based on cost–benefit analysis and advises managers to choose the action that has the great-est net benefit to society. This type of analysis is complicated by the task of calculating the full social loss and gain of any management decision.

The second mode of analysis recommends that managers take account of people's rights when they make decisions. Here the difficulty in applying the rules is that people claim different kinds of rights—the liberal civil rights to be left alone, the political rights to participate in group decisions, and the economic rights to a satisfactory standard of living. These rights overlap and conflict; managers need to make priorities and pick which rights come first if they are to use this mode of reasoning.

Many companies try to help their managers make ethical decisions by putting together company codes of conduct. It is easy to be cynical about such codes, to see them as pompous and insincere. In many organizations, the lofty words in these documents are not taken seriously and do become the object of ridicule. At other times, a devotion to the organization that goes beyond narrow economic concerns proves critical. So we should not dismiss the idea of developing a formal statement of company ethics.

Still, such private and voluntary rules are no substitute for public and involuntary commands. They reinforce public policy to make market society work, but they cannot support trade and industry on their own, as we will see in Chapter 5.

Questions

1. What are an organization's stakeholders? Who are they? Which one is the most important?
2. Give an example of utilitarian thinking. How can it help a manager solve an ethical question?
3. What are the three types of human rights?

How do these affect managers' decisions?
4. To what extent does corporate social responsibility conflict with responsibility to stockholders?
5. What is your opinion about corporate codes of conduct?

End Notes

1. Peter F. Drucker, *Concept of the Corporation*, rev. ed. (New York: John Day, 1972), p. 209.
2. See Robert C. Solomon, *Ethics and Excellence: Cooperation and Integrity in Business* (New York: Oxford University Press, 1993).
3. Adam Smith, *The Theory of Moral Sentiments* (1790; reprint, Oxford: Clarendon, 1976).
4. Walter W. Manley II, *Executive's Handbook of Model Business Conduct Codes* (Englewood Cliffs, NJ: Prentice Hall, 1991), p. xiii; and Walter W. Manley, *The Handbook of Good Business Practice* (London: Routledge, 1992), p. 2.
5. John Donaldson, *Business Ethics: A European Casebook* (London: Academic Press, 1992), pp. xx–xxi.
6. Francis P. McHugh, *Business Ethics* (New York: Nichols Publishing, 1988), pp. 7–9.
7. John Braithwaite, *Crime, Shame, and Reintegration* (Cambridge: Cambridge University Press, 1989).
8. Archie B. Carroll, *Business and Society: Ethics and Stakeholder Management* (Cincinnati: South-Western Publishing, 1993), p. 34.
9. Quoted in David Vogel, "Ethics and Profits Don't Always Go Hand in Hand," *Los Angeles Times,* December 28, 1988), part II, p. 7.
10. Adam Smith, *An Inquiry into the Nature and Causes of the Wealth of Nations* (1776: reprint, New York: Modern Library, 1937), p. 423.
11. Andrew Stark, "What's the Matter with Business Ethics?" *Harvard Business Review,* May–June 1993, pp. 38–48.
12. Discussions of the pros and cons of utilitarian thinking in management can be found in most business ethics texts. A lucid account is Manuel G. Velasquez, *Business Ethics: Concepts and Cases,* 3rd ed. (New York: Prentice Hall, 1992), Chap. 2.
13. Many experts in business ethics prefer to classify duty-based and rights-based theories as separate, for example, Kenneth E. Goodpaster, *Ethics in Management* (Boston: Harvard Business School 1984), pp. 7–8. Since respect for rights involves a duty, for sake of exposition, I have collapsed the two categories of ethical systems.
14. The most ambitious attempt to develop a rights-based theory of ethics is John Rawls, *A Theory of Justice* (Cambridge, MA: Harvard University Press, 1971).

15. T. H. Marshall's essay is reprinted in his collection, *Class, Citizenship and Social Development* (Garden City, NY: Doubleday, 1964).

16. The idea of negative and positive rights comes from Isaiah Berlin. See *Four Essays on Liberty* (London: Oxford University Press, 1969). Also see Albert O. Hirschman, *The Rhetoric of Reaction* (Cambridge, MA: Belknap, 1991).

17. Robert Nozick, *Anarchy, State, Utopia* (Oxford: Basil Blackwell, 1974).

18. The term began to appear in management texts in the 1970s and is now widely used. See, for instance, R. Edward Freeman, *Strategic Management: A Stakeholder Approach* (Boston: Pitman, 1984). The intellectual origins of the stakeholder concept can be traced to James G. March, "The Business Firm as a Political Coalition," *Journal of Politics* 24, no. 4 (1962), pp. 662–78.

19. James W. Kuhn and Donald W. Shriver, Jr., *Beyond Success: Corporations and Their Critics in the 1990s* (New York: Oxford University Press, 1991), p. 31.

20. For details, see Arthur Sharplin and Aseem Shukla, "Union Carbide of India Limited," in *The Corporate Social Challenge,* 4th ed., ed. Frederick D. Sturdivant and James E. Stacey (Homewood, IL: Richard D. Irwin, 1990), pp. 277–301.

21. Randolph Ryan, "Forum Explores Lawless Business Landscape in Russia," *Boston Globe,* November 19, 1994, p. 5.

22. Milton Friedman, "The Social Responsibility of Business Is to Increase Its Profits," *New York Times Magazine,* September 13, 1971.

23. See Elaine Sternberg, *Just Business* (Boston: Little, Brown, 1994), for development of this argument.

24. Talcott Parsons, "Suggestions for a Sociological Approach to the Theory of Organizations," *Administrative Science Quarterly* 1 (1956), pp. 63–85.

25. This is perhaps the main lesson in the best-seller by Thomas Peters and Robert Waterman, *In Search of Excellence: Lessons from America's Best Managed Companies* (New York: Harper and Row, 1982).

26. Rogene A. Buchholz, William D. Evans, and Robert A. Wagley, *Management Response to Public Issues,* 2nd ed. (Englewood Cliffs, NJ: Prentice Hall, 1989), pp. 277–95.

27. Laura Nash, *Good Intentions Aside* (Boston: Harvard Business School Press, 1990).

28. M. Cash Matthews, *Strategic Intervention in Organizations: Resolving Ethical Dilemmas* (Newbury Park, CA: Sage, 1988), p. 78.

29. Angela Baron and Mike Walters, *The Culture Factor: Corporate and International Factors* (London: Institute of Personnel and Development, 1994).

P A R T

III GOVERNMENT ECONOMIC INTERVENTION

5 PUBLIC POLICY AND THE RISE OF BUSINESS ENTERPRISE

Historical Dimensions

*We may observe that the government in a civilized country is much more
expensive than in a barbarous one . . . There are many expenses necessary in a
civilized country for which there is no occasion in one that is barbarous.
Armies, fleets, fortified palaces, and public buildings, judges, and officers of
the revenue must be supported, and if they be neglected, disorder will ensue.*
Adam Smith[1]

Business counts on and uses the state. This reliance on public policy is not new;
it goes back at least to the beginning of the **Industrial Revolution,** that period
of rapid technological change in the 18th and 19th centuries when modern business began to emerge in the West. By the same token, capitalist states have rarely
been content to sit back and let the market work by itself. To the contrary, they
used their political power to nourish and protect favored companies and industries.

Chapter 5 traces the business–government relation over time. We will see
that government (in its rule-making and umpiring modes) sets the preconditions
for capitalism by making and enforcing the framework for competition. Then
we will turn our attention to the role of the state in economic progress. Here
we will find government not the passive observer of business, but business'
active supporter through its roles of promoter, buyer, producer, and (sometimes)
regulator.

The Industrial Revolution

Today's mass-consumption society is a recent development. As late as the mid-
1800s, the United States was still an agricultural economy, though a prosperous
one by the standards of the time. Most Americans, like people everywhere,

dwelled in rural areas and made a living by farming. They produced and refined the majority of goods they used, and what manufactured goods they bought were made at home or in small firms.

It is hard to overstate the changes in lifestyles, working conditions, and material consumption that have shaken our society in the intervening years—change of such magnitude it has been called the "Great Transformation."[2] Now, three-quarters of the U.S. population live in areas classified as urban, and few people work the land any longer. Most goods are bought in stores. Work is dominated by formal organizations. A similar metamorphosis has taken place in all countries in the "North," and is going on now in some countries long thought of as backward or underdeveloped, particularly in the Far East.

Data on gross domestic product (GDP) give an idea of tempo and scale of the material progress of the past 175 years.[3] The per capita GDP in the United States in 1820 was only about $1,000 (in 1985 dollars)—roughly on a par with India today.[4] Low though this income level looks in hindsight, it was then higher than almost anywhere else. Yet within 50 years, U.S. per capita GDP had more than doubled to about $2,250. By 1989, it was over $18,000, 18 times greater than in 1820.

Other northern nations made analogous strides (see Table 5–1). Germany's per capita GDP rose 15-fold during the same period, from about $900 per head to $14,000. Japan had a 25-fold increase, from under $600 to over $15,000.

Putting a date on the start of any major social process is always a bit arbitrary. According to the economic historian Walt Rostow, however, the German economy began to take off into self-sustaining development around 1850, the Japanese economy, around 1880.[5] In the United States, the turning point came before 1860. Once under way, **industrialization** happened fast in the latecomer nations. They had the advantage of Britain's (and each other's) experience. By 1870, the United States and Germany together produced one-third of the world's industrial output—as much as Britain. Fifty years later, the Americans and the Germans accounted for more than half the world's much greater output, far more than Britain, the world's first industrial power.[6]

TABLE 5–1   **Real per Capita Income in the North Has Risen Enormously since the 19th Century**

	1820	*1870*	*1950*	*1989*
France	$1,052	$1,571	$4,149	$13,837
Germany	937	1,300	3,339	13,989
Japan	558	618	1,563	15,101
Sweden	947	1,316	5,331	14,912
United Kingdom	1,405	2,610	5,651	13,468
United States	**1,048**	**2,247**	**8,611**	**18,317**

Note: Figures are GDP per head at 1985 prices.

Source: Angus Maddison, *Dynamic Forces in Capitalist Development* (Oxford: Oxford University Press, 1991).

Rising Standards of Living

These dry numbers mask the material impact of the epic move of people from the countryside to the city, and from small- to large-scale enterprise. In the mid-19th century, the average American family spent nearly all its income on food, clothing, and shelter. The quality of these items was far below modern expectations. People ate mostly simple foods of questionable nutrition, such as lard, potatoes, cornmeal, and salt pork. Frozen and out-of-season fresh foods were unknown, even to the rich. Most clothing was handmade.

Nearly half the rural population lived in log cabins of one or two rooms. Living conditions in cities were worse. Boston in 1860 had only 31,000 sinks, 4,000 baths, and 10,000 toilets. City streets were poorly paved, if paved at all, foul, and overrun with animal scavengers. Goods and people moved only as fast as a horse or the wind allowed. A quarter of the population could neither read nor write. Due to poor diet, lack of hygiene, and primitive medical care, lives were short. A person born in 1855 could expect to live but 40 years.[7]

A century and a half later, Americans are better off in ways our ancestors could not have imagined. A far smaller share of income goes to necessities today, leaving more for education and play. Food—fresh, frozen, and canned—is readily available in dizzying variety. Inexpensive clothing is taken for granted, as are central heating, plumbing, electricity, and paved roads. Speedy travel and instant long-distance communication are mundane events. A constant flow of gadgets—color television, microwave ovens, personal computers, cellular telephones, compact disc players—enter the market and become the norm. Life expectancy has nearly doubled since 1855, to 76 years.

The biggest winners of **economic development** have been the poor and the middle class.[8] Not only did their incomes rise over the past century and a half, both absolutely and as a share of the total, but the cost of things they needed and wanted to buy also fell in real terms. Ordinary people now enjoy a level of material well-being that, in most respects, would have been beyond even the wealthiest families of the past.

Industrialization was not an outright blessing, of course. It uprooted people from familiar locales and routines. It forced them into crowded living conditions and made them work for long stretches at boring and dangerous jobs. Urban ills such as pollution, crime, and visible poverty deepened in the 19th century. Fed up with their lot, workers began organizing themselves for better wages and working conditions. The modern labor union movement resulted, as did socialist and other radical parties.

Post-Industrial Society

Internally, the northern economies' structure turned upside down because of industrialization (see Table 5–2). From a starting base in agriculture, they grew to be dominated by industry (defined as mining, manufacturing, construction, and energy). By the 1920s, most workers in Britain, and somewhat lower ratios

TABLE 5–2   **The North Has Changed in the Past 150 Years from Agricultural Economies, to Industrial Economies, and Now to Service Economies**

	Share of Labor Force		
	Agriculture	*Industry*	*Services*
Great Britain			
1851/61	20%	43%	37%
1921	9	59	32
1989	2	29	68
United States			
1839	64	16	20
1929	21	38	41
1989	3	27	70
Germany			
1852	54	27	19
1925	31	47	23
1989	4	40	57
Japan			
1872	86	6	9
1920	55	25	20
1989	8	34	58

Sources: Simon Kuznets, *Economic Growth of Nations* (Cambridge, MA: Belknap Press, 1971), pp. 250–52; *Historical Statistics 1960–1989* (Paris: Organization for Economic Cooperation and Development, 1991).

in Germany and the United States, worked in industrial pursuits. Japan, later to industrialize, then had about one-fourth of its labor force in industry.

Since the 1920s, the capitalist economies have continued to evolve, so that services (transport, trade, finance, and so on) make up the biggest sector. In the United States, for example, 70 percent of the labor force now works in services. Few people work in factories making things, and even fewer work on farms. Other countries are on the same trajectory. Even Japan and Germany, noted industrial powers, have more than half their labor force in the service sector.

Because of the move to services, some analysts contend that the capitalist world has moved into the **postindustrial** era, dominated by technocrats in control of ideas and other nonmaterial resources.[9] Postindustrial societies are paradoxical. They are marked by widespread affluence, but also by problems in producing enough well-paid jobs for everyone who wants them. They grow rich from the rapid movement of capital and information, though those same flows of resources also encourage the breakdown of families and communities.

Their label to the contrary, postindustrial societies remain heavily industrialized. While they have exported many of their dirtiest industries, they continue to manufacture many things. And they use sophisticated technology and machinery even when they produce services rather than goods.

Market-Driven Factors and the Industrial Revolution

How did this monumental change happen? How did we turn from a stable society based on tools to a dynamic one using machines? More importantly, how can progress be maintained into the 21st century? Economic development is ongoing. It requires constant attention, even in mature economies such as the United States. A nation can lose its economic edge if it is not careful. Thus, industrialization holds more than historical interest.

Revolution suggests sudden change, and the initial changes caused by the first Industrial Revolution left people reeling. In 1727, Manchester, England, was described by Daniel Defoe as "a mere village." Forty years later, 100 integrated mills were in the area, making it the center of world textile manufacturing.[10] Industrial production for the whole country went up 400 percent between 1701–1710 and 1803–1812.[11] Still, to think of economic development as a series of stages or discrete jumps is misleading. A more accurate description is a permanent sequence of decay and renewal, of old technologies and industries replacing or supplementing newer ones. Industrialization also entails **deindustrialization,** as Americans who have lost jobs in traditional lines of work have become acutely aware in recent years.

To account for economic progress, political economy leads us to look at both private enterprise and public policy. Private enterprise is one leg of the Great Transformation—companies large and small have been continually upgrading their methods and products since the 19th century and earlier. Their contribution to the economic betterment of the United States, and other northern countries, is central. As the business historian Alfred Chandler argues in his recent book *Scale and Scope*, without the ability and willingness of managers to invest in large-scale enterprises, the Industrial Revolution would not have pushed ahead.[12]

The other leg of development is public policy. Business competition and industrialization do not happen in a vacuum; they need a sustaining environment fashioned by the state. Too often in management education, the role of public policy in nurturing development gets overlooked, so we will direct our attention to it in this chapter.

Political Prerequisites for the Market

To understand the political economy of industrialization, let us begin by analyzing the political prerequisites for the market system. Most Americans take the market for granted. Yet, conditions for exchange have to be in place first, and many of these are public goods that must be provided by the state. An unfettered, competitive market is itself a public good and needs public action to be sustained.[13] As Susan Strange puts it: "Markets cannot play a dominant role in the way in which a political economy functions unless allowed to do so by whoever wields power and possesses authority."[14] Government action, not just individual drive, ushered in the market economy we know today by creating an environment favorable to investment and trade. There is nothing automatic or inevitable about this sequence.

Umpire and Rule Maker

As so often, Adam Smith states the case well. "Commerce and manufactures," he writes, "can seldom flourish long in any state which does not enjoy a regular administration of justice, in which people do not feel themselves secure in possession of their property, in which the faith of contracts is not supported by the law . . ."[15] Here, Smith has highlighted three public goods—basic law and order, the right to property, and the enforcement of contracts. Public goods, it will be recalled, are things produced by combined effort that benefit people despite whether they join in the effort. Each item on Smith's list is fundamental to business as we know it and worth a closer look.

Basic Law and Order. An industrial economy depends on large-scale commerce, on exchange between different towns, cities, regions, and countries.[16] Large-scale commerce needs lawfulness. For most of history, governments could not guarantee law and order, especially at night and in remote areas. Pirates and bandits flourished; goods moved slowly and at high risk. What 18th century philosophers called "commodious living" was hampered.

Lack of law and order is still a problem in many parts of the world, most dramatically where central states have completely broken down, as in the former Soviet Union. In Russia, gangsters are said to control half the private enterprise. Gangs operate freely, extorting payments from businesses with the threats of violence.[17] The resulting insecurity is compounding that country's economic meltdown and frustrating efforts to build an efficient, market-oriented economy.

We often forget that England established paid magistrates (judges) only in 1792 and set up a national system of full-time police only in 1856. Effective security came late to the New World, too. Volunteers did police work in colonial America until about 1750, when rising crime led communities to begin paying for wardens and watchmen. The first modern urban police force had to wait until 1844, when one was set up in New York. In frontier areas, unofficial "vigilance committees" of armed citizens continued to provide much local justice through the 19th century. Federal crimes, mainly mail and railroad crime, were covered by a relative handful of U.S. marshals (salaried only in 1896).

The emergence of these new public safety institutions had a profound impact. The rate of reported property crimes without violence in England fell by half between 1857 and the turn of the century. Property crimes with violence dropped by one-third.[18] Statistics are poor for the United States, but there are probably fewer murders per capita today than during the 1800s.[19]

Economic development needs laws that do more than physically protect, important though physical protection is. The sociologist Max Weber stresses the need for laws that are calculable. In preindustrial societies, Weber argues, systems of justice were subjective and changeable. They discouraged predictable conduct. Modern societies have evolved more formal and logical modes of legal reasoning.[20] Legislation, adjudication, and administration of laws are regular and dependable. By making the legal consequences of acts easier to foresee, the machinery of modern law reduces the risks of investing and trading. Weber probably overstates the coherence of modern law, but his main point cannot be denied. Commerce abhors uncertainty. All other things being equal, the more certain society's rules, the greater the volume of commercial activity.

Property Rights.   For early merchants and traders, the most important type of law and order may not have been to save their holdings from criminals, but to save them from the state. Monarchs and lords claimed the privilege to seize private assets whenever reasons of state required it. Their monopoly on force allowed them to exercise this privilege freely, checked only by their subjects' ability to move or conceal their possessions. Commerce was stifled by the need for secrecy.

As Smith recognized, the modern institution of **property rights** improved the climate for business. Property is a legal fiction. It refers to things that are owned. The right to ownership has four elements: (1) the right to use an asset, (2) the right to capture the benefit from that asset, (3) the right to change its form and substance, and (4) the right to transfer it to others at a mutually agreed price. Property is the bedrock for market exchange, since people cannot give and get assets they do not own.

In the 18th century, notions of property were shifting and ambiguous. Every trade had distinctive cheats and frauds, what we would today condemn as corruption, that the perpetrators considered customary rights to supplement their monetary wage. In Britain, tailors had their "cabbage" (stolen remnants), while tobacco workers practiced "socking" (pilfering from barrels) and dockworkers expected their "chips" (scraps and waste). Over time, employers got the state to label these acts criminal, a trespass of their property rights.[21]

Embezzlement, bribery, and other forms of corruption never fully died out in the West, but they have been pushed into the background. Corrupt practices are more prevalent in many developing countries and the transitional economies of eastern Europe. Not only are gratuities accepted modes of expediting business transactions, official corruption often runs so deep it is an impediment to commercial activity.

The idea of property, of possession, also is the basis of lawful, limited government. Historically, the claim of individuals to property grew with business's political influence. Over time, merchants and artisans in the West got the state to accept policies that limited its ability to encroach on private holdings. Property evolved into the realm of personal independence, largely beyond the rightful reach of government, that we know today.

John Locke (1632–1704) is the philosopher who made the most influential arguments for property rights. His ideas held sway on the framers of the U.S. Constitution and its first 10 amendments (1789–91).[22] Today, most Americans agree individuals ought to be left alone with the things they make and buy. We are prone to associate restraints on property rights with socialist thinking, forgetting how circumscribed is property even in the capitalist United States. Property is never more than the balance of things the state does not claim, and which the state permits us to call our own.

Eminent domain illustrates the point. Eminent domain entitles the sovereign to take property for a public use. It supersedes individual claims. Usually thought of concerning land, the power of eminent domain also applies to income and capital (taxation) and to labor (the military draft). We confine this power with many policy safeguards, but almost no one questions the state's right to seize property for the good of society, even in capitalist systems.

The limits to property—what individuals may own, use, and sell—are always a matter for public policy. Zoning laws are a good example. Zoning restricts land use for the good of the community: A landowner may not run some businesses or build certain structures on land because of neighbors' objections. In some historic districts, even the color paint used on the outside of a structure is subject to community approval. Price controls are another example. They specify for how much items can be sold and infringe on owners' rights to dispose of property as they wish. Like any public policy, the limits to property are subject to change. Zones can be changed and price controls lifted whenever the state so decides.

Contract Enforcement.   The third public good that Smith mentions is **contracts.** A contract is a binding agreement between two or more people to do something. It is the means by which people seek, specify, and guarantee exchanges. The central use of contracts is to hold down transaction cost, or the price of settling deals among diverse parties. Contracts reduce transaction cost by holding parties accountable—an unfortunate necessity because, in the view of political economy, people are opportunistic and will otherwise seek advantage.

Market economies cannot work without contracts for two reasons. First, contracts encourage exchanges that do not take place at the same time. The parties to an exchange can be confident that money spent today will result in goods being delivered tomorrow. Contracts thus promote large-scale commerce. Second, contracts aid people to deal with strangers, with businesses beyond their immediate community, and to buy and sell goods of which they have seen only samples or descriptions.

According to Sir Henry Maine (1822–1888), the great English jurist, before the invention of contracts, people had to rely mainly on social status to secure agreements. A reputation for honesty is still an important asset in business, particularly where personal connections are important. Still, think how many fewer transactions would take place today if they had to be based mainly on honor and a handshake. Telephone and credit card purchases, for example, could never have developed.

Living up to contracts has become a habit in the United States and other northern countries. Yet it is a habit gained from routine enforcement by government. Without the state's pledge to punish broken contracts, the climate of trust necessary to capitalist exchange would break down. The pursuit and arrest of swindlers and cheaters is critical for maintaining business and consumer confidence.

People cannot enforce contracts by themselves. They need an objective third party to do it: the state. Smith explains why in his usual concise way: "As the violation of justice is what men will never submit to from one another, the public magistrate is under a necessity of employing the power of the commonwealth to enforce the practice of this virtue. Without this precaution, civil society would become a scene of bloodshed and disorder, every man revenging himself at his own hand whenever he fancied he was injured."[23]

From Exchange to Development

Law and order, property rights, and the enforcement of contracts only set the stage for business exchange. More needs to happen to trigger development—the process of expanding production and changing the economic structure to one where industry is dominant. By the 19th century, industrialization had made Britain the world's richest and most powerful nation. Inspired by the British example, America, Europe (including Russia), and Japan consciously tried to catch up.

Of the late developers, the United States probably had the most laissez-faire development strategy. Still, even here government's visible hand is always present. Let us look at how public policy affects several causal factors in industrialization: capital accumulation, technology, methods of organization and management, entrepreneurship, and cultural attitudes. These causal factors are usually thought to be matters of private concern, yet there is often a hidden public dimension.

Capital Accumulation.   **Saving** and **investment** are crucial for business to grow. Saving is the act of giving up current consumption. By not consuming resources today, people release resources for investment—to be used to make capital that will produce income in the future. By **capital,** political economists mean anything that enhances society's power to do work—the stock of tools, equipment, buildings. Included is so-called **human capital,** or investment in education and training to enable people to produce more.

Also included in a society's capital stock is **infrastructure,** the skeleton and the circulatory system of the economy that allow goods and services to move to market. Roads, tunnels, harbors, dams, sewers, and telephone lines are examples of infrastructure. Rostow uses the more colorful term "social overhead capital," because infrastructure is a cost of doing business that cannot be attributed to any particular economic activity.[24]

As private and public capital build up, as society acquires more capacity to produce, greater national income may follow. In Karl Marx's theory of society, the accumulation of capital is the force that turns the wheel of capitalist development. Accumulated capital leads to surplus production that is reinvested, leading to more production, more surplus, more capital, and so forth. Many non-Marxists agree, at least in part, that capital investment is the motor for industrial progress. We will later see that the efficiency with which capital is used counts more than the raw quantity of capital.

Government joins indirectly and directly in the buildup of capital assets. The indirect role is that of economic manager—providing a stable currency and supporting a financial system that can supply firms with funds to expand. In the early period of the American republic, Congress went as far as to bankroll (with minority government ownership) the Bank of the United States. Its purpose was to increase the supply of financial capital for the economy's priority sectors. Controversial due to its power, the bank was closed in 1811. Farmers were particularly critical of the national bank for being too powerful and for serving East Coast monied interests. A successor bank reopened in 1816 and then closed again in 1836.

Thirty years of chaotic wildcat banking followed, with no uniform national currency or national debt markets. Not until the National Banking Act of 1863, which laid the groundwork for the regulatory structure that exists today, was order brought to the banking industry. The resulting financial stability aided the industrialization of the last half the 19th century.

Government's direct involvement in building up the infrastructure—part of its promoter role—also is vital. Excellent illustrations are the railroads and telegraphs that helped unify the modernizing American economy, creating a continental market. Like most infrastructure, railroads and telegraphs have long periods of gestation (railroads take time to build and repay investors), and they cannot be made in small increments (part of a railroad is useless). Thus, government had to get involved.

Public finance was more than half the investment in U.S. railroads by the Civil War. Steam-powered railroads had been introduced in England in 1825. A year later, the first American line was built in Quincy, Massachusetts. The Quincy railroad was horse-drawn, but steam locomotion was started in the United States in 1830. By 1850, 9,000 miles of track had been laid in this country alone. By 1860, the national total was 30,000 miles.[25]

State and municipal governments sometimes took part directly in these ventures through outright ownership of rail companies. Cincinnati and Baltimore, for instance, owned railroads at one point. But it was the federal government that bore most of the burden. Its chief method of financing railroads was the land grant, which it had begun to make to states for specific internal improvements starting in 1823. Given a federal grant of land, states would raise funds by either selling the property or using it as collateral for loans.

This practice was expanded to build the railroad system. Between 1850 and 1872, 131 million acres were made available, most going directly or indirectly to the railroad companies, such as the Union Pacific Company, so they could push their lines west. Such generosity invited corruption, such as the notorious Crédit Mobilier scandal. The Crédit Mobilier was a construction company, owned by a few large shareholders in the Union Pacific, who made contracts with themselves for building the railroad. This arrangement depleted the congressional grants. To forestall investigation, the company assigned shares of Crédit Mobilier stock to members of Congress. Once the press found out, there was a public uproar roughly equivalent to our era's Watergate affair. In hindsight, abuses such as these seem a small price to pay for getting the railroads built. The federal government also helped the railroads by paying for federal engineers to survey the land before laying track.[26]

The spreading railroad network created a need for rapid, long-distance communication. The telegraph, patented in 1837 by Samuel Morse, seemed the answer. Again, government action proved important. The U.S. Congress in 1842 appropriated funds to build a demonstration telegraph line from Washington to Baltimore, to see if the invention worked. It did, and by 1848, 2,000 miles of telegraph wire were operating in the United States. Four years later, there were 23,000 miles.[27] Clearly, the growth of the nation's infrastructure would have been slowed without government action.

Technology.   Important though amassing capital is, technological progress has more effect on development. **Technology** means science applied to production. As technology advances, it lets people use capital more productively. At higher levels of technology, society can turn out more output per unit of effort. Rising productivity, and thus rising living standards, rest on technological improvements.

The paradigm innovation in the first Industrial Revolution was James Watts's improved steam engine (1769). Earlier, watermills and windmills had produced only 10 horsepower on average. By 1800, steam engines could produce nearly 20 times that amount. The harnessing of steam, and later other forms of power such as electricity, made possible huge savings in labor cost. It also permitted large cities, since factories could be placed far from energy sources.

Another critical discovery was Sir Henry Bessemer's cheap way to make steel (1856). Steel became a standard commodity and soon replaced iron and wood in many uses. More complex, durable, and larger equipment and structures became possible. Steel production exploded in the United States. Annual output went from 6,000 tons in 1850 to more than 11 million tons in 1900.

After the industrialized countries of the North had assimilated steam power, they went through two more technological revolutions. One occurred around 1900, sparked by electricity and the internal combustion engine. The second Industrial Revolution affected many science-based industries such as chemicals and petroleum and was devoted to mass production and mass marketing. The so-called third Industrial Revolution, based on computers and electronics, is taking place in our own day. It seems to put more premium on flexible production and special product features than it does on mass-produced items.

Throughout the first, second, and third Industrial Revolutions, new machines, building materials, and energy sources made farms, mines, and plants more productive. Output per person rose many times. In the 1880s, for instance, Singer Sewing Machine supplied three-fourths of the world's demand for sewing machines from two plants.[28] A cigarette-making machine developed in 1881 was so productive that 15 of them could supply the entire U.S. market for cigarettes.[29] Cheap, high-quality goods grew abundant.

Joseph Schumpeter (1883–1950), the great Austrian economist, put technology at the center of economic progress. He believed technological breakthroughs created long booms by making new horizons for business to expand. The era of railroad building in the mid-1800s was one such breakthrough, and it created a wave of activity that for years carried the whole economy forward. When this technology was spent, the economy lost its buoyancy. Later, the internal combustion engine and the automobile provided a new technological lift.[30] Though he did not live to see it, Schumpeter's followers think the process continues with computers and electronics.

Government had two hands in promoting technical innovation in the early United States. One was the patent system. The practice of granting patents— temporary monopoly rights for inventions—started in Renaissance Italy and spread to England and the colonies. One of the few powers the U.S. Constitution specifically granted Congress was the power to grant exclusive rights to inventors as a way "to promote the progress of science and useful arts." It seems to have worked. In the 1840s, fewer than 500 patents were granted in the United States annually; in the 1880s, the number was more than 20,000 annually.[31]

The second way government got involved as a promoter of improved technology was through direct engagement in research and development (**R&D**). The most important early example was in agriculture.

Improvements in farm technology freed labor from the land so it could work in industry. Much farm technology is a public good. Better farming methods are apt to be nonexclusive (open to all) and nonsubtractable (sharing does not lessen availability). One farmer's successful new technique, in other words, is liable to be copied by his neighbors, thus negating the competitive advantage of the innovation. Farming techniques change slowly because of the deterrent for private farmers to innovate.

The solution was to set up tax-supported agricultural experiment stations to do R&D in the public interest. The first public experiment station was founded in Germany in 1851. Connecticut was the initial American state to copy the German model in 1875. A dozen years later, the federal government provided financial backing for experiment stations in every state. Soon they began to generate technology, such as hybrid corn (mass produced at the Connecticut station in a 1917 breakthrough). These discoveries led to huge jumps in farm productivity, which allowed many farmers to move to cities and take factory jobs.

The experience with agriculture inspired direct government support for R&D in many other sectors. We will return to the modern use of technology policy in Chapter 16.

Methods of Organization.   Technology is more than new hardware. It is also the software of better methods of organization and management. No doubt the biggest step forward in organizational technique was when people first decided to break work into specialized tasks and divide them—a mode of organizing that began to spread in the 17th century. It made possible large increases in labor productivity.

From the division of labor, the next logical step was to use interchangeable parts. Eli Whitney is credited with perfecting this technique, in what became called the American System of manufacturing. Uniform parts led to sensational cost cutting in making firearms, clocks, and other products. The government's buyer role was important—Whitney felt the assured government market for weapons gave him the freedom to experiment with the American System.[32] So impressed were the British, Parliament sent a committee to the United States in the 1850s to see how the American System worked.

Another U.S. management innovation was the moving production line, pioneered by meatpackers in Cincinnati around 1815. A century later, Henry Ford refined these ideas—division of labor, standardized parts, moving assembly—in his automobile plants. He reduced the labor time for putting together a Model T chassis from 12½ hours to 1½ hours. Cost plummeted, bringing cars within reach of the average person and quickly creating one of the world's largest family fortunes.

Bureaucracy and Large-Scale Organization.   To take full advantage of the economies inherent in specialization, companies had to get much larger. The change started in England about 1750. Before, working men and women used hand tools to turn out articles in their homes or in small shops. With the Industrial Revolution, owners and managers brought people together under one roof in factories, where they operated complex, powered machines. The first industries affected were textiles and then metallurgy.

Still, in 1840, the largest firm in the United States was the Springfield Armory in Massachusetts, with 250 employees. Railroads, with government backing, made a quantum leap forward in organizational size—only 15 years later, for instance, the Baltimore and Ohio Railroad listed 4,259 employees on its roster.[33] Companies in other industries copied and improved on the railroad's organizational methods. By 1919, three-fourths of the wage earners in manufacturing in the Northeast worked in factories with more than 100 employees. Thirty percent worked in giants with more than 1,000 employees.

These new business organizations were **bureaucracies.** As analyzed by Max Weber, in what is probably his most famous contribution to social science, a bureaucracy has the following characteristics: a graded hierarchy, formal rules, written files, and salaried, full-time staff.[34] The 19th century business enterprise set itself up by function—finance, operations, sales, and so on. It perfected the use of shop-order control systems and rate-fixing departments. Eventually, these innovations were codified in the new discipline of **scientific management,** led by Frederick Winslow Taylor (1856–1915).

Bureaucracy and scientific management have bad names today, but, for all their drawbacks, these innovations in administrative techniques allowed unparalleled central control and accountability. Companies could grow larger than they had before, enabling them to reap the economies of scale and scope inherent in the machines available. Even socialists advocated the use of the capitalist tools of bureaucracy and scientific management. Writing in 1918, Vladimir Lenin (1870–1924), founder of the Soviet state, declared: "We must organize in Russia the study and teaching of the Taylor system and singlemindedly try it out and adapt it to our needs."[35]

It is obvious now that bureaucratic organizations fall far short of the well-oiled machine envisioned by Taylor and Lenin. Everyone has a favorite story of bureaucracy gone wrong, of abuses and irrationality in large organizations. The virtues of bureaucracy, however, often outweigh the defects. For many tasks, particularly those of a routine nature, no one has identified structures and procedures that work better.[36]

Corporations.   Business enterprises did not get big spontaneously. Often overlooked today is that public policy was the midwife for the growing scale of business when it began allowing companies to incorporate easily. A **corporation** is an organized entity that has been given a legal personality and is entitled to do certain things, such as own property and enter contracts. We take it for granted, yet this form of organization is a relative novelty and a key to the growth of large industry.

Through the Middle Ages, most business was done by kin group, and lack of resources confined family-based concerns mostly to smaller projects. To raise the funds for more ambitious ventures, group or social ownership is helpful. Yet the transaction cost of organizing an investment group is daunting without government approval. Beginning in the 16th century, England and other European countries found a way to foster group-owned activities. They began to grant charters to joint-stock companies. Individuals could own stock jointly in these companies, whose charters allowed them to conduct specific business with monopoly privileges.

Often the idea was to encourage colonies and foreign trade. The Virginia Company (1606), the Massachusetts Bay Company (1629), and the Hudson's Bay Company (1670) are examples. Many joint-stock companies also were chartered to build bridges, roads, and other public works. Two important points to remember:

1. As corporations, these groups had rights under the law and could carry on projects despite the fate of individual owners.
2. Owners were at risk only for their investment; creditors to the company could not come after owners' other assets.

In legal language, this protection to owners is known as **limited liability,** source of the British term *ltd.* (equivalent to the American term *inc.*). The French counterpart S.A. (*societé anonyme*) is also revealing—in the eyes of the law, a corporation is a society of nameless persons who cannot be held personally responsible for collective liabilities. There is what lawyers call a corporate veil that hides and protects shareholders.

Incorporation was initially a privilege, extended by government for certain ends. By the 17th century, merchants in England began to form companies on their own, without the privilege of incorporation. Shares in these unincorporated firms were freely transferrable, creating the possibility of a capital market. Liquidity made the shares attractive, but it only partly offset the obstacles created by the lack of a corporate charter. Without corporate status, these companies had to go through awkward ploys to enter contracts. Nor could they offer investors the safety of limited liability. Between 1800 and 1823, only 557 manufacturing establishments had been incorporated in New England, New York, and Pennsylvania.

With time, incorporation turned into a right, not a privilege. The charter became automatic to anyone who met minimum requirements for running a business. In the United States, by the 1830s, state legislatures were routinely granting charters that took limited liability for granted. In the years after 1845, most states adopted general incorporation laws, allowing companies to incorporate without special legislation. There was support for limited liability because it was seen as democratic—it would encourage dispersed ownership of companies and act as a counterweight to the power of individual fortunes.

Incorporation was one of government's most important rules that helped business develop. Once they had the go-ahead to incorporate freely, large business concerns quickly became the economy's dominant feature. By 1919, there were 91,000 manufacturing corporations in the United States.[37]

There are few unincorporated large commercial organizations left anywhere. Even Lloyd's of London, which is not incorporated and whose owners (called "names") did not have the protection of limited liability for the organization's first 305 years, recently agreed to a change in policy. Too many "names" were losing their personal wealth to insurance claims. To guard their other property, the "names" have agreed to make Lloyd's a corporation.

Entrepreneurship.   New methods of organization and new technology do not happen by themselves. Innovation is always a human act. Some person has to think up and want to use the new inventions. That is why Schumpeter, the theorist of technical change, attributes development ultimately to **entrepreneurs**—to individuals who can see and make new chances for business.

According to Schumpeter, economic progress is "creative destruction." Dominant firms are undermined and replaced by competitors that can take advantage of the sorts of technical and management discoveries we just saw. In Schumpeter's view, entrepreneurs push the economy forward. The quest for profit induces them to try to stay one step ahead of the competition. To gain a temporary edge, they introduce new methods and products. Using political economic terms, entrepreneurs create disequilibria in markets, which allow them to cash in on economic rents before rivals have time to react.

The Industrial Revolution is partly a history of outstanding private entrepreneurs—"captains of industry" to their admirers, "robber barons" to their detractors. In the United States, Rockefeller, Carnegie, Ford, Gould, Morgan, and other names from an earlier era are still well-known. New names, like Jobs, Perot, Gates, and Kapor, are always joining the list. Many of these enterprising individuals hit on a few good ideas. These ideas need not be profound; they are often so simple it is surprising no one previously had thought of them.

Entrepreneurship is not solely a feature of the private sector, however. Entrepreneurs are prevalent in the public sector, too, and their activities have added to economic development. The state agricultural experiment stations we discussed earlier prove the point. The drive for the first experiment station in the United States, in Connecticut, was led by Samuel Johnson, a Yale professor who became the station's second director in 1877. In New York, a public entrepreneur, E. Lewis Sturtevant, got the state legislature to set up an experiment station under his leadership in 1882. Similar stories repeated themselves in other states and other countries. Usually, a self-interested, yet also public-spirited, person stands behind new public organizations.[38]

Cultural Attitudes.   Also important in industrialization are culture and mental outlook. The most famous champion of this argument is Weber, the sociologist whose analysis of modern law and bureaucracy we discussed earlier in this chapter. Weber showed how habits of rational thinking and the belief that work is good foster the growth of business.[39] In his view, preindustrial societies are held back partly because people lack drive. Members of these societies consider themselves bound by fate and tradition and do not put much stock in material success. Their economies languish.

What shakes preindustrial people out of their torpor? Weber emphasized the spread of the Protestant faith, which encourages a set of values that motivate people to get ahead. Conspicuous among Protestant values are beliefs in thrift, honesty, experiments and criticism, reward based on merit, and idleness as a vice. Though of religious origin, these values have the accidental effect of promoting economic development.

Ambition and hard work are not solely Protestant virtues, of course. Many observers see a Confucian work ethic in East Asian societies. Around the world, minority groups seem to acquire values and skills that allow them to excel in business, perhaps because they do not fit into the larger society. Sikhs and Jains in India, Chinese in Malaysia and the West Indies, Syrians and Lebanese in West Africa, Jews in Europe and America, and Indians and Pakistanis in East Africa are examples of enterprising minorities that come readily to mind.[40] Americans of all religions have long been regarded as especially devoted to making money.

It is often forgotten that government, in its role as business promoter, has long been concerned with goading people to work. The policy in early modern Europe was simply to make work compulsory—a policy backed by vagrancy laws, debtors' prisons, and work houses. Colonists brought these rules to America. Communities appointed overseers of the poor to collect a poor tax and dispense relief to paupers. The English model distinguished between the deserving poor (the old, the sick, widows, and orphans) and the undeserving poor (vagrants and sturdy beggars). The last were treated harshly—unemployed persons in colonial America could be punished by beating. Anyone who could was expected to work. The first poorhouse for forced labor was established in New York City in the 1600s. Poorhouses became widespread in the 1800s in the United States, partly as a way to keep down the taxes for poor relief.

In the 1870s, state after state passed "tramp acts," making it a crime for people without visible means of support to travel about the country. Such laws remain on the books, though they are not much enforced anymore, and they helped foster labor discipline at critical periods in the past. We like to think that current laws are more enlightened, but some scholars contend that a social function of the modern welfare state is to stigmatize unemployment and shame people into working.[41]

Another way government promotes a work ethic is through public schools. Using its power to tax everyone, government provides free and compulsory education. In the United States, this practice dates from the 17th century, when colonial towns were made to maintain schools at public expense. Schooling became mandatory starting in 1852, when Massachusetts passed the nation's first compulsory attendance law. Other states soon followed the Massachusetts example, though the laws were widely ignored until around 1900. Education was deemed too important to the community to be left to individual choice.

The obvious reason for public schooling is to teach children basic skills so they can become productive members of the new industrial society. (The illiteracy rate of U.S. army enlistees, 35 percent in the 1840s, dropped to 7 percent by the 1890s.[42]) Less obvious, the public school movement was about values. With immigration to the United States surging in the 19th century, it excited fears about the attitudes and aptitudes of the newcomers. Universal and compulsory education seemed the cure. Nineteenth century schooling was consciously designed to instill in all children good work habits—punctuality, respect for authority, and self-discipline.[43] We come back to contemporary issues of education and training in Chapter 18.

Rising Regulation

Industrialization had many bad side effects, such as monopoly and consumer fraud. These market failures created pressure for regulatory policies. Looking back over the past century in the United States, we see a rising tide of regulation with three crests. Between 1900 and 1980, 131 major federal regulatory statutes were enacted. The number of federal agencies supervising those statutes increased from 6 to 56. Parallel regulatory expansion took place at the state level.

The first regulatory crest was in the progressive era (circa 1890–1920). Laws were enacted to reign in Big Business, which was popularly believed to have grown too powerful for the country's good. Significant were the Sherman Antitrust Act (aimed at controlling monopolies) and the Federal Trade Commission Act (aimed at ensuring fair trade). As a rule, progressive era regulation tried to regulate economic activity comprehensively, in all sectors of the economy, though the landmark Interstate Commerce Act (1887) was focused on the railroads.

The next crest was in the New Deal of President Franklin Roosevelt (1932–1945). The regulatory policy of that period was intended to fight the Great Depression, which analysts ascribed to excess competition. To combat the ill effects of what was labeled "economic cannibalism," policy makers began to regulate prices, entry, and conditions of service in specific sectors.[44] The Roosevelt era produced such agencies as the Securities and Exchange Commission (covering the stock market), the Federal Communications Commission (covering radio and, later, television), and the Civil Aeronautics Board (covering commercial aviation). Unlike the progressive era regulation, these bodies did not cover every industry in the economy. An exception was the National Labor Relations Act (1935), aimed at stopping unfair labor practices by all employers.

The last crest of regulatory policy was in the 1960s and 1970s. While the first two crests had focused on making business work better, this one tried mainly to mend the externalities created by modern industry. There were efforts to stop companies from polluting (the Environmental Protection Act), to get companies to protect consumers from danger (Consumer Products Safety Act), and to make companies provide safer jobs (Occupational Safety and Health Act). Like progressive era regulation, recent regulation is apt to cut across industries.

Due to its lofty goals, and to its lack of thought about the most cost-effective means of reaching those goals, the last crest of regulatory policy has earned the pejorative name of **social regulation** in the United States. This class of regulation stands in supposed contrast to earlier economic regulation, which focused on economic matters such as prices. The dichotomy is misleading, however, for the earlier regulation was also claimed to help society, while the new regulation obviously has economic impact. Clear and consistent distinctions between social and economic regulation do not exist. Undeniably, U.S. employers found the 1960s-style regulation less acceptable than older statutes because it was more intrusive, inviting extensive government control over production methods and the quality of goods and services. We will look at specific economic and social regulatory issues in detail in Parts V and VI of this book.

Conclusion

We have seen in this chapter that throughout the modern era, business and economic development have been considered too important to leave to businesspeople only. We have debunked the folklore that government was ever fully laissez-faire, even in the freewheeling early United States. To the contrary, government has used its power to grant favors and make exceptions to create an environment in which private sector growth can occur. There is nothing inevitable or natural about this train of events. Industrialization does not just happen; it takes risk taking by private investors *and* urging by government.

In Chapter 6 we bring this discussion further up to date. We turn to the topics of capitalism, socialism, and democracy, and discuss contemporary models of organizing political economies. We will see why communist systems collapsed in the 1980s and discuss how, with a different approach, some less-developed countries have propelled themselves into the industrial world.

We also will see that advanced capitalist economies are themselves tending to converge as global economic forces oblige them to learn from each others' practices.

Questions

1. Why did industry grow rapidly from the mid-19th century in the United States?

2. Describe the growth of business enterprises. What drove their development?

3. What purposes do contracts and private property serve in industrialization?

4. Do you think Americans have a strong work ethic? What evidence leads you to that conclusion?

5. Why is the right of incorporation so important?

End Notes

1. Adam Smith, *Lectures on Jurisprudence* (1762–64; reprint, Oxford: Oxford University Press, 1978), pp. 530–31.

2. The phrase is from the title of Karl Polanyi's classic work, *The Great Transformation* (Boston: Beacon Press, 1957).

3. GDP is a measure of national income. It differs slightly from GNP because it does not include investment income from abroad.

4. Angus Maddison, *Dynamic Forces in Capitalist Development* (Oxford: Oxford University Press, 1991), p. 25.

5. W. W. Rostow, *The Stages of Economic Growth,* 3rd ed. (Cambridge: Cambridge University Press, 1990), p. 38.

6. Ibid., pp. 52–53.

7. The data in this paragraph is mainly from William J. Baumol, Sue Anne Batey Blackman, and Edward N. Wolff, *Productivity and American Leadership* (Cambridge, MA: MIT Press, 1989), Chapter 3.

8. Nathan Rosenberg and L. E. Birdzell, Jr., *How the West Grew Rich* (New York: Basic Books, 1985), p. 27.

9. Seymour Martin Lipset, ed., *The Third Century: America as a Post-Industrial Society* (Chicago: University of Chicago Press, 1980). For a different outlook, see Stephen S. Cohen and John Zysman, *Manufacturing Matters: The Myth of the Post-Industrial Society* (New York: Basic Books, 1987).

10. Cited in Robert L. Heilbroner, *The Making of Economic Society,* 7th ed. (Englewood Cliffs, NJ: Prentice Hall, 1985), p. 78.

11. W. W. Rostow, *The World Economy: History and Prospect* (Austin: University of Texas Press, 1978), p. 661.

12. Alfred Chandler, *Scale and Scope* (Cambridge, MA: Belknap Press, 1990).

13. Paul Streeten, "Markets and States: Against Minimalism," *World Development* 21, no. 8 (1993), pp. 1281–98.

14. Susan Strange, *States and Markets: An International Political Economy* (New York: Basil Blackwell, 1988), p. 23.

15. Adam Smith, *An Inquiry into the Nature and Origins of the Wealth of Nations* (1776; reprint, New York: Modern Library, 1937), p. 862.

16. These points were suggested to me by Theodore J. Lowi. See his article "Risks and Rights in the History of American Governments," *Daedalus* 119, no. 4 (Fall 1990), pp. 17–40. Also see work by political economists of the public choice school on the importance of constitutional settings for capitalist development, for instance, Gerald W. Scully, *Constitutional Environments and Economic Growth* (Princeton, NJ: Princeton University Press, 1992).

17. Michael Specter, "As Terror Spreads, Yeltsin Declares War on Moscow Gangsters," *International Herald Tribune,* June 11–12, 1994, p. 1.

18. See V. A. C. Gatrell, "The Decline of Theft and Violence in Victorian and Edwardian England," in *Crime and the Law,* ed. V. A. C. Gatrell, Bruce Lenman, and Geoffrey Parker (London: Europa, 1980), pp. 238–370.

19. Ramsey Clark, *Crime in America* (New York: Simon and Schuster, 1970), p. 47.

20. Max Weber, *General Economic History,* trans. Frank C. Knight (Glencoe, IL: Free Press, 1950).

21. Keith Thomas, "How Britain Made It," *New York Review of Books,* November 19, 1992.

22. See Jennifer Nedelsky, *Private Property and the Limits of American Constitutionalism* (Chicago: University of Chicago Press, 1990).

23. Adam Smith, *The Theory of Moral Sentiments* (1790; reprint, Oxford: Clarendon, 1976), p. 340.

24. Rostow, *The Stages of Economic Growth.*

25. James R. Beniger, *The Control Revolution* (Cambridge, MA: Harvard University Press, 1986), pp. 208–11.

26. Stuart Bruchey, *Enterprise* (Cambridge, MA: Harvard University Press, 1990), pp. 201–202.

27. Robert Luther Thompson, *Wiring a Continent* (Princeton, NJ: Princeton University Press, 1947), pp. 16–17 and 241.

28. Alfred D. Chandler, *The Visible Hand* (Cambridge, MA: Harvard University Press, 1977), pp. 302–14.

29. Robert Reich, *The Work of Nations* (New York: Vintage, 1991), p. 26.

30. See Joseph A. Schumpeter, *Capitalism, Socialism and Democracy,* 3rd ed. (New York: Harper and Row, 1950).

31. Jacob Schmookler, *Invention and Economic Growth* (Cambridge, MA: Harvard University Press, 1966), pp. 228–29.

32. William Diebold, "Past and Future Industrial Policy in the United States," in *National Industrial Strategies and the World Economy,* ed. John Dinder (London: Allenheld, Osmun, 1980).

33. Walter Licht, *Working for the Railroad* (Princeton, NJ: Princeton University Press, 1983), p. 36.

34. H. H. Gerth and C. Wright Mills, eds., *From Max Weber* (New York: Oxford University Press, 1946), pp. 196–99.

35. V. I. Lenin, *The Lenin Anthology,* ed. Robert C. Tucker (Princeton, NJ: Princeton University Press, 1975), p. 449.

36. Charles T. Goodsell, *The Case for Bureaucracy* (Chatham, NJ: Chatham House, 1983).

37. Henry C. Dethloff and C. Joseph Pusateri, eds., *American Business History* (Arlington Heights, IL: Harlen Davidson, 1987), p. 184. The best source on the rise of the modern corporation is still Alfred Chandler's *Visible Hand.* Also see his *Scale and Scope.*

38. Arthur A. Goldsmith, *Building Agricultural Institutions* (Boulder, CO: Westview, 1990), Chapter 2.

39. Max Weber, *The Protestant Ethic and the Spirit of Capitalism,* trans. Talcott Parsons (New York: Scribner's, 1958).

40. One of the few economists writing on this subject is P. T. Bauer. See, for instance, his *Dissent on Development* (Cambridge, MA: Harvard University Press, 1972).

41. See Frances Piven and Richard Cloward, *Regulating the Poor* (New York: Vintage, 1971).

42. Lee Soltow and Edward Stevens, *The Rise of Literacy and the Common School in the United States* (Chicago: University of Chicago Press, 1981), p. 52.

43. See Samuel Bowles and Herbert Gintis, *Schooling in Capitalist America* (New York: Basic Books, 1977).

44. Richard H. K. Vietor, *Contrived Competition* (Cambridge, MA: Belknap Press, 1994), p. 7.

6   DEMOCRACY, CAPITALISM, SOCIALISM

Today's Political and Economic Systems

The death of command economies in the late 20th century, and with it the simplistic notion that the alternative was some pure alternative called "capitalism," cleared the way for the real debate. Which element from each version of "capitalism" should be melded together to form the most effective economic system?

C. Fred Bergsten[1]

Societies have constructed different political and economic systems, different sets of institutions to make collective decisions and to produce and disperse goods. The profile of state activity varies widely in these systems, though often more in theory than in practice. There are marked and lasting differences in how even self-professed democratic and capitalist countries organize their political and economic life.[2]

This chapter reports on and evaluates the main types of political and economic systems that are important to managers today. We will look at the meaning, both historical and contemporary, of democracy and dictatorship, capitalism and socialism. These terms denote less than they once did, but they still dominate in debates over public policy and business. A close look turns up many points of convergence among supposedly distinct modes of organizing society's productive power. In discussing rival systems, managers need to keep their eyes on facts and not get misled by semantics.

There are at least two competing models of capitalism: the Anglo-American, individualist model and the Continental-Asian, communitarian type. Table 6–1 summarizes their central tendencies. It is commonplace to note that the Anglo-American brand of capitalism plays down state intervention, whereas the European and Asian variants stress it. Mainstream American economic theory sees government as getting in the way of business growth, whereas the view overseas tends to be that government is an indispensable tool for growth.[3] It is also the

TABLE 6–1　　**Central Tendencies in the Two Main Modes of Capitalism**

	Anglo-American Type	*Continental-Asian Type*
System of capital allocation	Dispersed in financial markets; involving open sale of securities	Concentrated in institutions; closed to outsiders
Business oversight	Boards of laypersons	Boards representing creditors, major shareholders, sometime workers
Management goals	Profits first, social goals second	Concentrate on social goals; profits will follow
Role of government	More limited, regulatory state; smaller safety net for the needy	More active, developmental state, working for national firms; larger public safety net
Role of labor	Adversarial relationship with management; stress on mobility	Cooperative relationship with management; stress on long-term employment

standard wisdom that Anglo-American public policies favor the consumer, while in continental Europe and Asia, public policy favors the producer.

These familiar observations are still generally true. Yet, as we also will find, there is plenty of overlap among capitalist systems, too. And the likenesses are becoming more pronounced. Global integration is both the cause and the effect. Foreign competition is encouraging national governments to copy each other's economic policies, which lately have often been to step out of the way, to intervene in business life by removing obstacles, not by making them.

Liberal Democratic States

All the advanced industrial states are classed as **liberal democracies,** but this simple classification does not mean they are the same in all ways. The United States, Great Britain, Japan, and Germany are *liberal* because they guard civil liberties; they are *democratic* because they extend citizenship rights widely and allow popular input into the selection of political leaders. To the extent these democracies are stable and not subject to extreme shifts in public policy, they are often the preferred place for multinational companies to do business.

Most of the economically developed democratic states belong to the **Organization for Economic Cooperation and Development (OECD)**—the so-called rich man's club of nations. The OECD was formed after World War II to follow and examine economic trends in the world market economy. It is a forum for setting international codes of conduct and coordinating national economic policy. The 25 member countries account for two-thirds of the world's production of merchandise. No country may join unless it adheres to democratic and capitalist principles. Signifying how the world is changing, Mexico has joined the OECD, and South Korea, Poland, Hungary, and the Czech and Slovak Republics are negotiating for membership.

To be succinct, we usually will use the term *democracy,* without the modifier *liberal,* to refer to political systems that both allow people to have ideas and organizations separate from the state (are liberal) and permit people to join freely in picking leaders (are democratic). Beyond these minimum requirements, democracy can take more than one form—as we discuss shortly. First, however, we consider nondemocratic political systems.

Nondemocratic States

Communism is the traditional foil for liberal democratic politics. Starting in World War I, but in particular after World War II, communist regimes seized power in the sweep of countries people used to lump together as the East—the Soviet Union, Eastern Europe, and much of Asia. Even some African and Latin American countries tried to follow the soviet model. Communists also gained control of local and regional governments in countries such as France, Italy, and India. This trend reversed in the 1980s. China, North Korea, Vietnam, Laos, and Cuba are the only officially communist states left, and most have moderated their political practices.

Rather than stress civil and political rights as democratic states do, communist states put the accent on economic rights. Orthodox communists call the traditional civil rights a sham, set up to protect the interest of capitalists, not working people. Similarly, they allege that political rights are just a cover for rule by business. Election campaigns are a sideshow. Voting does not affect real political power. Communists believe the underlying function of politics in capitalist societies is to let the wealthy accumulate capital and to hoodwink the population into thinking the resulting class structure is right and proper.

People's Democracy

Communist states instead urge people's democracy—a top-down system of rule where the communist party makes policy in the name of the mass of ordinary people, not monied interests. Claiming special wisdom, the party elite decides what to do without much outside discussion. These regimes still seek the people's approval and hold noncompetitive elections to validate their rule. Such elections fulfill an entirely different function than those in liberal democracies. Ironically, the pretense for the vanguard party was as self-serving as any capitalist's argument for property rights.

Despite their professed animosity toward private enterprise, communist systems are often practical enough to welcome foreign investors. China, for example, received over $30 billion in direct foreign investment in the period 1985–1990 and received another $10 billion in 1991 despite its poor record on human rights. Because of their firm control, at least until recently, communist countries could be relatively easy places for outsiders to do business.

In any event, the verdict is now in on people's democracy, rendered by the people who lived under it. People's democracy did provide work and access to basic services, but these advantages could not offset the lack of personal freedom and opportunity to take part in politics. Communist regimes were swept away in Eastern Europe and the Soviet Union in 1989–1991, and they may be cracking in Asia and the Caribbean.

Third World Authoritarian Regimes

People's democracies account for only a few of the nondemocratic or authoritarian states in the world (though, due to China, they rule more than a billion people). Most authoritarian states are not communist. Examples include the traditional monarchies of the Middle East and the military dictatorships in Indonesia and Nigeria. As these examples indicate, authoritarian regimes are found mostly in less developed countries **(LDCs).**

The LDCs are the poor nations of Africa, Latin America, and parts of Asia, and often they are lumped together as the **Third World.** They also are called the "South" (as opposed to the developed North). These labels are misleading because the countries so designated are far from uniform. A desperately poor country like Haiti has little in common with dynamic Taiwan, though both do have histories as exploited colonies. Still, the common denominator is that LDCs seek to create for themselves a modern economy, with its promise of better living standards and greater national power and prestige. For convenience, we will freely use the terms *LDCs, Third World,* and *South* to denote late-developing nations as a group.

Few Third World authoritarian regimes are as well organized and pervasive as the communist systems. They are mostly *weak* states, as Joel Migdal points out, helpless to carry out coherent public policies.[4] The result can be an unstable, unpredictable setting for business, which makes the job of managing in these countries very challenging.

Authoritarian states, whether communist or not, are receding in number. This trend is neither inevitable nor irreversible, but liberal democracy is on the upswing as the 20th century draws to a close.[5] According to data assembled by Freedom House, two-thirds of the world's population now lives in "free" or "partly free" states, compared to about half the world's population two decades ago (see Table 6–2). The Freedom House ratings can be questioned in individual cases, but the tide of political events is beyond dispute.

Optimists think democracy is taking root in Latin America, Eastern Europe, Asia, and parts of Africa and the Middle East. Some 60 countries now hold meaningful fair elections and allow full freedom for political organizations.[6] Pessimists doubt the roots go deep and anticipate instability as countries oscillate between authoritarian and democratic regimes.

Which side of this argument is right will have implications for management. Business likes stable political environments. If representative government shows promise of becoming established in these new settings, it will likely attract new investors. But if the fledgling democracies look unstable, investors will take their money elsewhere.

TABLE 6–2   Democracy Is Spreading around the World.

Regime Classification	Percent of World Population Living under Different Regimes		
	1973	*1981*	*1991*
Free	32%	36%	39%
Partly free	21	22	28
Not free	47	42	33

Source: Freedom House Survey Team, *Freedom in the World: Political Rights and Civil Liberties, 1990–1991* (New York: Freedom House, 1991).

Pluralism and Corporatism

The Cold War, by focusing attention on the clash between democracy and dictatorship, often obscured the differences among democracies. Yet, if we look closely around the world, we see government can be representative while embracing a range of procedures and institutions. Every democracy by definition has to respond to and reconcile popular opinion, but it need not do so the same way. To organize and make sense of the differences among democracies, the categories **pluralism** and **corporatism** are useful. The categories refer to two modes of policy making.

The bases for representation in both types of democratic states, pluralist and corporatist, are **interest groups.** An interest group is an association of like-minded people who band together to press their cause with political representatives. Business is always an important source of interest groups. Political representatives compete for support from these groups by agreeing to policies the groups want. Elections are the feedback mechanism. They allow the democratic system to correct itself by ejecting incompetent or out-of-touch representatives.

Of the two types of systems, pluralist states have a more fragmented political structure. They are marked by multiple, decentralized, nonofficial interest groups that vie for influence. There are plural centers of power, frequently causing political stress or stalemate. Examples of pluralist democracies are the major English-speaking countries (the United States, Britain, Ireland, Canada, Australia, and New Zealand), France, and Italy. Sometimes, these states produce less friendly environments for business because they lack the capability to forge national consensus around public economic policy. We will discuss pluralist interest group political activity in greater detail in Chapter 8.

Other democracies, by contrast, are more corporatist. They have centralized interest groups that engage in continuous political bargaining with state bureaucracies and political parties. These countries are labeled corporatist because the interest groups and the state form a body (*corpus* in Latin)—institutions that often have origins in medieval guild systems. They are apt to avoid conflict and to stress consensus.[7] Table 6–3 summarizes the main distinctions between corporatist and pluralist states.

Historically, corporatism is associated with fascism, and many corporatist states were nondemocratic. This distinction has faded. Examples of corporatist democracies are the Nordic countries (Denmark, Finland, Norway, and Sweden), the German-speaking countries (Austria, Germany, and Switzerland), the Low countries (Belgium and Holland), and Japan.[8] The fast-growing Asian countries, such as South Korea, Taiwan, and Singapore, also exhibit corporatist tendencies, though with more authoritarian overtones.[9] In each case, interest groups encompass large fractions of the population (including usually industry and labor) and can collaborate on policy issues.

The norm of collaboration can give firms based in corporatist states an edge in the international arena. Consider Germany's self-proclaimed **social market economy.** Close relations between business and government help build consensus about national economic policies. Labor–management harmony is a critical component. Many firms own shares in each other; contested takeovers are rare giving managers the chance to focus on strategic goals.[10] The social market economy system has worked well for Germany, which has had low inflation, low unemployment, and a high standard of living for most of the postwar period.[11]

There are drawbacks to the corporatist approach, however. An important one is that the search for national consensus may sometimes stifle creativity and adaptability to the global market. Firms may find themselves losing foreign markets and having to move jobs overseas, both of which are apt to increase friction among the social partners. German politics became less consensual in the 1990s, according to many analysts.

As the recent changes in Germany show, the distinction between pluralist and corporatist democracies is messier than the simple typology makes out. Too much energy has gone into controversies over where given countries fit, because,

---

Table 6–3   There Are Several Points of Contrast between Pluralist and Corporatist Modes of Organizing Political Life.

	Pluralism	*Corporatism*
Organized interest groups	Tend to be competitive	Tend to be monopolistic
Access of groups to government power	Relatively open	Apt to be restricted to privileged groups
Membership in groups	Usually voluntary	May be compulsory
Regulatory activities	Rarely delegated to groups	Sometimes delegated to groups
Policy making	Sometimes an open process	Prone toward closed bargaining

Source: Adapted from Peter Williamson, *Corporatism in Perspective* (London: Sage, 1989).

at the margin, the two types of democracies blend into one another. Pluralism and corporatism are axes of political development, and countries can be more or less pluralist and corporatist. Rather than focusing on the categories themselves, it is best to recognize the underlying truth that some democratic societies have less conflict than others. The American system in particular assumes conflict and builds it into its constitutional structure (see Chapter 10). But this observation does not mean business, government, and labor collaboration is an impossibility in the United States.

Alternative Economic Systems

Paralleling the oversimplified political debate over which is preferable—pluralist or corporatist democracy—are economic arguments about the merits of **capitalism** and **socialism**. As all management students know, capitalism and socialism are rival theories about how economies *should* be organized. As with all theories, they only partly reflect reality. The capitalism/socialism dichotomy misrepresents the way economies are set up today and can create a mindset that is misleading.

Capitalism

Every economic system has two basic decisions to make: First is to choose who controls, and thus enjoys the proceeds of, the economy's productive units. Second is the question who decides what to make and how to make it. The capitalist response to the first decision, about ownership, is to give private individuals extensive rights over moneymaking assets **(capital).** The answer to the second question, about decision making, is to decentralize, to push decisions down to the firm or enterprise. Capitalism invites company managers to anticipate and meet their clients' needs **(consumer sovereignty).**

In sum, capitalism is a pattern of private enterprise responding to demand in the market. The idea is to allow networks of millions of people to grow, unconnected by any self-conscious organization. At least this is the theory. In practice, capitalist countries have taken varied approaches to private ownership and private decision making. We explore these nuances below.

Leaving economic life in private hands is a new notion—market-oriented economies became well established in the West only in the 1800s. The term *capitalism* was popularized 150 years ago by radical opponents to free-market economics.[12] Thus, it was originally an expression of reproach, directed against the emerging industrial society. Later, the market's defenders themselves began to speak of capitalism, though with a positive spin. The Left and the Right thus agreed that the Western economies illustrated capitalism in action. Still, as a label originating in partisan debate, capitalism means positive and negative things to different people. Caution is advised in using a term that carries the baggage of ideology.

Students should remember, in particular, that capitalism does not fully portray any real economy. It is, as the subtitle of the libertarian writer Ayn Rand's book has it, an "unknown ideal."[13] Neither the United States nor any other nation has ever been altogether capitalistic, in the sense that all assets are privately held and consumer demand is everywhere supreme. In real capitalist economies, some assets are owned publicly and government makes some decisions about what is produced. In real capitalist economies, the market does not pervade every transaction.

Many exchanges take place inside large companies and thus are administered, not based on competition. Companies grow partly to *avoid* having to face the uncertainties of the market.[14] Japan's *keiretsu,* its system of interlocking ownership and networks of supply arrangements, is another example of how private companies try to reduce the risk of operating in an open marketplace.

For practical purposes, capitalism is best thought of as something like a magnetic pole. Real national economies line up toward or against that pole, some countries using more private ownership and market competition, others using less. None represent capitalism in pure form.

Socialism

The opposite pole of capitalism, its theoretical antithesis, is socialism. Socialism and the related communism doctrine are branches of the same core theory. Socialist and communist economic thinking are as old as humankind. People have always speculated about arranging economic output by social needs (hence socialism) and setting up systems of communal property (hence communism). Plato (427–327 BC) discussed such themes in his *Republic.* Modern socialism and communism, however, grow mainly from the work of Karl Marx (1818–1883).

Writing amid the Industrial Revolution, Marx in fact admired much about capitalism. It had transformed the agrarian economy and rescued people from "the idiocy of rural life." It brought technological innovations and broke down antique national barriers. Yet Marx condemned capitalist development for benefiting owners and leaving out the workers. As he wrote in the massive study *Das Kapital*: "Along with the constantly diminishing magnates of capital, who usurp and monopolise all advantages of this process of transformation, grows the mass of misery, oppression, slavery, degradation, exploitation."[15] In Marx's view, tension is built into the capitalist system. He thought the strain, the "internal contradiction," would get worse until it broke the system and the working class would take over the means of production.

Marx and his followers first used the words socialism and communism interchangeably. The meanings diverged later, when a dispute emerged within the socialist movement over tactics. The radical wing was more open to revolution and willing to use arms if needed to overthrow the free-market system. Its adherents grabbed the name communist. After the Russian Revolution (1917), communism became associated with the policies and practices of the Soviet Union, where extremists had taken control.

Moderate leftists kept the name socialist to set themselves apart from the radicals. They embraced the idea of gradually reforming capitalism from within by legal means. These moderate groups have evolved into the social democratic parties that are common in Europe. The United States never developed a strong self-styled socialist movement. Socialism is a taboo word in U.S. political discourse, but the Democratic party was influenced by social democratic ideas. To muddle matters more, Communist party members never ceased using socialism as a synonym to depict their system of beliefs.

Marx believed that the state would eventually wither away. Before that event would pass, however, his followers usually reasoned that the state should lead the economy for the masses' benefit. Government, not private investors, should own society's factories, farms, mines, and other assets. Government, not market forces, should tell producers what to make and how much to charge for it. By thus replacing the unplanned market, socialism's hope was to solve the age-old economic problems of production and distribution. Government control was expected to release humanity's creative energy so people would produce more. Government control also was expected to lead to a fairer, less wasteful way to distribute the economy's output.

Socialism in Action.   Radicals and moderates differed on the proper extent of state ownership and planning. Communists wanted a larger part for the state, while socialists were willing to accept more private ownership and decision making. Wherever communists came to power, they tried to create **command economies.** Central planners controlled the volume of goods produced and consumed. Prices did not figure in production and investment decisions, and there was no role for private enterprise. That at least was the image communist leaders usually wanted to project.

Whether any economy is socialist has always been a matter of degree. The closest to a true command economy were probably the Soviet Union during the rule of Joseph Stalin (1928–1953) and China under Mao Zedong (1949–1976). This pair of regimes exerted vast authority to control production. They abolished private ownership of farms and factories. They drew up and executed five-year plans that plowed resources into priority areas.

Still, communists have always been pragmatic about central planning. The Russian communists, for instance, adopted the market-oriented New Economic Policy (1921–1929) soon after coming to power. During that time, the private sector rendered over half the Soviet national income.[16] Markets and private enterprise never fully disappeared, even under Stalin. Peasants were permitted to grow private food and own farm animals when agriculture was collectivized in the 1930s. Black or underground markets proved persistent. Such forms of illegality were tolerated in the Soviet Union as a way to introduce flexibility into national plans.

The socialist states produced impressive economic performance after World War II, especially in the area of military technology. The Soviets quickly mastered nuclear technology, exploding a hydrogen bomb in 1953. They shocked the

United States in 1957 by launching *Sputnik,* the first satellite. This last event awakened Americans to weaknesses in education and research, leading to major changes in public policy toward science and technology.

Socialism in Former Colonial Areas.   Socialist ideas had great influence in the less developed countries. While industrialization came with social cost, most LDCs were eager to join the industrial club in the postwar era. How could they make the forward leap?

Socialism showed one plausible way. Though dissimilar in culture and level of economic development, LDCs shared a colonial past and a lack of any manufacturing base. Their often painful exposure to Western capitalism made that system repugnant to many. They had little confidence in private enterprise for their countries, for foreign companies had already staked out seemingly unassailable positions in key industries.

In political economic terms, the problem in latecomer nations was that modern industry had huge externalities the market could not capture. An externality, readers will recall, is a nonpriced effect on third parties that arises as an incidental byproduct of another person's or firm's activity. In a backward economy, private investors would be too timid to finance, say, steel mills until they were sure of demand from steel-using industries such as machine tools. Yet private investors would not want to invest much in machine tools either if they could not count on steel supplies. It was a typical Catch-22. Relying mainly on private enterprise alone to create industry thus would take a long time.

Better to have a big push from government through public ownership of the means of production, socialists argued, and get the job done. Central planning of investment and controlled prices would telescope the process of industrialization. The Soviet Union showed how with striking economic feats under Stalin. The human cost to soviet development was huge, but then capitalist development had not been free from suffering, either. Anyhow, to many, the price seemed worth paying to get a modern industrial base. Once independent, many LDCs took on the trappings of socialism, such as public ownership of key industries and economic planning.

The Welfare State.   Some of socialism's best-liked proposals concerned the welfare state. Industrialization had presented factory workers and their families with risk from many quarters. They might lose income for any of several reasons—layoffs, injury or sickness, death of the major breadwinner. Because they worked in one place and often lived together in company towns, workers could get together to try to protect themselves from these risks. In 19th century Europe and America, sometimes they formed sickness funds and mutual aid societies. But they also backed militant parties devoted to overthrowing the capitalist system.

Governments' reflex was usually to suppress the socialist movement—especially where workers were not fully represented in the legislature. Some more flexible and enlightened leaders, however, saw the chance to co-opt the issue.

Why not take socialist ideas and use them *to preserve the capitalist system?* Workers would be offered an implicit social contract. The state would protect them against calamity in exchange for their willingness to work within the legal framework. Support for radical change would dry up, and the political economy would be made more stable.

The first country to go this route was Germany. When the conservative politician Otto von Bismarck was chancellor (1871–1890), workers received health insurance, accident insurance, and public pensions. Other European countries followed the German lead (see Table 6–4). Britain, for example, accepted moderate socialist ideas that were pushed by the influential Fabian Society (formed in 1884) of intellectuals and professionals. Over time, more social insurance programs were added (such as unemployment insurance and family allowances). Existing programs were made more generous, providing bigger benefits and covering more people.

As Table 6–4 also shows, the United States stands apart. It moved later than Europe, and less deeply than even Japan, into insuring its citizens against risk.[17] No one is sure why. One explanation focuses on the difference in political culture. Europe and Japan were once feudal societies, and collectivist or group-oriented traditions persist today. America's European settlers, on the other hand, were trying to escape the hand of government. A political economy explanation would lean more on the fact that American society has been prosperous and not marked by sharp class division. Thus, people had less need for government insurance. Anyhow, the underlying support for social spending in the United States was always shaky, based more on controversy than consensus.

To be accurate, the national U.S. pattern masks regional differences. Progressive states (mainly in the Northeast and Midwest) began to aid the destitute in 1890, sharing what had previously been a local charge. They enacted workers' compensation laws starting 20 years later. Yet other states, especially in the

TABLE 6–4   The United States Has Been Slow to Develop a Welfare State.

	Date Selected Social Programs Were Introduced				
	Work Injury Insurance	*Unemployment Insurance*	*Health Insurance*	*Public Pensions*	*Family Allowances*
France	1898	1905	1928	1910	1932
Germany	1884	1927	1883	1889	1954
Japan	1911	1947	1922	1941	1971
Sweden	1901	1934	1931	1913	1947
United Kingdom	1897	1911	1911	1908	1945
United States	**1911***	**1935**	**1965†**	**1935**	—

*First state-level program.

†Elderly and low-income people only.

Source: *Social Security Programs Throughout the World—1989,* Research Report No. 6 (Washington, DC: U.S. Department of Health and Human Services, Social Security Administration, May 1990).

South, avoided these programs. Regional differences in social spending persist today in the United States.

Socialism's Declining Fortunes.   Despite its deep influence on economic and social policy, socialism's reputation was in tatters by the 1980s. One reason was that the centrally planned, government-owned economies stalled over time. The socialist states' growth turned out to have been "extensive" (using more inputs) and not due to more efficient use of inputs. While all right at the simpler economic tasks of creating basic industries such as steel and coal, the socialist approach faltered at the more sophisticated challenge posed by high technology.

Growth in the Soviet Union had dropped off markedly in the mid-1960s. The planned economy never came close to providing the creature comforts enjoyed in the West. Shortly before the disintegration of the Soviet Union, Soviet consumers ate half as much meat, fruit, and vegetables as Americans; lived in one-sixth the housing space; and had one-tenth as many telephones, to take some examples.[18]

Another factor discrediting socialism was the dramatic success of East Asia's capitalist **NICs** (newly industrialized countries), which eclipsed most self-proclaimed socialist countries' rate of development. The economic feats of the four capitalist "tigers" are legendary, with spectacular gains in per capita GDP over the past two decades (see Table 6–5). Other LDCs could not touch these records.

The NICs' economic miracles cast doubt on the blessings of public ownership and central planning, and seemed to extol private ownership and competition instead. Readers should be aware, however, that these countries do not bank on the invisible hand. Like most other examples of "late" development (notably Japan and Germany), development in these countries has been led by the state (see Box 6–1). It was "revolution from above," to use Barrington Moore's term,

---

TABLE 6–5   The "Four Tigers" Have Had Phenomenal Economic Growth.

	GNP/GDP per Capita (1987 U.S. dollars)		
	1971	*1989*	*Percent Increase*
Hong Kong	$2,697	$9,593	256%
Singapore	2,855	9,713	240
South Korea	792	4,090	416
Taiwan	1,172	6,823	482
All other LDCs	444	710	60

Note: Converted to 1987 prices using implicit GNP price deflator, from *Economic Report of the President 1991* (Washington, DC: U.S. Government Printing Office).

Sources: World Bank, *World Tables 1991* (Baltimore: Johns Hopkins University Press, 1991); *Statistical Yearbook of the Republic of Taiwan, 1991* (Taipei: Directorate General of Budget, Accounting, and Statistics, 1991).

Box 6–1

Capitalism, East Asian Style

The NICs' capitalism is, for the most part, not the laissez-faire variety with little public sector involvement. Except for Hong Kong, the governments of these dynamos have intervened for decades, often aggressively, to alter the trade and industrial profile of the economy in ways it deemed desirable. They are what Chalmers Johnson calls *developmental states* that try to guide investment according to national ends, rather than letting private investors make most decisions about how to allot resources.[1] In this respect, their public policies toward business are more like those of Japan and, to some extent, Germany than of the United States or Great Britain.

With government leadership, the NICs rapidly underwent structural transformation, replacing agriculture with manufacturing. They passed through

---

[1]Chalmers Johnson, *MITI and the Japanese Miracle* (Stanford: Stanford University Press, 1982). On the role of the state in late industrialization in East Asia, see Alice H. Amsden, *Next Giant: South Korea and Late Industrialization* (New York: Oxford University Press, 1989) and Robert Wade, *Governing the Market: Economic Theory and the Role of Government in East Asian Industrialization* (Princeton, NJ: Princeton University Press, 1990).

this process while preserving a relatively flat distribution of income between towns and countryside, and between workers and managers. Business is mostly in private hands in these countries, but it is disciplined by public policies that encourage exports and exposure to international competition. Companies can get government subsidies, but only if they meet strict performance criteria.

Yet Hong Kong's success, gained under a minimal state, suggests that other factors, too, lie behind the success of the "four tigers." These other factors include high levels of education, political stability, and an entrepreneurial culture. Since so many influences on industrialization interact with each other, it is hard to assign priority to any one. But for U.S. firms, the combination of private enterprise and state encouragement represented by Japan, South Korea, Taiwan, and Singapore obviously has created some formidable foes.

The list of NICs in the region is going to get longer. Malaysia, Thailand, Indonesia, and China all are developing at breakneck speed, making the Pacific Rim the world's most dynamic economic region at the end of the 20th century.

---

as opposed to the bourgeois-democratic "route to modernization" in which the state stays more in the background.[19]

Government does not own many industrial facilities in the NICs; government does intercede with owners to give them bearing, guided by the national interest as interpreted by government officials. Favored industries are targeted for development, then exposed to international competition. Consumer welfare is not the chief aim of public policy; gaining world market share in the target industries is. East Asian development thus entails much economic planning by the state, which decides where to allocate capital.

Interestingly, the NICs have not been democratic until recently, leading some experts to draw the conclusion that an authoritarian government, shielded from popular demands, is needed for the East Asian model to work. Many experts also doubt that the state-led approach can work well in societies where government officials are less educated, and less honest, than they are in the NICs.

It is obvious that government intervention is not a *sufficient* condition for rapid economic improvement in the 20th century. Many poor countries have derived little from states trying to guide them to national wealth. At issue is the way government intervenes. India is a good example. India's development strategy was inward looking, aimed at self-sufficiency instead of export growth. Unlike the East Asian trading states, New Delhi tried to constrain domestic competition.[20] Also, India invested far less in human capital. The result was slow development. State-led modernization does happen, but only when conditions are favorable and government follows the right policies.

New Faith in Markets.   Faced with stunted development, the socialist world began to experiment with market-based reforms. Most successful was China's policy of "Four Modernizations," launched in December 1978. It broke up the collective farms, introduced new material incentives, and allowed peasants leeway to decide what to grow. Individually owned shops and self-employment received official endorsement. As a result, Chinese national income grew by almost 10 percent a year from 1980 to 1989. Failing completely was the Soviet Union's more timid *perestroika* (restructuring) scheme. Started in 1986, *perestroika* did not turn around the Soviet economy before the 1991 revolution swept away the entire edifice of communism and the Soviet state. For western businesspeople, the importance of the market-based reforms in the East has been to create major new trade and investment opportunities.

Noncommunist developing countries also began to rethink their policies toward markets. Sometimes they did so due to pressure from the **World Bank** and the **International Monetary Fund (IMF).** The World Bank is a lending agency, owned by the governments of its member countries. It lends and grants funds to developing nations for development projects. The IMF, which works closely with the World Bank, uses money contributed by its member governments to stabilize foreign exchange rates and discharge international indebtedness. Headquartered in Washington, DC, these two agencies opened shop in 1945. They are important and influential, particularly in the Third World.

The World Bank and the IMF have a neoliberal agenda. Whatever a country's particular economic problems, they always urge it to remove controls on business, to "get prices right," and to make state enterprises respect the law of the market. From 1980 to 1987, 51 developing countries had structural adjustment programs under the World Bank's auspices. These programs differed in detail, but all aimed to shrink government budget deficits, remove subsidies, free prices, and devalue national currencies. Countries carrying out major adjustments seem to have done better in aggregate economic activity, but with wide individual variation.[21] Again, one effect is greater outside business opportunities.

The Fate of Social Democrats.   Socialism's waning appeal also affected Western countries. To entice middle-of-the-road voters, social democrats have tempered their economic platforms and now offer only a small alternative to market-oriented parties. They rarely advocate government ownership of companies or claim much faith in economic planning. Some social democrats have backed away from the welfare state in the name of international competitiveness. They are apt to urge deregulation and privatization to increase the efficiency of national business.

Even so, moderate socialists find it difficult convincing the electorate that they can run the economy, as happened to the British Labour Party in 1992 in its surprise loss to the Conservatives—the fourth in a row.[22] Many voters switched their vote at the last minute despite a recession that could be blamed on the Tories' economic fumbling. France's Socialists also suffered a humiliating loss in 1993.

Though not a socialist party, the U.S. Democratic party has urged government intervention in the economy over the years. Like their European counterparts, the Democrats' poor record in national elections in the 1970s and 1980s pushed them to the right on economic issues. President Bill Clinton's successful campaign as a "New Democrat" in 1992 was based on a pro-business platform that advocated tax incentives and a close partnership between the private and public sectors.

But political opinion swings to and fro. Left-wing parties cannot be counted out permanently. Less than five years after the fall of the Berlin Wall, for example, there was a backlash against neoliberal economic policies in Eastern Europe. Disillusioned with free markets, voters returned ex-communists to power in Hungary, Poland, and Lithuania. Yet even these elections do not necessarily reflect support for the old orthodoxy of central planning and public ownership. Former communist politicians in Hungary, for example, derive support from local entrepreneurs by promising them tax relief and cheap credit.[23] Political labels do not mean what they used to. Socialist parties of the future probably will be more market friendly than in the past.

Mixed Economies

To some pundits, the eclipse of socialism signals the end of history.[24] Capitalism has won the war of ideas; socialism is a dead letter. Readers should by now be cautious about such sweeping judgments. Capitalism and socialism are abstractions; neither was ever fulfilled in pristine form. Americans were apt to neglect this fact because for so long they took the Soviet Union as their point of reference. The Soviet system was socialistic, therefore everything associated with socialism was by definition suspect. The categories capitalism and socialism took on lives of their own. The end of the U.S.–Soviet standoff perhaps makes it easier to see that capitalist (market) and socialist (state) elements coexist in all economies, though in different amounts.

When mingled, **market allocation** and state intervention yield a **mixed economy.** Every real system for producing and allocating wealth is this type. The difference is that some mixed economies favor the market and are more capitalistic. They incline toward private enterprise. Their industries are mainly owned by investors and most investment decisions are in private hands. Other mixed economies put more stress on the state and are more socialistic. Public policy plays a greater direct role in deciding what is produced. For convenience, and because it is common practice, we will stay with the term *capitalist* to identify actual mixed economic systems, such as the United States, Germany, and Japan. But students should keep in mind that we will be talking about points along a continuum.

The United States is at the far end of that continuum. Its private sector is unusually large and its public sector unusually small compared to other mixed or capitalist economies. Americans are apt to prefer more liberal (that is, laissez-faire) policies. Continental Europe is at the other end, with larger public sectors and national governments that prefer to be restrictive.

But all rich national economies are tending to converge, to grow more like each other. Three sets of data show this fact. One is simply the share of government spending. Another indicator of convergence is the proportion of state ownership of industry. The third indicator is the extent of government regulation of business. We analyze these three indicators below.

Government Spending

The easiest way to assess the weight of government in the economy is to look at the size of the public sector. How much does the government spend? How large is that sum compared to private spending? The answer is that governments spend huge amounts, but with interesting differences among countries.

The international comparisons show the United States is atypical, but the deviation between it and other countries is waning. Government spending (federal, state, and local) started from a lower base than in Europe in the 19th century. Table 6–6 reports that consumption by all levels of government accounted

TABLE 6–6   **Government Spending Has Been Rising in the Industrialized North for a Century, with the United States and Japan Always on the Low End.**

	Government Expenditure as Percent of GNP/GDP						
	1890	*1913*	*1932*	*1960*	*1980*	*1990*	*1994 est.*
Germany	13%	15%	37%	32%	48%	46%	51%
Japan*	7	8	11	18	33	32	36
United Kingdom	9	12	29	32	45	42	45
United States	**7**	**9**	**21**	**27**	**33**	**36**	**34**

* Pre-1960 data are nearest available year and refer to general government consumption, excluding investment, using constant price data.

Sources: Richard A. Musgrave, *Fiscal Systems* (New Haven, CT: Yale University Press, 1969), pp. 94–95; Kazushi Onkawa and Henry Rosovsky, *Japanese Economic Growth* (Stanford: Stanford University Press, 1973); *Historical Statistics 1960–1990* (Paris: Organization for Economic Cooperation and Development, 1992); *OECD Economic Outlook* (Paris: Organization for Economic Cooperation and Development, June 1993).

for only 7 percent of U.S. national income in 1890. That share was about the same as Japan's at the same time, somewhat below Britain's, and about half the share in Germany.

There has been a persistent upward drift in public spending since then. Nowhere in the world was the growth of public spending smooth; it ratcheted upward due to war and other crises. In America, public spending spurted in the early 20th century to fight the First World War, then fell in the 1920s. It leaped again in the 1930s because of the Great Depression and in the 1940s because of the Second World War. U.S. government spending stayed high after the war's end and continued creeping upward through the 1980s. It has converged on, but never reached, European heights. Today, the government's share of national income is about one-third of U.S. national income. In major countries, only the Japanese government spends as little.

The rate of increase in public spending everywhere has slowed, however. All democratic states are finding it harder than before to raise their outlays, though the resistance has kicked in at different levels. Most European countries continue to tolerate public sectors that Americans would find crushing. But their governments want to hold the line on government spending to help their economies do better in the global economy. Despite effort, no advanced country has made much progress in *reducing* total government spending. We will return to the issue of fiscal policy in Chapter 7.

State-Owned Enterprise

All governments have gone into commerce with state-owned enterprises, even in allegedly capitalist societies. A **state-owned enterprise** is a government entity that administers a self-paying activity. The rationale for government entering into such a business is to protect jobs and provide goods and services the private sector will not provide in an amount or at a price deemed acceptable.

Many state-owned companies sell services in the natural monopolies (posts, telecommunication, local transit systems, and so on) we mentioned briefly in Chapter 3. State-owned companies also can include sectors of strategic national importance—for instance, steel or defense. The government takes them over (**nationalizes** them) to keep a key industry under domestic control or to prevent it from closing. (Excluded from the category of state-owned business are government services that are not sold, such as education or police and fire protection. Because public schools and public safety agencies do not try to cover their cost by charging fees, they are not listed as state-owned enterprises.)

People sometimes joke that state ownership is "lemon socialism," because often the companies are money losers. But state-owned enterprise is not a uniquely socialist idea. Right-wing governments in Europe often have taken over companies for reasons of national prestige and power. The U.S. government got into the rail transport business (Amtrak and, until 1987, Conrail) to preserve the operation of the railroads when private enterprise seemed unwilling. At one time, the largest holder of property in America was the Resolution Trust Corporation, a federal entity set up in 1989 to liquidate the assets of failed privately owned thrift institutions.

Most American government corporations are at the state or local level. There may be as many as 35,000 public authorities generating electricity, treating waste products, supplying drinking water, maintaining highways, even selling wine and spirits, among other economic activities. Some giants, in terms of outstanding debt, are the $4.2 billion Municipal Electric Authority of Georgia, the $6.2 billion New Jersey Economic Development Authority, the $8 billion State of Washington Public Power Supply System (WHOOPS), and the $7.3 billion New York State Municipal Assistance Corporation (Big MAC).[25]

The federal level includes another 50 huge public corporations, such as the Postal Service and the Tennessee Valley Authority in power. The number of public authorities is up, as government bodies seek ways to put spending programs "off budget," so they do not add to budget deficits or the tax burden. Many of these government corporations would be listed in the Fortune 500 if that list was not restricted to profit-making firms.

While public enterprise is not trivial in the United States, it has never been as widespread as in Europe. This country, to an unusual degree, has favored regulated, subsidized, and risk-underwritten private enterprise over state-owned companies as a means to provide many public goods.[26] AT&T and the "Baby Bells" that supply phone service, for instance, are all private companies, something unheard of in Europe until recently.

The State: Getting Out of Business?

The economic borders of the state are always changing, however. As recently as 1980, public enterprise accounted for 10–20 percent of annual investment in Europe and Japan, compared to 4 percent in the United States.[27] Foreign state-owned businesses made up 59 of the firms in the Fortune 500, and they were growing faster than similar investor-owned U.S. firms. Benefiting from government as a banker and owner, state-owned businesses were seen as imposing competitors.[28]

Things look different today. For a decade and more, governments have been rushing to get out of many lines of business, to sell nationalized industries to private investors (to **privatize** them). The motives for privatization are many. Governments want the cash and to be relieved of the pressure to pour funds into these companies. There also is a belief that public companies are not nimble enough to compete with private firms in the international economy.

During the 1980s, more than 8,000 firms were privatized in the world.[29] The trend continues in the 1990s (see Table 6–7). European governments planned to sell their stakes in many blue-chip companies, such as Renault, Air France, and Lufthansa, raising perhaps $150 billion.[30] For comparison, that amount is equal to one-tenth the market value of all companies traded on the New York Stock Exchange (1991). Many national postal services and telephone companies are on the block.

The most dramatic cases of privatization are in the former communist states.

TABLE 6–7   **There Has Been a Sharp Increase in Privatization, Especially in Developing Countries.**

	Major Worldwide Sales of State Enterprises ($ billions)				
	1988	*1989*	*1990*	*1991*	*1992*
Industrial countries*	37	21	18	31	24
LDCs	2	4	7	17	23

*Excludes United States.

Source: Gerd Schwartz and Paulo Silva Lopes, "Privatization: Expectations, Trade-Offs, and Results," *Finance and Development,* June 1993, p. 15.

They are selling their industries by issuing vouchers to all citizens. The vouchers can be used to bid for shares in privatized companies, or they can be sold to other investors. Russia used vouchers to privatize 70 percent of its industrial enterprises by 1994, creating a shareholding class of some 40 million people. A second round of cash-based privatization was planned to dispose of most of the rest of the state's businesses.

Selling state-owned enterprises has not been as important a policy in the United States, because government has fewer such companies in its portfolio in the first place. The biggest public entity sold to private investors so far is Conrail, the federal government's freight railway that was auctioned in 1987.

Regulatory Policy   The numbers reported thus far do not show the reach of authority over economic decisions. To what extent do public officials, as opposed to private individuals, choose how resources will be allocated, used, and enjoyed? The answer need not correspond directly to government spending or ownership. An apparently small government, as determined by share of GNP, might intervene a lot in economic decisions, and vice versa. Such government activities are hard to measure.

The U.S. government is more deeply engaged in business affairs than the customary, quantitative indicators show. We rely on regulation to police private activities, to make sure they conform to rules prescribed, at least outwardly, in the public interest. James Q. Wilson points out that

> appointed officials can decide, within rather broad limits, who shall own a television station, what safety features automobiles shall have, what kinds of scientific research shall be specially encouraged, what drugs shall appear on the market, . . . what fumes an industrial smokestack may emit, which corporate mergers shall be allowed, what use shall be made of national forests, and what price farmers and dairymen shall receive for their products.[31]

These rules are often a legacy of the populist and progressive tradition in the United States. The underlying reason for so many rules is that Americans fear centralized power, in both government and business. Business sins needed to be controlled, but not if that meant letting elected officials do it. Thus, Congress has often seen fit to delegate its responsibilities to bureaucratic agencies that could supposedly act more objectively and professionally in the public interest.

Economic and social controls can be just as pervasive in other advanced countries. The Japanese government, for example, has a lot to say in guiding Japanese business. There are an estimated 10,000 economic regulations in Japan, many of which are used to protect small businesses from large competitors, and domestic producers from foreign imports. These regulations do not include many informal arrangements that are not scrutinized by the law, so the full reach of government authority is even greater (see Chapter 17).

As a rule, though, other advanced countries rely less on formal regulation to reach social goals than does the United States. Instead of setting up an agency with powers to supervise industry in society's interest, they have often preferred the more direct route of nationalization, as discussed above. Other governments work with companies to plan private sector investments and to reorganize industries so they can be more efficient.

The Regulatory Backlash   Regulation has become a dirty word. By the 1970s, many people became convinced that excess government intervention was more of a problem than excess competition. Too many rules did not work or had backfired; it was better to let the market sort out matters. Starting with President Jimmy Carter (1977–1981) and continuing under President Reagan, **deregulation** became a thrust of public policy in Washington. As Table 6–8 shows, many regulations were repealed to allow companies greater leeway to decide what to do, for example, in the airline and trucking industries. The idea was to get government out of the way of business in the hope that the resulting free-for-all would make companies more productive and produce more jobs.

One of Reagan's first acts in office was to issue an executive order requiring the Office of Management and Budget to review all new and proposed regulations, all of which had to pass a cost–benefit test. The thrust of the Reagan administration's strategy for regulatory relief, however, was simply to encourage inaction by regulators. This do-nothing strategy was carried out by downgrading enforcement, appointing people to top agency jobs who were hostile to regulation, leaving important regulatory posts vacant, and not initiating rule-making procedures.[32]

In the global economy, industry regulation is no longer a purely domestic matter. Fearing that deregulated U.S. firms were gaining an upper hand in important sectors, other countries were tempted to follow suit by cutting their companies loose. Eleven years after the United States deregulated its securities market, for instance, Britain made the countermove of opening up its securities market.[33] British policy makers hoped by that to avoid losing business to Wall Street.

In Western Europe, deregulation also has been driven by the region's international trading community, now called the **European Union (E.U.).** (See Box 6–2.) The European Union is based on the free movement of goods and services among member states. Such economic openness is at odds with economic and social regulation.[34] As Europe moves toward a single market, countries have

TABLE 6–8 **Many Business Activities Have Been Deregulated in the United States since the Late 1970s, but New Regulations Have Been Imposed at the Same Time.**

Date	Act or Ruling	Effect of Deregulation
1978	Air Passenger Deregulation Act	Progressive and ultimately total deregulation of rates and entry
1979	Federal Communications Commission	Radio program content rules dropped
1980	Motor Carrier Act	Increased entry and rate freedom and reduced role for rate-fixing bureaus
1981	Decontrol of Crude Oil and Refined Petroleum Products (Executive Order)	Complete lifting of crude oil price controls
1982	Garn-St Germain Depository Institutions Act	Removal of restrictions on thrift institutions
1983	Federal Communications Commission ruling	Television program content rules dropped
1984	Cable Telecommunications Act	Virtually complete deregulation of cable TV
1985	Supreme Court ruling on interstate banking pacts	Banks in one state are allowed to control banks in another state
1994	Interstate Banking and Branching Efficiency Act	Allows banks to set up networks of regional or national branches

Date	Act or Ruling	Effect of New Regulation
1978	Fair Debt Collection Practices Act	Provides for the first nationwide control of collection agencies
1980	Comprehensive Environmental Response, Compensation, and Liability Act (CERCLA)	Creates fund to pay for cleanup of hazardous chemical spills
1981	Cash Discount Act	Prevents merchants from imposing a surcharge on credit card sales
1984	Insider Trading Sanctions Act	Increases penalties for trading securities while in possession of material nonpublic information
1986	Age Discrimination in Employment Act	Abolishes mandatory retirement
1988	Employee Polygraph Protection Act	Prohibits use of lie detectors by employers engaged in interstate commerce
1989	Financial Institutions Reform, Recovery, and Enforcement Act (FIRREA)	Imposes capital standards on thrift institutions
1990	Americans with Disabilities Act	Prohibits discrimination against those with physical disabilities
1991	Civil Rights Act of 1991	Amends the 1964 law to give victims of intentional discrimination a right for larger compensation
1992	Cable Television Consumer Protection Act	Reregulates cable TV

dismantled many confining rules. Customs checks and immigration controls, for example, were eliminated in the 1990s. By 1997, European airlines will have complete freedom on what routes they want to serve and, within limits, what fares to charge.

Reregulation?   Deregulation has captured a lot of attention. Yet, look again. There is a political undertow moving the other way. Much as governments argue for liberal policies, they often prefer to be restrictive.

Box 6–2

Europe's Common Market

The leading countries of Europe formed a common market in 1958. The association of these states has been broadened and deepened in the years since. By 1995, there were 15 member countries (Austria, Belgium, Britain, Denmark, Finland, France, Germany, Greece, Ireland, Italy, Luxembourg, The Netherlands, Portugal, Spain, and Sweden). Their combined population and purchasing power are greater than those of the United States.

This group of countries, now called the European Union, gradually reduced internal customs duties on industrial goods. By 1968, goods could move without tariffs among the members. The E.U. also applied a common external tariff to goods imported from nonmembers. Progress was made in the 1970s to allow the freer movement of capital and labor within Europe.

In 1986, the European community decided to create a unified market by 1993. They reasoned that remaining trade barriers hurt consumers and prevented European firms from competing with American and Japanese firms. The single market was designed to harmonize regulations and further liberalize the movement of factors of production within Europe. For example, border controls were eliminated and plans laid to establish a single currency. Some American and Japanese businesses feared the creation of a Fortress Europe, and made effort to set up shop on the continent for fear of being locked out later.

The Maastricht Treaty codified some of these decisions and set up political procedures that would give the European Commission, headquartered in Belgium, greater power. This threat to national sovereignty, however, triggered a backlash in many countries. By the mid-1990s, the rush to European union and integration had been slowed.

In the United States, many *new* regulations have been promulgated over the past several years. Contrary to the popular impression, real spending for regulation went up during Reagan's presidency.[35] The size of the *Federal Register,* where federal regulations are published, did shrink about one-third under Reagan. But it swelled again under President George Bush (1989–1993). The number of federal regulatory personnel also rose, and many new regulatory policies were enacted during the period. Republicans who took control of Congress in 1995 vowed to reverse matters again. So, while the effort to deregulate business gets the most attention, the full story of business regulation is complicated.

The same is true in the European Union. According to the European Commission, 230 measures need to be put into national legislation to implement a single European market. These involve Europewide standards for testing and certification, packaging and labeling, product safety and consumer protection, and company behavior, among other things. But countries are lagging in adopting the new rules.

More to the point, E.U. members often ignore the spirit of the deregulations they do adopt. They bend or break the rules for domestic reasons, as when Germany banned British beef to protect its citizens against "mad cow disease," though the European Commission's health experts detected no danger.[36] And members continue to expand regulations in new areas, such as the law passed by France in 1994 calling for fines for businesses that use unnecessary English words in their advertisements.

For the future, business managers will have to deal with both the liberalization of old regulations *and* the imposition of new regulations. We will look at the conflicting trends in specific policy areas in Chapters 11 through 17. They cover policies governing owner, worker, and consumer rights; product and job safety; exploitation of the natural environment; domestic and foreign economic competition; and technology—all of which are crucial areas of interest to business.

Conclusion

We have reviewed different types of political and economic systems in this chapter and have seen that the traditional contrast between democratic capitalism and undemocratic socialism or communism has lost its relevance. Markets and states are not opposed forms of social organization; they are linked. Subtle variations divide today's mixed economies, many of which are organized on a cooperative or corporatist footing or encourage the state to guide the economy. In relation to those countries, the United States has a more restrained government. These alternative forms of democratic capitalism, not old-fashioned socialism, pose the main economic and political options in the 1990s and beyond.

Corporatist states seem to gain from low conflict and high cooperation among business, labor, and government. They appear to benefit from real wage moderation, making their goods more competitive on world markets.[37] They can perhaps decide more quickly on public policies, and execute them better, than pluralist states. Several corporatist states, notably Japan and Germany, have followed policies of pro-business, government guidance of market competition that have proven highly successful throughout most of the post–World War II period.

How important are the different models of democratic capitalism as the 20th century comes to a close? Some analysts think that the world's mixed economies are converging. They stress the unity of capitalism, not its diversity. In the global economy, no government can make autonomous and binding decisions for any society marked by territorial borders. International competition is forcing countries to become more like each other. Even Japan is facing economic restructuring, which may force Japanese corporations to abandon cherished practices such as lifetime employment and the pursuit of market share over profits. The Japanese system is thus losing its distinctiveness.[38]

Other analysts disagree and emphasize the variance among capitalist systems. With their unique traditions and histories, countries will continue to have different political economic systems, to adopt different public policies, and to do differently in the economic arena.[39] These two views are not necessarily inconsistent; the issue is one of degree.

What is beyond dispute is that all advanced countries have had economic problems such as slow growth and rising unemployment since the end of the 1980s. Each is trying to learn from the others how to cope with these changes. The old models for public policy look increasingly passé, and it is not clear what will work to build globally competitive industry in the 21st century.

The solution will not be to choose between government and markets; it will be to strike a balance between the two. While no government can assure a country's global competitiveness, that fact does not argue for blindly cutting the scope and reach of government. Finely tuned public policies, not formulas and slogans, are needed for success in world markets.

Whether such fine-tuning is probable is another question. Political dynamics in democracies lead government officials to speak in slogans, and sometimes to take action based on reasoning they know to be untrue. The resulting policies may not help business to compete in international markets and may hold business back. We begin to look at the evidence of government mishandling of the economy, as well as of wise decisions, in Chapter 7, where we see how government raises and spends money.

Questions

1. What are the main differences between socialism and capitalism? How relevant are these differences today?

2. What is corporatism? Pluralism? How does public decision making take place in corporatist countries as opposed to pluralist ones?

3. Describe different types of democratic capitalism. Where does the United States fit?

4. Discuss privatization and deregulation. Why are they happening?

5. Are countries in the world becoming more alike? More different?

End Notes

1. C. Fred Bergsten, "The Rationale for a Rosy View," *The Economist,* September 11, 1993, p. 57.

2. See, for example, Charles Hampden-Turner and Alfons Trompenaars, *The Seven Cultures of Capitalism* (New York: Doubleday, 1994).

3. James Fallows, *Looking at the Sun: The Rise of the New East Asian Economic and Political System* (New York: Pantheon, 1994).

4. Joel S. Migdal, *Strong Societies and Weak States* (Princeton: Princeton University Press, 1988).

5. See Samuel P. Huntington, *The Third Wave: Democratization in the Late Twentieth Century* (Norman: University of Oklahoma Press, 1991).

6. Michael Coppedge and Wolfgang H. Reinicke, "Measuring Polyarchy," in *On Measuring Democracy,* ed. Alex Inkeles (New Brunswick, NJ: Transaction Books, 1991), pp. 59–60.

7. A good summary of the literature on corporatism is Alan Cawson, *Corporatism and Political Theory* (Oxford: Basil Blackwell, 1986).

8. These groupings are based on Arend Lijphart and Markus M. L. Crepaz, "Corporatism and

Consensus Democracy in Eighteen Countries," *British Journal of Political Science* 21, pt. 2 (1991), pp. 235–46.

9. Harmon Zeigler, *Pluralism, Corporatism, and Confucianism* (Philadelphia: Temple University Press, 1988).

10. Philip Glouchevitch, *Juggernaut: The German Way of Business* (New York: Simon and Schuster, 1992).

11. Michel Albert, *Capitalism versus Capitalism,* trans. Paul Haviland (New York: Four Walls Eight Windows, 1993).

12. The term's first known use in English was in 1854 by William Thackery, the English satirist.

13. Ayn Rand, *Capitalism: The Unknown Ideal* (New York: New American Library, 1966).

14. See Oliver Williamson, *The Economic Institutions of Capitalism* (New York: Free Press, 1985). Also see John Kenneth Galbraith, *The New Industrial State,* 4th ed. (Boston: Houghton-Mifflin, 1985).

15. Karl Marx, *Capital: A Critique of Political Economy,* trans. Samuel Moore and Edward

Aveling (New York: Modern Library, 1906), p. 836.

16. Alec Nove, *An Economic History of the U.S.S.R.* (London: Pelican, 1976), p. 137.

17. As Theda Skocpol points out in a recent study, Americans have been more receptive to public insurance against misfortune than is commonly thought. See *Protecting Soldiers and Mothers: The Political Origins of Social Policy in the United States* (Cambridge, MA: Belknap Press, 1992).

18. See Igor Birman, *Personal Consumption in the USSR and the USA* (New York: St. Martin's Press, 1989); and A. S. Zaychenko, "United States–USSR Individual Consumption (Some Comparisons)," *World Affairs* 152, no. 1 (Summer 1989), pp. 8–11.

19. Barrington Moore, Jr., *Social Origins of Dictatorship and Democracy* (Boston: Beacon Press, 1966).

20. John Stopford and Susan Strange, *Rival States, Rival Firms* (New York: Cambridge University Press, 1991), p. 12.

21. Vinod Thomas, Ajay Chhibber, Mansoor Dailami, and Jaime de Melo, eds., *Restructuring Economies in Distress: Policy Reform and the World Bank* (Oxford: Oxford University Press, 1991).

22. See Adam Przeworski, *Capitalism and Social Democracy* (Cambridge: Cambridge University Press, 1985).

23. David B. Ottaway, "In Hungary, the Socialists Return, but Which Ones?" *International Herald Tribune,* May 31, 1994, p. 1.

24. Francis Fukuyama, *The End of History and the Last Man* (New York: Free Press, 1992). For similar themes expressed in the 1950s, see Daniel Bell, *The End of Ideology* (Glencoe, IL: Free Press, 1960).

25. Donald Axelrod, *Shadow Government* (New York: John Wiley & Sons, 1992), p. 17.

26. Edward S. Herman, *Corporate Control, Corporate Power* (Cambridge: Cambridge University Press, 1981), p. 167.

27. Robert H. Floyd, Clive S. Gray, and R. P. Short, *Public Enterprise in Mixed Economies* (Washington, DC: International Monetary Fund, 1984).

28. Douglas Lamont, *Foreign State Enterprises: A Threat to American Business* (New York: Basic Books, 1979).

29. "Russia under the Hammer," *The Economist,* November 28, 1992, pp. 69–70.

30. "Europe for Sale," *Business Week,* July 19, 1993, pp. 38–39.

31. James Q. Wilson, *American Government,* 3rd ed. (Lexington, MA: D.C. Heath, 1986), pp. 364–65.

32. Susan Rose-Ackerman, *The Reform of the Regulatory State* (New York: Free Press, 1992), p. 150.

33. David Audretsch, *The Market and the State* (New York: NYU Press, 1989), p. 22.

34. John G. Francis, *The Politics of Regulation: A Comparative Perspective* (Cambridge, MA: Basil Blackwell, 1993), p. 34.

35. "The Iceberg's Tip," *Regulation* 12, no. 3 (1988), p. 12.

36. "Something Dodgy in Europe's Single Market," *The Economist,* May 21, 1994, pp. 69–70.

37. See Michael Bruno and Jeffrey Sachs, *The Economics of Worldwide Stagflation* (Cambridge, MA: Harvard University Press, 1985).

38. Steven Brull, "In Japan, a Mature Economy Must Reinvent Itself," *International Herald Tribune,* May 19, 1993; and "A Survey of Japan," *The Economist,* July 9, 1994.

39. J. Rogers Hollingsworth, Philippe C. Schmitter, and Wolfgang Streeck, eds., *Governing Capitalist Economies* (New York: Oxford University Press, 1994).

7　FISCAL POLICY

Taxing and Spending

Taxes not only helped to create the state. They helped to form it. The tax system was the organ the development of which entailed other organs. Tax bill in hand, the state penetrated the private economies and won increasing dominion over them.

Joseph Schumpeter[1]

The conservative or neoliberal critique of government has deeply influenced contemporary views on public policy. Starting in the late 1970s, countries everywhere, in the industrialized North and the nonindustrialized South, have tried to put their public sectors on a diet. They have attempted to slash taxes and public spending. They have looked for ways to lighten the regulatory load on business. They have tried to shift traditional government tasks to the private sector or to abandon them altogether.

The effort to slim down the state has had mixed results. In Britain and Germany, for example, government's share of GNP fell during the 1980s, but only marginally. In the United States, government spending actually rose a few points of GNP that decade. Public employment also rose: there were 1.5 million more U.S. public sector employees in 1989 than in 1979. These things happened despite two conservative presidents, Reagan and Bush, occupying the Oval Office.

Why is Big Government so stubborn, so difficult to cut? This is a central question of the business environment, whose answer is critical to managers. Part of the explanation is rent seeking by business and other organized groups as they try to minimize the economic resources they give to government to pay for programs, and to maximize the benefit they receive from government. Government is big because, rhetoric aside, powerful private interests want it that way. Another factor is that the state itself resists having its powers cut.

To understand the political economy of the modern capitalist state, this chapter discusses from where these states get resources. Equally important, it looks at where those resources go. We will consider direct spending and more subtle forms of government expenditure. The underlying concern is how taxes and spending both hinder and help business.

Where Does the Money Come From?

Whether they are pluralist or corporatist, capitalist democracies have had to search without let up for revenue to pay for the Big Government all have established. This is not the invisible hand, some quip, but the "grasping hand."[2] Fiscal policy—who pays for government and how much—always has been a central, and contentious, issue in political economy. The main reason for the controversy is that taxes are involuntary. Compared to a consumer in the market, a taxpayer in the political arena has less control over what he or she is buying. Taxpayers also have an incentive to shift the cost of policies from themselves onto other taxpayers, which creates more controversy. Tax policy is doubly important for business. Not only does business itself pay for the support of government, it also collects many taxes from individuals for the state.

The mobility of capital and the growing flexibility of production technologies are forcing all countries to rethink their tax systems. Global firms can spread different activities among nations with the most favorable fiscal policies. To avoid losing business, in the 1980s, OECD members have tried to lower their tax rates and simplify their tax codes. The extent to which they achieved these goals varies widely.[3]

In 1991, an American taxpayer paid an average of $6,745 in a bewildering array of federal, state, and local taxes. It took from January 1 to May 3 to earn enough money to cover this obligation.[4] Figure 7–1 shows how this money is taken, by which type of tax.

The American system is unusually complex due to its federal nature. But as Figure 7–2 shows, the total tax burden is low by international standards. The type of taxes favored in America also is unusual, with far less reliance on consumption taxes than in rival European nations.

Many politicians like to take credit for tax cuts in the United States. Yet the tax burden did not change much from 1980 to 1990 (it was about 30 percent of GDP in both years). What has changed is who collects taxes and who pays them. Federal taxes dropped slightly in recent years, but not state and local taxes. States, cities, and towns now get about 45 percent of government revenue in the United States. Let us look at the trends in more detail.

Traditional Taxes

Before the rise of democracy, the West's mostly absolutist governments had taken funds from three main places: **property taxes, excises,** and **customs duties.** These remained the main revenue sources through the 1800s. They still are used, though their importance has shrunk.

FIGURE 7–1

Total government revenue by source in the United States, fiscal year 1990

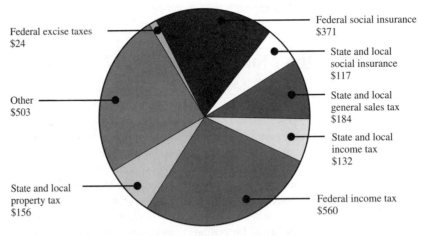

Federal excise taxes $24

Other $503

State and local property tax $156

Federal social insurance $371

State and local social insurance $117

State and local general sales tax $184

State and local income tax $132

Federal income tax $560

($ billions) (total revenue $2,047)

Source: Chris R. Edwards, Stephen Gold, Michael Fleming, and Karen Paisley, *Facts and Figures on Government Finance,* 28th ed. (Washington, DC: Tax Foundation, 1993), p. 13.

The property tax was broader then than now. We associate it with real estate, but early modern governments imposed property tax on movable effects also. These last taxes were hard to collect. Few people willingly admitted their full wealth to tax authorities. Under the *anciens régimes,* people without property did not get away, either. They were subject to taxes in kind and had to donate labor to public service every year.

Excise taxes are levies on specific commodities. Kings of the past taxed many basic goods—for instance, grain, sugar, salt, and, notoriously in the American colonies, tea. Customs duties (taxes on imports and exports) also generated much revenue and were an important instrument of mercantilist policies designed to promote national economic development.

The traditional taxes fell widely, on rich and poor. The poor, however, paid a higher proportion of their limited income. Why? Because the commodities subject to tax loomed large in their family budget. Adam Smith objected. In his view: "The subjects of every state ought to contribute towards the support of government, as nearly as is possible in proportion to . . . the revenue which they respectively enjoy under the protection of the state."[5] The rich, in other words, should pay more.

One maxim of political economy is that nobody likes paying taxes. Because of their position at the top of the social hierarchy, the rich could twist the revenue system in their favor. Tax evasion was common in the early modern period. People hid or understated their property. They bootlegged to avoid excises and smuggled to avoid tariffs. On occasion, people even rebelled rather than pay money to government. The American Revolution (1776–1783) was at heart a tax rebellion against the British state.

Still, even revolutionary governments need taxes to operate. The newborn American republic was no exception. Like its colonial predecessor, the federal government continued to levy tariffs and excises. One of the latter, an impost on spirits, sparked the Whiskey Rebellion in the Allegheny Mountains in 1794. It was the last major challenge to federal authority until the Civil War, though people in that region still make moonshine and try to avoid revenue agents.

Through the 19th century, tariffs and excises usually gave Washington enough money to run its affairs. But the revenue was too little to support the new demand being put on government as industry matured and citizenship expanded. Officials needed more sources of funds. As we will see shortly, the **income tax** was the answer.

Government rarely and reluctantly gives up revenue sources once it taps them. Washington continues to collect tariffs. These no longer yield much income, mainly because international treaties since World War II have compelled the United States to lower most tariffs. In quest of export markets, the signatories of the treaties have agreed to hold down import duties on each others' products. (We return to this topic in Chapter 17.)

Excise taxes on individual products (for example, on alcohol, tobacco, and gasoline) also exist still. They generate about $100 billion a year, or less than 5 percent of all tax revenue in the United States. In other Western countries, the take from excises is usually proportionately greater, due largely to much higher charges on fuel.[6] In the early 1990s, motorists in the United States paid only 38 cents of tax per gallon of gasoline; in Japan and the large European countries, however, they paid $1.68 to $3.64.[7] Ross Perot has advocated raising the U.S.

FIGURE 7–2

Advanced countries differ widely in the way they raise government revenue

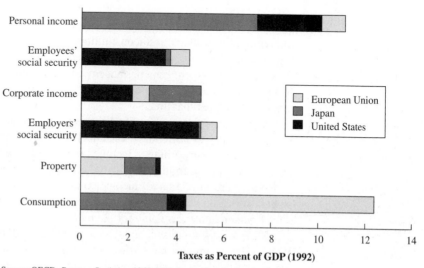

Taxes as Percent of GDP (1992)

Source: OECD, *Revenue Statistics, 1965–1993* (Paris: Organization for Economic Cooperation and Development, 1994).

tax by 50 cents, but few Americans back such an idea. Congress could barely muster the votes for a nickel increase in 1993.

Sometimes excises get earmarked for specific uses (gasoline taxes for roads, airplane fuel taxes for airports, cigarette taxes for antismoking campaigns, and so on). The U.S. interstate highway system, for example, is financed by motorists who purchase gasoline.

To the extent they are "sin taxes," which will be paid only by people who indulge in a "vice" such as smoking, drinking, or gambling, excises can be politically palatable to the majority. But that does not mean they can always get approved. President Clinton proposed helping to pay for health care reform with a $1-per-pack cigarette tax—still only about one-quarter the level of cigarette taxes in Denmark. The idea met resistance from tobacco interests and died with the rest of his health care plan in 1994.

Personal and Corporate Income Tax

As economies developed and became based on money, not barter and subsistence, a logical idea was to tax the income of people and companies. Britain started taxing income in 1799. Japan started in 1887, Germany, in 1891. The United States was the last major industrial country to go this lucrative route. Almost everywhere in the capitalist North today (France is an exception), the income tax leads all other sources of government revenue.

Washington imposed a temporary income tax during the Civil War but dropped it after defeating the Confederacy. The issue was revived by the **progressive movement** in American politics, which was influential from 1890 to 1920. Stimulated by the growth of vast and untaxed private fortunes such as Rockefeller's and Carnegie's, progressives wanted to subdue the nation's business elite. Their goal was to control the economy so as to distribute its benefits more widely.

The U.S. Congress voted a tax on personal income in the 1890s, but the Supreme Court declared it unconstitutional. Corporate income was taxed starting in 1909. Not until the Sixteenth Amendment to the Constitution (1913) did the federal government get a permanent tax on personal income. Under pressure from progressives, Congress also imposed assessments on capital gains and on inherited wealth at that time.

One reason progressives liked the personal income tax was that it can be based on ability to pay. They felt the rich could, and should, be made to pay more of their higher earnings. Income tax thus became a means for social leveling. It took money from the well-to-do and left the poor alone. The 1913 law levied a 1 percent rate on all incomes over $3,000 for a single person, with a 6 percent surtax on very high incomes. Because average income was about $600, only 1 person in 50 was liable for payment.

Rates were soon raised, and the income threshold lowered, to pay for World War I. The income tax burden was reduced after the war, though not as low as the prewar level, but it edged up during the Great Depression and World War II.

By 1944, rates ranged from 23 percent of earned income in the lowest tax bracket ($1,500) to 94 percent of adjusted gross income in the highest bracket ($200,000 and over). Starting in 1942, withholding of income tax from paychecks ("pay as you earn") made the income tax a regular, and hard to escape, source of revenue. Withholding also put new record-keeping requirements on employers, who had to keep track of employees' earnings and tax payments.

The personal income tax has been under continuous fire for killing the incentive to work or start a business. Why should people exert themselves if they have to give most of the proceeds to government? The tax on wages and salaries is particularly rankling because it is easy to see and hard to avoid—people know exactly how much they pay each year and they have few legal ways not to pay. Pay stubs provide a regular and irritating reminder that government is taking away "their" hard-earned money. These taxes are collected by the Internal Revenue Service, a bureau in the Treasury Department.

Congress dropped rates in the years after World War II, most dramatically with the Reagan tax reforms of 1981 and 1986. The Reagan reforms also made the tax flatter, eliminating most tax brackets. The president's goal was to let high-income people keep what they earn, and so foster investment and economic growth. Sometimes this approach is called **supply-side economics** or **Reaganomics** (or, more pejoratively, the trickle-down theory). It was highly popular, since every taxpayer got a break, though most of the benefit went to those with higher income.

By 1989, the U.S. federal personal income tax had only 3 brackets, compared to 25 in 1975. The top rate was 35 percent, down from 70 percent in 1975. (These are nominal rates; the effective tax rate is always lower due to exemptions or so-called **tax expenditures.** We will look at tax expenditures shortly.) Businesspeople have usually supported this flattening of the income tax rate, which is apt to be particularly helpful to them to the extent they have higher-than-average incomes.

Other industrialized countries moved in the same direction in the 1980s, though none went as far as the United States. Japan, for example, cut the number of brackets to five and reduced the top tax rate to 50 percent. Britain eliminated all but two income brackets and reduced its maximum rate to 42 percent of personal income.[8] The majority leader of the U.S. House of Representatives, Richard Armey, has proposed going still further, with a single, flat tax on all income.

Controversy has surged around the tax treatment of **capital gains.** If an asset increases in value and is sold, how should the profit (the capital gain) be treated for tax purposes? In most of Europe and Japan, capital gains are not fully taxed. The United States used to follow the same practice, but since 1986 it has become unique in counting capital gains as ordinary income. President Bush, during his term, repeatedly sought to bring back special treatment of capital gains, but the Democrat-controlled Congress never agreed. Bush's argument was that this change in the tax code would help business raise new funds. The new Republican majority that took over Congress in 1994 promised to revisit the issue.

A more immediate concern to business is the corporate income tax. As legal persons, corporations are liable for tax on their profit. Companies have used their political clout to get this tax cut, arguing that it reduces economic growth. The corporate income tax rate has been dropping in the United States and in most other industrial countries (see Table 7–1). Only in Japan does it represent a big slice of the total take in taxes.

American corporations, like individuals, are also subject to state and local income tax. Wisconsin was the first state to impose an income tax, in 1911 (two years before the federal government). Forty-five states, and some 3,500 municipalities, now claim a share of individual and corporate income. State and local revenue from taxing incomes is currently about $132 billion, compared to about $560 billion at the federal level (see Figure 7–1).

Social Insurance Payments

Income gets taxed another important way. In most industrial countries, employees and employers each must pay payroll taxes (often euphemistically called "contributions") for **social insurance.** Social insurance refers to compulsory programs run by government to protect workers and managers alike against income losses inherent in an industrial economy—especially losses arising from accidents, illness, or retirement. These programs are the heart of the government's guarantor role, a function introduced in Chapter 3. The payroll taxes to support social insurance are contributions in the loose sense that taxpayers are giving money to a common purpose and will be repaid later.

Social insurance schemes are not like private insurance plans, for no fund builds up from which to pay the future obligations. All so-called contributions become part of government's revenue stream. In fact, everywhere government adds money from general taxes to pay social benefits—about one-third the total in the United States.[9] Stripped of the rhetoric about insurance, money is simply

---

TABLE 7–1   **The United States Has Cut Corporate Income Tax, and so Have Other Countries.**

	Corporate Tax Rate		Percent of Central Government Revenue
	1984	*1990*	*1992†*
France	50%	39%	4%
Germany	56	50	4
Japan	55	50	30
Sweden	52	42	4
United Kingdom	45	35	9
United States*	**51**	**39**	**9**

*Federal only.

†Or nearest available year.

Sources: B. Guy Peters, *The Politics of Taxation* (Cambridge, MA: Basil Blackwell, 1991), pp. 24–25; and International Monetary Fund, *Government Finance Statistics Yearbook 1993* (Washington, DC: IMF, 1993).

being transferred from workers and businesses to beneficiaries of the system. It is "pay as you go."

During the Reagan presidency (1981–1989), U.S. workers' tax burden for social insurance rose by half in constant dollars. In 1990, the average taxpayer contributed about $2,200. The rise in social insurance contributions more than offset the income tax reduction for low- and middle-income people. Thus, contrary to popular belief, federal taxes (income plus payroll) did not fall for most individuals in the 1980s.[10]

Companies also have been hit by rising social insurance in the last decade. Their payment for these programs went up a third from 1979 to 1990 (adjusted for inflation).[11] Almost one-sixth the total U.S. tax revenue is now employer social insurance contributions. That is twice the amount obtained by corporate income tax. High though social insurance cost is to American companies, they pay less of GNP than do companies in Europe, and about the same as companies in Japan (see Chapter 12 for more details).

General Consumption Taxes

Supply-side theory prefers consumption-based taxes to income tax, because they are more likely to spur saving and investment. By raising the price of consumer goods, consumption taxes depress sales and get people to put money aside for the future. Consumption taxes have a work incentive, too. They make people work harder to maintain a given amount of consumption (the opposite of income taxes), though they penalize the poor (unlike progressive income taxes), because the poor usually spend a larger share of their income on consumption than do the rich.

With the switch to more conservative public policy in the 1980s, consumption taxes have been rising in most OECD countries. One type of consumption tax is the excise, as we discussed above. A far more important levy on consumption in the United States is **general sales taxes,** which merchants add as a percent of retail sales. First introduced in Mississippi in 1932, general sales taxes are imposed by all but five states and by many local governments (but not by the federal government).

Consumers pay the tax when they buy a good or service (usually with exceptions for necessities such as food or medicine). Merchants collect the money and periodically pay it to the appropriate authority, often using the funds as working capital meanwhile. Sales taxes now produce about $184 billion a year, or around 9 percent of all tax revenue. (States round out their income with a variety of licenses, user fees, and other charges.)

European countries tax consumption with the **value added tax (VAT).** It differs from a sales tax because it is imposed at every stage of production, not the retail level alone. The VAT is paid only on the difference between the price of materials that go into a product and the price received for it—that is, on the value business adds. In Europe, the VAT accounts for between 13 percent and 25 percent of all tax revenue—two to four times as much as the American sales tax (see Figure 7–2). The VAT's share has been going up, partly to compensate for the drop in income tax. Japan long avoided taxing consumption, but, in 1988, it did introduce a 3 percent national sales tax.

Governments like the VAT—it is less visible than a retail sales tax, since it is figured into the price of things rather than being added after a sale. Thus, the VAT is potentially less a political liability: to the extent people are unaware they are paying it, they are apt to be more amicable about government. For business, the VAT has the disadvantage of creating a greater recordkeeping challenge than the sales tax usually does. A federal VAT was discussed early in the Clinton administration for the United States as a way to finance national health care. The idea met stiff resistance and went nowhere.

Property Tax

Compared to other OECD countries, except Britain, the United States relies more heavily on imposts on property. These generated $156 billion in 1990, an average of $626 per capita.[12]

For American cities, towns, and counties, property tax is the leading revenue source. In contrast to their counterparts overseas, U.S. local governments have to raise more money themselves, and they get fewer grants from the central government. (They also have more functions than local governments do in most countries.) Property tax has always been important at the local level in the United States, though, since the 19th century, communities have moved away from hard-to-tax (that is, movable) property. Land and buildings are the base for the modern property tax. Real estate is easy for government to monitor and assess, and thus makes a good target for taxing. So do large items such as automobiles and trucks. Often, commercial and residential property are charged differently, with the heavier weight on business.

Like income and general sales taxes, property taxes are plain for taxpayers to see. Their visibility makes them a lightning rod for political opposition, especially when rising property values push up homeowners' wealth faster than their income. Since the late 1970s, several taxpayer revolts in the United States have been aimed mainly at reducing residential property taxes. Similar hostility by property owners to the property tax, or rates, in Britain led in the late 1980s to a short-lived and even less popular (and since repealed) poll or head tax.

Taxpayer revolts are easy to mount in the United States because Americans often get the chance to vote directly on local taxes (and on state taxes, too). Many state constitutions require voters to approve increases in local property tax rates. Often, local and state governments need a popular vote to borrow money with bonds. Voters in several states also may put issues on the ballot for popular vote (see Chapter 10). This last procedure allowed Proposition 13 in California (1979) and Proposition 2½ in Massachusetts (1981), bellwether instances when state residents voted to reduce their property taxes. In the Massachusetts case, the high-technology industry led the fight with an expensive public and behind-the-scenes lobbying effort. Executives argued that exorbitant property taxes prevented them from hiring and retaining skilled workers.[13]

Regulatory "Taxes"

Thus far we have been discussing ordinary taxes, which are resources taken from people and organizations at the government's behest. A hidden tax is government regulation of business. As we have seen, regulations are constraints put on employers: Activities thought to be harmful to society (polluting the air, false advertising, racial discrimination in hiring) are prohibited; activities thought to be helpful (publication of interest rates on loans, installation of safety devices on cars, on-the-job accident insurance for employees) are required.

These **employer mandates** are taxes in the sense that they are government-ordered payments, though no money passes through the government treasury. They require an outlay of funds just as any tax does. Companies pass the cost of conforming to employer mandates onto the consumer by raising the price of their products. We all pay more for things because of regulatory policy, though few consumers are aware of it. Owners and managers complain that these mandates discourage them from hiring people, and thus cost society jobs.

As noted in Chapter 5, there has been a drive to deregulate business in recent years, to lighten the load of employer mandates. This drive is part of the larger political movement against taxes and government that has caught fire around the world. Deregulation has met with mixed success, like the anti-government movement generally.

Nontax Revenue

Because voters resist taxes, government at all levels and in all OECD countries are turning more to nontax revenues. The leading source, measured by the amount of money raised, is borrowing. In the United States, per capita gross public debt (adjusted for inflation) nearly doubled in the 1980s. By 1991, the total (federal, state, and local) was about $18,279 for every person.[14] Most other OECD countries also have been borrowing heavily. The U.S. public debt is proportionately less than in Japan, but somewhat above the level in Germany (see Figure 7–3).

Government invests some money it borrows in infrastructure and other facilities. (Public assets in the United States are worth $4.7 trillion, which is $700 billion more than the equity that Americans have in their homes!) Presumably, government's capital outlays will generate future income and thus pay for themselves over the long run. Like a company's purchase of a factory or office building, it makes sense to spread the payment for capital outlays over many years. This is the reason many foreign countries divide their expenditures into a current budget (for ongoing expenses) and a capital budget (for long-term investments).

Unfortunately, most borrowing at the federal level goes for current consumption—health care, pensions, and so forth. The 1993 U.S. budget had a $311 billion deficit on operations versus $26 billion for capital transactions.[15] (To put these figures in context, Americans spent $260 billion on food in 1991.) The current deficit gets used up right away and does not lay a base for future revenue.

FIGURE 7–3

*The United States'
outstanding public
debt is neither high
nor low compared
to other countries*

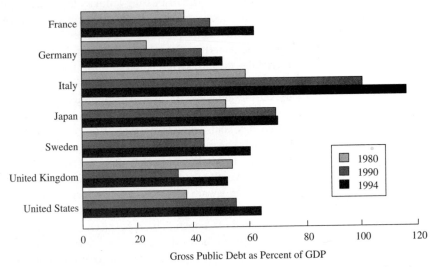

Source: *OECD Economic Outlook* (Paris: Organization for Economic Cooperation and Development, December 1993), p. 154.

Washington will repay its consumption loans, but with higher real taxes, fewer government services, or both. It is this side of government borrowing that lies at the center of the U.S. fiscal crunch.

Governments also exact **user fees** and other charges, such as licenses, from their citizens, often for services they once gave away to constituents. Due to their position as service providers, cities and towns are most likely to find ways to impose user fees. Examples where local authorities collect receipts directly include trash collection, resident parking permits, and admission to town beaches.

User fees have several advantages. They help government keep a lid on involuntary taxes. They free people who do not use a service from paying for it. They sometimes force people who live outside the boundaries of a political unit to contribute to it, lifting the tax burden on residents (that is, voters). Fees are also a way to ration public facilities that might otherwise be used excessively or unwisely. They now account for about $1 for every $20 collected by government in the United States ($1 in $4 at the local level).

Still, user fees do not preclude taxpayer revolts. In metropolitan Boston, for instance, residents have mobilized against skyrocketing water and sewer rates charged by the Massachusetts Water Resources Authority, a public body. Already paying among the highest rates in the country, Bostonians can expect their rates to double by the end of the century due to mandated antipollution measures in Boston Harbor. The harbor cleanup has been scaled back in response to these complaints.

Where Does the Money Go?

Government spending can be divided between outright purchases and **transfer payments** (Figure 7–4). About half the public budget in the United States is for final goods and services—a category that includes everything from paper clips to nuclear submarines. Purchases of final goods by all levels of government have held steady at about 20 percent of U.S. GNP for decades.[16] That amount is split between salaries for government workers and acquisitions from private contractors. Government buying (less employee compensation) in the United States was $470 billion in 1993—a huge market but less important than transfer payments, which are nearly twice as great.

Transfer payments are where all relative growth in federal government spending has happened since the 1950s.[17] In contrast to final purchases, with transfer payments the government does not expend the money for itself; it takes money from one person or company and gives it to another person or company to do with as seen fit. Transfer payments often are branded handouts or giveaways by people who do not like them (usually because they do not receive them).

Transfer payments also make up most of the difference among countries in how much their governments spend. The United States and, even more so, Japan spend much less on this function than do European countries (see Figure 7–5).

"Welfare" for Business

Transfer payments are central to the welfare state. Most often we associate welfare with people programs; we are apt to disregard how modern government transfers resources to business through a wide variety of subsidies. A **subsidy** is a payment to business or individuals for which government gets nothing in return. They are not entitlements. There is a quid pro quo: the recipient must do

FIGURE 7–4

Spending by all levels of U.S. government, fiscal year 1993 ($ billions)

Source: *Survey of Current Business* 74, no. 1 (July 1994).

Figure 7–5

*Government spends
for different
priorities in different
countries*

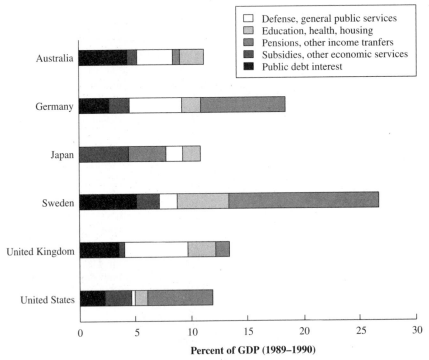

Source: *OECD Economic Outlook* (Paris: Organization for Economic Cooperation and Development, December 1993).

something to get the payment. These are classic distributive policies (see Chapter 1).

Direct handouts equal less than 1 percent of U.S. GNP, lower than in France, Germany, and Britain, and marginally higher than in Japan.[18] The E.U. countries doled out some $135 billion in 1990, according to one source. The biggest beneficiaries were the railroads, the coal industry, and agriculture, in that order.[19]

Subsidies are critically important to some economic sectors, in particular agribusiness. Table 7–2 shows that about one-third of U.S. farm income derives from government support. The figures are even higher in Europe and Japan, accounting for half to three-quarters of farm income. In the United States, large agribusinesses reap most of the subsidies.

Explicit cash subsidies to business in the United States date mainly from the New Deal. The Agricultural Adjustment Act (1933), for example, established the agribusiness subsidy programs. These programs include price supports, marketing quotas, acreage allotments, the soil bank scheme, and other endeavors to hold down farm production and hold farm prices up. Another example is the Merchant Marine Act (1936), which empowered the federal government to pick up

TABLE 7–2   **Producer Subsidies Loom Large in Farming.**

	Percent of Farm Income Derived from Government Support				
	1986	*1987*	*1988*	*1989*	*1990*
Australia	16%	11%	9%	10%	11%
Canada	49	48	42	37	41
E.U.	50	48	46	41	48
Japan	75	76	74	71	68
United States	**42**	**40**	**34**	**29**	**30**

Source: John M. Breen, *The GATT Uruguay Round, Agriculture* (Deventer, Netherlands: Kluwer, 1993), p. 2.

the difference in cost between constructing a vessel in the United States and abroad. It also subsidized the cost of shipping on American-owned ships.

There was a political counteraction to direct handouts for business in the late 1970s. As always, the talk of reform and austerity exceeded what was done. Under President Reagan, the shipping subsidy program and some other direct subsidies were repealed. Still, in 1995, House Budget committee members were able to identify some $85 billion in direct aid going to business.[20] The majority of these subsidies went to agriculture, transportation, energy, and natural resource companies.

Indirect Subsidies

Because of the stigma against giving money directly to companies, the United States has turned in recent years to indirect subsidies, especially to **tax expenditures** and **loan guarantees.** These two policy vehicles have the same effect as a cash payment, though no money changes hand. As a rule, indirect subsidies are more important in today's political economy than old-fashioned direct subsidies.

We analyze some public policies that provide indirect subsidies in the next two sections of this chapter. Students should bear in mind that any subsidy for business has second-round benefits for individual workers, managers, and owners, too. If they help a large or influential constituency, both direct and indirect subsidies prove difficult to trim.

Loan Guarantees.   One type of indirect subsidy is loan guarantees. Because they are offered free or at low charge, loan guarantees have the effect of boosting the profit of every firm that receives them. Most famous are the bailouts of Lockheed Aircraft Corporation (1975) and Chrysler Corporation (1979). In both instances, two large American companies were on the verge of bankruptcy and could not borrow money to reorganize themselves. On the grounds that there was a public interest in these companies, the federal government agreed to repay their creditors should either company default. With Washington standing behind them, Lockheed and Chrysler could go to the credit market and raise funds. Fortunately for U.S. taxpayers, both companies survived and repaid the loans.

These spectacular loan guarantees are only the tip of the iceberg. Government routinely steps in to underwrite loans when private lenders provide too little credit to produce a desired level of economic activity. By shifting the risk to itself, government induces lenders to make loans they would otherwise deny. The avowed purpose is to redirect resources to socially useful purposes, for example housing, college education, or small business. Loan guarantees are hidden subsidies because they do not appear as outlays in the regular budget.

Like many facets of the state's guarantor role, credit insurance dates mainly from the 1930s. Mortgage guarantees are the classic example. They revived the housing industry during the Depression by calming lenders that were leery of offering home buyers long-term, low-down-payment mortgages. Small business loans are another example.

As political economy predicts, loan guarantees are popular with legislators because they provide aid with apparently little pain. The guarantees cost the taxpayer not a penny except in cases of default. This may explain why new federal loan guarantees tripled during the 1980s. No cash outlays do not mean no opportunity cost. Society may still lose, for the guarantees distort the way resources are used. Too much capital may go, say, into vacation homes and not enough into new factories.

Loan guarantees expanded with the rest of government in the postwar period, though the rate of growth slowed under President Reagan. The federal government put its "full faith and credit" behind more than $115 billion in new loans in 1992. That amount was in addition to $15 billion in *direct* federal government loans, made at more favorable terms than private lenders would allow. The states make substantial low-interest loans to business, too. Outstanding state debt for private purposes was about $166 billion in 1990.[21]

Washington also stands behind several enterprises it sponsors to influence credit markets. The most important of these are in the home finance industry— the Federal National Mortgage Association (Fannie Mae), established in 1938, and the Federal Home Loan Mortgage Association (Freddie Mac), established in 1970. U.S. government–sponsored entities such as Fannie Mae and Freddie Mac obligated an estimated $470 billion in loans in 1993.[22] That amount is more than all federal spending on social insurance.

Deposit Insurance.   Since the 1930s, another important kind of government insurance covers financial assets. Included are such assets as deposits at banks, savings and loan associations, and credit unions, and contributions to pension funds. These are insured by organizations such as the Federal Deposit Insurance Corporation (established in 1933) and the Federal Savings and Loan Insurance Corporation (established in 1934). More than $2.7 trillion in deposits were insured in 1988. The federal government also insures against floods, crop failure, and other financial risks, worth another $1 trillion.[23]

Financial institutions pay premiums for such insurance, but the premiums do not cover costs fully. Thus, when the savings and loan (S&L) industry got into serious trouble in the late 1980s, the deposit insurance fund ran out of money. The federal government had to pick up the tab, estimated at $500 billion over 40 years, or about $2,000 for every man, woman, and child in the United States.

The proximate cause of the S&L fiasco was deregulation. To help them compensate for losses due to inflation, the thrift institutions had been cut loose from close government supervision in the 1980s and were allowed to make riskier investments. There was an incentive for them to speculate recklessly because deposit insurance would make good all losses. The predictable result was mass insolvency of the S&L industry.

A Capitalist Safety Net.   Combining the public credit activities—direct loans, guaranteed loans, and loans from government-sponsored agencies—government underwrites 10 to 25 percent of all funds loaned in U.S. credit markets each year. Through financial insurance, government also protects much of the nation's capital. The combined effect is a kind of capitalist safety net, equivalent to (and by some measures larger than) the individual safety net of the welfare state. The potential liability the federal government has accrued from these guarantees exceeds the GNP in value.[24]

Too often, these well-intended programs create moral hazard—that is, they tend to encourage the behavior they are trying to prevent. A good illustration is federal flood insurance, which spurs housing development near exposed beaches, river basins, and similar sites. These homes (often occupied by the well-to-do) are periodically damaged or destroyed by storms and then repaired or replaced at public expense. In fact, each time the government raises the insured-value ceiling, people build closer to the water—raising the cost for taxpayers with every flood.[25]

In an unbiased market, fewer resources would be pulled to waterside development, leaving more for other uses. The social loss created by flood insurance passes unnoticed by most individuals, however. Meanwhile, the homeowners directly benefiting are highly motivated to demand that the subsidized flood insurance program be kept in place. This is why subsidies and loan guarantees are such a prevalent form of public policy.

Tax Expenditures.   Another type of hidden subsidy results from not taxing certain activities. Whatever the government shelters from taxes, it encourages. Tax shelters have been labeled tax expenditures because they equal the revenue government *does not get* when it extends special relief to persons and firms.

Tax expenditures (loopholes to those who do not benefit) are not new, but they have become an important tool in the modern political economy. Politicians like them because they are a way to help constituents without having to spend money directly, thus providing cover from political opponents' possible charges of budget-busting. Like regular expenditures, tax expenditures in the United States have risen briskly in recent years. In 1968, Washington had fewer than 50 national tax expenditure programs; by 1985, there were 100.[26] They were pruned substantially in 1986. Still, three years later, tax expenditures were equivalent to 28 percent of federal tax revenue, almost twice as big as the annual federal budget deficit.

The most popular tax expenditure in the United States is the right to deduct home mortgage interest from income for federal tax purposes. The mortgage interest deduction (and the deduction for residential property tax) was part of the original 1913 tax code. These two deductions were worth $33 billion in 1990. All industrial countries (except Canada) offer taxpayers the same break, though most have more restrictions on it.

The mortgage deduction obviously benefits homeowners—hence, its popularity. Ross Perot correctly notes that the benefit accrues disproportionally to the rich, which is why he advocates a cap on mortgages over $250,000 and for second homes.[27] It is easy to overlook that the mortgage deduction also is an indirect subsidy to the construction and real estate industries. The effect of the subsidy varies from country to country, of course, depending on tax rates, limits on the exemption, coverage of second homes, and further factors.

Other important tax expenditures are for pensions (an indirect subsidy to banks, insurance companies, and brokerage firms), medical expenses (a subsidy to the health-care industry), and charity (a subsidy to universities, museums, and other institutions). The United States also helps subnational governments by allowing taxpayers to deduct state and local income taxes and shelter interest earned from state and local bonds.

Business receives other breaks in the federal income tax code (and also state codes). Since 1946, for example, companies have been allowed to write off assets by an accelerated depreciation schedule. They also are allowed to take a tax credit for investment and R&D. This pair of tax expenditures was worth $21.6 billion and $2.9 billion, respectively, in 1989.[28]

Over the years, the U.S. tax code has accumulated many other special deductions for particular industries. Business was apt to like these breaks—in particular if not in general—and to want more of them. Many citizens came to think the code unfair, however, for they could not take advantage of these deductions themselves. Tax authorities did not like the code either, because it had gotten too complex to administer.

These last pressures led to the Tax Reform Act of 1986. Over vigorous opposition from the affected industries, Congress agreed to shut most loopholes in exchange for the lower average income tax rate discussed earlier. Federal tax expenditures for corporations were only $39 billion in 1990, compared to $95 billion in 1985.[29] But Washington is under heavy pressure to open new loopholes to appease business—this is one reason the tax laws are rewritten so often. The 1994 Republican Contract with America, for example, promised several important new breaks for companies.

State Bidding Wars

While tax expenditures have been falling at the federal level, they have been growing at the state and local levels. To retain existing industries, and to attract new ones, states and communities go out of their way to make tax concessions. Thirty-one states, for example, offer qualified companies exemptions from corporate income tax. Thirty-five states offer companies abatements on land or capital improvements. More than 30 states even have offices in Tokyo to recruit companies from Japan.[30] Many other incentives are available, amounting to a "War between the States" for business.

These bidding wars can be costly. To lure Mercedes-Benz, which wanted to build a 1,500-employee plant in the United States, over half the states offered financial enticements. Alabama, South Carolina, and North Carolina made the final cut. Mercedes skillfully played the states off each other to get the best deal possible for itself. Alabama won the contest with a package that included donated land and site preparation, state allowances to the company to use money for income tax to pay debt, exemption from state and local property taxes for 10 years, a state training program to pay workers' salaries while in training, and an agreement by the state to buy 2,500 Mercedes vehicles for state use. The package was worth over $300 million.[31]

The rub is that too many giveaways can imperil a jurisdiction's capacity to provide services, which may later push companies away again. States, cities, and towns have a pressing need to improve schools, fix roads, and hire safety personnel; tax concessions make it harder to meet these needs. Meanwhile, existing companies complain the incentives give newcomers an unfair advantage, which creates pressure for governments to create more programs to help them, too. The competition among state governments and cities need not mean net gains in business and jobs for the nation. Companies often plan to locate new facilities *somewhere* in the United States anyway; state and local incentives only affect investment in particular sites, not its overall level in the country. When everything is summed, the social cost of business incentive packages can sometimes be greater than the return.

The National Governor's Association has tried to declare a truce to break this cycle, which costs states billions of dollars per year. But the temptation to attract jobs, and the pressure for other states to fight back, has made it impossible to stop the escalating battle.[32]

Tax concessions do not guarantee a company will keep a plant open, as Ypsilanti, Michigan, discovered. The town gave General Motors $13 million in tax relief to reinvest locally. Shortly after the agreement, the company decided to move production to Texas anyway. Ypsilanti sued to get its money back. It lost, on the grounds that tax abatements do not obligate a firm to guarantee employment.

Privatization and Contracting Out

A new boost for business is the delegating of public duties to private organizations—what Americans call **privatization.** (We ran across another meaning of privatization in Chapter 6. The term also refers to the selling or denationalization of state-owned enterprises. Still a third meaning of privatization exists—to import market incentives into the public sector by giving beneficiaries a choice of service providers. An example is a voucher system for choosing which town school to attend.)

Privatization in the American sense involves contracting out for services. Public funds continue to pay for the service (sometimes supplemented or replaced by user fees), but the government no longer furnishes the service itself. Usually, a profit-making firm takes over, for example, when a contractor assumed management of the Minneapolis public schools in 1993. The contracting can also embrace volunteer and not-for-profit organizations. A church group, for instance, might be given resources to run a feeding center for the destitute or a shelter for runaway children.

Why shift public services to the private sector? Four reasons are usually given:

- Those who want goods provided by government should pay the full cost of them.
- Production by the private sector is likely to be less costly.
- Consumers are likely to be more satisfied when given a variety of providers.
- Unlocking the innovative gifts of entrepreneurs will lead to new technology.[33]

Donald Kettl points out the trend toward privatization does not signify a shrinking government, but the opposite. It represents the quest by government for new ways to handle its increasing responsibilities. Turning to private management is, in his terms, the "governmentization" of the private sector.[34] Business approves because new opportunities are created for companies that want to compete for government contracts.

Privatization/hiring out has been embraced most warmly at the local level. As of mid-1987, there were 28,000 recorded instances of U.S. local governments engaging private firms to provide public services.[35] According to one study, 30 percent of American cities and towns use private firms to run hospitals, 35 percent contract for trash collection, 49 percent for legal services, and 80 percent for vehicle towing and storage.[36] As should be expected, research finds that contracting out is not a panacea for inefficient or costly services. Sometimes the services deteriorate and are run *less* efficiently than when under public control.[37] Privatization also creates opportunities for bribery, which pushes up cost.

The United States is turning to private sector service providers faster and further than other industrial countries. Contracting out public services is far less evident elsewhere. Even in Britain, less than 12 percent of local councils retain private contractors for services. Surprisingly, given the antigovernment, pro-business stance of the Thatcher government, the number of councils contracting out dropped in the latter 1980s.[38]

Government contracting often becomes a hidden subsidy for domestic businesses. Most countries use official and unofficial methods to block foreign companies from winning government contracts, preferring to reserve the work for their own citizens. Japan is thought to be particularly effective at subsidizing home-based companies this way.

Miscellaneous Subsidies

We have only touched the surface of indirect subsidies to business. There are many other government activities that have the effect of a subsidy. Take tariffs, which we discussed earlier. Besides their obvious purpose of providing the government with revenue, tariffs also subsidize domestic companies by raising the price of foreign products (thus allowing domestic companies to charge more). Publicly supported R&D is similar. It helps some firms more than others. The same is true of regulations that control competition in an industry: existing competitors gain, potential entrants lose.

We will return to these assorted indirect subsidies in greater detail in Chapters 15, 16, and 17.

Conclusion

This chapter has reviewed several aspects of government's effects on business in the United States and other mixed economies. We have looked at the sources of public revenues (that is, how government extracts funds from business organizations and people) and the objects of public expenditure (that is, how government gives cash, or its nonmonetary equivalent, to companies and individuals). Since early in the 20th century, and particularly since the Great Depression, the state has been taking in and disbursing more resources than before. These activities illustrate again the interdependence of government and capitalism, a theme we have been tracking throughout this book.

Public officials have tried to use their authority to take resources away from individuals and firms (and their power to give resources back) to guide the private sector. But the effects often did not correlate with the stated goals. Some taxes had adverse effects on investment and innovation and were seen as a drag on American companies that put them at a disadvantage in world markets. Subsidies and incentives were believed to have similar distorting effects. Sometimes private

interests found ways to profit from being regulated, defeating the purpose.

By the late 1970s, many independent observers concluded governments had gone too far in trying to manipulate their markets with taxes and incentives. Efforts followed to shrink the state. Specific policies have included giving up government functions (canceling programs), turning public functions over to the private sector (contracting out or privatization), limiting the scope of intervention (deregulation), and selling off public assets (another form of privatization). These policies were linked to tax cuts, intended to dry up government's resource base.

Deeds have never matched words, however, and the state has not been pushed back as far as conservatives (neoliberals) hoped. The reasons can be found in political economy—laissez-faire rhetoric aside, neither business nor government is keen to kill public policies that help them both. And the public likes many types of subsidies and tax breaks, too. How business and other interest groups fight for favorable policies is the main theme in Part IV.

Questions

1. What are the major sources of revenue for government? Why are some sources relied on more heavily than others?

2. Compare and contrast the financial burden of government on business in different countries.

3. How does social insurance work? What role does it play in the welfare state? Are these expenditures justified?

4. How is regulation a hidden tax? Is this hidden tax worth paying?

5. Is there an adversarial relationship between business and government in the United States? In other economically advanced countries?

End Notes

1. Joseph Schumpeter, "The Crisis of the Tax State," in *The Economics and Sociology of Capitalism,* ed. Richard Swedborg (Princeton: Princeton University Press, 1991), p. 108.

2. Mancur Olson, "Dictatorship, Democracy, and Development," *American Political Science Review* 87, no. 3 (1993), p. 569.

3. Sven Steinmo, *Taxation and Democracy* (New Haven: Yale University Press, 1993), pp. 159–60.

4. Chris R. Edwards, Stephen Gold, Michael Fleming, and Karen Paisley, *Facts and Figures on Government Finance,* 28th ed. (Washington, DC: Tax Foundation, 1993), pp. 17 and 19.

5. Adam Smith, *An Inquiry into the Nature and Causes of the Wealth of Nations* (1776; reprint, New York: Modern Library, 1937), p. 777.

6. The dollar figures in this section are from *Statistical Abstract of the United States 1991* (Washington, DC: U.S. Department of Commerce, 1991), p. 280. I have also relied on Carolyn Webber and Aaron Wildavsky, *A History of Taxation and Expenditure in the Western World* (New York: Simon and Schuster, 1986) and B. Guy Peters, *The Politics of Taxation* (Cambridge, MA: Basil Blackwell, 1991).

7. Peter G. Peterson, *Facing Up* (New York: Simon and Schuster, 1993), p. 162.

8. Wallace C. Peterson, *Transfer Spending, Taxes, and the American Welfare State* (Boston: Kluwer Academic, 1991), pp. 277–79.

9. Margaret S. Gordon, *Social Security Policy in Industrial Countries* (Cambridge: Cambridge University Press, 1988), p. 30.

10. Peterson, *Transfer Spending,* p. 128.

11. Edwards, et al., *Facts and Figures,* p. 29. Figures were adjusted with the implicit GNP price deflator presented in *The Economic Report of the President 1992* (Washington, DC: U.S. Government Printing Office, 1992).

12. Edwards, et al., *Facts and Figures,* p. 193.

13. Dekkers L. Davidson, *Massachusetts High Technology Council* (Boston: Harvard Business School, 1982).

14. Edwards, et al., *Facts and Figures,* p. 21.

15. *Budget of the United States, Fiscal Year 1993* (Washington, DC: U.S. Government Printing Office, 1992), part 3, p. 54.

16. Peterson, *Transfer Spending,* p. 20.

17. Ibid., p. 25.

18. Howard Oxley, Maria Maher, John P. Martin, and Giuseppe Nicoletti, *The Public Sector: Issues for the 1990s,* Working Paper No. 90 (Paris: Organization for Economic Cooperation and Development, Department of Economics and Statistics, 1990).

19. "Aidez-moi," *Forbes,* April 15, 1991, p. 43; and "Survey: Business in Europe," *The Economist,* June 8, 1991, pp. 15–17.

20. Christopher Georges, "House Republicans Draft Plans to Cut Billions in Subsidies for Large Firms," *The Wall Street Journal,* March 30, 1995, p. A2.

21. Edwards, et al., *Facts and Figures,* p. 276.

22. Ibid., p. 87.

23. *Special Analyses, Budget of the United States Government, Fiscal Year 1990* (Washington, DC: U.S. Government Printing Office, 1989), Special Analysis F.

24. David P. Calleo, *The Bankruptcy of America* (New York: William Morrow, 1992), p. 46.

25. Peterson, *Facing Up,* p. 112.

26. Paul R. McDaniel, "Tax Expenditures as Tools of Government Action," in *Beyond Privatization,* ed. Lester M. Salamon (Washington, DC: Urban Institute Press, 1989), p. 168.

27. Ross Perot, *United We Stand* (New York: Hyperion, 1992).

28. Murray Weidenbaum, *Business, Government and the Public,* 4th ed. (Englewood Cliffs, NJ: Prentice Hall, 1990), p. 277.

29. Peterson, *Transfer Spending,* p. 66.

30. Roger Wilson, *State Business Incentives and Economic Growth: Are They Effective?* (Lexington, KY: Council of State Governments, 1989), pp. 4–5. On innovative ways states are encouraging economic development, see David Osborne, *Laboratories of Democracy* (Boston: Harvard Business School Press, 1988).

31. E. S. Browning and Helene Cooper, "Ante Up," *The Wall Street Journal,* November 24, 1993, p. A1.

32. Jerry Ackerman, "What Price Good Jobs?" *Boston Sunday Globe,* April 2, 1995, pp. 75–76.

33. Calvin A. Kent, "Privatization of Public Functions: Promise and Problems," in *Entrepreneurship and the Privatizing of Government,* ed. Calvin A. Kent (New York: Quorum Books, 1987), p. 10.

34. Donald F. Kettl, *Sharing Power: Public Governance and Private Markets* (Washington, DC: Brookings Institution, 1993).

35. John D. Donahue, *The Privatization Decision* (New York: Basic Books, 1989), p. 135.

36. E. S. Savas, *Privatization, the Key to Better Government* (Chatham, NJ: Chatham House, 1987), pp. 70–71.

37. Office of Management and Budget, *Interagency Task Force Report on the Federal Contract Audit Process* and *Summary Report of the Swat Team on Civilian Agency Contracting* (Washington, DC: Executive Office of the President, 1992).

38. Timothy Ba nekov, Robin Boyle, and Daniel Rich, *Privatism and Urban Policy in Britain and the United States* (Oxford: Oxford University Press, 1989), p. 164.

IV   MAKING PUBLIC POLICY

8 BUSINESS, INTEREST GROUPS, AND POLITICAL INFLUENCE

[T]he most common and durable source of factions has been the various and unequal distribution of property. Those who hold, and those who are without property, have ever formed distinct interests in society. . . The regulation of these various and interfering interests forms the principal task of modern legislation . . .

James Madison[1]

Business competes in a political marketplace, just as it competes in the more familiar economic marketplace. Since the modern state's birth, companies—collectively and individually—have sought public policies that enhance their material gains while diminishing their losses. As government has grown in scale and scope in recent decades, business everywhere has redoubled its effort to sway policy its way. According to a recent Conference Board report, one-third of 185 CEOs the Board questioned spent 25–50 percent of their time trying to influence legislation and to comply with regulation.[2] At the same time, other groups have organized for policies that cost business, leading to conflict in the political marketplace.

The ways business goes about competing in politics—its strategies and tactics—are the subjects of this chapter. There are several contrasts with ordinary economic competition. The political marketplace gives companies more chances to form alliances with other, like-minded companies to seek shared advantage. Compared to many business activities, political action thus can be more cooperative.

Yet, the political marketplace simultaneously creates strife. While private economic exchanges are apt to be mutually beneficial, and thus done freely, public economic transactions often involve the unwanted transfer of resources from one party to another. There are winners and losers, and, depending on the stakes, the losers may choose to fight back. The result is that political competition sometimes makes companies clash with other sectors of the business community, not to mention with labor groups, consumer organizations, and other organized stakeholders.

To understand business and political competition, we start by discussing the idea of the public interest. Next, we look at the status of business in modern democracies and how companies organize themselves into interest groups that contest in the political arena for favorable public policies. Then we turn to techniques used by interest groups to raise money and exercise influence, followed by a brief review of proposals for making political competition more fair and open.

The Public Interest

Politics is about making social or collective choice; it is the way society chooses public policy, including public policy toward business. Yet, society is an abstraction; it does not think and act in unison. In democratic states, the foundation for public decisions is supposed to be the individual citizen. Democracy's main tenet is that citizens—and their voluntary associations—should select their leaders and hold them to account for public policies.

The stated goal of policy making is invariably to serve the **public interest,** that is, to advance the general welfare of the population. People defend or oppose policies in the name of their impact on the public interest, and it seems obvious that public policy should further the good of the whole. The trouble is that the public interest is a theoretical construct, to which different individuals and groups lay claim to legitimize their policy preferences. People disagree, often strongly, on what government should and should not do, but they rarely see themselves working against the public interest. Far more likely is for people to convince themselves that *their* policy choices are the best for everyone. There is no obvious way to separate the claims and counterclaims, to find a transcendent public interest that exists apart from the declared preferences of the people who make up society.

Business is not exempt. Adam Smith argued long ago:

> The proposal of any new law or regulation of commerce which comes from this order [dealers in trade or manufactures] ought always to be listened to with great precaution . . . It comes from an order of men whose interest is never exactly the same as the public, who have a general interest to deceive and even oppress the public, and who accordingly have, upon many occasions, both deceived and oppressed it.[3]

The implication of Smith's observation is that firms will make expenditures to seek government failure so they can capture the benefits.

Since no policy ever receives unanimous support in a nation, some method has to be found to choose among the options. Most businesspeople, as well as people in general, would agree that majority rule is the right way to settle policy disputes. Through debate and compromise, interested parties reconcile their disagreements to arrive at a course of action acceptable to most. The public interest is what a majority wants. Yet, as MIT's Kenneth Arrow proved, individual preferences need not yield consistent social choices. His "impossibility theorem" shows that the wishes of the majority can be cyclical, given certain reasonable assumptions about individual people's desires.[4] The public interest cannot be found by adding up private interests to find the most widely acceptable alternative.

Arrow's theorem has bleak implications. If there is no clear majority interest, let alone public interest, the rules for choosing among policies get foggy. Policy making can become a question of might more than right, of who gets to control the policy agenda and the alternatives considered.

Business and Democracy

Business is one participant in policy making, and corporate leaders help frame the issues that come up for public debate. Their ample resources and pivotal place in the economy give corporations leverage over public policy. Even in a liberal democracy such as the United States, where citizens have wide latitude to press demands, business is apt to have lopsided advantages to be heard and to get its way.

Businesspeople seldom see things this way and feel they are fighting an uphill battle. According to a recent study:

> Executives believe that corporations are constantly under attack, primarily because government simply doesn't understand that business is crucial to everything society does but can easily be crippled by well-intentioned but unrealistic government policies. A widespread view among the [business] people . . . interviewed is that "far and away the vast majority of things that we do are literally to protect ourselves from public policy that is poorly crafted and nonresponsive to the needs and realities and circumstances of our company."[5]

Because of this perceived assault from government, companies have redoubled their political activities in recent decades. Advocates of democracy have long feared that business has corrosive effects on the body politic. Thomas Jefferson (1743–1826) was among the earliest in a long line of observers to worry about the imbalance of economic power, and thus political power, that grows out of industrialization. Jefferson was optimistic about the new United States, but only because it was a farm society of small property owners. Should wealth and economic might become concentrated as they did under the British factory system, he worried, democracy would be put at risk.[6]

Jefferson's agrarian society disappeared by the mid-1800s. Business grew to vast size in America, alarming large segments of the electorate in the process. At the turn of the 20th century, populists and progressives mounted political challenges to the large corporations, creating a raft of public policies intended to restrict their freedom of action. Later, in the New Deal and again during the 1960s and 1970s, these challenges to corporations were renewed. Repeatedly, corporations have fought back, and, by the 1980s, corporate political influence was on the upswing again.[7]

Group-Based Politics

It is obvious that the United States today is not the type of democracy Jefferson foresaw. Political practices have followed a different track than the old town meeting and its direct citizen participation in policy making. As Joseph Schumpeter points out, modern democracies are no longer systems in which the public initiates policy and elects representatives to implement it.[8] Often, the modern electorate is uninformed about issues and apathetic about getting involved in political action. Few people even take the time to vote, and many are alienated from politics.[9]

This fact does not mean that public opinion counts for nothing. On occasions, an angered electorate has made its will felt, especially if the press has taken up an issue. In America, "throw the bums out" always has a popular appeal, even though Americans regularly do reelect incumbent officeholders. Still, popular involvement in public decisions is intermittent and often ineffective.

Who, then, if not the people, runs the country? The mainstream view is that the United States is today a group-based democracy. No one elite group (take your pick from Wall Street financiers, Big Business owners, or East Coast intellectuals, to name a few possibilities) always rules; rather, there are many **interest groups** whose degree of influence varies according to the particular policy area involved.

Interest Group Competition

Interest groups are formed to further the political and economic goals of the group's supporters, which they do mainly by communicating with the authorities responsible for public policy. The leaders of an interest group act as agents for the members and try to move decision makers on the group's behalf. Interest groups, often vilified as special interest or pressure groups, have a bad reputation. But the "right of the people peaceably to assemble, and to petition the Government for a redress of grievances," as the First Amendment to the U.S. Constitution quaintly defines interest group activism, is assured under American law. The founders felt it was essential for people to be free to organize and to say what they want their government to do. Thus interest group rivalry is at least as old as the American republic.

The first person to identify and discuss in detail the advantages of group representation as the basis for democracy was James Madison (1751–1836). According to Madison, the Constitution should encourage many interest groups (he called them factions) so that no one group could oppress the others. The idea was to promote competition among interest groups to produce a balance, with all interests canceling each other. Madison's argument is the political counterpart to Adam Smith's justification for unfettered markets. Madison contended that group competition would create a similar invisible hand that would lead people unconsciously to seek the public good while pursuing their individual interests.[10]

Following Madison, group rivalry is often seen as the practical successor to Jefferson's agrarian democracy. According to this line of reasoning, in today's complex societies, it is not possible, and perhaps not even desirable given the level of expertise needed, for citizens to take part continuously in governance. Interest groups replace individual citizens in making public policy, and democracy turns into the struggle among organized groups for favors from government. As these groups bargain with each other, winning on some issues and losing on others, an equilibrium is reached that approaches the public interest. The results, while not perfect, are about as good as one can expect in a large, industrial state.

Most political economists today do not make the same positive assessment of interest group activity that Madison did. Instead, they see the conflict among interest groups threatening the ability of the state to respond to problems with policies that help society in general. Nearly all interest groups are focused squarely on getting benefits for group members, and they encourage government to take a narrow view of its job. The result is muddled and deadlocked public policy, not a desirable equilibrium.[11]

Is Business on Top?

Critics of group-based democracy also point out that the political contest is not fair. The effectiveness of interests is determined neither by the size of the memberships nor by the merit of their goals. Some interests are, in George Orwell's phrase, more equal than others, with the well-organized (and business groups are among the best organized) having disproportionate influence. A good example of a powerful set of business interests is the military-industrial complex that President Dwight Eisenhower warned about in his farewell address. Defense contractors, he argued, had twisted American public policy so it favored the acquisition of more advanced weapons than were safe to have or really needed to protect the country.

Political economists suggest several reasons why companies often have the edge in a competitive political system. The obvious reason is that companies have money. With deeper pockets than other groups, they can sustain long-term political fights. Competing groups do not have as much money and are less capable of mounting effective political campaigns.

Motivation may be as important as the amount of resources. Companies are usually fewer than potential adversaries, such as consumers or workers. There is a transaction cost for organizing large groups, which gives companies the head start in getting together for political purposes. A handful of producer organizations has a much easier time identifying common interests than do more numerous countervailing interests.[12]

Also, producers, as opposed to consumers, are apt to feel the greater impetus to get involved in interest group politics. Consider the example of voluntary export restraints on steel with the European Community (now the European Union), Japan, South Korea, and other countries. Started in 1982, the restraints were intended to protect the U.S. steel industry until it could compete internationally. By the mid-1980s, these were costing the consumer $7 billion a year, or roughly $37,500 for each person engaged in the industry. Steel owners and workers had a strong motive to get and keep these measures. The same public policy was irrelevant to the average person; $7 billion divided by the U.S. national population is only $30 per head.[13] Similarly, policies to raise milk prices or to put passive restraints in automobiles mean much more to dairy farmers and carmakers than to milk-drinkers and drivers.

In each case, an obscure (from the average person's point of view) change of public policy can wreak major changes on the industry in question. The group with the more concentrated interest, usually the producer, has more incentive to join the political fray. The outcome is not a balance of all society's special interests, but a systematic bias toward business.

A more extreme view is that big companies hold hegemony over the U.S. political process.[14] Hegemony refers to a cultural world view and set of institutions that structure how people think and coerce a particular way of life. In capitalist societies, business allegedly is different from other interest groups because of its pervasive influence on society. The business point view is accepted without question on fundamental matters, which no one thinks to challenge.

This last characterization can be misleading, if taken absolutely. To the extent it exists, business hegemony is far from absolute. Industrial interests are not all-powerful, winning on every issue. The expiration of steel export restraints in 1992 refutes that unsophisticated argument. As in most things, sensible claims are not matters of one or the other, but of more or less. Firms are apt to have disproportionate influence on policy making, though they can lose on specific issues.

One reason firms do lose political battles is the interests of all firms are not uniform. Different industries can have different concerns that propel them to take opposite stands on policies. Consider the struggles in the United States over R&D tax credits. Major companies prefer the tax credits, but high-tech start-ups do not like them because new companies usually have no taxable profits. They prefer a capital gains tax cut to make it easier to raise funds. The two sides have ended frustrating each other.[15]

As a rule, companies are most likely to get their way on narrow questions that attract little public attention, say a tax expenditure that helps a particular industry. They also are likely to prevail on broad policy issues affecting the entire economic system, such as a change in income tax rates, where they can enlist widespread support for their stand. That leaves a broad range of contested issues. In this middle ground, where many safety and environmental regulations lie, nonbusiness interest groups carry the day.

While American business power is not absolute, it is stronger than in many other countries.[16] Business here has an unusual degree of influence on politics, probably because Big Business predates the rise of Big Government. Europe and Japan had powerful states before modern capitalism emerged. These states remain somewhat less open to interest group pressure and somewhat more capable of making independent decisions.[17]

Corporatist Alternatives

Interest groups are found in every society. What sets off American interest groups are their independence and self-reliance. Though Washington and the state capitals are often forced to heed interest groups, government neither sponsors these bodies nor officially recognizes them. American interest groups do get indirect support through tax expenditures and legal recognition, but they are still mainly private organizations. One consequence is a cacophony of voices trying to be heard in the legislatures and executive offices.

So-called corporatist states are less neutral about organized interests. As we alluded in Chapter 6, those societies include interests groups such as business and labor in decision making through formal arrangements for consultation and negotiation. This setup, which has medieval origins, is sometimes called **functional representation.** It is based on the idea that the community is divided into various strata, each performing a unique function, and that these strata should be represented in the polity. Some evidence suggests that corporatist modes of representing interests are more efficient and fair. Corporatist arrangements are alleged to help governments adjust to changes in the world economy, and they offer the possibility of turning economic policy making into a non–zero-sum game, so everyone is better off.[18] Lately, though, the model seems to be losing its relevance (see Box 8–1).

The United States experimented with corporatism and functional representation in the 1930s, but their constitutionality was challenged and they were dropped. Britain also tried to involve labor and capital in formal decision making until the Thatcher government stopped the practice in 1979.

Types of Interest Groups

Interest groups can form around any issue, from abortion to euthanasia, from peace to war, but the interest groups that occupy us in this book are ones devoted mainly to economic matters. There are three main clusters of economic interest groups: those associated with business, those with labor, and those with the social or public interest. All are pledged to getting government to take the right steps, *as they define them,* on behalf of their members.

These groups also do things that are not aimed chiefly at influencing public policy. They help members by performing many other tasks that members find uneconomical to do themselves, such as providing research and educational services. But lobbying is our principal concern in this chapter. Let us look at the three clusters of interest groups, one at a time.

Box 8–1

Corporatist Policy Making

Countries generally considered corporatist include Germany, Sweden, Norway, Austria, Holland, and Denmark. All these countries use a system of representation in which monopolistic organizations express the major interests in society, business and labor in particular. These monopolistic organizations, recognized and encouraged by the state, may bargain over public policy. The idea is to generate consensus, so the government does not take steps unacceptable to the important interests. For their part, the interest groups accept responsibility to help the government carry out its policies. Compared to interest group activity in the pluralist United States, the relationship with government is more formal and structured, carried out through well-established institutions.

In Germany, for example, meetings between government and the "social partners" were held from the 1960s to the 1980s to achieve agreements on economic policy. Before any federal ministry submits a bill for consideration, it must by law consult with the chambers or interest group peak associations. Thus, interest group pressure is funneled through an institutionalized process of consultation. Arguably this process helped Germany cope with the oil shocks of the period better than a country such as the United States, which lacks consultive procedures.[1] The corporatist countries have done well in other respects, maintaining very high standards of living. Germany, however, has been stepping away from the corporatist model. Corporatism is being challenged in other countries, too.

Why the dissatisfaction with functional representation and consensual bargaining? One problem is doubt about the fiscal viability of corporatism, as it often fuels the growth of an abundant welfare state to buy off the workers. Also, there is a breakdown in the consensus in these societies, a fragmentation of interests as in the United States. Finally, international competition is making it more difficult for interests to reach compromise on tough issues. Some German (or Dutch or Swedish) companies have done well, others poorly in recent years, and one policy no longer suits all.

[1]Graham K. Wilson, *Business and Politics: A Comparative Introduction,* 2nd ed. (Chatham, NJ: Chatham House, 1990), p. 98.

Business Self-Representation

Today, many companies see political activism as a major part of their strategy for dealing with their environment. Large firms can represent themselves. Citicorp, for example, employs eight registered lobbyists in its Washington office. They spend most of their time blocking and blunting policies that could hurt Citicorp's credit card business, student loan business, and other activities.[19] Citicorp is far from alone. A total of 1,300 firms maintained offices in Washington in 1986, as opposed to 100 in 1968.[20]

Three-quarters of large companies employ outside private lobbyists, too, according to a Conference Board survey. More than half the 300 companies queried had increased their internal government relations staff or use of outside lobbyists during the 1980s.[21] Citicorp is typical. In addition to its own people, it retains six law firms to represent its interests on Capitol Hill.

Business Interest Groups

Smaller companies may lack the resources to participate in politics by themselves. They may choose instead to work with alliances of similar companies to push their interests. Large companies also see advantages in working with competitors toward whatever goals they happen to share.

To fill this widespread need for common representation, thousands of business groups have emerged in the United States. Some are umbrella organizations, known as general purpose business groups or **peak associations,** that claim to speak for large categories of companies. Others are **trade associations** representing specific lines of trade. There are 46 different associations for the U.S. iron and steel industry, for example, including associations of producers, importers, and users.

Table 8–1 shows the scale and growth of these groups. In 1980, there were already some 3,100 national trade, business, or commercial associations; 12 years later, there were more than 3,800. Membership is voluntary, but companies like to join to get services and influence public policy. The associations have multiplied largely in response to perceived challenges to trade and industry from other interest groups.

Peak Associations.   Important peak business associations are listed in Table 8–2. The oldest is the National Association of Manufacturers (NAM), founded in 1895 largely to counter antibusiness policies being pushed by Progressive Era reformers. Later, the NAM became a platform for attacks on the New Deal and the labor movement. It currently has a membership of 12,500 companies, who together account for about three-fourths the nation's manufacturing production and employment.

The NAM was a low-key operation in the 1950s and 1960s, when business interests were comparatively secure. In 1974, it moved its headquarters to Washington, DC, to increase its political influence, and a year later it registered with Congress as an organization whose main activity is lobbying.[22] Today the NAM

TABLE 8–1   **Business and Professional Associations Have Been Proliferating in the United States.**

	Number of National Nonprofit Associations		
	1968	*1980*	*1992*
Trade, business, commercial	2,832	3,118	3,851
Agriculture	508	677	1,082
Scientific, engineering, technology	548	1,039	1,365
Health, medical	791	1,413	2,290

Source: U.S. Bureau of the Census, *Statistical Abstract of the United States* (Washington, DC: U.S. Government Printing Office, various years).

TABLE 8–2   There Are Several Peak Associations that Claim to Speak for Broad Segments of the American Business Sector.

	Year Founded	*Member Firms*	*Staff Size*	*Budget ($ millions)*
Business Council	1933	276	3	n.a.
Business Roundtable	1972	1,100	16	n.a.
Chamber of Commerce	1912	180,000	200	65
National Association of Manufacturers	1895	12,500	200	14
National Federation of Independent Business	1943	560,000	225	52

Source: *Encyclopedia of Associations 1993,* 27th ed. (Detroit: Gale Research, 1992).

maintains an active presence in the nation's capital, with a staff of 200 and a budget of $14 million.

Also dating from the Progressive Era is the Chamber of Commerce (established in 1912). It represents a federation of 2,800 local and state chapters, plus thousands of individual companies and industries, and is now the largest business interest group in Washington. Between 1974 and 1980 its membership more than doubled, and it currently has 1,100 staff members and a budget of $65 million. Traditionally, the Chamber of Commerce has stressed opposition to Big Government and the welfare state.[23]

The Business Council started during the New Deal period. Interestingly, the Business Council was originally attached to the Department of Commerce as President Roosevelt dabbled with corporatism during the Great Depression. The Business Council declared its independence in 1962, partly due to suspicion about its quasi-governmental status. The membership is limited to current and former CEOs of large corporations, who maintain liaison committees that connect with various government departments.

The newest peak association for employers is the Business Roundtable. Established in 1972 following the most recent surge of regulatory activity, the Business Roundtable is composed of the CEOs of 200 major corporations. Membership is by invitation, and the chief executives agree to join directly in the group's meetings. Because it represents Big Business primarily, the Business Roundtable has sometimes had a less antagonistic view of labor unions and government regulation than either the NAM or the Chamber of Commerce.

Representing just smaller businesses is the National Federation of Independent Business, established in 1943. It has nearly half a million members, two-thirds of whom employ fewer than 10 people. This organization mushroomed (it had but 500 members in 1975) in reaction to small companies' view that new regulation was causing them particular hardship. The National Federation of Independent Business works with Congress, the 50 state legislatures, and administrative agencies to make sure the needs of small employers are considered in new laws and regulations. A rival voice for small business is the National Small Business Association (founded in 1937), which claims 50,000 member companies.

These peak associations have many resources they can use to influence government activity. All are handicapped, however, by their assorted membership. When companies big and small, manufacturers and service providers, importers and exporters, get together, they find it hard to agree on positions and present a united front. Small business members of the Chamber of Commerce revolted, for example, over the Washington headquarters' temporary decision to support employer-mandated health insurance premiums. The group fired its top lobbyist over the issue in 1994.[24]

The Business Roundtable is generally viewed as the most potent of the major national general purpose employers associations, which may be due to the similarity and smaller number of the members. Even this organization is seen as having become less effective in the 1980s than it had been earlier.

Trade Associations.   Specialized trade associations, which coalesce around the needs of specific groups of companies, usually have more influence compared to the more diffuse peak associations. The number of industry-specific groups in the United States is huge and growing. A sample is shown in Table 8–3.

Prominent groups such as National Automobile Dealers Association or the American Bankers Association can have thousands of members. Other industry groups, such as the American Petroleum Institute, the Iron and Steel Institute, or the Motor Vehicle Manufacturers Association, represent large sectors of the economy. Their budgets and staffs may rival those of the general business groups. Most trade associations, however, are small. They represent specialized lines of work and have a narrow range—for example, the Peanut Butter and Nut Processors Association, the Bow Tie Makers Association, and the Frozen Potato Products Institute. There even is a trade association for people who work for trade associations—the American Society of Association Executives.

TABLE 8–3   **There Is a Bewildering Array of Specialized U.S. Trade Associations, as this Sample Shows.**

	Year Founded	Member Firms	Staff Size	Budget ($ millions)
Air Transport Association of America	1936	22	125	8
American Bankers Association	1875	10,000	400	62
American Trucking Association	1933	4,100	291	35
Association of Battery Recyclers	1976	45	1	n.a.
Bow Tie Makers Association	1952	10	1	n.a.
Chemical Manufacturers Association	1872	185	246	36
Frozen Potato Products Institute	1958	12	n.a.	n.a.
Motor Vehicle Manufacturers Association	1913	7	109	14
National Association of Broadcasters	1922	7,500	165	17
National Automobile Dealers Association	1917	19,600	405	10
Peanut Butter and Nut Processors Association	1969	180	3	n.a.
Pharmaceutical Manufacturers Association	1958	93	90	10

Source: *Encyclopedia of Associations 1993,* 27th ed. (Detroit: Gale Research, 1992).

Because of their focus, trade associations may find it easier to define their members' interest compared to the general purpose groups; because they are less well-known, they also may avoid the pitfalls of excess publicity that larger umbrella groups can attract. They are apt to be particularly forceful on the small issues about which their members care greatly but that do not touch the wider public.

It is safe to say that no significant commercial interest goes unrepresented today. Political economists see in these trends clear evidence of increased rent seeking by business. As David Vogel of the Haas School of Business (Berkeley) points out, corporations, in effect, now treat their Washington offices as another profit center.

> Companies originally came to Washington in the early 1970s primarily to defend themselves. But, once having invested so much in learning how the political process works, many decided to use their political skills to help them gain advantages over their competitors, domestic as well as foreign. As a result, the political agenda became increasingly dominated by the requests of particular firms and industries for changes in public policies that would enhance their competitive positions.[25]

With the expansion of state government, businesses also have greatly increased their political activity at the state level. The percentage of associations monitoring state issues grew from 35 percent in 1982 to 70 percent in 1987. There were 42,000 registered lobbyists in state capitals in 1990.[26] Whether corporations are heard and receive responses is another question, which we will look at shortly.

Business Organizations Overseas. Employers' political associations are prevalent in other countries. In Germany, over 70 percent of all but the smallest employers belong to trade associations, which in turn are affiliated with the German Federation of Industry. In France, the Comité National du Patronat Français is the umbrella organization for large employers. Japan has the *Keidanren*, the Federation of Economic Organizations, which groups together more than 1,000 of Japan's largest companies. As in the United States, there is movement back and forth between these private organizations and the government—what the Japanese call *amakudari* or "descent from heaven," where retired officials in the Ministry of Finance or the Ministry of International Trade and Industry take over top jobs in politics or business.

The major difference is that in democracies with corporatist overtones, the relation between business political organizations and the state is usually more centralized and more formal than in the United States. In Germany, one organization, the National Association of German Employers, handles labor negotiations. The boundary between the public and private sectors is correspondingly less clear in such countries.[27]

Japan is the best example. Japanese peak associations are stronger than in the United States, and some government assistance is provided in Japan, which is not true in the United States.[28] Companies in a particular sector must belong to the respective Japanese trade association, which is endowed with extralegal powers that curtail independent corporate decisions. These groups are linked to the government bureaucracy and often act on the behalf of the government.[29] Thus Japan's "voluntary" agreement not to sell as many cars as it can in the United States is carried out by the trade association representing Japanese automakers (see Chapter 17).

The corporatist setup often is preferred by government as a matter of convenience. It is an advantage to have a single body to consult for broad sectors of the economy. Also, public officials like differences of opinion within an industry to be worked out by a business association before a question is brought to their attention. The resulting cooperation and coordination are thought by many to play a key role in Japan and Germany's economic success since World War II.

Labor Unions

Workers have long sought representation in public policy making, usually as a counterweight to business. Their vehicle has been labor unions. Unions join the political fray to get government to make business act more favorably to employees. In describing American democracy in the 1950s, John Kenneth Galbraith called this mechanism the principle of countervailing power. According to the analysis in his book, *American Capitalism,* business and workers tended to balance off one another.[30]

Labor union power in the United States probably was near its peak when Galbraith wrote *American Capitalism.* Unions then claimed about one-quarter of the work force, compared to less than one-fifth today. Their shrinking ranks have reduced their influence, as have their links to the Democrats, who held the presidency for only four years between 1969 and 1993. These and other factors have weakened organized labor's ability to further its cause in recent times. Symptomatic of organized labor's lack of clout was the passage of the North American Free Trade Agreement (NAFTA) in 1993. Despite an all-out lobbying effort on the Democratic Congress and the president, the trade unions could not block NAFTA.

Still, 235 unions remain in the United States today, with more than 16 million members. Important individual unions such as the Teamsters, the United Mine Workers, and the United Auto Workers stay active in American politics. They work on issues directly relevant to their members and can still affect public policy despite their dwindling numbers.

Many American unions belong to the AFL-CIO. A peak association parallel to the general-purpose business groups, it was formed in 1955 from the merger of two competing labor bodies, the American Federation of Labor and the Congress of Industrial Organizations. Today, the AFL-CIO has over 100 affiliated unions, representing everyone from teachers and plumbers to garment workers and meat cutters. The organization supports some 300 lobbyists who work for the member unions to influence national policy on matters such as social welfare, job training, minimum wages, child labor, and occupational safety.

Public Interest Groups

The rise of **public interest groups** is a significant event in recent U.S. politics, though their influence has generally waned since about 1980. Public interest groups are organizations that seek public goods, whose provision will purportedly help society as a whole. They profess to act on behalf of people other than the group's members. This trait sets public interest groups apart from special interests, such as business or labor, which admittedly speak for their members first and the public second.

Relying heavily on voluntary contributions of time and effort, public interest groups push for government policies to provide such collective benefits as less influence of money on elections, safer products and workplaces, and cleaner air and water. Their stance often makes them clash with business groups. Support for public interest groups comes mainly from professionals and intellectuals with organizational skills and educational resources, and they have had more impact than their modest finances would suggest.

Public interest groups claim to be motivated mainly by altruism, not self-interest. The claim is partly true, in the sense that members do not always have a direct material stake in the policies being pursued. But political economists point out that there is usually an element of self-interest even in seemingly selfless pressure group activity. Support for environmental groups, for instance, often comes from middle-class people who use the outdoors for recreation or whose property values will be enhanced by slowed economic development. The point is not to denounce public interest groups, only to note that enlightened self-interest and public spiritedness are not incompatible.

Common Cause is the most prominent general-purpose public interest group. Founded in 1970 to make office seekers be more honest and to hold them more accountable for decisions, Common Cause has focused on matters such as campaign financing, lobbying disclosure laws, and open hearings requirements in Congress. Its membership peaked during the Watergate crisis of 1973–74.

The best-known consumer groups are those organized by Ralph Nader, such as the Center for the Study of Responsive Law, the Auto Safety Center, the Public Citizen's Health Research Group, and the Public Interest Research Group. As we will see in Chapter 13, Nader made a significant impact on policy, particularly in the 1960s and early 1970s. Although he is known mainly as a consumer activist, Nader aims less at protecting consumers than at checking what he sees as overweening Big Business power. More than any other public interest group's efforts, his groups have scared companies into coming to Washington to protect themselves.

The environmental movement has spawned many public interest groups, too. The Environmental Defense Fund, for instance, urges concerned citizens to press for testing local fish for dioxin levels and to act as watchdogs for proposed solid-waste incinerators. The Sierra Club promotes citizen action to stop paper companies from clear-cutting timber in old-growth forests.[31]

The civil rights and women's movements have given rise to another class of publicly spirited interest groups, though, due to their ties to identifiable categories of people, they often get distinguished from the good government, consumer, and environmental organizations. The important point is that groups such as Jesse Jackson's Operation PUSH or the National Organization of Women have among their aims getting business to act more favorably toward their real or potential members, who in total make up most of the population.

Industry often sets up phony public interest groups as front organizations to combat true public interest groups. Typically, these industry-backed bodies take misleading names to create the impression of a grassroots movement. The biggest spending lobby in Washington in 1986, for example, was the Citizens for the Control of Acid Rain. The citizens in question were organized by coal and electric utility companies fearful of stricter controls on polluting emissions. Another example is the Coalition for Vehicle Choice, founded by Ford Motor Company and General Motors Corporation in 1990 to fight proposals for higher fuel standards.[32] Groups that pretend to represent the public are not illegal. No federal law requires any advertising or mail solicitations to identify their major sponsors.

It is worth mentioning so-called single-issue groups, too. There are many, such as the National Rifle Association (dedicated to stopping gun control) or Operation Rescue (devoted to ending abortion), whose activities have some economic impact. Usually, the impact is inadvertent or secondary to the group's main aims. Maintaining free commerce in firearms, for instance, obviously helps arms manufacturers and retailers, and the industry does provide important financial support to the National Rifle Association. Still, protecting the profits of companies such as Colt or Sturm, Ruger is not the association's reason for being. Similarly, Operation Rescue's goals are at odds with the financial well-being of the health care industry. Taking a source of income from doctors may be a subordinate outcome, but it is not why the anti-abortion group was formed.

Altruism and Public Policy

It is cynical and inaccurate to see egoism behind everything done by public interest groups, just as it is unduly distrustful to debunk every corporate profession of social responsibility. Self-interest, narrowly understood, is not the only motivator of human political and economic activity. The model of rational choice, employed in this book to account for most political behavior, should not be interpreted so narrowly as to deny the possibility of altruism, of genuine regard for other people's well-being.

What motivates men and women to support public interest groups or to look beyond profits? Part of their goal is to enhance personal power, income, and so on, but they obviously are not in every act shooting for the greatest net benefit to themselves. Human behavior is actuated by mixed motives. People find satisfaction in social networks that generate solidarity and mutual responsibility, not just in individual aggrandizement. They fulfill themselves through duty and obligation, as well as through power and prestige.

Steven Kelman of the U.S. Office of Management and Budget (formerly at Harvard) argues that there is in fact a high level of public spirit in much public policy making. By public spiritedness he means that some participants in the policy process—the interest groups and the politicians and bureaucrats—do make good faith efforts to obtain good policies. They do not simply pursue what is best for themselves. Public spiritedness thus may temper the painful side effects of interest group competition.[33]

There are at least two themes that run through the public spirit.[34] One is the idea of trusteeship, of separating business decisions from the personal realm. Like all business functions, government relations are a public trust and should not be exploited for particular advantage. A second theme is that of service to society. Public policies should be shaped to respond to societal needs as fairly as possible. Together, these themes form a professional ethos that moderates (not eliminates) the self-seeking of managers in all sectors.

Tactics for Interest Groups

As the previous discussion hints, the distinction between public and special interest groups is partly in the eye of the beholder. It has been said that a special interest group is one to which you don't belong, and there is truth in the statement. The reverse also can be true: public and special interests overlap. In capitalist societies, the representatives of business can make a strong claim that whatever helps business helps everyone by providing jobs, tax revenue, new products, and so forth. Few people disagreed with the famous statement made in 1953 by Charles "Engine Charlie" Wilson, president of General Motors, at his Secretary of Defense nomination hearings. Asked about possible conflicts between the national interest and that of his company, he replied no such conflict was possible: "[F]or years I thought what was good for our country was good for General Motors, and vice versa."[35]

Unwise would be a spokesperson for business who did not link the fortunes of his or her company or industry with the public good. Naked self-interest is not nearly as effective in attracting support. Assertions about the public good serve to build political alliances—the wider their benefit, the easier public policy proposals are to sell to other groups whose agreement is needed to make the proposal law. Many Americans in the 1960s and early 1970s became skeptical about arguments like Engine Charlie's, but they are more trusting of such reasoning today. One reason is that business interest groups have persuaded voters that the nation's long-term economic health (perhaps the most unifying public cause) hangs on giving companies a freer hand (the archetype self-serving interest).[36]

How did U.S. business interests go about making the case that they are the linchpin of the economy? Though the argument for pro-business policies seems self-evident to most management students, pro-business policies do not simply happen by themselves; they require lots of spadework by business interest groups. An enormous investment of political resources must be made to get government to do what business wants. In the next section, we review specific tactics that companies use to guard against damaging government decisions.

Public Issues Management

As they began to see themselves under siege in the 1960s, many firms expanded and strengthened their public affairs departments. An outgrowth of older public relations units, these public affairs departments seek to create favorable public perceptions of the firm and to promote its public policy goals. According to a 1987 Conference Board survey of 300 large American companies, half the companies surveyed had 10 or more full-time staff working in public affairs.[37] Only three companies assigned no full-time personnel to this area. Despite cutbacks in many corporate staff functions during the early 1990s, most public affairs units have grown or stayed even.[38]

Public affairs units have three main jobs: (1) communication, or efforts to articulate the company's interest to stakeholders inside and outside; (2) philanthropy, or efforts to influence the social, cultural, and economic conditions in company communities; and (3) government relations, or alerting the company to threatening political trends and devising ways to head them off. Let us look at each of these jobs (in which some other company units share) more carefully.

Communication.   Companies naturally want to put their best face forward, and they are sure to tell the media good news about their activities, or to try to put a spin on bad news. Rather than rely just on press releases and the like, many companies engage in image advertising as a defensive move. The purpose is to create a positive impression by presenting a company as caring about the environment, health, and similar issues. An illustration is Monsanto Corporation's Chemical Facts of Life campaign ("Without chemicals, life itself would be impossible."). U.S. companies reportedly spent more than $725 million on image advertising in 1985, triple the amount 12 years earlier.[39]

Increasingly, though, companies are taking stands on broader public policy issues that concern shareholders, managers, and employees. By the early 1980s, corporations were reportedly spending one-third their tax-deductible advertising budgets to influence people as citizens, not as customers.[40]

One approach is known as advocacy advertising. The idea is to convince a wide audience to support the company's position. Mobil Corporation illustrates this approach by buying space for editorials in the op-ed section of respected publications like *The Wall Street Journal* and *The New York Times*. The impact of advocacy ads is diluted, however, by the extent to which they are perceived as self-serving propaganda.

A more subtle way companies defend their interests is to commission strategic research to defend their interests. A good example was Procter & Gamble's paying for a 1990 study of disposable diapers by Arthur D. Little, the consulting firm. The Arthur D. Little study proved that disposables (an important Procter &

Gamble product) were no worse for the physical environment than cloth diapers. This finding effectively ended the environmentalist campaign against disposable diapers.[41]

Another indirect way that U.S. business sways public opinion and government action is by underwriting think tanks or public policy research institutions. Think tanks are a 20th century phenomenon. Endowed with private funds, they began to appear in the United States around 1900 to bring science and reason to government. Today, public policy research institutions number 115, not including those sponsored by universities or attached to government. Paralleling the growth of corporate interest groups, nearly half were founded in the period 1976–1990.[42] Most are headquartered in Washington, DC, where they have access to national policy makers.

Their scope is diverse, but many think tanks specialize in policies meaningful to business and industry. Prominent older institutions with an economic focus are the National Bureau of Economic Research (1920), the Brookings Institution (1927), and the American Enterprise Institute (1943). Influential newer organizations include the Heritage Foundation (1974), the Cato Institute (1977), and the Institute for International Economics (1981). Much of their research is of a very high order. With the exception of the Brookings Institution, all the think tanks just mentioned lean toward producing studies with a conservative slant, doubtful about government interference with the economy.

The recent explosion in the number of public policy research institutions, especially conservative ones, has been financed largely by corporations and wealthy investors. The Coors brewing family is a major benefactor of the Heritage Foundation. The Cato Institute lists such donors as Coca-Cola, Citibank, Shell Oil, Philip Morris, and Toyota.[43]

As noted earlier, U.S. business was appalled by many public policies in the 1960s and 1970s. From business' vantage point, too much red tape was being imposed on them without sufficient regard for the consequences. The justification for these "bad" policies came from government agencies and universities, which were believed to be unsympathetic to business needs. At the time, the corporate community lacked the intellectual artillery to fight back with reasoned objections and ideas for "good" policies.

The think tanks gave business a means to sponsor applied research into its problems, such as overregulation. Business also began to fund more studies on such issues by scholars in universities and business schools. These endeavors to change the grounds of the debate over business and public policy in the United States were largely successful. The liberal/social democrat paradigm of activist government, dominant in the 1960s, was replaced by a laissez-faire paradigm in the 1980s.

Today, many Americans agree with President Reagan's statement at his inaugural that "government is not the solution to our problem. Government is the problem." Rather than more regulation to compel business to act in the public interest, people are predisposed toward deregulation and privatization. The shift in popular and informed opinion was bolstered by high-quality academic studies emanating from the think tanks and from some university faculties—often financed by corporate interests.[44] The conservative think tanks also supply many commentators for television—usually presented as objective experts, not spokespersons for a particular set of interests.[45]

Another way companies influence public opinion is through educational programs, often targeted at public schools. More than half the Fortune 500 firms provide readings, videos, speakers, and other teaching material to classrooms around the country.[46] A less obvious, but maybe more potent, influence is through the acquisition of equity positions in the media, such as General Electric's purchase of NBC. Corporate ownership likely has a dampening effect on critical news stories about the parent company. The same can be said of corporate sponsorship of news programs, which may deflect some reports.

Philanthropy.   Charitable donations are another important means corporations use to try to make a favorable impression on key stakeholders. These donations often are aimed at the local community in which the plants and offices are located. As good citizens, companies give away significant amounts to worthy causes—paying for scholarships, underwriting plays and concerts, beautifying parks, and the like. Skeptics call this practice mere symbolism, encouraged by public policy that allows a tax write-off for the donations.

While U.S. corporate income taxes have been dropping in recent years, philanthropy has been increasing—though not nearly enough to offset the tax loss. Based on a survey of 333 U.S. companies, charitable donations were $5.6 billion in 1989. That was more than twice as much as was donated in 1980, and represented nearly double the share of corporate pretax income. About one-third of that money went to health and human services activities, one-third to education, and the rest to the arts and community activities.[47] Tokenism or no, corporate philanthropy is helpful for society and does put a good face on a company's other activities.

Government Relations.   The most important facet of corporate public affairs is government relations. This activity includes keeping abreast of policy changes. One of the growth areas of corporate public affairs departments is regulatory work, according to a 1992 survey.[48] Government relations also covers attempts to convince decision makers to support policies a company wants.

Large companies often lobby themselves. They also may lobby indirectly through their trade associations, or through law, consulting, and public relations firms hired to act as intermediaries. In Washington, federal legislation since 1946 has required that professional lobbyists register with Congress. The city is now home to some 80,000 lobbyists of one kind or another.[49] Not all of them are formally registered, since the registration requirement applies only to people whose principal activity is lobbying. For instance, Lee Iaccoca, like other top industry executives, often testifies before Congress or has private meetings with White House officials. Because such political activities represent only a fraction of his job, Iaccoca is nowhere listed as an official lobbyist.

Special provisions cover lobbyists working for foreign governments and international corporations, who are required to register as foreign agents with the Justice Department. Japanese organizations reportedly employed 140 U.S. lobbying and public relations firms in 1990, at a price of $100 million, to influence Washington policy making.[50] The government of Mexico spent nearly $30 million over three years to push for NAFTA, according to the Center for Public Integrity. Naturally, there is controversy over the danger such foreign lobbying may represent to U.S. national interests.

Labor unions and public interest groups also lobby. In fact, most Americans belong to one or more organizations that try to influence public policy makers.

Lobbyists do not try to affect all policies, but specialize in the ones they or their clients consider most important. Most lobbying effort is spent on defensive activities such as tracking and trying to block undesirable proposals. The U.S. way of making public policy is deliberative, with many checks and balances, so preventing action is generally easier than making something happen. Lobbyists work the points in the system where policies bad for their clients can be stalled, altered, or defeated. By blocking one another's efforts, the lobbyists add to the much decried Washington gridlock (to be discussed further in Chapter 10).

How Lobbying Is Done

Information is the lobbyist's greatest asset. Due to his or her links to interest groups, a lobbyist often has exclusive information that elected officials and their staff want or need. In fact, officials seek out lobbyists for briefings on issues and for help in drafting rules. Why? Because they want to know what harmful impact new policies may have on constituents before making up their minds. For lobbying to convince a politician to take a particular stand, the information must be high quality. Special pleading by itself is unlikely to get far if not backed up with solid data and analysis. Misleading information will be exposed by other lobbyists, thus damaging the interest group's credibility and clout.[51]

Most lobbying traditionally takes place out of the public eye. In recent years, however, lobbyists have started to arouse voters to support their position. They encourage influential constituents to bring pressure to bear on decision makers or organize grassroots mail campaigns. Companies can pitch in by asking their employees to write their representatives. These orchestrated efforts can lead to a barrage of mail and phone calls, forcing legislators to change their minds on issues that matter to the interest in question.

An excellent example of the new style of lobbying is the U.S. banking industry's 1983 campaign to overturn an amendment to the tax code. The amendment would have required them to withhold taxes from customers' interest and dividends. While the average citizen did not like withholding, it was not a salient issue for most people. To jolt the public's apathy, the American Banking Association produced 15,000 repeal kits for member banks, complete with drafts of letters to congressional representatives and prepackaged op-ed articles to be submitted to local newspapers. The banks were instructed to give customers preprinted, preaddressed postcard protests with their monthly statements, which caused an avalanche of protest mail on Congress. Support for the withholding amendment withered. Two weeks before the law was to take effect, the Senate reversed itself and voted 86–4 against tax withholding.[52]

Similar events occur at the state level. In Massachusetts, the tobacco industry formed the Fair Tax Coalition to fight an initiative petition to hike the cigarette excise in 1992. The Philip Morris Company, the Smokeless Tobacco Council, and other organizations spent $675,000 to lobby state lawmakers and administration officials. They also ran a $7.1 million media campaign, outspending an antismoking coalition led by the American Cancer Society by more than 10 to 1.[53] Here the lobbying did not work and the cigarette excise passed easily.

Most lobbying is quieter, however. The object is to head off adverse decisions before they become widely known, and while politicians' positions are still fluid. Once elected officials have fixed their positions, getting them to change is more difficult.

Lobbying in Other Political Systems

Business lobbyists in other nations usually avoid the kinds of public campaigns that are becoming prevalent in the United States, preferring a more confidential approach. Coalition building often occurs through industry associations and peak organizations, like Japan's *Keidanren.* As noted in Chapter 6, the consultation and bargaining are apt to be more formal and systematic than in the freewheeling United States.

Still, we should not exaggerate the differences. Even in corporatist states, there is an informal side to lobbying that is not unlike what American firms do. In Japan, for example, firms use their personal contacts to keep abreast of developments and to express their policy preferences to the bureaucracy, the dominant political party, and the Diet (legislature). Many times, the connections are based on school ties, since many top executives and bureaucrats attended the same prestigious universities. To maintain access to politicians, companies make regular campaign contributions—legal and tax deductible under Japanese law.[54]

Also as in the United States, lobbyists in Japan try to diversify their relationships and points of access. Japanese firms focus on the legislative committees and the bureaucratic agencies that are most important to their concerns.

The Ethics of Lobbying

The U.S. policy-making system works reasonably well for single companies and industries. Given the system's fragmented structure and the opportunities for endless dickering, they can often neutralize unwanted policies—especially narrowly drawn regulatory policies. Lowi once called the result governing by "universalized ticket fixing."[55]

But the business community is more than the total of its parts. A system that works for companies and industries at the individual level need not work for private sector as a whole. The granting of one favor or exception may do little harm to the economy, but, when everyone receives such favors, the whole economy can be hurt. Subsidies encourage inefficiencies that can have a large opportunity cost for society, since the resources could have been used elsewhere. Corporate executives usually recognize this principle in the abstract, but do not refrain from special pleading on the grounds that everyone else is doing the same thing.

Business ethics does not give much guidance on this issue, since management's responsibility is usually to the firm's stakeholders, not to a social abstraction. Executives might be considered remiss by owners, by employees, and perhaps by customers and suppliers if they fail to use public policy as a strategic weapon to preserve and enhance their company's competitive position.

There is also the moral issue of how far companies and their lobbyists ought to push to block changes in the law—changes that might hurt the company but would help some of its stakeholders in society. The tobacco companies, for instance, have fought hard against all legislation aimed at them in the United States, for instance, proposals to raise cigarette taxes to punitive levels. High taxes would discourage smoking, especially among nonsmokers, and contribute to the population's health. But the taxes also would mean less cigarette consumption and lower profits, and ultimately harm for its owner and worker stakeholders. Is it legitimate for the tobacco industry to use its vast resources to promote policies that hurt consumers but help its bottom line? In fact, cigarette companies have never even admitted that science has proved a link between smoking and health, out of fear that such an admission would open them to product liability suits.

The example of tobacco products brings up another point about short-term and long-term gains. Lobbying can bring political victory, but such victories are sometimes temporary and merely delay the day of reckoning. Shareholders and employees at Philip Morris and RJR/Nabisco, for instance, might in the end have been better off had those companies opted years ago, when the hazards of smoking became evident, to begin pulling out of the tobacco industry. Instead, and despite major diversification programs, both companies remained dangerously dependent on tobacco sales in the 1990s. They even renewed their overseas efforts in attempts to find less regulated environments in newly industrialized countries. As the tobacco industry dwindles, however, Philip Morris and RJR/Nabisco are finding their cash cow is no longer reliable. Lobbying and litigation postponed but did not prevent the transition in that industry.

Political Action Committees

Getting a company's message across requires an entrée to the centers of power. The best way is by helping friendly legislators get elected and hostile ones get defeated. Since elections run on money, campaign donations play a critical role in lobbying. The money does not usually "buy" a candidate's vote with a direct quid pro quo. What is bought is access. Prominent donors get to plead their case with the politician, and they obviously stand a greater chance of being heard than people who do not get through the door.

In the United States, companies earn access mainly through **political action committees (PACs).** Political action committees are voluntary groups of individuals organized to support political candidates. The rapid growth in the number and influence of PACs is one of the most significant developments of the past 25 years in American politics. PACs have displaced political parties as the main source of campaign contributions. Anyone can set up one of these voluntary groups, but business has been particularly active.

In 1974, there were 516 federally registered PACs in the United States; by 1992, the number had jumped to nearly 4,200. Corporations directly sponsored nearly half that total. Those corporate PACs donated about $68 million to federal candidates in 1991–92, compared to about $11 million in 1977–78 (see Table 8–4). AT&T PAC was the biggest, with contributions of nearly $1.5 million in 1989–90. There are also nearly 800 national PACs sponsored by commercial or professional membership associations, such as the realtors, doctors, or trial lawyers, and they gave away $51 million to federal candidates in 1991–92.[56]

Other PACs focus on state or local issues. In Massachusetts, 26 new state PACs were organized in 1992–93. Included were the Professional Tow Operators of Massachusetts PAC, the Political Committee for Responsible Massachusetts Growth (representing commercial developers), and the FBMA/PAC (associated with Fleet Bank, the state's largest).[57] These organizations gave thousands of dollars to state politicians. In New York State, PACs contributed half the money raised by legislative candidates in 1992, reinforcing the notion that special interests have a stranglehold on state government.[58]

Not all PACs are connected to business. Labor unions, for example, have set up political action committees, too. Citizen groups, such as the American Asso-

---

TABLE 8–4   **Corporate PAC Contributions Have Been Climbing Steadily, Though at a Slower Pace since the Late 1970s.**

	Corporate PAC Contributions ($ millions)
1979–80	$21.6
1981–82	29.4
1983–84	39.0
1985–86	49.6
1987–88	56.3
1989–90	58.1
1991–92	68.4

Source: U.S. Bureau of the Census, *Statistical Abstract of the United States* (Washington, DC: U.S. Government Printing Office, various years).

ciation of Retired Persons, and special interest organizations, such as the National Rifle Association, also form these organizations to support friendly political candidates. Labor PACS contributed $40 million in 1991–1992, other nonbusiness PACs gave about $20 million—in both cases the amounts are much less than given by business PACs to national campaigns.

Corporate PACs were legitimized by the Federal Election Campaign Act of 1971. Before, corporations had funneled campaign contributions through executives' individual gifts, which were unlimited and unregulated. Direct corporate contributions to federal campaigns had been illegal since the 1907 Tillman Act, but companies got around this rule by paying bonuses to managers, which they simply redirected to candidates. The campaign reform act put a ceiling of $25,000 on individual campaign contributions, thus ending the era of the large political donor. The Federal Election Commission is the government agency charged with regulating these practices.

Under the 1971 act, as amended in 1974 and 1976, companies may collect uncoerced donations from employees, shareholders, or their families and distribute them through a PAC to candidates for political office. Easing the task of maintaining a corporate PAC, employee contributions can be made through a payroll deduction plan and company funds can be used to organize and pay administrative costs. The corporation, for example, is permitted to pay for printing and mailing PAC solicitations, for salaries of PAC employees, for rent and other expenses of maintaining PAC offices, and for attorneys, accountants, and other professional advisors to the PAC.

The amounts solicited and donated are not large in isolation. No one may contribute more than $5,000 to a particular PAC in a year, and the PAC cannot give more than $5,000 to any federal candidate per election (primary and general), or over $20,000 to a national party committee. However, PACs can spend for their own campaigns that are indistinguishable from official ones. The conservative NICPAC, for instance, spent millions to defeat several liberal senators in 1980. Since these funds did not pass through any candidate's campaign, there was no limit on spending.

Bundling is another method PACs and individual companies use to get around the legal limits. Bundling is when an organization appeals to executives for individual contributions to a congressional representative, senator, or other candidate. The PAC or company acts as the collection point for the donations, which do not count against its $5,000 limit. It puts the checks together and delivers them to the politician, reaping the political credit for raising the money. In 1985, for example, the insurance industry PAC bundled $215,000 in individual contributions for Senator Bob Packwood of Oregon.[59]

Yet another practice that makes a mockery of U.S. campaign finance laws is soft money. There are no reporting requirements or ceilings for contributions given to political parties instead of candidates. In 1988, nearly 400 people, including the notorious swindler Charles Keating, each appear to have given $100,000 or more in soft money to the participants in the presidential elections.[60] Other loopholes allow companies to donate staff and equipment to party conventions, and to sponsor parties and receptions for candidates. To help pay for Bill Clinton's 1993 inauguration, for example, corporations ranging from tobacco firms to Japanese subsidiaries gave $5 million in gifts and $7 million in unsecured loans.[61]

The Cost of Campaign Finance

The main charges against current U.S. campaign practices are two. First, the flood of money into politics helps push the cost of running for office to unacceptable levels. In 1988, the average winning candidate for the House of Representatives spent $388,000; for the Senate, $3,745,000.[62] Candidates for the California legislature in 1986 spent $60 million altogether. Office seekers have to spend far less in other countries. Compare these figures with the $10.3 million spent on the entire British general election in 1983.[63] American politicians get caught on a treadmill of fundraising that leaves them too little time to focus on issues, and that leads them to take money wherever they can find it.

Second, the diverse sources of campaign funds tear apart cohesive influences in U.S. politics by pressing politicians to act parochially. Fred Wertheimer, former president of Common Cause, contends:

> PAC money is like a laser beam. It helps a particular interest group play out very powerful influences on the issue that it cares about, while the general public is kind of diluted and left out of it . . . What are the balance wheels? The issue is one of weighing. That whole balancing process is done by representatives. . . If they are not free to balance, then our system's not working.[64]

Reforms

Many reforms have been proposed to reduce money's debasing influence on American public policy and create a better balance between business and other interest groups.[65] Similar methods have long been the practice in Europe, with mixed results (see Box 8–2). Whether they would work in the United States is not clear.

One set of reforms focuses on campaign finance. Many have suggested that tighter limits be put on donations, for instance, by eliminating soft money or limiting the amount of money politicians can earn in honoraria for speaking engagements before interest groups. History suggests, however, that interest groups and politicians will push the envelope of spending limits and find ways around them. The incentive for candidates to raise more money than their opponents is too strong.

Another idea is to put a ceiling on campaign spending. To stop the escalating race for funds, candidates would be barred from spending above a certain amount for election. However, the Supreme Court in 1976 declared it unconstitutional for the law to set any limit on candidates' expenditure of their money and on overall spending in a campaign, unless they voluntarily accepted public financing.

Box 8–2

Many Countries Limit Spending on Political Races and Provide Public Money to Finance Them

Germany was the first country to finance its parties, starting in 1959. Political contributions from trade unions are illegal, and the country's conservative parties also wanted to be less dependent on donations from industry. Currently, the parties in the Bundestag get about $150 million per year.

The Scandinavian countries follow the German model. Since the 1960s, they have paid subsidies to parties based on their share of the vote. Parties must publish information revealing their major donors.

In Italy, state financing was introduced in 1974. But the practice did not stop electoral abuses, and Italians rejected state financing in a referendum in 1993. Italian parties also are required to publish details of how they get money and the names of big contributors.

Great Britain is an exception, with even less regulation than America. It provides no money for parties' election expenses. It does not limit what they spend. And it does not have strict disclosure requirements.[1]

[1]"Only in Britain . . . ," *The Economist,* June 26, 1993.

Public financing exists now for the presidency. Some reformers propose expanding this practice for House and Senate races as a way to break the money cycle. One of the two main parties, the Republicans, has resisted this suggestion. They charge that public financing does not level the playing field, but blatantly favors incumbent officeholders. Incumbents have advantages in campaigns because they are better known, so they do not have to spend as much as their challengers to have the same effect. As a minority party with fewer incumbents in Congress for most of the postwar era, Republicans felt they would be further disabled by public financing.

Because of the difficulty in getting the campaign finance system improved, several states have passed term limits for officeholders to reach the same goal of cleaning up politics. The idea of term limits is to force turnover among politicians and prevent them from becoming too cozy with interest groups and lobbyists. It is the other major party, the Democrats, that is apt to be opposed to this reform. Just as public financing threatens Republicans more, because they usually have fewer incumbents, this one threatens Democrats, because they often have the most members with long tenure in office.

Term limits could have the reverse effect intended and might increase the influence of special interests. Veteran politicians, with knowledge and experience, can be less dependent on lobbyists for information compared to rookie politicians. In the 1993 budget debate, for instance, lobbyists specifically targeted freshmen in Congress on the assumption that they are the easiest to influence.[66] By lowering the experience level in Washington and the state capitals, term limits would bare the government to more outside pressure than now.

Conclusion

This chapter has reviewed the role of interest groups in determining public policy. We have seen that many groups compete in the political marketplace for influence, and that business interests are among the most active and effective. Policy results are skewed toward the powerful, and business tends to be powerful—though its power is neither constant nor monolithic.

For firms to get the policies they want, they have made public affairs and especially govern-ment relations critical areas of modern corporate strategy. These activities have not been without cost to the larger society, as they have tended to balkanize decisions and stall change. Some countries seem to have done better than the United States in focusing political energy and making hard choices, partly because they have different political institutions and procedures. These institutions and procedures are our main subject in the next two chapters.

Questions

1. Does business make most critical decisions that affect the United States economy? Or is business just another special interest in a group-based political system?

2. What are the major organizations that represent the business point of view in public policy matters? How do they differ? Which have the most clout? When?

3. Describe how PACs work. Analyze the problems that result. How might these be corrected?

4. Discuss the organizations that exist to offset business influence on public policy.

5. What tactics do businesses use to sway policy makers? Which are the most important?

End Notes

1. Alexander Hamilton, James Madison, and John Jay, *The Federalist,* ed. Max Beloff, 2nd ed. (1787–88; reprint, Oxford: Basil Blackwell, 1987), p. 43.

2. Cited by George Cabot Lodge, *Comparative Business–Government Relations* (Englewood Cliffs, NJ: Prentice Hall, 1989), p. 32.

3. Adam Smith, *An Inquiry into the Nature and Origins of the Wealth of Nations* (1776; reprint, New York: Modern Library, 1937), p. 250.

4. Kenneth J. Arrow, *Social Choice and Individual Values* (New York: John Wiley, 1951).

5. Don Clawson, Alan Neustadtl, and Denise Scott, *Money Talks: Corporate PACs and Political Influence* (New York: Basic Books, 1992), p. 25.

6. Mark S. Mizruchi, *The Structure of Corporate Political Action* (Cambridge, MA: Harvard University Press, 1992), p. 14.

7. Thomas Ferguson and Joel Rogers, *Right Turn: The Decline of the Democrats and the Future of American Politics* (New York: Hill and Wang, 1986).

8. Joseph Schumpeter, *Capitalism, Socialism, and Democracy,* 3rd ed. (New York: Harper and Row, 1950).

9. See William Greider, *Who Will Tell the People?* (New York: Simon and Schuster, 1992).

10. Steven Kelman, *Making Public Policy* (New York: Basic Books, 1987), p. 214.

11. The classic critique of interest group democracy is Theodore Lowi's, *The End of Liberalism,* 2nd ed. (New York: Norton, 1979), recently voted the political science book with the most lasting influence in the past 20 years.

12. This point was first made by Mancur Olson, Jr., in his classic, *The Logic of Collective Action* (Cambridge, MA: Harvard University Press, 1965).

13. "Protection's Stepchild," *The Economist,* May 16, 1992, p. 98.

14. Clawson et al., *Money Talks,* p. 23.

15. Jeffrey H. Birnbaum, *The Lobbyist: How Influence Peddlers Get Their Way in Washington* (New York: Times Books, 1992).

16. Sanford M. Jacoby, *Masters to Managers: Historical and Comparative Perspectives on American Employers* (New York: Columbia University Press, 1991).

17. Thomas K. McCraw, "Business and Government: The Origins of the Adversary Relationship," *California Management Review* 26, no. 2 (1984), pp. 33–52.

18. Wyn Grant, ed., *The Political Economy of Corporatism* (New York: St. Martin's, 1985), p. 25.

19. Kenneth H. Bacon, "For Citicorp, Which Has Largest Lobbying Force in Banking Industry, Victories Are Won Quietly, *The Wall Street Journal,* December 14, 1993, p. A13.

20. Lodge, *Comparative Business–Government Relations,* p. 34.

21. Seymour Lusterman, *Managing Federal Government Relations* (Washington, DC: Conference Board, 1989).

22. Sar A. Levitan and Martha R. Cooper, *Business Lobbies* (Baltimore: Johns Hopkins University Press, 1984), pp. 14–15.

23. David Vogel, *Fluctuating Fortunes: The Political Power of Business in America* (New York: Basic Books, 1989).

24. Jeanne Saddler and Rick Wartzman, "Chamber of Commerce Is Roiled by a Revolt within Rank and File," *The Wall Street Journal,* April 15, 1994, p. A1.

25. Vogel, *Fluctuating Fortunes,* p. 287.

26. Alan Rosenthal, *The Third House: Lobbyists and Lobbying in the States* (Washington, DC: Congressional Quarterly Press, 1993), pp. 3–4.

27. Graham K. Wilson, *Business and Politics: A Comparative Introduction,* 2nd ed. (Chatham, NJ: Chatham House, 1990).

28. Leonard H. Lynn and Timothy J. McKeown, *Organizing Business: Trade Associations in America and Japan* (Washington, DC: American Enterprise Institute, 1988), p. 4.

29. Karel von Wolferen, *The Enigma of Japanese Power* (London: MacMillan, 1990).

30. John Kenneth Galbraith, *American Capitalism: The Concept of Countervailing Power,* rev. ed. (Boston: Houghton Mifflin, 1956).

31. Murray Weidenbaum, *Business, Government and the Public,* 4th ed. (Englewood Cliffs, NJ: Prentice Hall, 1990), p. 417.

32. "Public Interest Pretenders," *Consumer Reports,* May 1994, pp. 317–18.

33. Kelman, *Making Public Policy.*

34. I borrow these themes from Milton J. Esman, *Management Dimensions of Development* (West Hartford, CT: Kumarian, 1991), pp. 150–51.

35. Cited in Robert B. Reich, *The Work of Nations* (New York: Vintage, 1992), p. 48.

36. See, for example, Ferguson and Rogers, *Right Turn,* pp. 89–94; and Vogel, *Fluctuating Fortunes,* pp. 228–32.

37. Seymour Lusterman, *The Organization and Staffing of Corporate Public Affairs,* Report No. 894 (New York: The Conference Board, 1987).

38. *National Directory of Corporate Public Affairs* (Washington, DC: Columbia Books, 1994), p. 6.

39. Rogene Buchholz, *Business Environment and Public Policy,* 4th ed. (Englewood Cliffs, NJ: Prentice Hall, 1992), p. 530.

40. Frances Fox Piven and Richard Cloward, *The New Class War,* rev. ed. (New York: Pantheon, 1985), p. 9.

41. Cynthia Crossen, *Tainted Truth* (New York: Simon and Schuster, 1994).

42. James G. McGann, "Academics to Ideologues: A Brief History of the Public Policy Research Industry," *PS* 25, no. 4 (December 1992), pp. 733–40. Also see David M. Ricci, *The Transformation of American Politics: The New Washington and the Rise of the Think Tanks* (New Haven: Yale University Press, 1993).

43. John J. Fialka, "Cato Institute's Influence Grows in Washington as Republican-Dominated Congress Sets Up Shop," *The Wall Street Journal,* December 14, 1994, p. A16.

44. Vogel, *Fluctuating Fortunes.*

45. Paul Steidlmeier, "Institutional Approaches in Strategic Management," *Journal of Economic Issues* 27, no. 1 (1993), p. 201.

46. Buchholz, *Business Environment,* p. 530, citing "Industry's Schoolhouse Clout," *Business Week,* October 13, 1980.

47. Anne Klepper, *Corporate Contributions, 1989* (New York: Conference Board, 1989).

48. *National Directory of Corporate Public Affairs,* p. 6.

49. Birnbaum, *The Lobbyist,* p. 7.

50. Pat Choate, *Agents of Influence* (New York: Knopf, 1990).

51. A good guidebook to the practical details of lobbying is Bruce C. Wolpe, *Lobbying Congress: How the System Works* (Washington, DC: Congressional Quarterly, 1990).

52. Hedrick Smith, *The Power Game* (New York: Random House, 1988), pp. 243–45.

53. Frank Phillips, "Over $800,000 Spent in '92 on Hill by Tobacco, Gambling Interests," *Boston Globe,* January 20, 1993, p. 21; and "Factions Spent $16 million on '92 Ballot Initiatives," *Boston Globe,* January 26, 1993, p. 14.

54. David P. Baron, *Business and Its Environment* (Englewood Cliffs, NJ: Prentice Hall, 1993), pp. 395–96.

55. Quoted in Greider, *Who Will Tell the People?* p. 108.

56. Edward Zuckerman, *Almanac of Federal PACs* (Arlington, VA: Amward Publications, 1994).

57. Craig Sandler, "The Price of Power," *The Brookline TAB,* October 12, 1993.

58. Kevin Sack, "Study Lists Political Action Groups' Spending," *The New York Times,* December 3, 1992, p. B11.

59. Smith, *Power Game,* p. 260.

60. Frank J. Sorauf, *Inside Campaign Finance* (New Haven, CT: Yale University Press, 1992), pp. 148–50.

61. Michael Kranish, "Corporate Cash Paves Way for Inaugural," *Boston Sunday Globe,* January 17, 1993, p. 1.

62. Ibid., p. 7.

63. Lewis Lipsitz and David M. Speak, *American Democracy,* 2nd ed. (New York: St. Martin's, 1989), p. 259.

64. Quoted in Smith, *Power Game,* p. 263.

65. See, for example, David B. Magleby and Candice J. Nelson, *The Money Chase* (Washington, DC: Brookings Institution, 1990).

66. Joel Brinkley, "A Strategy on the Budget: Round up the Greenhorns," *The New York Times,* July 23, 1993, p. A1.

9 POLITICAL INSTITUTIONS
How the Policy Process Is Organized

The separation of powers between the legislative and executive branches, whatever its merits in 1793, has become a structure that almost guarantees stalemate today.

Lloyd N. Cutler[1]

Governments are large and complex entities, and their policy-making structure is correspondingly mystifying to outside observers. Government policy making becomes more transparent and easier to grasp when one realizes that a government as a whole seldom acts on any one specific issue. While business leaders like to talk figuratively about a government taking this position or that, sophisticated ones know policy making is a decentralized activity.

Governments are composed of separate entities that specialize in different policy areas. In the U.S. Congress, for example, small groups of that body make most of the important decisions about any given government program. In the federal executive branch, public policy is crafted separately in the hundreds of bureaus and agencies that make up the branch. Congressmen and bureaucrats talk to each other and to the handful of interest groups and lobbyists wanting to influence a particular piece of legislation. Other countries often look different, with different patterns of political institutions, but they are like the United States in that their governments are never as unified as appears on the surface.

Policy-Making Systems

In stable polities, the pattern of interaction among key decision makers is not random. Policy making in the United States is orderly, despite being decentralized; it usually is done by the same people, who probably know each other and the issues well. The sum of people who control what government does in a specific policy area form a **policy-making system.** There may be hundreds of policy-

FIGURE 9–1

Hundreds of policy-making systems comprise the U.S. federal government

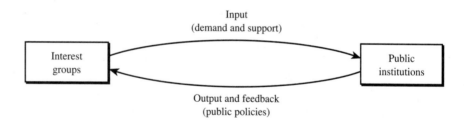

The purpose of this chapter is to provide a road map to the structure of the

making systems within the larger public sector. Political economists describe these decentralized groups as systems, because they are predictable and involve a high level of interaction and feedback (see Figure 9–1).

The presence of informal policy-making systems is helpful for business and other private organizations. It gives them points of entry to the political arena—a way to try to influence policies important to them. A. Lee Fritschler and Bernard H. Ross put it as follows:

> Government decision-making is not focused on abstractions. There is no decision-making system for something as broad or vague as . . . "commercial policy" or "agricultural policy." These are debatable political abstractions with little or no operational meaning. Instead, commercial or agricultural policies of the United States government are the sum of dozens of specific programs that are defined in specific terms in statutes and agency regulations . . . Rather than looking for operational decision-making systems for "agricultural policy," business executives should look for decision systems organized around specific agricultural programs, like price supports for various commodities, soil conservation, meat and grain inspection, and food stamps.[2]

The purpose of this chapter is to provide a road map to the structure of the U.S. policy-making systems. We will describe the branches of government—the legislative, executive, and judicial branches—and the different levels of government—federal, state, and local—with which business executives must deal. The formal institutions will be contrasted with the unofficial policy-making systems that have evolved alongside. We also will contrast American political institutions with those in other countries. While American institutions are unique, the method of desegregating public policy making by looking for the location of key decision makers can be used anywhere. The hope is to help readers be better at navigating the corridors of power in modern government. In Chapter 10, we will look at how these institutions, these policy-making systems, interact.

The Architecture of American Politics

A **government** is the institutions and processes through which binding decisions are made for society. Government activities include the making of laws, their execution, and their interpretation and application. The U.S. Constitution, now over 200 years old, created a distinctly American structure of government based on the **separation of powers.** Under the doctrine of the separation of powers, the major functions of government were dispersed to legislative, executive, and judicial institutions. The idea was to diffuse power horizontally. Any other arrangement, the framers of the Constitution reasoned, would produce concentrated political power—exactly what the War of Independence had been fought to escape.

As James Madison argued: "There can be no liberty where the legislative and executive powers are united in the same person . . . [or] if the power of judging be not separated from the legislative and executive powers . . ."[3] To protect the new republic against tyranny, the founders created an elaborate framework of checks and balances that gives each branch of government the means to take part in, and therefore the possibility to impede, the workings of the other branches. The assumption, in Madison's words, was that "ambition must be made to counteract ambition."[4]

The best known examples of checks and balances are the power of the president to veto legislation, the power of Congress to overrule a veto (by two-thirds vote), and the power of the judiciary to review legislation and presidential actions. Within the Congress itself, another check on policy making is the division of Congress into an upper and lower chamber, both of which must agree on legislation. The two chambers and the president are chosen in separate elections by different constituencies. These features are designed to prevent any one institution or group from accruing too much political power.

Federalism

The framers of the Constitution tried further to dilute power by dispersing it along a vertical axis. They created two layers of government: the federal government and the state governments. The states generally mirror the setup of checks and balances found at the federal level. A major objective of federalism was to spread the power to make decisions, to allow the needs and desires of people in the states to dictate diverse policies.

The Constitution reserves only a few powers exclusively for the federal level. For the business community, Washington's most important exclusive powers are to issue currency (resulting in a uniform nationwide monetary system), to impose tariffs (meaning all states have the same level of protection against foreign goods), and to regulate trade among the states (the interstate commerce clause). Beyond these limited functions, the central government made comparatively little policy during the nation's first 150 years. Until the 1930s, the states did most of it, including the bulk of policy making that affected business. Since then, Washington has encroached on the states' prerogatives. Thus, the level of government responsible for many economic policies is a gray area.

The Constitution encouraged federal–state (and state–state) competition that helped blunt policy changes. America's 18th-century leaders probably did not foresee, however, how much federalism complicates the job of business management, as companies have to conform to public policies from overlapping jurisdictions. Making the geographic distribution of power more complex, the states have delegated important responsibilities to local governments—counties, cities, towns, and special districts listed in Table 9–1. Much business regulation (health and fire inspection, for instance) takes place at the local level.

Nowhere is the Constitution's ambiguity more apparent than in the interstate commerce clause. Until well into the 20th century, the Supreme Court interpreted it to keep the federal government out of direct regulation of most businesses, on the grounds that events within factories and workplaces were inherently local. Federal regulation was allowed only in industries that obviously crossed state lines, such as railroads or gas pipelines. During the 1930s, however, the Court changed direction and began broadening its interpretation of interstate commerce to include matters such as collective bargaining, minimum wages, and unemployment insurance, which now came under federal jurisdiction.

Weak Government

The shape of the U.S. political system—its several branches, its various levels, its two parties—contributes to the much criticized gridlock in Washington and in many state capitals and city halls. It is no accident that government seems to act timidly, tardily, and in piecemeal manner. Madison and his colleagues intended the checks and balances to be conservative, in the sense of conserving the status quo. By setting up obstacles for policy makers to navigate, the idea was to force them to review carefully all angles of any new policy and thus avoid taking ill-considered decisions.

Thus, what looks like immobilized government to one person may look like prudent policy making to someone else. Conservative Republicans, for example, pointed to the blocking of health care reform in 1994 as their greatest accomplishment of the legislative term. When government inaction or nondecision is pursued consistently over time despite counterpressure, as is true of health care,

TABLE 9–1   Businesspeople Have to Deal with Many Governments in the United States.

Level	Number
National	1
State	50
County	3,042
Municipal	19,200
Township	16,691
School district	14,721
Special district	29,532

Source: U.S. Bureau of the Census, *Statistical Abstract of the United States,* 1990 (Washington, DC: U.S. Government Printing Office).

it becomes public policy.[5] In many matters, the unannounced government program of the United States is to do nothing.

This cautious system of divided government served the country adequately through much of its past, but critics think it is too cumbersome to deal with the challenges of the 21st century. The system was designed when the republic had maybe 1 percent its population today, and when government had far fewer responsibilities. Today, we cannot afford as easily to postpone decisions and let pressing problems, like the cost of health care, get out of hand. The U.S. system also encourages a lack of accountability, permitting officials to duck responsibility by blaming others for inaction.

Paul Kennedy, a historian at Yale University, raises the question on many observers' minds:

> [I]t ought to be honestly asked whether the much vaunted American Constitution, deep-frozen in the late 18th century when "checks and balances" were a more important consideration than national efficiency, does not hinder—or nowadays even paralyze—the taking of unpopular but necessary reforms. Elsewhere in the world, matters are often arranged differently . . . [A]t the least, other democratic constitutions—not just Britain's, but those of France, West Germany, and Australia—do permit governments to govern . . . The division of powers, however attractive in theory, reduces national policy making to a crawl and sometimes to a complete halt.[6]

While public attention has focused on the national government, paralysis is acute at the state level, too. In the largest state, California, elective power is dispersed among 58 counties, 447 cities, and more than 5,000 special districts covering everything from schools to sewerage. California is also a laboratory for direct democracy, thanks to the ballot initiative that has allowed citizens to vote on such matters as their car insurance rates and the share of the state's general fund that must be spent on education. The state is widely seen as ungovernable, with its multiple layers of government serving as a complicated channel for "passing the buck."[7]

Foreign Political Systems

The separation of powers and federalism are special features of the United States. Other industrial democracies do not fragment their governments so deeply, and instead favor greater coordination among lawmakers and other officials. In a **parliamentary democracy,** where the executive and legislature are one, there is a fusion of powers. Elections are held for the parliament, and whichever party or parties control parliament forms the government (the administration, in U.S. parlance). Due to party discipline, the governing party usually can pass its basic program as presented to the voting public. Most European states and Japan follow the parliamentary model. Box 9–1 describes briefly how this model works.

Most other advanced countries are also unitary states—no powers are constitutionally reserved for the lower tiers of government. The center has ultimate authority and can supersede regional decisions.

Box 9–1

Policy Making in Parliamentary Systems

The parliamentary or Westminster (site of England's parliament) model of democracy differs in many particulars from the U.S. presidential model. Instead of separating powers, the parliamentary model fuses executive and legislative power. The national legislature is the supreme authority. Some variation of the parliamentary model is practiced in all developed countries save the United States. The U.S. presidential model is more popular in LDCs.

General elections take place at various times, not on fixed dates as in the United States. Parliamentary elections are valid for a maximum period, usually five years, when a new contest must be held. But campaigns can take place early, and usually do.

The institutional structure of a parliamentary system is usually of a lower and an upper legislative chamber, with the lower chamber (the House of Commons in Britain) having most power. The upper chamber (the House of Lords in Britain) typically has an advisory role and can be overridden. The executive branch is divided into a head of government—the prime minister or chancellor—and a largely formal head of state—sometimes a monarch and other times an elected president.

The lower house chooses the prime minister, who in turn chooses the executive heads of government ministries (the cabinet). The prime minister and the cabinet, known together as the government, hold office only as long as more than half the members of the legislature support them. The remaining legislators form the opposition and have the chance to question government policies and to propose alternatives.

The members of the legislature regularly show their support through votes of confidence. A government can stay in office only temporarily without legislative support for its policies. If defeated on a vote of confidence, the prime minister and cabinet must resign and try to organize a new government that can claim majority support. Sometimes they have to call a general election to try to secure the confidence of a new majority in parliament.

In countries with multiple parties, such as Italy or France, coalition governments are the rule. Party leaders in the lower house negotiate for cabinet posts in exchange for their followers' support. Sometimes minority governments are possible, if the opposition is too disorganized to mount a successful challenge on a vote of confidence. Coalition and minority governments are apt to be unstable. Italy, for instance, averages one new government a year. But public policy need not shift as much as might be implied. Many ministers stay the same. Also, the bureaucrats who help write law and carry it out do not turn over with every government change.

The different institutions used elsewhere reflect less fear of concentrated political power. Of course, parliamentary systems have their drawbacks. The lack of a clear-cut majority, for instance, can lead to gridlock and lack of accountability in its own right. There are reasons to be skeptical that Britain, not to mention other parliamentary systems like Italy, does a better job of making public policy than the United States.[8] Also, unitary states can err by having too much top-down control that stifles initiative. As in most things, no magic bullets exist in politics. Still, many observers think the unwieldy framework of its government helps put American business and industry at a competitive disadvantage in the world economy.[9]

Having described the logic behind the architecture of the U.S. policymaking system, we now turn to a more detailed description of its constituent institutions. The point that needs to be kept in mind is that, whatever its other drawbacks, this elaborate framework offers business abundant opportunities to influence the course of public policy. There are many choke points at which policies damaging to a company or an industry can be annulled, delayed, or amended. It is also a stable system. Business can rest assured that elections will happen on time, policies will seldom change radically, and most decision makers will obey the law. This stability, which is reproduced in most other advanced countries, is the base of a good business climate.

Legislative Branch

The U.S. Congress has 435 representatives and 100 senators elected from the 50 states. Such large groups of elected officials are too unwieldy to develop public policy. The situation calls out for a division of labor, and the House and Senate long ago began to work through committees and subcommittees. Almost all legislation begins the road to enactment in a subcommittee, with most of it dying there without ever being considered by either full chamber. The same is true in legislatures at the state level, which use analogous committee systems.

Committees.   Anyone wanting to watch or influence policy needs to focus on the applicable committee or subcommittee. The committee system in Washington has been reorganized and streamlined several times, notably in 1946 when the number of standing or permanent committees was cut from 48 to 19 in the House and from 33 to 15 in the Senate. There are permanent or standing committees that deal with agriculture, banking, commerce, energy, and small business, to cite some examples particularly important to business (see Table 9–2). The number of subcommittees has increased markedly since 1946, canceling any gain in efficiency—though the House's new Republican majority that took office in 1995 streamlined that body's committee system somewhat.

Members of Congress with a distinct interest in the subject matter of a committee are expected to seek membership on it. A representative of a coastal district, for instance, might seek placement on the Merchant Marine and Fisheries Committee, but probably would not be attracted to the Agriculture Committee. The opposite would likely be true of someone representing a farming or ranching district. Lawmakers may serve on only two standing committees in the House, and three in the Senate—but they usually average four or five subcommittee assignments. Lawmakers also may be assigned to select, special, or joint committees. It is often physically impossible for them to be present at all the meetings of these various panels. Once on a subcommittee, however, most members stay because seniority determines who becomes the chair. A subcommittee or committee chair is a particularly influential position that gives its occupant leverage to set the legislative agenda.

In committee or subcommittee, members can give close attention to bills and

TABLE 9–2   **There Are Many Important Congressional Committees for Business to Worry About (100th Congress)**

House—Standing	Number of Subcommittees	Senate—Standing	Number of Subcommittees
Agriculture	8	Agriculture	6
Appropriations	13	Appropriations	13
Armed Services	7	Armed Services	6
Banking	8	Banking, Housing, and	
Budget	9	Urban Affairs	4
Education and Labor	8	Budget	0
Energy and Commerce	6	Commerce, Science, and	
Foreign Affairs	8	Transportation	8
Interior	6	Energy and Natural	
Merchant Marine	6	Resources	5
Public Works	7	Environment and Public	
Science and Technology	7	Works	5
Small Business	6	Finance	7
Ways and Means	6	Foreign Relations	7
		Labor and Human Resources	6
		Small Business	6

Joint—Standing	
Economic	8
Taxation	0

Note: List excludes several committees that are not immediately relevant to business.

learn areas of expertise. Lacking the same specialized knowledge, the rest of Congress is likely to defer to committee members' judgment on issues within their purview. The result is that most congressional decisions about public policy get made at a low level in the hierarchy of the legislative branch. Actions of subcommittees are upheld about 95 percent of the time by full committees, which, in turn, are upheld about 90 percent of the time on the floor of the House or Senate.[10] Thus, business and other lobbyists wisely concentrate their attention at the foot of the congressional hierarchy, not on the top.

Even the committee system has proved unable to keep pace with the increasingly complicated and technical nature of public policy. While the issues grow more complex, there is less time to study them, as lawmakers are forced to spend more time than they used to raising campaign funds, planning reelection campaigns, and so forth. A recent study by the House of Representatives found the typical member spent only about 4½ hours a day on legislative matters. The study concluded that "rarely do Members have sufficient blocks of time when they are free from the frantic pace of the Washington 'treadmill' to think about the implications of various public policies . . . the splintering of his or her time into so many bits and pieces hampers the effective conduct of lawmaking, oversight, and constituent service functions."[11]

Congressional Staff.   Professional staff have stepped into this vacuum. Representatives and senators together employ nearly 11,000 staff, and they rely on these employees' know-how in arcane policy areas. Increasingly, staff are responsible in their areas of special competence for drafting proposals, organizing hearings, and negotiating with lobbyists. Because they control the information the legislators receive, they can sway legislative outcomes.

The personal staffs of individual lawmakers are not the only unelected people engaged in policy making on Capitol Hill. Another 3,000 staff are attached permanently to the committees. Unlike the personal staff, they stay despite turnover in Congress. Because they provide the body's institutional memory, committee staff can play key roles in policy making. Congress also has several permanent agencies to help it make policy: the Congressional Budget Office, the Congressional Research Service of the Library of Congress, the General Accounting Office, and the Office of Technology Assessment. Not surprisingly, lobbyists quickly identify the influential congressional staff and try to work with and through them to affect policy.

Critics of Washington decry the shift of power to these unelected, unaccountable experts.[12] The Republicans who took majority control of the House of Representatives in 1995 cut the number of staff by one-third on the doubtful grounds this brings the legislature closer to the people who elect it. (The real reason may have been to weaken Democrats, who bore the cuts, while Republican legislators got a net increase in staff helpers.) In fact, any reduction in professional staff is more likely to enhance the power of organized interests and lobbyists and inhibit the capacity of Congress to make independent judgments about public policy. Without their own experts as a filter, elected officials will have to rely more than ever on pressure groups for information and ideas about how to vote.

Executive Branch

Like the rest of the U.S. government structure, the executive branch is composed of separate institutions sharing power. The operational centers of the executive branch include the Executive Office of the President, the cabinet departments (divided in turn into bureaus), and the almost independent executive agencies (see Figure 9–2). Each of these centers of power has its own bailiwick, with its own set of clients outside the formal government. The departments and agencies organize and guide the government's programs, including the critical programs that affect business profitability.

The president's office, often called simply the White House, is probably the most familiar to ordinary people. It is staffed at the top by the president's chief aides, who may be hired or fired at will. Several units directed by the president are concerned mainly with foreign affairs, while others are responsible for economic policy and thus have major effects on business. The business-oriented units include the Council of Economic Advisors, the Office of Science and Technology Policy, the Council on Environmental Quality, the Office of Special Rep-

FIGURE 9-2

Structure of executive branch

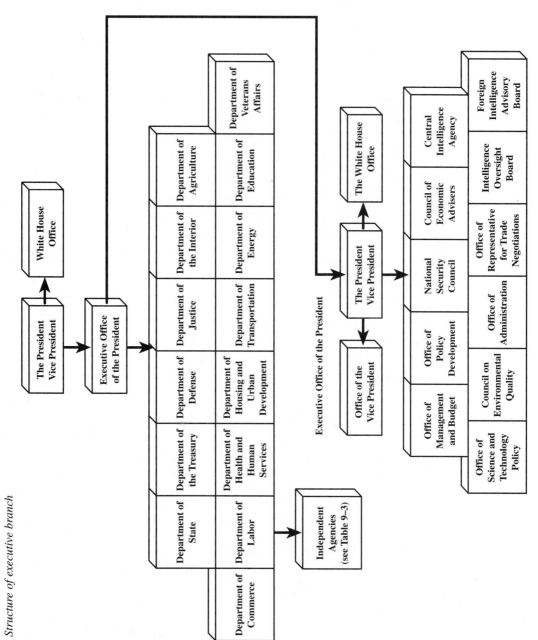

resentative for Trade Negotiations, and the Office of Management and Budget (OMB). This last office, the OMB, is especially important. Its two main functions are to prepare the federal budget and to clear all legislation submitted to Congress by executive agencies. There are currently about 1,000 people working directly for the president (not including 800 employees of the OMB and the U.S. Trade Representative). That is several hundred fewer than in the 1980s.[13]

Cabinet.   The president's cabinet is a separate group of officers, called secretaries. They are the equivalent of government ministers in other countries. The cabinet secretaries, in turn, head the major administrative departments, or what most countries term the government ministries. As the list of U.S. cabinet departments makes clear, they touch every facet of business and industry: Agriculture, Commerce, Defense, Education, Energy, Health and Human Services, Housing and Urban Development, Interior (i.e., natural resources), Justice, Labor, State (i.e., foreign affairs), Transportation, Treasury (i.e., finance), and Veterans' Affairs.

Presidents find the cabinet difficult to manage because it reflects competing interests—employers (Commerce) and employees (Labor), rural residents (Agriculture) and urban residents (HUD), diplomats (State) and soldiers (Defense). All the departments have an incentive to expand their budgets and thus increase their clout, except Treasury, whose interests lie in fiscal moderation. Their organizational imperialism, or desire for autonomy, brings the departments into conflict with each other and with the president himself.

The departments themselves are far from monolithic. Within each are subunits known as bureaus that are the real seat of power in the executive branch. These bureau-level units have a variety of designations besides bureau; they also may be called a service, an agency, or other names. Examples in the Department of Agriculture include the Forest Service, the Soil Conservation Service, the Food Safety and Inspection Service, the Agricultural Marketing Service, the Agricultural Research Service, and the Commodity Credit Corporation. The collective, often pejorative, label for the departments and their bureaus is the *bureaucracy*. The president is nominally in charge of these units, but his ability to make them carry out new policies is surprisingly limited.

Civil Service.   The president of the United States is a powerful office, one that has become more powerful since the 1930s. President Franklin Roosevelt started a practice of strong, often unilateral action on economic policy matters that his successors have followed. Still, the president is far from omnipotent in the economic realm. How can the bureaucracy frustrate the president's will?

Part of the explanation is that the top officials the president appoints to the executive departments usually lack prior experience in that unit, and rarely remain in office for more than a few years. Before civil service reform, in the days of the "spoils system," presidents could make patronage appointments deep into the executive branch. To the extent their loyalty was unquestioned, politically appointed officials could be counted on to carry out the president's program. Today, however, the president's appointees number only 1,350. Around 650 are cabinet secretaries, assistant secretaries, and other high-level appointments that require Senate confirmation; below them are another 700 political appointees who do not need to be confirmed by the Senate.[14] The president's handpicked deputies are too few and too unseasoned to carry out the president's program without cooperation from the permanent bureaucracy.

Just below the political appointees are 6,200 upper-level career bureaucrats whose experience is vital to the smooth functioning of the departments. Holding key management positions in the federal service, these professionals have a great deal of pull due to their numbers and their expertise.[15] Members of the Senior Executive Service, they sit at the pinnacle of the competitive civil service, meaning they had to pass examinations and meet objective criteria to obtain their post. Protected by the civil service's merit system, they do not owe the president or his appointees personal allegiance. The idea behind the competitive civil service was to take the politics out of policy making and make government a more efficient and scientific enterprise. But a price has been paid in weakened executive power.

Underneath the elite civil servants are another 2.78 million civilian employees, of whom only 350,000 are in Washington, D.C., reflecting Americans' like for decentralized government and their dislike of concentrated power.[16] Most of these employees handle routine matters and do not have much of a role in choosing public policy. Still, they can affect how policy is implemented. Completely controlling this sprawling empire is a hopeless challenge for every president.

While the U.S. federal bureaucracy is influential, its influence lies more in preventing changes in policy than in starting them. At the top, bureaucracies in other advanced industrial countries usually have a larger *creative* role (see Box 9–2). High-level foreign bureaucrats' greater positive power is due in part to the state's prestige and its consequent ability to recruit the "best and the brightest" to public service. The American higher civil service, object of historical misgivings, carries lower status compared to the equivalent posts in countries such as France or Japan. It does not attract as talented individuals or win the same deference from other participants in policy making.

Also, the U.S. executive's 1,350 political appointments cut deeper into the organs of government than is true elsewhere. Most other developed countries do not permit the executive to make nearly as many appointments. The need in the United States to recruit appointees is one reason for the extended transition period (November until January) between the president's election and the inauguration. Parliamentary systems turn over authority much more promptly, and such quick turnaround is only possible because few executive positions change hands. In Britain, for instance, just the new cabinet ministers are appointed to their office. The next immediate tier, the permanent secretaries in the ministries, are professional civil servants who serve the government whichever party controls it. Thus, the bureaucracy in most parliamentary systems probably has a more important advisory function than in the United States.

The main point to remember is that intradepartment and interdepartment

---
Box 9–2

Civil Service "Mandarins" Have a Powerful Influence over Business in Many Countries

The bureaucracies in many countries play a more direct role in economic management than is true in the United States. France, for instance, has long practiced *dirigisme* (state planning). It recruits the best students from two elite schools, the Ecole Nationale d'Administration and the Polytechnique, to serve in top government posts. They work closely with business to plan investment strategies. *Dirigisme* seemed to pay off in the 1950s and 1960s, when France's economy took off. The country's economic troubles in the 1990s (high unemployment and slow economic growth) have called the system into question in recent years, however.

An even better example of bureaucratic policy making is Japan. Two organizations are particularly important—the Ministry of International Trade and Investment (MITI) and the Ministry of Finance. Both these organizations cream off the nation's best university graduates and have enormous prestige and expertise.

MITI traces its origins to the Meiji Restoration (1868), when Japan first began its planned effort to industrialize. After World War II, MITI emerged as the government sponsor of high-speed economic growth. Practicing what was known as "administrative guidance," MITI's task was to guard and nourish Japanese industries until they could survive in any market in the world. For example, in the 1950s, MITI could forbid the import of foreign goods and force domestic firms into cartels. It used these powers to rationalize local industry. Most analysts give MITI much of the credit for Japan's commercial rebirth in the postwar period, though some dissenters think its contribution is exaggerated.

Japan's Ministry of Finance is less well-known than MITI, but it is perhaps even more powerful. It uses its financial clout and expertise to steer private and public capital into chosen areas and away from investments that are deemed low priority, often with an eye to promoting national competitiveness.

The ability of these agencies to control Japan's economic destiny has eroded in recent years. Japan's companies are big enough so that they no longer need MITI's protection as much and they can defy the Ministry of Finance. Pressure from trading partners like the United States also has weakened the policy tools available to the bureaucrats (see Chapter 16). So the old image of "Japan, Inc." is no longer valid.[1] Still, Japanese businesspeople and government bureaucrats cooperate more than is generally true in the United States.

---

[1]Kent E. Calder, *Strategic Capitalism* (Princeton, NJ: Princeton University Press, 1993).

---

rivalry in Washington means the executive branch of the U.S. government is not the unified pyramid often pictured. Sometimes the parts of the pyramid fit together, sometimes they pull apart. The president at the top is not in full control on many policy issues; he needs the cooperation of the bureaucracy around him and has to make accommodations to get that support. Internal debates within the executive may lead to impasse and can even cause important policies to be shelved. The same thing happens in most state capitals between the governor and the state legislature. Such fragmentation is nothing new, though the public is more aware of it due to media coverage.

Independent Regulatory Commissions

Several federal agencies with the most profound effect on American business have been set up outside the major cabinet departments. Today, there are about 60 autonomous federal agencies, comparable in size and power to department bureaus. Some, like the Environmental Protection Agency, report directly to the president, bypassing the cabinet secretaries.

Twenty agencies, however, do not report to the president. These, the **independent regulatory commissions,** include the Interstate Commerce Commission, the Federal Trade Commission, the Securities and Exchange Commission, the National Labor Relations Board, and the Federal Reserve System. Such commissions carry out much of the U.S. government's regulatory policies that require companies to keep their conduct within allowable bounds. Congress explicitly removed the independent regulatory commissions from presidential control. They thus occupy a peculiar place in the government due to the lack of continuing supervision by any of the formal branches of government. A list of the major independent commissions is in Table 9–3.

The independent regulatory commissions have so much authority they have been called a "headless fourth branch of government" beside the executive, the legislature, and the judiciary.[17] In principle, Congress has regulatory authority: only it can make the rules governing a sector of the economy or a type of commercial activity. Since such matters are highly technical, lawmakers have delegated much of their regulatory authority to bureaucratic experts in the regulatory commissions.

Rules made by the regulatory commissions have the force and effect of an act of Congress. Because these agencies wield tremendous influence over the economy, and because their rules are a form of legislation, Congress was reluctant to turn them over to the executive branch as ordinary agencies under the president.[18] Instead, Congress made them independent.

TABLE 9–3   **There Are Many Independent Establishments and Government Corporations in the U.S. Federal Government that Affect American Business in One Way or Another.**

Commission on Civil Rights	Federal Trade Commission
Commodity Futures Trading Commission	Interstate Commerce Commission
Consumer Product Safety Commission	National Labor Relations Board
Environmental Protection Agency	National Mediation Board
Equal Employment Opportunity Commission	National Transportation Safety Board
Federal Communications Commission	Nuclear Regulatory Commission
Federal Election Commission	Occupational Safety and Health Review
Federal Maritime Commission	Commission
Federal Mediation and Conciliation Service	Securities and Exchange Commission
Federal Reserve System	

Another reason for putting some regulatory agencies outside the normal channels is to break ties with interest groups. Congress, for example, considered creating the Consumer Product Safety Commission within the Commerce Department, but decided that would expose the CPSC to too much pressure from business interests. To free the CPSC, it was made an independent agency. Such arrangements have not truly allowed the independent regulatory commissions to keep interest groups at arm's length as intended.

The independent regulatory commissions are designed to have plenty of administrative discretion. They usually have broad, vague mandates. The Federal Communications Commission, for instance, is charged with regulating U.S. wireless communications for the "public interest, convenience, and necessity."[19]

To assure their independence, the regulatory commissions are headed by odd numbers of commissioners. The commissioners' terms of office do not match the president's, and they report directly to Congress. Naturally, these arrangements create tension with the White House and can lead to problems of policy coordination. When Bill Clinton took over the presidency in 1993, for instance, he had to court Chairman of the Federal Reserve Alan Greenspan, who had been nominated a year earlier by President Bush. In his position as head of the nation's central bank, Greenspan had the potential to undo many of Clinton's economic policies. Yet, Greenspan's term would not expire for another three years. The president went to great lengths to get Greenspan on board, even seating him in the front row next to Hillary Clinton during his first State of the Union Address. (See Box 9–3 on the Federal Reserve System.)

The separation of powers no longer applies to the independent regulatory commissions as individual units. As we will see in greater detail in Chapter 10, the typical agency exercises legislative, executive, and judicial authority. This amassing of power by unelected officials is the reason for the charge that the agencies are a fourth branch of government. The structure of the independent administrative system has been accused of being unconstitutional, but the courts have not upheld this point of view. Still, the independent agencies have plainly gained a degree of influence over the economy that the framers of the Constitution did not foresee.

Other countries do not use independent agencies to the same degree. They are more likely to regulate business through the regular government ministries, or through interministry commissions. As a consequence, regulations are apt to be less rigid overseas.[20]

Other Types of Regulatory Agencies.   To make the organization of the U.S. federal government more confusing, not all regulatory bodies are independent; there are additional agencies lodged in the regular cabinet structure that also direct regulatory policy. Examples include the Antitrust Division (Justice), the Bureau of Alcohol, Tobacco, and Firearms (Treasury), the Food and Drug Administration (Health and Human Services), the Office of Federal Contract Compliance (Labor), and the Mine Safety and Health Administration (Labor). It is important for business leaders to understand where in the government each

Box 9–3

The Fed

The Federal Reserve System, known colloquially as the Fed, is the central bank of the United States. Created in 1913, the Fed is among the public agencies with the greatest power to affect business. Yet it is a secretive and politically unaccountable organization.

The Fed is responsible for the nation's **monetary policy** by its influence on the amount of credit available and currency in circulation. The Fed also is a lender of last resort to the nation's banks and establishes banking policies. It is run by a seven-member board of governors, appointed by the president and confirmed by the Senate. The governors conduct 12 regional banks. The regional grouping was created to allay fears of a central bank that might become captive to the financial interests of its location.

The Fed's activities are critical to business, because they directly affect price inflation, interest rates, and, indirectly, the level of economic activity. Loose money policies are used to fight recession by making money and credit more available; tight money policies are used to restrain booms and fight inflation.

There are periodic calls to make the Fed less

autonomous and more accountable. In 1993, to placate critics in Congress, Chairman Greenspan offered to make minutes of the Open Market Committee meetings, where monetary policy is decided, available to the public within a month. But most bankers and businesspeople prefer an independent Fed. It is felt that this arrangement bolsters the credibility of anti-inflation policies. Otherwise, the Fed might be tempted to engage in political mischief, say, by turning to easy money before an election.

Not all governments have been willing relinquish control of the money supply to unelected central bankers. The Bank of England, for example, takes its cues from the British cabinet. Yet, the trend is toward central bank independence as a way to guarantee the integrity of monetary policy.[1] Germany's Bundesbank has long been known for being even more independent than the Fed. The Maastricht treaty requires all E.U. members to give their central banks similar full control.

[1]Marjorie Deane and Robert Pringle, *The Central Banks* (New York: Viking, 1995).

---

regulatory agency fits. The department agencies usually have closer ties to industry and are seldom charged with functions hostile to their clientele. As a result, department regulatory agencies issue twice as many rules as independent regulatory commissions.[21] The independent regulatory agencies, by comparison, are apt to be somewhat more antagonistic toward business. Thus, they issue fewer rules due to industry opposition.

There are also state regulatory agencies whose functions overlap with the federal agencies. Many states have stricter rules regarding the environment, safety, and other matters than the U.S. government has. They are not allowed to have less strict rules, but they usually can go beyond federal limits.

Regulatory commissions are not the only type of independent administrative entity important to American business. Another is the government corporation, established mainly to carry out distributive policies to help companies. Examples of government corporations involved in distributive policy are the organizations that insure deposits: the Federal Deposit Insurance Corporation, the Federal Savings and Loan Insurance Corporation, and the National Credit Union Administration. To isolate the government corporations from politics, they are usually headed by boards with bipartisan membership and long terms of office. There are also several independent foundations within the federal government, such as the National Science Foundation and the National Endowment for the Humanities. These are given a separate administrative structure to avoid censorship in activities like research.

How Much Autonomy?   The limitations on the president's capacity to direct the independent agencies are obvious. Congress is supposed to exercise oversight, too, but its capacity is also limited for reasons discussed in the next section. With neither the executive nor the legislative branch fully in charge, allegations of too little accountability haunt the entire system for regulating business. The bureaucracy, it seems, does not have to answer fully to the public for its actions.

The lack of offsetting influence from elected officials has meant that the agencies charged with regulating a single industry—the ICC and trucking, or the FCC and broadcasting, for example—have sometimes been captured by the industry they are supposed to regulate. Instead of working impartially, the agency becomes an advocate for the industry's views. Sometimes, it is the industry itself that sought regulation in the first place to shelter itself from market forces.[22] The newer regulatory bodies, such as the EPA or OSHA, are probably less prone to being captured, since they deal with many industries. It is harder for their diverse constituencies to get organized and agree on common goals.

Three factors have enabled companies to turn some regulatory policies to their advantage. First, agency personnel are often drawn from the regulated industries and return to them—the so-called revolving door. The expertise of professional lobbyists makes them logical candidates for agency appointments and vice versa. Second, the regulatory agency has to rely on the regulated industries for information about whether the industry is complying with rules. Third, regulated industries provide most expert witnesses at agency hearings where new regulations are formulated.[23] To the extent they share interests, regulators and companies may agree more than they disagree. Again, this observation is less true for environmental regulation, safety regulation, and other regulations that cut across industries.

The Congressional Connection

According to the separation of powers, the legislative branch is supposed to be the watchdog to stop relations between regulators and businesspeople from becoming too snug. Congress has several tools to help it assure the departments, bureaus, and commissions administer public policy fairly and in the national interest. These tools include committee investigations of agency actions, hearings, and the passage of legislation delimiting tasks and responsibilities. The

General Accounting Office performs between 50 and 100 audits a month for Congress. Congress's most important lever is its authority to provide the money to support every agency's programs and personnel. It also can rewrite the basic law of the agency. In recent years, the Congress has abolished the Civil Aeronautics Board, the Law Enforcement Assistance Administration, and the Community Services Administration—but these were exceptional events. Rarely are government programs eliminated due to the vested interests they create.

To avoid fights with Congress, independent and ordinary agencies alike engage in what is called legislative liaison. The focus is on the committees and subcommittees most important to the agency's mission. Liaison activities include drafting bills, preparing reports, and doing research to support legislative proposals. Much of this work is planned to maximize congressional support for the agency.

Most of us do not follow regulatory policy closely, making these policies politically irrelevant to the majority and leaving the field open to the concerned interest group. Individual senators and representatives seldom establish their reputations by policing federal agencies, as opposed to passing new legislation. The issues are too obscure or uninteresting to voters. Further, members of Congress lack the motivation to get into an adversarial position with an agency. A member who expects his constituents to benefit from an agency does not want to jeopardize those benefits.[24] Even if Congress did have an interest in overseeing the activity of the agencies to which it has delegated regulatory authority, it is cramped by staff shortages. Thus, Congress is apt to avoid probing the particulars of bureaucratic decisions, and the agencies can evade scrutiny. The result is that most regulatory agencies do get to run with autonomy most of the time.

Exceptions exist, of course. The National Highway Traffic Safety Administration sets safety standards for motor vehicles. But in 1974, responding to vast complaints from drivers, Congress decided the safety standards could not include a seatbelt/interlock system. Similarly, in the early 1980s, Congress vigorously investigated the EPA with great public fanfare. Following leaks about lax environmental regulation, dozens of hearings were held into the administration of Ann Gorsuch (formerly Buford). Revelations led to the appointment of a new administrator for the EPA and a shift toward tougher environmental policy. Events like the interlock controversy or the Buford scandal are rare; more often Congress does not make control of the bureaucracy a high priority.

The Judiciary

The last major branch of the American government is the courts. Their purpose in the political system is to settle controversies by applying established rules. Cases can arise from disputes between individuals (including corporate "persons"), from efforts by the government to punish wrongdoing, or from efforts by citizens to change public policy. The judiciary branch is often the last resort of interest groups trying to get a public policy voided.

Civil and Criminal Cases.   A dual structure of courts—federal and state— operates in the United States. Most litigation involving businesses are civil cases and do not entail violations of criminal statutes. A **civil law** case is usually a dispute between two private parties, one of whom claims to have suffered some harm from the other. An example is General Motors' suit (quickly settled out of court) in 1993 against NBC for a televised exposé it ran on the alleged danger of GM pickup trucks. NBC used an incendiary device while filming a crash test, causing the truck to explode in flames before the cameras; GM demanded, and received, an apology and compensation for having aired this misleading story. The government also can bring civil suits, and is doing so increasingly. Civil suits always involve monetary awards and damages for the plaintiffs who bring the charges, not fines or jail time for the defendant.

Companies regularly engage in civil litigation. According to a study that looked just at federal courts, Fortune 1000 companies were involved as plaintiffs or defendants in nearly 460,000 civil suits from 1971 to 1991. About half the cases appear to be contract disputes—business disagreements among individuals and corporations.[25] Such suits can be an important weapon for competition.

Intel Corp. and its rival Advanced Micro Devices, Inc., illustrate just how important. For seven years starting in the late 1980s, the companies sued and countersued over production of various microprocessors—developed by Intel and cloned by AMD. Intel claimed AMD's chips breached earlier agreements between the companies; AMD denied the charge. Different courts ruled for one company, then the other. With each ruling, the share prices of Intel and AMD seesawed. Investors recognized that the fortunes of each company turned on the courts' decisions, which determined to what extent Intel had the sole right to manufacture a pervasive technological commodity. The two companies did not call a truce until 1995.

Criminal law cases are different. They involve infractions of the penal code—the body of law that declares what conduct is criminal and provides punishment to protect society from harm. Government lawyers, not attorneys hired by an aggrieved private party, always bring criminal cases to court. Criminal cases usually focus on individuals, but companies can be held liable for criminal acts. Penalties include fines and, for individuals, imprisonment.

Most illegal acts involving businesspeople are white-collar crimes such as embezzlement, fraud, or insider trading. Among the more notorious recent cases is that of Michael Milken, the "junk bond" king, who pled guilty to six felony counts of securities and tax fraud in 1990. He agreed to a fine of $600 million and was sentenced to 10 years in prison. Milken's employer, the investment banking firm Drexel Burnham Lambert, also agreed to plead guilty in 1988 to violations of federal securities laws and to pay a fine of $650 million. A year later, Drexel filed for bankruptcy.

Corporate law-breaking is not uncommon. One study tracked the 70 largest U.S. corporations over a 45-year period. During that time, the corporations were involved in many suits. They lost 158 criminal cases and 296 civil cases and had 526 other adverse settlements. Every company had at least one decision against it; one had 50 negative decisions.[26] At present, 20 to 30 percent of offenses prosecuted by the federal government involve violations of antitrust law (see Chapter 15). Environmental prosecutions (see Chapter 14) account for 10 to 15 percent, and another 10 to 15 percent are private fraud cases. Currency violations, tax fraud, import and export violations, and food and drug violations make up the rest.[27]

Civil and criminal cases can be heard in both sets of courts, the federal and the state. Each has several tiers. In the state system, serious cases involving business usually enter through a general jurisdiction trial court. There also are specialized state courts, such as the small claims courts that handle minor civil disputes.

Above the court of original jurisdiction are courts of appeal and a state supreme court. These appellate courts can reverse or uphold decisions made at lower levels. Defendants who lose a case can ask for a review. Cases get winnowed out at each level, however, as litigants run out of resources or because the higher court refuses to get involved in a case.

The federal judiciary mirrors the pattern of the state systems. At the bottom are specialized federal courts of particular importance to many businesses (Tax Court, the Court of International Trade, and the Claims Court, for example), but the bulk of cases enter through the federal district courts. At the intermediate level are the Circuit Courts of Appeal. The U.S. Supreme Court is the highest court in the federal system and the nation. Under the Constitution, the Supreme Court has the power to decide which system, state or federal, has jurisdiction of a case and can decide whether state actions violate the superior federal law. The Supreme Court also exercises what is known as judicial review, by which it can revoke any public policy it determines conflicts with the Constitution.

Types of Laws.   Many cases at the state or local level arise under the Anglo-Saxon tradition of **common law.** (At the federal level and in Louisiana, there is no common law.) Common law lacks basis in legislation; it is determined by judges who apply to new cases the precedent set by previous judges' decisions. Because of its evolutionary character, common law is diverse and sometimes contradictory. Different judges can set conflicting precedents at various times in assorted jurisdictions. Common law is particularly important in the area of torts (civil wrongs or injuries) and contracts.

Many non–English-speaking countries instead follow the principles of Roman law, as codified in Napoleon's Code Civil (1804) and later modified. Roman law is particularly important in the laws that govern business transactions. In Europe, there is a separate system of courts to handle commercial laws. England, and later the United States, adopted the commercial aspects of Roman law in the 17th century and incorporated it into the common law tradition. The United States does not maintain a separate system of commercial courts, however.

The opposite of common or judge-made law in the United States is **statutory law.** Cases in this domain are governed by bills that legislatures have approved, often to clarify or modify the common law. Of special note for American business is the Uniform Commercial Code, which standardizes the hodge-podge of judge-made and legislature-made laws for commerce. All states except Louisiana have adopted the entire UCC, which facilitates the flow of trade through the nation.

The courts' main role in statutory cases is to interpret existing statutes and apply them to the case at hand. Because legislatures rarely draw statutes with enough precision to avoid ambiguity, once again the courts have leeway to make public policy themselves. Legislative enactments are not free of constraints. Federal laws must be in harmony with the U.S. Constitution, and state laws have to be consistent with both federal law and the state and national constitutions. The courts have an important role in determining whether legislatures have overstepped these boundaries.

The courts never act on their own; someone must bring a case to them. Americans are far more likely than other nationalities to settle disputes over such matters as product liability in the courts (see Chapter 13). Interest groups often use the opportunity of a legal case to advance their larger cause. Generally, they approach the judiciary by starting lawsuits that probe an issue that affects them, and then arguing these test cases in formal courtroom procedure. Besides bringing test cases before the courts, interest groups may appear as *amici curiae* (friends of the court) and offer arguments on appropriate cases in which they are not parties. Given the appeals structure, and the parallel state and federal systems of courts, interest groups can pursue a test case for years. Even if they do not win in the end, they may have temporary victories that delay the implementation of an undesired policy.

Environmental law groups have been particularly successful in using the courts. During the 1970s, approximately 1,000 suits were filed against federal agencies for violations of the National Environmental Policy Act. These suits helped prevent several large projects, such as Walt Disney Company's plan to develop a ski resort at Mineral King Valley, though more often the outcome was to hold up or modify projects that won eventual approval. Environmentalists had even greater success with lawsuits filed under the Clean Air Act.[28]

Political Parties

The last pivotal set of political institutions lacks foundation in the U.S. Constitution: the political parties. In his farewell address, delivered in 1797, President George Washington warned the nation against the "baneful effects" of political parties. These are private associations of citizens who come together to win political power. They recruit and support candidates for office under a common label with the expectation that these candidates, if elected, will champion the party's goals. While anyone is free to start a party, two such associations monopolize political competition in the United States—the Democrats, formed in the 1820s, and the Republicans, organized in the 1850s.

The two major political parties are well entrenched. They organize Congress, with each party having a quota on the committees according to the total number of seats it holds. The majority party gets to chair all the committees. Only one member of Congress, a representative from Vermont, is currently sitting who belongs to neither party bloc. The president uses party mechanisms for choosing candidates for appointment to federal office. Similarly, the two main parties control most state and local governments. In recent years, just Alaska, Connecticut, and Maine elected independent governors. However, none had notable success working with the partisan groups in the state legislature.

Efforts to start third parties, such as Ross Perot's United We Stand America movement, have never cracked the Democrat and Republican grip on power. This is partly the result of the single-member district, first-past-the-post system of balloting. In most states, for most offices, the candidate with the largest number of votes wins, even if the combined total of the opposition candidates is greater. Unlike the system of proportional representation, which many parliamentary systems use, the U.S. method gives no seats to second- or third-place winners. These rules encourage the creation of broad, moderate political parties.

Ideological vs. Catch-All Parties. Parliamentary systems are apt instead to develop more narrow, ideologically pure parties than exist in the United States. France has five major political groupings, ranging from the Communist Party on the left to the neo-fascist National Front on the right. These parties often do not win enough seats to control parliament and form a government alone. Germany has long been governed by Socialists and Christian Democrats with the small Free Democrats as a junior partner. Japan is an exception. One party, the mainstream Liberal Democrats, held office from World War II until 1993, when it was briefly replaced by a coalition government.

Potentially, catch-all parties can compensate for the fragmenting and stand-off built into the U.S. political system. As organizations that cut across electoral districts, they have the possibility to build coalitions out of diverse interests in the country. The Republicans, for instance, have won most presidential elections since 1968 by appealing to upper-income groups wanting *less* government involvement in the economy and to middle-income groups advocating *more* government involvement in social issues such as abortion and gay rights. Democrats chipped away at that coalition in the 1992 campaign, picking up support among professional women, for instance, while holding on to such traditional backers as urban blue-collar workers. To the extent the parties stand for a program, they can be held accountable by the voters for the results.

Unfortunately, the U.S. parties do not fulfill the promise of mobilizing public opinion for concerted action. Compared to parties in many countries, the Democrats' and Republicans' grassroots organizations and their national leadership are weak. So as not to offend potential supporters, neither party likes to advocate strong official positions on many issues. They are umbrella organizations that try to be all things to all people. Even when the national parties do take a stand, it does not mean much; the professional politicians who run for office under the party banners are individual entrepreneurs. They raise most funds themselves, and they do not feel themselves bound to support official party positions.

It is true that Republicans tend to be to the right (more suspicious of government intervention) and Democrats to the left (more skeptical about the market's efficiency) on economic issues. The Republicans have sharpened the ideological contrasts in recent elections, while the Democrats have tried to blur it. Many conservative true-believers were elected to the House and Senate in the 1994 elections.

But as catch-all groups, both parties attract candidates from across the political spectrum. William Weld, the successful 1990 Republican nominee for governor of Massachusetts, was widely seen as more liberal than his Democrat rival, John Silber (at least on so-called social issues). American voters accordingly feel free to split their tickets and vote for the "best" candidate despite party affiliation.

Whatever their public stance as conservatives or liberals, most elected officials are more pragmatic than doctrinaire on the bulk of pocketbook issues that come before them. Interest groups know this fact and are willing to work with officials of any political stripe. Political philosophy does not usually stand in the way, resulting in surprising alliances. Charles Keating, for instance, got senators from both sides of the aisle to intercede for him with bank regulators. Four Democrats and a Republican helped Keating, who was later convicted of swindling depositors and investors out of $2.5 billion.

The same trend is seen in other industrial democracies. Labels like "social democrat" and "Christian democrat" do not mean what they once did. Whatever they call themselves, all parties find themselves pulled to the center on economic policies, with little room to maneuver, whenever they take office. It is not the "end of ideology" sometimes identified, for there are nuances among parties. But implacable international pressure and domestic financial constraints have tended to homogenize public policies.[29]

Criticisms of the Two-Party System.   Few Americans are happy with their party system. As long ago as 1950, a committee of the American Political Science Association published a document calling for making the U.S. political parties more disciplined and programmatic.[30] In criticizing the Democrats and Republicans, the authors listed many deficiencies: the parties did not offer citizens distinct choices, they were not united on basic principles, they did not carry through their programs. These criticisms apply just as well today. Rather than stress issues, critics complain the parties have turned to the politics of scandal, character assassination, and empty imagery. The Perot movement in 1992 was driven by people's perception that, compared to the conventional party politicians, the Texan was not afraid to speak the truth, ignored the advice of pollsters and professional handlers, and was going to "lift up the hood" and really fix things. (Whether that perception was accurate is another question.)

On the other side of the ledger, the existing party setup has advantages. Because U.S. parties are not radically different or grounded in ideological principles, they encourage compromise and conciliation. This helps to create a stable, predictable policy environment. While many business leaders are too close to the public policy process to recognize the fact, government actions affecting business do not lurch back and forth as much as they might in a more polarized party system.

The difficulty is that too often the bargain struck is to push serious problems under the rug, only postponing the eventual day of reckoning. A disturbing example is the savings and loan crisis of the 1980s. During the 1988 election campaign, the Republicans and the Democrats made a tacit agreement to hide the scope of the crisis from the public. Both parties shared blame for the S&L crisis, and neither wanted a detailed airing of their actions toward the thrift industry while they maneuvered for advantage in the election. Meanwhile the crisis deepened. When officials got around to devising an effective rescue plan for the S&Ls, after the election, the cost had risen by tens of billions of dollars.

Conclusion

The task of this chapter has been to explain the structure of the U.S. government, particularly the places where it intersects with business interests and other interest groups. There are multiple access points to the system, and many points at which a policy proposal can be stopped. Most of these veto points are constitutionally established in the system of checks and balances among the various units of government.

Congress has a highly decentralized and fragmented decision-making structure. Most of the legislative work is performed by specialized committees and subcommittees—increasingly by their staff acting as surrogates for elected members. Frequently, legislators of a certain region or representing a specific constituency dominate a particular committee, and like-minded members may wind up supporting consistent policies. Interest groups try to develop close relations with the committees and staff. The outcome is that Congress is apt to serve many small constituencies, such as particular industrial trade associations, and finds it hard to adopt a larger view. Congress often gets deadlocked over issues.

Similarly, the executive branch is splintered into competing bureaucratic units, including many that are formally independent of presiden-

tial control. The important agencies for business have the power to make regulations that have the effect of law. Finally, the judicial branch often speaks its own mind, with judges also having the ability to make laws that affect business decisions.

This structure shows several tendencies. One is a bias toward incremental decisions—new policies usually do not differ much from previous ones. Another is a preference for vague decisions by elected officials, with the real task of policy making falling on the bureaucracy, and sometimes the courts, for interpretation. A third result is that many issues get hidden, and decisions about them are made without much public scrutiny. Last, the structure sometimes seizes up and takes no decisions at all—in effect, a decision to preserve the status quo.

The structural characteristics of the government are justifiably criticized. Yet, there are virtues for business in so byzantine a structure, especially when alternatives are considered. A more streamlined system might make fewer errors of omission, but perhaps make more errors of commission. In Chapter 10, we will see what business and other interest groups do to make the policy process respond to their needs.

Questions

1. How is Congress set up? What ought the savvy businessperson know about its structure?

2. What is the function of the president in policy making? How much control does he have?

3. Discuss regulatory commissions. What are the two main types? How do they differ?

4. What are policy-making systems? Who belongs to them? Why are they important for business?

5. Describe the U.S. judiciary. What types of law are there? How do companies use the legal system for competitive advantage?

End Notes

1. Lloyd N. Cutler, "To Form a Government," *Foreign Affairs* 59, no. 1 (Fall 1980), p. 127.

2. A. Lee Fritschler and Bernard H. Ross, *Business Regulation and Government Decision-Making* (Boston: Little, Brown, 1980), p. 74.

3. Alexander Hamilton, James Madison, and John Jay, *The Federalist,* no. 47, ed. Max Beloff, 2nd ed. (1787–88); (reprint, Oxford: Basil Blackwell, 1987).

4. Ibid., no. 51.

5. Arnold J. Heidenheimer, Hugh Heclo, and Carolyn T. Adams, *Comparative Public Policy,* 3rd ed. (New York: St. Martin's, 1990).

6. Paul Kennedy, "Fin-de-Siècle America," *New York Review of Books,* June 28, 1990, p. 40.

7. See "Government in California," *The Economist,* February 13, 1993, pp. 21–23.

8. See James Q. Wilson, "Political Parties and the Separation of Powers," in *Separation of Powers—Does It Still Work?,* ed. Robert A. Goldwin and Art Kaufman (Washington, DC: American Enterprise Institute, 1986), pp. 18–37. Also see the readings in James H. Thurber, ed., *Divided Democracy* (Washington, DC: Congressional Quarterly Press, 1991).

9. See, for example, George C. Lodge, *Comparative Business–Government Relations* (Englewood Cliffs, NJ: Prentice Hall, 1990).

10. Fritschler and Ross, *Business Regulation,* p. 78.

11. Commission on Administrative Review, cited in Lynne O. Cabot, *The Role of Congress in the U.S. Government Decision-Making Process* (Boston: Harvard Business School, 1981), pp. 17–18.

12. Hedrick Smith, *The Power Game* (New York: Random House, 1988).

13. Michael Kranish, "Clinton to Reduce White House Staff," *Boston Globe,* February 10, 1993, p. 3.

14. A. Lee Fritschler and Bernard H. Ross, *How Washington Works* (Cambridge, MA: Ballinger, 1987), p. 60.

15. Hugh Heclo, "In Search of a Role: America's Higher Civil Service," in *Bureaucrats and Policy Making,* ed. Ezra Suleiman (New York: Holmes and Meier, 1984), p. 14.

16. Kenneth J. Meier, *Politics and the Bureaucracy,* 2nd ed. (Monterey, CA: Brooks/Cole, 1987), p. 30.

17. The phrase was coined in the famous Brownlow committee report: *Administrative Management in the Government of the United States* (Washington, DC: U.S. Government Printing Office, 1937).

18. Theodore J. Lowi and Benjamin Ginsberg, *American Government: Freedom and Power,* 2nd ed. (New York: Norton, 1992), p. 338.

19. See Theodore Lowi, *The End of Liberalism,* 2nd ed. (New York: Norton, 1979).

20. Giandomenico Majone, *Deregulation or Reregulation? Regulatory Reform in Europe and the United States* (New York: St. Martin's, 1990).

21. Meier, *Politics and the Bureaucracy,* p. 84.

22. This is the thesis forwarded by the University of Chicago Nobel-laureate, George Stigler. See "The Theory of Economic Regulation," *Bell Journal of Economics* 2, no. 1 (1971), pp. 3–21. Most commentators think Stigler overstates the case. Political scientists had earlier made similar observations about how independent agencies get captured by interest groups. See, for example,

Grant McConnell, *Private Power and American Democracy* (New York: Vintage, 1966).

23. Lowi and Ginsberg, *American Government,* p. 339.

24. Meier, *Politics and the Bureaucracy,* pp. 148–49.

25. Mike Geyelin, "Suits by Firms Exceed Those by Individuals," *The Wall Street Journal,* December 3, 1993, p. B1.

26. Edwin Sutherland, "White Collar Crime," in *Corporate and Governmental Deviance,* 4th ed., ed. M. David Ermann and Richard J. Lundman (New York: Oxford University Press, 1992), pp. 51–73.

27. John M. Holcomb and S. Prakash Sethi, "Corporate and Executive Criminal Liability," *Business and the Contemporary World* 4, no. 3 (1993), p. 84.

28. David Vogel, *Fluctuating Fortunes* (New York: Basic Books, 1989), p. 110.

29. The phrase was coined by the sociologist Daniel Bell, *The End of Ideology,* with a new afterward (Cambridge, MS: Harvard University Press, 1988).

30. Committee on Political Parties, "Toward a More Responsible Two-Party System," *American Political Science Review* Supplement, September 1950.

10   COLLECTIVE DECISIONS
Muddling Through

Issues are like snakes—they just refuse to die. They keep coming back, time after time.

Howard Baker[1]

There is no mystery in the public policy-making process. It is complex and convoluted but not hard to grasp once one knows the basics about it. In most policy areas, few interests are engaged. These policy areas are characterized by continuity of the groups involved (both inside and outside the formal government), and often of the policy outcomes. The relationship between private interests and government does vary among the policy areas, a fact likely to be missed unless one looks at each case closely.

While Chapter 9 concentrated on the structure of government institutions, on *where* policy is made, in Chapter 10, we look at the mechanics of government, *how* policy is made. We begin with the tortured route a bill follows on the way to enactment as a federal law, centering on the way business interests make their wishes known. The procedures are those of the federal legislature, but analogous procedures are followed in most states. Next, we turn to the rule-making process within agencies, which parallels the normal legislative process. Finally, we generalize about how different kinds of policies tend to give rise to different kinds of political relations.

Decision-Making Systems

The U.S. government is a vast apparatus, but the key players are not many in a nation of 250 million. As we saw in Chapter 9, they include several thousand lobbyists, elected officials, political appointees, congressional staff, and managers in the civil service. Even this relative handful of people do not make most public policy; that responsibility falls on smaller subsets of players. We call these policy-making systems or policy networks: small, stable groups of people who control the operating decisions of specific government agencies for specific programs. They are the meaningful interface between business and government.

Impossible to define rigorously, there may be 800 to 1,000 policy systems in Washington. Each revolves around a core of only 30 to 50 people, depending on the policy area. These systems are formed to make focused demands and influence particular programs. Their power is narrow yet deep in the given policy domain. The effective business executive learns to discriminate between broad, often immaterial, policy discussions and the concrete activities taking place within the circle of people concerned with a program area.[2] While dealing with the government is an impossible task, working with a policy-based decision system is manageable.

Sometimes these decision-making systems are so strong and resistant to outside pressure that they are called **iron triangles.** An iron triangle is a three-way alliance among a set of interest groups, a portion of the federal bureaucracy, and a congressional committee. The three sides of the triangle reinforce one another with mutual, protective influence. (See Figure 10–1.) An example is the mili-

FIGURE 10–1

Iron triangles are stable, powerful decision-making systems in Washington

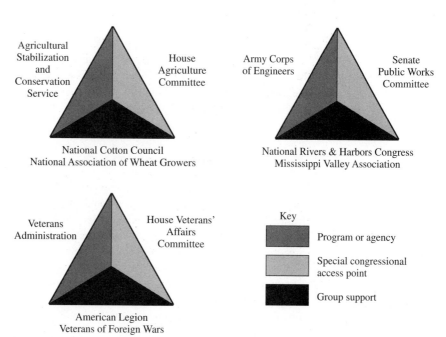

Source: Adapted from U.S. Congress, House of Representatives, *Report of the Subcommittee for Special Investigations of the Committee on Armed Services,* 86th Congress, 1st session (Washington, DC: U.S. Government Printing Office, 1960), p. 7.

tary industry, the Defense Department, and the House and Senate defense committees. The iron triangles in Washington have been broadly successful in shielding their program areas against drastic change.

Comparable policy networks of politicians, bureaucrats, and interest groups exist in other democracies, too. Great Britain's political system, for example, is becoming more fractured. There are many divisions in government and a growing number of pressure groups. Policy making takes place within a variety of networks marked by close relations among particular interests and different sections of government.[3]

An Overview of How Policy Systems Work

Businesspeople are inclined to complain about government's "irrational" decisions—decisions that run counter to their economic interest. Why do we seem collectively to muddle through with half-baked, inconsistent plans and programs? The conventional explanation is to blame politics for tainting the public policy process, but this explanation is tautological. It begs the question of why political processes do not yield more suitable policies than they do.

Political economists have a better answer: Government is not a unitary decision maker, and policy makers do not base decisions on a lucid, thorough review of alternatives. As Adam Smith pointed out long ago, it is unrealistic to expect of a legislature "that its deliberations could always be directed, not by the clamorous importunity of partial interests, but by an extensive view of the general good."[4] The same is true of government's other branches. No large formal organization is monolithic. Although, when they are seen from afar, governments sometimes appear to be homogeneous entities, the people who know them well usually perceive a different reality. Looked at up close, every government is revealed as a patchwork of subunits, each with its own interests and perspectives.

Simplistic versus Realistic Explanations for Public Policy

For convenience, economic and administrative theories often rely on the fiction that organizations are unitary and unified, that they are completely controlled from above, that their various offices move in lock step. It is easy to speak of decisions and actions taken by an administration, a ministry, a bureau, or a public corporation. Such shorthand is usually misleading. Because of their hodgepodge makeup, no government organization ever behaves as purposefully as the simplistic, unitary model implies. Muddling through is the norm.[5]

Standing in sharp distinction to conventional policy analysis, political economy teaches us to concentrate not on the whole of government but on its parts.[6] As we learned in Chapter 9, the formal decision system of the United States is intentionally fragmented. Informal policy-making systems have evolved to bridge the gaps required by the Constitution. Most of the participants in these policy-making systems are not elected: they are lobbyists, professional staff, and full-time bureaucrats. Outcomes are driven by the interests of participants, who, either individually or united into subunits, are striving to fulfill their personal and group ambitions. The policy-making systems are not the passive instruments of voters and taxpayers but are composed of active agents who engage in the tactical use of power to retain or obtain control of resources, whether real or symbolic.

Given these facts, the government can hardly practice textbook-style analysis of options before it takes action. Policy makers' mobility and survival are rarely a solitary venture. They must negotiate, bargain, and form coalitions. Even within the public bureaucracy, interest groups emerge. They may coalesce around a professional connection, a common workplace, old school ties, or any other consideration. These small combinations of people are the actual substance of government, especially in the United States. As surely as day follows night, they come into conflict with one another, and also with the goals espoused by the nominal leadership. In striving to enhance their members' position, interest groups within the bureaucracy often end up undermining directives coming from the top or creating informal codes of conduct that are not synchronized with the president's avowed mission.

Self-promoting activities like these make sense from each individual's point of view, though they can be counterproductive when aggregated for a branch of government, an executive department, or a government bureau as a whole. Because self-promotion also may overlap with and reinforce competing ideas about where the total organization should be heading, policy making does not have to be completely without altruistic intent, either. The important point is that the needs and desires of individuals and small groups are at least as important for public policy as transcendent values are. Public organizations may present a unified face to the outside world; that face is really a mask that always hides some internal tension and rivalry.

Government's Limited Capabilities. It follows that the government, writ large, makes equivocal decisions based on an imprecise evaluation of the available options. It picks policies partly through competitive gamesmanship and not purely through a comprehensive search for the best solution. We are not being cynical to say that the players are driven by diverse group and personal concerns, instead of just the will of the people or party leaders' objectives. Above all, the decision-making systems that make up government are held together by the fear of what would happen to those responsible for programs should they disintegrate.

Students should note that imperfect decisions need not be impulsive decisions. Outcomes can often be estimated with confidence. Precedent and prior alignments strongly affect the rules of the policy-making game. Change is incremental: last year's budget is the base for this year's, current rules are the stepping stone for new rules.[7] To win, players engage in bargaining and subterfuge, the intention being to maximize their standing. On what an established body finally settles, the collective decision, is neither the selection of a unified group nor the aggregation of leaders' preferences. Rather, it is the result of individuals pulling and pushing to advance their particular conception of social, group, and personal interests. Such outcomes look illogical from the macro level, yet are easy to grasp from the micro level.

Much the same is true of implementation. Political economists expect government not to carry out policies exactly as planned; government's fractured structure and divergent goals prevent such a happy outcome. Unintended consequences abound, for those who are responsible for enacting any program have an incentive to bend it according to their preferences. Bureaucrats can come up with ingenious and subtle strategies to pursue their private purpose, the byproduct of which may be to frustrate their organization's public aims. Even people at the bottom, those with no formal authority, enjoy some latitude to interpret rules and regulations in self-serving ways. If a new directive has potential benefits for him, the average employee will try to capitalize on those benefits; if a directive penalizes him, he will take steps to minimize the cost. The logic of the existing pattern of behavior is never ironclad, but it makes the whole organization difficult to budge. Thus do government's authorized plans frequently go awry.

Such a system of making public policy has advantages. Incremental change is predictable change. The odds of making a big, irreversible mistake are small. As a rule, business and many other interest groups prefer evolutionary adjustments in public policy to sweeping, revolutionary shifts. They also like the stable, small-scale decision systems that are easier to deal with than the larger institutions of government. For decades, the U.S. economy thrived under a regime of small steps and mutual adjustment.

How a Bill Becomes Law

Today's business leaders must understand well the process of policy making. The discussion that follows focuses on Washington, but similar processes exist in the 50 states. Most policies begin formally in the legislature. The main exception is with executive orders—proclamations by the president that are legally binding. Many executive orders are used to establish or change practices of administrative agencies. One of President Reagan's first acts in 1981 was to issue an executive order freeing the price of crude oil. But the Congress is where most federal policies start. Congress can even pass a law overturning an executive order if it so chooses.

Every law begins as a bill. All bills have to be introduced by members of the legislature. When presidents present their programs to Congress they need members to sponsor the legislation. Congress considers many bills but passes only a fraction. In 1991, for instance, members submitted 7,758 bills and resolutions during the session; just 243 bills cleared Congress to become public laws.[8]

Despite formal labels that suggest otherwise, the president is in effect the chief legislator today. Most successful legislation comes from the White House, which gets introduced on the president's behalf in Congress. Thus, many bills are first written by executive branch officials. When Congress begins to act, however, congressional staff members or sometimes interest groups draft alternate legal language.

Businesspeople pay special attention to the president's budget that he delivers to Congress each January. The budget, prepared by the Office of Management and Budget, spells out the activities of government and reconciles expenses and income. Congress can and always does change the budget, but its size and specificity tend to limit the choices. The president thus puts a stamp on spending priorities. Interest groups naturally work unseen to influence the budget proposal.

Not all the original bills are serious proposals. Some are introduced for symbolic reasons, to appease an interest group, or as a trial balloon to generate debate on an issue. Congressmen frequently engage in the "blame game"—maneuvers that have little chance of adoption but that dramatize their side's goodness and the other side's failing.[9] These motives partly explain the high mortality rate of bills. Perhaps more importantly, getting a substantive law enacted simply takes too much work for it to happen often.

As Figure 10–2 shows, passage of a bill is the last stage in a laborious process that starts in a subcommittee and works its way through the House of Representatives and the Senate.

Most bills are introduced simultaneously in the two chambers, though some undergo consecutive consideration, passing through one chamber then being considered in the other. In each chamber, the proposal is given a number, referred to the proper standing committee, and then usually sent on to the specialized subcommittee with jurisdiction over its subject matter. As we have seen, the subcommittee stage decides the fate of most bills. The industry associations to which most companies belong are paid to monitor subcommittees and committees that affect them.

Hearings

Members of the subcommittee choose whether to hold hearings on the bill. Hearings are formal meetings where witnesses, including representatives of affected interest groups, testify for and against the proposal. Usually, hearings are open to the public and the transcripts are published. Astute business leaders or their hired lobbyists pay close attention to subcommittee hearings and will try to make a formal presentation when necessary. Time constraints allow only a fraction of the bills to be aired this way, which is why the bulk of bills die in subcommittee.

When the hearings are over, the subcommittee meets to decide if there is support to mark up the bill. If there is, the subcommittee goes over the bill in detail, often rewriting it based on what the members believe the full committee will agree to. Input from the proponents and opponents of the bill during the hearings helps reshape the legislation.

FIGURE 10–2

Bills become law through a tortuous process

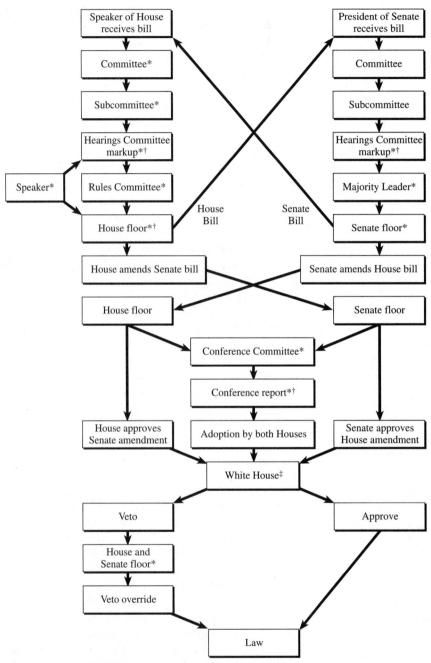

*Points at which bill can be amended.

†Points at which bill can die.

‡If there is no action by the president, either signing or vetoing the bill, after 10 days it becomes law.

Next, the subcommittee sends the marked-up bill to the larger committee with a favorable or unfavorable recommendation. If the committee votes to approve the bill, it goes to the full chamber. The committee is not bound to follow the subcommittee's lead, but it usually does since the subcommittee members know more about the issues involved. There is an unspoken agreement among all participants not to second-guess each other on noncontroversial matters. This understanding lets each representative and senator move his or her favored proposals forward without the threat of too much probing at later stages.

Debate

Once a bill has been reported out of committee, it must be scheduled for floor debate. The Senate arranges debate through informal consultation between the leaders of both parties. In the House of Representatives, setting the timetable for a floor debate is more complicated. Most bills have to pass through the Rules Committee—a powerful standing committee in the House whose main job is to decide the rules by which bills will be debated. Most important, the House Rules Committee decides whether and to what extent amendments can be offered to the bill.

Bills normally can be amended at any step on the way to final passage. Usually, amendments aim to strengthen or weaken the bill. In Washington, legislators also can attach nongermane amendments, called riders, to bills. Once a rider has been attached, it can be hard to separate it from the main legislation, and the rider can be approved as part of a larger package. Legislators often use the rider system to promote pet projects that help their home state or district. Sometimes, proposals become so loaded with additions their sponsors reject them. Many bills have been killed this way.

The U.S. Senate has evolved an unusual mechanism for delaying decisions or extracting concessions from the majority—the **filibuster,** or unlimited debate. Senators can hold up or kill pending legislation by talking at great length, offering numerous amendments, or making dilatory motions. It takes three-fifths of the full Senate to cut off debate and bring an issue to vote, a hard number to muster. The filibuster is being used more frequently—in the 1970s, 52 times; in the 1980s, 90 times; and in the 1990s, 200 times if the current pace holds.[10]

To build support for a bill, legislators can engage in logrolling. **Logrolling** is a political relation among two or more parties who have nothing in common. Their agreement is to exchange support on issues of individual interest: "I will help you with a policy you want, if you will help me get the policy I want." Logrolling is common with distributive policies. Coalitions often form in Congress whose members are joined solely by the prospect of each member getting a public works project earmarked for his or her constituents.[11]

The actual debate on many bills is usually a formality. Members of Congress are too busy to justify spending several hours to hear a measure discussed about which they know little or that does not interest them. Also, when a bill reaches the floor, most of the serious argument has already happened. Necessary compromises have been worked out privately. Few of the members may be present for speechmaking, which is aimed at television audiences, not at undecided colleagues.

Vigorous, exciting floor debate does take place for some controversial, closely fought bills. An example is the Senate debate over the balanced budget amendment to the Constitution in 1995, the negative outcome of which was not known until the last votes were cast. Some minds may have been changed by the speeches. Events like that are the exception.

Voting on bills may take place repeatedly before they are finally approved or denied. Votes can be cast on procedures and on amendments, whose outcome can be a more revealing test of the bill's support than the last vote on the measure. Opponents use these opportunities to gut the legislation. Majority support is needed to block unfriendly changes and eventually to pass the bill itself. Not all bills that get this far come up for a final vote; if not voted on during the current legislative session, a bill has to be reintroduced for consideration when the legislature convenes again. Such a delay can prove fatal.

Any tendency to rush to decisions on a bill is tempered by the party system. Starting in 1956, the first time this century that a newly elected president faced a Congress controlled by the opposition party, Republicans won 6 of 10 presidential elections. Until 1994, Democrats always controlled the House and usually the Senate, so, more often than not, national politics entail Republican presidents having to deal with Democratic Congresses. In 1994, the roles reversed, and Democratic President Clinton found he now had to work through a Congress dominated by Republicans. These partisan divisions increase the friction between the two branches.

Further, there is little party discipline in the United States. Since representatives and senators are free to disregard their party's platform, single-party control of both ends of Pennsylvania Avenue does not guarantee that the legislative and executive branches will work together smoothly—as Clinton found during the first half of his term when conservative Democrats often joined with Republicans to thwart his proposals.

Reconciling House and Senate Versions

After one chamber has acted positively on a bill, it is sent to the other chamber. The second body may accept the bill as is, reject the bill, send the bill to one of its committees, or ignore the bill while continuing to work on its version. Always, much informal bargaining among staff, lobbyists, and politicians is involved. Frequently, the second body approves a version of a bill that departs greatly from the one passed earlier. Such was the fate of President Clinton's first budget.

The House accepted one version with an energy tax. A powerful coalition, including the National Association of Manufacturers, the Chamber of Commerce, and the American Petroleum Institute, was determined to kill the tax. A handful of Democratic senators from oil-producing states agreed that the tax would hurt business for their constituents. Since they held swing votes, these senators, with interest group help, could block the energy tax in the Senate. The bill that emerged looked very different from the House's version. (See Box 10–1.)

When legislation has gone this far, a conference is organized to reconcile the conflicting House and Senate language. Senior members of Congress from the committees that managed the bills staff the conference. The goal is to find compromise language that a majority of each full chamber will accept. As they do at every step, lobbyists bring pressure to bear on the conferees. Haggling over details can take days or even weeks; sometimes, uncertainty or brinkmanship leads to an impasse and the bill dies in conference, though it was approved in each sponsoring chamber. When the conferees do reach agreement, they issue a report that both House and Senate must approve on a yes/no vote with no amendments.

Seldom does Congress reject a conference report, though the negotiated set-

---

Box 10–1

Lobbyists at Work

A cadre of lobbyists began to plot the death of President Clinton's energy tax in December 1992—a month before Clinton took office and two months before he submitted the tax plan to Congress. Clinton's idea was to create a broad-based tax on the British thermal unit (Btu) content of fuels, thus raising money and discouraging energy use. Jerry Jasinowski, president of NAM, said, "We had a very single-minded coalition . . . The administration never got out into the field." Jasinowski is a former Carter administration Commerce Department official who joined the traditionally conservative NAM in 1980.

He helped organize a group of 1,400 lobbies, dubbed the American Energy Alliance. The NAM, the U.S. Chamber of Commerce, and the American Petroleum Institute footed most of the bill. But the large number of participants created the impression of a mass movement. In the states of two key senators on the Finance Committee, the alliance spent about $100,000 mobilizing public opinion. They ran full-page ads and set up a toll-free phone number residents could use to call their senators and complain about the tax.

Behind the scenes, groups lobbied successfully for exemptions. First, coal was left out to appease Senator Robert Byrd of West Virginia, a coal-producing state. The National Corn Growers Association and the Renewable Fuels Association got the administration also to exempt ethanol, which is made from corn. Next, the administration agreed to leave out home heating oil. The Chemical Manufacturers Association used calls and visits by executives to get an equalizer tax imposed on competing imports, and the American Gas Association got the cost shifted from pipeline operators and onto consumers. Aluminum smelters and barge operators also got a break.

By June, what had been a fair, across-the-board tax was riddled with loopholes that would make it very expensive to administer. Lacking any clear popular support for the Btu tax, and facing defeat in the Senate, the White House threw in the towel and withdrew its proposal.[1]

---

[1]Michael Winer, "Energy Plan's Foes Poured on the Coal Starting Last Year," *International Herald Tribune,* June 15, 1993.

tlement on President Clinton's 1993 deficit reduction package came close. It passed by only two votes in the House of Representatives and one vote in the Senate, despite arm-twisting and cajoling by the president. The last step in the legislative process (not the policy-making process) is when the final, compromise legislation is sent to the White House for action.

The President's Role

If the president approves the bill, he signs it. Should he choose not to sign it, the bill becomes law 10 days later (not including Sundays), provided Congress is in session. A president turns down or vetoes a bill by refusing to sign it and sending the bill back to Congress before the 10 days expire. An alternative, the so-called pocket veto, can happen at the end of a congressional session. If Congress adjourns before the 10-day grace period, an unsigned bill does not become law. For the bill to be considered again, it has to work its way through the same sequence of subcommittee and committee meetings at another session of Congress.

At the state level, most governors have a line-item veto, meaning they can reject parts of a bill while accepting others. They find the line-item veto is a useful means to eliminate riders and costly pork barrel amendments. Despite requests for this power from the White House, as of 1995, Congress has never agreed and the president cannot veto part of a bill. He must either accept or reject the whole package. (This is likely to change. Republicans promised the line-item veto in their Contract with America, and were poised to pass it into law as this book goes to press.)

Circumstances often present the president with a cruel choice. The Tax Reform Act of 1981 had so many amendments tacked on to help different interests that critics compared the bill to a Christmas tree, full of ornaments. President Reagan may not have wanted these giveaways, but he had to tolerate them as the price of getting the tax cuts that were his main goal.

Congress can try to override the president's veto and enact the bill anyway. Overriding a veto requires a two-thirds vote of those present in both chambers. Should either chamber fail to garner the two-thirds needed, the veto is sustained and the bill dies. Due to the partisan division of Congress, the votes to overrule the president are hard to muster. President Bush used the veto 46 times in four years, losing but once when Congress enacted cable television reregulation over his objection.

Laws passed by Congress and signed by the president are added to the *U.S. Code*. This document is a compendium of legislation and can be used to find out which agency is charged with administering the program. Still, the laws in the *U.S. Code* are usually drafted in broad terms, the result of political compromise. The details are left to the professional bureaucrats.

Legislators make laws vague on purpose. Vague laws permit them to please the general electorate with the impression that a well-known problem is being solved, while simultaneously winking at special interests to reassure them that the details can be further negotiated and adjusted to their favor. Legislators thus pass the buck to the regulatory agencies, shifting difficult decisions to a less public arena than Congress. The Clean Air Act of 1970 is a good example of unclear legislation that got watered down at the regulatory level, as the Environmental Protection Agency repeatedly changed emission deadlines and made exceptions that gutted the law. In 1990, Congress passed a new clean-air law that started anew the laborious process of regulating toxic air pollution.[12]

Authorization and Appropriation

The president's signature is still an early step in the policy-making process. Before they can take effect, most policies have to go through the legislative cycle twice. The first cycle is called *authorization;* here, Congress approves a program and empowers a government agency to take steps to stop or encourage some behavior in society. But authorization is meaningless without funds. There is a separate *appropriations* cycle where Congress allocates the money to carry out the policy. Many federal programs affecting business receive funds for two years at a time. Appropriations entail the same process of committee hearings, amendments, floor debate, conferences, and presidential approval that takes place with authorization. The fact that a policy has been authorized does not mean it will be funded. Congressional representatives have been known to use the separate funding cycle as a way to play both sides of an issue: they placate one faction by voting to authorize a certain policy and mollify the other faction by not voting to appropriate money needed for implementation.

Students should be aware that many large government programs are nondiscriminatory—that is, they get funded automatically without close review by Congress. Most programs in this category are the so-called **entitlements**—like social security, Medicare, veterans' benefits, and food stamps. An entitlement program is a payment to individuals or households that does not represent compensation for a good or service. People who qualify have a legally enforceable right to get these benefits. By enacting an entitlement program, Congress in effect mandates later appropriations to pay for it. Often, cost increases are built in, say, to compensate for inflation. Entitlements now account for 60 percent of federal spending, leaving only 40 percent for allocation through the normal budget process.

Business leaders show little respect for the "do nothing" Congress, with its endless inside games and seeming inability to grapple with tough issues. Yet, given the multiple hurdles over which legislation has to go, it may be unreasonable to expect more output from Congress. Policy making through the legislative process is a most laborious, time-consuming endeavor. The wheels of Congress move slowly and are not likely to jolt with policies that displease important interest groups such as business. To an extent, Congress also mirrors public opinion, which is far from homogenous in a large, complex country like the United States. On many complicated issues, gridlock simply reflects the people's wavering attitudes.

Power to the People?

At the state and local levels, there are other processes that sometimes bypass the normal legislative process. These are the **initiative** (by which citizens put a proposal on the ballot) and the **referendum** (by which citizens can vote directly on a piece of legislation). These are forms of direct democracy that supplement or go around the representative institutions of government. People have the power to present measures to voters and to approve or reject the policy. The outcomes often are important to business.

Citizens vote on 10,000 to 15,000 local referenda a year, mostly dealing with local bonds, tax rate changes, and school financing.[13] A far smaller number of state-level questions come up each year, but the volume has been swelling since the 1980s. State-level issues are likely to be about taxes and environmental problems, and often carry significant implications for companies. The United States is unusual in having no national referenda. Most countries put significant national issues to the people, for instance, the recent question in Scandinavia and Austria about whether to join the European Union.

Companies often mobilize to use sophisticated techniques to sway the public on ballot questions. When Missouri voters were presented with a referendum that would have halted construction at one of its nuclear power plants, the Union Electric Co. quickly organized a campaign committee to fight the referendum. The company donated more than $1 million to a media blitz, orchestrated by public relations consultants and pollsters for maximum impact.[14]

How Rules and Regulations Are Made

The legislative stage (including referenda) marks just the start of the policy process. The next two stages are administrative. A bureaucratic agency has to clarify the law, making it workable by eliminating ambiguities and developing well-defined procedures for implementation. Then the agency must administer the law and, in doing so, interpret and reinterpret it. Policy making is unending.[15] The post-legislative stages of the policy process are important, for they can define the policy's actual impact on business, workers, consumers, and others in society. These stages, illustrated in Figure 10–3, invite additional deal making, beyond what was worked out in Congress and the White House. Business executives naturally observe the emerging policies closely and try to seek favorable interpretations.

The Power of Civil Servants

Civil servants have administrative discretion—that is, they can make policies that are not spelled out in advance. One vital job of the federal bureaucracy is to fill the gaps in the written law, and armies of experts have been hired to do it. The federal government alone employs 150,000 engineers, 31,000 lawyers, 14,000 scientists, and 10,000 physicians.[16]

FIGURE 10–3

Rule making in the bureaucracy

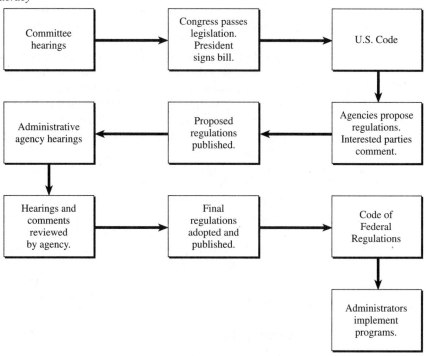

For instance, the Internal Revenue Service has wide discretionary power to write rules affecting tax policy within the boundaries voted by Congress. It decides mundane but important matters such as what a home office is, or whether receipts are needed to justify certain types of deductions. Similarly, the FDA issues rules and guidelines for the types of laboratory tests that pharmaceutical companies must perform to prove a new drug safe and effective. Congress normally does not get into this level of detail.

In theory, civil servants are supposed to be apolitical and to administer the law objectively whatever their personal feelings. Yet, they always enjoy some latitude in deciding exactly how to carry out policies, since neither Congress nor the president can foresee all contingencies and completely tie the hands of the bureaucracy.

Besides giving bureaucrats political power, administrative discretion provides interest groups more chances to influence policy by bargaining directly with the agency involved. Just as they identify and work with the relevant congressional committees and staff, business lobbies seek out the relevant bureaucrats with whom to talk and to try to sway. The relationship is reciprocal. The agencies look to organized interests for technical data and political intelligence. Prohibited by Congress from lobbying themselves, agencies depend on outside interests groups to lobby for them.

We discussed in earlier chapters the principal–agent problem. It applies to the regulatory agencies in the federal executive branch. Despite their theoretical neutrality, the professional bureaucrats often find themselves at odds with the espoused objectives of their titular boss, the president. Political economists note that every organization holds both formal and informal goals. One informal goal, which most departments and bureaus share, is to avoid change. They see it as a means to protect the organization's members. Yet, presidents usually say they want the opposite and try to initiate new ways of doing things. Due to their expertise and contacts, the bureaucrats rather than the president may have the determining impact on public policy. James Q. Wilson quips that "What is surprising is not that bureaucrats sometimes can defy the president but that they support his programs as much as they do."[17]

A major reason for bureaucratic conservatism is the **sunk cost** of innovation. Without compelling arguments to the contrary, employees generally prefer to economize and not incur additional costs by trying to innovate. It is easier and cheaper to maintain current practices. Reforms may suit the purpose of the president. Yet, the people on the receiving end are understandably reluctant to make the investment needed to master new techniques, especially if there is no clear individual payoff to them. Employees in any bureaucracy are apt to organize themselves informally to sabotage novel ideas being promoted from the top. By tacit agreement, they make sure the innovation fails.

Making the Rules

Federal agencies must announce in the *Federal Register* any changes planned in existing rules and proposals for new ones. This publication codifies all official actions of agencies and is published five days a week, except during holidays. It tells how and where comments on pending rules and regulations can be sent. Agencies have to receive the written comments of interested parties on these matters, so lobbyists keep tabs on the *Federal Register*. The document has had upwards of 70,000 pages annually in recent years. Despite some progress with deregulation under President Reagan in the 1980s, federal regulatory agencies continue to issue an estimated 30,000 pages of new or amended rules every year.

According to Wilson, the underlying reason for so many rules is that bureaucracies are risk averse: They prefer independence to growth, security to conflict, stability to change. Their dislike of risk does not mean they are passive. To the contrary, bureaucracies have a strong motivation to make and enforce rules related to their mission. This motivation is fortified by their want for autonomy and a stable environment. Thus, threat-avoiding impulses in the bureaucracy foster the proliferation of rules, as they try to "cover their flanks."[18]

Administrative procedures ordinarily require that agencies hold public hearings before promulgating new policies. The hearings are publicized in the *Federal Register*. These sessions look like the ones run by congressional committees. The politically appointed directorate or the agency staff preside. Expert witnesses are called to testify, submitting written testimony ahead of time and answering questions posed by the hearing officers. A written transcript is kept and used by the agency to reach its decisions. The lobbying at this stage can be as intense as in Congress itself. Businesses and trade associations devote about one-fifth of their staff to the rule-making process.[19]

Hearings are followed by discussion within the agency to revise the proposed rules. After a final draft is completed that satisfies agency personnel, it is formally submitted to the bureau leadership for approval, then the rule becomes law. Final, authorized regulations are then published in the *Federal Register.* They also will appear in the *Code of Federal Regulations,* published quarterly. Comprised of about 140 volumes, this document is a codification of the current, general, and permanent rules of the federal agencies. It is a comprehensive reference for anyone who needs to know the exact text of a U.S. regulation.

The process does not end here. Many agency rules are subject to constant review. Frequently, the recommendation is that rules be modified or replaced to make them more cost effective or fair. This again sets off the whole cycle of public announcements and formal hearings.

While the policy-making activities of the federal agencies are officially open to public view, few people have the time or inclination to concern themselves with these matters. The networks and major newspapers do not routinely report on agency hearings. Most changes in policy do not attract much attention and are generally invisible to outsiders. The same can be said about policy making in Congress and the White House. Most of it goes on unnoticed by the media or the average citizen. This lack of public scrutiny helps add to the stability of the process and increases the leverage of special interests and lobbyists.

As in congressional lobbying, productive contacts are often informal. A friendly staffer can give advanced warning about likely administrative action. Personal relations may allow the lobbyist to comment off the record on policy changes incubating within the agency.[20]

Who wins these lobbying battles? Often it is the companies or industries with the most to lose. As the 1992 *Economic Report of the President* observes: "Because all interest groups must make similar expenditures to seek government failures, the regulatory process tends to favor those groups or businesses that can capture the greatest benefits from a protected position. Once achieved, a protected position must be defended against competitors trying to dislodge the incumbent firm."[21]

Getting the Rules to Stick

Besides their rule-making power, the federal agencies also have law enforcement duties. To carry out their policies, the agencies inspect companies to verify compliance and take steps against companies that do not follow the rules. These steps include the following:

- Revocation—withdrawal of a license to do something or the refusal to grant one.

- Fines levied for infractions of rules.
- Cease-and-desist orders—directives to someone to stop doing something.
- Bad publicity.

The agencies also have quasi-judicial powers called adjudication. Administrative law empowers federal agencies to resolve disputes through hearings, based on the theory that the regular court system is too slow and uninformed to handle administrative cases. There are over 1,100 special examiners, called administrative law judges, who run these hearings.

Both enforcement and adjudication give the regulatory agencies further opportunities to make public policy. The agencies, for instance, may decide on selective application of rules, vigorously enforcing certain rules while turning a blind eye to others. With respect to the Clean Air Act mentioned above, for instance, many companies successfully negotiated with sympathetic enforcement agents to be allowed more lenient pollution emission levels. Similarly, hearings allow for policy to be adjusted. During hearings over product recalls, manufacturers often can bargain about the scope and content of the recall. Unlike rule making, the adjudication process affects only the single case being heard by the administrative judge. Some analysts think the agencies prefer to adjudicate rather than make rules because it arouses less controversy among the regulated industries.

When an unfavorable policy has been adopted despite objections, business and other interest groups still can use litigation to block the policy. They can sue the government or private parties for violating the law, using either the regular courts or the administrative courts. Also, they can file a friend-of-the-court brief in support of another group's suit. Interest group litigation has mushroomed at both the federal and state levels in recent years.

Criticisms of the Regulatory Process

The U.S. regulatory process is often reproached for being undemocratic, for failing to respond to majority demand, and for giving too much power to narrow interest groups. While the news media concentrate on the conventional activity of passing new laws, the more important issue is whether and to what extent new laws are enforced. One critic, the reporter William Greider, concludes:

> Those interests that have the resources and the incentives to stall the law's application do not always succeed, of course, but their persistent efforts keep government authority always in doubt . . . The transactions where this [bargaining over the law] occurs are mostly submerged in the Executive Branch, scattered across hundreds of bureaus and agencies and focused mainly on the esoteric language of federal regulations and enforcement. The regulatory government is a many-chambered labyrinth, staggeringly complex and compartmentalized in its thousands of parts.[22]

Greider sees the result as a form of "random lawlessness," which he believes undermines the reliability of the law in the citizens' eyes.

Yet the pattern is not random. It is just slow to take action. The operating assumption, dating from 1789, is that no decision is better than a bad one. Delay is built into the system. There is a risk to companies from such a fragmented system. An agreement once made can be overruled or rendered moot at a later time, interfering with planning. But the advantages are greater.

According to Lloyd Cutler, a top lobbyist in Washington, the diffusion of authority suits corporate interests because they are best equipped to take advantage of it. "If you're against something, you're much better off in this diffuse world. It's harder to pass a law than to stop one. On the whole, I would say the professional lobbyists and lawyers prefer to live in this world where there are so many buttons to push, so many other places to go if you lose your fight. In a cohesive government, once you lose, it's over."[23]

Other criticisms target the bureaucrats themselves. Officials in the regulatory agencies are accused of abusing power, of acting in arbitrary and high-handed ways. Charges range from inefficiency to outright corruption. Ronald Reagan summed up the feelings of many business leaders in the phrase "waste, fraud, and abuse," which he saw as endemic in the bureaucracy.

There is a germ of truth in such accusations, but it is important to see it in the larger context. All bureaucratic organizations, in both the private and public sectors, are prone to isolate themselves from the outside world and to sanction featherbedding, goldbricking, and other unproductive behavior. Most Fortune 500 companies are finding they, too, have fat in their middle-management ranks as they restructure to become more competitive on international markets. While it is true that private companies are usually quicker to downsize, public organizations are being forced to do the same thing across the country—and around the world in competing states that are finding they can no longer support government on the scale to which they are accustomed.

However unsatisfactory American bureaucratic performance is to business leaders, it is better than what is found in most nations. Studies of European bureaucracies, for instance, repeatedly identify them as rigid, overcentralized, impersonal, and officious. Civil servants there are accused of delays in dealing with public, of lacking imagination, and of unwillingness to make decisions. Developing country bureaucracies are even worse. Public opinion surveys show that Americans are apt to have a better opinion of their administrative systems. Eighty-three percent of U.S. respondents in one survey expect equal treatment from government officials. Only 65 percent of Germans and 53 percent of Italians had the same expectation.[24]

The incidence of outright bureaucratic (and elected officials') corruption is also blown out of proportion in the public mind. Scandals such as the dope ring in the House of Representatives Post Office attract attention precisely because they are not everyday events. Occasional bribes and kickbacks aside, government bureaucrats hardly have a monopoly on crime—witness the extravagant rip-offs in the financial securities industry in the 1980s, for instance.

Bureaucrats, and the politicians with whom they work, are probably no more honest in most other countries. In 1993, to take two recent examples, both Japan and Italy were shocked by revelations of official wrongdoing. The scandals touched the highest levels of government. Dozens of prominent Italian politicians were found to have connections to the Mafia, and one former prime minister was indicted for actually being a member. In Japan, the entrenched Liberal Democratic Party was defeated in election for the first time in over 40 years, following charges of rampant corruption. These cases make even the U.S. Watergate affair look tame.

Policies and Politics

Public policies shape politics. By altering the cost and benefit of government, public policies produce a political reaction from the affected parties. Many analysts see distinctive patterns in policy making: different types of policies have unique political patterns. In other words, it is possible to predict roughly the politics that will surround changes in a particular public policy. Such predictions are helpful to managers trying to understand and make use of government programs.

Wilson suggests that the important defining attribute of a policy is the perceived distribution of its cost and benefit.[25] The cost and benefit can be nonmonetary, and the value assigned to them can change, but all policies have winners and losers. Some groups and individuals in society expect to gain from a given government action or inaction; others (sometimes, but not usually, the same groups and individuals) think they are going to suffer. It is the way that the cost and benefit are shared that has political significance, by shaping the kinds of political coalitions that form.

Four Types of Policies and Politics

A policy's cost and its benefit can both be widely distributed (spread over most citizens) or narrowly focused (limited to an identifiable group). Income taxes, for instance, are widely distributed because almost everyone pays them; regulations imposing cost on a specific industry are narrowly concentrated. Though there are many cases between, four political situations (shown in Figure 10–4) can be classified by combining the dichotomous cases.

Majoritarian Politics.   In the interplay over policies, interest groups and government agencies follow patterns that flow from the four cost–benefit relationships. When both cost and benefit are widely distributed, what Wilson calls majoritarian politics exist. All or most people expect to gain, and to pay for it themselves. Here, interest groups have little motivation to involve themselves because no segment of society will get an extra share of the benefit of the policy, or will bear an uneven share of the burden. Such policies are often widely popular, "apple pie and motherhood" issues. An example is the Social Security Act of 1935.

FIGURE 10–4

There are different categories of public policy that depend on the distribution of the policy's cost and benefit.

Policy benefit

	Concentrated	Dispersed
Concentrated	Interest group politics	Entrepreneurial politics
Dispersed	Client politics	Majoritarian politics

Policy cost

Client Politics.   When the benefit of an anticipated policy is concentrated but the cost is widely distributed, client politics are likely to result. Some small group—often a business or an industry—stands to profit and thus has strong reason to organize and lobby for the policy. No one is likely to work as hard against the policy: The cost is distributed at a low rate over too many people, many of whom will not even know of the policy's existence. Experience shows that it is very hard to get rid of any policy that benefits a small, well-organized producer group at the expense of the larger society (see Box 10–2).

Client politics are typical of regulatory policies. Quiet lobbying, logrolling, and the quick passage of rules with little public discussion characterize this type of politics, which has often served regulated industries well, if not the wider public. The resolution of the S&L crisis is a good illustration. Early in the Bush administration, the Treasury Department planned to resolve the crisis by imposing a fee on S&L deposits. The industry adamantly rejected this plan and compelled the administration to disown it in favor of a plan financed with general tax revenues. In this way, the S&L industry shifted the burden of a major federal program, designed to help it, from itself to the public.[26]

Industry domination of client politics may be diminishing, however, due to the rise of public interest groups that monitor changes in regulatory policies. Public interest groups can raise an effective voice of opposition even when they are not affected materially. The greater scrutiny that ensues can offset the clout of the business or other special interest.

As a rule, government bureaus have the most liberty with distributive policies, like pork barrel projects for favored constituents. Because such policies appear politically painless, at least in the short run, they are the most common form of federal action to solve public problems. In this policy arena, bureaucratic influence is the result of strong clientele support, which can often counter diffuse opposition.

Box 10–2

Client Policies, such as the Subsidy to Wool and Mohair Producers, Take on a Life of Their Own[1]

The United States began to subsidize wool and mohair during World War II and the Korean war, when the military faced a shortage of fabric for uniforms. These commodities were placed on the Strategic Reserve List, and the 1954 National Wool Act authorized payment to producers. The military removed wool and mohair from the strategic list in 1960, but large sheep and goat ranchers got Congress to save the subsidy.

By 1993, the wool subsidy was worth $190 million a year. According to the National Performance Review, put together under the supervision of Vice President Al Gore, the top 1 percent of sheep raisers received one-quarter of the money—about $100,000 each. Half the funds went to ranchers who raised Angora goats for mohair, about 80 percent of which was exported—in effect subsidizing the price of mohair sweaters overseas.

Wool and mohair subsidies were widely seen as an archetype of spendthrift government, yet stopping

the program proved arduous. Senator John Kerry of Massachusetts (notably a state with few sheep or goats) spearheaded a drive in 1991 to kill the aid to sheep and goat ranchers. Predictably, officials from Texas and other wool-producing states fought doggedly to keep the subsidies alive. Often, the officials kept their struggle in the backrooms, while simultaneously posturing in public against the budget deficit and Congress's reluctance to cut the fat from government.

Kerry and his supporters won a key vote to end the subsidy in the Senate in 1993, then had it overturned on a technicality. The anti-wool forces later won two more votes, but House negotiators in the House–Senate conference stripped the amendment from the bill. After a series of parliamentary maneuvers, the amendment was reinstated, then dropped again on the floor of the House of Representatives. With the two houses at an impasse, a deal was finally cut. The wool and mohair programs would be phased out over three years. Kerry remarked: "I'm stumped. If it is so difficult to kill this program, how do we take on the really tough ones?"

[1]"Trimming Mohair Subsidies: Key Battle Won on Budget Waste," *Boston Globe,* October 22, 1993, p. 12.

Interest Group Politics.   Where cost and benefit are narrowly concentrated, as with redistributive policies that help one group at the expense of another, interest group politics are likely to follow. Each side has an incentive to try to exercise influence on policy makers, but people at large are indifferent because they do not think the policy touches them. An illustration is the policies of the Federal Communications Commission. Were the FCC to decide, say, to allow cable television companies to provide phone service over their lines, it would help cable companies but hurt the local phone companies. Similarly, a decision to permit the local phone companies to provide interactive video services would be good for them but not for cable companies. In fact, these two industries are lobbying over just these issues as the nation moves toward an information superhighway. As long as good telecommunications services are available, the average consumer does not care much about these turf battles.

Entrepreneurial Politics.   The last combination of cost and benefit is entrepreneurial politics, when society or a large part of it gains from a policy that harms a small segment of society. The antipollution and safety requirements that were imposed on automobile manufacturers illustrate distributed benefit and concentrated cost. Policies of this sort are rare in the United States because the political system creates so many opportunities for blocking the action of others. Any organized group that faces some new penalty or the loss of a privilege has a strong motive to resist the threatened change. The larger group of potential winners, on the other hand, may see the benefit as too small to be worth fighting for—what we discussed in Chapter 3 as the free-rider problem. The result is that no one in the larger group wants to make the necessary sacrifices, and their common interest is not fulfilled.

A good example of how hard it is to get policies with distributed benefit and concentrated cost was the failure of President Clinton's health care reform program in 1994. Despite putting his prestige on the line, the president's plan to trim the nation's health bill (a distributed benefit) by requiring that a business buy health insurance for its workers (a concentrated cost) collapsed. This bill should have had wide appeal, and it did at first. However, small business interests, the insurance industry, drug firms, and others who stood to lose the most under the plan mobilized for an effective negative publicity campaign. The potential winners under the proposed health care system did not feel the same intensity and did not organize an effective countermovement. The majority's passiveness can be explained because the alleged economic gains (slower growth in insurance premiums, lower inflation, reduced budget deficits) were remote, uncertain, and spread thinly over the population. The opponents of health care reform raised enough doubts about the risk and cost of health care reform that popular support for the bill vanished.

Still, policies with distributed benefit and concentrated cost do happen. As Wilson notes, an important causal element is people who work for the unorganized or apathetic public. These people have been labeled *policy entrepreneurs.* Ralph Nader and Ross Perot are two examples from opposite ends of the political spectrum. Policy entrepreneurs can dramatize an issue of widespread concern (car safety, the federal deficit), and thus pull together a legislative majority for interests who are not well represented in government. These coalitions are not common. All political systems have a hard time forcing losses on some groups for the greater good, but the United States is especially flabby.[27]

In sum, the politics of policy making follow four basic patterns, and have four different outcomes, depending on the proposed policy's distribution of cost and benefit. In these political patterns, the economic interest of key actors is paramount—especially in client and interest group politics when cost/benefit is concentrated. Each category of policies has a distinct shape to which managers should be alert as they try to predict and perhaps influence public policy.

How the policy turns out depends, of course, on other factors. One is the level of effort the different sides put into the policy-making process, which is influenced by how big the cost and benefit are. The greater the effort, the greater the likelihood of success. Another factor is how easy it is for supporters and opponents of a policy to get organized.

Business leaders can use this information to plot corporate political strategy. For example, if business losers from a policy can portray it as having a widespread cost for society, they stand a good chance of blocking it. This would argue for a grassroots strategy to stir up worries among citizens, as the insurance industry did with Clinton's health care package. Such a strategy would probably be unnecessary or unworkable for a policy that did not have widely distributed cost. For such a policy, backroom lobbying might be more promising.[28]

Conclusion

Policy was defined earlier as the purposeful and deliberate side of government, its attempt to control society for a predetermined purpose. Writ large, government hardly looks purposeful and deliberate. It is necessary to disaggregate government, to break it into smaller parts to see the logic of policy making.

This chapter focused on informal policy-making systems where most decisions get made about public policy that affects business. Composing these informal systems are lobbyists, bureaucrats, and politicians. The players in these networks are stable and well-known to each other. Together they engage in what has been called the dance of legislation and rule making. It is no exaggeration to say that public policies are never finally decided, that there is always room for further compromise and adjustment. American business fully employs the opportunities available for securing a milieu of policy favorable to its interests.

The evolution of public policy is an inexact science, and it is hard to know what government decisions will look like at any given time. Still, we saw that the distribution of a policy's benefit and its cost does create some regular patterns of policy making. The likelihood of influencing a decision is greatest for groups that stand to bear a heavy loss or to make a large gain from the result. Groups with a more dispersed interest have a lower probability of influencing the output of the policy-making process.

In the remaining chapters of *Business, Government, Society,* we will inspect the policy outputs more closely. Social policy will occupy us in Part V. Then we will turn to economic policy in Part VI, remembering that all government policies have both social and economic consequences.

Questions

1. Describe the way a bill becomes a law. What are the main points a businessperson needs to know about the process?

2. How does rule making work? What is the significance for business?

3. Discuss lobbying. Where and when does it happen during the making of public policy? Is lobbying a legitimate mode of business activity in your view?

4. What powers do the regulatory agencies have to enforce their authority? How do they use these powers? How effective are they?

5. In what ways do the cost and benefit of a public policy help determine the type of politics that result?

End Notes

1. Quoted in Hedrick Smith, *The Power Game* (New York: Random House, 1988), p. 652.

2. A. Lee Fritschler and Bernard H. Ross, *How Washington Works* (Cambridge, MA: Ballinger, 1987), pp. 70 and 75.

3. Bernd Marin and Renate Mayutz, eds., *Policy Networks: Empirical Evidence and Theoretical Considerations* (Boulder, CO: Westview, 1992), and David Marsh and R. A. W. Rhodes, *Policy Networks in British Government* (New York: Oxford University Press, 1992).

4. Adam Smith, *An Inquiry into the Nature and Origins of the Wealth of Nations* (1776; reprint, New York: Modern Library, 1937), p. 437.

5. See Charles E. Lindblom's classic article, "The Science of 'Muddling Through,'" *Public Administration Review* 19, no. 1 (1959), pp. 79–88.

6. For a good summary of this school of thought, see Graham Allison, *Essence of Decision* (Boston: Little, Brown, 1971), especially Chapter 5.

7. See Aaron Wildavsky, *The Politics of the Budgetary Process,* 4th ed. (Boston: Little, Brown, 1984).

8. *Congressional Quarterly Almanac* (Washington, DC: U.S. Government Printing Office, 1991), p. 11.

9. Smith, *Power Game,* p. 657.

10. Hendrik Hertzberg, "Catch XXII," *New Yorker,* August 2 and 29, 1994, pp. 9–10.

11. Theodore J. Lowi and Benjamin Ginsberg, *American Government: Freedom and Power,* 2nd ed. (New York: Norton, 1992), p. 657.

12. Ibid., pp. 128–29.

13. Lewis Lipsitz and David M. Speak, *American Democracy,* 2nd ed. (New York: St. Martin's Press, 1989), p. 322.

14. Joseph L. Badaracco, Jr., *Proposition 11(A)* (Boston: Harvard Business School, 1981).

15. Fritschler and Ross, *How Washington Works,* p. 95.

16. Ibid., p. 65.

17. James Q. Wilson, *Bureaucracy* (New York: Basic Books, 1989), p. 275.

18. James Q. Wilson, "The Politics of Regulation," in *The Politics of Regulation,* ed. James Q. Wilson (New York: Basic Books, 1980), pp. 376–77.

19. Cornelius M. Kerwin, *Rule-Making: How Government Agencies Write Law and Make Policies* (Washington, DC: CQ Press, 1994), p. 197.

20. Kay Schlozman and John Tierney, *Organized Interests and American Democracy* (New York: Harper and Row, 1986), p. 33.

21. *Economic Report of the President 1992* (Washington, DC: U.S. Government Printing Office, 1992), p. 168.

22. William Greider, *Who Will Tell the People?* (New York: Simon and Schuster, 1992), p. 106.

23. Ibid., p. 134.

24. For a review of these studies, see Charles T. Goodsell, *The Case for Bureaucracy,* 2nd ed. (Chatham, NJ: Chatham House, 1985), pp. 55–60.

25. This typology is based on one that first appeared in James Q. Wilson, *Political Organizations* (New York: Basic Books, 1973), Chapter 16. For a similar fourfold typology, see Theodore Lowi, "American Business, Public Policy, Case-Studies and Political Theory," *World Politics* 16, no. 4 (1964), pp. 677–715.

26. Theodore Lowi and Benjamin Ginsberg, *Democrats Return to Power* (New York: W. W. Norton, 1993), p. 48.

27. Bert A. Rockman and R. Kent Weaver, eds., *Do Institutions Matter?* (Washington, DC: Brookings Institution, 1993).

28. A good discussion of how the Wilson model can be adapted to development of political strategies is David P. Baron, *Business and Its Environment* (Englewood Cliffs, NJ: Prentice Hall, 1993), pp. 142–58.

V BUSINESS AND SOCIAL REGULATION

11 PUBLIC POLICY AND CORPORATE GOVERNANCE

The directors of such [joint stock] companies, however, being the managers rather of other people's money than their own, it cannot well be expected, that they should watch over it with the same anxious vigilance with which the partners in a private copartnery frequently watch over their own . . .
Negligence and profusion, therefore, must always prevail, more or less, in the management of the affairs of such a company.
Adam Smith[1]

Big companies are one of modern capitalism's strengths, but that same strength is also a source of controversy and disapproval. In formal terms, all but a handful of large corporations are private organizations. Yet, they have public effects that make them a matter of social and political concern. Who controls these firms? Do they answer to anyone other than themselves? Can and should they be held more accountable for their actions? These have long been important questions facing public policy makers.

To answer them, this chapter looks at companies' relationship to their three important stakeholder groups. We will review how corporations deal with what may be the most critical constituency—their owners. We will go over recent moves by government to empower owners, to make them active participants in corporate governance, not mere spectators. Finally, we will turn to corporate dealings with two other very important sets of stakeholders—creditors and employees.

Shareholders' Rights

Owners are the traditional leading constituency of business. They are the ones who stand to make the most profit if the business succeeds, and to suffer the financial consequences should it fail. Proprietary (that is, privately owned) business firms come in many forms, with a few to many owners (see Chapter 1). Different modes of governance have evolved to protect and promote owners' interests. The complexity of these arrangements turns on how many proprietors the business has.

For corporations, the corporate charter designates shareholders or stockholders the right of ownership. According to the logic of economic rationality, the shareholders' object is to gain a material advantage through a return on their investment in the corporation. By buying shares, they receive legal claim to the firm's residual assets (that is, all assets that would remain after paying off creditors). Shares are a negotiable instrument and can be transferred to someone else, for example, through sale on a stock exchange. Shareholders, of course, also get to stand behind the screen of limited liability.

Private sector corporations fall into two categories. Some are closed or closely held, often involving family ownership. The shares are not sold to the public, and usually the owners have the right to buy back any departing members' stock. Such corporations often are on the small side, but not always. Both Fidelity Investments, the nation's number one family of mutual funds, and Bechtel, at one time the world's largest construction company, are privately held corporations, for example.

The other kind of private corporation is publicly traded. Their shares can be purchased by anyone with money who is willing to pay the going price. (Readers should not confuse this type of public corporation with the public sector or state-owned corporations discussed in Chapter 5—where government holds some or all shares.) Publicly traded corporations are what Americans usually have in mind when they speak of Big Business or corporate America. These businesses are private collectivities. They have thousands of owners, whose relation to the firm is apt to be remote, impersonal, and often temporary. Unlike sole proprietorships, partnerships, and even closely held corporations, the distant relation between the owners and their property creates a problem of control.

Whether a corporation is closed or publicly traded, it usually hires professional managers for day-to-day management. The professional managers, in turn, are entrusted to make decisions on the owners' behalf, including the hiring and firing of other employees. The legal term for their role is that of a **fiduciary,** meaning they are supposed to set their interests aside and manage the organization impartially. The highest ranking officer can have several titles, but is most often called the **chief executive officer (CEO).** The CEO has responsibility for setting strategic direction for the firm.

Standing between shareholders and management is the **board of directors.** This body is delegated the job of watchdog for the owners' interest. Besides choosing the management team, the board's most important responsibilities are setting executive compensation and approving major strategic moves, such as a merger or acquisition. Nonprofit organizations have similar boards of trustees or overseers, who are charged with assuring that resources are being used in line with the organization's charitable or public service mission.

Problems with the Corporate Form of Organization

Judging from how common it is, the widely held corporation is a winning species of economic organization. It will be recalled from Chapter 5 that a major reason for the spread of the corporate form is capital formation. Capital is any company's lifeblood. Getting access to capital is critical for firms to get started and grow, and the corporate form has unique advantages because it pools the funds of many people. The result is that corporations can undertake huge projects beyond the means of most sole proprietorships and partnerships—projects such as designing and building the Boeing 747 or the Trident submarine. (Some undertakings, such as the Eurotunnel under the English Channel or the development of high-definition television, are beyond the capacity of even the largest corporations, so today companies are often combining resources in **joint ventures.** We will look at joint ventures more closely in Chapters 15 and 16.)

If the corporate form yielded nothing but benefits, however, no other type of business organization would exist. So, these vast enterprises must have some drawbacks. The most important, many critics contend, is their lack of accountability. Corporations are seen as rogue elephants, unbeholden to society. They do what they want even when it harms many stakeholders. From this point of view, new public policies are needed to tame these large entities.

Unfortunately, according to political economy, some lack of accountability is inevitable in corporations. The main reason is agent misdirection—a problem of human behavior we first encountered in Chapter 3. Given agent misdirection, even government action can only go so far in bringing corporations to bay. Let us see why.

Conflicts of Interest

In theory, the managers of corporations (agents) are the mere instruments of the owners (principals). Generations of business students have learned that managers' first responsibility *should* be to maximize the wealth of shareholders. Whether this moral precept is right, it is a dubious description of the real world. Too often, the interest of managers, who want to make as much money as possible and to keep their jobs, conflicts with what is best for shareholders.

Since the 1930s, it has been a truism that shareholders have lost control of most publicly traded U.S. corporations. According to the commonplace analysis, corporate governance represents the form, not the substance, of private ownership. While legal authority flows forward, from the owners, real power seems to run the other way, from the managers backward. A managerial revolution has taken place in many companies, with paid executives seizing control from the capitalists who ostensibly employ them.[2] Similar trends are seen in every kind of organization—the professional managers tend to dominate.[3]

Exceptions are where a person or family owns a major block of shares, as, for example, Bill Gates, who still controls Microsoft, the company he founded. But heavy ownership does not guarantee control, as Stephen Jobs, founder and principal shareholder of Apple Computer, discovered. He was removed from Apple's board of directors while out of the country in a coup orchestrated, ironically, by the CEO he originally hired, John Sculley. The rule is that the more dispersed the ownership of a corporation, the more dominant is management's position. That position need not be unassailable, however, as Sculley himself learned several years later when Apple's board sacked him.

Executives—Out of Control?

Salaries and Perks.   One symptom of owner/management conflict of interest is executive salaries. In the 1980s, executive salaries rose four times faster than factory worker wages in the United States, and three times faster than profits. The pace continued in the early 1990s despite hard times. According to one survey, earnings of CEOs at the largest firms took a 56 percent leap in 1992 over 1991. Total annual pay of these particular executives is about 85 times the pay of the average factory worker.[4]

U.S. executive compensation is much higher than in other industrial countries.[5] As reported in Table 11–1, the average CEO of a large American company earned a salary of about $750,000 in 1991—twice as much as his or her Japanese and German counterparts. The gap between CEO pay and workers' pay is also far wider in the United States. Michael Eisner of Walt Disney Co. holds the record, with total direct compensation of $203 million in 1993, most of it a gain on stock options. The data do not include executive perks, such as stock options, company cars, and country club memberships, which raise true executive earnings much higher but do not change the top rank of U.S. bosses.

A similar pattern is beginning to be seen with nonprofit organizations. University presidents and the heads of major foundations, for example, can earn upwards of $300,000 a year. John Silber, president of Boston University, makes

TABLE 11–1   CEOs of U.S. Companies Make More Than Their Counterparts in Other Countries.

	Average Remuneration of CEOs (1991)	*Ratio—CEO to Average Manufacturing Worker*
United States	$747,500	25
France	448,500	16
Switzerland	424,100	11
United Kingdom	399,600	16
Japan	371,800	11
Germany	364,500	10
Sweden	335,600	10

Source: *Worldwide Total Remuneration 1991* (Valhalla, NY: Towers Perrin, 1991).

about $750,000. That includes a $62,000 raise plus a $300,000 bonus in 1993—a year when he was under investigation for conflict of interest.[6]

The fringe benefits can be lavish in nonprofit organizations, too. William Aramony, head of the United Way, always flew first class, often on the Concorde, and charged United Way $20,000 a year for chauffeurs, among other benefits. Aramony had to resign in 1992 when his actions became public, sparking new scrutiny on heads of nonprofit organizations. He was later found guilty of having taken advantage of contributors.

Some defend high executive pay as the price that must be paid to attract talented people. This argument is unfounded, for no one can show a clear link between executive pay and company performance.[7] Kenneth Olson of Digital Equipment Company, for example, was paid more than $1 million in 1992 while the company lost millions. Further, why can foreign corporations hire skilled managers for less money? Many critics conclude that CEOs and other corporate officers are abusing their position to line their pockets—a clear case of an agency relation gone wrong.

Defense against Corporate Raiding.   Other signs of owner/manager tension are the heroic measures managers use to fend off corporate raiders or takeover artists. As we will discuss at greater length in Chapter 15, a surge of hostile takeovers of companies started in the 1980s. Raiders such as T. Boone Pickens, who forced Gulf Oil to merge with Standard Oil of California, and Carl Icahn, who took over TWA, began to mount many more campaigns than before to buy whole companies and install new management. Pickens claims to be leading a grassroots shareholders' movement and has formed the United Shareholders of America to lobby for public policies to give owners more power.

Naturally, managers of the takeover targets fight back. No one wants to give up the prestige and power of a high executive position. To defend their position, endangered managers have discovered a variety of "shark repellent" tactics with colorful names such as **poison pills, greenmail,** and **golden parachutes.** The incidence of these and other questionable practices is up (see Table 11–2).

A poison pill is a shareholders' protection plan, designed to make a company

---

TABLE 11–2   **There Is Plenty to Reform in U.S. Corporate Governance.**

	1990	*1993*
Number of Top 1,000 Firms with		
Golden parachutes	441	535
Poison pills	495	643
Staggered board elections	550	594
Unequal voting rights	67	92
Confidential ballots	35	94

Source: "Shareholders Call the Plays," *The Economist,* April 24, 1993.

too expensive for an unfriendly suitor. The way a poison pill works is by giving shareholders purchase rights to dilute a suitor's holding and discourage a takeover bid. Most large U.S. corporations have put poison pills in their bylaws. Greenmail involves buying back the company's stock from an active or potential bidder at a premium over the market price. Fifty or so U.S. companies a year were paying greenmail in the mid-1980s. Many went deeply into hock, making them vulnerable to any drop in sales and forcing them to sell assets or to restructure—actions with major effects on such stakeholders as labor and local communities.

A golden parachute is a contract in which the corporation agrees to pay key officers if the corporation changes hands. Whereas poison pills and greenmail are designed mainly to block takeovers, golden parachutes are intended more to ease the way for departing executives. Staggering sums may be paid. Frank Lorenzo, for example, was awarded a severance package of $30 million when he surrendered his post as head of Texas Air. The late Ross Johnson of RJR did even better, taking away $53 million when he left that company.[8]

"Shark repellants" undoubtedly benefit corporate officers. They get to keep their jobs or, failing that, to retire in luxury. Whether making a pitched defense against takeover bids serves shareholders' interest is another question. According to a series of publications by the Securities and Exchange Commission in the 1980s, the antitakeover devices erode the value of shares. They do not add to owners' wealth, which is the stated goal.

None of these doubtful practices prove CEOs and other managers are *always* untrustworthy or negligent in their fiduciary role. There are many examples of executives who do excellent jobs for modest pay. Philip Knight, CEO of the sports shoe company Nike, earned just over $1 million in the three years ending in 1990; Nike shareholders earned a return of 323 percent during the same period.[9]

Remember, too, that most corporate officers have much of their personal wealth tied up in the companies they manage, and their annual income is usually tied to profit and share price. These are two good reasons for seeing shareholders prosper. Further, executives have to maintain their reputations if they ever need a promotion or job with another firm, giving them an incentive at least to create the impression of diligence and ability.

Still, a pattern of misuse of office exists in many large companies and other organizations that has caught the public's eye. The perceived corruption or incompetence by managers has led owners to try a variety of means, including the passage of new public policies, to bind corporations more closely to their will. Results have been mixed.

Governing the Publicly Traded Corporation

To understand the effort to make the corporation more accountable, let us first compare the formal governance of these organizations with the substance of how they really work. Then we will look at some public policy reforms.

Two Models of Governance

In capitalist societies, the law affirms that shareholders should have final say over what corporations do. Beyond that basic tenet, different countries have evolved two broad types of corporate governance.[10] One, which is practiced in the United States and Britain, stresses liquidity in the stock market. Firms depend on the stock exchanges and over-the-counter markets for capital. Shareholders check up on managers by watching share prices, whose movements are a barometer of managers' performance. This market-based system is underpinned by laws requiring that financial information be made public, and by insider-trading laws to stop managers from profiting from secret information.

The second model is followed in Germany and Japan. This insider system plays down liquidity for small shareholders. Capital is obtained mostly from banks, insurance companies, and other firms. Rather than monitoring managers through the stock market, these shareholders watch managers directly—sometimes by having an intermediary such as a bank do it for them (see Box 11–1). The owners and financial intermediaries forge close, long-term relationships with companies by buying large stakes and holding them. They often sit on boards of directors. In the course of these relationships, the intermediaries glean information about the managers, which is more important than the scant financial data that officially have to be revealed. There is only limited protection against insider trading.

At several points in the 20th century the United States was headed in the direction of this second model, with large institutions taking a large equity interest in other firms and paying close attention to how they are managed. Each time, public policy stopped this change. In 1906, insurance companies were banned from holding shares; in 1933, the Glass-Steagall Act separated commercial banking (making loans) and investment banking (organizing the issuing of stocks and bonds for corporations).[11] In the 1990s, the country seems again to be moving away from fragmented, apathetic ownership. The vehicle is mutual funds and pension plans. This time, public policy seems to be encouraging powerful owners who will take a hand in corporate governance. We will return to this question shortly.

Which Model Works Better?

Many people argue that the fast growth of Germany and Japan has been helped by long-term relationships between owners and managers. The insider model allows managers and owners to make valuable long-term commitments to each other. The slower growth of the United States and Britain since World War II gives credence to these arguments.

One of the most common complaints leveled against U.S. and British companies is that they have a short-term perspective. They make fewer long-term investments than firms in continental Europe or Asia. Many explanations have been given for American industry's impatience, but one is that managers need to

---

Box 11–1

Banks Have a More Important Equity Position in German and Japanese Companies Than They Do in the United States

Germany has a so-called universal banking system. It allows German banks to engage in all kinds of financial activities. The German system is distinct from the American approach, which is far more restrictive of banking. All the top banks hold large ownership shares in German companies, and bankers dominate the ranks of corporate boards. Germany's leading bank, Deutsche Bank, for example, holds a 28 percent stake in Daimler-Benz, Germany's largest industrial company. Banks also get to vote shares kept on deposit with them by small shareholders, giving them more power over corporations.

The close relationship between banking and industry in Germany goes back over 100 years. Equity markets did not exist, and banks stepped in to provide the capital needed by sprouting German industry.[1] Even today, only half the top 100 German companies are quoted on the stock exchange. Many observers think the banks' large role is a reason capital is more patient in Germany compared to the United States. German managers do not have to react to every move up or down in stock prices and have more latitude to take a longer-term view.[2]

Japan has similar institutions. Bank loans are a major source of capital for Japanese firms, most of which are more highly leveraged than American companies. Banks in Japan also maintain significant equity positions in their client companies—a practice from which U.S. banks have been barred by the Glass-Steagall Act since the Great Depression. Japanese banks also are expected to provide more business services than is the case in the United States, such as helping clients find customers.[3] Again, the tight, long-standing relationship among bankers and businesspeople is suspected of making it easier for Japanese companies to plan for the future.

Proposals have been made to reform U.S. banking policy, to give commercial banks greater flexibility. President Clinton, for example, called for Congress to repeal the Glass-Steagall Act in 1995. It is anticipated that such reforms might make American capital less impatient and reduce the pressures for quick returns that companies feel now. After the fiasco of the S&L industry deregulation of the early 1980s, however, Congress has been skittish about experimenting with commercial banks.

[1]Philip Glouchevitch, *Juggernaut* (New York: Simon and Schuster, 1992), pp. 72–75.

[2]Michael T. Jacobs, *Short-Term America* (Boston: Harvard Business School Press, 1991), Chapter 5.

3Michael L. Gerlach, *Alliance Capitalism* (Berkeley: University of California Press, 1992), pp. 114–18.

---

pump up current earnings to keep investors happy.[12] This may not be wise. A blue ribbon panel put together by the Twentieth Century Fund concluded that financial markets are a poor guide for managers' decisions, because securities investors are too swayed by passing news.[13]

Also, in the Anglo-American model of corporate governance, managers are hesitant to cut dividends when earnings slide. They fear shareholders will drive down the price of the company's stock. With extensive cross-holding of shares in the German and Japanese model of governance, managers can more easily trim the payment to shareholders. That leaves more funds for investment during down periods and may put German or Japanese companies in stronger positions when business picks up.

The insider system does have some drawbacks, though. It may lead to *over-investment*—the opposite problem of the market-based system. Since companies buy shares in each other to cement their broader business relationships, they may be more interested in capital gains or supply contracts than in dividends. Similarly, the banks are mainly interested in making loans to their clients. They may not care whether those loans are used for the most profitable investments, so long as they earn enough to repay the loans. In short, the insider system may not encourage the efficient use of capital.[14]

The market-based approach has corresponding advantages. Some observers prefer it because it is more fluid, and thus potentially more adaptable to changing circumstances. It also is less prone to becoming an ingrown, old-boy network and thus more open to new ventures. Both the United States and Britain have good records as business incubators. It is easier in these countries to be entrepreneurial than in the more closed corporate world of Germany or Japan.

But perhaps we are overstating the differences between the two models. Recent scandals and widespread privatization of government holdings in Europe are pushing continental firms closer to the Anglo-American model. Compared to before, shares are more widely held, shareholders wield more power, and outside directors are more likely to challenge management.

German companies, for example, are moving away from inscrutable German accounting standards. Sensing that German capital markets are too narrow for their future funding requirements, they hope the accounting changes will be a prelude to listing on the Big Board in New York.[15] This trend is another example of how different national political economies are converging due to new public policies, global competition, and economic change.

Annual Meetings

An element in all systems of corporate governance is the annual meeting. Shareholders are entitled to gather at least once each year to discuss the firm's performance and strategy. They may vote on various resolutions of importance to the owners. Harvard's John Kenneth Galbraith, with his usual irony, calls these meetings a corporate ceremony designed to give owners the impression of power.

> They are presented with handsomely printed reports . . . Products and even plants are inspected. During the proceedings, as in the report, there are repetitive references to *your* company. Officers listen, with every evidence of attention, to highly irrelevant suggestions of wholly uninformed participants and assure them that these will be considered with the utmost care . . . No decisions are taken. The annual meeting of the large American corporation is perhaps our most elaborate exercise in popular illusion.[16]

Beyond the universal right to an annual general meeting, shareholders' rights vary from country to country. As Table 11–3 shows, national law gives

TABLE 11–3   Shareholders' Rights Vary from Country to Country.

	France	*Germany*	*Japan*	*Sweden*	*Switzerland*	*United States*
Percent of shares to call extraordinary shareholders' meeting	5%	5%	3%	10%	10%	Varies by state
Minimum notice for meeting	45 days	30 days	14 days	14 days	10 days	21 days
Percent of shares to put item on agenda	5%	None	1%	None	10%	1%
Management must provide accounts	Yes	Yes	Yes	No	No	Yes
Shareholders can inspect books	NA	Yes	Yes*	Yes*	No	NA

*For holders of more than 10 percent of outstanding shares.

Source: Joseph Lufkin and David Gallagher, eds., *International Corporate Governance* (London: Euromoney Books, 1990), p. 3.

Swedish and Swiss investors fewer chances to call special meetings, to be told of meetings, to put items on the agenda, and to get detailed information about company operations. Owners of French, German, and Japanese stock have generally more rights regarding these items. U.S. shareholders fall in the middle.

Boards of Directors

Besides attending meetings and voting on resolutions, shareholders get to control the corporation by picking the board of directors, whom they delegate to oversee the business. Voting is proportionate to the number of shares owned. A shareholder with 100 shares has 100 votes, one with 10 shares has only 10 votes. Whoever controls 50 percent plus one of the shares gets to name the board of directors. Since shareholders rarely can attend shareholders' meetings, they are given the opportunity to vote by absentee ballot (called a *proxy*).

Corporate boards are legally permitted to vary in size and structure. In the United States, for example, the average board of a manufacturing concern has 13 members, with a range of 8 to 22. German and Japanese corporate boards are generally larger, having up to 50 members in Japan. Most U.S. board members have a three-year term of office. They usually convene quarterly, for two to three hours, though some boards in the United States gather as rarely as twice a year, while others meet twice a month.[17]

There are two kinds of board members: inside directors (people serving as managers of the companies that employ them) and outside directors (prominent people whose principal employment is elsewhere). Inside directors have the advantage of knowing the company intimately, and the disadvantage of being so close to operations they may not be objective. The opposite is true of the outside directors. They tend to be less informed, but perhaps can be more impartial.

Different countries have a different balance between inside and outside directors on corporate boards. As Table 11–4 shows, all boards in France and Sweden, and most in the United States, have a majority of outside directors. By contrast, in Germany and Japan, no boards have a majority of outside directors.

The push in the United States has been to get even more outsiders on the boards to avoid the conflict of interest inherent to inside directors.

There are also differences in the kind of person chosen to be director. Some countries stipulate that workers be represented on the board of directors. This method of tapping employees for ideas and support is most common in corporatist states, notably Germany and Sweden. The Germans call their system **co-determination.** It is a form of **industrial democracy,** under which employees elect representatives to seats on the board of directors of the companies for which they work (see Box 11–2). In the United States, workers rarely get a seat, even in employee-owned firms. (We will return to this issue of worker ownership and participation shortly.)

Nowhere do corporate boards match closely the general population. Members are older, more male, and less diverse in ethnic background than would happen at random. To stem criticism that their boards are unrepresentative, U.S. companies have been bringing a more diverse group into the boardroom over the past decade. By 1989, for example, 18 percent of corporate boards in manufacturing industries had at least one minority group member. The United States is unusual in having more women corporate directors than other countries have.

Stronger Boards?

Corporate boards only have time to consider broad policy issues, not the nitty-gritty of day-to-day company operations. The intent is for corporate boards to dismiss any management team judged to be doing a poor job and to hire a new team of managers. Yet, as we have seen, corporate boards are seldom an effective check on management in the United States. Why?

A pair of reasons stands out. First, under the American system, management usually controls the proxy machinery. Shareholders have neither the time nor the interest to inform themselves about the details of internal corporate affairs. Why should they? Shareholders see themselves mainly as investors and have no particular loyalty to any one company. Their main worry is the value of their equity in terms of earnings, appreciation, and salability. Thus, shareholders are apt to turn their proxies over to the company's executives, allowing the executives usu-

TABLE 11–4   **Corporate Boards of Directors Are Composed Differently in Different Countries.**

	France	*Germany*	*Japan*	*Sweden*	*United Kingdom*	*United States*
Percent with majority of outside directors	100%	0	0	100%	30%	83%
Workers sit as voting directors	No	Yes	No	Yes	No	No
Percent with women directors	1.5%	NA	0	10%	4%	28%

Note: Refers to manufacturing companies only.

Source: Jeremy Bacon and James K. Brown, *The Board of Directors: Perspectives and Practices in Nine Countries* (New York: Conference Board, 1977), p. 22.

Box 11–2

Germany Has Instituted a Model of Industrial Democracy

In Germany, employers and unions are known as social partners, reflecting a different attitude than the more antagonistic one prevailing in American firms.[1] German managers prefer to manage by consensus, and public policy has helped create the mechanisms to do so.

By German law, workers of every company with five or more employees can elect representatives to a works council. The council must be consulted about important organizational changes, and they have veto rights over company personnel decisions. The works councils are tightly linked to the labor unions. For large firms (more than 2,000 workers), the law goes further. It mandates that employees be represented on corporate supervisory boards, in numbers equal to the representation of shareholders. Ordinary work-

ers, in other words, have a say in overseeing the work of their bosses. Other countries, such as Sweden, have copied aspects of this system of codetermination.

Some advocates of codetermination attribute Germany's industrial calm to it. There are few strikes, and output per worker is high, giving German firms an advantage in international competition. Skeptics, however, point out that German firms have an unusual structure, with two boards. It is the second, management board that has most of the power, so the gulf between the U.S. and German systems is not as wide as appears on paper.

Further, the workers on the supervisory boards are apt to be docile, not the source of much criticism. The cooperation between workers and managers in Germany probably is due mainly to historical and cultural factors, not to the formal structure of organizations. From this point of view, codetermination is more the effect of social harmony than its cause.

---

[1]Kirsten S. Wever and Christopher S. Allen, "Is Germany a Model for Managers?" *Harvard Business Review,* September–October 1992, pp. 36–43.

---

ally to outvote dissident shareholders. (Some readers will observe that shareholder passivity is another instance of free riding. The payoff of organizing a shareholders' revolt is less than the personal costs they would have to bear. Such revolts are usually led by a corporate raider who stands to make a huge personal return from organizing shareholders.)

The second source of management power results from mastery over the board of directors. A board is supposed to supervise the executives, but it is the executives who control the information available to the board, and it is they who can set the agenda for discussion. The dynamics of small groups and the pressure to get along cause controversial issues to be buried. Frequently, boards are little more than rubber stamps for the managers' proposals, unable or unwilling to be an independent counterweight.

Still, things may be changing. Lately, U.S. corporate boards seem to be taking their responsibilities more seriously. One reason is shareholder suits against negligent directors. While directors are protected by the corporate shell from personally meeting the financial obligations of the corporation, they are not protected for failing to carry out their fiduciary responsibilities. Legal actions against directors have become more common in recent years. About 300 U.S. firms were subject to 713 claims against directors and officers in 1993—23 percent more than five years earlier.[18] Companies provide liability insurance to their boards, but the threat of a legal action keeps members on their toes. (It also deters some qualified people from wanting to serve as corporate directors.)

Because of scandals and public scrutiny, many corporate boards also have begun to form committees to do their work more professionally. The most important is the audit committee, made entirely of outside directors, to monitor accounting methods and ensure the accuracy of information in the annual report.

The same forces for greater accountability are being felt in the nonprofit sector. Under pressure from the state attorney general, for instance, the trustees of Boston University grudgingly agreed to change their procedures. Previously, a small subcommittee set executive compensation, and they had made John Silber the highest paid university president in the country. Now, the full board must vote on top university officers' pay. Also, the trustees accepted safeguards to prevent financial conflicts of interest between themselves and the university. And they agreed to term limits and to let nonuniversity employees join in choosing new trustees.[19]

Boards seem more willing to flex their muscles and to reject management. A good example is the decision by the directors of GM in 1992 to fire CEO Robert Stempel, because he had not removed enough executive deadwood and not moved quickly enough to turn around the troubled automaker. GM's boardroom coup was engineered by dissident outside directors. Similarly, outside board members in 1993 forced out Kay Whitmore, the chairman of Eastman Kodak Co., for not moving fast enough to improve the company's financial performance.

Such events are still the exception, not the norm. As Harvard's Jay Lorsch found in a recent study, boards of most companies remain only minor participants in corporate affairs. Lorsch thinks U.S. boards' small role impedes the ability of American companies to compete abroad.[20]

Exit and Voice in Corporate Governance

Owners in the United States have two basic ways to reassert dominion over corporations. Albert O. Hirschman, an economist at the Institute for Advanced Studies, calls these the *exit option* and the *voice option.* Hirschman points out business and other formal organizations often give below-par service. Disgruntled stakeholders have a choice. They may leave the organization and take their business elsewhere (the exit option), or they may stay with the organization but express their unhappiness through petition, protest, and other political activities (the voice option).[21] Economists, because of their admiration for market mechanisms, usually like to see organizations disciplined through exit; political scientists, with their interest in democracy, are prone to prefer voice. Hirschman points out, however, that neither option is inherently superior.

In the United States, as we noted earlier, dispersed corporate owners have traditionally favored exit. If they are unhappy with the company's record, they simply sell their stock and invest somewhere else. For the Anglo-American model's enthusiasts, exit is a sufficient restraint on managers. When enough owners dump a company's shares, or threaten to do so, they will force down the value of those shares. The theory is that a prolonged fall in share value will alert managers to try a new strategy, or signal the board of directors that a change in leadership is in order.

For the exit mechanism to get managers' attention, there obviously must be a broad and deep market for corporate shares, as exists in the United States and Great Britain. Exit will be less potent in countries such as Germany and, to a lesser extent, Japan, where securities markets are not as well established and most shares are held by (or voted by) a few banks and other institutions. But even in the United States or Britain, one may doubt whether the roundabout mechanism of "voting with dollars" is adequate to express specific gripes about company activity.

In recent years, U.S. shareholders have been taking up the voice option more often. Two trends are driving the switch toward voice: the rise of activist shareholders and the spread of institutional ownership.

Activist Shareholders

Not all owners care exclusively about profit. Contrary to a simplistic political economy view, owners can put other values—the environment, justice, public health and safety—at the same level or above profit. In fact, public interest groups sometimes buy shares specifically to force a change in company policy with no design to make money on their holdings. Since their ownership is often token, the best way these new stakeholders have found to convey their preference is via internal political action. From the late 1960s, therefore, activist shareholders have been using annual meetings to push their social agenda.[22] Many companies have put church or civic leaders on their boards as a way to appease, or perhaps co-opt, activists.

The activists' most common goal has been to fight apartheid in South Africa. The pressure was sufficient to get most U.S. firms with business in South Africa to sign the Sullivan Code, agreeing to desegregate their workplaces and recognize black unions. During the 1980s, about half the U.S. firms with business in South Africa went further and ended their activities in that country. Most, however, simply licensed South African firms to continue the same business, raising doubt about corporate sincerity. The apartheid problem is now moot, and activists are turning more to environmental and health issues.

Institutional Owners

The second factor driving the increased use of voice is the spread of institutional ownership of shares. Such institutions as pension funds and mutual funds have increased their part of corporate equity from 8 percent of the total in 1950 to nearly 60 percent in 1990, according to Michael Porter.[23] These institutions own so much stock that, for them, the exit option is becoming less and less workable. When institutional ownership was insignificant, it was easy to sell off poorly performing stock and buy shares in a more attractive company, but no longer. Simple arithmetic makes it harder and harder to do better than average, creating an inducement for institutional owners to become directly involved in management decisions as a way to protect the value of their assets. The term coined for this approach is "relationship investing."[24]

The two trends—socially conscious shareholding and institutional investing—have begun to blend. Through their pension funds, for example, the Teamsters and the United Food and Commercial Workers have been leaders to get Philip Morris to split its food and tobacco units. Some mutual funds now invest only in companies deemed socially responsible, a category that usually excludes gambling, tobacco, and alcohol companies, among others. In 1984, less than $40 billion was professionally managed in the name of socially responsible investing; by 1992, the total was $700 billion, according to the Social Investment Forum.[25] If accurate, that figure is the equivalent of half the net assets in all U.S. mutual funds.

Institutions still turn over their portfolios—the average holding period of stocks has fallen from more than seven years in 1960 to less than two years today. They are encouraged by laws and regulations to be prudent and spread their investment risk by taking small stakes in many different companies. Still, the large institutional owners are being led, whether they want to or not, to become more involved in corporate governance. Public sector pension funds, such as those in New York and California, have taken the lead. Private institutional investors have been more conservative about challenging management, though Fidelity Investments, the nation's largest mutual fund group, is working behind the scenes to overhaul many large companies.[26] Unlike the individual investor, investment institutions have the potential clout to make their voice heard. Thus, the United States may come to look more like Germany and Japan in terms of who controls large companies.

As U.S. institutional investors move toward having more voice in corporate affairs, their calculus probably will force them also to think further into the future than has been customary. Edward C. Johnson, head of the Fidelity group of mutual funds, argues, "For too long institutions have failed to act as long-term owners of the equity they hold. They have failed to use their influence as shareholders."[27] If institutions have less flexibility to abandon dullard companies, they are apt to insist on long-run restructuring and turnaround programs.

Shareholders' Bill of Rights

In 1985, several public sector funds banded into an umbrella group, known as the Council of Institutional Investors. With more than 50 members and assets of $300 billion, the council has promulgated a Shareholders' Bill of Rights, which states:

American Corporations are the cornerstones of the free enterprise system, and as such must be governed by the principles of accountability and fairness inherent in our democratic system. The shareholders of American corporations are the owners of such corporations, and the directors elected by the shareholders are accountable to the shareholders. Furthermore, the shareholders of American corporations are entitled to participate in the fundamental financial decisions that could affect corporate performance and growth and the long-range viability and competitiveness of corporations.[28]

Specific items in this Bill of Rights include giving all shares of common stock equal voting rights, requiring majority shareholder approval of significant transactions, and approving independent directors for annual compensation of chief executives. Groups such as the Council of Institutional Investors and the United Shareholders of America, mentioned earlier, may represent a shift in the balance of power of major corporations.

Enhancing Shareholder Voice with New Public Policy

In response to owners' demand for checks on management power, the Securities and Exchange Commission (the federal agency regulating the securities industry) in 1992 introduced a slate of reforms that could equip institutional investors to contest seriously the way companies are run. The reforms include:

- Lifting the restrictions that bar investors from talking to one another.
- Easing access to companies' lists of shareholders.
- Relaxing the process of circulating proxy campaign material.
- Requiring greater disclosure of total executive pay, including the value of stock options.[29]

The SEC's actions are having an impact. According to the Investor Responsibility Research Center, for example, labor unions sponsored 70 proxy battles in the first half of 1994, versus only 16 in all of 1992.[30]

Similar policies are being considered or enacted around the world. In Britain, the *Cadbury Report* on corporate governance recommends having a majority of outside directors and more completely divulging executive pay. Shareholder revolts have forced out the top executives at Barclays Bank, British Aerospace, and British Air in recent years. In Japan, the Ministry of Justice is proposing rules to allow suits against directors for poor performance. Helping push these reforms overseas is the $70 billion California Public Employees' Retirement System (CALPERS), which has holdings around the world. CALPERS has launched an international corporate governance program aimed at foreign companies.

Creditor Stakeholders

A company's creditors have little to say about internal governance in normal times. When a company gets into financial trouble, matters change. Creditors have first claim on a company's assets. They will want to find ways to use those assets to raise cash to pay off its debts to them, as quickly as possible. The threat of insolvency often brings creditors into sharp conflict with shareholders and employees, who are interested in a different question: how to keep the firm going, in the hope of turning the business around, even if that means not paying off debt.

Bankruptcy law provides the framework for working out these clashing interests, which are of such overwhelming public importance that the U.S. Constitution specifically empowers Congress to enact uniform bankruptcy legislation. These rules are yet another example of the public character of private property. As Theodore Lowi puts it: "Just as there have to be legal procedures for acquiring and exchanging property, there have to be procedures for liquidating it. Property is private as long as it is successful. When it fails, it becomes public, either permanently or temporarily through the process of receivership."[31]

Chapter 11

American bankruptcy law was last reformed in 1978. This change in public policy triggered a wave of voluntary bankruptcies under its **Chapter 11** provisions (see Figure 11–1).

Designed to give breathing room to firms with a cash flow problem, Chapter 11 provides temporary respite from creditors while a rescue plan is negotiated with shareholders and creditors. Usually Chapter 11 is voluntary, chosen by the existing management team to retain control of the bankrupt firm. Once in Chap-

FIGURE 11–1

Voluntary bankruptcy filings of U.S. corporations exploded in the 1980s

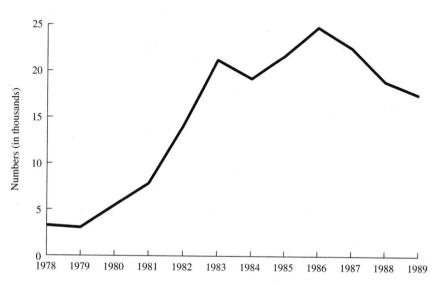

Source: Michael Bradley and Michael Rosenzwigh, "The Untenable Case for Chapter 11," *Yale Law Journal* 101, no. 5 (1992), p. 1090.

ter 11, managers have 120 days to submit a plan to the bankruptcy judge. A plan usually includes debt rescheduling and equity transfers, and it must be approved by two-thirds of the shareholders and two-thirds of the creditors. Negotiations can go on for much longer. LTV, a steelmaker, was in Chapter 11 for seven years starting in 1986.

Chapter 11 is controversial.[32] The legal and accounting fees can run into the millions. Allowing the executives who ran a company into the ground the chance to save it seems a doubtful policy. Healthy companies also complain that Chapter 11 inhibits the market from weeding out inefficient players.

Chapter 7

The other important part of U.S. bankruptcy law is Chapter 7, or straight bankruptcy. Here, a court-appointed trustee takes charge of the company, sells the firm's assets, and pays off its debts. Chapter 7 liquidation proceedings may be either voluntary, with the debtor seeking relief from creditors, or involuntarily compelled by the creditors. More than 650,000 companies wound up under Chapter 7 in 1991. Many of these were formerly in Chapter 11 (80 percent of firms in voluntary bankruptcy fail to reorganize and are eventually liquidated).

Creditors versus Owners

The outcome of a U.S. bankruptcy proceeding seems weighed against creditors, because the law gives shareholders a veto over rescue plans. Any delay hurts creditors, who lose money every day negotiations drag on, much more than it hurts shareholders. The threat of stalling thus enables shareholders to force concessions from creditors. This may drive up the cost of borrowing for all firms. Drawn-out negotiations can also give bankrupt firms an unfair edge against better-run competitors, who are not relieved of interest payments meanwhile.

Most other countries—Japan, Germany, and France, for instance—also favor owners in bankruptcy (Britain is an exception). But in Japan and Germany, at least, the stress is on voluntary proceedings that avoid the high transaction cost of going through the courts.

Because of pressure from two stakeholder groups—creditors and solvent competitors—Congress is contemplating changing the bankruptcy law. Reforms are also likely to help another stakeholder group, retirees, whose pension rights often are not protected in bankruptcy proceedings. Congress seems set to establish deadlines for rescue plans, after which time an independent arbitrator could be brought in to resolve the conflict between shareholders and creditors.[33]

Listening to Employee Stakeholders

Employees, who can spend a lifetime working for an employer and who come to depend on it for their livelihood, clearly have a legitimate right to some say in what their employers do. In the United States, the tradition is for employees to exert influence on companies through labor unions. The unions organize employees and bargain with management over pay and working conditions, backing up their bargaining position with the threat of strikes.

Labor relations in the United States assume strife. Unions (representing workers) and managers (representing owners) fight over surplus resources. Often, this fight becomes a win–lose situation by which one stakeholder gains at the other's expense. Productivity and profits may suffer.

Labor relations are not so confrontational in every country, especially in countries that have a corporatist background. For example, Germany's labor market resembles the medieval guild system, in which craftsmen set wages, defend quality standards, and discourage outside competition. Employees belong to trade unions, employers to industry associations. They negotiate wages across whole industries. Firms that belong to an industry association may not pay less than the negotiated minimum. Workers like this practice of wage bargaining because of the high benefits it generates; managers like it because it minimizes the threat of strikes. It is a win–win situation, in which everyone gains.

"Workers' Capitalism"

American public policy has tried to foster more cooperation within firms. One way is by laws encouraging worker ownership. The idea is to give workers a stake in a company's profitability. Not only should ownership induce unsupervised workers to work harder themselves, it also should encourage them to stop fellow workers from free riding.

Fully worker-owned firms are rare in the U.S. industrial sector—an exception is the plywood industry where production cooperatives account for perhaps 10 percent of plywood output. Partial ownership is a different matter. Many corporations have been encouraging workers' ownership through **ESOPs (Employee Stock Ownership Plans).**[34] These are also known as Kelso plans, after Louis Kelso, the attorney who popularized the idea. The shares in the ESOP are exempt from federal taxes until distributed on retirement.

Typically, ESOPs are set up as a deferred compensation plan. The employer deposits stock in a trust fund that holds the stock for participating employees. Sometimes, the idea is to get employees to accept pay cuts so a company can become more competitive. The tax incentive, available since 1974, has made this form of worker ownership popular. Today, roughly 9,500 companies have ESOPs—representing about 10 percent of the nation's workforce. Another 5,000 firms have other kinds of worker ownership schemes.[35]

Kelso plans rarely give workers a voice in governance of the firm, however. About half the stock ESOPs hold is nonvoting. Only a handful of the big employee-owned firms, including TWA, Northwest Airlines, and Republic Engineered Steels, have nonmanagement employees sitting on their boards. The ESOPs, thus, bear little resemblance to European industrial democracy, which mandates codetermination.

In the 1980s, management increasingly began to turn to ESOPs as another weapon in the anti-takeover arsenal, using the plans to buy out companies under siege. Such uses of worker ownership were not what the law intended and are widely seen as an abuse. ESOPs also have been criticized for exposing participants to undue risk, by tying up their assets in one company. According to this argument, workers would be better served by a diversified pension fund and a profit-sharing compensation plan—an approach that offers most of the advantages of an ESOP in giving workers a sense of belonging and shared responsibility, witho ut the attendant risk. For these reasons, the U.S. Congress is considering repealing the tax subsidy given to ESOPs.

Quality Circles

A different approach to listening to employees is through **quality circles.** An idea originated in the United States and perfected in Japan, the circles include shop-floor workers in finding ways to enhance quality and raise productivity, on the assumption that they are in the best position to know how to innovate. In continental Europe, similar bodies for routine consultation with employees are called works councils.

American public policy does not require this kind of participation, though many companies have experimented with it. The situation is different in the European Union. Works councils are mandated for large companies in all member countries except Britain.[36] The intent is to improve competitiveness through communication. American subsidiaries in Europe have vowed to resist the directive to have works councils.

Getting workers and managers to cooperate has proven difficult in the United States due to the deep-seated adversarial tradition in industrial relations.[37] Yet, companies that can carry out worker participation schemes seem to pull ahead of their rivals, especially if participation is combined with worker ownership, according to one federal study.[38] Famous examples are the Lincoln Electric Company, a manufacturer of arc welding equipment, and Nucor, a mini-mill steel company, both of which maintain high output by soliciting workers' ideas and allowing them to buy company shares. (Lincoln Electric later got in trouble for an ill-advised overseas expansion program, but that is a different story.)

Conclusion

The American corporation is typified by strong managers and weak owners. U.S. corporate managers have preserved much of their autonomy despite criticisms that such independence does not fit in a democratic society. Management decisions about investment, employment, and product development affect everyone, not just owners, yet other corporate stakeholders still have little say in picking corporate leaders or in approving their policies.

The American approach to corporate governance is different than in Japan or Germany. In the United States, control shifted more than 50 years ago from fragmented shareholders, none owning more than a small share of the company, to managers, who became expert professionals. In Japan, groups of firms and banks are woven together through complex webs of cross-ownership; in Germany, large banks oversee companies in a dual position as shareholder and lender. The American system gives little formal role to workers in determining corporate policy; the German and, in a different way, Japanese systems give workers more input.

The balance may be shifting, however. New public policies are in the pipeline in the United States that promise to add to the countervailing power of some stakeholders, especially owners of corporate equity, and also creditors and employees. Management is likely to keep the whip hand, however, due to its key position in the corporate hierarchy. Employees are asserting their rights in other domains with the corporation, too, and often are meeting with more success. That is our topic in Chapter 12.

Questions

1. What are the main issues in corporate governance? Why have they developed? What are the remedies?

2. How does corporate governance differ in Germany or Japan?

3. Explain how corporate raiding relates to corporate governance.

4. What are the types of bankruptcy? What ethical issues do they raise?

5. Describe industrial democracy. Is it a good idea?

End Notes

1. Adam Smith, *An Inquiry into the Nature and Origins of the Wealth of Nations* (1776; reprint, New York: Modern Library, 1937), p. 700.

2. The classic works are Adolf A. Berle and Gardiner C. Means, *The Modern Corporation and Private Property,* rev. ed. (New York: Harcourt, Brace & World, 1967); and James Burnham, *The Managerial Revolution* (1941; reprint, Westport, CT: Greenwood Press, 1972).

3. See, for example, Robert Michel's classic analysis of the "iron law of oligarchy," *Political Parties,* trans. Eden and Cedar Paul (Glencoe, IL: Free Press, 1962).

4. See "Executive Pay: The Party Ain't Over Yet," *Business Week,* April 26, 1993, pp. 56ff; and "Bosses' Pay," *The Economist,* February 1, 1992, pp. 19–22.

5. John A. Byrne, "The Flap over Executive Pay," *Business Week,* May 6, 1991, p. 90.

6. Alice Dembner, "BU Gave Silber $300,000 Bonus during AG Probe," *Boston Globe,* May 13, 1994, p. 23.

7. "Executive Pay," *Business Week,* March 30, 1992, pp. 52–58.

8. Dan Dalton, "Let the Punishment Fit the Corporate Crime," *Business Month,* November 1990, p. 100.

9. Byrne, "Flap over Executive Pay."

10. "Watching the Boss: A Survey of Corporate Governance," *The Economist,* January 29, 1994. Also see Nicholas Dimsdale and Martha Preveyer, eds., *Capital Markets and Corporate Governance* (Oxford: Oxford University Press, 1994).

11. Mark Roe, *Strong Managers, Weak Owners: The Political Roots of American Corporate Finance* (Princeton, NJ: Princeton University Press, 1994). On the Glass-Steagall Act, see George J. Benston, *The Separation of Commercial and Investment Banking* (New York: Oxford University Press, 1990).

12. Michael Porter, "Capital Disadvantage: America's Failing Capital Investment System," *Harvard Business Review,* September–October 1992, pp. 65–82.

13. *The Report of the Twentieth Century Fund Task Force on Market Speculation and Corporate Governance* (New York: Twentieth Century Fund Press, 1992).

14. "Survey of Japan," *The Economist,* July 9, 1994, p. 13.

15. Peter Grumbel and Greg Steinmetz, "German Firms Shift to More Open Accounting," *The Wall Street Journal,* March 15, 1995, p. C1.

16. John Kenneth Galbraith, *The New Industrial State,* 4th ed. (Boston: Houghton Mifflin, 1985), pp. 88–89.

17. Jeremy Bacon, *Membership and Organization of Corporate Boards* (New York: Conference Board, 1990).

18. "Boardrooms: The Ties that Bind," *Business Week,* May 2, 1994, p. 113.

19. Alice Dembner, "BU Trustees Agree to Increase Control," *Boston Globe,* December 15, 1993, p. 33.

20. Jay W. Lorsch, *Pawns or Potentates: The Reality of America's Corporate Boards* (Boston: Harvard Business School Press, 1989).

21. Albert O. Hirschman, *Exit, Voice, and Loyalty* (Cambridge, MA: Harvard University Press, 1970).

22. See David Vogel, *Lobbying the Corporation* (New York: Basic Books, 1978), especially Chapter 3.

23. Cited in Steve Lohr, "Fixing Corporate America's Short-Term Mind Set," *The New York Times,* September 2, 1992, p. D3.

24. See Judith H. Dobrzynski, "Relationship Investing," *Business Week,* March 15, 1993, pp. 68ff.

25. "Socially Responsible Investing on the Rise," *Boston Herald,* October 18, 1993, p. 26.

26. Allen R. Meyerson, "The New Activism at Fidelity," *The New York Times,* August 8, 1993, p. F15.

27. Ibid.

28. James E. Heard, "Institutional Investors and Corporate Governance: The US Perspective," in *International Corporate Governance,* ed. Joseph Lufkin and David Gallagher (London: Euromoney Books, 1990), p. 246.

29. Judith H. Dobrzynski, "An October Surprise that Has Shareholders Cheering," *Business Week,* November 4, 1992, p. 144.

30. "Labor Flexes Its Muscles—as a Stockholder," *Business Week,* July 18, 1994, p. 79.

31. Theodore J. Lowi, "The Public Character of Private Markets," unpublished manuscript, Cornell University (July 1985), p. 5.

32. "When Firms Go Bust," *The Economist,* August 1, 1992, pp. 63–65. Subsequent paragraphs draw heavily on this article.

33. "A New Page for Chapter 11?" *Business Week,* January 25, 1993.

34. Henry Hansmann, "When Does Worker Ownership Work?" *Yale Law Journal* 99, no. 8 (1990), p. 1758.

35. "A Firm of Their Own," *The Economist,* June 11, 1994, p. 61.

36. "EU to Require Works Councils," *International Herald Tribune,* June 23, 1994, p. 13.

37. Michael L. Dertouzos, Richard K. Lester, Robert M. Solow, and the MIT Commission on Industrial Productivity, *Made in America: Regaining the Productive Edge* (New York: HarperPrennial, 1989), pp. 150–51.

38. Dunlop Commission, *Report of the Commission for the Future of Worker/Management Relations,* Draft (Washington, DC: 1994).

12   PUBLIC POLICY AND WORKERS' RIGHTS

A successful industrial nation—which means a nation with a future—doesn't allow itself to be organized as a collective amusement park.
Helmut Kohl[1]

Markets do not define or enforce rights; states do. Rights mean little in the abstract. They are won or lost mainly in the public policy arena. Since before the emergence of capitalism, employers and employees, managers and workers, have fought over their relative rights and relative obligations.

In all democracies, employees have won new rights at the expense of employers over the past century. They have taken many traditional prerogatives away from their bosses, a process that is continuing. Compared to earlier times, employers today have more duties toward their workers. Though some cooperative and enlightened employers freely embrace many employee rights, it is public policy that gives these rights their bite.

The job-related rights we explore in this chapter include varieties of civil, political, and economic rights—categories we introduced in Chapter 4. Many of these rights originated in the public sector and spread, in different form, to the private sector. Workers, for instance, now make claims to privacy, free speech, equal treatment, and other civil liberties in the workplace, claims that are parallel to those they make as citizens in the political arena. Workers also have earned a type of political rights on the job in the sense that they can participate in labor unions. Finally, they have won economic or social rights in employment, such as the right to minimum wages, shorter hours, and fringe benefits.

Workers have done still better for themselves in Europe and Japan. There, complex legal provisions and customs favor permanent employment and secure job tenure. Workers are apt to have more input into corporate governance, and more protection when they do get laid off.

We will look first at the common law basis for labor relations in the United

States. Then, we will learn how changing interpretations of the law, plus the passage of new laws by legislatures, gradually ate away at owners' and managers' power. While public policy is always changing, we will take a snapshot and see what employers' current obligations are toward the people who work for them.

Employment-at-Will Doctrine

In the United States, employer–employee rights are governed by a body of common law called "agency." The central precept in agency law is **employment at will.** Framing employment as a master–servant relationship, this long-standing doctrine holds that the employer can set the terms and conditions of the job. Agency law also maintains that the agreement between employer and employee is voluntary. By common consent, the employer gets to control the employee's actions. Either party can end these agreements at any time: Employees are free to quit their jobs, and employers are free to discharge those who work for them. The thrust of the employment-at-will doctrine was to create a free market for labor, breaking the older bonds of feudalism that tied workers to the land or to a guild.

Though the employment-at-will doctrine looks evenhanded, critics note that it really favors employers. Supervisors and subordinates do not come to the workplace as equals. Their relationship is asymmetric, at least when unemployment is high. Finding a new worker is easier than finding a new job. Under these circumstances, an individual worker's implicit threat to quit is little restraint on a manager's authority.

Through the 19th century, U.S. courts interpreted the employment-at-will doctrine strictly. As a judge ruled in Tennessee in 1884: "All may dismiss their employees at will, be they many or few, for good cause, for no cause, or even for cause morally wrong without thereby being guilty of legal wrong."[2] In this laissez-faire interpretation, the state can put no limit on employers' right to hire and fire whom they please. As long as workers are willing to go along, employers can set any terms for employment. Even the basic constitutional safeguards, for example, the right to due process or to free speech, do not apply at the workplace.

Continental Europe's policies were more benevolent at the time. Employment was viewed in the spirit of tutelage, a carryover from medieval practices that were more thoroughly purged in the common law of England (and by extension in America). Employers had obligations that protected their workers' jobs, but workers had reciprocal obligations that constrained their liberty to move from post to post.[3] So the paternalistic European approach had its drawbacks, too.

American workers were not entirely happy with being subjected to the rigors of the labor market, which made them rely on the goodwill of their employer. They began trying to use the policy process to protect themselves in personnel matters. The state has responded over the last century or so by trimming employers' freedom to do whatever they want with their employees. As we will see, employers never accepted the challenge to their authority passively, and they retain important privileges.

Child Labor Laws

Among the earliest workplace regulations were those that governed the employment of children. Factory owners liked children for many jobs because children could be paid less. As any reader of Charles Dickens' novels knows, working conditions were brutal. It seemed to many onlookers unfair and heartless to take advantage of young people this way.

Connecticut passed the nation's first state-level child labor law in 1813, though all it did was require that children working in factories be given instruction in reading, writing, and arithmetic. By 1899, 28 states had some kind of protection for child workers. The minimum employment age was usually 12 years, with no more than 10 hours of work allowed per day.[4] During the Progressive Era, these policies were strengthened significantly and enforcement beefed up. Women also got special protection from long hours. Factory owners resisted these policies, which drove up adult male wages and made it harder to turn a profit.

The controversy has faded, and few today dispute the need for the state to step into the workplace and block young people from working. There is a market failure due to young people's inability to make a free and informed choice about taking a job. Putting them to work is inherently an abuse of employers' power. All industrial nations have effective policies regulating child labor.

The basic U.S. statute is the Fair Labor Standards Act, passed in 1938 and later amended. With certain exceptions (mainly in agriculture), children under 14 years of age may not be employed, and hours are restricted for children under 18. Still, infractions occur. In 1993, for instance, A&P stores agreed to pay $490,000 in fines for illegally employing more than 800 minors since 1987. Violations involved allowing youths under 18 to work with hazardous equipment, employing 14- and 15-year-olds during prohibited times, and hiring 12- and 13-year olds. The same year, Red Lion, the fast-growing food chain, agreed to pay $16.2 million for violations of child labor laws—the largest such accord ever with a private employer.[5]

Conditions are much worse in the Third World. Most LDCs have child labor laws on the books, but enforcement is lax. An estimated 100 to 200 million underage workers in the Third World toil on farms, in textile factories, and in other pursuits. Many of their products find their way into the hands of American consumers.[6] The Child Labor Deterrence Act, banning the import of anything made by children, has been proposed to stop this practice. We discuss trade and public policy in detail in Chapter 17.

Wages and Hours

Adult workers in the 19th century also pushed for the right to shorter hours. Twelve- and 14-hour days were common in many industries, and workers wanted policies to allow them more leisure time. With some exceptions, business opposed these demands, too. A shorter workweek makes labor scarcer, making it easier for people to quit their jobs and harder for companies to recruit replacement workers.

Eventually, workers won the right to shorter hours in the United States, with a 10-hour day becoming the norm during the Civil War and the 8-hour day during World War I. The Fair Labor Standards Act, mentioned above, specifies that wage earners be paid "time and a half" for work over 40 hours a week. (Professional, administrative, and executive employees are exempt from the overtime provisions of the Fair Labor Standards Act, and many of them work longer than 40 hours without extra pay.) At one point during the Great Depression, 30-hour-week legislation passed the Senate. The idea was to pull even lower the ceiling on weekly hours to prompt companies to make more jobs. Business threw up fierce opposition, and President Roosevelt abandoned his support.

Most European countries have statutory weekly hours similar to those in the United States—though Germany and Italy allow 48-hour weeks. Still, because of collective bargaining agreements, the effective workweek for Europeans is often 35 to 37½ hours. In 1991, the average German manufacturing worker clocked but 31⅔ hours a week (including vacation weeks), the average Italian worker, 34¼ hours. Their Japanese and American competitors put in an average of 35¾ hours and 36⅔ hours a week.[7]

The work gap is widening, with Americans working even more than they did 10 or 20 years ago. This is often by choice, as, unlike their European counterparts, many Americans say they prefer extra income to extra leisure. It is not clear that more work is better for society, due to stress and "burnout." Productivity may be enhanced by working more efficiently for less time.[8] There also can be other social cost from working too much, measured in the slighting of children and the decay of voluntary community activities.

The last important part of the Fair Labor Standards Act covers minimum wages. To ensure workers a modest standard of living, Congress required that they be paid at least $0.25 an hour. The amount has been raised several times since then, to its current level of $4.25. Inflation has risen faster, so the minimum wage is no longer enough to keep a full-time worker's family above the poverty level.[9]

Figure 12–1 shows that other industrial countries are more generous about minimum wages. In the United States, the statutory minimum is less than one-quarter the median wage. In the European Union, by contrast, the statutory minimum is often the equivalent of half or more the median wage, perhaps adequate to feed, cloth, and house a person in modest comfort. Britain is the only member without a statutory minimum.

Whether minimum wage policies work is controversial. Many economists maintain that minimum wages only add to unemployment, particularly among the young, whose skill levels may not warrant even $4.25. Rather than hire a menial worker at the statutory base, employers may choose to forgo hiring anyone at all. But recent research by the National Bureau of Economic Research

FIGURE 12–1

Statutory minimum wages in the United States are low by international standards

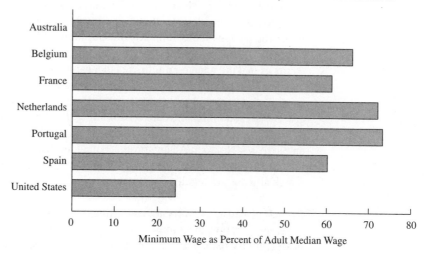

Source: Institute of Personnel Management, *Minimum Wage* (London: Institute of Personnel Management, 1991).

suggests otherwise. Increasing minimum wages in low-wage labor markets does not cost jobs, and it can increase them.[10]

The fast food industry, among others, has pushed to be relieved from the minimum wage. In response, Congress passed a temporary provision allowing employees aged 16–19 to be paid a lower "training wage" for three months. The easiest course, to which Washington seems implicitly to have agreed, is simply to let the rising cost of living render the legal minimum beside the point for most jobs.

The Right to Fair Treatment

Another set of restrictions on employers' freedom in the United States involves fair treatment of workers. These restraints are the result mainly of changes in common law, mostly at the state level. Judges have ruled with growing frequency that employees can sue for unjust dismissal or wrongful discharge. Every year more than 25,000 such suits are filed, versus a mere 200 or so in the late 1970s.

Under the guidelines emerging from state courts, aggrieved employees may be entitled to back pay and punitive and compensatory damages if successful in court. Few people who have been passed over for a promotion or been fired make a legal case of the matter. The transaction cost is too high. Yet enough employees do sue for wrongful discharge that companies need to take precautions. Judgments may be awarded to employees under the conditions discussed next.

Contractual Obligations.   Employment at will could always be superseded by a labor contract, where an employee and employer agreed to a fixed working relationship. Now, the courts are beginning to protect workers who argue that they have an implied contract with the employer. Judges are holding companies liable for pledges the companies did not know they had made. Statements in company literature, and even oral statements, are being interpreted by some courts as making legal commitments that cannot be put aside. One employee, for example, won a case by proving in court that he was told, "Nobody ever gets fired around here without good reason."[11]

As a result companies are reexamining their procedures to remove implicit promises of job tenure. One employer stopped using the term "permanent employees." Not to make any promise of a long-term job, it now calls them "regular employees."[12] Many firms are asking hirees to sign disclaimers, though it is not clear these are legally enforceable.

Breach of Faith.   Courts are restricting American employers' freedom to fire if the employers breach an implied covenant of good faith. Companies may not act in an arbitrary manner in personnel matters and must give employees reasonable opportunities to improve their performance. Employees have the right to appeal decisions against them.

To protect themselves from suits based on breach of faith, careful employers now try to ensure that they use **due process** to handle complaints about employees. By due process in the workplace, the courts mean a visible, regular procedure that is in place to review employee grievances. Unless there is a union contract to the contrary, companies are generally free to choose how to get due process. Some use ombudsmen, a third party designated to investigate employee complaints. Others use a peer review panel, where an aggrieved employee can appeal to a board of fellow workers. Also common is the use of a management grievance committee.

Public Policy Exceptions.   Judges in most states have decreed that public policy can override the employment-at-will doctrine, though they have said it with less vigor in the South. These public policy exceptions protect employees who refuse to commit crimes or who try to exercise privileges they are legally due. For example, a worker was fired for testifying honestly before legislative committees about his employer's labor practices. He sued and won on the grounds that there is an overriding public interest in getting truthful testimony at public hearings.[13]

Among the most important public policy exceptions are union organizing and membership. Employers usually defy unionization because it reduces their control over their workers. Due to the National Labor Relations Act of 1935 (NLRA), however, firms are formally forbidden to punish workers for union activities. This statute has not stopped them from firing union organizers anyway during one-third of organizing campaigns in the late 1980s.[14] We will discuss the NLRA and labor unions below.

An emerging public policy exception is whistle-blowing—reporting some wrongdoing by the employer to outside parties, for example, the press or a government agency. Most whistle-blowers seem motivated by conscience, though some are disgruntled employees seeking revenge on a supervisor or company. However pure their motives, whistle-blowers are usually punished by their organization for being disloyal. They may be fired or, more subtly, passed up for promotion, not given raises, reassigned to less desirable jobs, or given more work.

Most state courts recognize whistle-blowing as a public policy exception. Still, proving employer retaliation in these cases is not easy. Michigan has gone further than other states, backing common law with legislation in 1981 to protect employees against reprisals for reporting violations of the law to authorities. Few states have followed Michigan's lead, due to employers' lobbying. Federal employees also have specific legislative protection under the Whistle-Blower Protection Act enacted in 1989.

Plant Closings and Corporate Restructuring.   The workers' rights just discussed pertain mainly to individuals in continuing positions, that is, to jobs that will be refilled. Often, firms eliminate whole categories of positions permanently as they "rationalize," "downsize," or "restructure," to use various euphemisms for permanent layoffs. Foreign competition, corporate debt, and labor-saving technology are among the factors driving companies to become smaller and stay there. Corporate America announced over 600,000 layoffs in 1993—a record.[15] Even companies such as IBM that prided themselves for offering lifetime employment are being forced to radically trim their workforce. The computer giant planned to eliminate 85,000 jobs in 1993 and 1994, on top of another 100,000 jobs it had cut since the mid-1980s.

The trend is worldwide. Table 12–1 shows that Europe's best-known firms are similarly slashing their payrolls by the thousands. The goal: to push down their break-even point so they can stay profitable. Japanese companies are not immune, either. In 1993, Nissan became one of the first major Japanese manu-

TABLE 12–1   **Massive Job Cuts Are Under Way Everywhere in Europe.**

Company	Country	Period	Number
Philips	Netherlands	1990–93	75,000
British Telecom	United Kingdom	1992–93	39,800
Daimler-Benz	Germany	1992–93	33,000
Fiat	Italy	1993	20,000
Michelin	France	1991–94	20,000
Electrolux	Sweden	1990–91	15,000
Ciba-Geigy	Switzerland	1991–93	5,000
Iberia	Spain	1992–93	4,700

Source: Terrence Roth, "Jobs Crisis," *The Wall Street Journal Europe,* June 28, 1993.

facturers in modern times to shut a factory. Nowhere are corporations the secure or stable places to work as they were not long ago.

In the United States, courts are reluctant to intervene in plant closings and layoffs. A handful of states have passed some form of plant closure legislation, including Massachusetts, California, and Illinois. In response to popular concern about the fairness of corporate restructuring, Congress also passed the Worker Adjustment and Retraining Notification (WARN) Act in 1988. It requires employees be given 60 days' notice of layoffs. But the federal law is weak. Small firms are exempted, so WARN covers less than half the private sector workers, and exceptions are granted for firms with major losses.

As a rule, neither Congress nor the state legislatures have rushed to impede managers' discretion in downsizing. They reason that bids to curb plant closings or layoffs would make matters worse, by creating an incentive for companies to set up shop in less restrictive business environments. The United States is an odd man out; Europe and Japan are apt to have better coordinated and more comprehensive policies providing for advance notice of shutdowns, income guarantees for those made redundant, and worker retraining.[16]

Employees' Right to Privacy.   For managers to dismiss or otherwise discipline a misbehaving employee they, of course, need information about the wrongdoing. Managers have traditionally enjoyed wide leeway to investigate their workforce. Workers had little right to privacy on the job, and could not expect to keep personal information to themselves. In the 1920s, for example, the Ford Motor Company set up a sociology department under a Detroit minister. It sent teams of investigators to workers' homes to certify the morality of their private lives. Ford also set up a service department to watch workers at the plant so they did not drink, smoke, or criticize the company. Violators often were summarily fired.[17]

Companies' ability to gather, store, and use information on their workers is far greater today than in the 1920s, due to the explosion in computer power. Yet, like other facets of the employment relationship, management prerogatives here have ebbed under pressure from worker stakeholders. Increasingly, workers are suing companies for invasion of privacy, alleging improper collection and use of personal data. There may be 1,000 such suits a year in the United States.[18]

Employers do not lose all these cases, of course, but the threat of suits has made many of them take employees' right to privacy seriously. Rather than wage costly legal battles, the pragmatic, not to mention socially responsible, choice is often to take anticipatory safeguards. IBM, for example, has had a privacy code for 20 years that allows it only to collect information needed to hire someone and to make periodic performance evaluations. IBM does not pry into off-the-job behavior unless it interferes with the job. Such a policy may pay other dividends in worker loyalty and contentment.

Lie Detectors.   Employee stakeholders also have lobbied successfully for legislative shelter of their privacy. One milestone was the Employee Polygraph Protection Act of 1988. The polygraph or lie detector was widely used in the United States to screen prospective employees or to catch employees suspected of theft. Polygraph tests are not 100 percent accurate, so some honest individuals will register a false positive and be wrongly faulted. Also, the line of questioning used in the lie detector tests usually delves into personal zones such as sexual preferences, finance, religion, and political beliefs.

Congress banned about 80 percent of polygraph use in the United States. The device may not, with limited exceptions for private security firms and drug manufacturers, be used for screening. Random polygraph tests are forbidden, although they can be used to investigate a specific infraction. Employees may not be disciplined for refusing to submit to a polygraph test. Nor can tests include questions about personal beliefs or sexual activities.

Drug and Alcohol Testing.   Employee stakeholders have had less success in shielding themselves from drug tests. Substance abuse costs American industry $100 billion a year in absent workers, job turnover, and rehabilitation.[19] To protect themselves, companies routinely test for drugs. According to the Conference Board, more than half of 681 companies surveyed have drug testing programs.[20]

As with polygraph tests, critics claim that drug tests violate employees' rights to due process and privacy. They see due process being violated because of false positive readings, privacy because of the attempt to police off-the-job activities. In these disputes, the courts have been apt to disagree with the critics, especially in industries where mistakes can cost the lives of bystanders. In an important decision in 1989, the Supreme Court ruled that federal authorities could order drug and alcohol tests for transportation workers. The Teamsters Union and railroad workers had sought to block a plan for drug testing, adopted after an Amtrak train wreck. To the unions' disappointment, the court reasoned along utilitarian lines that public safety outweighs the Constitution's guarantee against unreasonable search and seizure.

There are few federal restrictions on drug testing in the private sector. Some states and cities, however, have enacted or are considering enacting laws to restrict the practice. These laws limit drug testing to situations where employers have reasonable cause to be suspicious, and they define disciplinary action employees may take.[21] But there is wide variation. Utah illustrates another extreme by allowing the firing of employees who refuse to submit to drug testing.[22]

Electronic Monitoring.   Many companies go beyond testing, and monitor workers in the office or on the shop floor. Supervisors have always tried to keep tabs on employees, but new technology has vastly expanded the options. With modern video and audio equipment, they can spy and eavesdrop in unprecedented ways. Computers hold the greatest potential. Anyone using a terminal can be monitored for productivity. The result is that millions of American workers labor under electronic surveillance.

To date, these practices are largely unregulated. Unions and civil libertarians have been pushing for public policy to restrict monitoring. Some states have enacted legislation, but the federal government has not taken similar steps. In 1987, the telemarketing industry blocked a bill for a mandatory beep when supervisors were listening to calls. Yet, the issue is far from dead. In 1991, the Senate began hearings on a bill to regulate electronic monitoring. Observers think some regulation is inevitable.[23]

Organized Labor

The common law doctrines and legislation we have been discussing can be supplanted by an employment contract. Public policy sets minimum rights and obligations, but, as we remarked earlier, employees can seek to negotiate a higher standard of security and benefits for themselves. Most individual workers have too little bargaining power to negotiate employment contracts on their own, so they often group together to seek collective pacts. As a rule, union contracts supersede the presumption of employment at will. The agreement usually sets up specific guidelines that must be followed in personnel matters. These collective guidelines normally tie managers' hands more than common law does.

The unions have used their group bargaining power to get contracts with favorable work rules, grievance procedures, guarantees of seniority in layoffs, and so on. These workers' rights are besides unions' more well-known function of garnering high wages and fringe benefits for members. Managers have an interest in minimizing the nonwage rights resulting from collective bargaining agreements. They want to keep their flexibility and authority so they can more easily keep their organizations' costs in line.

Public policy was not always friendly to union contracts. In the 19th century, American courts held that labor unions were illegal criminal conspiracies. Employers also used civil courts to combat unions through injunctions. If a group of workers began picketing a factory, the owner could easily get a court order to stop them. The legal argument was that both parties were free to negotiate and that strikes were an unlawful form of intimidation. Many workers of the day had to sign "yellow dog" contracts that prohibited them from joining a union. Still, through political action, workers gradually expanded their rights to organize and to strike against employers. In 1887, states began to pass laws banning "yellow dog" contracts. In 1888, Congress prohibited employers from discharging employees because of union membership, though the Supreme Court later declared this policy unconstitutional.

The main U.S. labor law affecting current practices is the NLRA, mentioned above. This act requires employers to bargain with unions acting as the agent for workers. Certain classes of workers are excluded, notably agricultural workers, domestic help, independent contractors, and supervisors or managerial employees. There has been much litigation concerning the last two exclusions—for contractors and for managers. The key issue is how much freedom the employee has, how much authority to exercise independent judgment on the job. Faculty unions in private universities, for example, have been declared ineligible for collective bargaining because professors join in so-called management decisions such as who to hire to teach and who to promote to tenured posts.

The NLRA established an independent regulatory agency, the National Labor Relations Board, in 1935 to administer the labor act. The board has five members, appointed by the president and approved by the Senate, who serve five-year staggered terms. Under the NLRA, two types of requests can be filed with the board: requests for representation or decertification by a union, and charges of unfair labor practices.

Business managed to get the NLRA weakened in 1947, when Congress passed the Taft-Hartley Act. It lets states outlaw labor contracts that make union membership a condition of retaining employment. These right-to-work laws are prevalent in the South and the Southwest. By banning compulsory unionization, they weaken the hand of organized labor. The anti-union climate in the Sunbelt may be a factor in the migration there of many manufacturing jobs.

With common law and legislation moving along a parallel track, toward more workers' rights, unions' appeal has been diluted. Today, American workers can assert many rights independent of collective bargaining agreements, and without having to pay union dues. Workers are increasingly rejecting attempts to organize them. In 1950, unions won three-quarters of union elections; today, they win less than half. Similarly, the number of decertification elections increased fivefold, and unions were more likely than not to lose these.[24]

Another factor in the decline in union membership is that the National Labor Relations Board fell under control of board members who favored management during the Reagan/Bush period. Thus, for example, the NLRB sought court injunctions against employers only 142 times in 1991, compared with 309 times in 1983.[25]

The hostile public policy environment helped frighten workers away from unions. As Figure 12–2 shows, union membership in the United States fell by 6 percentage points in the 1980s, dropping to less than one-sixth the work force.

The United States is not alone in having union membership decline. The same trend is seen in other OECD countries, though usually off a higher base, and the influence of organized labor is on the wane everywhere. The reasons for this trend are many, but the most important is probably the decline of older, large-scale industries, such as steel and coal, that were heavily unionized. Still, as Figure 12–2 also shows, all is relative. Despite worldwide shrinkage of union strength, more of the workforce belongs to unions in Europe and Japan than they do in the United States.

Discrimination on the Job

A very important exception to the employment-at-will doctrine is **discrimination**—that is, the freedom to make decisions against employees (or prospective

FIGURE 12–2

Union membership is falling in most advanced nations, but is lowest in the United States

*Or nearest available year.
Source: Clara Chang and Constance Sorrentino, "Union Membership in 12 Countries," *Monthly Labor Review* 114, no. 12 (1991), p. 48.

employees) based on their membership in a certain group. Discrimination in employment means judging people because they belong to a particular category of people, not as individuals on their ability. It involves treating them differently in hiring, promotion, and pay based on stereotypes of how well they can do jobs.

Under the old common law rules, employers were at liberty to discriminate. If a company was prejudiced, say, against blacks or women, that was its business. No matter how foolish or incorrect the prejudice, the state lacked authority to intervene in private employment practices. An employer could choose to hire only white males, or to reserve the best jobs for them, if it wanted. Victims of discrimination in employment had no recourse other than to look for a more open-minded boss.

The United States is a varied society. Almost everyone is of immigrant stock. The workplace is correspondingly diverse, and becoming more diverse. Projections are that 4 out of 10 new entrants to the labor force by the year 2000 will be nonwhites or immigrants. Six out of 10 new entrants will be women (including native-born whites).[26]

The groups that make up the United States have had different success fitting in and being accepted in the job market, particularly in higher status jobs like management. There has always been resentment against minorities, which was sometimes reflected in public policies to keep particular ethnic groups from

full participation in the economy. The old Jim Crow laws in the South are a good example. Demographic trends would undoubtedly force employers to become more tolerant of people who seem "different." But, in a democracy, it is certain that unassimilated groups will also try to stop discrimination through public policy.

Discrimination represents a failure of the market. For the market to work, there needs to be a **meritocracy.** Workers must be judged on merit, not on group stereotypes. In a meritocracy, each person can offer his or her skills to society despite skin color, religion, national origin, or other irrelevant criteria. Otherwise, the mutually beneficial transactions that are the market's reason for being will be blocked. Everyone loses.

Some market enthusiasts think the market will eventually purge itself of prejudice. A firm that is intolerant arbitrarily deprives itself of human talent, and it will be impaired as a result. As William Baumol argues: "All will be forced to knuckle under to the market's commandment: Thou shalt not discriminate (socially). Those who refuse to do so will simply find themselves ejected from managerial ranks as their firm disappears or stockholders replace them with successors more willing to go along with the dictates of the market."[27]

Marxists disagree entirely and see discrimination as fundamental to capitalism, as a way of holding down wages. Even granting the point that capitalism is at heart a system based on merit and that discrimination cannot last in the long run, there is a problem. To paraphrase another economist, John Maynard Keynes, in the long run, we are all dead. History teaches that prejudice runs deep and is slow to change. Stakeholder groups are not so patient to test the theory that discrimination will go away by itself.

The fact is that discrimination is apt to be self-perpetuating, unless public policy counteracts it. Even under competitive conditions, large systematic differences can persist in the skills and incomes of groups over time.[28] People who are the object of discrimination usually have the same average native intelligence as the perpetrators (an exception is those who are mentally disabled). What they do not have are the same opportunities to develop their latent skills. Poorly educated parents who lack self-esteem are prone to have poorly educated children who lack self-esteem. Second and third generations caught in this trap are unlikely to have great success in the job market. Until marginal groups can fulfill their potential and compete on an equal footing, the play of market forces is not going to break the cycle of discrimination.

Government intervention to stop discrimination is thus justified by political economists on the grounds of market failure. As we have seen in other cases in this book, government does not act spontaneously in such matters. Interest groups need to coalesce around the issue and compel the government to act. This was what happened in the United States when the civil rights movement used civil disobedience and the courts to gain more equal treatment under the law. The movement's greatest legislative achievement was the Civil Rights Act of 1964, passed during the political honeymoon created by President John Kennedy's assassination.

Protected Groups

Since humans are disposed to fear or dislike those they judge to be different, discrimination can occur on any distinguishing characteristic. The Japanese are said to be biased against left-handed people. In West Africa, some ethnic groups in the past were hostile to twins. For American companies, however, the differences that count most are ones that have been defined in U.S. public policy. These government-designated groups enjoy legally enforceable rights to be treated as equals in hiring, promotion, pay, and layoffs. Members of these groups also are protected against discrimination in their roles as consumers, residents, and citizens, topics we do not discuss in this chapter.

U.S. public policy acknowledges the following protected categories, although with varying degrees of stringency:

- Women.
- African-Americans.
- People of Spanish, Asian, Pacific Island, American Indian, or Eskimo ancestry.
- Vietnam-era veterans.
- The physically challenged, including obese people and sufferers of chronic illnesses such as AIDS and alcoholism.
- Workers over 40 years of age.
- Members of religious or ethnic groups.

TABLE 12–2   Major U.S. Equal Job Opportunity Laws and Executive Orders

Law	Effect of Law	Year
Executive Order 10925	Prohibits job discrimination by government contractors.	1961
Equal Pay Act	Requires equal pay for equal work.	1963
Civil Rights Act	Created EEOC. Forbids job discrimination by race, color, gender, religion, and national origin.	1964
Executive Orders 11246 and 11375	Requires written affirmative action programs by most government contractors.	1965, 1967
Age Discrimination in Employment Act	Forbids job discrimination against people 40 to 65 years old.	1967
Revised Order No. 4, Department of Labor	Requires results-oriented affirmative action, with goals, timetables, and statistical analysis.	1970
Equal Employment Opportunity Act	Strengthened enforcement powers and expanded jurisdiction of EEOC.	1972
Vocational Rehabilitation Act	Requires affirmative action for handicapped persons by government contractors.	1973
Pregnancy Discrimination Act	Expands definition of sex discrimination to include pregnancy and child rearing.	1978
Americans with Disabilities Act	Bans discrimination against disabled people in employment, public accommodations, transportation, and telecommunications.	1990
Civil Rights Act of 1991	Overturns several Supreme Court decisions that had made it difficult for plaintiffs to win discrimination suits.	1991

The categories overlap. Though we often use the shorthand expression *minority* for the protected classes, in aggregate, they cover most of the population.

The list of protected categories of employees has grown since the 1960s when public policymakers began to mandate against intolerance in the workplace. The landmark Civil Rights Act of 1964 focused on protecting blacks from discriminatory practices. Its famous Title VII (named for a chapter in the bill), however, mentions "race, color, sex, religion, or national origin" as the critical groupings. Title VII applies to companies involved in interstate commerce that have 15 or more employees. Most states have similar laws for smaller firms, so almost no business is immune from civil rights laws. Table 12–2 lists the most important federal laws and executive orders affecting job discrimination.

Other industrial countries similarly try to ban racism and bigotry at work. The number of protected categories, however, varies widely, as reported in Table 12–3. There also are wide differences in how rigorously antidiscrimination statutes are enforced overseas.

The policy umbrella is likely to be spread wider in the United States. Some state and local laws already forbid arbitrary mistreatment based on sexual orientation. The federal government has yet to order private employers to ignore homosexuality and bisexuality in employment decisions, though pressure is building in that direction. Some jurisdictions also are beginning to ban discrimination based on physical appearance, for instance, if someone is slovenly. "Lookism," like racism or sexism, is not allowed in these jurisdictions. Such statutes call into question employers' freedom to impose dress codes.

TABLE 12–3 **With the Exception of Race and Sex, Countries Protect Different Categories of People against Discrimination in the Workplace.**

Discrimination Forbidden on Following Grounds:	*France*	*Germany*	*Japan*	*United Kingdom*	*United States*
Race	Yes	Yes	Yes	Yes	Yes
Color	No	Yes	No	Yes	Yes
Ethnic origin	Yes	No	No	Yes	Yes
Social origin	No	Yes	Yes	No	No
Sex	Yes	Yes	Yes	Yes	Yes
Marital status	Yes	No	Yes	Yes	No
Sexual orientation	Yes	No	No	No	No
Age	Yes	No	No	No	Yes
Handicap	Yes	No	No	No	Yes
Religion	Yes	No	Yes	No	Yes
Political opinion	Yes	No	Yes	No	No

Source: R. Blanpain, ed., *Comparative Labour Law and Industrial Relations,* 3rd ed. (Deventer, The Netherlands: Kluwer, 1987), p. 460.

The Antidiscrimination Agencies

Government responsibility for ending job discrimination in the United States rests mainly with two agencies: the Equal Employment Opportunity Commission (EEOC) and the Office of Federal Contract Compliance Programs (OFCCP) in the Labor Department.

The EEOC is a five-member commission appointed by the president with the advice and consent of the Senate. It has about 3,200 employees. Anyone who feels he or she has been discriminated against can file a charge with the EEOC. The commission received nearly 88,000 job bias claims in 1993. More than one-third alleged race discrimination, followed in frequency by allegations of sex and age discrimination. After receiving such a claim, the commission investigates. If it finds sufficient evidence of discrimination, the EEOC files suit in federal court. The commission has no enforcement power but relies on the court system, so judicial interpretations are critical determinants of U.S. public policy toward discrimination.

Successful litigants can win backpay for two years before filing charges. Under the 1991 Civil Rights Act, workers can collect punitive damages for sexual harassment, too. The 1991 act also makes it easier for plaintiffs charging discrimination, because employers have to prove their hiring practices are not discriminatory. Defending even against frivolous or unfounded charges is expensive. The publicity also is bad. So companies are apt to avoid going to court if they can.

The Labor Department's OFCCP oversees the antidiscrimination programs of federal contractors. Employers with contracts of $50,000 and up, or 50 or more employees, are covered—about one-fifth of the workforce in all. The OFCCP illustrates the potent use of government's role as buyer. To be eligible to do business with the federal government, organizations have to have approved policies for hiring and promoting minorities, women, physically challenged workers, and veterans. Many other employers cooperate, even if they are not bidding for government contracts.

Defining Illegal Discrimination

Job discrimination is easy to grasp in theory. It means using race, sex, or similar characteristics for treating people unequally. Unfortunately for managers, defining discrimination in practice is not easy. Legislators, agency personnel, and especially judges have been working for decades to clarify what it means to discriminate unfairly. Their conclusions are sometimes inconsistent.

The most obvious kind of discrimination is intentional. A company has a stated policy that purposely excludes a protected category of people from work for no good reason. Few blatantly discriminatory policies survive. The old policy of airlines only hiring young, single, female flight attendants is a good example. This was the traditional practice, but it was indefensible under the civil rights code. There is no legitimate reason to keep men or older and married women from competing for these posts. Similarly, the exclusion of women from many police forces and fire departments was quickly determined illegal. Gender per se is irrelevant to whether one can be a good police officer or fire fighter.

This form of discrimination is often called *disparate treatment.* It is ended by treating all groups alike in the workplace—that is, by giving them an equal chance to compete for jobs and raises. Job criteria need to be gender-free and color-blind, and based only on relevant traits. Weight or height regulations for flight attendants, male or female, are acceptable because they affect a person's ability to do the job. So are strength or endurance tests for police and fire ser-vices. More men than women might pass such tests, but the employer ought not to make blanket presumptions before the fact. What counts is who can do the job. Everyone deserves the same shot at proving his or her ability.

Screening employees in a gender-free, color-blind way is trickier than it seems. Since different groups of people have different skills and proclivities, they will not do the same on many tests. A subtle form of discrimination can develop, often unintentionally, where employers use what seem objective crite-ria to eliminate some groups from their workforce. This kind of discrimination is known as *disparate impact.*

While disparate treatment concerns the employer's intentions, disparate impact looks at the consequences of the employer's actions: Do they have an unequal effect on men and women, whites and blacks? The courts have ruled that employers need to refrain from both types of discrimination, disparate treat-ment and disparate impact. In the historic *Griggs v. Duke Power Co.* (1971) decision, the Supreme Court disallowed the use of high-school diplomas to select menial workers. Since blacks were less likely to have graduated, they were excluded out of proportion to their numbers from working at Duke Power. The Court was not convinced the diploma was relevant to the jobs in question. "The Civil Rights Act proscribes not only overt discrimination but also practices that are fair in form, but discriminatory in operation. The touchstone is business necessity."[29]

Disparate impact means employers have to do more than hire qualified workers without regard to race, gender, ethnicity, or membership in other protected categories. Employers need to pay close attention to the qualifications themselves to make sure they do not have unequal effect. As the *Griggs* ruling suggests, an exception can be made for "business necessity." The courts allow the use of what they call "bona fide occupational qualifications" that might ordinarily be deemed discriminatory but that can be proven necessary to the job. No one expects universities, law firms, or hospitals to ignore education levels in hiring professional staff. The *Griggs* case probably would have turned out differently had the high-school diploma been required for more skilled jobs.

Disparate impact also opens companies to charges of discrimination based on statistical analysis. If a company has disproportionate numbers of white males in jobs, this is *prima facie* evidence that the company discriminates. At first, the courts generally said that such businesses must produce tangible changes in their workforce. By the 1980s, conservative judges appointed by President Reagan began to issue conflicting opinions, ruling for example that intent to discriminate must be proven. Business saw the new judicial opinions as gains because they made companies less vulnerable to discrimination lawsuits. The Civil Rights Act of 1991, however, reversed several conservative court decisions and placed more of a burden back on employers to prove they treat women and minorities in an evenhanded way.

Sexual Harassment

The Civil Rights Act also covers **sexual harassment.** This term refers to unwanted sexual advances in the workplace, to sexual attention forced on someone who is not in a position to stop it. The EEOC is empowered to investigate charges of sexual harassment because it is a misdeed based on the gender of the individual.

Most men think sexual harassment at work is greatly exaggerated; most women do not.[30] Public policy largely ignored this issue when most paid workers were male, but as women moved out of homemaking and into formal jobs, sexual harassment became the object of legal remedies. Men can be victims of sexual harassment, too, though this is less common.

The law says supervisors (typically, male) may not request sexual favors from subordinates (typically, female) as a condition for employment. The target of harassment, however, need not suffer financial loss to make a complaint. And sexual harassment goes beyond overt pressure for sex; courts have interpreted the offense liberally to include off-color jokes, pats on the rear, and the like. The corporate environment, rather than the actions of an individual, has also been found sexually harassing—for example, if suggestive cartoons or pictures are present at the office. Companies can be made financially responsible unless they take active countermeasures.

The hard part about dealing with sexual harassment is its subjective nature—it may only be clear to the receiver and, thus, be hard to identify objectively. Where does, say, a request for a date end and illegal pressure for sexual favors begin? How does one draw the line between reciprocal affection of a boss and worker, on the one hand, and sexual exploitation of a position of power, on the other? Some companies, such as Wal-Mart, try to avoid these ambiguities by forbidding all sexual relations among employees. But such company policies raise other legal problems, for they may step over the line of employee privacy. As we have seen, companies are generally permitted to interfere in employees' personal lives only in matters that influence work performance.

The issue is serious for American business. One-third of Fortune 500 companies have been sued for sexual harassment.[31] Sexual harassment complaints resulted in $25 million in backpay, damages, promotions, and reinstatements in 1993.[32] The cost of settling complaints that do not get to the stage of formal review is far greater.

Illegal Aliens

The 1980s were the decade of greatest immigration to the United States, with nearly 10 million legal arrivals. Perhaps 300,000 more illegal immigrants also arrive each year. Many newcomers are from the Caribbean, Latin America, or Asia and, thus, likely fall into Title VII's protected ethnic categories. The ones who enter the United States without proper papers may not be hired legally.

Employers often engage aliens for dangerous, unpleasant, or low-paid jobs that are otherwise hard to fill. Some unscrupulous companies violate the law on purpose and deny aliens their legal rights since no one will protest for fear of risking their resident status. Before 1986, employers were free to hire anyone, even foreigners who were in the country without permission. Only citizens and legal residents were entitled to work, but employers did not have to check. The Immigration Reform and Control Act (IRCA) changed the rules. It holds employers accountable for documenting their employees' immigration status. Violators are subject to fines.

Minority interest groups voice fear that IRCA spurs unlawful discrimination by encouraging employers to shun all immigrants. Rather than risk fines, they may err on the side of caution and only hire people who are obviously born in this country. These fears are exaggerated, for the law has not been very effective due to lax enforcement and the use of counterfeit immigration papers. Under IRCA, employers do not have to verify a worker's documents.

Affirmative Action

The notion of disparate treatment underlines the policy that Americans call **affirmative action.** Affirmative action means going beyond removing barriers in employment to take positive steps to correct the effects of past discrimination. The term first appeared in a presidential order in 1965, which required major government contractors to have written plans for promoting more equality on the job. In 1970, President Richard Nixon made the requirement for affirmative action stronger. Government contractors now had to submit results-oriented plans with specific goals and timetables for integrating their workforce.

The OFCCP monitors these results-oriented plans to make sure they conform with the current law. Also, the EEOC may make companies adopt affirmative action plans to settle legal suits against them. Even when they were not required to by law, many other companies voluntarily embraced affirmative action as a matter of social responsibility or as a way to head off discrimination suits from employees. Still, business leaders have long been uneasy about mandated affirmative action, with its inevitable government red tape.

The plans focus on equality of outcome more than equality of opportunity. They commit the employer to specific efforts to recruit, train, and hire minorities (specifically African-Americans, Asians, Hispanics, and Native Americans), women, the disabled, and veterans. The other classes of people protected by civil rights laws—religious groups, most ethnic groups, and the middle-aged and elderly—do not now qualify for special help in employment.

The expectation is that every company's workforce should roughly mirror the labor pool on which it draws. A plant in Texas should have lots of Mexican-Americans; a plant in California should have lots of Asian-Americans. To satisfy public policy, government contractors need to do the following:

- Conduct a utilization analysis that compares the employer's workforce with the available labor supply.
- Find out what company policies are leading to the "underutilization" of the target groups.
- Set up goals for increasing the use of the "deficient" groups in areas where they are scarce.
- Make a good faith effort to meet the goals.

As Table 12–4 shows, the OFCCP and EEOC can accept a variety of specific actions for making the workforce more diverse.

Other countries, too, practice affirmative action. It is most prevalent in highly diverse societies, for example, India, Nigeria, and Malaysia, where civil service jobs, university seats, and even seats in parliament are set aside for minorities.[33] Several European countries take special steps to assure preferential treatment of women. Everywhere the policy is controversial. In India, more than 160 young people set themselves on fire in 1990 to protest a plan to reserve 49 percent of central government jobs for "backward" castes and tribes. The suicides and accompanying riots were driven by despair of higher-caste students at the prospect of unemployment. India's government fell partly because of the unrest.

Other Programs to Help Minority Business and Employment

The U.S. government has other policies to assist minority-owned companies directly. There is an Office of Minority Business Enterprise that provides financial and technical services to approved firms. The Minority Business Develop-

---

TABLE 12–4   Affirmative Action Plans Can Involve a Variety of Activities.

Recruitment and training	The company makes an extra effort to hire and promote minorities, women, and other excluded groups by advertising jobs in new places, using minority recruitment firms, offering special training, and so on.
Preferential hiring	The company gives preference to minorities, women, the physically challenged, and veterans in hiring and promotion decisions.
Employment goals	The company sets rough numbers or proportions for excluded groups to be hired or promoted.

ment Agency in the Department of Commerce runs similar programs. Winners of federal contracts are required to do their best to find minority subcontractors. This contracting program is parallel to affirmative action in hiring and promotion, as described above. The Small Business Administration runs the so-called 8(a) set-aside program to award federal contracts to minority-owned small businesses. Predictably, this last scheme has been the object of major fraud by white-owned firms posing as minority businesses.

A different approach is to subsidize any company willing to build plants in economically depressed areas where many minorities live. Employers are given special breaks on state and local taxes to locate in designated enterprise zones. Since 1982, 38 states have created 600 enterprise zones in inner cities. Washington is considering making these state programs more attractive with the addition of federal tax incentives. Still, many experts are skeptical that federal help will make a big difference. The added cost of doing business in poor neighborhoods is apt to offset any possible tax savings.[34]

The Ethics of Affirmative Action

The rationale for affirmative action is the principle of compensatory justice—to make up for past wrongs. Lyndon Johnson, who signed the first presidential order mandating affirmative action, used the following analogy to justify the policy:

> Imagine a hundred-yard dash in which one of the two runners has his legs shackled together. He has progressed ten yards, while the unshackled runner has gone fifty yards. How do they rectify the situation? Do they merely remove the shackles and allow the race to proceed? Then they could say that "equal opportunity" prevailed. But one of the runners would still be forty yards ahead of the other. Would it not be the better part of justice to allow the previously shackled runner to make up the forty-yard gap or to start the race once again?[35]

There is a tension in the public policy fight over discrimination. On the one hand, employers may not act against individuals because of race, gender, and the like. On the other hand, employers have to recruit, hire, and promote individuals who fall into legally defined categories such as race and gender. It is hard to reconcile the two positions, hard to give some people an edge without being unfair to others.

Critics of the second policy call it "reverse discrimination" and say it makes a mockery of the first policy. It simply introduces a new double standard to replace the old one. They note that the burden of compensating for past injustice falls on a class of people—mostly white males—and not just on individuals who in the past acted in a racist or sexist manner. Defenders of affirmative action say there is a difference between discriminating against someone and discriminating for them. Whatever temporary unfairness may occur, they argue, it is necessary for the greater long-run good of making society fairer.

If we look at affirmative action on utilitarian grounds, evidence of success is mixed. Women have made gains in the workplace but have not reached parity with men. In 1990, for example, women held 40 percent of the executive, administrative, and management jobs, versus 32 percent in 1983. But their earnings were only 65 percent of men's earnings, essentially the same as in 1983.[36] Some movement of women into higher-status jobs would have happened anyway, without the benefit of public policy, so it is hard to know the effect of affirmative action programs alone (or of affirmative action versus equal opportunity rules). Moreover, women's lower pay may be partly due to lower seniority, less education, and other factors that have little to do with discrimination in employment.

The picture is just as cloudy for ethnic minorities. Better educated, upwardly mobile blacks have improved their standing in the workforce in the past 30 years, but blacks as a group lag far behind whites on every social indicator. The hard-core underclass of blacks has made little or no progress in getting better jobs, or even in finding any jobs at all. Asian-Americans, on the other hand, have been moving quickly into good-paying, responsible positions. Again, the effect of affirmative action (and of equal opportunity policies) cannot easily be isolated from other causal factors. Probably, antidiscrimination public policies are hastening trends that are already under way, but they obviously are not the panacea for inequality in the workforce.

Whatever one's evaluation of affirmative action, this public policy toward business has been bitterly disputed. Though Fortune 500 companies usually have been willing to live with race and sex preferences, many white workers and small business owners resented a one-sided policy they saw as working against them. These people expressed their anger in the courts and at the ballot box. Even some potential beneficiaries of affirmative action questioned the policy on the grounds that it cast a shadow on their genuine achievements as individuals.

Answering the complaints, the Reagan administration EEOC began to play down the use of class action suits on behalf of large numbers of people. Clarence Thomas, later named to the Supreme Court and an outspoken critic of affirmative action, was made head of the EEOC. The commission took the view that discrimination was usually an individual problem that affects particular people. The EEOC thus put less stress on statistical evidence of discrimination and demanded evidence of purposeful bias. The courts, with more and more Reagan or Bush appointees, also watered down the rigorous interpretation of affirmative action, ruling against strict quotas for hiring members of protected groups.

These steps did not go far enough for many Americans, and, by the mid-1990s, a grassroots movement had emerged demanding an end to most special treatment of employees or companies based on race or sex.[37] With most Republican politicians promising to eliminate traditional affirmative action, even many Democrats wanted to replace racial and sexual preferences with ones based on income.

Where do these events leave employers? Public policy pulls in different directions, and the inconsistencies have yet to be sorted out fully. The safest stance for a manager is to try to treat all employee stakeholders fairly. Special effort can be made to recruit and train members of protected groups, but rigid rationing of jobs should be avoided. Affirmative action programs cannot displace existing workers. Above all, managers need to keep abreast of court decisions and other policy changes in this controversial area.

Mandated Social Benefits

Unions and other workers' interest groups also have pressured the government to require business to guarantee employee social rights, rights that range from pensions to health care to mandated vacations. As Table 12–5 shows, these political efforts have met modest success in the United States; E.U. workers have won many more social rights. A watershed event in Europe was the acceptance of the Charter of Fundamental Rights for Workers in 1989. Only the United Kingdom declined to endorse the Social Charter, preferring, like the United States, to leave workers' social rights a private matter to be negotiated between employer and employee. (As we observed at the beginning of this chapter, these differences between the European approach and the Anglo-American approach go back centuries.)

• *Paid vacations and holidays.* American workers do not enjoy the right to paid vacations or paid holidays, while their foreign counterparts have these perquisites written in law. By common practice or union contracts, most U.S. employers do allow their employees to take national holidays. Most also offer their full-time employees paid leave—typically two weeks after one year of service, rising to three weeks after five years. Employers do not have to offer the holiday benefit, so it is not portable. When a U.S. worker changes jobs, he or she usually must build up vacation credits again. (In the European Union, labor

TABLE 12–5   **Employers Have to Provide More Fringe Benefits outside the United States.**

Statutory Benefit	France	Germany	Italy	Japan	United Kingdom	United States
Annual leave (weeks)	5	3	none	2	none	none
Public holidays	11	11–15	11	12	8–11	10
Medical insurance	Yes	Yes	Yes	No	Yes	No
Sick leave	Yes	Yes	No	Yes	Yes	No
Long-term disability insurance	Yes	Yes	Yes	Yes	Yes	Yes
Maternity leave	Yes	Yes	No	Yes	No	Yes
Unemployment insurance	Yes	Yes	Yes	Yes	Yes	Yes
Severance pay	No	No	Yes	No	Yes	No
Pension	Yes	Yes	Yes	Yes	Yes	Yes

Sources: R. Bean, ed., *International Labour Statistics* (London: Routledge, 1989); Mary E. Horn, *International Employee Benefits: An Overview* (Brookfield, WI: International Foundation of Employee Benefit Plans, 1992); and *The OECD Jobs Study,* Part II (Paris: Organization for Economic Cooperation and Development, 1994).

agreements go beyond the mandated level so that many workers have five or six weeks of leave a year *plus* national holidays.)

• *Health care.*   Most full-time U.S. workers receive health insurance through their jobs, paid for mostly by their employers. Health insurance is not required by law, however, and part-time, minimum wage, temporary workers, and unemployed or laid-off persons are usually not covered. This situation is unique in the developed world. President Harry Truman first proposed compulsory medical insurance for American workers in 1945, to be paid with a 4 percent health tax on the first $3,600 in wages. Due to opposition from the American Medical Association and other interest groups, the law never passed. National health insurance was an intermittent issue over the next 50 years. A major bill to provide universal coverage was proposed in 1993, but the bill was gutted when Congress dropped the key provision to make companies provide paid health insurance to their workers. Business antagonism to this "employer mandate" was again too strong to surmount, and health care reform died the next year without coming to a final vote.

• *Sick leave.*   There is no law in the United States making employers pay workers who are ill, and 30 percent of full-time workers in larger companies (more than 100 workers) do not have sick leave.[38]   Again, this situation is unusual. Most counterpart countries mandate sick leave, a right critics claim is abused by malingerers.

• *Long-term disability insurance.*   U.S. employers *do* have to underwrite their workers against the loss of wages resulting from an on-the-job injury. This compulsory insurance is provided through state-level workers' compensation schemes. (It does not replace income lost due to a long-term illness or injury that is not job-related.) The relevant statutes generally force employers to buy private insurance, insure themselves, or pay into a state workers' compensation insurance fund. Injured employees are entitled to one-half to one-third of their average weekly wage, depending on the state, usually after a one-week waiting period. Again, other countries tend to be more liberal in granting employees this benefit. We discuss workers' compensation more fully in Chapter 13.

TABLE 12–6   **The U.S. Unemployment Insurance Program Is Relatively Restrictive (1989).**

	Initial Benefit as Percent of Pay	*Duration*
France	59	30 months
Germany	58	12 months
Japan	48	30 weeks
United Kingdom	16	12 months
United States	**50**	**26 weeks**

Source: Ronald G. Ehrenberg, *Labor Markets and Integrating National Economies* (Washington, DC: Brookings Institution, 1994), p. 62.

- *Family leave.* In 1993, the Family and Medical Leave Act went into effect, requiring U.S. employers to grant up to 12 weeks of unpaid leave a year for births or other medical emergencies. The law, passed over the strenuous objection of business and after two presidential vetoes, makes many exceptions for small companies and critical employees. In the European Union, all countries except Britain are far less scrimping about family leave and mandate extended *paid* time off for workers.
- *Unemployment insurance.* As first remarked in Chapter 6, the United States does require employers to insure their workers against unemployment. The U.S. program is tighter than elsewhere, with lower benefits and shorter payment periods (see Table 12–6). (Again, Britain, and to a lesser extent Japan, is a partial exception to the rule.)
- *Pensions.* All developed country governments require employers to help pay for their employees' retirement. Table 12–7 shows the benefit level is stingier in the United States than elsewhere. The typical public pension (Social Security stipend) of an American middle manager is only 20 percent of preretirement income. In European countries, the levels are two or three times higher.

Many American companies supplement the meager public pension system with private retirement plans. Over three-fourths of full-time employees in medium and large companies receive private pensions (less than half the full-time employees in small companies get this benefit).[39] To protect the rights of participants in private retirement plans, Congress passed the Employee Retirement Income Security Act (ERISA) in 1974. Enforced by the Department of Labor and the Internal Revenue Service, ERISA requires employers to fund fully the annual cost of the retirement program so money will be there when participants retire. The law also requires vesting, which entitles the employee to benefits even if he or she leaves the company before retirement. Employees are usually vested after five years.

TABLE 12–7   Public Pensions Are More Generous outside the United States . . . and Employers Pay More for Them.

	Public Pension as Percent of Final Pay	*Employer Contribution as Percent of Salary*
France	59%	41%
Germany	29	12
Italy	73	41
Sweden	63	44
United Kingdom	28	10
United States	**20**	**9**

Note: Figures are for a typical middle manager.

Source: Howard Foster, ed., *Employee Benefits in Europe and the USA,* 5th ed. (London: Longman, 1992).

Workers' Rights and National Competitiveness

Workers' rights, especially the rights to social or fringe benefits, do not come free. Firms have to pay for time off, pensions, and insurance programs. They also have to pay for affirmative action officers, special recruitment programs, labor negotiators, ombudsmen, and other guarantors of workers' social and political rights. Ability to compete internationally can be affected. No nation is an island, and when one country mandates more job security and privileges than do rival countries, it may put domestic firms at a disadvantage. Many Germans, for instance, worry about the "German disease" of excess wages and fringe benefits, which they fear is driving business away from their country. (See Box 12–1.)

Box 12–1

Is Germany's Powerhouse Economy Too Generous to Workers?

The bargain between labor and management in Germany is founded on the idea that workers will be handsomely rewarded for cooperating. They are well paid and enjoy three times the vacation time of their American competitors. They have numerous other generous benefits guaranteed by German public policy, such as sick leave, health care, and pensions. Many companies implicitly or explicitly promise long-term employment.

This so-called social market economy has many advantages. For example, stable employment encourages both firms and workers to invest in skills and training—something they might be less inclined to do in a pluralist state like the United States, where there is more friction between firms and workers. Germany's skilled labor force is among that country's greatest economic strengths. The high wages also reward German firms that shift to higher-value goods, promoting innovation.

Some observers think the German model has run its course. Germany's centralized method of setting wages, for example, has come under fire for being too rigid. A troubled firm cannot respond by reducing wages below those of its competitors, and a low-profit industry must have the same working conditions as a more profitable one. By the 1990s, German companies may have priced themselves out of world markets. American workers, not to mention Korean or Taiwanese workers, will do the same job for less money. Unemployment was up and output, down. Germany, according to this view, can no longer afford to be so lavish.

Already many companies, particularly small and medium-size firms, are rebelling against the centralized system of wages. Cutbacks are planned in social benefits. Such changes will not come easily, and pessimists reason that they will poison labor–management relations. The social contract between management and labor in Germany works only as long as the economy is growing and competitive.

The German system ought not to be written off so quickly, however. German workers remain a rich resource meriting good pay. There may be reservoirs of goodwill that companies can tap as they solicit their employees' help in boosting productivity. Unit labor costs have been cut without much disruption to production.[1] The social market economy's troubles of the 1990s may prove to be just temporary setbacks.

---

[1] "A Survey of Germany," *The Economist,* May 21, 1994.

FIGURE 12–3

U.S. nonwage costs are low, bringing total hourly compensation below many competing countries (1992)

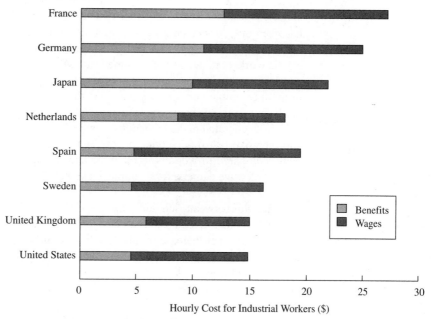

Hourly Cost for Industrial Workers ($)

Source: Institute of German Industry, cited in *The New York Times,* December 26, 1993, p. 14.

Seen from a comparative perspective, American companies appear to have an edge in the labor market over rivals based in most other developed countries. Despite the maligned reallocation of rights to employees by courts and legislators, American employers still possess broad liberty in relation to their workers. They have more flexibility to hire and fire, and they do not have to support as generous social benefits.

The exception in Europe is Britain, whose relaxed labor laws resemble America's. Unlike other E.U. countries, Britain does not restrict the number of hours worked. Wages are low, and so are nonwage labor costs. Britain's laws on sacking workers are loose. Boosters of the British model tout the flexibility of the labor market, and note more of the working-age population have jobs than in other European countries.

The competitive advantage of U.S. and U.K. firms shows up clearly in the comparative cost of hiring a worker. Manufacturing wages are average by international standards. But fringe benefits are low—less than half the level in Germany and Sweden, for instance. Thus the *total* cost of industrial labor in America and Britain is cheap compared to Europe and Japan (see Figure 12–3).

The Quest for Flexible National Labor Markets

The more supple U.S. labor market is one reason unemployment is far lower in the United States (but not in Britain) than in western Europe (see Table 12–8). While the number of American jobs has doubled since 1960, E.U. employment has risen only 10 percent. Labor's mobility also makes it easier for the American economy to respond to global competition and technological change, as excess workers in one sector become available to work in another.

Unfortunately, no country in the late 20th century has found public policies to produce ample *good-paying* positions for the people who want them. There has been a trade-off between the quantity of new jobs and their quality. Much of the work generated in the United States and Great Britain is in poorly paid, dead-end jobs like fast-food service or retailing. The poorest American workers do badly compared to workers in other advanced countries: men in the lowest 10 percent of wage earners, for example, make half what their counterparts make in Italy.[40]

The gap between rich and poor grew wider in America and Britain during the 1980s, which critics see as a direct outcome of their flexible labor markets. Inequality did not increase in other leading countries (see Table 12–9). Part of the reason is that high minimum wages and greater government social protection offset market trends. Also, in societies with a corporatist orientation, the practice of countrywide (rather than company-level) collective bargaining helped level income differences. When groups of unions and employers negotiate national wage settlements, low-skilled workers are more apt to keep pace. But these same societies have paid a price in rising joblessness, as noted above.

To fight unemployment, continental European governments are looking for ways to make their labor markets more fluid—in effect copying the United States and Britain. The OECD recommends such steps as easing employment protection rules or cutting minimum wages for young workers.[41] Governments' leeway is limited, though, because the losing groups organize to keep their privileges. France, for example, backed down quickly on its plan for a special starting min-

TABLE 12–8   **Unemployment Is Higher in the United States than in Europe, but Is Lower Still in Japan.**

	Unemployment Rate (percent of labor force)				
	1975	*1980*	*1985*	*1990*	*1992*
European Union	4.2%	8.0%	11.2%	8.7%	10.6%
Japan	1.9	2.0	2.6	2.1	2.2
United States	8.3	7.2	7.2	5.5	7.4

Source: *OECD Economic Outlook* (Paris: Organization for Economic Cooperation and Development, June 1993).

TABLE 12–9   **Inequality Has Widened Significantly Only in the United States and Britain.**

Ratio of Average Hourly Pay of Men in the Top 10 Percent of Wage Earners to Those in the Bottom 10 Percent

	1980	1992
France	3.3*	3.2
Germany	2.9†	2.7
Japan	2.6	2.5
United Kingdom	2.5	3.4
United States	4.8	5.6

*1984.

†1985.

Source: "Inequality," *Business Week,* August 15, 1994.

imum wage in 1994 after students began to demonstrate nationwide in protest. The plan was to encourage French companies to hire more young people, admittedly at lower pay, but French youth wanted nothing of it.

The Challenge from Developing Countries

Trying to compete in the world economy with loose labor laws is risky. LDCs can undercut any developed country on workers' rights as well as on wages. Critics call this practice "social dumping," by which they mean LDCs sell goods for less than it would cost to make them if those countries protected workers' rights the way western countries do. It is one of many unfair trade practices, which are discussed in detail in Chapter 17.

Under pressure from organized labor, the United States is trying to safeguard the rights of its workers by pushing LDCs to extend more protection to their workers. The LDCs object that the United States is meddling in their affairs, acting like a colonial power. It is not likely that the U.S. effort to equalize labor conditions between the First and the Third World will get far. Mass production jobs will continue to migrate to the poorer countries because of lower cost.

Longer-term competitive advantage in rich countries must be based on something other than a mobile labor market. The more important factor is how skilled and versatile workers are. Here, the U.S. edge is less clear. Loosening the bonds between employer and employee by making it easier for a company to trim its workforce may have the unintended effect of reducing the adeptness of workers over the long term. If companies are free to hire and fire, they have less reason to invest in training for risk of losing their investment. Workers have less time and motivation to build teamwork, all of which hurt, not help, a company's competitiveness.[42]

Japan makes an interesting comparison. That country values labor stability over mobility. One of the hallmarks of Japanese management is to cultivate the loyalty of workers—to try to include them as partners in devising ways to get more output from existing resources. The Japanese approach cannot work when people are forced onto the unemployment rolls to protect profits. Not only does it antagonize workers, but treating people as a disposable resource denies them the same chance to develop their expertise.

Japanese managers conclude that it is better to keep workers on during slow periods, even if it means sacrificing profits. The consequence is an unemployment rate that is even lower than in the United States (see Table 12–8). It is questionable whether the Japanese approach is pertinent to other countries, however. Lifetime employment is easiest to offer in a rapidly growing economy. As economies mature, their growth slows, making it harder to soak up the excess labor. Japan retains many make-work jobs in distribution and other sectors, and even so unemployment has been creeping upward in recent years. Skeptics doubt the lifetime employment system is sustainable.[43]

New Forms of Work

Partly as a reaction against the encroachments on their workplace prerogatives, employers are experimenting with new forms of work. Included are such novel practices as greater use of temporary workers, part-timers, independent contractors or consultants, and home-based teleworkers. Today, many firms retain consultants on fixed-term employment contracts to do particular jobs—often hiring back experienced people they have previously let go. There were more than 15 million such workers in the United States in 1992, plus another 22 million part-time workers—30 percent of the workforce.[44] Public policy has yet to catch up with the trend away from traditional full-time, permanent workers. This is as true in the European Union as in the United States.[45]

These new-style workers are often self-employed in the eyes of the law.[46] Or they may be considered just partly employed. Their status denies them the rights of regular employees. Public policy does not shield the new-style workers from arbitrary dismissal, nor does it guarantee them a minimum wage. They often cannot claim paid holidays or vacation time. They are excluded from other fringe benefits in certain countries, particularly in the United States. Employers like the new working arrangements because they give employers much greater flexibility to increase or reduce their labor force without having to worry as much about employees' civil rights. The new arrangements also allow them to escape paying for employees' social rights, leading to major cost savings.

Conclusion

This chapter has focused on employee rights, broadly defined. We saw that the employment-at-will doctrine, which, in effect, gave employers more rights than the people they hired, has been greatly eroded. Modern public policy restricts employers' freedom in the workplace and extends many new privileges to workers as a matter of law. These policies limit the hiring of children, require payment of minimum wages, make necessary fair treatment of workers, permit workers to organize and bargain collectively, forbid forms of job discrimination, and require the payment of many fringe benefits.

Employers have always complained about granting employees more rights and have fought the drift of history in legislatures and the courts. These rights are expensive, and companies, as a rule, would prefer not to pay for them. Lest one feel too sorry for U.S. employers, however, it is important to put employee rights in a global perspective. Compared to European workers, Americans have few rights, which may give U.S. firms an international cost advantage. Comparing the United States with the NICs, however, looks different. The cost advantage lies with the latter.

These trends underline the fact that employee rights are not just a burden on employers, a debit on the income statement. Employee rights also have a positive role. By increasing workers' sense of security and feelings of worthiness, these rights can help to raise and maintain productivity. That, in turn, contributes to employers' profits. The public policy quandary is to find the correct balance between justifiable and necessary employee rights, and needless and excessive privileges.

Questions

1. What is the employment-at-will doctrine? How has it evolved over time? Do you think the direction of change has been good?

2. Compare mandated social benefits in the United States and other countries.

3. How do workers' rights affect national competitiveness?

4. Analyze discrimination in the workplace. What must companies do to end discrimination? What should they do?

5. What rights do trade union members have on the job? What are employers' obligations toward unions?

End Notes

1. Helmut Kohl, quoted in Daniel Benjamin, "Losing Its Edge," *The Wall Street Journal Europe,* May 7–8, 1993.

2. Quoted in David P. Baron, *Business and Its Environment* (Englewood Cliffs, NJ: Prentice Hall, 1993), p. 617.

3. Andrew Shonfield, *Modern Capitalism* (New York: Oxford University Press, 1965), pp. 116–17.

4. John Clayton Drew, *Child Labor and Child Welfare,* Ph.D. dissertation (Ithaca, NY: Cornell University, 1987), p. 89.

5. "A&P Fined for Child Labor Violations," *Ithaca Journal,* July 29, 1993, p. 10A; and Kurt Eichewald, "Food Lion Still Faces Troubles, Despite Its Government Accord," *The New York Times,* August 5, 1993, p. D8.

6. Bureau of International Labor Affairs, *The Sweat and Toil of Children: The Use of Child Labor in American Imports* (Washington, DC: U.S. Department of Labor, 1994).

7. "Maybe We All Deserve Raises," *Business Week,* August 2, 1993.

8. Juliet Schor, *The Overworked American* (New York: Basic Books, 1991).

9. Tony Horwitz, "The Working Poor," *The Wall Street Journal,* November 12, 1993, p. A1.

10. Edward Balls, "US Research Causes Rethink on Pay Theory," *Financial Times,* September 30, 1994, p. xi.

11. Archie B. Carroll, *Business and Society,* 2nd ed. Cincinnati: South-Western, 1993), p. 423.

12. George A. Steiner and John F. Steiner, *Business, Government, and Society,* 6th ed. (New York: McGraw-Hill, 1991), p. 626.

13. Ibid.

14. "The State of the Unions," *Business Week,* May 23, 1994, p. 78.

15. John Byrne, "The Pain of Downsizing," *Business Week,* May 9, 1994, p. 61.

16. H. A. Stafford, "Geographic Implications of Plant Closure Legislation in the USA," in *Government Policy and Industrial Change,* ed. David Gibbs (New York: Routledge, 1989), pp. 96–116.

17. John D. Dahlinger, *The Secret Life of Henry Ford* (New York: Bobbs-Merrill, 1978), cited in Steiner and Steiner, *Business, Government, and Society,* p. 623.

18. Jeffrey Rothfeder and Michele Galen, "Is Your Boss Spying on You?" *Business Week,* January 15, 1990, pp. 74–75.

19. "Privacy," *Business Week,* March 28, 1988, p. 61.

20. Randal Poe and Emily L. Baker, "Fast Forward," *Across the Board,* May 1990, p. 7.

21. John Fay, *Drug Testing* (Boston: Butterworth-Heineman, 1991).

22. Baron, *Business and Its Environment,* p. 633.

23. Michael Allen, "Legislation Could Restrict Bosses from Snooping on Their Workers," *The Wall Street Journal,* September 24, 1991, p. B1.

24. See Robert J. Flanagan, Lawrence M. Kahn, Robert B. Smith, and Ronald G. Ehrenberg, *Economics of the Employment Relationship* (Glenview, IL: Scott Foresman, 1989), Chapter 11, for a good discussion of the regulation of union–management relations.

25. William B. Gould IV, *Agenda for Reform: The Future of Employment Relationships and the Law* (Cambridge, MA: MIT Press, 1993).

26. William B. Johnston and Arnold E. Packer, *Workforce 2000* (Indianapolis: Hudson Institute, 1987), p. 95.

27. William Baumol, *Perfect Markets and Easy Virtue: Business Ethics and the Invisible Hand* (Cambridge: Basil Blackwell, 1991), p. 18.

28. Gary Becker, *The Economics of Discrimination* (Chicago: University of Chicago Press, 1957).

29. William C. Frederick, James E. Post, and Keith David, *Business and Society,* 7th ed. (New York: McGraw-Hill, 1992), p. 165.

30. Alfred A. Marcus, *Business and Society* (Homewood, IL: Richard D. Irwin, 1993), p. 158.

31. William H. Shaw and Vincent Barry, *Moral Issues in Business,* 6th ed. (Belmont, CA: Wadsworth, 1995), p. 433.

32. *International Herald Tribune,* May 26, 1994, p. 3.

33. Thomas Sowell, *Preferential Policy: An International Perspective* (New York: William Morrow, 1990).

34. "Enterprise Zones: Do They Really Work?" *Business Week,* May 25, 1992, p. 29.

35. Quoted in Robert A. Fullinwider, *The Reverse Discrimination Controversy* (Totawa, NJ: Rowman and Littlefield, 1980), p. 95.

36. "Women in the Marketplace," *The Wall Street Journal,* October 18, 1991.

37. Paul M. Barrett and G. Pascal Zachary, "Race, Sex Preferences Could Become Target in Voter Shift to Right," *The Wall Street Journal,* January 11, 1995, p. A1.

38. U.S. Department of Labor, Bureau of Labor Statistics, *Employee Benefits in Medium and Large Private Establishments* (Washington, DC: U.S. Government Printing Office, 1993).

39. Joel S. Piacentini and Jill D. Foley, *EBRI Databook on Employee Benefits,* 2nd ed. (Washington, DC: Employee Benefit Research Institute, 1992), p. 123.

40. Richard B. Freeman, ed., *Working under Different Rules* (New York: Russell Sage Foundation, 1994). Also see the Report of the Commission for the Future of Worker/Management Relations (Dunlop Commission) and the Report of the Center for National Policy Research.

41. *The OECD Jobs Study: Evidence and Explanation* (Paris: Organization for Economic Cooperation and Development, 1994).

42. Michael J. Piore and Charles F. Sabel, *The Second Industrial Divide* (New York: Basic Books, 1984).

43. Christopher Wood, *The End of Japan Inc.* (New York: Simon and Schuster, 1994).

44. Mario Shao, "New US Workers: Flexible, Disposable," *Boston Sunday Globe,* April 3, 1994, pp. 1ff.

45. *New Forms of Work* (Luxembourg: European Foundation for the Improvement of Living and Working Conditions, 1988). Also see the Report of the National Commission for Employment Policy (Anthony Carnevale, chair).

46. Robert Aronson, *Self-Employment* (Ithaca, NY: ILR Press, 1991).

13 PUBLIC POLICY AND SAFETY

All substances are poisons; there is none which is not a poison. The right dose differentiates a poison and a remedy.

Paraclesus[1]

Modern capitalism exposes consumers and workers to many safety and health hazards. The federal government estimates that consumer products contribute annually to 29,000 deaths in the United States.[2] Ten million U.S. workers per year are injured on the job, and many more catch occupational diseases.[3] Some of these risks are unavoidable in an industrial society. People move at high speed, use powerful machines, and handle dozens of new and untested materials—activities that pose potential danger. A risk-free world is beyond reach; the best we can work for is an optimal level of product and workplace safety.

In a fully competitive market, with the usual assumptions of perfect knowledge, no uncertainty, and so forth, the law of supply and demand would produce the right amount of protection from dangerous goods and jobs. Consumers and workers would bear the cost of accidents. The prices of dangerous goods would be lower, and the wages for dangerous jobs higher, than for safer alternatives. These lower prices and higher wages would compensate consumers and workers for assuming risk. If the cost to producers of preventing a hazard was less than they lost in lower prices and higher wages, they could raise their profits by taking preventive steps. Thus, the market theoretically minimizes the cost of averting and compensating for hazards.[4]

The theory is wrong, of course, because real consumers and workers have far from perfect knowledge. They do not always know what products are safe to use, or what jobs pose a risk, especially given rapid technological change and the constant development of novel products and new types of work. For health hazards, there is a problem of uncertainty, too, due to the difficulty of detecting a cause-and-effect relationship between a product/procedure and an illness. People may eventually learn by experience, but experience is a costly teacher when the price is serious injury or death. Some people also question the fairness of asking a few members of society to bear catastrophic losses so the rest of us can discover health or safety hazards through their ill fortune.

Since the idealized market model does not work in reality, a strong case can be made for government intervention to make consumer products and the workplace healthier and safer. This chapter considers the real public policies that have evolved to compel business to take greater precaution in designing and manufacturing goods and services. We look first at consumer protection and product liability, then at occupational safety and health. The underlying question is whether U.S. policies strike the right balance between risk and the cost of reducing it, particularly in light of international developments.

Consumer Safety

Two sets of public institutions in the United States compel companies to try to keep customers free from harm: the courts and the regulatory agencies. The courts are the older and more important institution, so we start with them and the common law doctrines they have evolved. As always, it is hard to generalize about U.S. common law due to the great diversity of the courts. Decisions in one state can have little bearing on what happens in the other 49 states, the District of Columbia, or the federal courts. Yet, like other facets of the common law analyzed in this book, the pattern is of a gradual erosion of the rights of business over the past century.

Consumer Safety under Common Law

No respectable firm wants its products to hurt people. A reputation for shoddy or dangerous goods is bad for business. That is why private organizations such as the Underwriters' Laboratory or the Better Business Bureau have evolved, as a voluntary way to certify product quality and safety so that firms can protect their good name.

Still, accidents and injuries will happen. When they do, the question of **product liability** arises. Who ought to pay for the damage? Product liability falls within the law of accidents or tort law. A **tort** is a private wrong or injury, other than a breach of contract. When a tort is committed, the injured party has the right to collect damages from the wrongdoer.

In the early capitalist era, judges followed the principle of *caveat emptor* ("let the buyer beware"). This axiom meant sellers were not responsible for defects in their products; it was the buyers' task to take proper precautions. There was no thought of product liability, as we know it today, as a way to compensate victims for medical bills and lost wages.

Later, sellers began to lose their carte blanche as courts started weighing the role of negligence, or sellers' failure to take due care in designing, producing, and distributing a product. By the mid-1800s, a negligent firm could be held to account for the harm done by its product and be made to pay for the damage. Still, negligence was difficult to prove because courts found firms not guilty if they acted like a "prudent man," in the jargon of common law. To parry consumers' allegations, firms merely had to prove they had taken "reasonable" caution with the product.

Legal actions based on negligence were restricted further by the ancient doctrine of privity. *Privity* means a direct contractual relationship between parties. Under the doctrine, a buyer could sue for personal injury or property damage, but only against the immediate seller. Most manufacturers were shielded from negligence claims, since they usually sold through middlemen and did not have first-hand contact with consumers. They also could defend themselves by arguing that (1) the injured party was aware of the dangers and still chose to use the product (assumption of risk) and (2) the plaintiff did not use enough care in using the product (contributory negligence).

Modern Interpretations of Common Law

In the 20th century, the courts began to move away from concern with manufacturers' negligence and to develop the new doctrine of **strict liability** (liability without fault). It puts much more of a burden on firms. Under strict liability rules, firms have a duty to be more than careful; they actually must make safe products. If they produce something that is judged less than safe, they can be held liable for harm it causes. Strict liability extends to suppliers, contractors, and assemblers—all who contribute to the final product.

As applied by the courts, strict liability is an exacting standard. Firms can take every safeguard and still be forced to repay consumers for damages. Strict liability is far more sweeping than the older negligence doctrine, which absolved firms that took reasonable care. Now it is "seller beware." Whenever a product is proved to have a defect in design or manufacture, and to have caused injury, the firm must pay. Many courts will reject the assumption of risk and the contributory negligence arguments when applying the strict liability rule. These practices ease the way for plaintiffs to prove personal injury from a product. All but four states (Massachusetts, North Carolina, Virginia, and Wyoming) have officially adopted strict liability rules.

Strict liability can produce bizarre results. In one recent case, Ford Motor Company and Goodyear Tire & Rubber Company were sued for a traffic fatality. The driver killed in the crash was legally drunk and traveling more than 100 miles per hour when a tire failed. The courts ruled both companies were liable for the death and had to pay damages. Why? Because the car had a powerful engine and could reach high speed, higher than the safe operating speed of the tires, and thus it was inherently dangerous.[5] In another case, a plaintiff won a case against Fabergé after she tried to make a scented candle by pouring perfume over a lit candle. The product was ruled defective for not having a warning about the flammability hazard.[6]

Lately, some courts have been moving even further to the consumers' side, to a theory of **total liability** or absolute liability. This theory recognizes almost no mitigating circumstances that a firm can use to escape blame. Responsibility for the harm caused by its product is unlimited. A product that is safe for most uses is defective if it fails to work safely for things it was never meant to do. Even the fact that a hazard was unknown by science is no defense in some jurisdictions.

A man, for example, recently sued successfully a power tool manufacturer for injuries he received while using a lawnmower to trim hedges. In another contemporary case, a worker won $50,000 in damages from the original manufacturer of a bench saw. The saw had been delivered in 1942, was later sold and rebuilt without a safety guard, and was sold again. Still, the original manufacturer was held liable for injury caused by the modified machine.[7] The lone defense a firm has under the doctrine of total liability is to prove the product did not, in fact, cause the injury. Happily for firms, only about 2 percent of product liability cases are based on total liability, and this theory probably will continue to play but a small role.[8]

Injured consumers also have the right to make claims against manufacturers based on a breach of warranty. A **warranty** is a guarantee arising out of a contract. Sellers often offer consumers express warranties about the quality of goods. Under consumer law, however, there is also an *implied* warranty that goods are safe and fit for the purpose for which they are sold. This implicit contract is a powerful tool for consumers seeking to recover damages.

The Logic of Product Liability

Most people find strict liability and total liability outlandish, because they seem so patently unfair to firms. How can a company be expected to find out about every unknown danger and every reckless use to which its products may be put? The business community has objected to the erosion of its rights and put pressure on both Congress and the state legislatures to reform tort law in its favor.

Yet, there is a logic to the way common law has evolved. The judges who devised the stringent rules were not thinking as much about fairness to firms as they were making a utilitarian calculation about how to promote the general welfare. Holding sellers mainly responsible for product-related injuries makes some sense because they are in a better position to know about a product and to invest in making it safer. Buyers, whose contact with most products is far more cursory, do not have the same opportunities. Also, sellers are apt to have "deep pockets." Compared to buyers, they can better absorb the loss caused by an accident.[9] They simply spread the cost to all consumers, who in effect buy an insurance policy with each product that covers them if they have an accident.

To put it differently, public policy forces firms to internalize an external cost. By making companies compensate anyone hurt by their products, tort law spurs them to look for ways to reduce the likelihood of people hurting themselves. If companies can cut their product liability insurance premiums or their legal fees by taking extra care with the product, they will do that. Companies will pick a combination of insurance coverage and built-in safety that costs them the least—which, in theory, is the level of safety that also minimizes the cost to society. In effect, strict liability is a substitute for perfect consumer information.[10]

Flaws in the System

Things do not work that smoothly, critics of this policy note. The transaction cost of running the product liability system is far from negligible. That makes many openings for people to gain at society's expense—that is, to capture economic rent.

Lawyers' fees are much of the transaction cost. The legal system in the United States, like all others based on the British common law system, places emphasis on the private practice of law, creating opportunities for litigation. Since 1971, the number of attorneys in the United States has nearly tripled, to 780,000. Of every three lawyers in the world, one is American—though the profession is growing much faster in other rich countries. Not every U.S. lawyer practices product liability law, but the large number who do put upward pressure on the number of claims and the expense of settling them.

The legal system in other countries is usually based on the Napoleonic Code, which relies on a comprehensive set of laws, not precedent, to guide judgments. These countries are prone to have many fewer lawyers. Germany has about two-thirds as many lawyers per capita as America has, Japan has about one-third as many. (See Table 13–1.) This saves them money on lawyers' fees.

The adversarial U.S. approach to product liability also fosters inequitable awards. While spectacular, million-dollar settlements attract public attention, the truth is that most product liability rewards are small. The Vietnam veterans who were compensated for Agent Orange exposure, for instance, only received $12,000 per claimant, hardly a windfall for injuries as severe as terminal cancer.[11] Product liability litigation has become a kind of lottery, with the chance of huge payoffs for a few lucky participants, but little or nothing for the majority.

The possibility of jackpot verdicts also creates an impetus for frivolous lawsuits, producing more friction in the liability system. Many firms will settle these

---

TABLE 13–1   The United States Has Plenty of Lawyers . . . and Many Civil Suits.

	Lawyers per 100,000 People	*Civil Cases per 100,000 People*
Germany	190	2,340
Japan	102	1,170
United States	**312**	**4,400**

Sources: "Guilty," *Business Week,* April 13, 1992; and "A Survey of the Legal Profession," *The Economist,* July 18, 1992.

nuisance claims out of court rather than bother with a trial. Other common law countries have found ways to reduce the number of frivolous suits. Britain simply makes losers pay winners' fees. The United States gives no such disincentive because each side pays its own legal cost, despite the outcome.

It is alleged that the contingency-fee method of billing (plaintiff's lawyers have an equity interest in the monetary rewards) makes matters worse in the United States by encouraging plaintiffs to hold out for large settlements. This problem is probably exaggerated—lawyers' financial stake in the settlement is more likely to be a sobering influence, since they get no money if they lose the case. It is hourly billing that has a greater likelihood of increasing transaction cost by creating incentives for endless litigation.

A different drawback of strict and total liability is that tilting the scales of justice so far in the consumers' direction distorts the incentives for people to be careful with products—a form of moral hazard. If they know they can sue manufacturers, they may be lulled into paying less heed than they should, leading, in turn, to a rise in needless accidents. Society might be served better by a system that obliges consumers to take greater responsibility for their behavior.

Product liability has the potential to help national economic competitiveness by acting like a sophisticated buyer to encourage better products. According to Michael Porter, the U.S. system does not fulfill this possible function because it is too capricious.[12] He is backed up by a majority of executives in a 1992 *Business Week*/Harris poll, who blame the civil justice system for hampering American companies as they vie with Japanese and European firms.[13] Dan Quayle, head of the short-lived President's Council on Competitiveness, calls it a "self-inflicted competitive disadvantage." He claims that the indirect cost for product liability reaches $300 billion. Others dispute Quayle's figures as overstated, but even more conservative estimates are around $140 billion. That is about 2.5 percent of GNP, three times more than any other rich country spends on product liability.[14]

American business can take some comfort because the scope of consumers' rights is increasing around the world. The European Commission issued a directive in 1988 for member countries to move to strict liability. Despite domestic business opposition, by 1990, Britain, Denmark, Germany, Greece, Italy, and Luxembourg as well as non-E.U. Austria, Norway, and Sweden had changed their laws so injured consumers do not have to prove fault.[15] New Zealand has tried a radically different approach, eliminating all tort liability from accidental personal injury and replacing it with a government-administered system of compensation.[16]

Japan, too, is introducing greater protection for consumers. Foreign companies are pushing for this, preferring lawsuits to the high cost of complying with Japanese safety regulations. *Keidanren,* the business lobbying group, is fighting the changes, which it claims will hurt its members' ability to compete with foreign companies. (Box 13–1 describes consumer protection in Japan.) Still, the growth of consumer rights overseas suggests that any acute handicap the United States has in international markets is likely to be short-lived.

Box 13–1

The Japanese Approach to Product Liability Favors Producers

Japanese companies face far fewer legal challenges for faulty products than do American companies. Part of the reason is cultural. Japan is a homogenous society whose traditions stress group obligations. Suing is frowned upon; people's distaste for personal confrontation helps ensure that many legal disputes are resolved privately.

There also are sound economic reasons people do not sue. The shortage of lawyers (only about 14,000 for the whole country) causes delays and makes legal action expensive. Plaintiffs have to pay an upfront fee to their lawyers of up to 8 percent of the damages sought; contingency-fee arrangements are not allowed. Plaintiffs also have to pay a nonrefundable filing fee to the courts of .5 percent of damages. They do not have the right of access to potential evidence held by an opponent, as they do in America, which makes it hard for consumers

to win. When they do win, the awards rarely exceed $150,000. Japan does not have juries, so judges set the awards according to well-established formulas.

Japanese consumers thus have strong incentives to settle disputes with companies in an amicable way. The strong position of industry vis-à-vis its clientele lightens the burden of legal and insurance fees, and frees cash for research and product development. Whether it is fair to the consumer is another question. There is pressure, some of it coming from foreign companies, to rewrite product safety laws to favor consumers more.[1]

---

[1]"Guilty," *Business Week,* April 13, 1992, pp. 64–65; and J. M. Ramseyer, "Reluctant Litigant Revisited: Rationality and Disputes in Japan," *Journal of Japanese Studies* 14, no. 1 (1988), pp. 111–23.

The Cost of Liability Insurance

Business never liked the shift away from *caveat emptor* rules. In the 1980s, however, the situation became intolerable for many companies because of what they saw as an explosion in liability insurance. As Table 13–2 shows, the number of personal injury product liability suits almost tripled in federal court between 1980 and 1988, and the average award tripled to over $1.5 million. Systematic data are not available for the states, which account for just over half the product liability cases, but the trend is the same. Giant settlements are possible, such as the $105 million fine an Atlanta jury levied against General Motors in 1993 for the death of a teenage driver in one of its pickup trucks.

The cost of liability insurance followed pace, and, by 1988, net premiums had grown to three times the 1980 sum. According to one report, product liability insurance costs 15 times more in America than in Europe, and 20 times more than in Japan.[17] Some companies cannot get insurance at any price due to their business's risk. They also face hidden administrative and opportunity costs in trying to reduce liability exposure.

There is some dispute about the scale of this insurance crisis. It affects some

TABLE 13–2   **The Explosion in Product Liability Suits Caused an Insurance Crisis in the 1980s.**

	Personal Injury Product Liability Suits Filed in Federal Court	*Product Liability Suits, Average Verdict Award*	*Net Premiums Written for General Liability Insurance ($ billions)*
1975	2,393	$ 394,000	$ 3.1
1980	6,876	563,000	6.4
1985	12,507	1,091,000	11.5
1988	16,166	1,536,000	19.1

Source: W. Kip Viscusi, *Reforming Products Liability* (Cambridge, MA: Harvard University Press, 1991), pp. 17, 27, and 96.

industries, in particular pharmaceuticals, more than others. According to one study, for instance, asbestos, the Dalkon shield (an intrauterine device), and Bendectin (a drug for morning sickness) accounted for a third of the federal cases from 1974 to 1986.[18] The number of product liability suits against Fortune 1000 companies in federal court has dropped, from a high of 3,500 in 1985 to 1,500 in 1991.[19]

Still, in a Conference Board survey of large and small companies, 4 out of 10 companies said product liability was having an adverse impact on them. The most important repercussions were discontinued product lines and decisions against introducing new products.[20] Of course, if these products were truly faulty, they should have been withdrawn. The fear is that too many risky but valuable products will be stillborn, for instance, promising new medical therapies. Pharmaceutical companies are routinely faced with liability cost greater than the market value of a medicine, which has a chilling effect on innovation. Sometimes, a useful product may disappear. An illustration is the soaring liability cost of private airplanes, which led Beech, Cessna, and Piper almost to stop making them by the mid-1980s.

The Political Reaction

The business community, including the insurance and medical industries, has put pressure on state legislatures and Congress to step in and reform the judge-made product liability laws. Despite opposition from other interest groups, including the Association of Trial Lawyers of America (who recently changed their name to Consumer Lawyers) and Consumers Union, they have made headway. The low profits and poor financial health of the insurance industry (which has to pay off product liability settlements) have been an impetus. They embrace the following demands:

- Put a cap on punitive damages (money charged to punish a wrongdoer) to stop excessive settlements.

- Allow a state-of-the-art defense, to prevent the retroactive application of current technology to past production.
- Eliminate joint and several liability, which can hold many parties to blame for an injury but often makes the one with the most resources pay to mend it.
- Strengthen the assumption-of-risk and the contributory-negligence defenses, putting more of the burden on consumers to act responsibly.
- Bring back the reasonable-person standard, so sellers only have to exercise normal prudence.
- Create loser-pays rules to discourage frivolous suits.

Many states have adopted some of these proposals since the mid-1980s. At the federal level, the House of Representatives has passed the Common Sense Legal Reform Act (1995) to weaken federal product liability laws. So, the public policy pendulum is clearly moving back toward business's side on the tort law issue.

Some industries have responded by expanding production of risky products. Small airplanes, mentioned earlier, are a good example. The General Aviation Revitalization Act, passed in 1994, limited lawsuits involving airplanes over 18 years old. Soon after, Cessna announced it would build a new plant and hire 1,500 people to make single-engine aircraft. Piper Aircraft Corporation also geared up production due to the new product liability limitations.[21]

The Consumer Safety Agencies

Due to the faults in tort law as a means for forcing firms to make safe products, consumer activists, public interest groups, and other concerned parties also have pushed for direct government intervention to keep consumers from harm. The U.S. Congress has created several regulatory agencies that focus on specific hazards and mandate particular safety standards for business to follow. The most important consumer safety agencies are listed in Table 13–3.

TABLE 13–3 **Several Federal Agencies Try to Ensure Consumer Safety.**

Consumer Product Safety Commission (1972)	Safety standards for consumer products not specifically covered by other agencies
Federal Aviation Administration (1958)	Sets standards of airworthiness for all civil aircraft
Food Safety and Inspection Service (1907)	Inspection and labeling of meat, poultry, and eggs
Food and Drug Administration (1931)	Safety, effectiveness, and labeling of food, drugs, food additives, and cosmetics
National Highway Traffic Safety Administration (1966)	Motor vehicle safety standards, fuel economy standards
National Transportation Safety Board (1962)	Investigates accidents involving air, water, railroads, highways
Nuclear Regulatory Commission (1974)	Inspects nuclear power plants and monitors their safety procedures and security measures

The logic behind these agencies is the public's worry about *hidden* product risks. Some risks are plain to see. The potential danger posed by, say, a handsaw is obvious to most users, even beginners. Other risks are not as obvious. The danger multiplies with new, more powerful products that people use infrequently. Compared to a handsaw, a chainsaw is more complicated. Casual users can easily fail to see the nuances of how to work a chainsaw properly, with fatal results. People are particularly afraid of invisible dangers in things of which they eat, breathe, or put on their skin, things they may have no knowledge of at all.

When people lack data, they cannot make an informed, voluntary assessment of product risks. Risks are imposed on them whether they like it or not. To correct this market failure, they have, in effect, asked government to make judgments for them. Government regulators do research to evaluate product hazards, set guidelines for product use, require warnings and instructions for users, and monitor companies to make sure they abide by the regulations.

Among the earliest laws to protect consumers from unseen peril were statutes against adulterated food and drugs in Virginia in 1848 and Ohio in 1853. Today, the federal Food and Drug Administration (FDA) requires complete testing of new drugs to make sure they work and are safe. The FDA also has the power to outlaw chemicals that are added to food. Similarly, the Consumer Product Safety Commission (CPSC) and the National Highway Traffic Safety Administration (NHTSA) have authority to ban products, and to recall items and force manufacturers to fix them. The CPSC focuses expressly on children's goods, because children have less capacity to examine goods for concealed threats. In theory, getting the government involved in the area of hidden product risks costs society less than relying on consumers' trial and error.

Another justification of regulation is on the grounds of limiting moral hazard. We saw in Chapter 3 that moral hazard arises when one party to a transaction cannot observe another participant, who in turn may have reasons to do things the first party does not like. Insurance illustrates the consequence. Insurance sometimes alters the behavior of insureds, encouraging them to gamble or be careless, but insurers will rarely learn about it. The cost of insurance goes up for everyone. By analogy, the product liability system creates incentives for consumers to use products in dangerous ways that manufacturers do not want.[22] They may take chances if they know they can sue for any injury that follows. Society picks up the tab. From this perspective, it is better to have government force manufacturers to build more safety into their products, thus protecting people from themselves.

Usually, the catalyst for consumer safety regulation is a tragedy or controversy that captures the public's imagination and gives leverage to political entrepreneurs eager to change public policy. Upton Sinclair's graphic account of the Chicago stockyards, *The Jungle* (1906), sparked the modern system of meat and poultry inspection. Reputable canners supported the policy as a way to protect their reputation from damage by shady competitors.[23] Similarly, Ralph Nader's indictment of Detroit automakers, *Unsafe at Any Speed* (1965), helped push through more stringent automobile safety standards in the United States. A 1989 report on *Sixty Minutes,* the television news program, about residue on apples of a pesticide, Alar, forced the FDA and other federal agencies to reevaluate their spraying regulations. Though apples later got a clean bill of health, the apple industry lost many sales because of frightened consumers.

Pitfalls of the Regulatory Approach

Government regulation of product safety is well-intended, yet critics note it can have unwitting bad results—what we have earlier called government failure. One is regulatory excess. A study of 27 major product regulations found a wide variation in the cost per life saved. The NHTSA's steering column protection regulation, for instance, cost only $100,000 per life saved and was clearly worthwhile. But 13 of the 27 regulations studied cost more than $25 million for each life saved, confirming that the consumer protection agencies have not done a systematic search for cost-effective remedies.[24]

Especially controversial is the Delaney Clause, a 1958 amendment that bans all cancer-causing food additives. The clause has been interpreted to mean zero tolerance. There is no threshold below which carcinogens are deemed safe, no matter how small the hazard to human health. Improved toxicology testing has allowed scientists to identify many weak carcinogens, but the FDA is not allowed to consider the tradeoff to banning these substances. When the FDA proposed banning saccharine as a potential cancer threat, for instance, no thought was given to the negative impact on diabetics or on the obese. (There was so much popular outcry that Congress overruled the FDA on saccharine.) At the same time, the Delaney Clause makes no mention of natural cancer agents in food, some of which pose a graver threat than most artificial ingredients.

Another problem with trying to regulate product safety is the lulling effect.[25] By concentrating on technological solutions, not behavioral ones, safety regulations encourage people to ignore the consequence of their actions. Rules and procedures can backfire, prompting careless or even reckless behavior that nullifies the safety gains. Airbags in automobiles, for example, may make people feel oversecure so they stop using seat belts. Safety caps on medication may increase poisoning. The caps were meant to prevent accidental harm to children, but they simultaneously invite parents to let their guard down about keeping medicine out of children's reach. Also, many people find child-resistant caps hard to use and leave them off, creating a worse safety hazard than existed before.

The focus on technological solutions is also apt to lock in current technology and cramp firms from finding new ways to solve safety problems. It also limits their flexibility to find the cheapest method for reaching a given measure of safety. Instead, regulators like to specify exactly what firms need to do, even if it is sometimes more expensive. Every consumer, whether they want or need the added protection, has to pay for it.

Finally, like any regulatory policy, safety regulation is bound to produce rent-seeking behavior that is at odds with the policy's stated purpose. Consider the narrow specifications for bicycles mandated by the CPSC. Many observers think the main goal was not protecting consumers but keeping inexpensive bicycles from Taiwan out of the U.S. market. Similarly, the Japanese are alleged to use safety standards to block U.S. automobile and other exports to Japan.

Despite these problems, product safety regulations do have a collective payoff, though how much is difficult to say. Accident death rates dropped by one-quarter in the United States from 1950 to 1980.[26] The improvement in automobile safety is particularly striking, with fewer people dying in road accidents in 1992 than in 1961, despite more than twice the cars on the road. American drivers are far less likely to be killed (on a mile-traveled basis) than European or Japanese drivers. Many factors account for these gains in safety, but one has to be better-designed and built products. Whether the same result could have been had at lower cost is another question. The answer is almost certainly yes.

Reform and Deregulation

Because companies have to shoulder the direct cost of consumer safety regulation, they have naturally resisted the trend toward greater regulation. Since the 1970s, reform of the consumer safety agencies has been an important item on the business community's political agenda. Many of their proposed changes have become public policy. President Carter put procedures in place to review the economic impact of important safety (and other) regulations. The Reagan administration went further and issued an executive order that no regulation should be permitted if its cost outweighed its benefit unless there was an express law to the contrary.

Under pressure from corporate interest groups, cutbacks also have been made at the safety agencies, making it harder for them to carry out their regulatory duties. Take the CPSC. To placate the business community, it was set up as a small organization in 1970. Though the CPSC has authority over some 15,000 products, it has never had more than 900 staff. Still, at President Reagan's urging, Congress slashed the CPSC's budget by 30 percent in 1981. Its budget continued to dwindle during the decade and, by 1989, equaled only 58 percent of its 1980 budget in inflation-adjusted dollars.[27] (See Figure 13–1.)

New policies have been launched to streamline some procedures for ensuring safety. The FDA has been a focus. Approving a new drug can take 7 to 13 years. The drug lag is partly an offspring of the thalidomide affair in the early 1960s, when a sedative widely used in Europe proved to cause terrible birth defects. In response to public outcry about thalidomide, the FDA required that new drugs be proved safe before they could be marketed, a step that added several years to the approval process. While erring on the side of caution looks sensible, it has an opportunity cost to American consumers who are denied early access to beneficial medication. There may be no net gain for society. Further, most other developed countries have quicker review times, which give their drug firms an edge in international competition.

The cost of getting new drugs registered became so high that no company

FIGURE 13–1

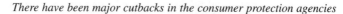

There have been major cutbacks in the consumer protection agencies

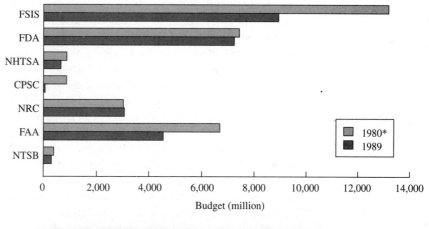

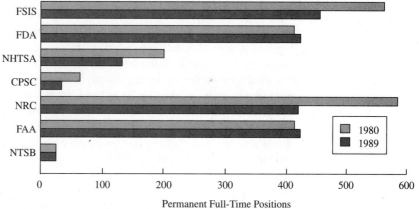

*1989 prices.
Source: W. Kip Viscusi, *Fatal Tradeoffs* (New York: Oxford University Press, 1992), pp. 253–54.

was willing to produce them unless the potential market was large. The effort to ensure safety thus meant that drugs for rare conditions were in danger of not being developed at all. Such drugs are called "orphans" because they have no corporate parent. To deal with the problem, Congress passed the Orphan Drug Act in 1983, providing federal aid for developing and marketing medicine that otherwise would not be commercially viable. To qualify, the disease must affect less than 200,000 people. In the first five years, 61 products were registered under the Orphan Drug Act.

In 1987, the FDA also began an accelerated drug approval process for drugs aimed at fatal illnesses such as Acquired Immune Deficiency Syndrome (AIDS).

This was less the result of pressure from the business and medical communities than from well-defined constituencies of patients. Advocacy groups pointed out the absurdity of the FDA's forbidding terminally ill people to try unproven treatments. They were going to die anyway, and there was a chance the treatments might work. Why not leave the decision to them?

Under the FDA's "fast-track" approval procedure, drugs intended for severe disease may not have to pass through full-scale clinical trials before approval. Experimental drugs also may be released early, as happened with the AIDS treatment AZT. The FDA is also more willing to use foreign research data as the basis for approval. Since 1987, there has been a marked increase in the rate of drug approvals for life-threatening diseases.[28]

The business response to the consumer movement is not just reactive and political. Some companies have sought to get ahead of the threat to their autonomy posed by consumer safety regulation. Recognizing that consumers are a critical stakeholder, they often set up consumer affairs offices to deal with product safety and the broader issue of product quality. Trying to keep close to customers and grasp their needs are basic sound business practices.[29] Many firms, especially carmakers, have learned that safety is an important selling point for their merchandise. Advertisements now stress that some car models surpass the legal minimum of safety, providing features such as passenger airbags, side-impact protection, and antilock brakes that are not yet required by law.

While business can point to numerous victories in annulling government's product safety rules, the tide is not always running their way. In 1993, for instance, the FDA and the USDA stiffened the labeling requirements for food to make it easier for consumers to compare ingredients, calories, and fat content. There also are more restrictions on health claims, concerning assertions that a product is "lite," "no-fat," or "low in cholesterol." The FDA has moved to tighten up regulation of the vitamin business. These changes in public policy have been supported by consumer activists and the medical community, but opposed by most food processors. Managers can anticipate further give-and-take in the domain of consumer safety regulation.

Occupational Safety and Health

Just as consumer products can be dangerous, so can the act of making those products. Some jobs are more dangerous than others. A coal miner runs a far greater risk of death or injury on the job than, say, a bookkeeper. The invisible hand theoretically holds the sum of workplace dangers to a minimum. As Adam Smith observed two centuries ago, workers demand extra pay for jobs they see as risky or unpleasant. Wages are adjusted for hardship "by the higgling and haggling of the market, according to that sort of rough equality which, though not exact, is sufficient for carrying on the business of common life."[30]

According to this line of thought, cautious workers turn down hazardous jobs; less risk-averse workers take these jobs, but only for high wages to compensate for the danger. To avoid paying this "risk premium," employers look for ways to take the danger out of jobs. Products that remain dangerous to make will carry a higher price tag, discouraging consumers from buying them. Under the right conditions, therefore, economic competition creates a suitable balance between safety and risk on the job. Unfortunately, conditions never are right and the market fails to deliver the amount of protection people truly want.

The familiar problem is lack of information. Because of it, workers and managers can underestimate workplace risks. The efficient matching of workers and jobs does not take place. People are most likely to miscalculate health hazards in the workplace, where a long latent period often separates the exposure to a harmful substance from the resulting disease. It was decades, for instance, before shipworkers who had been exposed to asbestos began to succumb to lung cancer, or before rubber workers who used vinyl chloride began to get liver disease. People find it easier to gauge external safety risks, such as the danger of falling off scaffolding, because they are more evident. But, even here, errors in judgment are common.

Due to the imprecision of workers' information, they also will systematically prefer jobs where the risk is not fully understood. On-the-job learning and the right to quit do not guarantee efficient outcomes, because often the workers' welfare will be irreversibly harmed while they gain knowledge of workplace perils.[31] There is a strong case for government involvement to make up for the market's shortcomings.

Like consumer safety, two sets of public institutions have evolved to furnish worker safety in the United States: the **workers' compensation** system and direct regulation. Workers' compensation, which requires bosses to pay workers who are hurt on the job without having to prove who is to blame, has some resemblance to the product liability scheme discussed above. Direct regulation of job safety and health is mainly the job of the Occupational Safety and Health Administration (OSHA), an agency similar to the CPSC and the NHTSA.

Workers' compensation is the more significant policy. Employers' premiums for the system are 1,000 times as much as the penalties levied by OSHA in any year. And workers' compensation is estimated to have a vastly greater effect than OSHA in reducing injuries.[32] We discuss this policy of recompensing injured workers first, then federal risk regulations.

Workers' Compensation

Workers paid with life and limb for industrialization. Fatalities on U.S. railroads reached a peak of 28 per 10,000 employees in 1904. The death rate for coal miners was still higher—33.5 per 10,000, or about three times higher than in France or Britain.[33] Serious accidents were even more prevalent than fatal accidents. Factories were unsanitary and often filled with choking dust, and many workers developed chronic illnesses, for example, black lung and brown lung. Employers during the first and second industrial revolutions had little economic incentive to take precautions due to the abundant supply of labor. It was cheaper to hire replacements for the injured and the ill than to put in safety equipment and train employees in safety, especially since so few factory jobs were skilled.

American workers who got hurt could sue their employers for tort. They rarely brought such cases, however, because injured workers had to surmount three powerful defenses under common law. As with legal action brought against them by consumers in the 1800s, companies could assert contributory negligence and assumption of risk, claiming the plaintiff was at least partly responsible for the injury and should have recognized the potential for harm at the workplace. Employers also could invoke the "fellow servant rule" and try to prove that the accident was caused by a coworker. Workers were barred from recovering damages if their negligence, or that of another worker, was even a small factor in an injury. Standing on shaky legal ground, only about one injured worker in six could receive compensation for work-related injuries.[34]

The working class everywhere faced similar problems, and they mobilized to force government to create a more prompt and certain means of receiving reparations. Germany adopted the first workers' compensation law in 1884, and, within several years, all European industrialized states had some public policy for workers' compensation, levied on employers. With these laws, government purposely changed the focus from fault to the simpler question of whether the accident or illness arose from employment. Neither worker error nor employer precautions mattered; any injury automatically entitled the victim to a payment. Workers' compensation does not preclude a negligence suit against an employer, but often makes it needless.

Due largely to the political power of business, the United States came late to workers' compensation. In 1908, the Federal Employers' Liability Act was enacted, but this landmark piece of legislation only affected common carriers engaged in interstate commerce, such as railroads. Wisconsin and New York are generally credited with establishing the first true workers' compensation programs in 1911. By 1949, every state had some type of workers' compensation law. These laws vary from state to state, but, in all but three states (Texas, New Jersey, and South Carolina), they require employers to insure against workplace injuries. Some states maintain a state fund for this purpose, others allow companies to insure themselves or buy private insurance. About 90 percent of U.S. workers are now covered. There is a schedule of benefits that includes hospital and medical payments and compensation for lost wages. Disabled employees who cannot go back to work are eligible for long-term benefits.

Again, these payments are an entitlement and are not affected by who is to blame. During a slow time at work, for instance, a 16-year-old showed a friend a "trick" in which a match is tossed into oil, gasoline, and grease without exploding. The trick did not work and the volatile mixture did explode, wounding the worker. The New York Workers' Compensation Board agreed this accident was covered since it was "related to his employment."[35] Rather than filing a civil lawsuit in situations such as this, workers simply apply for benefits based on injury, illness, or death.

As with product liability rules, the main rationale for workers' compensation is that it makes firms internalize a social cost. Work-related injuries and diseases are an unwanted byproduct of the creation of goods and services. Making firms pay the full cost of this negative externality gives them a strong incentive to cut their accident and illness rates. Workers' compensation insurance premiums are tied to safety records, meaning firms can receive a competitive advantage by making their facilities less risky. The significance of this public policy is that it pushes companies to invest in safety, and not solely that it creates a social insurance program.

Workers' compensation has the additional feature of reducing transaction cost. As with any form of no-fault insurance, it reduces the volume of litigation. Thus, the system is economical to run. It should bring the sum of the cost of injuries and the cost of preventing them as low as possible. Still, civil suits are possible when workers are denied benefits, or when they choose to start a separate legal action based on employer negligence. Litigation has been increasing, helping to drive up the cost of workers' compensation. We will return to this problem shortly. In rare instances, there even can be criminal charges for maintaining an unsafe workplace. In 1985, the parent company of Film Recovery Systems in Chicago was found guilty of manslaughter after a worker died of inhaling cyanide fumes. Three company officers were convicted as individuals of murder.[36]

Dramatic improvements in job safety have taken place this century, and workers' compensation shares some credit. There is under 1 death per 10,000 factory workers per year today. The rate of job-related accidents fell to less than 8 per 100 workers, compared to 10 per 100 in 1973.[37] Comparative statistics are hard to find and may be unreliable due to different reporting methods in countries. But the data available indicate the United States has an ordinary accident and illness rate for an advanced country (see Table 13–4.)

Other factors that help account for the progress in job safety include the shift to a service economy (where jobs are less dangerous on average), rising living standards (pushing up the price of pay for hazardous duty), union contracts (bar-

TABLE 13–4   **The Occupational Death Rate in the United States Is Not out of the Ordinary.**

	Deaths as a Result of Accidents at Work and Occupational Illnesses (1986–90 average per 100,000 workers)		
	Mining	*Manufacturing*	*Transport*
Canada	64	6	15
Finland	25	4	9
Switzerland	61	4	13
United States	**22**	**4**	**14**

Source: *World Labour Report* (Geneva: International Labor Organization, 1993).

gaining for health and safety provisions), and changing ethical standards among businesspeople (recognizing employees as a valuable human resource). Less significant are OSHA's rules, as we will see below.

The Workers' Compensation Crisis

Businesspeople, particularly owners of small businesses, are not happy with workers' compensation. They detect problems that are similar to the weaknesses of product liability, discussed above. One is the possibility of moral hazard, as workers may be tempted to take more chances than they might without insurance against accidents. Another is rent-seeking, as unscrupulous workers take advantage of the system by making false claims. Also, the part of workers' compensation that goes to medical treatment has been skyrocketing with all health care costs. The result is a workers' compensation "crisis" akin to the product liability crisis.

Employers spent an estimated $62 billion on workers' compensation in 1992, triple the amount a decade earlier.[38] About 40 percent is for medical treatment; the rest, mostly to replace lost wages. According to a 1993 survey, this cost is a leading factor undermining U.S. firms' effort to compete globally.[39] Meanwhile, many state programs are deep in the red. At the same time, labor groups charge that workers' compensation does not create sufficient incentive to prevent accidents and disease. Coverage is spotty, and maximum benefits are often below the poverty level. Injured workers also face many bureaucratic barriers to making claims.

Relief is coming. Over 200 reform bills were submitted in state legislatures in 1993. Most propose to overhaul administrative procedures and redefine benefits. California, a bellwether state, passed a reform package that makes it harder to collect for job-related stress, puts limits on the number of medical opinions allowed, and toughens law enforcement to fight fraud.

These new public policy measures should slow future rises in the price for covering workers hurt on the job. In Massachusetts, for example, legislative reforms led to a 10 percent drop in compensation rates in 1994. That was the first decrease in the cost of workers' compensation insurance in more than 20 years.[40]

Direct Regulation of Worker Safety

Workers' compensation encourages job safety through incentives; by turning accidents and illnesses into a cost of doing business, companies are induced to find safer methods of production. Policy makers do not tell companies how to reach this goal. However, government also takes part more directly in company decisions about job safety. Instead of leaving managers to decide the way to reduce occupational risk, policy makers create regulatory policies that explain in detail things managers must do. This second approach is far more controversial with business.

As with workers' compensation, direct regulation of employee safety started earlier in Europe than in the United States. In 1802, England established regulations requiring employers to ventilate and whitewash workplaces. In 1844, machine guards were mandated. American workplace safety standards emerged later, and then only at the state level. Massachusetts created a Department of Factory Inspection in 1867 and passed a law 10 years later requiring guards on textile machinery.[41] Following a catastrophic fire at the Triangle Shirt Factory in New York in 1911, there was a national movement toward stricter safety regulations. Without federal guidance, however, state and local standards were a hodgepodge of rules, with many gaps.

To deal with the problem, the Occupational Safety and Health Act of 1970 set up OSHA. This legislation was organized labor's main legislative goal at the time. In light of later debates, it is surprising that President Nixon supported the bill and that there was near unanimous backing in Congress.[42] OSHA has two main tasks. First, it proclaims regulations about workplace conditions deemed important to employee safety and health. These regulations cover equipment and exposure to chemicals, radiation, and other harmful agents. Second, OSHA inspects workplaces to determine whether they conform with the regulations. The new agency was expected to lead to a 50 percent decline in workplace injuries.

The OSHA Controversy

OSHA soon became one of business's favorite objects of complaint. The gripes centered on the agency's meddlesome and picayune rules, many of which lacked safety benefit. The rules could be a hardship for business to follow. OSHA came to symbolize all that was wrong with government and bureaucracy, and turned into a rallying point for the conservative political movement that has dominated U.S. politics since the 1980s.

Part of the problem was that, within one month of its creation, OSHA adopted 4,400 standards from voluntary safety codes, such as those set by the American National Standards Institute and the National Fire Protection Association, and from existing federal standards for maritime safety. Careful review was not possible. Thus, too many of OSHA's standards were trivial or obsolete and became the target of ridicule.

OSHA required that toilet seats be split, not round. Spittoons were to be cleaned daily. The handrail regulation laid out in minute detail their required height, spacing, thickness, and clearance. There were 140 standards covering ladders. OSHA produced a brochure for farm workers warning them about the hazard of stepping on manure. Many regulations were baffling, such as the definition of an exit ("A means of egress is a continuous and unobstructed way of exit travel from any point in a building or structure to a public way . . . and comprises the vertical and horizontal ways of travel . . .").[43] Because of the jeering that resulted, the agency revoked 928 nitpicking rules in 1978.

More serious in the eyes of many observers was OSHA's preference for engineering controls rather than personal protective equipment to abate health hazards. As Steven Kelman points out: "Reducing exposure to health hazards (such as noise or chemicals) by engineering controls is often horrendously expensive, especially when the new controls must be fitted onto existing machines at existing plants with fixed layouts. By contrast, personal protective equipment—ear plugs, earmuffs, and respirators—costs a tiny fraction of what engineering controls cost."[44] Business much prefers the cheaper method. But OSHA engineers, trained in industrial hygiene, do not trust people to wear safety equipment and prefer to have safety built in to plants and machines.

OSHA conducts surprise inspections. The employer can refuse to admit the inspector to the work site but rarely does so because OSHA can obtain a search warrant easily. Once admitted, the inspector does a walk-around tour, looking for infractions of safety standards and checking the employer's records. If violations are found, citations can be issued. Penalties of up to $10,000 can be levied for willful or repeated violations. Fines are not a major factor in a company's calculations, however. They plummeted during the Reagan and Bush administrations to less than $10 million per year. By contrast, higher worker wages generated by hazard pay are $70 billion.[45]

More important than OSHA's fines for companies is the cost of meeting OSHA's standards. The price tags of proposed new occupational safety regulations in 1988 and 1989 were estimated to be $12 billion and $10.5 billion.[46] These government-mandated expenses, plus the charge for workers' compensation and other compulsory benefits, are encouraging some companies to relocate their more hazardous operations in LDCs, where occupational safeguards are far less burdensome.

Even rival industrial countries may have a cost advantage in worker safety. All have public agencies that do the same functions as OSHA, but the corporatist democracies are apt to make regulation less adversarial and more cooperative. In Sweden, for example, compulsory health and safety committees coordinate with unions and have veto power over company decisions that affect occupational safety and health. With its advanced welfare state, the stress is more on worker wellness and preventive measures than it is on inspecting and punishing employers.[47] Austria, Norway, Finland, and, to a lesser extent, Germany have similar features. Congress has considered bills to make employers form labor–management safety and health committees, which many executives oppose as a pretense for union organizing.[48]

Since OSHA did not perform a systematic analysis of the cost and benefit of its various remedies for safety problems, the offsetting gains are small. According to a 1988 study, only about 1 injury in 10 can be prevented by OSHA standards.[49] Not surprisingly, the consensus among researchers who have investigated OSHA during its first years is that any effect on safety was negligible at best. More recent evidence, however, suggests improved performance as the agency has changed its behavior, putting more emphasis on cost–benefit analysis and allowing companies more leeway to choose how to reach safety goals.

The Political Fight over Occupational Safety Regulation

Business's campaign against OSHA soon bore fruit. Under the Carter administration, the number of inspections was scaled back by one-third. President Reagan allowed the agency to dwindle in size, further cutting inspections. So few take place now that the average employer is likely to see Halley's comet before he sees an OSHA inspector.[50] Part, but not all, of the decline is from OSHA trying to focus on large companies in particularly dangerous industries. Thus, from being a lightning rod for controversy, OSHA has become something of an irrelevance. It is no longer the prying, pushy force business once perceived. Unfortunately, during the same period, there has been a rise in work time lost to injuries, on a per-employee basis, that may be tied to lax enforcement by OSHA.

OSHA's inactivity also pushed many states to fill the void. Prompted by events such as the Union Carbide accident in Bhopal, India, for instance, workers began clamoring for more information about toxic substances with which they work. By 1985, 20 states had passed right-to-know laws, compelling companies to provide this sort of information. To preempt the states, OSHA in 1987 issued a revised standard requiring chemical manufacturers to alert workers to the effects of hazardous chemicals through labeling and training.

There are other signs of a counterreaction to the inertia of OSHA. A fire at a poultry processing plant in North Carolina that killed 25 workers in 1991 underlined for the public the infrequency of safety inspections. The plant had no fire exits (they were padlocked to prevent pilferage), sprinkler system, or fire drills, and had not been inspected in 11 years. Political demand is building to increase the inspection rate so such outrages will not be repeated.

As more Americans turn to work in the service sector, public attention has also begun to focus on hazards in the office. OSHA has always put most of its energy into more obviously dangerous work sites, but offices may not be as harmless as they seem. One possible threat to office workers is video display terminals, which may emit harmful radiation. Another risk is repetitive motion injury, such as carpel tunnel syndrome, caused by typing. There is also "sick building syndrome," associated with poor ventilation and indoor contaminants from photocopying machines, cleaning liquids, and plastic furnishings. Under the Clinton administration, OSHA is drafting more health and safety regulations for the office setting.[51]

Conclusion

This chapter has shown how American managements' freedom in the domain of safety has been narrowed over the past century. Where managers once had few legal duties to protect customers and employees from harm, they now have many such duties. These two stakeholder groups have asserted their rights through the courts, which have grown more willing to take the side of consumers and workers in disputes with management over safety. These stakeholders also have increased their rights through legislatures, especially by encouraging lawmakers to set up bureaucratic organizations to oversee the safety practices of companies.

The result is two public policy approaches for protecting consumers and employees. One is to create economic incentives that make it a company's interest to be safety conscious. This is the approach of product liability law and the workers' compensation system. Both encourage companies to try to minimize their insurance payments by having fewer accidents. The other approach is direct regulation, where a government agency simply tells companies how to design and manufacture products in a safe way. Most economists think the incentive system gets more results, and empirical studies support them.

The American business community complains that public policy to reduce the risks of industrialism has gone too far and is hurting the nation's ability to compete in the global market. Inflated though the protests are, there is waste in federal and state safety-seeking policies. Companies in other countries do not have the same weight of product and worker safety regulation. Business has pressed its case with success and has had some of the regulatory load lifted. Still, the struggle is not over, and there is some evidence the scales are beginning to tip the other way.

Questions

1. Why does unrestrained economic competition not provide the "right" degree of protection to consumers and workers? Can the market be mended so it does provide a socially desirable level of safety?

2. Discuss product liability. How has public policy in this area changed in the last century? What is your evaluation of the changes?

3. Describe the workers' compensation system. Why was the system established? What problems does it have today? Discuss any parallels you see with product liability.

4. How does direct regulation of product or workplace safety work? In what ways is this different from an incentive-based approach? Which method of assuring safety works best?

5. Detail the ways that safety regulations can affect national competitiveness. Is excess regulation a major problem? If so, what should be done about it?

End Notes

1. Quoted by Aaron Wildavsky, *Searching for Safety* (New Brunswick, NJ: Transaction Books, 1988), p. 149.

2. George A. Steiner and John F. Steiner, *Business, Government, and Society,* 6th ed. (New York: McGraw-Hill, 1991), p. 560.

3. Rogene A. Buchholz, *Business Environment and Public Policy,* 4th ed. (Englewood Cliffs, NJ: Prentice Hall, 1992), p. 352.

4. Nina M. Cornell, Roger G. Noll, and Barry Weingast, "Safety Regulation," in *Setting National Priorities: The Next Ten Years,* ed. Henry Owen and Charles L. Schultze (Washington, DC: Brookings Institution, 1976), pp. 464–65.

5. Cited in William C. Frederick, James E. Post, and Keith Davis, *Business and Society,* 7th ed. (New York: McGraw-Hill, 1992), p. 352.

6. W. Kip Viscusi, *Reforming Products Liability* (Cambridge, MA: Harvard University Press, 1991), p. 1.

7. Cited in Archie B. Carroll, *Business and Society,* 2nd ed. (Cincinnati: South-Western, 1993), p. 297.

8. Viscusi, *Reforming Products Liability,* p. 45.

9. W. M. Landes and Richard A. Posner, *The Economic Structure of Tort Law* (Cambridge, MA: Harvard University Press, 1987), pp. 438–39.

10. A. Mitchell Polinsky, *An Introduction to Law and*

Economics (Boston: Little, Brown, 1983), p. 99.

11. Viscusi, *Reforming Products Liability,* p. 2.

12. Michael E. Porter, *The Competitive Advantage of Nations* (New York: Free Press, 1990), p. 649.

13. "The Verdict from the Corner Office," *Business Week,* April 13, 1992, p. 66.

14. "A Survey of the Legal Profession," *The Economist,* July 18, 1992; and "Not Guilty," *The Economist,* February 13, 1993, pp. 63–64.

15. Warner Freedman, *International Product Liability* (Charlottesville, VA: Mitchie, 1990), p. 402.

16. Robert Cooter and Thomas Ulen, *Law and Economics* (Glenview, IL: Scott, Foresman, 1988), p. 463.

17. David Fraun, "High Noon," *Forbes,* September 14, 1992, p. 478.

18. Cited in David P. Baron, *Business and Its Environment* (Englewood Cliffs, NJ: Prentice Hall, 1993), pp. 286–87.

19. Milo Geyelin, "Suits by Firms Exceed Those by Individuals," *The Wall Street Journal,* December 3, 1993, p. B1.

20. E. Patrick McGuire, *The Impact of Product Liability* (New York: Conference Board, 1988).

21. Barbara Carton, "Cessna Says It Will Make More Small Airplanes," *The Wall Street Journal,* March 14, 1995, p. B1.

22. Viscusi, *Reforming Products Liability,* p. 76.

23. James Harvey Young, *Pure Food: Securing the Food and Drug Act of 1906* (Princeton, NJ: Princeton University Press, 1989).

24. John F. Morrall III, "A Review of the Record," *Regulation* 10, no. 2 (1986), pp. 25–34.

25. Viscusi, *Reforming Products Liability,* pp. 123–24.

26. R. E. Litan, ed., *Liability: Perspectives and Policy* (Washington, DC: Brookings Institution, 1988).

27. Baron, *Business and Its Environment,* p. 298.

28. W. Kip Viscusi, John M. Vernon, and Joseph E. Harrington, Jr., *Economics of Regulation and Antitrust* (Lexington, MA: D.C. Heath, 1992), p. 732.

29. Thomas Peters and Robert Waterman, *In Search of Excellence* (New York: Harper and Row, 1982).

30. Adam Smith, *An Inquiry into the Nature and Causes of the Wealth of Nations* (1776; reprint, New York: Modern Library, 1937), p. 31.

31. W. Kip Viscusi, *Risk by Choice* (Cambridge, MA: Harvard University Press, 1983), p. 77.

32. Viscusi, *Reforming Products Liability,* pp. 178–79.

33. Carl Gersuny, *Work Hazards and Industrial Conflict* (Hanover, NH: University Press of New England, 1981), p. 20.

34. Charles Noble, *Liberalism at Work: The Rise and Fall of OSHA* (Philadelphia: Temple University Press, 1986), p. 54.

35. Tony McAdams, *Law, Business, and Society,* 3rd ed. (Homewood, IL: Richard D. Irwin, 1992), p. 513.

36. Buchholz, *Business Environment and Public Policy,* pp. 369–70.

37. Murray Weidenbaum, *Business, Government, and the Public,* 4th ed. (Englewood Cliffs, NJ: Prentice Hall, 1990), pp. 146 and 151.

38. Peter Romeo, "Broke," *Nation's Restaurants,* April 10, 1993, pp. 70–80.

39. Angela Carlisle, "RMs Call Tort Reform, Health Care Top Concern," *National Underwriter,* May 24, 1993, pp. 35–36.

40. Kimberly Blanton, "Regulators Slash '94 Comp Rates," *Boston Globe,* January 14, 1994, p. 65.

41. Noble, *Liberalism at Work,* p. 31.

42. Steven Kelman, "Occupational Safety and Health Administration," in *The Politics of Regulation,* ed. James Q. Wilson (New York: Basic Books, 1980), pp. 238–42.

43. Cited in Buchholz, *Business Environment and Public Policy,* p. 365.

44. Kelman, "Occupational Safety and Health Administration," p. 251.

45. Viscusi et al., *Economics of Regulation and Antitrust,* p. 709.

46. W. Kip Viscusi, *Fatal Tradeoffs* (New York: Oxford University Press, 1992), p. 276.

47. Steven Kelman, *Comparing Countries, Comparing Policies* (Cambridge, MA: MIT Press, 1980).

48. "Stepping into the Middle of OSHA's Muddle," *Business Week,* August 2, 1993, p. 53.

49. Weidenbaum, *Business, Government, and the Public,* p. 147.

50. Viscusi, *Fatal Tradeoffs,* p. 11.

51. Diane E. Lewis, "OSHA Finishes Draft of Strain-Injury Rules," *Boston Globe,* November 5, 1994, p. 23.

14 PUBLIC POLICY, POLLUTION, AND RESOURCE CONSERVATION

What belongs in common to the most people is accorded the least care; they take thought for their own things above all, and less about things in common . .
Aristotle[1]

People have always inflicted damage on their physical surroundings. The results are sometimes hardly noticeable, sometimes inconvenient, sometimes catastrophic. Ancient civilizations such as the Sumerians in the Middle East and the Mayas in Central America may have perished because they exhausted their natural resource base. The Roman empire was weakened by lead that leached from public water pipes and poisoned the population. In the cities of medieval Europe the populace regularly succumbed to epidemics caused by crowding and poor sanitation. Later, in the early industrial period, society fouled rivers with industrial and human waste, cut down whole forests for fuel and building material, and hunted entire animal species to extinction.

A Global Problem

While ecological distress is nothing new, its scale today is unique. The planet has more people to support now—over 5 billion, as opposed 1.6 billion in 1900, and heading toward 8.5 billion in 2025. The burgeoning population alone adds pressure on the world ecosystem. Yet, due to industrialization and rising living standards, each of the world's inhabitants uses more resources on average than in the past. Since Thomas Malthus (1766–1834), experts have speculated about when the limit to growth would be hit. Technological change and rising productivity have multiplied the earth's carrying capacity thus far, but many wonder whether it can continue to sustain so vast a population without a decrease in consumption.[2]

The past may not be a good indicator of the future because the ecological ill-effects of industrial development are accumulating, and sometimes pushing past a threshold to overload the natural environment. Poisons that were dumped into landfills decades ago are just now beginning to leach, menacing underground water supplies. Chlorofluorocarbons (CFCs), used as a coolant, have built up in the atmosphere and are alleged by many scientists to be eating the ozone shield; so many old refrigerators and air conditioners have been buried in landfills that CFC pollution is guaranteed to worsen for decades. Most ominous, CO_2 emissions, the byproduct of burning fuel, may have reached a critical level and be helping to raise the earth's temperature. Scientific opinion is not unanimous, but the results might be devastating, including the flooding of much of the world's prime farmland and its coastal settlements.

Pollution's negative externalities thus look heavier than ever. The degradation of nature has long injured third parties who have not been consulted by the people doing the polluting, and whose injuries are not incorporated in the price system. Yet, humankind's larger numbers, and the larger potential ecological impact of such new technology as nuclear power, make the world a more interconnected place today. We all are affected by decisions made many miles away by people of whom we have never heard.

When Brazilian ranchers choose to burn rain forests to clear grazing land, they can hardly be aware that the smoke and loss of CO_2-using trees may help trigger floods or drought years later in the American Midwest, forcing some farmers out of business. When Midwestern power plants throw smoke out of tall smoke stacks, designed to limit local air pollution, they do not intend to produce acid rain in New England and eastern Canada that kills trees and poisons lakes. When Asian fishermen use drift nets to sweep parts of the ocean clean of fish, they do not seek on purpose to cause subsequent shortages of seafood, making it hard for fishermen anywhere to make a living. There is no escaping these external effects.

Trends in the physical environment are not entirely grim. Rising living standards also mean more resources ready for fighting ecological problems. There have been measurable improvements in air quality in many urban areas in developed countries. More lakes in the United States can be used for fishing or swimming than 20 years ago. Forest acreage is expanding rapidly. The plight of some endangered animals has stimulated major efforts, funded mainly by well-to-do people, to protect them. A few species, for example, the bald eagle, have made a comeback. Some toxic substances, for example, PCBs and DDT, are no longer widely used.[3]

Also, scientific opinion is uncertain about some apparent dangers to the biosphere. The Congress's $500 million National Acid Precipitation Assessment Program, for instance, concluded in 1990 that there is no evidence of widespread forest damage from acid rain. The evidence is inconclusive about the extent of global warming, and about the role of man-made pollution in it.[4] It is not clear what, if anything, can be done to stop the natural process of climate change. A warmer earth might also have positive effects that mitigate the harm, for example, by extending the growing season in northern latitudes.

Still, public opinion in the West remains anxious that the balance of nature is being upset permanently with dire effects.[5] Many government studies and reports have highlighted the danger, for example, *The Global 2000 Report to the President,* submitted in 1980, or the World Commission on Environment and Development's *Our Common Future* (the "Brundtland Report") completed in 1987. So-called green political parties and nonpartisan ecological activists around the world are using public policy and other forms of influence to change the way business and consumers treat the physical environment.

Governments have the capability to make all firms minimize the negative externalities of production, to reduce the harmful effect of economic activities on people other than those undertaking them. Firms are made to pay for pollution through regulations and taxes. They, in turn, pass the cost to consumers who use the goods that caused the pollution, and not to the larger society. In this chapter, we examine how, and how well, public policy does limit pollution and protect nature. As with other facets of safety, the trend has been toward greater restriction of business's behavior. We start with an analysis of what the threats to the natural world are and why they happen. Then, we turn to the agencies and public policies that have evolved to combat these problems. We will see that, as usual, it is much easier to identify the need for government intervention than to specify how it should intervene.

Threats to the Physical Environment

Threats to the environment are often broken into two categories: pollution and the excessive depletion of natural resources. **Pollution** refers to the undesirable contamination of nature by the manufacture or use of commodities. (There is natural pollution, too, such as volcanic ash and radon, but it will not concern us in this chapter.) **Resource depletion** is the using up of the earth's natural wealth.[6] The two problems are conceptually the same, though, since pollution destroys some finite resources and is therefore a form of resource depletion.

A part of the natural resource base is *renewable.* Forests will grow back, farmland will regain its fertility, lakes will purify themselves. Still, nature's restorative powers cannot work if people are impatient, if they do not leave the resource alone. Societies run the risk of doing irreversible damage to their renewable resource base. Other natural resources are *nonrenewable.* Once used they are gone. Minerals and fossil fuels are examples of nonrenewable resources. There is a limited stock of these raw materials, and, though more reserves can be found for a while, eventually they will be exhausted. Modern societies are apt to wear out renewable resources and to use nonrenewable resources too fast.

Some resource depletion is part of the human condition. So is some pollution. As the Second Law of Thermodynamics states, every process generates waste as a byproduct. By extracting raw materials and transforming them into useful goods, business produces waste. The excess, which often has undesirable properties, has to be reabsorbed by nature.[7]   "Spaceship Earth" is a closed ecosystem, and there is no place else to find raw materials, no place else for waste products to go.

The most important forms of pollution are toxic substances that taint the air and the water, because the pollutants readily find their way into our bodies when we breathe or drink. Pollution of soil also can be a major hazard, by contaminating food that is grown on it or people that work or play near it. Air, water, and soil pollution can have *point sources* (a pipe, stack, or other distinct place of origin) or *nonpoint sources* (for example, chemical runoff from farms and roads). Point sources are easier to identify and therefore to control.

Some pollutants are *biodegradable.* They break down into harmless substances and are reabsorbed into the natural environment, provided they are not disposed of in excess quantity or concentration. Other toxic pollutants do not change this way or do so slowly. They carry longer-term cost. Still, many of these undesirable byproducts of human activity can be *recycled,* being used over directly or being reprocessed to extract usable elements.

Not all pollutants threaten people with disease. They may just be annoying. This is the case of much visual pollution, such as billboards on rural highways or modern buildings in historic urban centers. Visual pollution is offensive mainly for aesthetic reasons; people object to it because it lowers their quality of life, not because it imperils their health. Excess noise is similar. In some urban areas or places near major transportation facilities, the din is irritating and can reduce property value. There can be health effects, too, such as hearing loss and stress-induced sickness.

Sometimes the victims of pollution are not human. As people push into new places to settle, they modify ecosystems and jeopardize the species that live there. Some plants or animals do not yield useful economic products (or contain products that have yet to be discovered, as is alleged to be true of tropical forests), and the market usually ignores them. Other natural life may be considered so valuable it is used faster than it can be replaced. The rhinoceros is being slaughtered for its horn, the elephant for its ivory, and, eventually, these animal products may no longer be available at any price.

Among the most intricate environmental issues is energy use. Cheap energy is the basis of postindustrial society, but also a threat to it. America, which consumes 10 times as much oil as Britain or Canada, is singularly hooked on cheap energy. Since the quadrupling of oil prices in 1973, Americans have been uneasy about their dependence on fossil fuel. The Arab oil embargo showed how vulnerable our and other modern societies are to breaks in energy supplies. In 1990, the United States led an international coalition to war in the Persian Gulf largely to assure access to the world's main stock of oil.

Still, the day of reckoning will come when the West must adjust to a lack of traditional fossil fuel. That adjustment has some helpful implications for the physical environment, for most fossil fuel is dirty. Unfortunately, the replacements, for example, nuclear or hydroelectric power, create environmental problems of their own. (Fusion power is an exception. It is clean, but not yet technologically feasible.)   Conservation can buy time, but it requires people to change habits (especially regarding private automobiles) in ways they find disagreeable and they are apt to protest.   How to reconcile these factors is a Promethean dilemma.

The issue for mixed economies such as is found in the United States is not to end all industrial waste or to stop all use of fixed resources but to keep these activities at an acceptable level.   In the language of political economy, pollution and the waste of energy and similar assets are allocation problems.   Some destruction of natural habitat is tolerable as long as the benefit exceeds the cost.   Too much destruction happens when one use of the physical environment diminishes other, more worthwhile uses.

Tragedy of the Commons

The ruin of our natural surroundings is frequently a result of market failure.   It happens not because businesses or consumers like polluting, but because businesses and consumers are misled by economic incentives.   In a market, resources are allocated by prices.   Pollution has social cost, a clean environment social value, that is not reflected in the price of things.   Economic signals thus point in the wrong direction.   By suggesting that air, water, and the like are free or very cheap, the invisible hand of economic competition encourages producers and consumers to squander them.

One reason the market discounts these resources is that the physical environment is a *common property good*.   Common property goods are things we consume collectively.   Once they are supplied to one person, they cannot be withheld from others.   Unlike pure public goods, however, common property goods do dissipate.   After one person uses them, there is less to go around for others.   These two aspects of the physical environment create a framework for overuse.

Common property goods cannot be reduced easily to private ownership.   The low degree of excludability makes limited access infeasible, and that undermines the basis of individual property rights.   It is hard to assign ownership to, say, the atmosphere or the ocean because of the difficulty in controlling trespassers.   The problem is that something that belongs to no one is no one's responsibility.   People are thus apt to use common property resources more wastefully than their individual property.

Why should a factory owner worry about the residue his factory empties into the ocean?   It does not cost his company much.   Consumers are part of the problem, too.   When we drive rather than take mass transit, we use an unpriced resource (the air) to dispose the emissions our car produces.   The single person has little motivation to incur the cost of cleaning up an environmental problem, because most of the benefit will be for others to enjoy.   To the contrary, the individual has some reason to exploit the cheap resource as much as possible, knowing that, if he does not, someone else will.   This is another example of the free-rider problem, which impedes individuals from pursuing their joint welfare.

Such a situation cannot last forever, for if everybody treats the physical environment as a free good, it will get used up. The phrase often used to describe this bind is the **tragedy of the commons.**[8] Consider herders who have access to communal pasture land. Each herder receives a direct benefit from his sheep or cattle but bears only part of the cost of overgrazing. All the herders feel pushed to increase the number of animals under their care, though the long-range effect is to destroy the pasture and impoverish everyone. The logic of individual self-interest locks everyone into a free-for-all of self-destructive behavior. Examples of the tragedy of the commons are many, from overfishing off the New England coast to the decision of parents in developing countries to produce large families as insurance for their retirement.

Environmental Ethics

Appealing to people's ethical sense and feeling of community sometimes can preclude the tragedy of the commons and encourage the thrifty use of common property resources. Few people want to hurt nature. Many societies in the past have believed individuals ought to act as trustees toward the earth, to preserve and respect it as a matter of duty. They have found ways to manage common property resources.[9] Today, through moral suasion, human beings can learn to take steps that lower their ecological impact, for example not littering or avoiding disposable merchandise.

Many firms are profiting from consumers' compassion for the physical environment by marketing "green" products, such as biodegradable detergent or plastic. Other firms try to earn the public's goodwill through open displays of their ecological sensitivity. McDonald's has replaced foam containers with paper packaging. Kodak is recycling its disposable cameras. Du Pont has committed to phasing out the production of freon, a CFC, by 1999.[10] The tuna industry agreed on its own in 1990 to change its fishing methods to avoid accidently drowning the dolphins who travel with tuna schools, though this makes catching tuna fish harder.

Some stockholders are beginning to demand that companies address environmental problems. There are specialized mutual funds today that buy shares only in green companies. A group of bankers, investors, and brokers have organized the Social Investment Forum that controls about $150 billion in pension and mutual funds.

Together with several environmental groups like the Sierra Club and the National Wildlife Federation, these investors have formed a Coalition for Environmentally Responsible Economies (CERES) and written a statement called the Valdez Principles (named after the gargantuan Exxon oil spill in Alaska). This statement (since renamed the CERES Principles) is modeled after the Sullivan Principles, which had been put together earlier to get companies to work against apartheid in South Africa. CERES has called on 400 companies to endorse the 10-point code of conduct, which commits them to protect the biosphere, make sustainable use of natural resources, reduce waste, and minimize environmental risk, among other steps. Many companies have indicated interest, but few have been willing to sign.

Government Intervention

Voluntary, market-based endeavors such as this to maintain the harmony of nature are not enough to block the market forces that are pushing the other way. To remain competitive, companies must minimize all cost to themselves, and fighting pollution is liable to add to their cost. Luckily, people have created government agencies to regulate and correct the market's deficiency, its tendency to despoil the earth. Individuals need not blindly, automatically foul their natural environment. The state sets up rules on how to conserve common property resources and tries, imperfectly, to make people use these resources in their best interest. Otherwise, nature is too meagerly protected.

Governments do not have to do a better job than the unregulated market. Terrible pollution occurred in the Soviet Union and its satellite countries because of public, not private, decisions.[11] There is one site in the Ural Mountains that may be the most polluted place on earth. At the shore of Karachay Lake, the radiation at a weapon factory's outlet pipe is so intense, an hour's exposure is enough to kill a person within weeks.[12]

The explanation for so much environmental mistreatment in the eastern bloc is that those states were indifferent to public opinion. When Soviet planners approved an unsafe design for a nuclear power plant in Chernobyl, they did so without having to consult Ukrainian residents, let alone the Poles, Germans, and others who also stood in the path of possible radioactive leaks. The socialist systems thus were free to take huge ecological risks in their economic development plans, posing heavy health burdens on their citizens.

Less authoritarian states could not have gotten away with using natural resources so thoughtlessly on such a scale, making those resources unusable for other, better purposes. In the West, when people become mindful of an environmental hazard, they are apt to demand protection or compensation. Ultimately, the socialist states could not get away with mass pollution either, as popular discontent with the domestic ecological crisis fueled the anti-Soviet revolutions of 1989–91.

Democratic states are by no means innocent of encouraging pollution and the waste of resources, however. A case in point is the U.S. nuclear arms industry. Operating under the cloak of national security, atomic bomb factories were not subject to ordinary environmental regulation. Now that the Cold War is over, the secrecy is being lifted, and we are learning of reckless, casual disposal of nuclear waste at such sites as Rocky Mountain Flats, near Denver. Lack of accountability can lead to terrible pollution in any political system.

Water gives another good example of how public policy can stumble in a democratic society. The United States heavily subsidizes irrigation, paying up to

90 percent of the supply cost of water in California. The subsidy induces extravagant use of this scarce resource, causing soil to become waterlogged and saline, lowering water tables, and altering the flow of rivers. Wealthy farmers reap most of the benefit. These wealthy farmers form an imposing lobby for keeping irrigation subsidies in place despite the harm to the physical environment.[13]

The Costs and Benefits of Environmental Protection

Public policy in capitalist democracies is powerless to abolish all pollution, but, in theory, it can help bring pollution down to the "right" level. From a utilitarian vantage point, the right level takes full account of the damage from industrial waste (not omitting the damage to future generations) and the cost of averting or cutting down the damage. Pollution that is not too costly to prevent (including opportunity cost) should be prevented. Any remaining ecological harm has to be tolerated as the price of commercial society. Alas, as the example of underpriced irrigation cited above proves, governments may have as much trouble as the market does finding this socially efficient degree of pollution.

Many business leaders and their allies argue that the United States has overinvested in environmental protection. They focus on the cost side of the ledger. According to a study by the Environmental Protection Agency (EPA), the nation spent $115 billion on pollution control in 1990, or 2.1 percent of the GNP. The sum may rise to $185 billion (1990 prices) by the end of the century.[14]

Some of this money, critics say, could be better spent on other purposes. Because of environmental controls, consumers have to pay higher prices for energy and other products. A typical car, for example, carries $800 worth of equipment to curb pollution.[15] When producers are forced by the regulations to divert resources from moneymaking investment, it adds to inflationary pressure.

Hit hardest are the older, basic industries such as steel, paper, and electricity. Pollution control faces diminishing returns. During the 1970s, for instance, the paper industry reduced about 95 percent of its pollutants for $3 billion. The next 3 percent of pollutants were expected to cost the industry $4.8 billion. Is it worth the money to squeeze out the last traces of pollution? Faced with towering cleanup charges, many dirtier factories have closed. The former Lakeway Chemical Company in Michigan is one case. It folded because it could not afford the $60 million (twice its annual sales) needed to clean a single polluted site.[16]

The drag of pollution abatement is feared to tilt the balance of trade against U.S. firms, as foreign competitors in less-regulated business settings have a cost advantage in producing some goods. These fears are exaggerated. Environmental protection probably does not handicap the nation's ability to compete with other OECD countries. As Figure 14–1 shows, the percent of gross fixed capital formation that goes to investment in pollution abatement and control in the United States is ordinary. Companies in all industrial countries have to pay for cleaning up the physical environment. A handful of American firms have moved abroad to countries, mostly in the Third World, with less severe environmental regulations, eliminating American jobs. These lost firms mostly make highly toxic products or process minerals.[17]

What about the other side of the environmental balance sheet? Ecological activists are apt instead to look more at the gains from pollution control, which usually lead to a different conclusion about the worth of government intervention. To them the United States spends far too little on protecting nature. The activists note how frequently business influences government to water down or delay regulations. They say arguments about inflation, unemployment, or national competitiveness are beside the point. Of course, undoing man's pollution has social cost, but this is lower than the social opportunity cost of *not* acting. Most Americans seem to agree. According to a 1990 *Wall Street Journal*/NBC News poll, six out of seven say they want to protect the physical environment even if they have to pay higher prices to do so.[18]

Outlays to fight pollution also beget new industries and new jobs that partly offset losses in other sectors. Mandatory recycling in Massachusetts and other states has created an important trade in converting trash into usable products. Firms such as Clean Harbors have sprung up to clean polluted dumps and toxic waste sites. Publicly funded R&D in such novel technologies as electric cars or nuclear fusion may be the basis for vast industries in the future. In Western Europe, the market for environmental goods and services was worth $94 billion in 1992.[19] Not surprisingly, the companies that sell such items press for stiffer environmental regulations.

Sometimes a country's green industry becomes internationally competitive

FIGURE 14–1

Industrial countries invest a lot to limit pollution

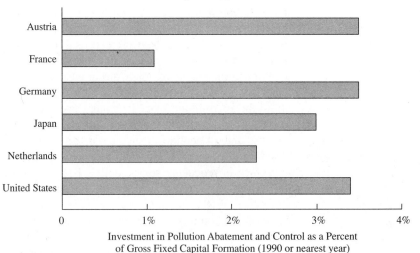

Investment in Pollution Abatement and Control as a Percent
of Gross Fixed Capital Formation (1990 or nearest year)

Source: OECD Environmental Data Compendium 1993 (Paris), p. 295.

precisely because government encouraged early demand for its services, giving it first-mover advantages in global competition.[20] Stringent standards for SO_2 and nitrous oxide in the United States, for example, created the biggest market in the world for gas scrubbers to clean the emissions from power plants. When foreign orders for gas scrubbers began to take off later, due to tightening air quality standards overseas, American firms capitalized on their early lead to become the foremost suppliers of this technology to other countries.[21] It is noteworthy that American firms do not have an edge overall in air pollution control equipment, 70 percent of which is imported from Europe or Japan, where many regulations are just as strict.[22]

The quarrel over environmental regulations is hard to resolve with cost–benefit analysis. There is great scientific uncertainty about the short- and long-term effects of pollution. The pluses and minuses of controlling it are so hard to measure we cannot easily determine who is right, and whether society is a net winner or loser of environmental rules. But perhaps the question is framed too roughly. Some regulations (for instance, banning lead from gasoline) have a big payoff and are clearly worth doing, even if the result is job loss or declining national competitiveness. Others are ineffective and a waste of resources. The challenge for public policy makers is to craft policies that walk the line between doing too much and doing too little.

Earth Rights

In the view of some ecological activists, and many ordinary people, the matter goes deeper than cost–benefit analysis. Access to a livable environment is a basic human right. Efforts have been made to develop legal theories of rights for animal species and even plants. According to opinion polls, roughly four Americans in five think the air, water, and land should be protected at any price. If one accepts this view, then companies have a duty to act as a guardian of nature that overrides cost. U.S. environmental law seems to agree, for it does not rest on utilitarian analysis. As we will discuss below, it often imposes absolute bans on pollution with no thought to the price.

The difficulty with the rights-based approach to pollution is that it lacks nuance. Given that a pristine physical environment is not feasible with any conceivable technology, partial controls on pollution are unavoidable. Mechanisms are needed to choose both the acceptable level of industrial cleanliness and the best means to reach that goal. Thus, we can agree that a clean environment is an irreducible right and still need public policies to weigh the tradeoffs of different antipollution measures.

Public Policy toward Nature

Government effort to protect the physical environment is not new. In the 14th century, Londoners who disobeyed that city's smoke pollution ordinances could be beheaded.[23] Before the American Revolution, the Massachusetts Bay Colony had regulations to prevent pollution in Boston Harbor.[24] Hundreds of years later, Michael Dukakis, governor of Massachusetts and presidential candidate, may have wished the Puritans' regulations, like London's, had called for capital punishment. By then, Boston had the nation's dirtiest harbor, and his opponent during the 1988 campaign, George Bush, blamed Dukakis for the pollution. The hapless governor's plight, as he struggled to defend his environmental record, illustrates how hard it can be for public policy to fix ecological problems in the face of relentless population growth and economic development.

In the 19th century, science identified the link between filth and disease, and concerned citizens began to demand pollution control to safeguard the public health. Before 1860, no American city had a comprehensive sewer system, but, after the Civil War, many cities began constructing sewers to remove waste. Municipal garbage collection and street cleaning also were undertaken in a bid to prevent disease. Sometimes, these cleaning efforts created the worse problem of contaminating the domestic water supply, and, by around 1900, public investment was begun in sewage treatment plants, purification plants, and other facilities to assure clean drinking water.[25] It was during this period that government also began to take a more active stand in conserving woodlands, wetlands, and other wild areas.

To enforce public health regulations, boards of health were established by cities and states, with broad authority over quarantines and the improvement of sanitary conditions. Massachusetts was the first state to set up a board of health in 1869. These government bodies could issue orders for abatement of health nuisances and could bring civil and criminal action against violators. Later, in the 20th century, public health officials began to identify industry as the major source of pollution. There was little federal government involvement until 1948,

TABLE 14–1   There Was a Flurry of U.S. Environmental Policy in the 1970s.

Policy	Year	Purpose
National Environmental Policy Act	1969	Mandates environmental impact statements for federal projects.
Clean Air Act (and amendments)	1970	Authorizes clean air standards, auto emission limits, and air quality regions.
Noise Pollution and Control Act	1972	Authorizes limits on noise from industrial activity.
Water Pollution Control Act	1972	Sets national goal of eliminating all pollutant discharge into water.
Federal Environmental Pesticide Control Act	1972	Requires registration of pesticides, permits pesticides to be banned.
Endangered Species Act	1973	Creates program to identify animals and plants on verge of extinction.
Safe Drinking Water Act	1974	Authorizes enforcement of national standards for drinking water.
Energy Policy and Conservation Act	1975	Provided detailed price structure for domestic crude oil (expired in 1981).
Resource Conservation and Recovery Act	1976	Establishes regulation of solid and hazardous waste disposal.
Toxic Substances Control Act	1976	Establishes national control policy for chemicals.
Comprehensive Environmental Response Compensation and Liability Act	1980	Identifies dangerous dumpsites; establishes Superfund for cleanups.

when the Water Pollution Control Act empowered the surgeon general to mediate disputes about pollution between parties in neighboring states.

Modern environmental regulation in the United States dates mostly from the 1970s. Rachel Carson's book *The Silent Spring* (1962) had warned many Americans about the pesticide hazard for the first time and roused them to other ecological hazards, too. Rising income and changing taste also piqued interest in the outdoors, and the environmental movement was spawned. The first annual Earth Day was held in 1970. At about the same time, the U.S. Congress started to create a broad statutory base for tightly controlling pollution, greatly limiting managers' discretion in disposing of waste.

Putting a spotlight on the looming shortage of energy, OPEC's actions led Congress during this period to invoke mandatory conservation measures for fuel use, for instance, maximum cooling temperatures in air conditioned buildings. These energy policies also limited managers' freedom of action. The more important environmental statutes are recorded in Table 14–1.

Political Clashes

All public policies create an arena for political conflict. Environmental policy is no exception. To take an example, green activists have used the Endangered Species Act to fight the logging industry. The threat posed to the spotted owl in the Pacific Northwest led to large areas of federal primal forest being declared off-limits to loggers in 1989. The lumber industry protested, and a compromise was later worked out to allow a limited timber harvest in the owl's habitat. No one was happy with the outcome.

The friction is not always between companies and environmental groups. Public policy is an adaptable weapon that one firm can turn against another. Established companies in slow-growing industries may push for tighter environmental rules, knowing these will affect new entrants more. Electrical utilities and smelters have used this tactic against younger rivals in the United States. Companies also may lobby for standards that they can meet but that will put a burden on competitors. That is why Chrysler, which specializes in small cars, supported high fuel-economy standards in the 1980s while its rivals opposed them.[26]

National Environmental Agencies

Table 14–2 lists the main federal government bodies responsible for enforcing the environmental policies that affect business. The most important is the EPA, established in 1970 by President Nixon. An independent agency in the executive branch, the EPA sets standards, enforces compliance, and does research in air, water, solid waste, toxic substance, radiation, and noise. Unlike many other regulatory agencies at which we have looked, the EPA's budget and staff grew

TABLE 14–2   A Host of U.S Agencies Carry Out Environmental Policy

Forest Service	Administers forest reserves and grasslands.
Bureau of Land Management	Leases federal land for mineral exploitation.
National Marine Fisheries Service	Monitors ocean fishing.
National Parks Service	Administers areas designated places of historic or scientific interest.
Council on Environmental Quality	Sets national pollution control policy.
Office of Surface Mining	Enforces reclamation of surface mines.
Environmental Protection Agency	Carries out clean air and water regulations.
Fish and Wildlife Service	Protects endangered species.
Department of Energy	Coordinates federal government's energy programs.
Department of Transportation	Sets and enforces fuel economy standards for automobiles.

in the 1980s. (We discuss why below.) It currently has more than 14,000 employees.

Another agency is the Council on Environmental Quality, which serves as an advisor to the president. The council collects information on the environment and develops legislative proposals for Congress. A very small body (13 employees), its primary influence is through environmental impact statement requirements. Most federal projects, and many private-sector actions, require a report analyzing the effect on the environment before they are approved.

The U.S. Forest Service executes environmental policy through its administration of national forests and grasslands, which are used for lumber and grazing as well as recreation and preserving wildlife. The Interior Department, through its Bureau of Land Management, supervises mineral exploration on federal land. Interior's Fish and Wildlife Service plays a role, too, through its power to declare plants or animals in danger of extinction. The department must ensure that actions it authorizes or funds do not jeopardize the continued existence of endangered species. A cabinet-level Endangered Species Committee (the so-called God Squad) can intervene to decide whether a form of life should be protected.

Energy policy is mainly the responsibility of the Energy Department, established in 1977. When created, mostly from preexisting agencies, it started with 18,000 employees and a $10 billion budget. The bulk of these resources were for distributive-type projects to investigate and invest in new energy sources, for example, solar and wind power or nuclear fusion. Billions of dollars were channeled through the Synthetic Fuels Corporation, an independent federal entity that dispersed money to private industry to develop oil shale, tar sands, and other oil substitutes. The rationale for getting government involved in developing energy technology was that the cost is so great, and the payoff so remote, the private sector will invest too little on its own. The Transportation Department has a hand in energy policy, too, through its responsibility for regulating the fuel efficiency of motor vehicles and setting speed limits on roads.

Other Institutions

Much environmental policy in the United States is made and enforced by state or local authorities. Several states, for example, have "bottle bills" requiring that consumers pay a deposit on bottles and cans to deter littering. At least 3,500 communities require that residents recycle their trash. Cambridge, Massachusetts, has special ordinances governing the practices of local biotechnology firms to prevent genetically altered organisms from escaping.

The courts, too, are used to control pollution through the common law tradition of suing for damages. Injured parties can win compensation from polluting firms, which in turn deters firms from polluting in the first place. This method of controlling pollution is impractical on a large scale, however, due to the high transaction cost and the trouble of ascertaining who is responsible for many types of pollution.

A good example is from Woburn, Massachusetts. Eight families took years to win an $8 million judgment against W. R. Grace in 1987 for contaminating town well water, which they alleged had given family members leukemia. A similar action against Beatrice Foods was unsuccessful, the appeals being exhausted in 1990. The litigants had a hard time proving Beatrice's role in polluting the ground water, and that the ground water had caused the cancer. In a parallel case brought by the EPA under the Superfund statute, Beatrice ultimately did accept responsibility for contaminating Woburn's water. With W. R. Grace and two other chemical firms, Beatrice agreed in 1991 to pay $69 million to clean the toxic waste dump that was the source of the Woburn pollution.

People also turn to the courts, and to direct political action, to stop projects that threaten the environment before any damage can occur. Often the focus is local, on blocking a proposed solid waste dump, power station, dam, or highway that is going to disrupt a community. People usually will admit that such facilities are necessary, but everyone naturally prefers they be put somewhere else. "Not in my backyard" (NIMBY) goes the saying.

The American policy-making system, with its checks and balances (see Chapter 9), has a hard time breaking the impasse caused by NIMBY attitudes. For years, lawmakers have been at a standstill over where to put nuclear waste. These byproducts of electricity production must be disposed of somewhere, but no one will willingly assent to having radioactive material near them, not even if it is buried in remote desert locations. Meanwhile, nuclear waste is stored in temporary sites at nuclear plants where it poses much greater risk to the environment.

Democracy's difficulty in coming to grips with the NIMBY problem is the mirror image of the old communist states, where officials arrogantly ignored people's concerns about radioactivity or toxic chemicals. Developers and government planners in a democracy often do get to build controversial projects eventually, though usually it requires lengthy arbitration and adjustment in their plans to account for local objections. This process can be frustrating to both sides and has a social cost, but it is definitely preferable to the alternative of rushing ahead with private or public venture schemes that threaten the natural environment.

Environmental Protection Overseas

The United States sometimes leads the world in trying to safeguard nature. The first national parks were set up here, starting with Yellowstone in 1872. Catalytic converters were required on U.S. automobiles to reduce hydrocarbons and CO_2 in the 1970s; they did not become standard in the European Union until 1993. Lead was phased out from American gasoline by 1982, a decade ahead of the European Union. American road speed limits also are much lower than in Europe—a conservation and a safety measure.

These deeds do not mean the United States sets the pace for protecting the environment. Because of their lifestyle, especially their heavy reliance on cars, the average American uses twice as much energy as a German or a Japanese, and about 12 times as much as a Chinese. Consequently, the United States produces far more CO_2 and other air pollutants than any other country (Table 14–3). Americans also generate more waste than other nationalities do—and they recycle a smaller share of it (Table 14–4).

Still, there is convergence in environmental public policy among the economically advanced countries, all of which face similar ecological challenges.[27] The French national government has had legal authority to control air pollution since 1961 and water pollution since 1964. England established the Department of the Environment in 1970 with responsibility for alleviating pollution. Germany set up its Federal Environmental Office in 1974, modeled on the U.S. EPA.

TABLE 14–3   **Despite Environmental Regulation, the United States Is a Voracious Consumer of Energy . . . and Has Pollution to Show for It.**

	Per Capita Energy Use (kg of oil equivalent) in 1990	*CO_2 Emissions (million tons of carbon) in 1989*
China	598	652
India	231	178
Germany	3,491	175
Japan	3,563	284
United Kingdom	3,646	155
United States	**7,822**	**1,329**

Source: *World Development Report 1992: Development and the Environment* (New York: Published for the World Bank by Oxford University Press, 1992), pp. 204 and 226–27.

TABLE 14–4   **Americans Also Generate Lots of Waste . . . and Do Not Recycle Much of It (1990)**

	Municipal Waste (kg/capita)	Recycling rate	
		Glass	*Paper and Cardboard*
France	328	29%	46%
Germany	333	45	40
Sweden	374	44	43
Switzerland	441	65	49
United Kingdom	348	31	21
United States	721	20	29

Source: *OECD Environmental Data Compendium 1993* (Paris: Organization for Economic Cooperation and Development, 1993), p. 149.

Ecological political parties are active in many European countries, such as the Green party that has won seats in the German national legislature. These parties play a function similar to that played by environmental interest groups in the United States, of keeping pressure on government to speak to problems in the natural environment.

These trends do not mean all countries at a similar level of development do things the same way. Most of them have more informal and cooperative modes of environmental regulation. There is nothing comparable in Germany and Japan to the court litigation and liability exposure in the United States. The American style of legalistic, command-and-control regulation tends to drive up compliance cost. Nations with more flexible approaches can have the same level of protection at less cost—which may be an advantage in international competition.[28]

The situation is different in the Third World, where strict regulation of pollution is seldom regarded with the same urgency. Pollution laws are apt to be weaker in LDCs, and enforcement laxer, often as a carrot for enticing foreign investors. Third World leaders argue, accurately, that their residents' impact on the earth is low compared to citizens in the United States, Europe, or Japan. They go on to conclude, with less justification, that fairness dictates that the rich countries should make most of the sacrifice of protecting the earth. The argument is specious because pollution has plenty of cost for Third World residents themselves, such as the many diseases they catch from unsanitary water. If they had a political voice, these poor people would ask for a cleaner habitat just like people in developed countries do, though they might settle for a lower level of cleanliness.[29]

LDC pollution has consequences for the First World, too. Imported food products, for instance, can have residue of pesticide that is banned in the United States. Many Americans object to the North American Free Trade Agreement because they think it will propel American companies to relocate operations to

Mexico, where the physical environment is less well-protected than in the United States—what might be called "eco-dumping." They fear the increase in pollution will affect the United States, too. The Clinton administration negotiated with the government of Mexico to beef up its enforcement, but the environmental movement was not satisfied that the agreements went far enough in limiting Mexican pollution.

International Cooperation . . . or Lack Thereof

As the dispute with Mexico illustrates, many threats to the natural world are beyond the reach of nation states to solve by themselves. Worldwide cooperation is needed. So, various international institutions and treaties have been created to try to deal with those threats to the earth's resources that do not respect national frontiers. The United States entered 11 multilateral environmental treaties in the 1980s, compared to 10 in the 20 years from 1960 to 1979.

The International Whaling Commission (IWC) is an illustration. It was established in 1948 to manage global stocks of whales—a classic common property resource. The IWC set national harvesting quotas to be sure that enough whales would be left to reproduce and be replenished. Faced with an alarming drop in the whale population, members agreed after years of debate to phase out all commercial whaling over a three-year period starting in 1982. Protecting the whales hurt the whaling industry, but, like most public policies, it benefited another industry, in this instance, tourism. Whale-watch voyages are now an important source of revenue in many seaside communities.

Another notable international agreement is the Montreal Protocol (1987). Since 1974, scientists have believed that CFCs are destroying ozone in the earth's atmosphere, which is likely to provoke a rise in skin cancer, among other ill effects. No international action was taken until the discovery some dozen years later of the ozone hole over Antarctica. At one point, the Reagan administration suggested that ozone depletion could be addressed via the market for personal protection products such as skin lotion and sunglasses. This idea was ridiculed for failing to deal with the root problem of managing a common property resource (the ozone layer), and the United States and most other industrial nations committed themselves in Montreal to cap production of CFCs. In 1990, the Montreal Protocol was extended to include more chemicals and a pledge to end CFC use altogether.

The problem with such treaties is enforcement. The IWC was weak from the start, for member nations had the right to veto any rule they felt too restrictive, and there were no powers to use against members who disregarded rules. Also, whaling nations such as Brazil, Peru, and Chile refused to join the IWC. Since the ban, illegal whaling still takes place, and Norway in 1993 decided to ignore the treaty and exercise its sovereign right to resume for-profit hunting of whales. In the Montreal Protocol, developing countries received a 10-year grace period to increase CFC production for their domestic needs, such as refrigerators.

These countries argued that it was unfair to deny them technology that was already standard in the West, but the exemption aggravated the damage to the ozone layer.

International agreements about pollution are no stronger than their weakest link, which may not be strong at all due to the free-rider problem. Without the domestic political will to support them, or some external force to compel compliance, international pacts are little more than sheets of paper. Interestingly, the United States backed a total ban on CFCs after Du Pont came out in support. Part of the reason the company wanted the treaty was probably to protect its investment in developing and producing substitutes for CFCs.[30] Banning CFCs would drive up their price and create a price umbrella for Du Pont's new product line.

The challenge of reaching global unanimity was made clear at the United Nations Conference on Environment and Development (the Earth Conference) in Rio de Janeiro in 1992, attended by representatives from 178 countries. One main objective was to agree on the terms of intergovernmental conventions on grave global issues, such as climate change and the extinction of species. But due to conflict among commercial interests in the different countries, language was usually left ambiguous and enforcement mechanisms were not included.

The United States wanted a legally binding forest treaty. LDCs with important logging industries such as Malaysia refused to be constrained by such a treaty, so the conference settled for a vague Statement of Forest Principles. Similarly, oil-exporting nations blocked language from another document, called Agenda 21, to foster energy conservation and the development of different fuels. Most delegations endorsed the Biodiversity Treaty to protect threatened plants and wildlife. The United States did not sign because of fears the treaty would impair the patent rights of U.S. biotechnology firms.

Given all the hedging, many observers are skeptical the Earth Conference will have much practical effect. In particular, it soon became apparent that greenhouse gas emission targets would be missed. Three years later the international community met again at a UN climate conference in Berlin, where a new negotiating procedure to curb emissions was agreed on. Still, squabbling among the various countries in attendance made concerted global action unlikely, for now.

Direct Controls versus Incentives

As with the consumer and worker safety agencies we discussed in Chapter 13, the EPA mainly uses direct controls, not indirect economic incentives, to curtail pollution. Because of fear the agency would be captured by industry, the legislative acts it carries out are detailed and include timetables. The statutory language for the EPA Act was designed to be specific to combat the weak, highly discretionary model of most independent regulatory agencies. Because it was written so specifically, there is less a pattern of "agency capture" than is found in other policy areas. But this has created a new problem of unrealistic regulations, leading to delays and special treatment of different companies and localities.

The EPA has established standards for air quality, meant to remove visible pollutants and protect the health of sensitive groups in the population. The EPA also sets emissions standards for new sources of air pollution, for example, a new factory. Under the Clean Air Act of 1990, factories must install "maximum achievable control technology" to reduce the release of many toxic chemicals by 90 percent in 10 years. Similarly, the EPA sets standards for the discharge of pollution into water by industry or municipalities—again based on the use of state-of-the-art control technology.

After deciding the desired level of environmental quality and the abatement methods to be used to reach that level, the EPA monitors how companies comply. The agency has the power to take enforcement action against violators. Penalties for air or water pollution include a maximum $25,000 a day in fines and possible criminal prosecution of corporate executives. In 1989, fines for environmental crimes totaled $13 million, versus only $600,000 in 1985.[31]

Direct regulation has drawbacks. Critics note that this top-down technique often bogs down in red tape and courtroom fights. It is apt by statute to lock in technology and freeze innovation, and it may mandate an expensive method when cheaper methods are available. Direct regulation also gives manufacturers no incentive to go *below* legal limits of pollution. There may be better ways to protect the natural environment.

Pollution Taxes and Permits

Many economists think a **pollution tax** (or tax subsidy) is the answer.[32] Instead of dictating remedies, the government charges a business for the units of pollution it discharges (or gives it a tax write-off for pollution it stops), setting the fees (or the awards) high enough to encourage firms to reduce emissions. Prices thus reflect more closely the full social cost of pollution. A pollution tax is a subtler policy tool than direct regulation. It encourages companies to discover superior means to reduce pollution, for example, by reformulating a product or changing the manufacturing process.

A public policy that works on the same principle is to issue **pollution permits** that companies can buy or sell. While a pollution tax sets the price companies must pay to pollute, a permit system sets the quantity of pollution allowed and lets the market establish the price of pollution rights.[33] The goal of freely marketable pollution rights is again to push producers to find the means of cutting emissions that cost society the least, whether it means closing a dirty plant or continuing to run some dirty facilities.

The policy works as follows: The government puts limits on the amount of pollution that a company can legally discharge. Companies that go below regulatory requirements can bank and sell pollution credits to other companies seeking to build or expand. The price of the pollution credits varies according to supply and demand. Each management team decides themselves whether it is cheaper to invest in pollution control equipment, and sell the unused right to pollute, or to save on equipment and buy pollution credits. Green lobbyists could raise cash to buy pollution permits and then sit on them.[34] While some companies pollute more under such an arrangement, others pollute less. Air or water quality is maintained, but at low opportunity cost.

What these two approaches—the pollution tax and the pollution permit—have in common is that they try to get firms to internalize an external cost. The tax is a liability, the permit an asset, that managers have to consider in making business decisions. Once pollution represents a cost of doing business and the environment is no longer a place to unload waste for free, the market can begin to allot resources appropriately. By seeking their firms' best interests, managers collectively will reduce pollution in the cheapest way possible. With government prodding, in other words, the invisible hand can be revived and used to clean the environment in an efficient manner. Managers are likely to prefer incentive systems to direct regulation since they provide flexibility that cannot be had under centralized government edict.

Policy Experiments

At first, U.S. lawmakers disliked these market-oriented or incentive-based solutions, partly because of the difficulty of metering emissions. Without accurate and dependable metering devices, the tax and permit systems will not work. Also, Congress is dominated by members who have legal backgrounds, and they feel more comfortable with specifying rights and duties than with an incentive-based approach to pollution control.[35] Still, several European countries successfully introduced pollution taxes. Germany has set uniform fees for water pollution throughout the country since 1973, but the choice of pollution control technology is left to the individual polluters.[36]

Under President Carter, official opinion began to change in Washington about the merits of direct controls versus incentives. In 1979, regulators introduced the bubble concept. Under the bubble concept, an entire plant is treated as if it were surrounded by an invisible shield. Instead of measuring the pollution coming from each pipe or smokestack, regulators measure the total emissions going into the imaginary bubble. One or more pipes or stacks may emit more pollutants than the law allows, as long as the whole plant stays within acceptable bounds. The EPA has approved about 100 bubbles, with cost savings of $435 million.[37]

Even earlier, in 1977, the EPA had begun to try so-called pollution offsets. The idea is to permit a new source to pollute, provided that old sources reduce their pollution by the same amount. For example, a company might be allowed to construct a new incinerator if it closed down an old one to offset the new pollution. By 1985, over 2,500 offset transactions had taken place.[38] Most of these involved internal trades rather than outside exchanges.

In 1979, the EPA started allowing firms to store the rights to pollution allowed at a plant or to trade them to other firms, an idea the Reagan administration naturally embraced when it took office in 1980. In essence, public policy is being used to create property rights to the physical environment on the assumption that this will create better incentives for companies not to pollute wantonly. Companies can treat a pollution offset as an asset, little different from cash or a security, to be bartered, sold, or even given away. The 1990 Clean Air Act calls for greater use of tradable pollution rights. Thus, Northeast Utilities of Connecticut in 1993 donated to the American Lung Association the right to release 10,000 tons of emission allowances, worth $3 million. The Lung Association planned to use the rights to sell symbolic "pollution retirement" certificates to raise money.[39]

The Clinton administration envisions extending this market-oriented approach to help contain gases that may be warming the world's climate. The cheapest chances for reducing emissions of these gases lie outside the United States. So the plan is to allow U.S. companies to meet their domestic legal obligation to curb greenhouse gases by paying for reductions in developing countries. A U.S. power company might help modernize electricity generation in China, for example. This would have a positive effect on the environment by curbing the burning of coal in inefficient plants. Similarly, a simple way to control emissions would be for an American firm to help Russia repair leaks in its natural gas lines. If this approach catches on, public policy might eventually lead to an international trade in pollution allowances.[40]

Still, for now, the EPA continues to rely mainly on direct control, not incentives. Controls are easier to set and monitor, though they are a blunt instrument of public policy. Also, the green movement has objected to the idea that companies have a right to pollute and has fought the incentive-based approach in the courts and other policy forums.

The Reagan Revolution and Its Aftermath

The Reagan administration took office in 1981 with a negative agenda for environmental policy, part of its larger program of regulatory relief for business. Reagan spoke for the "Sagebrush Rebellion" of commodity interests in the western states, who were reacting to the inroads made by environmentalists during the 1970s. James Watt was appointed head of the Interior Department; Anne Gorsuch, head of the EPA. Neither had sympathy with the environmental ethic, nor were they competent administrators.

The Reagan administration submitted legislation that would cripple the Clean Air Act and the Clean Water Act. But its negative program did not rest on new legislation as much as on weakening the existing statutes. The EPA's budget was cut by $400 million between 1980 and 1982, making it hard for the agency to do its job and easing the pressure on business. The EPA also reduced the stringency of its existing standards and did more rigorous analysis before promulgating new standards.

In the energy field, Reagan's objective was to get the federal government out of this sector of the economy. The working assumption, supported by oil, coal, and electric utility industries, was that many untapped conventional energy sources were available in the United States. By letting market players decide what to do, production of oil, gas, and coal would surge. There was no need for government to second-guess the market by encouraging energy conservation or the use of renewable fuels.

One of Reagan's first acts in 1981 was to decontrol oil and, later, natural gas prices. Subsidies for solar energy and other less common sources of power were cut. More federal land was leased for exploration. That this shift in policy often helped the "hard" energy interests, and hurt the smaller "soft" energy sector, was no coincidence given Reagan's support from the Sagebrush Rebellion. During the election campaign, he had pledged to dismantle the newly formed Department of Energy. He did not carry out this pledge, but the department was cut back (except for nuclear energy).

The attempted Reagan revolution provoked a lively political backlash. For example, between 1983 and 1989, membership in the Sierra Club, the Audobon Society, the National Wildlife Federation, and the Wilderness Society soared from 1.7 million to 7.2 million.[41] Interior Secretary Watt got into trouble repeatedly for making inane or offensive statements, such as his belief that conservation was not needed because the world was in its final days. EPA Administrator Gorsuch was accused of timing the release of Superfund money for toxic waste cleanups in a way to help Republicans in the 1982 elections. Both Watt and Gorsuch were forced to resign.

The average U.S. citizen did not buy the argument that government should leave the natural environment to private interests. To the contrary, people demanded action from government to deal with what they saw as a rapidly decaying global habitat. Congress resisted gutting the EPA and allowing developers to have free run of wilderness areas. By the end of the 1980s, the EPA had recovered to its earlier size. The Reaganites thus did not leave as deep an imprint on environmental regulation as they did on other public policies toward business.

Business kept on the heat, however, and by 1995 was winning the fight in Washington to overhaul the clean air and water acts. One far-reaching proposal would compensate property owners for losses in land value as a result of wetlands regulation. Another would require detailed cost–benefit analysis of new environmental rules. The business victory in these and other regulatory areas was so complete that some executives worried corporations might have overplayed their hand. Ford Vice President Peter Pestillo urged his colleagues: "Let's seek only what we need, not what will make us feel good."[42]

Conclusion

We have seen that a major bloc of the public is deeply worried about pollution and the waste of natural resources. Abuse of the physical environment is partly a consequence of market failure. Because it is a common property resource, the environment produces externalities, discrepancies between private and social cost. Thus, investment or consumption decisions taken on the individual level produce less than an ideal ecological outcome for society, and economic activity makes the earth more polluted than we want.

A completely clean environment is a utopian goal, but public policy has made the environment cleaner by making business pay to use what had been a free dumping ground. Business has thus often resisted clean air rules, clean water rules, and similar regulation. Resistance is stiffest among companies the most affected, such as power companies, chemical manufacturers, petroleum processors, timber and paper companies, and mining interests. Their leaders remind the public that government action, even if well-intended, does not necessarily yield benefits that exceed the cost to society. When regulation has been imposed, they have preferred incentive-oriented regulations to the command-and-control approach.

Still, as this book goes to press, the burden on U.S. companies of protecting the natural environment has not been lifted dramatically since the 1970s. To the contrary, some firms have tried to ride the crest of stakeholder opinion and regulate their pollution voluntarily. Others are exploiting the economic opportunities created by environmental regulation and energy conservation. Unfortunately, many problems of pollution and resource depletion, those that menace all civilization, are far beyond the ability of individual firms or nation states to solve. They are rooted in industrial development and humankind's accustomed mode of living. Finding constructive international answers to these problems is one of the main public policy challenges of the 21st century.

Questions

1. Describe the "tragedy of the commons." Give some examples of this type of behavior.

2. What are the cost and benefit of government action to protect the physical environment? Is society the net winner or loser? How can public policies be made more efficient in curbing pollution and conserving resources?

3. Do green regulations hurt or help U.S.

companies in international competition? How?

4. Discuss ways that companies use green regulations as a weapon in the economic marketplace. Do you think these are abuses of public policy?

5. How do international regulations influence threats to the physical environment?

End Notes

1. Aristotle, *Politics,* trans. Carnes Lord (Chicago: University of Chicago Press, 1984), p. 57.

2. For an optimistic view of the population crisis, see Julian Simons, *The Ultimate Resource* (Princeton, NJ: Princeton University Press, 1981); for a more pessimistic view, a recent treatment is Paul Kennedy, *Preparing for the Twenty-First Century* (New York: Random House, 1993).

3. Gregg Easterbrook, "Here Comes the Sun," *The New Yorker,* April 10, 1995, pp. 38–43.

4. About 25 years ago, scientists were worried instead about a coming ice age, based on an apparent downward trend in global temperatures.

Stephen Schneider, author of a well-known book, *Global Warming,* wrote one then about global cooling, *The Genesis Strategy.* Cited in Wilfred Beckerman, "Global Warming and International Action," in *The International Politics of the Environment,* ed. Andrew Hurrell and Benedict Kingsbury (Oxford: Clarendon Press, 1992), p. 257.

5. *The Environment: Public Attitudes and Individual Behavior,* a study conducted by the Roper Organization, July 1990, New York.

6. Manuel G. Velasquez, *Business Ethics: Concepts and Cases,* 3rd ed. (Englewood Cliffs, NJ: Prentice Hall, 1992), p. 214.

7. Alfred Marcus, *Business and Society* (Homewood, IL: Richard D. Irwin, 1993), p. 410.

8. The term *tragedy of the commons* became popular because of Garrett Hardin's influential article of the same name in *Science* 162 (1968), pp. 1243–48.

9. For an account of some institutional responses, see Elinor Ostrom, *Governing the Commons* (Cambridge: Cambridge University Press, 1990).

10. Rogene A. Buchholz, Alfred A. Marcus, and James E. Post, *Managing Environmental Issues: A Casebook* (Englewood Cliffs, NJ: Prentice Hall, 1992), pp. xii–xiii.

11. Murray Fesbach and Alfred Friendly, Jr., *Ecocide in the U.S.S.R.* (New York: Basic Books, 1992).

12. Reported in Tony McAdams, *Law, Business, and Society,* 3rd ed. (Homewood, IL: Richard D. Irwin, 1992), pp. 774–75.

13. Frances Cairncross, *Costing the Earth* (Boston: Harvard Business School Press, 1992), pp. 64–69.

14. *Environmental Investments: The Cost of a Clean Environment,* A Report from the Administrator of the Environmental Protection Agency (reprint, Washington, DC: Island Press, 1991).

15. Douglas E. Greer, *Business, Government, and Society,* 3rd ed. (New York: Macmillan, 1993), p. 488.

16. Amal Kumar Naj, "See No Evil," *The Wall Street Journal,* May 11, 1988, p. A1.

17. H. Jeffrey Leonard, *Pollution and the Struggle for World Product* (Cambridge: Cambridge University Press, 1988).

18. Cited in McAdams, *Law, Business, and Society,* p. 772.

19. "The Money in Europe's Muck," *The Economist,* November 20, 1993, p. 81.

20. Michael E. Porter, *The Competitive Advantage of Nations* (New York: Free Press, 1990), p. 652.

21. Maurice Samuelson, "Big Suppliers Chase Gas Scrubber Market," *Financial Times,* June 23, 1987, p. 20.

22. Cairncross, *Costing the Earth,* p. 303.

23. Stephen J. K. Walters, *Enterprise, Government and the Public* (New York: McGraw-Hill, 1993), p. 473.

24. Murray L. Weidenbaum, *Business, Government, and the Public,* 4th ed. (Englewood Cliffs, NJ: Prentice Hall, 1990), p. 84.

25. Nancy Frank, *From Criminal Law to Regulation* (New York: Garland, 1986), pp. 131–44.

26. "Regulate Us, Please," *The Economist,* January 8, 1994, p. 69.

27. Craig E. Reese, *Deregulation and Environmental Policy: The Use of Tax Policy to Control Pollution in North America and Western Europe* (Westport, CT: Quorum, 1983).

28. Richard B. Stewart, "Environmental Regulation and International Competitiveness," *Yale Law Journal* 102, no. 8 (1993), pp. 2039–106.

29. *World Development Report 1992: Development and the Environment* (New York: Published for the World Bank by Oxford University Press, 1992), pp. 83–84.

30. Cairncross, *Costing the Earth,* p. 159.

31. Archie B. Carroll, *Business and Society* (Cincinnati: South-Western, 1993), p. 314.

32. William J. Baumol and Wallace E. Oates, *The Theory of Environmental Policy,* 2nd. ed. (Cambridge: Cambridge University Press, 1988), p. 1.

33. Greer, *Business, Government, and Society,* pp. 494–95.

34. Cairncross, *Costing the Earth,* p. 101.

35. Allen V. Kneese and Charles L. Schultze, *Pollution, Prices, and Public Policy* (Washington, DC: Brookings Institution, 1975), p. 116.

36. Damodar Gujarati, *Government and Business* (New York: McGraw-Hill, 1984), p. 474.

37. W. Kip Viscusi, John M. Vernon, and Joseph E. Harrington, Jr., *Economics of Regulation and Antitrust* (Lexington, MA: D.C. Heath, 1992), p. 670.

38. Greer, *Business, Government, and Society,* p. 493.

39. Scott Allen, "Rights to Pollute Given Up," *Boston Globe,* March 20, 1993, p. 35.

40. Peter Passell, "For Utilities, New Clean Air Plan (A Swap May Lead to a Global Effort)," *The New York Times,* November 18, 1994, p. D1.

41. Greer, *Business, Government, and Society,* p. 479.

42. Bob Davis, "Business Is Big Beneficiary as 'Contact' Is Completed," *The Wall Street Journal,* April 7, 1995, p. A6.

VI   BUSINESS AND ECONOMIC REGULATION

15 PUBLIC POLICY AND COMPETITION

The day of the combination is here to stay. Individualism is gone, never to return.

John D. Rockefeller[1]

Free enterprise and free competition are not the same. The rhetoric of capitalism aside, enterprising people do not always wish to compete. They frequently see advantages in cooperating instead, in avoiding ruthless fights with adversaries. As Adam Smith observes, "People of the same trade seldom meet together, even for merriment and diversion, but the conversation ends in a conspiracy against the public, or in some contrivance to raise prices."[2]

Conspiracies and milder forms of cooperation can enable firms to wield market or monopoly power, to control prices and sometimes demand for their products. While expedient for the firms involved, market power can be bad for society. It violates the assumptions of competitive free enterprise, because sellers become price makers and because they can keep new firms from entering the market whenever they want.

Monopoly and collusion among companies are a class of market failure, with the free action of private decisions having socially inefficient consequences. Smith noted 200 years ago that the inhabitants of England had paid a high price for one important monopoly—the East India Company. Not only did the company earn "extraordinary profits," but there was "extraordinary waste which the fraud and abuse, inseparable from the management of the affairs of such a company must necessarily have occasioned."[3] The net result, in the language of political economy, is a "deadweight social loss" with firms producing less than the ideal equilibrium output. This hurts consumers, though it can serve the interest of producers, and should be avoided, according to Smith and his later followers.

What Is Antitrust Policy?

Governments try to block companies from gaining market power, and employ public policy to prod companies to contest one another in the marketplace. The goal is to protect the consumer. In the United States, the policies to prompt economic competition are called **antitrust laws** because they were originally enacted to stop corporate abuse of trusts—a legal device for securing assets. Intended for benign purposes such as managing a retirement fund, trusts were used in the 19th century as covert devices to halt economic struggles. Participating companies pooled their resources to fix prices, manipulate supplies, and carve out exclusive territories. The trust device is used no longer, but the name antitrust has stuck and is applied to any public policy designed to fight corporate market power.

Antitrust or competition policy has two sides. One is to force companies to oppose each other in the market so they do not take advantage of the public. Government tries to make sure an industry is not dominated by one firm or a few firms in league with each other. The second side of competition policy applies to cases where, for one reason or another, pitting firms against each other is thought to be a detriment, a source of harm for consumers. Here, government tries to act as a surrogate for competition, regulating the noncompeting industry so it does not take undue advantage of its monopoly status.

Regarding the first side of competition policy, the Reagan administration challenged the "big is bad" philosophy. Instead of trying to keep firms small, policy became likely to allow them to grow big if they could and to band with other firms if they so wanted. Given the global economy, the view was that policies to conserve atomistic domestic markets were self-defeating. Companies need to spread fixed costs over a vast level of production if they are to contest in the world arena with mammoth international firms.[4] Small firms cannot achieve a competitive advantage from economies of scale, or from their limited capacity to mount R&D programs.

While U.S. public policy was becoming more easygoing about enforcing antitrust provisions in some industries, it also was becoming less strict about using regulation as a stand-in for market competition in other industries. Regulated groups of firms (banks, for example) were deregulated and thrust into the marketplace. The result was apt to be similar to what happened in the rest of the economy—a smaller number of more powerful companies.

The Reagan policies were touted as helping consumers, but they may have helped big corporations more. At least some in the public think so, and the policy pendulum has swung back a little under President Clinton. The country remains far from the old trust-busting days, however. U.S. officials are still apt to give firms a freer hand to collaborate than under previous policies; officials remain less likely than before to try to regulate firms' decisions to enter or abandon new markets.

This chapter reviews competition policy in the United States, making brief comparisons to practices in Europe and Japan. We will discuss the major antitrust laws and how business interests sometimes exploited these laws in unforeseen ways. We also will see how efforts to fix these policies had other unintended consequences, for example, a rash of corporate raiding and big run-ups in corporate debt.

Big Business

Giant corporations hold what Lenin would have called the "commanding heights" of today's mixed economy. Few in number but imposing in size, firms such as General Motors and International Business Machines provide much of America's work, and most of its output. Large U.S. corporations are being tested by large foreign rivals and some smaller domestic firms. They are proving more vulnerable than once thought—GM alone lost $20.8 billion in 1992 and IBM posted a one-quarter loss of $7.9 billion in mid-1993. Still, such giants remain the economy's center of gravity and its most familiar characteristic.

Simple statistics make the case. In 1990, there were more than 20 million business enterprises in the United States. Of these millions of businesses, a mere 16,000 corporations (with sales over $50 million) accounted for *60 percent* of business receipts.[5] Contrary to the conventional wisdom, innovation is greater in industries dominated by large firms, particularly in capital-intensive industries. Also contrary to the conventional wisdom, Big Business creates most of the net new jobs in the U.S. economy, especially most of the good paying and secure jobs.[6] (Small companies do produce many jobs, but they also lose many of them because small companies are prone to go out of business, so the net gain is modest.)

Japan, Britain, Germany, and other nations boast many enormous companies also, and large corporations dominate their economies. Those countries' share of global Big Business has been rising and is likely to continue growing at the expense of American firms. The United States, nevertheless, remains home to more corporate giants than any other nation, as displayed in Figure 15–1.[7]

American public policy has been ambivalent about the large corporation. These behemoths are powerful and thus an object of suspicion. Yet, they also have obvious frailties, which make people apprehensive about their fate. As we mentioned earlier, laws are on the books, dating from the Progressive Era, to restrict the market power of Big Business and to encourage small-scale, atomistic competition. Today, however, the greater fear is that such companies cannot win in the world arena because government has tied their hands. Let us review the history.

The Legal Framework for Antitrust Policy

Restraints of trade are as old as trade itself. Merchants and tradesmen would enter covenants to refrain from competing, for instance, by not selling products

FIGURE 15–1

The United States has more of the world's 500 largest companies than any other country (1993)

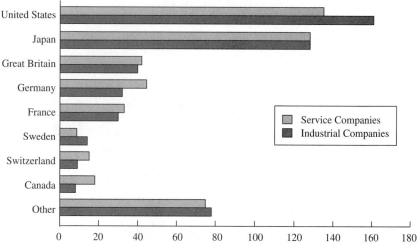

Source: *Fortune,* July 26, 1993, and August 23, 1993.

in each others' territory. Under common law doctrine, covenants to restrain trade were legal in the United States through the 19th century. They could be enforced in court as long as they were reasonable and went no further than was needed to protect the businesses involved. Consumers might pay the penalty of higher prices and fewer goods, but, because most producers were small, the windfall they garnered was not great.

By the 1880s, confidence in the self-sustaining character of competition was gone. Progressives began instead to call for government to underwrite competition.[8] The old common law heritage was felt to be inadequate to this task. What had happened?

At issue was the changing scale of capitalism. During the second Industrial Revolution, firms began to grow much bigger, and people became alarmed when these giants restrained trade. To avoid destroying each other, business leaders formed trusts in many industries, including petroleum, meat packing, sugar, and tobacco. These trusts came to control almost 100 percent of their respective markets.

Farmers and small businessmen were hurt by the resulting high commodity prices, and by the railroads' high freight charges. Their dissent helped pave the way for passage of the Sherman Antitrust Act in 1890. This law, and two subsequent laws, the Clayton and FTC Acts, are the framework for U.S. antitrust policy today. The antitrust laws fit with the nation's dislike of large, powerful institutions—be they public or private. Washington treated antitrust as the "Magna Carta of free enterprise," a "Bill of Rights" central to defense of economic freedoms.[9]

In other countries, government policy was apt to be more forgiving about attempts by firms to suppress competition and escape price warfare. (See Box 15–1.) Germany, with its strong historical tendency toward mutual organization, is a good example. German law long favored the creation of **cartels** (formal associations of firms that would otherwise be competitors). Under Adolph Hitler

---

Box 15–1

Antitrust Policies Overseas Are Usually Less Demanding than in the United States

All industrial countries have antitrust policies, but these policies often serve a different function than they do traditionally in the United States. They are as likely to promote rationalization of an industry as they are to encourage competition.

Germany, for example, enacted the Law against Restraint of Competition in 1958. In contrast to American policy, Bonn's policy does not see economic rivalry as a goal in itself. Rather, it sees rivalry as a means for making technical progress and efficient production. German law exempts from antitrust rules corporate agreements that expand foreign trade or meet other government goals, and 300 cartels have been approved by the government. The government can only take action against companies that abuse their monopoly privileges by charging excessive prices or restricting sales.

German firms also fall under international rules. Article 85 of the E.U. treaty bars most anticompetitive agreements between European companies—for example, price fixing, control of output, or sharing of markets. The E.U. Commission, which is responsible for carrying out Article 85, can level stiff fines—such as the $300 million penalty it imposed on European cement firms in 1994 for cartel activities.[1] Like most member nations' authorities, however, the commission is liable to be lenient in granting exceptions to antitrust enforcement. Joint ventures and other restraints of trade are deemed permissible if they encourage efficiency.

Japan enacted its Antimonopoly Law in 1947, under pressure from Occupation authorities. Through World War II, the Japanese economy had been dominated by *zaibatsu*—huge monopolies. The United States wanted to break the hold of the *zaibatsu*. Still, the Japanese never went along with the change imposed on them by the Americans. The law was not stringent, and it had loopholes for small companies, declining industries, and foreign trading firms to limit competition. Even when it does have statutory authority, the government seldom acts due to business and bureaucratic pressure groups. Japan's Fair Trade Commission, for example, has brought but one case a year since 1991. The result is that the economy looks remarkably similar to the way it did before 1947, with interlocking networks of corporate families (*keiretsu*) controlling much production.[2]

These types of policies have given some Japanese and, to a lesser extent, German firms an edge in world competition, even as they potentially harm consumers at home. Companies can pool their resources for research and product development. They also get to use their monopoly profits at home to sustain losses while they break into foreign markets. An important public policy question in Japan is how long local consumers will put up with high prices so domestic firms can win global market share.

---

[1]Charles Goldsmith and Julie Wolf, "EU Commission Metes out Heavy Fines against Cement Firms for Cartel Activity," *The Wall Street Journal,* December 1, 1994, p. A14.

[2]Richard Lehne, *Industry and Politics* (Englewood Cliffs, NJ: Prentice Hall, 1993), pp. 118–19.

in particular, membership in certain cartels was made compulsory in hopes of fortifying national industries.

Exceptions always were made to antitrust laws in the United States, too, in industries where it was felt cooperation or monopoly best served the public interest. Here, government supervision would replace government-enforced competition. During the 1930s, the National Recovery Act in effect copied features of German law to create mandatory cartellike arrangements for some U.S. industries. That law was declared unconstitutional and voided, but other efforts to limit competition in certain lines of trade (telecommunications and automobile insurance are examples) survive in American public policy to this day.

Sherman Antitrust Act

The Sherman Act has two main sections. The first one bars firms from making formal arrangements to curb their independent action; the second prohibits firms from taking steps to control sales in a market. As it emerged through the bargaining process of Congress, however, the act had fuzzy language. (See Table 15–1.) The task of defining such key terms as *restraint of trade* and *monopolize* was left to the judiciary. The courts thus play a leading role in deciding what are legal and illegal forms of market behavior.

Charged with enforcing the Sherman Act (and the subsequent Clayton Act) is the Antitrust Division of the Justice Department. The Antitrust Division is a bureau-level agency in the executive branch, whose head serves at the pleasure of the president. It prosecutes antitrust cases before the courts.

Progressives were irate with the first interpretations of the Sherman Act. The law was used mainly to prosecute labor unions, which were not the original target. There were no major decisions against large companies until 1911, when the Supreme Court handed down two important rulings. In the first, the Rockefeller brothers' Standard Oil Company was found guilty of monopolization and

---

TABLE 15–1   Key Statutes Promoting Competition in the United States

Sherman Act, Section 1	Every contract, combination in the form of trust or otherwise, or conspiracy, in restraint of trade or commerce among the several States, or with foreign nations, is declared to be illegal.
Sherman Act, Section 2	Every person who shall monopolize, or attempt to monopolize, or combine or conspire with any other person or persons, to monopolize . . . shall be deemed guilty of a felony. . . .
Clayton Act, Section 7	No corporation engaged in commerce shall acquire, . . . directly or indirectly, the whole or any part of the stock . . . .or any part of the assets of one or more corporations engaged in commerce, where in any line of commerce in any section of the country, the effect of such acquisition, of such stock or assets . . . may be substantially to lessen competition, or tend to create a monopoly.
Federal Trade Commission Act, Section 5	Unfair methods of competition in or affecting commerce, and unfair or deceptive acts or practice affecting commerce, are hereby declared unlawful.

TABLE 15–2   Horizontal versus Vertical Restraints of Trade

Horizontal

Price fixing	Two or more competitors agree to set the price for their products.
Division of markets	Competitors agree to divide up territories or customers.
Group boycott	A group of competitors jointly refuse to deal with another competitor or group of competitors.

Vertical

Resale price maintenance	Manufacturer tries to control the retail price of its product.
Territorial restrictions	Imposition of exclusive territories or customer divisions on buyers.
Exclusive dealing	Contracts that oblige the buyer to purchase all its needs for a commodity from the seller.
Price discrimination	One party sells substantially identical goods at roughly the same time to different purchasers at different prices.
Tie-ins	One party offers to provide a good or service only to those who agree to buy another good or service.

dissolved into 33 geographically separate companies. Two weeks later, James Duke's Tobacco Trust was also found guilty of monopolization and was split into 16 companies.

Significantly, both monopolies had attained their market power with predatory and abusive tactics. Among other acts, they had bribed railway employees for information and temporarily sold products below cost to drive competitors out of business. In the eyes of the courts, these are "per se violations" of antitrust laws; they are so harmful that no mitigating circumstances can justify them. Still, the list of inherently illegal trade restraints has become shorter as the populist philosophy undergirding antitrust has faded. Most firms' legal advisors can identify current per se violations and warn clients away. We will discuss some of these violations later.

It is helpful to think of restraints of trade falling along two axes. Horizontal restraints involve agreement between companies not to compete. They are aimed mainly at other competitors. Vertical restraints are agreements among two or more companies at different levels of the production process, for example, a manufacturer and a retailer. Vertical restraints target the firm's suppliers or its buyers. Table 15–2 lists specific types of horizontal and vertical restraints of trade.

The "Rule of Reason"

In another important case, brought against U.S. Steel in 1911, the Supreme Court acquitted the company on the grounds that the steel producer, while big, was a good corporate citizen. It had not competed with underhanded tactics and, thus, was not guilty of monopolistic practices. The *U.S. Steel* case illustrates what the courts have called the "rule of reason." According to the logic of the rule of reason, there are legitimate restraints on trade, and "good" monopolies. Some things a company might do to expand are illegal in some contexts, but reasonable and, thus, legal in other contexts. Unlike per se rules that brand business practices as wrong in themselves, the rule of reason uses a flexible yardstick. The test of legality is whether an act has harmful or beneficial effects.

Rule of reason violations of antitrust are harder to pin down than per se violations. The courts have not helped by issuing unclear or contradictory rulings in different cases over the years. In a landmark decision that broke with precedent, Alcoa (1945) was found guilty of monopolization though it had engaged in none of the aggressive tactics that marked earlier convictions. Alcoa controlled 90 percent of the market for aluminum ingots and, thus, had the potential to abuse its market power. That the company had cut prices, increased output, and made only normal profits was no defense. There was a latent threat to consumers, so to invite more opposition in the aluminum industry, Alcoa was forced to sell some facilities to other aluminum companies.

Recently, the courts have stepped back from the *Alcoa* ruling and its implication that size itself is a per se violation of antitrust. In 1979, for example, Kodak won a case in the Second Circuit Court of Appeals (the Supreme Court declined to review the decision), despite having 60 to 90 percent shares of most segments of the photography industry. Accused of shutting out rival film suppliers, Kodak was found merely to have earned its dominant position through superior performance.

Despite the limited number of successful prosecutions in the early years, the Sherman Act did affect the behavior of business. It triggered a wave of mergers, which were on safer legal ground than trusts or cartels. By 1900, after 10 years of enforcement of the Sherman Act, the number of industrial combinations with capital of $1 billion or more had exploded from 10 to 300.[10] The trust-busting law thus had the inadvertent effect of pushing firms to grow bigger.

Alfred Chandler, the Harvard Business School historian, thinks this was a lucky accident, which by the early 20th century produced giant corporations for the United States that could dominate international markets. In Germany, where the government tried to promote industrialization by making cartels legal, public policy inadvertently may have had the opposite effect of stifling German industry.[11]

The Clayton Act

President Woodrow Wilson wanted to make federal antitrust legislation stronger with more precise wording. In 1914, he signed the Clayton Act, which expressly forbids specific actions that lessen competition, such as tying arrangements (making retailers buy all their products from one supplier) or group boycotts (refusal of a group of firms to buy from or sell to other firms). These are per se breaches of the law.

In addition, the Clayton Act has a section meant to slow the merger movement that was creating large companies. A **merger** occurs when two or more business organizations blend their assets to make one new firm. (There is little practical difference from an acquisition, when one firm absorbs another.) The Clayton Act bars business combinations that "substantially lessen competition" in an industry—a vague notion open to the rule of reason. In one of the most important public policies toward business, the Justice Department gets to review and approve mergers and acquisitions.

The Federal Trade Commission

Congress passed the Federal Trade Commission Act the same year as the Clayton Act. The FTC Act is a catch-all statute that prohibits any anticompetitive behavior that does not fit under other federal laws. It created a powerful, independent regulatory agency, the FTC, to root out "unfair methods of competition" and "deceptive acts or practices" by business. Each of its five commissioners is appointed by the president (subject to confirmation by the Senate) for a five-year term. Only three commissioners can belong to the same party. Antitrust is the domain of the FTC's Bureau of Competition. Another unit, the Bureau of Consumer Protection, takes charge of unfair advertising and marketing (discussed at the end of this chapter). There are also FTC judges who hear cases brought up under the trade commission act.

Due to its broad mandate, the FTC's responsibilities overlap with the Justice Department's Antitrust Division. The president has less control over the FTC compared to the Antitrust Division, which is part of his cabinet. Congress exercises oversight of the FTC. Dissatisfied with the commission's performance, Congress curtailed the FTC's statutory authority in 1980, restricting several ongoing programs and promising continued scrutiny in antitrust.

Despite some effort to write more lucid language in the 1914 laws and subsequent legislation, the antitrust statutes are vague, leaving much room for civil servants and judges to put their stamp on policy. The 50 states also have antitrust laws that are enforced by state attorneys general.

Tensions in the Policy

Like many public policies, antitrust has multiple and sometimes conflicting goals. One goal is to protect consumers. Another goal is to protect small business. A third goal is to promote economic efficiency. The inconsistency is that small business is not necessarily efficient business, so consumer welfare can be hurt when small companies are protected. Some firms become large mainly because they are better at producing a desirable product at less cost, while other firms stay small because they are less productive. Policies that try to maintain a large population of producers thus can make consumers worse off, and vice versa.

A good example of the tension in antitrust is state fair trade laws, which were legal until 1976. Upset by price-cutting from discount stores, small retailers lobbied for protection. Starting in the 1930s, most state legislatures responded by allowing manufacturers to set list prices for products and to forbid any retailer from selling for less. Fair trade laws gave small retailers breathing room, but meant consumers had to pay inflated prices. Mail-order houses got around the law by shipping merchandise nationally from the few states with no such laws. And the growth of national discount chains and of the consumer movement changed the political balance. By the mid-1970s, most states had repealed or weakened their fair trade statutes when Congress made this kind of price fixing illegal. The American consumer gets to pay lower prices today, but small ma-and-pa stores are driven out of business, often destroying older, in-town business districts in the bargain.

Public policy in other countries has often been resolved the other way, against consumers and for small business. France, for example, has laws that force large stores to close on Sundays and allow small merchants to stay open. Japan uses public policy to nurture an inefficient retail distribution system that favors family firms. Indications are that these anticompetitive practices are on the wane overseas.

Most bids to mend flaws in the market produce some government failure, and competition policy is no different. In enforcing domestic competition, U.S. policy often weakened American companies overseas; in promoting harmony or even monopoly within select industries such as the airlines or trucking, policy simply allowed lucky companies to slack off, to the detriment of consumers. Critics see evidence of rent seeking. Instead of increasing consumer welfare, antitrust laws are alleged to have the opposite effect of protecting companies at society's expense.

Laissez-faire idealists think the dangers of market power and monopoly are exaggerated. Because of free riding, collusion among firms is hard to preserve, they argue. The temptation to cheat is too great. Cartels and other combinations are prone to break down on their own. The markets' true believers also think entry barriers (impediments to new firms coming into an industry) are seldom sustainable because of technical change. Many business leaders agree, and advocate little government control of competition so they can enter new lines of business as they see fit.

Under intellectual and political assault, the broad, bipartisan support for antitrust disintegrated around 1980.[12] It was replaced with a more laissez-faire attitude toward business competition. Companies, whether they liked it or not, were freer to enter or leave markets, to merge or divest, without needing permission from government first.

Exemptions from Antitrust

As noted in the beginning of this chapter, policy makers do not want to stir up competition in all industries, all the time. Sometimes, they want to foster cooperation instead. Thus, several exceptions exist to antitrust legislation. These allow economic actors to collaborate, or to act as monopolies, under certain circumstances, usually under government supervision.

An important exemption applies to labor unions, which the Clayton Act exempts. Labor unions were initially found by courts to be unlawful combinations, "conspiracies" against the public good in Smith's term. Now, U.S. workers are free to try to fix the price of their labor in ways that would otherwise be illegal. Their unions are allowed to form a monopoly to represent all employees of a company in salary negotiations with management.

In another important exception, competitors are not bound by antitrust law from working together for government lobbying and other political action. Under the First Amendment's right to free speech, competitors can join forces to influence legislators and administrative agencies, as we saw in Chapter 8. Patents, copyrights, and trademarks are also recognized as legitimate, government-granted monopolies.

Other exemptions to antitrust are regulated industries (insurance, utilities, banking, and so on), state economic activity (for example, New Hampshire's liquor monopoly), agricultural cooperatives, and, oddly, professional baseball. The loophole for baseball is rationalized because it is a game, not a business, though other professional sports are not exempted. Antitrust rules also have been relaxed for military contractors, to allow more consolidation in the troubled defense industry.[13] In most of these exceptions to antitrust, a government entity supervises the companies or organizations in question so they do not exploit their privileged position.

Why are some industries not forced to compete? Sometimes, it is for reasons of natural monopoly, a concept discussed in Chapter 3. It makes little sense to force competition onto, say, local utility companies that might only raise costs.

But there are many other industries that are not natural monopolies, but that still are (or have been) regulated, for example, airlines, trucking, and agriculture. Most such regulation goes back to the 1930s. The rationale was to avoid what was thought of as destructive competition. Washington gained broad control of prices (plane fares or freight rates, for instance) and productive capacity (airplane or interstate truck routes, for example). In exchange, the participating companies are shielded from new opponents or price competition. Exceptions to antitrust in regulated industries thus often worked to keep down the number of competitors. For the health of the industry, a few large firms are allowed to dominate, for example, the several dozen baseball teams—each a local monopoly.

Yet regulators do not always aim for consolidation and economies of scale. They may try instead to nurture many small competitors, as illustrated by the banking industry. For fear of too much influence by large banks, there is no nationwide system of branch banks in the United States. Interstate banking restrictions, which date from the 1920s, perpetuated a more fragmented banking industry than would exist otherwise. They are the main reason there are no U.S. banks in the world's top 20. The biggest U.S. bank is Citicorp, number 26 in the world ranked by assets, followed by Bank of America at number 54.[14] (Repealing the limits on interstate banks, as agreed by President Clinton, should reverse the pattern and lead to streamlining in the banking industry.)

Revoking the Exemptions

When people began to think that exempted sectors were using the immunity from antitrust rules for private gains, pressure began to build to deregulate and allow competition to sort out prices, routes, and the like. It seemed bad public policy to reward, say, the Teamsters Union and a few large trucking companies with artificially high wages and profits by keeping down the number of rival firms in the trucking industry.

The landmark legislation came during the Carter administration, with the Airline Deregulation Act of 1978, the Motor Carrier Act of 1980, and the Staggers Rail Act (also of 1980). Another milestone was the breakup of AT&T a few years later. The telecommunications giant had been tolerated as a monopoly since the 1920s, when it agreed to submit to regulation of its rates and services. AT&T lost its protected status in 1982, when it spun off its 25 operating companies, in exchange for government permission to get into new industries. Similar pressures have been building following the Major League Baseball strike of 1994–95 to take away that industry's exemption to antitrust in the hope that competition will solve its labor and financial troubles.

The deregulatory policies bore fruit in many ways. In 1985, before the AT&T breakup, the average one-minute long-distance rate in America was 41 cents. Seven years after the breakup, the cost was 14 cents.[15] In the airline industry, fares also fell, as new competitors such as New York Air, Texas Air, and People's Express entered the business. Consumers were better off.

There were costs to deregulation, also. Take air travel again. Within a few years, travelers began to question how much they had won, as service (and, some feared, safety) dipped in quality. Critics point out that air transport has never been a free market. There are constraints on airport capacity that limit entry into the business, so monopolization is inevitable. There was a shakeout among carriers, leading to greater consolidation than had existed during the regulated era. Yet, with few exceptions, the surviving companies still could not turn a profit in the early 1990s.

Not surprisingly, voices have begun to be raised for *re*regulation, for rules to assure competition, at least in air transport. The industry was reviewed by the National Commission to Ensure a Strong Competitive Airline Industry in 1993. Heavily influenced by the big carriers, the commission did not call for tougher antitrust standards. It advocated, instead, bailouts in the form of tax and regulatory relief and bankruptcy reform.

R&D Consortia

A partial antitrust exemption is granted for joint R&D ventures. Historically, corporate collaboration for research was banned in the United States. In 1969, for example, the Justice Department successfully sued U.S. auto manufacturers over joint work on pollution controls. The suit charged the companies with working together as a cover for delaying the development of antipollution technology.

Foreign competition forced U.S. policy makers to reevaluate their stand toward this type of collaborative capitalism. Neither Japan nor Europe play by the same rules. To the contrary, their governments are apt to support and force co-ordinated R&D among domestic firms. These orchestrated technology campaigns overwhelmed some U.S. industries. For example, Japan's Very Large-Scale Integrated Circuit project (1976–80), involving five companies, was instrumental in displacing American manufacturers in semiconductors in the early 1980s.

Under the National Cooperative Research Act of 1984, companies now can petition the U.S. Attorney General and the FTC for permission to pool resources to work on new technology. Inspired by the Japanese model, the idea is to allow companies to share cost and risk, and avoid wasting resources on duplicated effort. American industry has since surpassed Japanese companies in semiconductors, and the cooperative research law may have contributed to this accomplishment.

The first R&D joint venture to clear antitrust review (even before the law's passage) was the Microelectronics and Computer Technology Corporation (MCC) in Texas. An alliance of 103 companies, MCC runs an industrywide research center with 350 staff drawn from member companies. In a typical favor to business, local authorities paid $63.5 million in land, new university facilities, and an executive jet for the right to host the MCC.[16] About 30 percent of MCC's revenue comes from government sources.

MCC has been criticized for not being market-oriented and taking too long to produce usable results. Still, by 1990, over 100 similar R&D consortia had been organized nationwide, and they are increasing at a rate of one or two per month.[17] Meanwhile, MCC has been reorganized to concentrate more on technology that members want.[18]

Not to be outdone, Europe has been moving to speed up approval of joint ventures in research, purchasing, sales planning, and other business activities. Sweeping new antitrust rules are designed to make it easier for E.U. companies to coordinate their activities.[19] Over 100 firms have joined a pan-European program called RACE (R&D in Advanced Communications Technology in Europe), and about 250 firms are enlisted in ESPRIT (the European Strategic Program for R&D in Information Technology).[20] We will discuss R&D joint ventures further in Chapter 16, focusing on how government takes part in them.

Antitrust and Foreign Competitors

Foreign companies are *not* exempt from antitrust. The courts have generally held that U.S. antitrust laws apply to the operations of firms overseas if they have a substantial impact on domestic commerce in the United States. But the laws are hard to enforce. The United States, for example, has investigated de Beers, the South African diamond cartel, at least four times since World War II. As the organizer of monopolistic activities, de Beers cannot sell diamonds directly in the United States and must work through intermediaries instead. U.S. officials have never gotten de Beers executives to appear in American court, and they have had to drop antitrust charges.

Increasingly, antitrust policy is seen as a means to back traditional foreign trade policy (the main subject of Chapter 17). International trade talks often aim to unlock overseas markets. These talks do not always meet their objective. In Europe and Asia, local business practices can continue to shut out U.S. firms. Antitrust policy gives the United States another way to force an entrance into these countries.

Since 1992, Justice Department guidelines allow federal suits against foreign companies for violations abroad that hurt American exporters, as well as American consumers. The intent is to get foreign companies to cease practices that limit U.S. entry into their home markets. In the first successful action under this policy, the British company Pilkington PLC agreed to open to U.S. companies the construction of glass factories around the world. The settlement was expected to increase U.S. exports of high-tech services by up to $1.25 billion over six years.[21]

Since other countries seldom have as strict antitrust policies, this extraterritoriality is a source of friction. Some nations have passed retaliatory legislation, for instance, that makes it hard to gather evidence on antitrust violations or that encourage countersuits. They also make veiled threats of reprisals against U.S. exports. The U.S. courts have never assumed jurisdiction in suits involving a foreign government. This provision is one factor that protects OPEC, an otherwise illegal cartel, from an antitrust lawsuit.[22]

OPEC illustrates another feature of economic collusion—its inherent unsteadiness. The free-rider problem subverts most cartel agreements by tempting the participants to cheat. When world demand for OPEC's oil slackened in the 1980s, OPEC's member countries tried to preserve their earnings by secretly exceeding their individual production limits. Despite its best effort, the organization could not control the cheating, which helped drive weak prices even lower and further increased the pressure for each member to betray the others. Events such as these make conservative critics wonder whether public policy efforts to prevent economic collusion are worth the effort.

Joint Ventures

In another sign of a more relaxed position on antitrust, the Justice Department tolerates more joint ventures now than in the past. A joint venture is an undertaking by two or more firms for a limited purpose. They are a popular mechanism for U.S. companies that want to break into foreign markets, where it is helpful to have a local partner with contacts and knowledge of business and political conditions. Joint ventures are also a way to increase manufacturing capacity at lower cost, to learn new methods, and to share the cost of R&D. Texas Instruments is an example of a firm that relies heavily on these strategic alliances, having formed partnerships with the Italian government, the Taiwanese PC maker Acer, Japan's Kobe Steel, and a consortium with Canon and the Singapore Economic Development Board.[23] The disadvantage is that discord can disrupt the joint venture, with the partners feeling a loss of control.

Domestic joint ventures are less common. "Partnering" among U.S. competitors gives them the chance to connive in restraining trade, and runs the risk of antitrust prosecution. According to Michael Porter, antitrust policy deters U.S. firms from forming alliances with each other and prompts them to work with foreign firms because that is less likely to raise antitrust problems.[24] The result may be to hurt U.S. national competitiveness. Under recent guidelines, though, the Justice Department is receptive to all joint ventures (including ones in highly concentrated industries) that hold the promise of efficiency gains. Rivals IBM and Apple even have a joint venture now.

A new model is for government to enter these ventures as a partner. In 1993, for instance, the federal government joined the United States Council for Automotive Research (USCAR), an auto research and development consortium of the Big Three automakers. The goal of federal participation is to triple fuel efficiency within a decade. By 2000, USCAR intends to have practical technology for an 80 mpg car. We will discuss business–government combinations again in Chapter 16.

Suits and Penalties

About 9 out of 10 antitrust suits are private. Consumers or businesses that believe they have been harmed by price fixing or other breaches of the law on competition have the right to sue the offending firm. Antitrust thus can be a strategic weapon that firms use against competitors. The number of private cases has been decreasing since the peak of 1,600 in 1977, due mainly to court decisions that favor defendants in antitrust suits.[25]

Government brings the rest of the antitrust cases in the United States. Though fewer (about 100 per year recently), these tend to be the more significant, trend-setting legal disputes. Private cases also can have wider meaning beyond the immediate parties and lead to changes in common law that affect decisions on subsequent cases. Sometimes, the government cases are brought at the urging of injured companies, so the distinction with private antitrust cases is not airtight.

A good example of the blurring between public and private interests in an antitrust case is the FTC's investigation of Microsoft, launched in 1990. Microsoft was suspected of using its dominance of personal computer operating systems to shut out rival software firms. Two years into the probe, one of Microsoft's competitors, Novell, began to aid the FTC. Novell's CEO was angry with Bill Gates of Microsoft following the collapse of secret merger talks in 1992. After the FTC's Bureau of Competition could not decide whether to prosecute, it turned the case over to the Antitrust Division for further thought. Novell also filed an antimerger case against Microsoft with the European Union, and it discussed with Lotus and Borland the possibility of a joint civil antitrust suit.[26]

Government cases usually end with consent decrees, where the defendant agrees to take certain actions. To continue the previous example, after lengthy negotiations, Microsoft agreed to stop requiring computer makers to pay royalties on every computer they sold, regardless of whether the computers included the Microsoft operating system. In return, the Justice Department and the E.U. agreed to end the monopolization case. Rival firms thought Microsoft got off lightly. A federal judge agreed, and refused in 1995 to approve the consent decree negotiated with Microsoft.

Consent decrees can stay on the books indefinitely. IBM, for example, still operates under a 1956 agreement that forced it to offer computer services separately from its manufacturing and sales business. General Electric remains confined by an agreement it signed in 1911 to refrain from making generic lighting products. There may be other 100 decades-old decrees controlling corporate behavior in the United States. Business leaders complain these antitrust agreements are obsolete and make no sense in today's global economy. The FTC decided in 1994 that its consent decrees would lapse after 20 years.[27]

In criminal antitrust cases, fines or prison sentences may be imposed. Such severe penalties are usually reserved for price fixing, as occurred in the electrical equipment industry in the 1960s. Then, the judge sent seven defendants to jail and fined General Electric, Westinghouse, and two other firms several million dollars.

In private antitrust disputes, plaintiffs can obtain judgments equal to three times their actual damages. Treble damages produce a strong incentive to file antitrust suits. Critics think the potential rewards are too great and prompt abuses of public policy, or what we earlier called rent-seeking behavior. Firms are tempted to invest too much in legal action against competitors and to neglect product development and customers' needs. Society suffers.

Chrysler and Ford offer a good illustration of how companies use antitrust to gain strategic advantage, but to the detriment of the larger society. In 1983, General Motors and Toyota proposed a joint venture (NUMMI, or New United Motor Manufacturing, Inc.) in California. GM hoped to learn Japanese manufacturing techniques, and Toyota wanted more access to the American car market. Chrysler and Ford protested to the FTC and asked that the joint venture be blocked for violating the antitrust laws. The FTC ultimately agreed to let NUMMI proceed, but, as a compromise, it limited production to 250,000 vehicles per year.[28] It is hard to see how the FTC's decision increased competition or maximized consumer welfare, but easy to see how it helped Chrysler and Ford.

Private antitrust actions are rare in other countries. Most do not provide multiple damages and attorney's fees to those who bring antitrust suits. These differences in public policy discourage plaintiffs overseas from trying to stop anticompetitive behavior through their courts.[29]

Structure, Conduct, and Performance

In looking at market power and monopoly, political economists like to talk about three ideas: a market's structure, its conduct, and its performance. For a long time, the hypothesized link was that the structure (number of sellers, ease of entry) of a market determines the conduct (pricing policy, cooperation) of the participant in the market, which in turn affects the performance of the companies (efficiency, degree of technical progress). Thus, an industry with a few sellers would be expected to charge excessive prices and be inefficient.

Today, however, there is dispute over these links. Differences among industries are too great to make simple generalizations about the relationship between industrial structure, company behavior, and results.[30] Consider the fast-changing computer industry. The Justice Department charged IBM in 1969 with monopolizing the market for mainframe computers. The company's annual revenues then amounted to 70 percent of the industry's total. Government attorneys pursued the case for 13 years while, counter to the theory about monopolistic industries, computer prices dropped and the pace of technical change quickened. By 1982, the industry had changed beyond recognition with many new competitors and novel products, including minicomputers and PCs. The Justice Department, by then controlled by Reagan appointees, found the IBM suit without merit and dismissed it. Policy makers today are still reluctant to make a mechanistic connection between structure and performance.

Measuring Monopoly

The key structural feature of an industry is the degree of monopoly or concentration. Textbooks make the measurement look easy: the fewer the number of sellers, the greater the degree of monopoly. A simple index is often used to access industries. It is made by calculating firms' market shares and adding the shares of the top four sellers. This is the four-firm concentration ratio.

Take the U.S. airline industry, which had a four-firm concentration ratio of 61 in 1990. The combined market share of the top four companies was

American	18%
United	17
Delta	14
Northwest	<u>12</u>
Total	61

Source: W. Kip Viscusi, John M. Vernon, and Joseph E. Harrington, *Economics of Regulation and Antitrust* (Lexington, MA: D. C. Heath, 1992), p. 55.

By this measure, the airline industry is highly concentrated or monopolistic, dominated by four large companies. From 1968 to 1982, the U.S. Antitrust Division used a simple rule that a merger was suspect if it produced an industry with a four-firm concentration ratio of more than 60, the postulate being four dominant companies will work together to muffle competition.

The trouble is that the relevant market for calculating the concentration index is rarely obvious. In the example above, should we limit the analysis to domestic U.S. passengers, or should we look at the whole world? If the latter, and foreign carriers are included in the calculations, the airline industry looks far less concentrated. Even the product market is murky. There always are goods or services that can substitute for each other. Flyers often can choose instead to take a train, a boat, a bus, or an automobile to get where they are going. These varied modes of conveyance all serve the same end. Airlines, seen from this vantage point, are just a segment of the larger transportation market.

Determining the right base of measurement is more than academic. The stakes are high for the businesses affected. Define a market narrowly, and you will find evidence of monopoly; define it loosely, and the monopoly disappears. It is not surprising that in the Justice Department case against IBM, about half the six-year trial was spent presenting evidence on market definition.[31] In 1982, the department stopped using the four-firm formula in favor of a more sophisticated measure of industry concentration. Two years after that, it revised its merger guidelines to give more weight to judgmental factors such as efficiency and imports.[32]

This simple change in public policy opened the gate to a flood of enormous mergers. The number of billion-dollar deals went from 10 in 1982 to 36 in 1989—including the biggest deal ever, the purchase of RJR Nabisco in 1989 (see Table 15–3).[33] These megadeals captured the public's imagination and were the emblem of the free-wheeling policy environment for business in the 1980s. There was a parallel but smaller rise in mergers overseas, too (see Figure 15–2).

The wave of takeovers in the United States was made possible partly by the ownership structure of U.S. firms. As we noted in Chapter 11, ownership is fragmented by public policy that discourages shareholders from participating in management decisions. The scattering of shareholders set the stage for the widespread buying and selling of whole companies.

TABLE 15–3   There Have Been Many Multibillion Dollar Mergers in the United States since the Mid-1980s.

Buyer	Target	Value ($ billions)	Date
KKR	RJR Nabisco	$30.6	1989
AT&T	McCaw Cellular	17.6	1994
Time, Inc.	Warner Communications	14.1	1990
Philip Morris Co.	Kraft Inc.	13.4	1988
Standard Oil	Gulf Oil	13.4	1984
Bristol-Myers	Squibb Corp.	12.1	1989
Texaco	Getty	10.1	1984
Viacom	Paramount	10.0	1994

Source: *Boston Globe,* October 14, and December 23, 1993.

FIGURE 15–2

Mergers and acquisitions have become more common in recent years

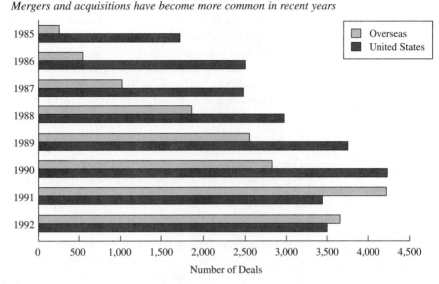

Source: *Mergers and Acquisitions,* May/June 1993.

The merger binge could not be sustained at such a tempo, and activity dropped off in the more somber economic conditions at the end of the decade. It picked up again in the mid-1990s, however.

Types of Mergers

Mergers have three structural forms: horizontal, vertical, and conglomerate. A **horizontal merger** is the union of companies that sell the same product, for example, when *The New York Times* bought the *Boston Globe* in 1993 for $1 billion. A **vertical merger** is between firms in buyer–supplier relationships, such as the $6 billion acquisition of Medco (a drug distributor) by Merck and Co. (a drug maker) in 1993. All remaining mergers are **conglomerate,** when the companies bear little or no working relationship to each other. International Telephone and Telegraph is the classic example of a company that emphasizes conglomerate mergers, having bought such varied companies as Hartford Insurance, Continental Baking, Sheraton, and Ceasars World.

Horizontal mergers are usually motivated by an urge to increase a company's market share. The Antitrust Division has customarily focused on horizontal mergers, since they have the most immediate effect on competition. The unification of two firms making the same thing adds to the level of concentration in the industry. As noted above, the rules governing horizontal mergers are now more lenient than they were.

Companies merge vertically to gain control over supplies or to move forward to the more value-added aspects of a business. Vertical mergers have no direct effect on concentration, but they have come under scrutiny because they can foreclose new entrants to the market. They are rarely litigated today.

Conglomerate mergers are even less likely to be the subject of an Antitrust Division suit. One study showed that from 1951 to 1977, the government challenged one out of four horizontal mergers and one out of seven vertical mergers. Only 1 conglomerate merger in 50 was contested.[34] Partly as a result, most mergers are conglomerate. Managers might choose independently to acquire companies in unrelated product areas to spread risk, but the antitrust laws reinforce the practice.

Friendly or Hostile?   Mergers and acquisitions can be either friendly or hostile. In friendly transactions, all sides see some advantage in uniting their assets and liabilities. Bargaining among the parties produces a mutually agreed structure of the successor firm.

In **hostile takeovers,** the voluntary, mutual agreement is lacking. Only one side wants to consolidate; the directors and managers of the target company object, so the outsiders try to buy a controlling amount of stock to force the merging of assets. If successful, they also displace the original management team, which is why the takeover is resisted in the first place.

Hostile takeovers were sporadic in the 1970s, but became everyday occurrences in the 1980s due partly to the Reagan administration's hands-off attitude toward antitrust. As we discussed in Chapter 11, target company managers have devised a range of "shark repellant" strategies to defend their firms from unwanted suitors.

A public policy that can make takeover battles more difficult is the Williams Act of 1968. It stipulates that any person who owns more than 5 percent of the outstanding shares of a company must file a disclosure form with the SEC, thus giving advance warning of a possible takeover attempt. It also says that tender offers must be open for 20 business days. A *tender offer* is when the party who seeks control of an organization asks owners of the target firm to sell or tender their shares for a specified price. The legal waiting period gives current managers time to start a defense campaign.

Leveraged Buyouts.   Sometimes the investor group is made of managers of the company itself—in essence, an internal corporate raid. Because they typically use borrowed money to turn the acquired firm into a privately owned company, the internal takeover is called a **leveraged buyout** or **LBO.** In an LBO, the original management stays, but the original board of directors is removed.[35] No longer traded on the stock market, the new company is not subject to public disclosure requirements. As long as it is privately held, the company is also protected from future hostile takeovers.

Eventually, the investor group hopes to resell the streamlined company at a large profit. Huge amounts of money can change hands. The LBO of Owens-Illinois, the glass manufacturer, netted the company's chairman $10 million. The consultants who organized the deal pocketed $60 million in fees. Thousands of workers lost their jobs, however, and the new Owens-Illinois was a gaunt reflection of its old self.[36]

Controversial Financing. Corporate raiding and LBOs take vast sums of money; much of it comes from high-interest debt **(junk bonds).** To finance hostile takeovers, raiders borrow against the takeover target's assets. They offer to buy outstanding shares at a premium price, paying for them with money raised from the issue of junk bonds. Investors will be paid back later, once the target company has been bought. In essence, the corporate raider uses the company that is raided to pay for its own takeover. Since there is no guarantee the takeover bid will work, junk bonds are very risky and pay duly high interest rates.

Public policy unwittingly subsidizes debt-financed takeovers through the tax code. By taking on huge new loans, firms get to write off more interest payments. Corporate interest deductions soared in the 1980s to $92.2 billion—half again as much as they paid in corporate income tax.[37] Firms that are taken over also benefit from higher depreciation charges, since they get to carry assets on their books at the new purchase price, not at the (usually lower) historical cost.

Whether a takeover is carried out by outsiders or insiders, the target company finds itself owing a lot of money. It is not a coincidence that corporate debt per employee in the United States went from under $19,000 (in 1990 prices) in 1980 to over $23,000 in 1990.[38] Interest payments have prior claim over investment, which may sacrifice long-term growth. Not surprisingly, research finds that companies that have gone through LBOs cut R&D and plant capital expenditures.[39]

The new owners must pare their cost to carry interest charges and begin paying back the principal on junk bonds and other borrowed funds. They usually begin selling parts of the company to cut its liabilities. They also try to close stores or factories and to lay off employees to increase profits. Even so, the weight of new debt can become crushing during economic downturns.

Deep in the hole, scores of once prominent companies were forced into bankruptcy in the 1990s, or had to make fire sales of subsidiaries they had recently bought. Some companies seem to have restructured to the extent they are too frail to stay in the running.[40]

Foreign Takeovers

A growing volume of takeovers and mergers, both friendly and hostile, are mounted by foreign investors, including the controversial purchases of Columbia Pictures by Sony in 1989 and of MCA by Matsushita Electric in 1991. Most foreign takeovers are not Japanese, but British, Canadian, German, and French, though these have attracted less attention. As Figure 15–3 reports, the investment flows run two ways, but U.S. companies are not making foreign acquisitions at the same rate. This imbalance is probably due partly to tougher takeover laws overseas.

FIGURE 15–3

Foreign buyers acquired U.S. companies at an accelerating rate in the 1980s . . . far outpacing U.S. acquisitions overseas

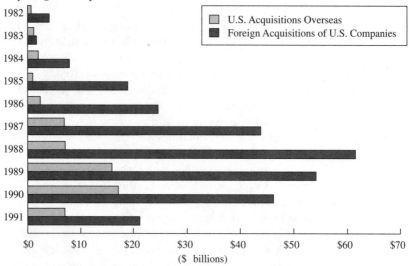

Source: *Mergers & Acquisitions,* May/June 1992, p. 54.

The buying of "trophy" assets by overseas investors has hit a political nerve in the United States and generated demand for public policies to arrest the trend. Probably of greater long-run importance are purchases of U.S. cutting-edge firms, particularly by Japanese companies. Critics worry these mergers will strip the United States of the latest technology. The Treasury Department's Committee on Foreign Investment in the United States monitors foreign purchases of strategic assets, but it rarely takes action. We will return to government protection of critical industries in Chapter 17.

Alarmed by Washington's hands-off approach, more than 30 state governments have stepped in with statutes intended to repel corporate raiders, whether foreign or domestic. State antitakeover laws often force raiders who accumulate a specified percent of stock to obtain approval from the remaining shareholders before voting these shares, and impose a moratorium on the sale of acquired assets to finance the takeover. Pennsylvania has the nation's strictest antitakeover law, which forces raiders to surrender short-term profits. These laws are one reason the takeover boom slowed in the late 1980s.[41]

The Market for Corporate Control

Laissez-faire liberals like to look at takeovers and LBOs as part of the market for corporate control. In this view, there is use in threatening managers and board members who fail to maximize their shareholders' wealth. The prospect of an unwanted takeover reduces agency problems and makes managers watch closely the threats and openings facing their companies. It also keeps boards of directors on their toes. After a takeover, or a successful defense, the large debt service payments allegedly force managers to generate cash and prevent them from spending money unproductively. The wheeling and dealing of the 1980s was thus part of a process for weeding out incompetent corporate leadership, and for putting companies on a firmer footing.[42]

The stockmarket bought this argument, bidding up the shares of such companies. But a blanket endorsement of corporate raiding and buyouts does not stand up to scrutiny. Many corporate executives contend that fear of takeovers makes them seek short-run gains rather than plan for the long term. Studies find that takeovers are frequently motivated by executives' dream for empires, less by sound business analysis. There is little gain in economic efficiency in merged entities—mainly a redistribution of the tax burden or wealth from some shareholders (or bondholders) to others.[43]

The critics prefer to characterize these activities as "casino capitalism," where fortunes are gambled but no new assets are created. To be sure, the individual investment bankers, lawyers, and CEOs who put companies into play sometimes reap bonanzas. According to Treasury Undersecretary Lawrence Summers (formerly chief economist at the World Bank) and Harvard University's Andrei Shleifer, these winnings are a transfer of resources from workers.[44] It is doubtful that society makes net gains. The contrary may be true; society may be a net loser because of the enormous transaction cost of moving corporate assets from one company to another.

Peter Drucker remarks:

> What emerged from this frantic decade was a redefinition of the purpose and rationale of big business and of the function of management. Instead of being managed "in the best interests of stakeholders," corporations were now to be managed exclusively to "maximize shareholders' values."
>
> This will not work, either. It forces the corporation to be managed for the shortest possible term. But that means damaging, if not destroying, the wealth-producing capacity of business.[45]

Which side is right? Asking whether allowing these takeovers and financial restructurings was good public policy or bad is too simple a question. Takeovers had a positive effect on some poorly run or inefficient companies; they had a negative effect on other companies.

It is instructive, however, to note that Japan follows a different path to mergers and acquisitions. The sale of companies is not rare, but usually involves much smaller entities than in the United States.[46] Large companies there are almost never subject to hostile takeover bids due to the intertwined network of share ownership discussed in Chapter 11. These facts may allow Japanese managers to focus better on long-term issues without fear of being penalized by a corporate raider.

The Clinton Administration Approach

The election of a Democratic president in 1992 caused a modest upswing in the pace and vigor of antitrust investigations. Among the high-profile investigations were probes into price fixing at the NASDAQ over-the-counter stockmarket, into the way car dealers set prices, and into the methods used by carmakers to sell fleet vehicles to rental firms. Most of these cases would not have attracted attention under the more laissez-faire regime of the 1980s.

As a result of the new scrutiny, firms such as AT&T and MCI have altered their business practices or restructured deals. Many companies are incorporating antitrust considerations more deeply into their strategic plans to avoid trouble later with mergers and acquisitions.[47]

Still, as the 1994 consent decree with Microsoft shows, Clinton administration officials are apt to be pragmatic in their negotiations with offending firms, and to handle them gently if jobs are at stake. There is little wish to bar mergers that could advance U.S. competitiveness. Combinations that lead to concentration within industries are likely to be approved if they boost efficiency or R&D spending.[48] Above all, the thrust of Justice Department and FTC activities is to try to foster private-sector innovation.

Looking at Conduct

Whatever the structure of a firm or an industry, some conduct is considered a per se violation of U.S. antitrust laws. Commentators and experts of all political stripes usually agree that price fixing is wrong. Price fixing entails overt collusion among firms to set prices, for instance, an arrangement to rig the bids on a government contract, with each firm taking a turn to submit the lowest bid. The Reagan administration doubled the number of price-fixing cases it pursued.

Price fixing is illegal in the nonprofit sector as well. In an important case, the Antitrust Division went after the Ivy League colleges and other elite universities for sharing budgeting and other financial information. The schools arranged for their tuition increases and faculty raises to be similar and to make identical financial aid packages to star students. Observers suspect the Bush administration started the Ivy League probe because of upper-middle-class complaints about soaring college expenses and the lack of scholarship funds earmarked for that group.

All the schools except MIT agreed to stop the financial aid practice, known as "overlap." MIT went to court, claiming an exemption to antitrust. The school insisted that its financial aid was charity and thus not commerce. The goal of the overlap meetings, MIT said, was not to maximize revenue but to stretch scholarship money. An appeals court agreed with MIT in 1993, finding that the rule of reason did merit an exception to antitrust law. The Justice Department later dismissed its suit, thus allowing the elite universities again to share information on student financial need.

Another practice, known as price discrimination, is against the law, too.

Discriminatory pricing is when a producer sells the same product at different prices to harm its competitors. This practice was banned during the Great Depression largely to protect independent retailers from emerging chain stores. Price discrimination can take many forms, one of which is predatory pricing. Firms with several products or points of sale can temporarily lower prices at one outlet, while subsidizing the low prices with profits from another outlet. In this way, they can drive smaller competitors out of business. But the antitrust law has been interpreted as holding any price difference unlawful, despite cost differences, if it causes injury to competition.[49] A volume discount, for instance, might be illegal even if it is warranted by the lower cost of selling in bulk. Still, proving discriminatory pricing is hard. Sellers defend themselves by arguing that discrepant prices are due to a good faith effort to meet the price of a competitor.

Deception and Fair Competition

As we have seen repeatedly, competition works only if information about goods and services is handy to buyers. Yet, sellers have an incentive to circulate false information. Incomplete or distorted information may spur sales, thus boosting profits. Deceptive advertising is another instance of agent misdirection, the market failure we first discussed in Chapter 3. Reputable firms will not make flagrantly untrue claims; consumers would find out and the tactic would backfire. But, if the harm done to the consumer is small, or if consumers cannot easily verify a seller's assertions about a product, there are subtle pressures on firms to stretch the truth.

Accordingly, government tries to assure that companies do not go overboard in misleading their customers. The FTC is the main federal agency carrying out this function in the United States. Similar agencies exist at the state level. Under the FTC Act, illegal practices include fraudulent advertising, the spreading of falsehoods about competitors' products, bait-and-switch selling techniques, coercive marketing systems, and deceptive guarantees.

Still legal is puffery. The FTC did not move against Newman's Own Virgin Lemonade in 1989 when it claimed that the drink restores virginity. The claim is so exaggerated that it is obvious that the company is not serious. The line between permissible and impermissible exaggerations, however, is unclear. Under Reagan, the FTC became more forgiving about overstated advertising than before, and took action mainly when there was evidence of injury to consumers. The National Coffee Association, for example, was allowed by the commission to continue using its message that coffee "let's you calm yourself down," though caffeine makes such an effect most implausible.[50] Disturbed by the FTC's passivity, states' attorneys general picked up the slack and began vigorously pursuing cases like these in the 1980s.

The FTC has several tools to use against a false advertiser. Accused firms can try to negotiate a settlement informally or go to trial before an FTC administrative judge. If the accused is found guilty, a cease-and-desist order is issued, demanding that the firm halt the offending message. Civil penalties of $10,000 can be sought if the firm fails to comply. The commission also can order corrective advertising. An illustration is the Listerine incident in 1975. The maker of the mouthwash was required to make clear in future advertising that Listerine does not prevent colds, as past advertising had declared. The FTC, however, is strapped by limited resources that prevent it from checking the claims in all but a fraction of the advertising messages communicated.

Public policy also has positive disclosure requirements. Revealing full information is particularly important when consumers have trouble corroborating a seller's claims about a product. The Consumer Credit Protection Act of 1968, for example, requires truth in lending. Before this policy was enacted, few borrowers could calculate the real cost of their loans. The law mandates fully reporting finance charges using a common format, so borrowers can compare services. Another example of a positive disclosure requirement is the Fair Packaging and Labeling Act of 1966. It requires companies to disclose package contents on labels so consumers will know accurately what is inside. Readers will recall from Chapter 13 that accurate information about food, food additives, medicine, and cosmetics is certified by the USDA and the FDA.

Conclusion

Our review of U.S. competition policy has found an ebb and flow in government action, with the policy running on two tracks. One track is to encourage marketplace competition and fight monopoly throughout the economy. The other track is to diminish the intensity of competition in certain sectors of the economy and to promote monopolistic elements there.

In the past, the working hypothesis of policy makers was apt to be that, for either track, government intervention was necessary to ensure a healthy diversity of companies or, when a diversity of companies was impractical, to protect consumer welfare directly through regulation of prices. Now, policy makers are prone to think that government should not intervene in these matters. The current theory is that, as a rule, government should sit more on the sidelines because innovation and international rivalry will do a better job of checking corporate power than government can. Monopoly and allied problems will go away by themselves. Therefore, the United States is apt to let companies get big so they can reap economies of scale by themselves, or to cooperate with other companies when they want to pool resources.

Today's world is not like the 1890s when antitrust moves in the United States led automatically to gains for other American firms. In today's world, traditional antitrust may impair American firms vis-à-vis foreign companies. Most other countries have not been satisfied with trying to promote local competition. They are more likely to try to use public policy to build national champions and promote corporate teamwork, at least among domestic firms. Antitrust thus needs to be seen in light of efforts to promote national competitiveness. We will revisit this important topic in Chapters 16, 17, and 18.

It is not clear whether the lower government profile in business competition has paid off for U.S. society in the past 20 years. The policy encouraged financial antics that weakened many U.S. corporations in the 1980s but strengthened others by forcing them to focus on core businesses. What is clear is that industry, consumer, and labor groups continuously try to use competition policies in ways that will help them.

Questions

1. What is a monopoly? How does one measure the degree of monopolization? What are the practical difficulties in doing so?

2. Describe the different types of restraints of trade. How does the so-called rule of reason apply to them? How vigorously should government try to stop companies from restraining trade?

3. What are the main categories of mergers? Why do companies merge or make acquisitions? When should government turn down mergers?

4. How does antitrust policy influence a country's ability to compete in the global economy? Should antitrust policy be reformed to promote national competitiveness?

5. Describe hostile takeovers and leveraged buyouts. Should government regulate these more rigorously?

End Notes

1. Allan Nevins, *Study in Power: John D. Rockefeller, Industrialist, Philanthropist,* vol. 1 (New York: Scribner's, 1953), p. 402.

2. Adam Smith, *An Inquiry into the Nature and Causes of the Wealth of Nations* (1776; reprint, New York: Modern Library, 1937), p. 128.

3. Ibid., p. 596.

4. George Garvey and Gerald Garvey, *Economic Law and Economic Growth* (New York: Greenwood Press, 1990), p. 123.

5. The calculation is based on business tax returns, as reported in U.S. Bureau of the Census, *Statistical Abstract of the United States, 1994* (Washington DC: U.S. Government Printing Office, 1994).

6. See Zoltan J. Acs and David B. Audretsch, *Innovation in Small and Large Firms* (Cambridge, MA: MIT Press, 1990); Charles Brown, James Hamilton, and James Medoff, *Employers Large and Small* (Cambridge, MA: Harvard University Press, 1990); and Bennett Harrison, *Lean and Mean* (New York: Basic Books, 1994).

7. See Lawrence G. Franko, "Global Corporate Competition," *Strategic Management Journal* 5 (1989), pp. 449–74.

8. Richard Hofstadter, "What Happened to the Antitrust Movement," in *The Political Economy of the Sherman Act,* ed. E. Thomas Sullivan (New York: Oxford University Press, 1991), p. 22.

9. Marc Allen Eisner, *Antitrust and the Triumph of Economics* (Chapel Hill: University of North Carolina Press, 1991), p. 2.

10. Martin Schnitzer, *Contemporary Government and Business Relations,* 2nd ed. (Boston: Houghton Mifflin, 1983), p. 149.

11. Alfred Chandler, *Scale and Scope* (Cambridge, MA: Belknap Press, 1990), pp. 423ff.

12. Donald Dewey, *The Antitrust Experiment* (New York: Columbia University Press, 1990).

13. Thomas E. Ricks, "Antitrust Pact Aims to Support Defense Mergers," *The Wall Street Journal,* April 12, 1994, p. A3.

14. *American Banker's Ranking the Banks 1991* (Naperville, IL: Financial Sourcebooks, 1991).

15. Peter Gammons, "Game of Monopoly May Be Over," *Boston Sunday Globe,* October 16, 1994.

16. Stuart Macdonald, *Technology and the Tyranny of Export Controls* (New York: St. Martin's, 1990), p. 55.

17. Robert W. Preer, *The Emergence of Technopolis* (New York: Praeger, 1992), p. 66.

18. "R&D, with a Reality Check," *Business Week,* January 24, 1994, p. 62.

19. Charles Goldsmith, "EC Easing Joint Venture Rules," *International Herald Tribune,* January 20, 1992, p. 9.

20. Andrew J. Pierre, ed., *A High Technology Gap?* (New York: Council on Foreign Relations, 1987), pp. 56–57.

21. "US Wins Antitrust Case," *International Herald Tribune,* May 27, 1994, p. 12.

22. Dan Bertozzi, Jr., and Lee B. Burgunder, *Business, Government, and Public Policy* (Englewood Cliffs, NJ: Prentice Hall, 1990), p. 130.

23. "TI Is Moving Up in the World," *Business Week,* August 2, 1993, pp. 46–47.

24. Michael Porter, *The Competitive Advantage of Nations* (New York: Free Press, 1990).

25. Two law professors who became federal judges, Richard Posner and Robert Bork, were especially influential in watering down antitrust. See Richard A. Posner, "The Social Costs of Monopoly and Regulation," *Journal of Political Economy* 83, no. 4 (1975), pp. 807–27; and Robert Bork, *The Antitrust Paradox: A Policy at War with Itself* (New York: Basic Books, 1978).

26. "The Microsoft Probe Looks Like a Bust for the Trustbusters," *Business Week,* May 3, 1993, p. 32; and "Novell vs. Microsoft: What's Behind the Hate," *Business Week,* September 27, 1993, pp. 121–28.

27. Linda Himmelstein, "Old, Onerous, and Still on the Books," *Business Week,* November 7, 1994, pp. 58–59.

28. William F. Shughart, *Antitrust Policy and Interest Group Politics* (New York: Quorum, 1990), pp. 160–61.

29. Joel Davidow, "The Worldwide Influence of U.S. Antitrust," *Antitrust Bulletin* 35 (Fall 1990), pp. 619–20.

30. W. Kip Viscusi, John M. Vernon, and Joseph E. Harrington, *Economics of Regulation and Antitrust* (Lexington, MA: D. C. Heath, 1992), p. 54.

31. Stephen J. K. Walters, *Enterprise, Government, and the Public* (New York: McGraw-Hill, 1993), p. 138.

32. Murray Weidenbaum, *Business, Government, and the Public,* 4th ed. (Englewood Cliffs, NJ: Prentice Hall, 1990), pp. 182–83.

33. *Mergers & Acquisitions,* May/June 1992. A good popular account of the RJR Nabisco case is Bryan Burrough and John Helyar, *Barbarians at the Gate* (New York: Harper and Row, 1990).

34. Cited in Walters, *Enterprise, Government, and the Public,* p. 230.

35. Paul Krugman, *The Age of Diminished Expectations* (Cambridge, MA: MIT Press, 1990), p. 154.

36. George Anders, *Merchants of Debt: KKR and the Mortgaging of America* (New York: Basic Books, 1992).

37. Donald L. Barlett and James B. Steele, *America: What Went Wrong?* (Kansas City: Andrews and McMeel, 1992), p. 40.

38. Ibid., p. 85.

39. William F. Long and David J. Ravenscraft, "Decade of Debt: Lessons of the LBOs of the 1980s," in *The Deal Decade,* ed. Margaret M. Blain (Washington, DC: Brookings Institution, 1991), p. 222.

40. G. Hamel and C. K. Prahalad, *Competing for the Future* (Boston: Harvard Business School Press, 1994).

41. Rogene Buchholz, *Business Environment and Public Policy,* 4th ed. (Englewood Cliffs, NJ: Prentice Hall, 1992), p. 253.

42. Among the defenders of hostile takeovers and leveraged buyouts is Harvey N. Segal, *Corporate Makeover: The Reshaping of the American Economy* (New York: Viking, 1989).

43. Alan R. Beckenstein, "Merger Activity and Merger Theories: An Empirical Investigation," *Antitrust Bulletin* 24, no. 1 (Spring 1979), pp. 105–28; and David Ravenscraft and F. M. Scherer, *Mergers, Sell-offs, and Economic Efficiency* (Washington, DC: Brookings Institution, 1987).

44. Lawrence Summers and Andrei Shleifer, "Breach of Trust in Hostile Takeovers," in *Corporate Takeovers,* ed. Alan Auerbach (Chicago: University of Chicago Press, 1988), pp. 33–56.

45. Peter Drucker, *Post-Capitalist Society* (New York: HarperBusiness, 1993), p. 80.

46. W. Carl Kester, *Japanese Takeovers* (Boston: Harvard Business School, 1991).

47. Viveca Novak, "NASDAQ Investigation Showcases New Moxie at Justice Department," *The Wall Street Journal,* October 20, 1994, p. Al.

48. "Another Tough Cop for the Antitrust Beat," *Business Week,* November 14, 1994, p. 49.

49. Viscusi et al., *Economics of Regulation and Antitrust,* p. 279.

50. Douglas F. Greer, *Business, Government, and Society,* 3rd. ed. (New York: MacMillan, 1993), pp. 257–58.

16 PUBLIC POLICY, INNOVATION, AND TECHNOLOGY

America already has an industrial policy, and it's a bad one.
Lee Iacocca[1]

Every nation's economic future depends on its ability to adjust to changing economic conditions. Industries rise and industries fall. To keep jobs and a good standard of living, countries must shift factors of production from the declining industries and into the ascendant ones. Labor, capital, and other resources need to move to uses that produce the greatest return, even if that means shrinking some important sectors of the economy. Managers and workers must embrace the latest technological advances or be pushed aside by others who will.

This cycle of economic decay and renewal is an old one. Manufacturing displaced farming as the U.S. economy's base in the 1800s and was succeeded in turn by services. Within these broad economic sectors, new methods and products continually uproot older ones. Yet, while industries have always risen and fallen, the pace of change is quicker now. In the turmoil created by economic globalization, it is not always clear what will replace the jobs in the older industries that die or migrate abroad. Many Americans fear a loss of national economic sovereignty. If the leading industries of tomorrow are dominated by companies based in foreign countries, wages and investment income may accrue overseas, not to people locally.

Industrial Policy

To assure their share of high-paying industries, all modern governments engage in **industrial policy.**[2] They target certain companies or groups of companies for special assistance, the objective being to hold on to or seize a lead in the world's economic races. Industrial policy is about trying to coordinate and concentrate government programs to improve global economic competitiveness. Supporters of industrial policy believe that government, using sharply focused programs, can help industries that have lost their luster to downsize quickly and help other industries take the early steps they need to be competitive in the future.

Industrial policy is distinct from government's macroeconomic policies that treat all companies the same way. Taxes and interest rates alter national competitiveness, but they do not entail the planned development of new sectors or the organized retrenchment of old ones. Industrial policy, by contrast, is based on the view, somewhat controversial, that market forces alone are too slow to reshape national economies. Thus, government should intervene on purpose to help certain firms while ignoring others. Trade policy, regulatory relief, special tax incentives—any public policy aimed at a particular segment of the economy—can be considered part of industrial policy. Several of those topics have been considered in earlier chapters. Here we focus on business–government collaboration in technical innovation.

The Japanese Example

Japan is the country with probably the best organized industrial policy. As we have seen throughout this book, it has had great success in a stream of target industries. In Japan's high-growth period after World War II, the Ministry of International Trade and Industry (MITI) tried to orchestrate the rationalization of traditional industries such as cement, chemicals, machine tools, and shipbuilding. During those years, MITI also encouraged companies to invest in emerging sectors such as electronics and computers. How much of Japan's economic accomplishment is due to the planned development of industries is controversial; most observers give the business–government alliance some credit.

The American Style

The United States practices a form of industrial policy, though the term is seldom used by officials. The contrast between the United States and other countries is that they go about making industrial policy in a more open and systematic way.[3] Less wedded to laissez-faire ideas, people overseas tend to view the notion of government and business teamwork favorably. They expect the public and private sectors to collaborate on improving national competitiveness. In this country, cooperative capitalism of the Japanese or continental European variety is mistrusted. Americans think in terms of government *versus* business, not government working with commercial enterprises for common ends. Still, the U.S. government, in its promoter and its buyer roles, furnishes aid selectively to national corporations to give them a headstart in chosen industries.

We have touched on aspects of America's hidden industrial policy throughout this text. We saw that soon after the American Revolution, states and local governments aided specific companies with "bounties" (special premiums) and release from taxes. They awarded franchises, or monopoly rights, to companies to protect them during their early growth. Franchising was particularly important in arranging the building of internal improvements such as bridges, aqueducts, and mills. Without such subsidies, private firms usually could not undertake these projects due to the risk and large investment needed.

These government actions continue in an unbroken, if largely unacknowledged, thread today. The decision to build the federal interstate highway system in the 1950s, for example, gave a giant boost to the automobile, tire, and gasoline industries—and helped kill private passenger train service and local masstransit systems. This was an industrial policy of far-reaching consequence, even if no one called it that.

Because it is kept out of sight, America's industrial policy is poorly coordinated and sometimes works at cross-purposes. Yet, it can be credited with many accomplishments. Chapter 16 takes up these issues as they pertain to up-and-coming industries, in particular, to the development of hopeful technologies. We compare the American approach to promoting technical modernization with what other countries do. We discuss help for mature industries, too, and weigh the odds for making U.S. industrial policy less of a patchwork.

Sunrise and Sunset Industries

As suggested above, industrial policy has two sides. One is anticipatory; the other, defensive. The anticipatory side of industrial policy aims to beat other nations at cultivating sunrise industries, particularly those using high technology. To keep ahead in the global arena, the public sector works in partnership with domestic business to keep foreign competitors from monopolizing emerging technologies. Government even may use the levers of public power to discourage private investment in ventures deemed to lack promise.

Some writers use the term **technology policy** for public efforts to move a nation forward in technology.[4] Recalling the brief discussion in Chapter 5, technology is the engine of higher productivity and, ultimately, higher living standards. When better ways of doing things are found, the same number of people can make more goods provide more services with less effort. Government patronizes technology on the premise that the social returns to high-technology industries are much better than the private returns. The positive externalities are too great to trust matters to the market alone. (Not all technology policy is marked for specific industries, however, as will be discussed below. Some of it aims at more generalizable technology.)

Industrial policy's second, defensive side addresses the trials of sunset industries.[5] Governments are inclined to try to guide the modernization of (or the orderly withdrawal from) mature sectors of the economy. In alliance with business, they aim to cushion the effect of industrial decline. The intent is to help companies and workers adjust to shrinking markets and retool for growing ones.

A Debate Full of Sound and Fury

While America's hidden industrial policy is nothing new, open discussion of the issue began in earnest in the 1970s, when the nation's competitive problems first began to surface. The Japanese experience seemed to hold lessons that America could learn. Following a thorough cabinet-level study, Jimmy Carter went as far as to propose the Economic Revitalization Plan, a comprehensive industrial strategy. *Business Week* and many business leaders supported the idea of a federal effort to revive industry.[6] Carter backed away from his proposal as he faced Reagan in the 1980 election campaign, seeing that it exposed him to too much reproach from his conservative foe.

Reagan's free-market creed was hostile to any national industrial strategy. The road to national competitiveness did not lie in government seeking to pick winners or to revive flagging industries, but in tax cuts and deregulation to unleash private enterprise. Market forces should be allowed to figure out the direction of technological change. When several years of Reaganomics failed to boost the country's ability to compete as expected, interest in industrial policy began to reemerge.

By the early 1990s, a flurry of blue ribbon studies were calling for government and business to cooperate to recapture the lead in the global economy.[7] Though most official reports avoid the words *industrial policy,* that is what they recommend. The Clinton administration embraced the idea as a key to economic revival.

The irony of the controversy is that the federal government never was a mere spectator to industrial change. Industrial policy was always being used sub rosa, even under Reagan. As we have observed throughout this book, labels are misleading in discussions of business and government relations. Smart managers judge public policy by what it does, not by what it is called. Efforts to promote national competitiveness in key industries deserve to be rated on pragmatic grounds, not by reflex.

Government Incompetence

What is the complaint against industrial policy? There are two main arguments. One is that industrial policy does not work. Government is too ham-handed to "pick winners and losers," the critics say. They doubt the public sector can guide the early development of technologies that will help national firms contend in world markets. Bureaucrats making economic decisions are bound to get things wrong; businesspeople are quicker and nimbler.

To support their reasoning, critics point to the duds. There are many. In the 1980s, Washington spent $1 billion to help several military contractors develop high-speed integrated circuits. Intel got there first without federal financing.[8] The Synfuels Corporation did not develop synthetic fuels to replace fossil fuels despite billions of dollars of congressional appropriations (Chapter 14). Even MITI has made bad industrial policy decisions in Japan (see Box 16–1).

Box 16–1

Japanese Industrial Policy Is Not Invincible

Japan's attempt to build a nuclear power industry around new breeder reactors is a cautionary tale for industrial policy. Three decades ago, Japanese planners decided the country would develop a new generation of reactors that would produce as much fuel as they used. They would be powered by plutonium—a highly dangerous energy source that also can be used in nuclear weapons.

In 1967, the Power Reactor and Nuclear Fuel Development Corporation was formed. It forged an alliance among private utility companies, MITI and other government agencies, and research laboratories and universities. Britain, France, Germany, and the United States started rival programs at around the same time, and a race was on to create what seemed at the time like a breakthrough in energy production.

In succeeding years, however, technical problems forced other nations to rethink the breeder reactor. The technology uses sodium, not water, to carry away heat, and the piping must be thin to transfer the heat quickly. The reactors are thus extremely hard to build. Plutonium also caused giant problems. It is made from reprocessed aluminum. Moving and stockpiling this fuel is a logistic and security nightmare. Meanwhile, the price of uranium has plunged, so electricity derived from plutonium costs 5 to 15 times more.[1] To date, Japan has not been willing to admit a mistake and write-off its investment in breeder reactor technology.

Another big mistake in Japanese industrial policy occurred with high-definition television. Japan's

government-owned broadcaster started research into HDTV in 1968. It paid for development of HDTV technology and encouraged Japanese electronics firms to put $1.3 billion of their money into it. The Japanese bet on an analog system, an extension of conventional television. Test transmissions began in 1979. Yet, Japanese HDTV did not catch on, partly due to the high cost of the receivers. Meanwhile, American companies came up with a new generation of technology using a digital system for transmitting data (See Box 16–3). Despite its first-mover advantages in HDTV, Japan was left with an expensive white elephant that was outmoded before it was marketed. The fate of the American system, which was not formally adopted until 1993, proves that victory in international competition can go to late starters, who can learn from others' mistakes.[2]

A recent study suggests these false steps are more than anecdotes. MITI and other government agencies may have supported more losers than winners over the years.[3] In the early postwar years, when Japan was catching up with the West, it was easier to determine into which industries to move next. Once Japan was no longer a follower, the task of spotting winners became much harder. This is why MITI is pulling back from industrial policy.[4]

[1]David E. Sanger, "Japan's Nuclear Fiasco," *The New York Times,* December 20, 1992, Section 3, p. 1.

[2]"Do Not Adjust Your Set," *The Economist,* February 27, 1993, p. 65.

[3]Richard Beason and David Weinstein, *Growth, Economies of Scale, and Targeting in Japan (1955–90),* Discussion Paper 1644 (Cambridge, MA: Harvard Institute of Economic Research, 1993).

[4]"MITI's Identity Crisis," *The Economist,* January 22, 1994, pp. 65–66.

Still, for every botched effort, there are successful instances of public support for technical innovations. Consider the computer industry. In the 1940s and 1950s, most computer R&D in the United States was launched by federal agencies.[9] A half-century later, U.S. firms still dominate software and many aspects of hardware production. Of course, bureaucrats err; so do private managers and investors. There is no reason to be starry-eyed about either side's ability to make early calls about winning technologies. Industrial policy is no panacea, but, in today's global economy, it is hard to picture companies in many fields staying at the frontier of knowledge on their own, without a boost from government. This does not mean government should make technology and investment decisions itself. The point of modern industrial policy is to capitalize on alliances between the private and public sectors.

The Technological Pork Barrel

The second major objection to industrial policy is that it stimulates rent-seeking behavior. Funds will flow to the industry that lobbies the hardest, not necessarily to the one that has the best technology or the brightest prospects for growth. Even if an industry is worthy of support, the public money creates its own constituencies, thus corrupting the process by which subsidies are allocated. These constituencies will fight to keep any privilege they once receive. Once government starts down this slippery path, it is unable to stop and industrial policy will lose most links to reason. It is better, therefore, for government to remain neutral and let companies fight it out by themselves.

This point of disapproval seems utopian. The fact that a public policy is subject to abuse is not sufficient grounds for rejecting it altogether. Assuming the private sector will not make as many improvements on its own, without government encouragement, the opportunity cost of public investment in R&D is probably low even when the nominal cost is high. If industrial policy is sometimes squandered, the failures could be more than made up for by a few successes.

The value of computers, for instance, is inestimable. Does it matter that some early government money that helped establish the computer industry may have been wasted? Or that other research funds allocated at that time may have gone into some dead-end technologies? For now, we simply note that, even in the United States, business and government have proved they can work together, whether doing so fits the prevailing ideology.

Losing the Technological Lead?

What accounts for the ongoing domestic debate over industrial policy? The driving force is America's seeming loss of technological leadership. Following World War II, the United States was preeminent in the broad range of sophisticated products. Since then, overseas companies have been closing in on and sometimes overtaking American firms. America's share of the rich countries' high-technology exports slipped in the 1970s and 1980s, reflecting a loss of international competitiveness in these pivotal goods (see Table 16–1). There are several crucial technical areas where the United States is now an also-ran (see Table 16–2).

Another disturbing trend is the rate of innovation. It may be ebbing com-

TABLE 16–1   **The United States' Share of High-Tech Exports Has Been Shrinking.**

	Share of OECD High-Tech Exports*		
	1970	*1980*	*1990*
France	7.0%	7.9%	7.8%
Germany	16.1	15.9	14.6
Japan	12.0	15.3	19.1
United Kingdom	9.6	11.2	9.2
United States	**28.3**	**25.1**	**23.7**

*Aerospace, computers, electronics, pharmaceuticals, instruments, and electric machinery.

Source: *Industrial Policy in OECD Countries, Annual Review 1992* (Paris: Organization for Economic Cooperation and Development, 1992), pp. 150–51.

TABLE 16–2   **The United States Lags in Some Advanced Technologies.**

	Strong	*Competitive*	*Weak*	*Losing Badly*
Biotechnology				
Drug discovery techniques	X			
Genetic engineering	X			
Electronic Components				
Microprocessors	X			
Memory chips				X
Magnetic storage	X			
Optical storage				X
Screen displays				X
Silicon				X
Superconductors				X
Engineering and Production				
Total quality management			X	
Design for manufacturing			X	
Advanced welding		X		
High-speed machining			X	
Robotics				X
Engines and Propulsion				
Alternative fuel engines		X		
Electric motors and drives		X		
High-fuel-economy engines			X	
Rocket propulsion	X			
Information Technology				
Artificial intelligence	X			
Computers and software	X			
Database systems	X			
Fiber optics		X		
Operating systems	X			
Telecommunications	X			

Source: Council on Competitiveness, as reported by Steven Greenhouse, "The Calls for an Industrial Policy Grow Louder," *The New York Times,* July 19, 1992, p. 5.

pared to other countries. The National Science Foundation reports that the Japanese doubled their share of U.S. patents during the 1980s. Japanese patents appear to be valuable, too. In applications for new patents, patents from that country are cited more frequently than patents from any other country.[10] Such events have forced Americans to think about ways to improve their performance.

We should avoid taking a Chicken Little view of America's technological strength. The sky is not falling, for the nation has a rising trade surplus in high-technology capital goods. Americans sell more measuring and control instruments, computers and peripherals, semiconductors, telecommunications equipment, office machines, and scientific and medical equipment than they buy from overseas.

The United States still remains at the forefront of science. The federal government spent at least $68 billion on R&D in 1993. With government subsidies, the nation has built a huge base of researchers—950,000 in all. That is almost as many as in western Europe (580,000) and Japan (435,000) combined.[11] America excels at esoteric research. It continues to win the lion's share of Nobel Prizes and other scientific awards. According to the Council on Competitiveness, a private group of business, labor, and higher education leaders, U.S. firms have pushed ahead in many technologies that are crucial to the nation's ability to win in world markets.[12]

Yet, these same firms are prone to be less good at the more mundane task of figuring out how to use technology for practical purposes. A report from MIT's Commission on Industrial Productivity notes: "Prowess in research does not lead automatically to commercial success. New ideas must be converted into products that customers want, when they want them, and before competitors can provide them, and the products must be made efficiently and well."[13] Too often, U.S. firms find themselves lagging in the commercial exploitation of inventions.

The challenge is for business to capitalize on the latest discoveries. In the past, U.S. firms have often been willing to cede innovations to foreign firms. Flat-panel displays, videocassette recorders, and numerically controlled machine tools are just a few examples of products pioneered in the United States but now dominated by other countries. The same thing may happen with superconductivity, cold fusion, and other promising and long-shot technologies in the future.

Government's Role in Basic and Applied Research

The scientific knowledge that underlies such innovations is a public good. Discoveries are apt to spread quickly, and trailblazing firms find that rivals soon copy them. This fact causes a market failure. Since imitation costs less than innovation, R&D that might help a whole industry may not be worth any one company's time. Competition thus produces less R&D than is desirable for society.

The disincentive is greatest for studying fundamental scientific questions, or what is called **basic research.** Companies seldom want to put money into investigating matters that lack a clear and likely payoff. True, there are some outstanding private facilities in the United States that do basic research—Bell Laboratories, Xerox's Palo Alto center, and the David Sarnoff Research Center. These are exceptions—and industry spending on basic research fell 15 percent from 1986 to 1990, according to one estimate.[14] Few companies today feel they can afford long-term studies to explore basic phenomena.

Yet, basic research is the underpinning of technical progress. While false starts and dead ends are the norm in basic research, sometimes a small discovery has enormous, unanticipated consequences for the productive sector. Genetic engineering is a good illustration. A huge and promising industry today, it is the chance byproduct of basic research done years ago. Similarly, the laser and the transistor grew unexpectedly out of discoveries in quantum physics.

Due to the private sector's disinclination to support research for its own sake, government steps in to fill the gap. (See Figure 16–1.) The broadest program of basic research in the United States is funded by the National Science Foundation (NSF). It was created shortly after World War II. The National Institutes of Health (NIH) is another huge federal entity that funds basic research. The NSF, NIH, and other government agencies pay for most of the scientific work performed in the nation's universities and not-for-profit science centers. The federal government also runs a network of 700 national laboratories. Many scientists working in these facilities (not to mention the ones in industry) had their graduate training subsidized by government grants. The largest chunk of federal R&D, however, goes for military and space projects, as reported in Figure 16–2.

Applied research has different characteristics from basic research. This term refers to scientific inquiry that has a direct economic benefit. It is pragmatic

FIGURE 16–1

Who Pays for R&D in America (1993)

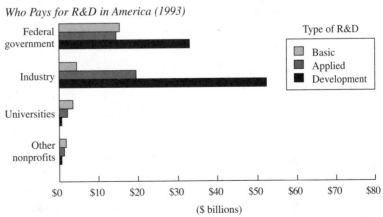

Source: *Science and Engineering Indicators—1993* (Washington, DC: National Science Board, 1993).

FIGURE 16–2

U.S. government agencies supporting R&D (1991) (amounts in $ billions)

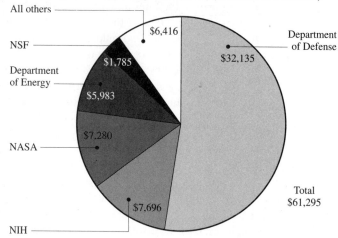

Source: *Federal Funds for Research and Development* (Washington, DC: National Science Foundation, 1993).

and closed-ended. Companies are naturally more prone to study concrete problems than they are to probe abstract issues. Today, business enterprises account for over half the applied research outlays in the United States, as they look for answers to immediate problems. The trouble is that business spending to turn ideas into product prototypes is even higher in Germany and Japan.[15]

Product development is the last stage in the R&D process. It entails turning prototypes into products and making existing products better. Development work focuses on improving manufacturing and meeting customer needs. Many U.S. companies lag in production techniques and innovative merchandise. Due to competitive pressures, they are now putting a greater share of R&D spending into product development than they did in the past.

A chief justification for industrial policy in America is that privately funded R&D is too meager. Government can perhaps help American business develop new products, engineer them, and bring them to market. These last steps are controversial. That government needs to support basic research is rarely disputed. The results are generic and available to everyone. Whether government also should move downstream to applied research and development is less clear. Is it fair to take sides with one company or group of companies over another? Do we really need government to help private organizations determine what products to make and how to make them pay? Many Americans say no, such action goes beyond government's legitimate ambit.

The fact that even practical ideas do not push themselves into the marketplace spontaneously is a compelling counterargument. Society has an interest in encouraging innovations that companies do not adopt on their own. Besides, rival governments are working closely with their firms to help them innovate. Everywhere in the capitalist world, one finds efforts to induce academic and research institutions to collaborate more with industry, to direct their research toward the needs of business.[16] Even newer rivals such as Taiwan and Korea have thorough industrial and technology policies (see Box 16–2). Thus, more and more, the U.S. government is getting drawn into industrial policy, and into working with companies on applied R&D.

Many observers are anxious, however, that the U.S. attempt to focus on near-term research goals not come at the expense of basic research. Congress, for instance, has recently ordered the NSF to spend 60 percent of its research budget on projects deemed relevant to national needs. That type of preapproval of research topics could stifle creative thinking and ultimately help dry up the flow of useful new ideas to be developed into commercial products. Meanwhile, Japan is boosting public spending on basic research, a decision that could give Japan an edge in technology in the 21st century.[17]

America's Hidden Industrial Policy

As noted at the beginning of this chapter, industrial policy is nothing new in the United States. The federal government has long been engaged in applied agricultural research, the fruits of which are an important factor in the farm sector's

---

Box 16–2

The Asian "Tigers" Also Have Active Industrial and Technology Strategies

Not to be left behind in the race for high technology, the NICs are trying to catch the industrial states. In 1991, Taiwan spent 1.6 percent of its GNP on R&D and plans to raise this to 2.5 percent in 1996. The public sector foots much of the bill, to compensate for lack of R&D by the private sector. Working with the private sector on long-term research programs, Taiwan is pouring billions of dollars into industries deemed priority areas. Half the funds go to basic research, the rest, to industrial applications.[1]

Korea has an even more ambitious plan. It wants to hike R&D spending to 5 percent of GNP by 2001. Major projects include HDTV and advanced computer chips.[2] These initiatives are the latest in Korea's effort to make the transition to knowledge-intensive industry—which its leaders think is better suited to a country with few natural resources. Much like MITI in Japan, the Ministry of Trade and Industry in Korea has pushed firms into such fields as industrial and consumer electronics.[3]

---

[1]*Industrial Policy in OECD Countries, Annual Review 1992* (Paris: Organization for Economic Cooperation and Development, 1992), p. 224.

[2]Ibid., p. 223.
[3]T. W. Kang, *Is Korea the Next Japan?* (New York: Free Press, 1989).

international competitiveness. Washington has also been a major patron of basic biological and medical research, which has helped make the U.S. biotech industry the best in the world. Japanese firms have stumbled in biotech despite pouring money into U.S. start-ups in the 1980s. A major reason is their weak basic research tradition in the life sciences that makes it hard for them to adopt American innovations.[18]

The most familiar instances of U.S. industrial policy, however, involve the armed forces. World War II's Manhattan Project to build the atomic bomb was an early success story. This project helped create a military and a civilian nuclear industry, though the second outcome was subsidiary to the main goal of deterring the Soviet Union. Years later, the Apollo Project to explore the moon won similar victories. The entire U.S. aerospace industry is the product of business–government partnerships. Though not part of a self-conscious industrial policy, U.S. defense and space programs had the effect of sowing globally competitive industries. No other country makes the same range of sophisticated military aircraft that U.S. defense contractors make today, to take an example.

A defense-based industrial policy has major liabilities, however. The government's bias toward arms has distorted the nation's industrial structure. The firms that dealt with the Pentagon became soft. They got used to a customer intent on performance at any price.[19] Other countries, meanwhile, had the advantage that their companies could concentrate on commercial products for more price-sensitive consumers.

Admittedly, military technology had spinoffs that aided civilian industries in the United States. Take the computer network built by the Pentagon in 1969 to ensure communications after a nuclear war; it has grown into today's Internet system. But gains such as these were haphazard. Germany and Japan (since World War II kept by their basic laws from building major military sectors) were free of this handicap. In total, they set aside far less of their income for military research than the United States does (see Figure 16–3). That means more money for R&D on consumer goods.

The German and Japanese advantage has increased in later years as the technological advances supported by U.S. industrial policy have grown less relevant for nondefense purposes. Take the stealth B-2 bomber. It is made of advanced material that renders it invisible to radar. This costly improvement is of no use to civilian aviation. At the same time, the market for sophisticated military goods is shrinking at home and abroad due to the end of the Cold War. Thus, the lines of business that were the nucleus of U.S. industrial policy are dwindling.

Postwar technological development did not come at a bargain price; many government-led projects were wasteful and, perhaps, could have been run more efficiently. An element of pork barrel spending crept into the process.[20] Congressmen like to earmark funds for research in colleges and universities in their home districts, as opposed to a blind review of who has the best capabilities. This shotgun approach to research is wasteful because it lacks economies of scale.

Going too far in the opposite direction toward megaprojects is also a problem. Congress has shown a bias for such showcase ventures as the Supercollider

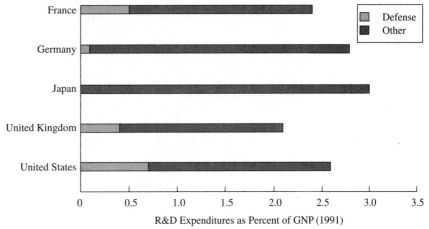

FIGURE **16–3**

The United States spends more of its national income on military R&D and less on civilian R&D than Japan or Germany

Source: *Science and Engineering Indicators—1993* (Washington, DC: National Science Board, 1993).

(killed in 1993) and the Space Station (since scaled back)—huge undertakings that drain funds from worthy, but less visible, smaller projects. Research money is likely to provide a greater return when spread more widely, though not so widely that it leads to duplication and underfunding.

For example, government support of basic research in computer science was critical to the rise of the American software industry. This success was not orchestrated according to a single, overarching plan. To the contrary, the government funded separate and sometimes rival technologies to see what worked. The bottom-up approach often works better than deciding things in advance and trying to impose order from above in the interest of avoiding waste.

Policies for Mature Industries

What about aging industries? These often supply basic materials such as steel or critical components such as machine tools. When such sectors lose ground to foreign competition, governments are liable to try to preserve them. As discussed in earlier chapters, the United States does much for declining businesses. It protects them from imports; it lends and grants them money; and it provides special unemployment benefits and job retraining for the workers who are displaced. The federal government also provides economic development assistance to communities and regions that suffer from aging industries.

In the 1980s, the distressed businesses that received the most government attention were steel mills and automobile makers. In the 1990s, attention has turned to salvaging the defense industry. The Pentagon has a $1.5 billion Technology Reinvestment Program aimed at helping communities and businesses cope with the shrinking military budget.

This defense conversion program illustrates a familiar problem with industrial policy measures. It is no coincidence that the biggest beneficiary is California, a swing state onto which Democrats need to hold to retain the presidency. Massachusetts, a solidly Democratic state, has received proportionally less defense conversion funds.[21] Industrial policy always has an element of partisanship in it. Waning, but politically connected, sectors may grab the lion's share of resources. Emerging firms, too small to have as much political clout or located in politically marginal parts of the country, are shortchanged.

Critics of U.S. industrial policy complain that it falls into this trap. Too much support goes to the sunset sectors; too little, to the sunrise sectors. They call for a more comprehensive, balanced approach.[22] Whether industrial policy can be immunized from interest groups in the pluralist U.S. political system is another question. We will return to it after we look at government's current efforts to help particular American industries.

Military Technology

Military support for new technology in the United States has been orchestrated by the Defense Advanced Research Projects Agency. In 1993, the agency dropped the word defense from its title to become just ARPA, reflecting a new stress on so-called dual-use technology. With a budget of about $1 billion, ARPA acts as a military venture capital firm. It funds scientists and engineers in universities and corporations to discover futuristic technology with potential military payoff.[23] By encouraging private research, ARPA works much as does MITI in Japan, which also organizes research projects and finances corporate participation in them. ARPA's budget is just the tip of the iceberg of R&D oriented toward U.S. national security. But it is more important than the numbers suggest due to ARPA's enterprising mission.

Semiconductors are a good illustration of the kind of dual-use technology being supported by ARPA as defense spending shrinks. In the early 1980s, the military became worried over the drop in the U.S. semiconductor industry. Japanese companies had taken the leading positions in many types of computer chips. A government task force looked into the problem and concluded a healthy domestic semiconductor industry was essential to national security. Shortly after that, the Semiconductor Industry Association proposed setting up the Semiconductor Manufacturing Technology Institute (Sematech), with partial government funding. The idea was for companies to pool their scientific resources, focusing on manufacturing processes. IBM, Intel, Motorola, Texas Instruments, and other large companies joined.

Sematech lobbyists pushed hard for congressional backing. Some smaller companies complained that the fees for joining excluded them and that the whole enterprise was a subsidy for big business alone. Disregarding these objections, Congress authorized $100 million for Sematech through the defense budget as a grant in 1988.[24] In subsequent years, the nation's share of the world semiconductor market did grow. By 1990, U.S. chips accounted for about one-fifth of Japan's domestic consumption. Many observers give credit to Sematech, though other factors may have been more important.[25] The consortium announced plans in 1994 to free itself entirely from government support within two years.

There are many similar examples of business and ARPA forming associations for R&D. In a notable move in 1992, ARPA gave $20 million to a consortium to push flat-panel displays, a technology of vast potential for both weapons and consumer products. Sales of this product may grow to $20 billion by 2000. Japanese firms control the market for passive-matrix screens, and the Pentagon fears its supplies could be jeopardized. U.S. companies have a chance to leapfrog the competition with active-matrix screens. The second-generation displays are larger and sharper but more expensive to make. Members of the U.S. Display Consortium include AT&T and Xerox. Like Sematech, the U.S. Display Consortium aims to move improved technology from lab to factory. The hope is to build on what the Japanese have learned—and avoid their mistakes.[26]

To encourage the U.S. display industry further, in 1994, the Pentagon pledged to spend as much as $500 million over the decade in matching funds for companies willing to mass-produce flat panels. These funds are on top of the $200 million the federal government had given for display research since 1989. Companies will compete for grants, with winners receiving about 30 percent of the cost of building a display factory. In the face of the Japanese lead, private capital is not willing to invest in manufacturing capacity. The carrot from government provides a hedge against defeat in the marketplace.[27]

As usual, there are fears the plan will be corrupted by pork-barrel politics. Earlier, ARPA gave $50 million to help Optical Imaging Systems, Inc., build a flat-screen factory—but only after the head of the defense appropriations subcommittee in the House of Representatives inserted language into a funding bill favoring the company. After a consortium of rival companies complained, they received assurance of another $50 million for themselves.[28] Critics also worry that ARPA here has "picked a loser"—that flat panels will soon be made obsolete by field emission displays. Time will establish whether ARPA has made the right bet.

Another recent effort to redeploy defense-oriented research involves the national laboratories. To compensate for their military contracts and avoid threatened staff cuts, many national labs are entering cooperative research and development agreements with the private sector. These agreements are instigated and in part paid for by industry. They are subject to review, they cannot last longer than 11 years, and their results eventually become common property. There were 460 public–private R&D pacts running in the national labs in 1990.[29]

Again, the skeptics wonder about this venture in industrial policy. It looks to them like an inefficient way of providing a subsidy to lucky firms. If the national labs have outlasted their original purpose, why not close them rather than cobble together a new function? The answer given is that these institutions are too valuable to waste that way. It is best to convert them from military to civilian production to conserve the talents of their research scientists and engineers, but many do not find that argument persuasive.

Civilian Technology

In spite of ARPA's good record of supporting dual-use technology, many officials in Washington advocated a parallel program solely for nonmilitary projects. They were wary whether military planners could adjust to fully commercial ventures. The expertise needed to work with the sheltered sector of American high technology, comprised of the Pentagon's customers, is probably different from what is needed in the exposed sector of civilian consumers.[30]

Accordingly, the Clinton administration designated the National Institute of Standards and Technology (NIST), an arm of the Commerce Department, to act like ARPA but with no military ties. The NIST, which used to be called the Bureau of Standards, received an 80 percent increase in budget in 1995, to $935 million.[31] Its new mission is to set trends for new technology in the civilian sector.

The NIST administers the Advanced Technology Program (ATP), which donates money to private companies or consortia for "precompetitive generic technology." Its goal is to fund technologies with wide benefits whose risks or costs are too high for single companies to bear alone, and to speed their delivery to market. The ATP aims to improve manufacturing processes, but not in a way that favors one company over another. The Omnibus Trade and Competitiveness Act of 1988 had forced President Bush to set up the ATP grant program, but funding was so small it hardly mattered. After the change in administration in 1993, the NIST picked five areas of technology to support with $745 million over five years. The priority areas include a national health care information network, DNA analysis techniques to diagnose disease, and methods for making automobiles weigh less.[32]

In a related move, Congress, in 1992, voted $1.1 billion for the Small Business Innovation Research program. It requires federal agencies to set aside a portion of their R&D budgets for small firms that are trying to produce new commercial technologies. Congress also has approved the federally funded Critical Technologies Institute. Started in 1992 with a $7.6 million budget, the institute is meant to give business a voice in Washington's R&D decisions.[33]

An Uncertain Future

The fate of recent federal industrial policy initiatives became unsure when Republicans took control of Congress. Elected on a "Contract with America" platform in 1994, the new majority party targeted the ATP, ARPA's dual-technology program, and the Technology Reinvestment Program for cuts. The flat-panel project, for example, seemed unlikely to survive intact.[34] Doubtful about government, few Republicans want to support any public policy that tries to pick winners in the high-tech marketplace.

Surprisingly, business leaders have not rushed to save these programs. When CEOs tote up the loss of research grants it does not compare with the gains from Republican plans to cut taxes and regulation and to put restrictions on lawsuits (see Chapters 7 and 13). Technology programs "aren't on anybody's list," according to Jerry Junkins, head of Texas Instruments. "It's small dollars."[35]

Perhaps the more acceptable model for industrial policy is just for government to stimulate demand for innovative ideas and let the private sector find the best solutions.[36] By using its buying power and regulatory authority, government can compel companies to come up with ingenious answers to technical problems. The recent development of high-definition television (HDTV) in America illustrates how government can play this catalytic role. (See Box 16–3.)

Box 16–3

The Development of HDTV Provides One Model for Successful Industrial Policy . . . or Does It?

America seems to have won the race to develop HDTV, a new generation of television with extra-sharp screens that its backers think could be one of the most important technologies in the 21st century. The country did so with a nuanced industrial policy where government played the roles of rule maker and umpire.[1]

The process of selecting an HDTV standard started in 1987 at the request of broadcasting companies that feared being left behind if cable or satellite competitors went ahead with HDTV on their own. The FCC set up an advisory committee of broadcasters and electronic firms to pick the best system in an open contest.

The FCC set the ground rules, such as requiring that any HDTV system be compatible with conventional television and that the winner agree to license its technology to other manufacturers at a fair price. The market was guaranteed; as early as 2009, all broadcasts using existing technology will have to stop. Still, a request for $1.35 billion in government aid was rejected; industry paid all costs for the HDTV competition—about $5 billion—including a test center in Virginia.

Twenty-three rival systems vied. By 1993, the testing had eliminated all but three systems. Each used digital signals similar to the ones used by computers. This technology was a quantum jump over the systems promoted by industrial policy in Europe and Japan (see Box 16–1). A new method of compressing digital signals made the breakthrough possible. It is likely that the rest of the world will be forced by circumstances to adopt whatever standard is picked in the United States.

The three finalists were controlled by rival consortia. As the technical contest came down to the final rounds, the consortia chose to form a grand alliance. That way, none would risk losing. The alliance partners include AT&T, General Instrument, Zenith, the Sarnoff Research Center, and MIT, as well as Holland's Philips and France's Thomson.

For now, the U.S. electronics industry appears to be the big winner. Time will tell if HDTV will fulfill its promise, or if it will be rendered obsolete before its time by some other innovation (satellite communication and multimedia computing are contenders). Broadcasters initially reacted with uninterest, and consumers seem not to care much about the improved picture quality. Meanwhile cable TV and telecom companies are preparing digital TV transmissions based on other technologies.[2] Even successful industrial policy can finally fall short if the market fails to develop as predicted.

---

[1]"Do Not Adjust Your Set," *The Economist*, February 27, 1993, pp. 65–66; and "All Together Now," *The Economist*, May 29, 1993, p. 74.

[2]"Screened Out," *The Economist*, September 24, 1994, p. 66.

State Government Activities

Industrial policy also takes place at lower levels of government. We saw in Chapter 7 how states, cities, and towns use incentives to attract and keep employers. There often are special government offices whose job it is to develop industry. Two examples from Massachusetts are described in Box 16–4.

State and local governments make a particular effort to get high-technology employers. Over 100 proposals were submitted by places wanting to become the site for Sematech, for example. Austin, Texas, won with a package that included a rent-free facility, free supercomputer time, employee moving assistance, and

---

Box 16–4

Massachusetts Is Just One State Where Public Agencies Try to Woo and Promote Business

The Massachusetts Office of Business Development tripled its staff during the first term of Governor William Weld, a Republican not known for support of activist government. With an annual budget of $4.5 million, the office recruits firms from elsewhere to come to Massachusetts, and works to keep other firms here. It claims to have created 7,000 jobs in two years, and to have saved another 17,000.[1]

A typical success story involved a 60-employee plastic food-wrap manufacturing plant. It was set to move south in search of a better business climate, and, especially, lower electric rates. Utilities in the South quoted rates almost half those in Massachusetts. The Office of Business Development, however, worked out a deal: a special subsidized electric rate available under state legislation for companies that agree to stay in Massachusetts.[2] The food-wrap company decided to stay where it was.

Another government agency in the state that engages in industrial development is the Massachusetts Port Authority's International Trade Development Unit. Established to generate business for MassPort,

which derives income from ships that use Boston Harbor, the unit works with importers and exporters to expand their trade.

An example is the trade unit's activities to promote the sale of modular housing from New England to Japan, with Boston as the natural port of exit. Officials from MassPort studied market conditions in Japan and saw an untapped market for New England wood products. Further investigation revealed the most promising market segment was in prefabricated homes, done in various traditional American styles. New England lumber and wood-product companies would be able to break into the Japanese market with a better-quality, lower-price product than Japanese companies made.

The trouble was that the New England industry, with its family-based operations, lacked the contacts and knowledge necessary to get into the export trade. Here is where MassPort stepped in. It organized a consortium of the small New England wood companies, developed a marketing strategy, and arranged for a middleman to serve as the contact point with Japan. The consortium was soon freestanding and selling its products well in Japan, creating jobs for Massachusetts and neighboring states, as well as more cargo fees for MassPort.

[1]Jerry Ackerman, "Attitude Adjustment," *Boston Globe,* November 22, 1994, p. 39.
[2]Ibid., p. 49.

free tickets to sporting events. North Carolina uses $82 million in taxpayers' funds to back a state Microelectrics Center.[37]

A favorite technique of state officials is to sponsor science parks. Over 200 state-supported science parks have been established in the United States, most built around a local university. The largest is the Research Triangle Park in North Carolina, started in the 1950s.[38] Science parks usually are run by a board representing the public and private sectors. The state government typically builds the infrastructure and allows strict zoning, with research-oriented companies picking up the rest of the tab. Policies such as these spurred the growth of vast technology districts such as California's Silicon Valley and Massachusetts' Route 128.

Other countries have similar programs, though usually with more leadership from the central government. There are at least 40 science parks in France, where they are called *technopoles*. The Japanese government has gone further with the vast Tsukuba Science City, which is home to about half the public-sector research institutes in Japan. This concentration of scientific talent has attracted 150 or so companies to Tsukuba. Taiwan has a similar complex in Hsinchu focused on computers and telecommunications. It attracts companies with prefabricated factories, tax exemptions, and duty-free imports of equipment.[39]

American state governments also try to encourage innovation directly. To help smaller companies, about half the states support technology extension centers at an annual cost of $50 million. The objective of these centers is to speed the spread of better manufacturing techniques. Japan spends about 10 times as much for similar industrial outreach programs, leading to calls for a greater federal role equivalent to the cooperative agriculture extension service.[40] The Clinton administration has responded, and asked Congress for $68 million for manufacturing extension centers in 1995.

Industrial Policy in a Comparative Perspective

The big role of the states in America's industrial policy is part of a larger issue: the way the United States is organized seems to guarantee haphazard assistance to critical industries. As the MIT Commission on Industrial Productivity notes:

> Responsibility for technology is dispersed widely throughout the executive branch and in Congress. No fewer than 12 federal agencies have responsibility for research and development. The White House Office of Science and Technology Policy could in principle provide a strategic focus and coordinate these agencies, but in recent years it has not done so. In Congress responsibility for the federal science budget is shared among 9 of the 13 appropriations subcommittees. Regulatory governance of commercial technology is dispersed still more widely.[41]

The result is a crazy quilt of contradictory individual decisions.

Other capitalist countries are more systematic. In Germany, for instance, there are two principal agencies carrying out industrial policy. The Ministry of

Economic Affairs subsidizes the traditional sunset industries such as coal, steel, and shipbuilding. The Ministry of Research and Technology assists the sunrise industries, including computers, aerospace, and nuclear energy.[42] Although German government support to industry is not coordinated by a single agency, the consensual temper of German politics assures a high degree of unity among policies. A National Technology Council is being created to call attention to German technological shortcomings.

Many people want to bring U.S. industrial policy out of the shadows and to put more order into it. Reagan's President's Commission on Industrial Competitiveness, for instance, recommended creation of a cabinet-level department of science and technology.[43] The idea was to provide an integrated framework to guide the nation's programs for promoting innovation in business firms. The new cabinet post also could create better cooperation among government, industry, and universities. Others have seconded this idea, but it has never been acted on.

Institutional reforms such as these might make industrial policy less disjointed. The American political system, however, is not hospitable to centralized, top-down policy making. Government in this country cannot easily orchestrate technological change. It will be subjected to competing demands from business and other interest groups, all clamoring for a piece of industrial policy. The outcome is unlikely ever to look as methodical as the industrial policy that emerges in the more corporatist states of Germany or Japan.[44]

We also should not blow out of proportion the effectiveness of industrial policy overseas. The Germans are going through a period of doubt and self-evaluation over their technological prowess. German companies lag in high-tech areas, with patents falling in microelectronics, computers, and lasers since the late 1980s. They, like Americans, have let others commercialize their innovations. The fax machine, for example, was invented in Germany by Siemens but was brought to market by the Japanese.[45] Public policy has not averted these failings by German industry.

Conclusion

We have reviewed industrial policy, or the effort by government to fine-tune support for chosen lines of business, and especially to encourage new technology. This area of public activity blends seamlessly into antitrust and foreign economic policies (discussed in Chapters 15 and 17). The thrust of industrial policy is twofold: to reap the benefit of technological change and to mitigate the social harm that results. To reach these goals, government may provide tax relief, cheap loans, trade protection, and, as emphasized in this chapter, public backing for R&D. We saw that it is probably not a good idea for government to promote any particular technology, as opposed to improving the environment for innovation and providing resources for research.

American business and political leaders do not like to use the term *industrial policy,* which violates free-market ideology. Yet, America has practiced a thinly disguised industrial policy for decades, directed mainly at military products. Because it is largely unplanned, this industrial policy does not reach its potential. It gets watered down and sidetracked, though it still has had an important impact on some high-tech industries.

We do not want to oversell the potential gains from a more orderly industrial policy. Other things government does—from setting tax rates to instituting new regulations—are often more important than targeting resources at a given group of companies. A high foreign exchange rate, for example, can easily undo industrial policy efforts to encourage home industry to be at the head of global competition. The whole issue of foreign trade and investment policy will be explored in Chapter 17.

Questions

1. What is industrial policy? Is it a good idea?
2. Describe the differences between basic and applied research. Should government be involved in both types? Why or why not?
3. What should government do for sunrise industries? For sunset industries?
4. Describe America's industrial policy. How does it compare with other countries' industrial policies?
5. Discuss ARPA. Should it be given a more prominent role in executing industrial policy in the United States? How is it different from the NIST?

End Notes

1. Lee Iacocca with William Novak, *Iacocca: An Autobiography* (New York: Bantam, 1984), p. 330.
2. For descriptions of several countries' approaches, see Robert E. Driscoll and Jack N. Behrman, eds., *National Industrial Policies* (Cambridge, MA: Oelgeschlager, Gunn, and Hain, 1984); and Graham Hall, ed., *European Industrial Policy* (London: Croom, Helm, 1986).
3. Ira Magaziner and Robert Reich, *Minding America's Business* (New York: Vintage, 1982).
4. This term has almost as much stigma as does industrial policy. See, for instance, Lewis M. Branscomb, "Does America Need a Technology Policy?" *Harvard Business Review,* March–April 1992, p. 24. For comparative discussion, see Richard Nelson, ed., *National Innovation Systems: A Comparative Analysis* (Oxford: Oxford Business, 1993).
5. The terms *sunrise* and *sunset* industries were coined by Lester Thurow, *The Zero-Sum Society* (New York: Basic Books, 1980).
6. Otis L. Graham, Jr., *Losing Time: The Industrial Policy Debate* (Cambridge, MA: Harvard University Press, 1992), pp. 46–47.
7. See, for example, *Gaining New Ground: Technology Priorities for America's Future* (Washington, DC: Council on Competitiveness, 1991); *Building a Competitive America* (Washington, DC: Competitiveness Policy Council, 1992); and Panel on Government Role in Civilian Technology, *The Government Role in Civilian Technology: Building a New Alliance* (Washington, DC: National Academy Press, 1992).
8. Steven Greenhouse, "The Calls for an Industrial Policy Grow Louder," *New York Times,* July 19, 1992, p. 5.
9. Graham, *Losing Time,* p. 184.
10. "The Bashful Giant," *The Economist,* May 22, 1993, p. 91.
11. "Europe's Technology Policy," *The Economist,* January 9, 1993, p. 19.
12. *Critical Technologies Update* (Washington, DC: Council on Competitiveness, 1994).
13. Michael L. Dertouzos, Richard K. Lester, Robert M. Solow, and the MIT Commission on Industrial Productivity, *Made in America* (New York: Harper, 1990), p. 67.
14. "Could America Afford the Transistor Today?" *Business Week,* March 7, 1994, p. 80.
15. *Technology and the Economy* (Paris: Office for

Economic Cooperation and Development, 1992), p. 31.

16. *Science and Technology Policy Outlook* (Paris: Office for Economic Cooperation and Development, 1988), p. 17.

17. "Who Says Science Has to Pay Off Fast?" *Business Week,* March 21, 1994, p. 110.

18. David P. Hamilton, "False Alarm," *The Wall Street Journal,* May 20, 1994, p. R14.

19. For evidence, see Seymour Melman, *The Permanent War Economy,* rev. ed. (New York: Simon and Schuster, 1985).

20. Linda Cohen and Roger Noll, *The Technology Pork Barrel* (Washington, DC: Brookings Institution, 1991).

21. Melissa B. Robinson, "Pentagon Project Slights Northeast," *Boston Globe,* May 19, 1994, p. 44.

22. See, for example, Magaziner and Reich, *Minding America's Business.*

23. Richard Saltus, "Defense Agency May Be Innovation Model," *Boston Globe,* March 17, 1992, p. 1.

24. George Cabot Lodge, *Comparative Business–Government Relations* (Englewood Cliffs, NJ: Prentice Hall, 1990), pp. 133–53.

25. "Uncle Sam's Helping Hand," *The Economist,* April 2, 1994, pp. 77–79.

26. "Flat Panels: Can the U.S. Get Back into the Picture?" *Business Week,* November 30, 1992, p. 36; and "Japan's Liquid-Crystal Gold Rush," *Business Week,* January 17, 1994, p. 77.

27. G. Pascal Zachery, "Road Toward Success at 'Flat Screens' Is Full of Bumps," *The Wall Street Journal,* April 29, 1994, p. B3.

28. Bob Davis and G. Pascal Zachary, "Electronics Firms Get Push from Clinton to Join Industrial Policy Initiative in Flat-Panel Displays," *The Wall Street Journal,* April 28, 1994, p. A14.

29. "American Technology Policy," *The Economist,* July 25, 1992, p. 23.

30. Jean-Claude Derian, *America's Struggle for Leadership in Technology* (Cambridge, MA: MIT Press, 1990).

31. Bob Davis, "An Old, Quiet Agency Has Suddenly Become a High-Tech Leader," *The Wall Street Journal,* April 5, 1994, pp. Alff.

32. Asra Q. Nomani, "U.S. Selects Five Areas of Technology to Back with Research Funds in the '90s," *The Wall Street Journal,* April 26, 1994, p. B6.

33. "A Think Tank for, er 'Competitiveness,'" *Business Week,* April 20, 1992, p. 90.

34. Michael Schrage, "GOP Sweep Will Take a Broom to High-Tech Agenda," *Boston Sunday Globe,* November 13, 1994, p. 84.

35. Bob Davis and Helene Cooper, "Big Business, Striking It Rich in GOP 'Contract,' Stands by as Clinton's High-Tech Plans Get Cut," *The Wall Street Journal,* March 7, 1995, p. A20.

36. Branscomb, "Does America Need a Technology Policy?" p. 25.

37. Graham, *Losing Time,* p. 201.

38. Robert W. Preer, *The Emergence of Technopolis* (New York: Praeger, 1992), pp. 12–14. Also see Jurgen Schmandt and Robert Wilson, eds., *Promoting High-Technology Industry: Initiatives and Policies for State Governments* (Boulder, CO: Westview, 1987).

39. "Yin and Yang in Asia's Science Cities," *The Economist,* May 21, 1994, pp. 93–95.

40. "Industrial Policy," *Business Week,* April 6, 1992, p. 73.

41. Dertouzos et al., *Made in America,* p. 113.

42. Andrew P. Black, "Industrial Policy in West Germany," in *European Industrial Policy,* ed. Hall, pp. 84–127.

43. President's Commission on Industrial Competitiveness, *Global Competition: The New Reality* (Washington, DC: U.S. Government Printing Office, 1985).

44. Kevin P. Phillips, "U.S. Industrial Policy: Inevitable and Ineffective," *Harvard Business Review,* July–August 1992, pp. 104–12.

45. Daniel Benjamin, "Some Germans Fear They're Falling Behind in High-Tech Fields," *The Wall Street Journal,* April 27, 1994, p. Al.

17   PUBLIC POLICY AND FOREIGN TRADE AND INVESTMENT

A merchant, it has been said very properly, is not necessarily the citizen of any particular country. It is in a great measure indifferent to him from what place he carries on his trade; and a very trifling disgust will make him remove his capital, and together with it all the industry which it supports, from one country to another. No part of it can be said to belong to any particular country.

Adam Smith[1]

Government is a key player in international trade and investment. As we have seen throughout this book, the world economy is growing ever more integrated. Countries are tied to each other with the thread of global competition; they have come to depend on each other for prosperity. Any nation's involvement in the world economy is pushed and pulled by public policy decisions made at home. An important factor driving the surge in cross-border business, for example, is the decision taken in many countries to lower the regulatory barriers to overseas investment and to imported products.

As with all policy making, decisions about international trade and investment are swayed by interest groups. Global competition touches them in different ways. Some groups win and other groups lose, creating political fissures over what government should do. Governments have responded with a hodgepodge of often-discrepant public policies toward foreign commercial activity.

The plan of this chapter is to review the major problems posed to today's managers by the international political economy. We start by discussing trends in the global system for producing and consuming goods, and follow with an analysis of the rationale for policies for trade promotion and trade protection. In the rest of the chapter, we will go over the major multilateral and national institutions that govern trading relations.

Growing U.S. Involvement in the World Economy

For most of U.S. history, American business did not have to bother much about foreign competition. Given the vast domestic market, inputs and customers could be found without having to look beyond the nation's borders. There were, however, large-scale international capital movements in the 19th century, so the United States was never as insular an economy as sometimes imagined. As Figure 17–1 shows, from 1970 to 1980 the share of GNP represented by merchandise imports and exports doubled, from about 8 percent to 16 percent, roughly the level today.

There is a myth that the United States is less engaged in international commerce than are other advanced countries. This is not true. By virtue of its size, the United States is the world's largest exporter. America accounts for around 18 percent of total exports among industrialized nations, more than any other nation. It is by far the leader in commercial service exports (not shown in Figure 17–1), as opposed to merchandise, with a market share equal to Germany, Britain, and Japan combined.[2] The top service exports are travel, passenger fares, port services, foreign transport, and education (foreign students paid $6.1 billion in tuition and fees to American schools in 1992).

Given the huge internal U.S. market, it might be expected that trade in goods would represent a smaller reported share of national income than in other countries. Even here the contrasts are less than imagined. Despite Japan's reputation as an export giant, merchandise exports do not weigh much more in the Japanese economy (about 9 percent of GNP versus 7 percent in the United States in 1990). In proportion to their size, European countries export more than either the United States or Japan. Yet, those figures are deceptive because of shipments within the European Union that may bear more similarity to a delivery between, say, New York and Illinois than to a true overseas sale. So, however one measures it, the United States cannot be considered a straggler in exports.

The Trade Gap

Still, Americans are alarmed about the yawning trade gap that has opened over the last decade or so. As recently as 1981, the United States exported as many manufactured goods as it imported; by 1984, the current account of the balance of payments (the broadest measure of foreign trade) was in deficit at an annual amount of $100 billion. Once-proud U.S. firms had their markets taken away in a broad range of manufacturing industries, from automobiles to high-fidelity equipment, from motorcycles to machine tools.[3]

The trade gap may not be as deep as the numbers suggest due to measurement problems and the growth of service trade (see Box 17–1). Still, the trend is troubling. The deepest imbalance is with Japan. Between 1981 and 1988, the cumulative trade deficit with that country alone was more than $300 billion. There is little likelihood that the trade deficit will drop much below the current level for years to come.[4] (See Figure 17–2.)

FIGURE 17–1

Foreign trade has risen briskly in the United States, but it is still more important in some other advanced capitalist countries.

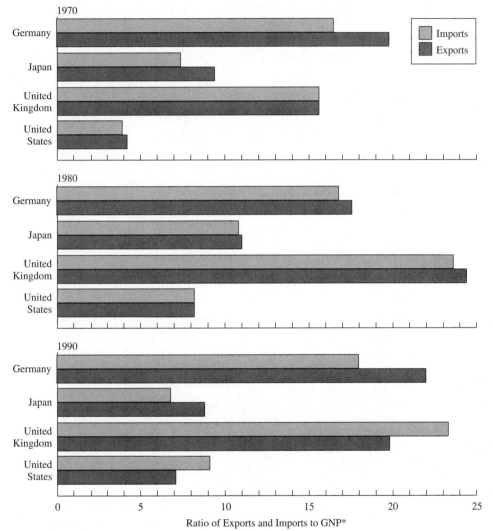

Ratio of Exports and Imports to GNP*

*Merchandise f.o.b.: comprises the market value of movable goods and related distributive services.
Source: World Bank, *World Tables* (Baltimore: Johns Hopkins University Press, various years).

When the United States or any nation buys more goods and services from abroad than it sells, it must somehow cover the difference. The only way to finance a trade deficit is by selling assets. Thus, foreigners are increasingly buying U.S. stocks, bonds, real estate, and sometimes whole companies. When a foreign company acquires a domestic firm, or sets up a new production facility of its own, the technical term is **direct foreign investment.** This is opposed to portfolio investment that produces income but not control. Japan is often assumed to be the biggest foreign investor in the United States, but this is a misperception due to Japan having made many high-profile purchases such as the Rockefeller Center (later in financial trouble) and the Pebble Beach golf course (since sold at a loss). Japan is the biggest creditor worldwide, yet, with less fanfare, other countries such as Canada and Britain have bought more U.S. assets.

Foreign Debt

Because of the surge in foreign investment made here, the United States became a debtor nation in 1985 for the first time since World War I. In simple language, Americans now own fewer assets abroad than other citizens own here (Figure 17–2). Again, there may be measurement errors traced to the accuracy of book values and market values of foreign assets. But these errors do not change the fact that, for the future, the United States must pay more dividends, interest, and rent to foreigners than it used to.

Box 17–1

The U.S. Trade Deficit Is in Part a Statistical Illusion

Official data on U.S. foreign trade are misleading. The Commerce Department has a pretty good record in tracking merchandise, though the trend toward intercompany transfers skews the numbers. By 1989, 28 percent of U.S. exports, and 19 percent of imports, were shipped between affiliates of American firms.[1] To a large extent, the price of these goods is arbitrary. To avoid taxes in the United States, multinational enterprises routinely report artificially low export figures and inflated import figures.

The more serious source of error is the difficulty in measuring trade in services, which is the fastest growing sector of international trade. Bank fees for making foreign loans are missed. So are money management fees for foreigners' holdings of U.S. stocks and bonds.

Imports and exports of services and manufactured goods can become hopelessly confused. If engineers working for an American firm design computer equipment that is later built by a foreign subsidiary, this transaction is not recorded as an export because no money changes hands. Yet, if the computer equipment is sold back to the United States, it is classed as an import and adds to the trade deficit though much of the value was produced by the American engineers.[2]

Correcting these accounting errors is not easy, but they suggest the foreign trade picture is brighter than sometimes thought. The miscalculations should not be a cause for smugness, however. Other countries probably are making similar mistakes, so the real position of the United States in world trade may not be much different from what the official figures show.

[1]David B. Yoffie, ed., *Beyond Free Trade* (Boston: Harvard Business School Press, 1993), p. xi.

[2]Mark Levinson, "The Great Trade Hoax of 1993," *Newsweek,* November 15, 1993, pp. 48–49.

FIGURE 17–2

The U.S. position in foreign trade and international investment has eroded in recent years

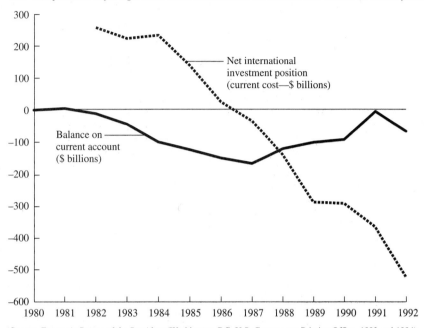

Source: *Economic Report of the President* (Washington, DC: U.S. Government Printing Office, 1992 and 1994).

Foreign payments sap American resources that could be used for other purposes, such as reinvestment in plant and equipment at home. The opportunity cost for U.S. society will grow bigger while the trade deficit persists.[5] Should foreign investors ever lose confidence in the United States, there could be a mass flight of capital. To adjust, Americans would have to cut their standard of living just as have Mexicans, Brazilians, and others when their debt crises broke in the 1980s.

The penetration of the U.S. market by foreign-made goods, the trade deficit, and the growth of foreign investment are important public policy concerns today. They have provoked a strong nationalistic reaction to "buy American," on the one hand, and to "bash Japan" and other trading partners, on the other. What is government to do?

Theories of International Trade

Free Trade

Two strongly held ideologies provide alternative answers to this question. One is the (classical) liberal view. It advocates **free trade.** As Adam Smith argued 200 years ago, "If a country can supply us with a commodity cheaper than we ourselves can make it, better buy it of them with some part of the produce of our own industry, employed in a way in which we have some advantage."[6] Smith's point was that different countries hold a leg up in different dimensions of foreign trade. The invisible hand makes an international division of labor, with each country concentrating on the set of products it is best suited to make. The proper role of government usually is to stand back and let this process work itself out naturally.

To illustrate, Smith pointed out that Scotland is poorly adapted to grow grapes and produce wine. The opposite is true of France. It would be folly for the Scots to try to be self-sufficient in wine. Foreign trade takes place because people want the specialized goods produced elsewhere. Scotland swaps its products, say, Scotch whiskey, for French wine, and residents of both countries enjoy a higher standard of living than if they only had local products from which to choose. It follows that foreign trade without restrictions is the best policy with which government can comply, because unfettered exchange fosters the most efficient use of resources on a global scale. Free trade is a positive-sum game where everyone wins. Efforts to improve on international market forces are unnecessary and probably counterproductive.

The liberal argument has been critiqued on several grounds. One objection is that it is not realistic. Governments are apt to treat foreign trade as a zero-sum game where gains come at the losers' expense, and not as the win–win situation described by liberals. No matter how persuasive the rationale for free trade is in the abstract, political pressure makes intervention hard to avoid in practice. Political leaders are leery of open markets if the result is to be the death of an important industry due to foreign competition. They will likely try to defend and encourage home industries at the expense of other countries', often as a means, other than military force, of expressing national power.

If one country closes its markets, the rest feel forced to respond in kind. Without reciprocity, free trade will simply give trading partners lopsided advantages. In Smith's words: "The very bad policy of one country may thus render it in some measure dangerous and imprudent to establish what would otherwise be the best policy in another."[7] He did not think as a rule that governments ought to open their national markets unilaterally.

Further, there is an issue of market failure. Markets do not always take account of long-run national competitiveness. For many lines of trade, a country's comparative advantage does not lie in its natural resources or location but in such manmade factors as human capital or infrastructure. In rising industries, the first country in the field has advantages to the detriment of latecomers. And in declining industries, private decisions may lead to too much reduction in capacity, since private firms do not bear all the cost of industry shrinkage.[8] The existence of market failure in international trade argues for public policy to relieve the problem.

Mercantilism

The main rival theory of international trade is related to **mercantilism,** the doctrine of activist public policy we mentioned in passing in Chapter 2. Mercantilism often is associated with France's finance minister Jean-Baptiste Colbert (1619–1683), though he never used the term and his brand of economic policy was not original but represented standard economic thinking from the 15th century onward. During the early modern period, France and other European powers wanted to promote national self-sufficiency in production, the formation of domestic manufacturing industries, and the domination of foreign trade. These goals led to public policies that tried to minimize imports and maximize exports. The objective was to maintain a trade surplus, or so-called favorable balance of trade.

Great Britain followed a mercantilist approach before and during its Industrial Revolution. The Crown (government in contemporary language) made grants of monopoly status to domestic companies and made foreign treaties to obtain exclusive trading privileges for these companies. It put taxes on imports (called **tariffs**) and paid "bounties" to encourage other countries to buy British products. Competition among domestic merchants was discouraged so they would not bid against each other and drive up prices. Under mercantilist policies, business and government became allies. Each sheltered line of trade generated income that business and government split.

Smith gave mercantilism a bad name. His foremost objection to this strategy was that, compared to free trade, it hurt consumers and thus was socially inefficient. The reason international trade is useful to society is to import the things people want; exports are just a means to pay for those imports. Exporting for exporting's sake makes society poorer over the long run, though it might help some particular firms get rich.

Still, Smith was a subtle enough thinker to make exceptions to his critique of mercantilism. The East India Company and other companies chartered by the monarchy opened markets around the world to British goods. Other grants of monopolies were designed to encourage new industries from abroad to start in Britain. For instance, the Navigation Acts, repealed only in 1849, gave the English shipping industry priority in world trade and stifled colonial manufacturing to the benefit of British firms. Thus, Smith could find helpful features in the Navigation Acts, once calling them "perhaps, the wisest of all commercial regulations of England," because they promoted national defense.[9]

The net effect of British mercantilism was to nurture companies that, when *The Wealth of Nations* appeared, were strong enough to exploit new markets and new technology, making England "the workshop of the world."[10] Of course, British consumers paid a price to build British industry. Goods cost more, and there were fewer from which to choose than would have been the case with unimpeded trade. Producers in other nations, especially colonies, suffered from British market power, too. But mercantilism did nurture in the British Isles an industrial base that would dominate world trade for decades.

We will never know if early British industry would have thrived the same way in an unprotected environment. Only after the Industrial Revolution was well-established did the British government feel confident enough to throw its market open to foreign trade. The Corn Laws, which sheltered agriculture, were annulled in 1846. Over the next 15 years, most tariffs were abolished in Britain.

As we will see in a later section of this chapter, most other western nations followed Britain's lead and did *not* open their markets before their economies were industrialized. They, too, usually waited until their industries seemed strong enough to stand the competition.

Mercantilism Today

Today, neo-mercantilists call for policies similar to those followed by Britain until 1846. On the defensive side, they advocate **protectionism** to stop imports and shelter domestic industry from foreign competition. On the offensive side, neo-mercantilists urge policies to help domestic industry crack foreign markets and sell more of its wares overseas. The reason is that no country's comparative advantage in international trade is fixed. Neo-mercantilism aims to move the designated country from low value-added activities (based on raw materials or simple labor) to sophisticated activities (using brain power) that are worth more in the global market. It also aims to shift the country from declining sectors (e.g., heavy industry) into growing ones (e.g., high technology). The protected home market is used as a profit sanctuary to launch export drives and seize a world lead in target industries. Japan and the East Asian NICs (except Hong Kong) have followed neo-mercantilist strategies in the post–World War II era.

Neo-mercantilist thinking has received an intellectual boost in recent years with the development of so-called new trade theory.[11] According to this theory, free trade works for industries that border on being perfectly competitive but does not necessarily fit industries with few sellers, few buyers, and many differences among products. Some imperfectly competitive sectors are *strategic,* meaning the social gains to the industry exceed the private gains because of external benefits.

For example, the industry may have technological spillovers that profit other groups of companies. Or it might provide a critical component that is used throughout the economy. There may only be room in the world for one, two, or three enterprises in the strategic industry. How many civilian aircraft makers can the global economy support, for example? It might pay a country to subsidize such an industry, especially if other nations are doing so.

This theory provides the base for a strategic trade policy. If a branch of the economy is strategic, and if competitors are being subsidized overseas, the national government should consider furnishing protection while the industry gets started. Especially where scale and learning economies exist, private investors may view investment in an emerging industry as too chancy unless government offers tariff protection.[12] This idea is not entirely novel. From the beginning of the American republic, many policy makers made the similar "infant industry argument," that emerging lines of business should be given a refuge while they get off the ground (see the next section).

New trade theory departs from this more familiar rationale for protectionism because it calls for focusing on critical sectors. Since there are often first-mover advantages in strategic industries, a short-term subsidy can create a lasting lead in the world economy. Once a few companies have established themselves, the cost of establishing a competing firm may be so daunting that no other country will dare sponsor a new entrant.

Japan may have been intimidated from entering the civilian aircraft industry, for example, by the large lead that American and European firms have, which makes it very expensive to catch them. Students should know, however, that the Japanese are breaking into this business by pursuing strategic alliances with Boeing. They are gaining knowledge about technology and production they hope will allow them to found an independent aircraft industry later.

The extent to which strategic trade policy works in the real world is another matter. As we have seen throughout this book, governments need not be wise or objective. Because political institutions are subject to lobbying, this brand of co-operative capitalism may simply reward the best organized lines of business, not the most deserving ones. Politicians also may be tempted to use the export subsidies, industrial licenses, and so on for political patronage, to reward allies and punish foes, instead of on the merits. For these reasons, even the originators of strategic trade theory are skeptical about its practical use.[13]

Strategic trade policy overlaps with other facets of the business–government partnership. Public aid to build world-class, critical industries goes beyond trade policy, narrowly understood. At the margin, it cannot be separated from industrial and technology policy—the topic addressed at length in Chapter 16.

Inevitability of Protectionism

Whatever the theoretical pros and cons of mercantilism are, governments have usually opted for some variant of it. American manufacturers benefited from mercantile protection for most of the republic's history. Favoritism toward domestic producers is reflected in the U.S. Constitution, which forbids taxes on exports and allows taxes on imports. The framers of the Constitution wanted no public policy to discourage exporters, but they envisioned the possibility of restricting the purchase of foreign commodities.

With this bias in place, the United States industrialized behind high tariff walls. Alexander Hamilton (1755–1804) was the most prominent early advocate of protectionism and state-led industrialization. As secretary of state, he proposed a systematic and comprehensive plan to encourage manufacturing and large-scale enterprise. Presented in his famous *Report on the Subject of Manufactures* (1791), the idea was for government to be the spearhead of modern industry. Europe, with its technical superiority and greater capital stock, he argued, would never allow American industry to grow up on its own. "[T]he United States cannot exchange with Europe on equal terms; and the want of reciprocity would render them the victim . . ."[14] Thus a strong federal state ought to subsidize domestic business, create a captive local market through import duties, and sponsor "internal improvements" in communication and transport.[15]

Hamilton's activist public policies were opposed by the farming community.

Political economy expects such a result. Farmers had no stake in protecting manufacturing. That policy hurt their business by making imported machinery more costly, and by inviting foreign countries to strike back against tobacco and other agricultural exports. Support for government activism came from ironmasters and merchants in New England, New York, and Pennsylvania—groups that benefited economically. Federal trade policy ebbed and flowed in the coming decades, as the political balance between East and West, North and South shifted. Protective tariffs reached a peak in 1828 and were reduced in a process ending in the Walker Tariff of 1846. After the Civil War, tariffs rose steadily through 1900, when they stood at 49 percent. (See Figure 17–3.)

A comparable pattern of protection held in Germany. Before unification, German industry was aided by a discriminatory customs union among German-speaking states (the *Zollverein*). After 1871, Germany put up high tariffs to shield domestic companies. On close examination, all of Europe save Britain pursued mercantilist policies during the late 1800s. They saw a link between economic strength and national political power, and regarded foreign trade as too important to be left to the private sector alone.[16]

Protectionism continued to be the reality of public policy around the world in the decades following World War I. In 1930, for instance, the United States passed the Smoot-Hawley Act that raised tariffs to historic highs. The driving force was to help special interests hurt by cheap foreign goods. Protectionism can trigger trade wars, and, within two years of the Smoot-Hawley Act's passage, 60 countries increased similar tariffs, both to retaliate against the United States and to help their industries. The tit-for-tat tariffs canceled each other and stifled

FIGURE 17–3

Tariffs were high for most of U.S. history, but they have been falling since the 1930s

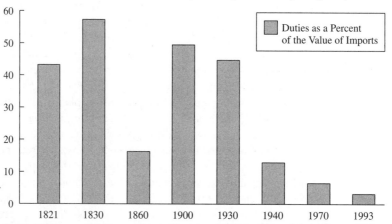

Source: U.S. Bureau of the Census, *Historical Statistics of the United States: Colonial Times to 1970* (Washington, DC: U.S. Government Printing Office, 1975); U.S. Bureau of the Census, *Statistical Abstract of the United States* (Washington, DC: U.S. Government Printing Office, 1994).

world trade. That ordeal led President Roosevelt to cut tariffs in 1934. Since then, all U.S. presidents have stood publicly for a more open world trading system, though, as we will see later in this chapter, they have selectively supported protectionism.

The experience of the 1930s illustrates a difficulty with the mercantilist approach—one that reflects the familiar problem of collectively unsound solitary action. While some countries can cut imports and boost exports, all countries cannot do so at once. On average, world imports have to equal world exports. It is mathematically impossible for every country to run a trade surplus. Should every country restrict imports, all will have trouble selling their exports. Thus, mercantilist or protectionist policies can prove self-defeating. This quandary has driven many countries in the postwar era to work for international coordination on import and export policies. As we will see later, they have signed a raft of reciprocal treaties to stop blocking each others' exports in the hope of selling more abroad themselves.

Government Vacillation

Political economy posits that governments are inclined to favor policies of unfettered trade mainly when they believe their home industry's position in the international economy is secure. This was as true of the United States in the 1940s as it was of Britain in the 1850s. Governments' ability to execute such policies, on the other hand, is hampered by the asymmetry in the internal distribution of the cost and benefit of freer trade. The gains (lower prices, better products) are apt to be diffused among all consumers. The pain (shuttered factories, layoffs) falls on a few communities and industries. In a political system that responds to constituent groups, as the pluralist American system does, these victims of free trade can make a strong claim for public help.[17]

Yet, the results of political pressure are hard to predict. Foreign trade is a redistributive policy area: some sectors stand to be hurt by the protection that helps other sectors. Thus, protectionist pressure does not go unanswered. Someone is bound to apply heat from the other side. Hard as the Big Three automakers and the United Auto Workers pushed for a restriction on the quantity of Japanese car imports in the early 1980s, for example, they did not speak for all economic interests. The American International Automobile Dealers Association, the Automobile Importers of America, and the Japanese Automobile Manufacturers Association were just some of the interest groups pushing the other way.[18] As with many redistributive policies, foreign trade issues are apt to drive a wedge between interest groups. The result often is a policy standoff in the United States, with the different sides creating cross-cutting political pressures on government that cancel each other.

The tendency toward political stalemate may explain the finding of many researchers that U.S. trade agreements do not correspond closely with the preference of interest groups. Tariffs are more than a function of who lobbies the hardest. Given some freedom to maneuver by the lack of consensus over foreign commercial policy, the president sometimes can take the high road and try to do what is best for the country—that is, he can work for freer trade. Even if one rejects such lofty motivation as unlikely, clearly, negotiators must sometimes rebuff entreaties for protection lest international trade talks unravel.[19]

In either case, political economy analysis helps explain the paradox of current foreign economic policy trends, when the U.S. and rival nations emphasize protectionism and open markets concurrently.[20] Sometimes, they yield to pressures from local producers that they be sheltered or aided in foreign competition; other times, they respond to other political pressure for cheap imports and tit-for-tat opening of foreign markets.

Fortunately, protectionism costs society less than many people realize. It does reduce the efficiency of the world economy, and it fragments markets so some firms cannot realize economies of scale. Many studies have tried to estimate the size of these losses. For the United States, the annual cost of import restrictions is usually found to be 1 percent or less of the GNP.[21]

Part of the reason the cost of protection is not that high is that market forces often are more powerful than public policy. Trade barriers are never impenetrable; businesspeople are inventive and will find ways around them. History teaches that even embargoes like the one put on Iraq in 1990 and enforced by military power are porous. Iraq continues to export oil and import essential goods despite United Nations' sanctions.

Foreign Investment

Business need not turn to smuggling to get around trade barriers, of course. Perhaps the favorite path is through direct foreign investment. Instead of trading with the target country, the company sets up or buys a business there. In the United States, the proportion of output held by foreign-controlled firms tripled in the 1980s.[22] By the end of the 1980s, U.S. subsidiaries of foreign enterprises employed about 3 percent of the U.S. labor force.[23] The boom in direct foreign investment was driven by companies trying to hurdle over trade obstacles (actual or potential) to have secure access to the U.S. market. This experience illustrates an irony of protectionist trade policy: the effort to slow the pace of imports can deflect the energy of foreign competitors onto another, more aggressive track. Having Japanese, German, and other rival firms producing within U.S. borders presents an even greater challenge to domestic producers than do foreign products alone.

As with trade, public policy toward direct foreign investment is ambivalent. The free movement of capital around the world is the corollary of free trade in goods and services. The theory is that, if government stands back, investment resources will go where they produce the greatest return. The reality is that, as with trade, capital is not always allowed to move unencumbered from one country to the next.

In the popular imagination, foreign-owned companies are often pictured as a Trojan horse. Their owners are suspect for lack of patriotism, for representing a potential threat to national sovereignty. Pressures are created to regulate foreign investment.[24] Yet, opinion is equivocal. People know also that foreign-owned companies possess valuable skills and technology. Japanese automakers have proved they can run efficient auto plants in the United States and have had a positive demonstration effect on Detroit. These transplant companies also have created employment. So people are not sure whether direct foreign investment is a good or bad thing. This uncertainty is reflected in public policy, with governments sometimes luring **multinational corporations (MNCs)** and putting strings on them simultaneously.

Multinational Corporations

MNCs are giant enterprises whose businesses span more than one country. They control more and more production, either by themselves or in partnership with other multinational companies. From 1983 to 1990, corporate investment across borders grew four times faster than world output. According to the United Nations, there are today at least 35,000 MNCs controlling 170,000 affiliates.[25] They manufacture one part in one place, another part somewhere else, and assemble them in a third place. The web of cross-border corporate investments and alliances blurs the distinction between what is domestic and what is foreign. "Made in America" (or in any other country) is a term that means less and less today.[26]

Consider the developing countries first. India, Mexico, and other late-developing countries have often tried to attract foreign investors with various carrots—tax breaks, access to foreign exchange, and so on. Yet, they also have employed sticks to control MNCs, such as mandating that there be majority local ownership of foreign subsidiaries, or that a high percent of parts be bought from local firms (so-called local content rules). As their economies stalled in the 1980s, many LDCs reluctantly concluded that such two-sided policies had outlived their usefulness. In the quest for more capital to modernize their moribund economies, many have recently liberalized their foreign investment rules, putting away the sticks to give MNCs greater discretion.[27]

Economically advanced countries have usually been less averse to foreign direct investment, though 20 years ago there was widespread worry in Europe about American MNCs. Those fears receded as the advantage of U.S. firms declined, and they resulted in no significant public policy in Europe to block American capital. To the contrary, European countries often bid for foreign investment with incentive programs.

According to a U.N. report, programs to woo specific companies are growing so fast that governments are overpaying. Incentives for a Mercedes-Benz Swatchmobile factory in France in 1994, for instance, cost $57,000 for each job won. Such giveaways can trigger similar responses by other countries that are counterproductive. The U.N. report suggests international cooperation may be needed to curb the excessive use of incentives for MNCs.[28]

As Chapter 7 reported, in the United States, the task of trying to entice foreign corporations has been picked up mainly by state governments. Those programs also have gotten out of hand and sometimes do more harm than good by subsidizing companies at the expense of essential government services.

The Exceptional Case of Japan

Outside capital now flows easily into the OECD member countries, with one exception: Japan. Unlike Europe and America, Japan is barely touched by foreign-owned firms. By legal right, Japan is open to overseas investment, yet foreign companies have a hard time getting into business in Japan. There were a mere 18 purchases of Japanese companies by foreigners in 1990![29] Just as they informally block foreign goods and services from entering their country, the Japanese put up many informal obstacles to MNCs investing locally.

Political support for free capital movement depends on a fair exchange. If one country—for example, Japan—is seen as playing by different rules, calls for it to make concessions are inevitable. In the United States and Europe, there is legitimate concern that their protected home base gives Japanese firms an unfair advantage. Pessimists worry that Japanese companies will use their investments abroad as an economic beachhead, sourcing most parts from Japan, not local suppliers. They may opt to keep the more value-added activities at home and farm out the menial activities overseas.[30] Evidence suggests that corporate domicile, particularly for Japanese firms, does have a ripple effect of making the U.S. trade deficit worse by increasing the demand for imported parts.[31]

The greater danger for Americans is that Japan may be made the scapegoat for the nation's economic woes. As we have seen throughout this book, American business and government have many self-inflicted wounds, and the nation's relative economic slide cannot be blamed mainly on others. The rising tide of Japanese investment in the United States can be traced to the deepening federal budget deficit and America's low savings rate, which together aroused an enormous appetite for foreign capital. Japan's biased investment (and trade) policies are not the pivotal issues. We come back to this topic in Chapter 18.

The General Agreement on Tariffs and Trade

Most governments today at least pay lip service to the virtues of open trade in goods, services, and capital. Since World War II, this doctrine has been the approved guide for public policy around the world. Determined to devise an international economic order that avoided the mistakes of the Great Depression, the United States and allied nations signed the **General Agreement on Tariffs and Trade (GATT)** in 1948. The goal was to minimize controls on cross-border economic deals on the assumption that doing so would generate greater affluence for all countries.

The GATT was technically an agreement, not an organization in the United Nations family like the IMF, though it had a permanent secretariat in Geneva. Plans for an official trade body, worked out in 1944 when the World Bank and IMF were set up, fell apart due to opposition from the U.S. Senate. Fifty years later, in 1995, a new **World Trade Organization (WTO)** finally was created with stronger powers to execute the GATT accords. With 121 nations participating, and more joining all the time, the organization covers most of the world's trade.

The guiding principle of the trade pact is that one-sided economic relations chill international trade. To stop that from happening, each country is supposed to bare its markets the same way to every other country. Parties to the GATT thus agreed to prohibit quotas on imports and to give most-favored-nation status to all contracting countries. Most-favored-nation status refers to an agreement between two countries to apply tariffs to each other at rates as low as are applied to any other country.

GATT Negotiations

The GATT has been renegotiated several times to reduce tariffs more. The reductions are worked out through long multinational meetings, called rounds. Eight tariff-cutting rounds have taken place so far. As a result, the average tariff in the United States fell to under 4 percent in the 1980s.

The latest session, the Uruguay Round, started in 1986 and ran for seven years. It was directed mainly at agriculture. The Uruguay Round also worked for the first time on a set of rules to cover cross-border services, a rapidly growing $900 billion form of trade, and it worked to protect intellectual property, including patents, copyrights, and trademarks. One of its most important items was to create the WTO. With so many participants, each with its own industries to worry about, the talks were painfully slow.

Agricultural commodities had been left off the GATT rules from the beginning at the insistence of the United States, which had large, subsidized agricultural surpluses. During the 1980s, the United States reversed itself to become a champion of freer trade in agriculture. No doubt, the fact that the U.S. farm industry was in strong shape compared to other countries' contributed to the change in policy.

The European Union and Japan became the objects of criticism for screening their farmers from global competition. American negotiators insisted that Europe change its Common Agricultural Policy and that Tokyo open its home market to American rice and other farm products. France, in particular, opposed giving ground on these issues, which it feared would ruin many rural French communities. With French farmers taking to the streets, Paris could not accept a compromise. The Uruguay Round of the GATT negotiations collapsed in 1990. Under U.S. pressure, the talks resumed later and finally ended in a rush of last-minute deals at the end of 1993. The deal was projected to increase global income by $500 billion over 10 years.[32]

Weaknesses in the GATT

Appearances aside, GATT's effect in liberalizing world trade is unfulfilled. Four fine points in the treaty weaken it in operation.

Escape Clause. One is the so-called escape clause. This clause is a safeguard provision that allows countries to protect a domestic industry that is injured by foreign trade. The United States has used the escape clause to help more than 30 industries since 1947, including ceramic tableware, nonrubber footwear, citizens band radios, clothespins, mushrooms, and motorcycles.

The escape clause also allows "orderly marketing agreements" to resolve trade disputes. These are formal deals by which exporting nations undertake to limit exports of sensitive products. The United States, for example, has had orderly marketing agreements with Korea, Taiwan, and Japan to limit shipments of color televisions. It is revealing that the agreements failed to save the U.S. television manufacturing industry.[33]

The escape clause is a powerful trade weapon. Still, countries are hesitant to invoke it due to the risk of provoking a trade war, whose results can be hard to foresee. In the 1960s, for instance, the American sheet glass, carpet, and rug industries received escape clause protection from European imports. Then, the European Common Market retaliated against U.S. chemical products, helping to set off a so-called Chicken War over frozen poultry exports. The GATT mediated the dispute and found the United States had a just grievance. The country was permitted to raise tariffs on brandy (hurting France), on potato starch and Dexedrine (hurting Holland), and on light trucks (hurting Germany). An importer of brandy challenged the ruling, but it was upheld by the U.S. Court of Customs and Patent Appeals.[34] Governments would prefer not be drawn into open-ended disputes such as this one and will use the escape clause mainly as a last resort.

Free Trade Areas. A second loophole in the GATT is for the creation of special free trade areas to encourage closer integration of participating countries' economies. Participants in free trade areas give each other preferences. This is legal, but it clearly contradicts the GATT's principle of nondiscrimination in international trade.

The best example of a free trade area is the European Union, where products of member countries have advantages. This arrangement has had a huge positive effect in boosting trade within Europe and in raising living standards there. The European Union also has helped its members avoid the warfare that was so much a part of European history in the first half of the 20th century.

The North American Free Trade Agreement (NAFTA) is similar, though too new to evaluate fully. Like the European Union, it removes most tariffs among the United States, Canada, and Mexico. But the name NAFTA is deceptive.

For one thing, Chile and other non–North American countries want to join NAFTA. More important, the idea of the accord is not to promote "free trade" (except among the participating states) but to construct a regional trading bloc that will be harder for European and Asian companies to enter. The three charter members invented NAFTA partly to offset the trend toward a single market in Europe. The European Union, in return, is considering creating a Euro-Mediterranean Economic Area in North Africa and the Middle East, which would be the largest free trade zone in the world.[35]

It is symptomatic that to line up the votes needed to get NAFTA passed in 1993, President Clinton granted protection to tomato growers, wheat farmers, corn syrup producers, and other narrow economic interests. Thus, even within the three-country area, trade is far from open. U.S. labor unions suspect the agreement is a cover for companies to move jobs to Mexico to take advantage of cheap Mexican labor—or to drive down U.S. wages by threatening to move.

Nontariff Barriers. A third factor that mitigates GATT's effect is that the treaty says little about **nontariff barriers** to trade. Countries have many ways to block imports without having to impose a formal tariff or quota. They may use import licensing procedures as a delaying tactic, effectively driving up the price of imports. They may grant preference to local suppliers in government contracts. They may employ official product specifications to hamper foreign suppliers. France, for example, restricts the import of British lamb ostensibly because of pesticides. Britain, for its part, restricts imports of French poultry, also on spurious health grounds.[36] These nontariff barriers help British and French farmers, but at a cost to British and French consumers.

Such practices are far from disappearing. According to one study, in 1983, 35 percent of U.S. consumption of manufactured goods was covered by major nontariff barriers. That was up from 20 percent three years earlier.[37] See Box 17–2 for a description of nontariff trade barriers used by Tokyo.

Bilateral Arrangements. A fourth factor that partly neutralizes the GATT is the prospect of individual deals between countries that bypass the treaty. These usually are called "voluntary restraint agreements"—informal pacts to limit exports. An example is the restriction on Japanese car shipments to the United States negotiated in 1981. It falls outside GATT's purview because it is officially a private arrangement with Japanese automakers. The initial quota was for 1.68 million vehicles, a cut of 140,000 vehicles from the previous year, and a gift to the U.S. car industry. Because it is "voluntary," this arrangement does not bind the United States to compensate Japan under the rules of GATT.

The automobile trade restraint salvaged some auto worker jobs, though at a cost to consumers of about $160,000 per job saved.[38] It may not have helped domestic automakers as much as thought either, for it encouraged the Japanese to import larger cars that would compete directly with Detroit's models. If a manufacturer must sell fewer cars, he can make each car more expensive to maintain the same cash flow. Also, as suggested above, the voluntary restraint sped up the decision by Toyota, Nissan, Honda, and others to establish assembly plants in the United States. The products of these Japanese transplants are not covered by the trade quota with Japan.

Anyhow, creative policies such as voluntary trade restraints enable countries to adhere publicly to the canon of free trade while continuing to practice protec-

Box 17–2

Japan Uses Many Nontariff Barriers to Trade, Though the Impact Is Fading

Japan is well known for its trade barriers. Under a 1949 law, all imports needed licenses, the granting of which was controlled by the Ministry of International Trade and Industry. Still, most import restrictions were dismantled by the 1960s under pressure from GATT. By the 1980s, Japan had lower tariffs and fewer quotas on its books than most industrial countries. These reforms did not mean Japan truly embraced free trade, however.

Officials found a variety of informal barriers to fill in for the lost formal barriers to imports. These included:

- Product standards that were deliberately set differently from foreign products.
- Testing and certification processes for foreign goods that required expensive and time-consuming individual inspection.
- Customs procedures that could involve delays and arbitrary actions by officials.

- Government procurement practices that were manipulated to serve domestic suppliers.
- Off-the-record advisement from officials to importers or users to inhibit imports.[1]

Recent evidence suggests, however, that these informal procedures are losing their punch, as the United States continues to apply political pressure to pry open Japan's markets. By 1990, Japan was the world's third largest importer. Measured per head, imports were pretty similar to the United States': $1,900 against $2,050.[2] Japan is still made the whipping boy for many American trade problems, but facts no longer warrant the same level of protest.

[1]Edward J. Lincoln, *Japan's Unequal Trade* (Washington, DC: Brookings Institution, 1990), p. 15.
[2]"Trade Made the Ship to Go," *The Economist,* January 11, 1992.

tion of home markets. One reason for the formal success of the GATT negotiations is exactly because countries have invented other ways to counter the effect of lower tariffs. Thus, they can work for less protectionism by other countries and still have the flexibility to shield their industries when pressed. Meanwhile, the GATT accords have produced public bureaucracies in member countries that act like local lobbies of producers and do not represent the interests of consumers.

The many flaws in the GATT accords do not mean the agreement is meaningless or, worse, damaging to the world economy. While it does not live up fully to its promise (no public policy ever does), the GATT has encouraged the boom in foreign trade since 1945, which, in turn, has made many countries prosperous. This is why, despite misgivings, almost every nation is a party to the trade pact and why, despite some lapses, progress is being made toward ever freer international trading regimes.

Export Promotion

The other side of the coin from protectionism is policies to encourage exports. Government subsidies that intentionally and directly help exports are explicitly proscribed by the GATT. But, as with import restrictions, there are ways around the spirit of the GATT accords in the export domain. All advanced nations give local companies billions of dollars of export credits, often at below-market interest rates. The Export-Import Bank, an independent government-established bank, provides this service for American firms.

Under the Clinton administration, the Ex-Im Bank has become more aggressive about financing U.S. exports in emerging markets. For example, in 1993, India received $60 million in financing to buy a modern air control system from Raytheon Corporation. The grant portion of the financing was 45 percent and was intended to fight off competition from the government-backed Thomson conglomerate of France, which tried to win the contract after bidding was finished, according to Raytheon.[39]

Hidden Subsidies

Many other hidden subsidies for exporters are possible. Consider the case of the European aircraft consortium, Airbus Industrie. It has had the advantage of direct subsidies worth perhaps $12 billion from European governments bent on building a company that can compete with Boeing and other U.S. firms. Airbus had ready access to government loans for new ventures that it did not always have to repay.[40] With government sponsorship, Airbus also can arrange for seemingly unrelated payoffs to the governments of its foreign customers (of course, many airlines are state-owned). In one case, Air India agreed to buy several Airbus planes in the mid-1980s. In exchange, France apparently promised the government of India technical assistance cleaning the Ganges River and accelerated delivery of French Mirage military jets for the Indian air force.[41]

Boeing, the world leader in civilian aircraft, complained about Airbus's subsidies. The Seattle firm pressed Washington to parley a settlement, but it was reluctant to file a formal grievance under GATT. Boeing feared reprisals from E.U. members that were major buyers of Boeing's products. The federal government was itself divided on the issue, partly because of the position of U.S. airlines, for whom the European subsidies for Airbus represented a windfall. The financially pressed U.S. carriers could ill afford to give up the chance to purchase Airbus jets at bargain prices. Besides, Boeing itself was not innocent; it received much aid from its government, too. The company shared technology developed under defense contracts with its civilian aircraft, giving it a strong competitive edge in international markets. This case is an emblem of the complexity and internal contradictions of foreign trade policy.

Trading Companies and Foreign Trade Zones

One step the United States has taken to promote exports was to allow the formation of export trading companies in 1982. This type of company has been in existence in the European Union and Japan for years but was subject to antitrust sanctions in America. An export trading company buys products from third parties for sales overseas, which offers the chance for price fixing and other forms of collusion. The new law makes an exemption to antitrust for these firms. It also allows banks to participate in export trading companies.

Another federal law allows the establishment of foreign trade zones (exempt from customs duties) to encourage export industries. The occupants of such zones receive tariff breaks on products they bring in. There are about 200 foreign trade zones in the United States, including one owned by Ross Perot. Perot's foreign trade zone is part of an airport complex in Texas, a spot where it is convenient to take advantage of the Mexican market. The value of this asset is diminished by NAFTA, which some people suspect is why Perot fought that trade agreement with such zest.

Unusual in the United States, much of the help with exports comes from state governments. Jolted by the trade shock of the early 1980s, most states now organize trade missions, sponsor trade shows, and have agencies that act as clearing houses on trade information. Nearly half the states have enacted export financing legislation. These laws permit the state to offer guarantees to encourage banks to make loans to small and medium-sized exporters. Unfortunately, many state initiatives are falling flat for lack of organization and follow-through.[42]

Licensing Strategic Exports

It is interesting that one thrust of federal policy has been to *discourage* exports that have military applications. Sensitive technology must be licensed for sale overseas for fear that it might fall into the wrong hands and become an armed threat. In the interest of national security, more than half the U.S. technology exports needed government permission to leave the country in 1993. Even simple exports may need more than two dozen licenses. The cost in lost foreign sales may be $20 billion a year.[43]

Relaxing the licensing procedures has become part of U.S. trade policy. With the end of the Cold War, the basis for export controls in sophisticated industries has diminished. Critics charge that the rules merely give away sales to non–U.S. companies and do little to protect the country. Under pressure from industry, the Clinton administration freed $37 billion in potential computer and telecom sales. High-tech exporters complained that these moves were too timid and demanded more freedom to sell their products abroad.[44]

The World Trade Organization

The GATT's inability to hold in check members' protectionist and promotional policies has been widely criticized. The new WTO agreed to during the Uruguay Round is a trade governing body that may prove more forceful than the GATT. It will have greater power to arbitrate trade disputes. Unlike the GATT, its decisions will be binding.

When a conflict arises between member countries, trade experts with the WTO will settle it. Under the old treaty, any country could block adverse rulings on trade matters. Not so with the WTO. Countries that win a case with the WTO will receive automatic permission to retaliate against the offending country if that country does not change its trade practices. Before, if the United States objected to being penalized for, say, refusing to import products made with child labor, it could vote no. Lacking unanimous consent, the penalty against the United States would be barred. Now, the situation is reversed: unanimous consent is required *not* to impose penalties.

An unlikely coalition of hard-right conservatives and consumer activists have expressed fear that the WTO will erode national sovereignty. Such fears are likely to prove unfounded. In reality, the WTO probably will be subject to the same give-and-take bargaining that characterized the GATT. The new organization cannot override any country's law unless the country itself agrees to it.

International Economic Cooperation

Linked to trade policy are a government's macroeconomic policies—taxing, spending, borrowing, and the expansion or contraction of credit. Deficit spending on the public account, for example, is likely to drive up interest rates as the government competes with private borrowers for funds. High interest rates, in turn, attract foreign investors seeking a good return for their money. As foreign funds flow into a country, increasing demand for its currency, the foreign exchange rate will rise. The rising foreign exchange rate will make the country's exports more expensive on world markets. It also will make it easier for the country to buy imports. Such a scenario hit the United States in the early 1980s. Mammoth public borrowing by the Reagan administration boosted the dollar to record levels and was the proximate cause for the sudden explosion in the trade deficit. (See Box 17–3.)

All countries recognize that international commercial issues cannot be separated from domestic macroeconomic policy. Therefore, they have evolved several international forums to try to coordinate their fiscal and monetary actions. The goal is for countries to avoid working at cross-purposes.

The most notable coordinating activity is the annual economic summit among the so-called Group of Seven (G–7). The G-7 are the largest industrialized economies—the United States, Japan, Germany, Britain, France, Italy, and Canada. (Russia is now a corresponding country.) At the formal meetings, the leaders of these countries focus on such issues as the degree and timing of economic stimulus. Other gatherings take place when circumstances dictate. In 1985, for instance, the G-7 finance ministers met in New York and agreed to take steps to reduce the dollar's value. That meeting worked, and the dollar plummeted over the next several years. The European Union and the OECD also provide mechanisms for international economic cooperation.

Often, the results disappoint. Just as countries have conflicts on matters of trade, so they have conflicts on macroeconomic questions. Bonn in the early 1990s kept interest levels high for internal reasons to dampen the inflation threat-

Box 17–3

Who Cares about Foreign Exchange Rates?

Foreign exchange rates are increasingly important to business. These rates are the ratio of one currency to another. They determine, say, how many dollars a U.S. company clears when it converts the marks, yen, or francs it has earned from selling a product in Germany, Japan, or France. Since 1972, the major currencies have been allowed to float, meaning that supply and demand set the foreign exchange rates. These rates waver up and down, making some firms suffer and others benefit.

As a rule, firms that export like their home currency to be weaker. Take the dollar. When the dollar falls compared to a foreign currency, dollar-denominated products become cheaper and, thus, more attractive to foreign buyers. That makes the job of exporting easier. Top policy makers often like a weak dollar policy, too. The cheaper U.S. currency makes imported goods more expensive and, thus, deters Americans from buying overseas products. In theory, therefore, a weaker dollar should reduce any trade deficit that exists. For these reasons, the Treasury Department is often under pressure to drive down the exchange rate.

But there is another side to the story. A low exchange rate creates many problems of its own. Domestic companies use imported items, too. A weak dollar makes their cost of doing business go up, encouraging them to pass along the higher cost to consumers. A weak dollar also tempts foreign companies that export to the United States to raise their prices to keep earning the same number of marks, yen, or francs from U.S. sales. The consequence is that a drop in the dollar can set the stage for a bout of price inflation. A dropping dollar also may scare foreign investors to liquidate their bond and equity holdings, making it harder to fund the national debt.

To stop these scenarios from unfolding, central banks may raise interest rates. The Fed has often followed this course in the United States. Higher interest rates make U.S. bonds and money market accounts more attractive to international investors, who must buy dollars to invest in them. The increased demand for dollars will push the exchange rate up again. Unfortunately, the Fed's actions also make loans more expensive and will cause the domestic economy to contract, risking a recession.

Every country faces such cruel choices, and finding the right level for a national currency is tricky. Central banks often intervene in foreign exchange markets, buying or selling dollars (or any other currency deemed out of line) to support particular exchange rates. Such intervention can have a psychological effect of calming markets, but it cannot work if investors as a group really think the exchange rate should be at another level.

ened by the huge cost of integrating East Germany. The country's main trading partners had lower rates, and they wanted Germany to bring its rates in line with theirs to boost demand for their exports and help them out of their business slump. Bonn would not go along. This incident illustrates how hard it can be for countries to coordinate their economic policy decisions.

U.S. Government Agencies

International trade requires diplomatic support. The Office of the U.S. Trade Representative (USTR) is a cabinet-level agency that takes the lead for America in the international negotiations over trade. It also is the main advisor to the president on international trade policy. The USTR's jurisdiction includes such issues as expansion of U.S. exports, protection of U.S. rights under international trade and commodity agreements, and unfair trade practices.[45]

International commercial relations cut across the conventional divisions of government, so the USTR is far from alone in working on these relations. Foreign trade and investment are important to the State Department and to the other cabinet departments. Within the departments, almost every large agency has a foreign economic policy concern, which can breed confusion and inconsistency in government programs. The main agencies and their functions are listed in Table 17–1.

The heart of the State Department's economic policy activities is the Bureau of Economic and Business Affairs. With about 150 professionals, this agency helps develop U.S. strategy in international trade and commercial affairs, international finance, trade controls, and related questions. Still, the clout of the Bureau of Economic and Business Affairs has eroded in recent years, as leadership in international economic matters has shifted to government units that are linked more closely to domestic interest groups.[46]

The Treasury Department is now the dominant player in international economic policy. Its chief worries in this domain are foreign exchange rates, the balance of payments, international capital markets, and international tax policy. Most of the relevant policy making is housed in the Office of the Assistant Secretary for International Affairs. This bureau has about 200 economists, probably the largest body of international economic expertise in the government, which gives Treasury weight in disputes with state and other bureaucratic units over U.S. international economic policy.

TABLE 17–1   An Array of Federal Agencies Work to Help U.S. Business in Foreign Trade.

Export-Import Bank	A government corporation, the Ex-Im Bank encourages exports by providing loans, guarantees, and insurance to exporters.
Foreign Agricultural Service	Part of the USDA, this agency helps to expand agricultural exports, manages the Export Enhancement Program of agricultural subsidies, and administers foreign sales of the Commodity Credit Corporation.
Foreign Commercial Service	A unit of the Commerce Department, this agency assists U.S. companies interested in overseas sales.
International Trade Agency	Also in the Commerce Department, this agency investigates foreign dumping.
International Trade Commission	An independent federal agency, the ITC sets tariffs and rules on dumping cases.
Overseas Private Investment Corp.	OPIC is an independent federal agency that insures U.S. investors against political risk in foreign countries.
U.S. Trade Representative	The USTR is a cabinet post responsible for negotiating international trade treaties.

Another important agency is the International Trade Commission (ITC). Called the Tariff Commission until the Trade Act of 1974, the ITC advises on tariffs. Under Section 201 of the Trade Act (the escape clause provision permitted under GATT), an industry that is injured by imports, or threatened with injury, may petition for relief (see Table 17–2). The ITC investigates these petitions. If a petition is found to have merit (roughly one petition in two), the commission advises the president what to do. Specific recommendations from the ITC may include import protection through higher duties, quotas, or marketing agreements.

The president may follow or modify the ITC's advice, and Congress can later overrule the president's decision. Interestingly, presidents agree to start protectionist measures less than half the time they are advised to, due to fear of retaliation that will hurt other sectors of the economy and make matters worse. President Reagan, for instance, denied import relief for the American shoe industry in 1985 despite an ITC recommendation. Unhappy with this decision, Congress later passed legislation that authorized quotas for imported shoes.

The ITC also may urge that the injured industry receive trade adjustment assistance—aid to retrain and relocate workers, to pay unemployment benefits, and to make loans to firms. The United States is unique among rich countries in having a program (started in 1962) designed specifically to help workers and firms hurt by import competition to shift to new activities. Much of the money was wasted because it focused on companies with the least chance of success. Under Reagan, this shock-absorber program was scaled back.

The U.S. system of checks and balances gives Congress the right to ratify major trade agreements negotiated by the president (or his emissaries). Because individual legislators are subject to pressures from constituents who may be threatened by a trade pact, approval often is in doubt. Senator Ernest Hollings (D–S.C.), for example, in 1994 tried to bottle up in his committee the GATT ac-

---

TABLE 17–2   U.S. Firms Can Call upon Their Government to Use Several Public Policies to Protect Them in International Trade.

U.S. Trade Laws	Problem	Remedy
Section 201	Injury to U.S. industry from foreign competition	Tariffs, quotas, or voluntary export restriction with offending countries
Section 232	National security	Protection for defense-related companies
Section 301	Unfair trade practices hurt U.S. exporters in foreign markets	Presidential retaliation against offending countries
Section 303	Foreign government subsidizes its exporters or domestic producers	Countervailing duties on the good when it enters the U.S. to compensate for the subsidies
Section 731	Material injury to U.S. industry from imports sold at below market value	Special duties to offset the price advantage of the foreign product

cord approved by the president a year earlier. He hoped to extort the administration into reopening the agreement to protect textile interests in his home state. The effort failed, but Hollings did delay a vote on the bill for many weeks, throwing it into jeopardy.

To reduce such a temptation to tinker with economic pacts, the Congress often gives the president "fast-track" negotiating authority, by which it agrees to consider trade agreements on a single, up-or-down vote without possibility of amendment. Otherwise, trade agreements would become hopelessly bogged down in pork-barrel politics.

Fighting Trade Wars

Washington often finds itself in dispute with its trading partners. The federal government has several trade weapons that it wields on behalf of domestic companies (see Table 17–2). The most important are antidumping penalties, the power to impose countervailing duties, and the Section 301 provision of the Trade Act of 1974. They are brandished dozens of times every year, as Table 17–3 shows. A fourth weapon, the Section 201 escape clause, is rarely invoked anymore—there were but three cases in the period 1986–90.[47]

Antidumping Activities

Dumping is one form of competition that is considered unfair and hence illegal under U.S. public policy. Dumping happens when a foreign company charges less for goods in the United States than in its home market, or when it sells goods below the cost of production (including a profit). Typically, the International Trade Agency (ITA) of the Commerce Department conducts the first investigation of dumping cases to see if the alleged action really happened. Then, the International Trade Commission examines the extent of harm to domestic firms. If the ITC finds dumping to have caused material damage, the Commerce Department directs the Customs Service to impose duties to provide relief to the embattled domestic industry. The duties are set to make up the difference between fair value and the actual sales price.

TABLE 17–3   Trade Cases Started in the United States, 1979–90

	Number
Antidumping cases	507
Countervailing duty cases	392
Section 301 investigations	67

Source: I. M. Destler, *American Trade Politics,* 2nd ed. (Washington, DC: Institute for International Economics, 1992).

TABLE 17–4   **The United States Resorts More Often to Trade Sanctions than Do Other Countries**

Frequency of Antidumping and Countervailing Duty Actions (1980–1986)

	Number
United States	631
Australia	436
European Union	287
Canada	241
Japan	1

Source: Pietro S. Nivola, *Regulating Unfair Trade* (Washington, DC: Brookings Institution, 1993), p. 72.

The United States has imposed more dumping penalties than any other country (see Table 17–4). In 1993, the Commerce Department issued over 80 rulings in dumping cases, finding foreign companies guilty most of the time.[48]

An illustrative case concerns flat-panel displays, which are an important new technology used mainly in laptop computers, but which have many other potential applications. Japanese electronics firms hold the lead over the tiny U.S. industry. American companies brought a dumping case to the ITA, charging the Japanese with unfair trade practices, and they won. Next, the ITC found there was material damage. So, the Commerce Department put an antidumping duty on imports of the displays, giving U.S. firms a respite and time to catch the Japanese.

As often happens with public policy, the victory for one U.S. industry was a loss for another. U.S. buyers of flat-panel displays, for example, Apple Computer, objected to having to pay a premium for imported components. They moved some operations offshore to get around the duty and put pressure on the Clinton administration to back off and stop protecting domestic flat-panel makers. The Commerce Department revoked the antidumping duties in 1993, probably because the computer industry's pull is stronger than the flat-panel industry's.[49]

Countervailing Duties

The Commerce Department also may put duties on imports that received subsidies from the exporting company's home government. If a subsidy is proven, and the International Trade Commission finds that U.S. firms have been materially injured, **countervailing duties** can be imposed. These duties are set at a level to cancel the subsidy and thus allow U.S. firms to compete on an equal footing. Again, as Table 17–4 reports, the United States is far more likely to use this trade weapon than are its trading partners.

Unfair Trade Practices

The Section 301 provision of the 1974 Trade Act is the most disputed trade weapon. It is designed to help U.S. manufacturers deal with unfair restrictions on their products in foreign markets. Section 301 requires the president to take reprisals against countries that breach the rules of fair trade. Although the president can start Section 301 investigations, usually they are launched following complaints from a company or U.S. industry association. Typically, the trade group works through the trade representative. This procedure saves him or her the effort needed to identify foreign trade barriers.[50]

First, the U.S. trade representative investigates the foreign nation's trade practices to see if they are "unreasonable." If a trade practice meets this test, economic sanctions can be imposed. The retaliation is supposed to be proportional to the damage caused. The idea is to "level the playing field" so U.S. firms have a fighting chance to stay in the market. For example, Section 301 was used in 1990 to help Allied-Signal Corporation sell metal alloys in Japan, whose buyers had previously been discriminating against this product under Japanese government auspices.[51]

The so-called Super 301 amendment to the 1988 Trade Act goes further and calls for the trade representative to designate the worst offending countries regardless of any specific industry complaint. The United States is obliged by Super 301 to strike back at these countries if they do not end the protectionist behavior.

Section 301 has stirred resentment abroad. America's major trading partners do not have matching policies on their books to fight trade wars. They complain that Section 301 gives the United States the upper hand and is a hypocritical use of naked economic power. There is pressure through the GATT to weaken this trade weapon, but Congress will not surrender it easily.

Multinational Corporations

When the U.S. computer industry moved overseas in reaction to the Commerce Department's initial ruling on flat panels, it revealed a general failing in foreign economic policy. The rise of MNCs that own or control production in more than one country can foil government regulators. MNCs can easily shift production to the least regulated national environment, parrying all attempts at controlling them with national-level public policy. In fact, a major reason companies become global is to gain leverage by playing one national state off against another.

As mentioned in Box 17–1, a rapidly growing share of international trade is made of intercompany transfers—shipments of parts and materials from one subsidiary to another. These are not imports and exports in the conventional sense. They do not reflect market prices and are simply recorded as internal accounting entries. Individual countries have a hard time measuring intracompany trade and, thus, have a hard time taxing MNCs. Many large companies use accounting techniques to move profits out of the United States, a high-tax country, to places with lower corporate taxes. Bermuda, Liechtenstein, and other tax havens specialize in attracting such business.

One interesting, yet probably futile, effort to regulate multinationals is the

Foreign Corrupt Practices Act (FCPA), passed by the United States in 1977. This law makes it a criminal offense under U.S. law for an American company to bribe or make other payoffs to obtain business in a foreign state, whatever legal standing the practice may have in that country. The FCPA also has accounting provisions that require U.S.–based MNCs to use bookkeeping procedures that will catch questionable overseas payments.

The business community vigorously opposed the FCPA on the grounds that it is a handicap for national competitiveness because no other country plays by the same rules. All OECD countries outlaw bribery of their own officials, but only the United States makes it a crime to bribe foreign officials. Many foreign MNCs even can deduct bribes as a cost of business. According to a White House task force appointed by President Jimmy Carter, the business lost due to the FCPA amounted to $1 billion a year. Because of the difficulty of enforcement, federal regulators have been indifferent about enforcing the FCPA. Since the law's passage, the SEC has brought only one criminal prosecution.[52]

Still, since 1989, the United States has been trying to get other OECD countries to accept strict antibribery laws so U.S. firms can compete on an even basis for overseas contracts. The reaction is tepid. Bonn, for instance, voted not to abolish tax credits for foreign payoffs by German companies. Few nations want to give up the freedom of their companies to use all means, even shady ones, to induce foreign sales.[53]

Conclusion

We have reviewed public policy for international economic affairs. Because of globalization, American managers can ill afford to ignore foreign trade and related issues today. We have seen that the U.S. and other governments have been working for freer trade since World War II, mainly under the GATT's auspices and through regional agreements such as the European Union.

These policies have many enemies. Businesses often want to spare themselves from foreign competition. Workers suspect their jobs will be wrested away by cheaper workers overseas. Popular sentiment is easily inflamed when a foreign power, for example, Japan or China, looks like it is stealing markets. The advocates of more liberal international trade are are not as loud, for the benefits are often so small to each individual consumer, they are invisible. Thus, the biggest winners in the global economy are apt to be the least motivated to enter the political fray.

The political pressures for and against protectionism tend to wash out. As companies and their home governments jockey for position in today's chaotic world economy, foreign trade policy has muddled, turning into a mix of liberalism and managed trade. Governments have found ways to get past the GATT accords and help their injured domestic industries. Yet, they also have been agreeable to lowering trade barriers and cooperating on trade problems. These contradictory things are done to create and preserve jobs, good wages, and high profits within their borders.

The quest for national competitiveness does not stop with foreign trade policy, however. It includes other efforts to enhance national productivity and output. In the concluding chapter to this book, we will put the U.S. economic performance in worldwide context to see how well these policies have worked.

Questions

1. What is the significance of the U.S. foreign trade deficit? Of direct foreign investment in the United States? Should Americans be worried about these things?

2. Summarize the arguments for and against free trade and protectionism. With which side do you agree?

3. What are the principles underlying the GATT? What are the weaknesses in how the treaty is put into effect?

4. Discuss trade wars. What public policies does the United States have for fighting these wars? Who carries them out?

5. What is NAFTA? What are its implications for U.S. business?

End Notes

1. Adam Smith, *An Inquiry into the Nature and Origins of the Wealth of Nations* (1776; reprint, New York: Modern Library, 1937), p. 395.

2. "A Guide to GATT," *The Economist,* December 4, 1993, p. 25.

3. For evidence, see the report by Michael L. Dertouzos, Richard K. Lester, Robert M. Solow, and the MIT Commission on Industrial Productivity, *Made in America* (New York: HarperPerennial, 1990), and the results of a colloquium at Harvard Business School, Bruce R. Scott and George C. Lodge, eds., *U.S. Competitiveness in the World Economy* (Boston: Harvard Business School Press, 1985).

4. Paul Krugman, *The Age of Diminished Expectations* (Cambridge, MA: MIT Press, 1990), pp. 35–36.

5. Ibid., pp. 40–41.

6. Smith, *Wealth of Nations,* p. 424.

7. Ibid., p. 507.

8. Robert Z. Lawrence and Robert E. Litan, *Saving Free Trade* (Washington, DC: Brookings Institution, 1986), p. 7.

9. Smith, *Wealth of Nations,* p. 431.

10. William Lazonick, *Business Organization and the Myth of the Market Economy* (Cambridge: Cambridge University Press, 1991), pp. 4–5.

11. See Paul Krugman, ed., *Strategic Trade Policy and the New International Economics* (Cambridge, MA: MIT Press, 1986).

12. David B. Yoffie, ed., *Beyond Free Trade: Firms, Governments, and Global Competition* (Boston: Harvard Business School Press, 1993), p. 17.

13. See, for example, Paul Krugman, *Peddling Prosperity* (New York: Norton, 1994), Chapter 10.

14. *The Papers of Alexander Hamilton,* Vol. X (New York: Columbia University Press, 1966), p. 263.

15. For a good summary of Hamilton's and others' ideas, see Frank Bourgin, *The Great Challenge: The Myth of Laissez-Faire in the Early Republic* (New York: George Braziller, 1989).

16. Harry Scott, *The Myth of Free Trade* (London: Basil Blackwell, 1985), p. 11.

17. Lawrence and Litan, *Saving Free Trade,* p. 23.

18. I. M. Destler and John S. Odell, *Anti-Protection* (Washington, DC: Institute for International Economics, 1987).

19. Stefanie Ann Lenway, *The Politics of U.S. International Trade* (Boston: Pitman, 1985).

20. For evidence of this trend, see Peter F. Cowhey and Jonathan D. Aronson, *Managing the World Economy: The Consequences of Corporate Alliances* (New York: Council on Foreign Relations Press, 1993).

21. See, for example, Gary Clyde Hufbauer and Kimberly Ann Elliott, *Measuring the Costs of Protection in the United States* (Washington, DC: Institute for International Economics, 1994).

22. Edward M. Graham and Paul R. Krugman, *Foreign Direct Investment in the United States,* 3rd ed. (Washington, DC: Institute for International Economics, 1993).

23. Raymond Vernon and Debora Spar, *Beyond Globalism* (New York: Free Press, 1989), p. 110.

24. Martin Tolchin and Susan Tolchin, *Buying into America* (New York: New York Times Books, 1988).

25. "A Survey of Multinationals," *The Economist*, March 27, 1993.

26. Robert Reich, *The Work of Nations* (New York: Vintage, 1991).

27. For a discussion of the incentives now being used to attract business to developing countries, see *World Investment Report 1993* (New York: United Nations, 1993).

28. *Incentives and Direct Foreign Investment* (New York: U.N. Division of Transnational Corporations and Investment, 1995).

29. "Japanese Mergers," *The Economist*, October 15, 1994, p. 103.

30. Clyde Prestowitz, *Trading Places* (New York: Basic Books, 1988).

31. Paul Magnusson, "Why Corporate Nationality Matters," *Business Week*, July 12, 1993, p. 142.

32. Peter Norman, "GATT Says Uruguay Round Worth $500bn," *Financial Times*, October 4, 1994, p. 5.

33. See Ira C. Magaziner and Robert B. Reich, *Minding America's Business* (New York: Vintage, 1983), Chapter 14.

34. John A. C. Conybeare, *Trade Wars* (New York: Columbia University Press, 1987), pp. 160–71.

35. David Gardner, "Brussels Urges Wider Trade Zone," *Financial Times*, October 20, 1994, p. 2.

36. Conybeare, *Trade Wars*, p. 174.

37. Theodore H. Moran, ed., *Multinational Corporations: The Political Economy of Foreign Direct Investment* (Lexington, MA: Lexington Books, 1985), p. 144, citing a study by Bela and Carol Belassa.

38. Moran, *Multinational Corporations*, p. 143.

39. "U.S. Bank Helps India Finance $89 Million Deal with Raytheon," *Boston Globe*, December 14, 1993, p. 51.

40. Wendy Coleman and Malcolm S. Salter, *Airbus versus Boeing (B)* (Boston: Harvard Business School, 1988).

41. Laura D'Andrea Tyson, *Who's Bashing Whom? Trade Conflict in High-Technology Industries* (Washington, DC: Institute for International Economics, 1992), p. 203.

42. James D. McGiven, "Challenge and Response: The Rise of State Export Development Policies in the U.S.A.," in *Export Development and Promotion,* ed. F. H. Rolf Seringhaus and Philip J. Rosson (Boston: Kluwer, 1991).

43. Jerry J. Jazinowski, "Removing U.S. Export Shackles Will Increase Profits and Jobs," *Christian Science Monitor*, July 18, 1994, p. 18.

44. "President Pitchman," *Business Week,* December 6, 1993, p. 43; and Asra Q. Nomani, "Business Criticizes Administration Plan to Speed High-Tech Exports Licensing," *The Wall Street Journal,* February 24, 1994, p. A2.

45. Robert E. Baldwin, *The Political Economy of U.S. Import Policy* (Cambridge, MA: MIT Press, 1985), p. 67.

46. Stephen D. Cohen, *The Making of United States International Economic Policy,* 3rd ed. (New York: Praeger, 1988), pp. 58–60.

47. I. M. Destler, *American Trade Politics,* 2nd ed. (Washington, DC: Institute for International Economics, 1992), p. 166.

48. James Bovard, "Clinton's Dumping Could Sink GATT," *The Wall Street Journal,* December 9, 1993, p. A16.

49. "Did Commerce Pull the Plug on Flat-Screen Makers?" *Business Week,* July 5, 1993, p. 32.

50. George Cabot Lodge, *Comparative Business Government Relations* (Englewood Cliffs, NJ: Prentice Hall, 1990), p. 207.

51. David P. Baron, *Business and Its Environment* (Englewood Cliffs, NJ: Prentice Hall, 1993), p. 485.

52. George A. Steiner and John F. Steiner, *Business, Government, and Society,* 6th ed. (New York: McGraw-Hill, 1991), p. 416.

53. Robert Keatley, "U.S. Campaign Against Bribery Faces Resistance from Foreign Governments," *The Wall Street Journal,* February 4, 1994, p. A4.

P   A   R   T

VII   CONCLUSION

18   THE REBIRTH OF AMERICAN BUSINESS?

The United States is losing its ability to compete in world markets. We are still the world's strongest economy. However, the question we must answer is where we will be tomorrow.

President's Commission on Industrial Competitiveness[1]

A major theme of *Business, Government, Society* has been to pinpoint public policies that allow the private sector to run productively. Contrary to some superficial assertions, the best thing government can do is *not* just to get out of the way. We have seen that there is a set of jobs that only government can carry out, such as maintaining a system of laws for economic exchange, setting macroeconomic policy, and protecting the physical environment. There are other areas where government has to take the lead, if not do the tasks itself, such as providing new technology, building infrastructure, and assuring mass education. These functions are essential to a productive business sector.

We also have seen that, unfortunately, many public actions distort markets and foster rent seeking, leading to the careless use of public and private resources. Such failures undermine business's and society's trust in public institutions. Appropriate public policy reduces government's shortcomings by focusing government energy on the things only it can do—and that it does best.

Public policy has never worked perfectly. Why, then, the bitter attitude of voters in the United States (not to mention other countries)? What accounts for the intense dislike of government evident today? A major factor is the global economy.

A train of events in the past two decades or so have hurt the nation's international prestige and undermined its self-confidence. The devaluation of the dollar and the oil shocks of the 1970s, the rising tide of high-quality imported goods in the 1980s, the permanent layoffs at blue-chip corporations in the 1990s—these and other incidents have shaken Americans. Opinion polls tap a shared feeling of malaise, a belief that the country has lost control over events, that things are going to get worse.

These trends are echoed in other rich countries. The world has entered a new era of instantaneous flows of capital, a global labor market, and floods of foreign-made products. Many people worry that they are being left out of the world economy as it evolves. Governments are called on to respond, yet we have seen how deepening international interdependence has made it harder for governments to manage their domestic economies. Lacking quick or painless solutions to voters' worries, government impotence breeds further frustration and disillusionment.

Given this background, it is no wonder that policy makers have become absorbed with national competitiveness, with how countries can assert themselves in the world economy. Throughout this book, we have seen ways that government both helps and holds back companies at home and abroad. During our investigation, we have likened the American business environment to what exists in other countries, finding important points of contrast and of parallel development.

Now, it is time to stand back and take stock of what we have learned about how the United States stands in the global economy—and what, if anything, government can do about it. Success in the global economy is primarily a business responsibility, of course, and good public policy is not a substitute for good management. As we discussed in Chapter 1, however, public policy is critical in creating an environment in which private firms can flourish.

We start this chapter with a short reexamination of the term *national competitiveness,* addressing its tie to productivity. Then, we will take a balanced look at the evidence of U.S. economic decline and find the situation complex and, thus, often oversimplified in the popular mind. Finally, we will look at the foremost public policy reforms needed to reverse the nation's major weaknesses.

Competitiveness and Productivity

There is much confusion about the meaning of *national* competitiveness. It is different from the competitiveness of a firm or industry, which can be measured by market share. All sectors of a nation's economy cannot be equally successful, for success in one industry will bid up wages and attract resources from other industries, thus reducing their ability to produce products of superior quality or lower cost.[2]

National competitiveness is not a matter of trade surpluses, either. The United States could have a trade surplus by slashing the foreign exchange rate, making U.S. exports very cheap for consumers in other countries to buy. But that also makes imported goods more expensive and reduces the standard of living at home. Being poor is not what most Americans have in mind when they think of being competitive.

Those who have thought deeply about these matters are prone to conclude that the only meaningful notion of competitiveness at the national level is productivity—the value of output produced by a unit of capital or labor.[3] Productivity growth is the engine that drives higher living standards, which keeps a country competitive.

American workers are the world's most productive. Counter to common belief, the average Japanese worker produces 22 percent less an hour; the average German, 14 percent less.[4] The average in Japan is pulled down by the inefficient service sector, which is overstaffed compared to the United States. Higher American productivity translates into larger homes, newer automobiles, more food, and better home electronics equipment. Thus, by many measures of material well-being, Americans produce more and live better than inhabitants of other advanced countries. In this sense, the U.S. economy as a whole is competitive.

The problem is with how fast output is going up compared to input; according to OECD data, in the United States, the rate of business productivity growth (labor and capital combined) fell from 1.6 percent annually in the 1960s to 0.5 percent in the 1980s. It also has fallen in other OECD countries, though not nearly as far. Japan's business sector productivity grew about four times as fast as America's in the 1980s; Europe's grew about three times as fast (see Table 18--1). (The figures are subject to dispute, but most data do point to a relative drop in U.S. productivity growth starting about 20 years ago.)

The slowdown in productivity growth, when combined with a shift in income distribution away from middle- and low-income individuals, has helped create what Robert Reich calls an "anxious class" of Americans. Americans are no longer as well off as they imagine they should be, and they are nervous about holding on to what they have. The example of other countries getting richer drives home the point that the United States is growing *relatively* less competitive.

Losing the Global Economic Race . . .

The sour national mood is reflected in, and has been reinforced by, the large volume of "declinist" writings that have appeared over the last 25 years.[5] These

---

TABLE 18–1   **Productivity in Other Countries Has Been Rising Faster than in the United States.**

	Productivity in the Business Sector* Percent Change per Year		
	1960–73	*1974–79*	*1980–91*
OECD Europe	3.3%	1.6%	1.3%
Japan	5.5	2.1	1.9
United States	**1.6**	**0.2**	**0.5**

*Total factor productivity (labor and capital combined).

Source: *OECD Economic Outlook 1993* (Paris: Organization for Economic Cooperation and Development, December 1993).

books and articles see things fundamentally wrong with the U.S. economy that, if not fixed, will prevent the United States from getting the best in global markets. They express fear of "deindustrialization," that the nation's manufacturing base is eroding.[6] Many corporations are said to have become "hollow," to have turned into the mere repackagers and marketers of products made elsewhere. As basic industries are dismantled and moved overseas, the income gap grows wider and the lower half of the nation is made to work harder for less pay. There is a growing "outer class" of homeless and unemployable people who do not participate in the regular economy. Some writings on these depressing subjects verge on the apocalyptic.[7]

From the average management student's perspective, the most ominous trend is the restructuring (that is, mass permanent firings) at large corporations that used to hire armies of business school graduates for middle management posts. In 1979, sales of America's largest 500 companies amounted to 58 percent of GNP, and they employed 16.2 million people. By 1989, sales were only 42 percent of GNP, and employment at the top 500 companies had shrunk to 12.5 million.[8] The traditional career path for professionally trained managers is thus far less certain than it was until recently.

Another strong thread in the declinist literature is the fear that corporations in rival countries such as Japan and Germany are pulling ahead, due partly to better business environments.[9] Often, these other countries are portrayed in the popular press as unbeatable, usually because they have been bending the rules of competition in their favor. One particularly apprehensive book, a bestseller in Japan, foresees U.S.–Japanese economic strife leading in the end to a shooting war.[10] The irony is that the recovery of Japan and Germany from World War II (and the development of South Korea and Taiwan) was an explicit goal of U.S. policy, intended to create counterweights to the Soviet Union. The policy may have been too successful; in many people's eyes, by helping our allies as part of the Cold War, we gave up our advantage on the economic front.

. . . or Coming Out on Top?

But the national mood, if such a thing can be said to exist, has a split personality. Anxiety about the global economy is not universal. For every pessimist, there seems to be an optimist who, usually looking at different evidence, sees proof of American greatness, not decay. They detect temporary downturns due to the business cycle and shifts from old to new industries, but no long-term slide in the nation's economic well-being. They believe the United States does not face an economic doomsday due to global competition since the bulk of American jobs and output are not directly affected by the foreign trade.[11] Crucial as globalization of the economy is, imports and exports in the United States account for just one-fifth of the GNP. The huge service sector is largely insulated from foreign rivalry because most services are produced and consumed locally.

Alongside the literature of decline, these writers have produced upbeat works that stress the U.S. economic strong points face to face with other countries.[12] Much of what is perceived as decline, they argue, is simply the convergence of advanced economies. America's postwar lead was not sustainable; Germany and Japan were destined to narrow the gap. Whatever its problems may have been in the recent past (and their existence often is denied), the United States is seen to be undergoing an industrial resurgence in the 1990s. The nation is, according to the title of one recent scholarly book, "bound to lead."[13]

Established firms have come back in a range of older industries, most dramatically in the bellwether automobile sector. In other established sectors, such as popular entertainment, fast food, and consumer goods, U.S. companies never did lose their lead. And there are also many rising American stars in such newer industries as biotechnology, computer software, and wireless communications. No other country comes close in economic diversity and vitality.

Writers from the optimistic school also are taking a second look at public policy and business in the other economic superpowers. In this revisionist literature, the industrial prowess of Japan, Germany, and other trading states turns out to have been overdrawn.[14] Their public policy and business systems were never as effective as commonly thought, and, anyhow, they have lost their punch. The economic momentum is still with the United States for the next century.

The optimists, not to mention most mainstream economists, scoff at the idea of deindustrialization. Employment in American manufacturing is shrinking, as it is in all OECD countries. But that just means fewer workers are making more products. The percent of U.S. GNP accounted for by the manufacturing sector has barely budged in decades. And the U.S. share of OECD industrial production is roughly unchanged since at least 1980.[15]

There has been a revival of U.S. productivity in the 1990s. Because workers produce more, unit labor cost in manufacturing declined an average of 6.4 percent a year in the United States in 1985–93, compared with a *rise* of 6.6 percent and 4.2 percent a year in Japan and Germany.[16] The good performance in the United States is partly a reflection of the restructuring in large corporations since the late 1980s—companies are squeezing more output from their employees—so even that trauma has a blessing. Companies in other countries have not done as much yet to downsize, and public policies are seen as a greater impediment to business efficiency than they are in the more freewheeling United States.

Experts are not sure if the rekindling of U.S. productivity growth is a new trend or just the normal upturn that happens after recessions, but it is a welcome change—except perhaps for those called upon to work harder.[17] (We will see below that there are underlying obstacles in the United States that, if not dealt with by public policy, make it likely the recent productivity surge will languish.)

Optimism Resurgent

By the mid-1990s, optimistic views of America's business prospects seemed to be gaining the upper hand in popular discussions. Consider the trend in data from the World Economic Forum in Switzerland. Every year, the forum puts together a scoreboard of how domestic environments help or hurt global competitiveness of entrepreneurs in different countries. For the scoreboard, global competitiveness is defined as the ability of entrepreneurs to design and make goods and services that are more attractive than competitors can produce. Using eight criteria, the leading industrial countries are then ranked from more to less competitive.

The scores reported in Table 18–2 suggest the United States has one of the best national environments for business in the world. It comes out near the top every year. Perhaps more important, the trend seems to have turned upward. The U.S. position had been slipping while Japan's and Germany's were improving, but the nation regained the top rating in 1994. Looked at over time, there is reason to take comfort in the environment for American business. Public policy and other factors have improved conditions relative to those of other industrial powers.

We should, of course, be skeptical about the effort to reduce something so complex as competitiveness to a simple ranking. Ranking countries also plays to the misplaced American fixation with winning.[18] The point of public policy for business should not be just to have world-class national companies. As mentioned earlier in this chapter, providing a good quality of life for ordinary people is a more important goal. Still, the competitiveness scoreboard does reinforce the general point made by many recent studies: U.S. companies can compete with the best foreign firms in many industries.

TABLE 18–2   The United States Remains among the Most Competitive Nations, According to One Study.

| | World Competitiveness Scoreboard (rank)* | | | |
	1985†	*1990*	*1992*	*1994‡*
United States	1st	3rd	5th	1st
Switzerland	2nd	2nd	3rd	6th
Japan	3rd	1st	1st	3rd
Germany	4th	4th	2nd	5th
Denmark	5th	8th	4th	7th
Sweden	6th	6th	8th	10th
Austria	7th	11th	7th	12th

*Based on analysis of eight factors of competitiveness: domestic economic strength, internationalization, government, finance, infrastructure, management, science and technology, and people.

†Calculated with slightly different method.

‡Developing countries included for the first time.

Source: *The World Competitiveness Report* (Lausanne: World Economic Forum and International Institute for Economic Development, various years).

Taking Stock

Fascinating though it is to follow, the debate over U.S. competitiveness has often been misleading. The two sides have been drawn into hyperbole to win debating points. Some participants in the polarized exchange of views have come to believe their own propaganda. As is often true, economic reality is not as dramatic as people like to assert.

American business and government have been adapting to international pressure since at least the 1970s, though the fact was often overlooked. The economy always has been powerful. Yet, despite how well U.S. business is doing now, holding onto that momentum will not happen naturally. The nation needs to take steps today to keep pace with its trading partners tomorrow. Bettering the U.S. business environment is a vast undertaking; it is cause for neither panic nor self-satisfaction.

Other advanced industrial countries face similar trials. World economic interdependence and technological change create deep political fissures in every society. Anytime the structure of an economy changes, the resulting upheaval is painful for the individuals whose lives are disrupted. Labor is not an abstract factor of production but people whose income may have depended on a declining industry. If a company makes something people no longer want (say, large automobiles) and closes a factory, the laid-off workers are theoretically available to make something people do want (say, computer software). The truth is that economic resources do not flow as easily to new uses as theory implies—after all, few automobile workers will ever become computer programmers.

The explosion of world trade has linked the U.S., European, and Japanese labor markets to those of developing countries as never before. Since Third-World imports are concentrated on labor-intensive sectors, they have a large impact on the demand for unskilled labor. As we discussed in Chapter 12, in the United States and Britain, the fall in labor demand has shown up as wage inequality. In Europe, unemployment has risen instead.[19] These social problems create political demand for government to do something.

Thus, the other major powers, as in the United States, are under similar pressure to dismantle their traditional ways of doing things. No one should console himself with this thought. Because change is buffeting the business environment everywhere is no reason for smugness. Japan and Germany, not to mention Switzerland and Sweden, Taiwan and South Korea, among other nations, have impressive long-term records. It is premature to project their contemporary troubles into the future, or to conclude that those societies will not learn to cope with these challenges. History suggests otherwise.

A great challenge for business and government in the 21st century is to produce enough jobs to soak up the new job seekers. Another challenge is to deal with the growing gap between people with good jobs and those without them. A third problem is to find ways to get people without skills to become more productive members of society. We should not discount the difficulties these tasks pose. To ignore them is to risk a further fraying of the social fabric.

Meaner . . . or Just Leaner?

To combat the slowdown in productivity and declining competitiveness, deregulation, privatization, and liberalization have been the centerpieces of policy making since about 1980, and not just in the United States. Where these policies deserve the most credit is where efforts by government to micromanage economic decisions are impractical or unnecessary. From Russia, to France, to Mexico, it is now widely recognized that society gains little from, say, having the state own steel mills and coal mines, or from having rules that keep new competitors from coming into the postal or telephone industries. Many reforms that aim to lessen government intervention in the economy have paid off in greater output produced with more efficiency. We have reviewed these issues throughout this book.

But the pendulum against the public sector and government intervention can swing too far. This has happened in the United States. Federal, state, and local tax cuts (and the political price politicians must bear for any increases) have sometimes had a paralyzing effect on government in this country. Simply put, the public sector is broke and unable to sustain all its programs. Not all these programs are equally effective, of course; the problem is that the budget ax falls in a haphazard way on good and bad activities alike.

Contrary to popular impressions, productivity gains across nations are not associated with tax cuts.[20] As we have seen throughout this book, a capable government is a sine qua non for a robust private sector. Given that the United States entered the 1980s with public spending at a low base compared to rival countries, the reduction of taxes has often meant too few funds were left over for government to take care of some critical needs. The policy decision in Washington to run budget deficits throughout the decade made matters worse by channeling marginal public revenue into debt service, leaving less and less for constructive activities.

The picture is somewhat brighter in other OECD countries, except possibly Britain, because they have not faced as much taxpayer resistance. These nations thus are likely to have an easier time finding funds for public investment, though all have analogous problems with public deficits and wasteful programs. In some cases, Italy and Sweden for example, the deficits are much deeper and even harder to reduce than in the United States due to the electorate's greater dependence on public spending.

To observe that the U.S. government has retreated too far from economic management is not to make a blanket endorsement of managed trade, industrial policy, or other types of business–government partnerships. The risk of government failure is often so great in these policies that they are better avoided—not that avoiding them is always possible given political dynamics. The preferred strategy is frequently for government just to create an enabling environment in which the private sector makes investment decisions, without government worrying too much about where the investment goes.[21] More intense government participation in opening foreign markets, developing given technologies, or promoting certain industries needs to be examined case by case before deciding whether it is worthwhile.

Readers also should not jump to the conclusion that productivity is mainly a public responsibility, or that protecting the U.S. position in the world economy has little to do with private sector action. To the contrary, private decisions are critical. American managers can—and fortunately do—learn from industrial practices that have been pioneered or used more fully in other nations.[22] Frightened by foreign competition, they have counterattacked by copying the best practices of other countries, and by building on their own core competencies.

Empowering workers, staying close to customers, creating flatter organization structures, using lean production methods, and other factors can boost productivity under the right conditions. Many U.S. companies have prospered in the 1990s by concentrating on the products and services in which they have a competitive advantage. Internal management techniques such as these are analyzed in other books and courses and are beyond the realm of *Business, Government, Society.* Here, the focus is public policy to support an environment that makes it worthwhile and easy to use state-of-the-art methods of managing.

The Role of Government

What is government's job? For government to help raise productivity—and thus assure good jobs, better living standards, and hardy local companies—three policy-related factors are pivotal: to promote public and private savings, to maintain society's infrastructure, and to provide primary and secondary education. We have touched on these public goods at several points in this book. They are essential to a supportive economic climate, and experience shows that it is mainly the government that renders them. Unhappily, in the United States, a lack of public attention is hurting the supply of savings, of infrastructure, and of human capital, with potentially grave ramifications for business firms over the long term.

Let us examine the record.

Saving and Investment

Americans do not save much. This is true of households and of government. Figure 18–1 shows the U.S. net national savings rate has been dropping for decades and is well below the level in most other advanced countries. It amounted to a paltry 2 percent of GNP in 1990.

The unwillingness of Americans to put money aside is serious because those funds are the source of investment, which is the prime long-run contributor to productivity growth.[23] America's lagging productivity performance is largely due to low capital formation, and that is due in turn to an absence of domestic saving. The shortage of funds may drive up interest rates, making it harder for

FIGURE 18–1

Americans do not save as much as most rival societies do

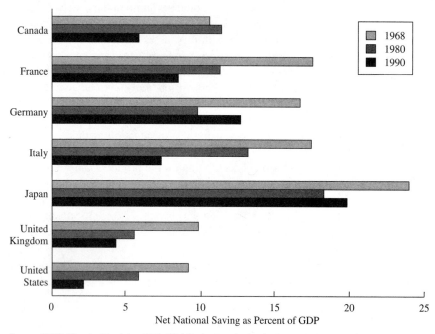

Source: *OECD Historical Statistics, 1960–1990* (Paris: Organization for Economic Cooperation and Development, 1992).

companies to raise funds to expand or replace outmoded equipment. And if companies do not purchase new plants and equipment, they will not become more productive and will suffer in international competition. There is evidence that the cost of capital is higher in the United States than in Japan, which may be a competitive disadvantage.

Americans' short-term solution to the lack of savings has been to borrow from foreigners. As mentioned in Chapter 17, depending on others for capital is risky. Foreigners could lose confidence in the U.S. economy and stop investing in and lending to American business. That scenario would drive the cost of capital even higher and probably provoke a recession. Another possibility is a drop in the foreign exchange rate and a corresponding fall in U.S. living standards as imported goods became more expensive. Anyhow, the capital inflows add to the trade deficit and make it even more necessary to boost productivity in export sectors to help pay back the foreign investment.

The shortage of American savings is a partial mystery. No one is sure why Americans are prone to spend so much more of their personal income than other nationalities do, though public policy adds to the problem. The tax code penalizes saving, and it encourages borrowing, especially for real estate. (This bias toward real estate does little for productivity.) Changes in the code might boost saving, though experience with individual retirement accounts (IRAs) in the

1980s raises doubts about that eventuality. The beneficiaries of such tax expenditures are typically already big savers. Besides, the decline in tax revenue would make public indebtedness worse.

The inability of government to save is easier to explain. As we have seen earlier, deficit spending is at least partly the result of people and firms insisting on public services, but hoping that someone else will foot the bill. Productivity growth is likely to be held back as investable funds are drawn off to cover the public debt. Reining in the public budget gap proves a heroic task. Yet, almost all analysts agree that progress in this area is essential to sustain a rising standard of living in the United States.

Public Works

The United States has been running down its physical infrastructure, the backbone of the national economy. As analyzed in Chapter 3, private investors have few incentives to build many kinds of infrastructure; it is largely a government job. In the face of taxpayer resistance, real investment in highways, railroads, sewers, bridges, tunnels, harbors, and the like dropped 75 percent in the 1970s and 1980s.[24] The United States has a rich stock of infrastructure assets, like the interstate highway system constructed as part of the Cold War effort. Lately, fewer new facilities are being built and, more ominously, maintenance of the existing infrastructure is often being deferred. When the bills for repair eventually come due, the price is bound to be higher than if a regular maintenance schedule had been followed.

Some have labeled the lack of public physical investment America's "third deficit" and consider it a problem as troubling as the budget and trade deficits. Meanwhile, other leading countries have not been as negligent about their infrastructures (see Table 18–3). By greater public investment, these countries may be making themselves more pleasing to MNCs looking for the best environment in which to conduct business. Because modern, flexible production methods are more vulnerable to bottlenecks, it is more important than ever to have good transport and communication links.

TABLE 18–3   America Lags in Improving Its Public Infrastructure.

	Expenditure on Civil Engineering Works (1990)	
	Percent of GDP	*Per Capita (dollars)*
France	3.3%	$658
Germany	3.2	656
Japan	4.8	996
United Kingdom	1.0	179
United States	**1.8**	**422**

Source: *Purchasing Power Parities and Real Expenditures 1990* (Paris: Organization for Economic Cooperation and Development, 1993).

The precise cost to U.S. business of the decaying infrastructure is not known, but it is real. Time lost in traffic or waiting for deliveries is time that could be used more productively. Thus, greater government spending on "social overhead capital" should bring gains in private sector output, though how much is controversial.[25] Building better transport and communication facilities also may have a low opportunity cost for society, measured in business decisions *not* to move to other countries.

Restoring and expanding the nation's infrastructure will require mammoth public investment, however. Like the problem of too little saving, the answer is more taxes or more cuts in "superfluous" public expenditures (if these can be identified)—neither of which is easy to do. The $150 billion public works bill of 1991 is a step in the right direction, but more will probably be needed.

Education ˙

The U.S. system of public education does a poor job for business. Executives complain that a shortage of skilled workers is holding them back. Every international study of educational achievement finds that American students rank near the bottom in math, science, foreign languages, and other subjects (see Table 18–4).[26] As work becomes more knowledge intensive, the economic handicap posed to society by bad education grows larger. Government reports confirm that U.S. workers' skills are not on par with those of European and Japanese workers.[27]

Education for undergraduate and graduate students is often better in the

TABLE 18–4   American Students Do Poorly in Basic Subjects.
Rank on Tests in Selected Countries—13-Year-Olds (1991)

Rank	Science	Math	Literacy*
1	Korea	Korea	Finland
2	Taiwan	Taiwan	France
3	Switzerland	Switzerland	Sweden
4	Hungary	USSR	New Zealand
5	USSR	Hungary	Hungary
6	Slovenia	France	Iceland
7	Israel	Italy	Switzerland
8	Canada	Israel	Hong Kong
9	France	Canada	**United States**
10	Scotland	Scotland	Singapore
11	Spain	Ireland	Slovenia
12	**United States**	Slovenia	Germany
13	Ireland	Spain	Denmark
14	Jordan	**United States**	Portugal

*14-year-olds in 1992.

Source: *Digest of Education Statistics 1993* (Washington, DC: U.S. Department of Education, 1993).

United States than anywhere else in the world. University teaching is the fifth leading American export industry, and more Americans go to college as a proportion of population than go to college anywhere else. Primary and secondary education is another story. Noncollege bound students receive mediocre instruction. Far more students drop out of school in the United States than in competing nations, and those that stay are likely to get a thinner curriculum. The U.S. school year is the shortest in the industrial world. American schoolchildren receive less than half the daily instruction than they would in Japan, Germany, and France, according to a blue-ribbon commission established by Congress (see Figure 18–2).

The United States does particularly poorly in vocational education. Young people who are not on the college track are apt to see no connection between schooling and work. There are just 300,000 apprenticeships; Germany has 1.7 million (see Box 18–1).[28] So, the average American student has less chance than his German counterpart to make contacts or learn practical skills that lead to a first job.

U.S. companies do spend about $30 billion a year on training. But private on-the-job training is marred by market failure. Companies are apt to invest too little money in workers' skills for fear that their investment will literally walk out the door, helping competitors, or that those employees who stay will capitalize on their higher market value to demand better pay. The Europeans and Japanese recognize these potential market failures. To reach a better result for society, their training systems are more centralized and have formal structure.[29] Government takes the lead in encouraging the delivery of general training, for example, through taxes and national accreditation schemes.

An ignorant labor pool makes it harder to attract or keep skilled, good-pay-

FIGURE 18–2

American students spend little time in the classroom

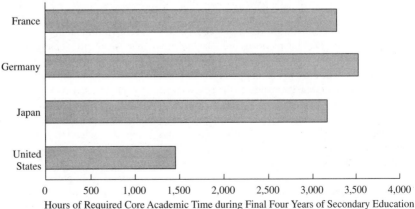

Hours of Required Core Academic Time during Final Four Years of Secondary Education

Source: National Education Commission on Time and Learning, *Prisoners of Time* (Washington, DC: U.S. Government Printing Office, 1994).

ing jobs. Rather than attempt to teach workers what they ought to have learned in school or in a publicly financed training program, many U.S. companies find it in their best financial interest to move production to other countries. They may go to Europe, Japan, or, increasingly, the NICs—where education has near cult status and where well-educated people will work for much lower wages than Americans.

Criticism of public education and demands for reform are perennial features of U.S. political life. Despite many experiments, little progress can be measured since the 1970s. A consensus is emerging, however, about the outlines of a more effective approach that borrows from other countries' systems. That approach usually includes a more consistent and rigorous curriculum, school-leaving tests, and more attention to the needs of the noncollege track.

These reforms will cost money, though money alone is not the answer without changes in the way education is delivered. The United States is currently in

---

Box 18–1

Education for the Noncollege-Bound under the German Dual System

Germany has a two-track system of education that turns out skilled workers as well as scientists and professionals. Switzerland, Denmark, and other northern European countries have similar programs.[1]

At 15, students who do not want to go to the university opt for a three-or-more-year apprenticeship. It combines theoretical education for two or three days a week in school and on-the-job training in a local factory. Most students are motivated for the classroom work, which is rigorous, because they can see the links with earning a living. The factory work exposes them to the real world and pays them a nominal salary. Successful apprentices are guaranteed a job after graduation. Companies like to participate because it enables them to identify good workers and train them at partial public expense (the government subsidizes the apprenticeship program).

Under the dual system, other students can select the university track. In higher education, science and engineering have greater status than in the United States or Britain, with their liberal arts tradition.

Many ambitious students choose to pursue technical degrees that give them links to firms upon graduation.

The dual system is far from perfect. Apprenticeships work best for large, established industries and not as well for small employers, many of which cannot afford the cost ($19,000 per apprentice). It also is more suited to manufacturing than to the more dynamic service sector. Critics think German education leads to overspecialization and is too rigid for the demands of today's fast-changing economy. The vocational-high-school track might not work the same in a society like that which exists in the United States where manual work is held in contempt and which lacks the Germanic tradition of revered master craftsmanship.

On balance, however, the dual-system approach works well, especially at easing the trauma of moving from school to job. Germany and countries with similar systems produce excellent engineers and technicians, and they do an especially good job with students who move on to blue-collar jobs. It is this highly skilled workforce that is probably these countries' greatest international competitive edge.

[1]"A Survey of Education," *The Economist,* November 21, 1992, pp. 11–13.

FIGURE 18-3

Americans spend less on nonuniversity education compared to some countries

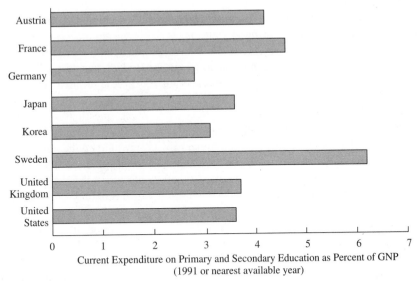

Current Expenditure on Primary and Secondary Education as Percent of GNP
(1991 or nearest available year)

Source: *UNESCO Statistical Yearbook* (Paris: UNESCO, 1993).

the mid-range of countries in how much of its national income goes to primary and secondary education (see Figure 18–3). But education in America is costly due in part to the nation's much more diverse population, with its different language and cultural backgrounds. The large proportion of children living in poverty puts further burdens on education that other countries do not always have. It would pay society to provide these kids with intensive day care and nursery school programs (standard in such places as France)—but we choose not to do this.

Mobilizing new resources for primary and secondary education in the face of pressure to economize public spending is a great challenge. Unfortunately, the payback would not be felt for decades. Investment in education has a lagged effect on productivity because schooling takes years to complete. To the extent that U.S. policy makers have a short attention span and are under pressure for quick results, the political system may not be capable of sustaining increased public investment in schooling. American business will suffer.

Conclusion

In this concluding chapter, we have reviewed the polemic about U.S. competitiveness. We saw that the truth is nuanced. The U.S. business environment does not look so bad when one looks around the world. Yet, this accomplishment should not be reason for solace, because the rest of the world is not standing still. Reformed and improved public policies, as well as changes in internal ways of managing, are needed to keep up productivity and living standards in the United States.

Many political economists concur that three pressing tasks for U.S. government and business in the 1990s are to boost saving, to upgrade the infrastructure, and, especially, to make the education system work better. The United States is not alone in facing this trio of problems, of course. There is disquiet about lack of investment, crumbling public works, and miseducated workers in all advanced countries. Yet, the problems often run deeper in the United States.

American companies have offsetting advantages, too. The United States is a traditional object for immigration. It can import the skilled manpower it needs more easily than most other nations and thus can avoid some education expense. The United States also has an entrepreneurial culture and is an outstanding incubator of new business. The venture capital market seems dynamic despite the lack of saving. The national infrastructure is still extensive due to earlier investment. But these positive features may not be sufficient to neutralize the long-term effects of recurrent shortages of domestic financial, physical, and human capital.

Redirecting the U.S. education system, increasing the saving rate, and improving the infrastructure are not the answers for every challenge to U.S. business. There are no magic bullets, even if these reforms do hold promise for boosting the nation's capacity to contend in world markets. The question is whether American society can mobilize to carry out improvements in public policy. Given the structure of the U.S. political system, it is hard to be reassured. Public opinion is divided over making the sacrifices needed to put the economy on a sounder footing, and it is not possible for a narrow majority to push through a bold program of reform, as is truer in other countries. The likely result will be stalemate, which could allow a continued, slow deterioration in U.S. relative economic standing.

Questions

1. Discuss the idea of national competitiveness. To what extent does it make sense?

2. What are the major problems facing American business in your view? What can be done about them?

3. How do you think the U.S. education system could be improved to help business? What specific steps could be taken?

4. What is productivity? Why is it important?

5. Is U.S. business in decline? On the rise? What do you think the future holds?

End Notes

1. President's Commission on Industrial Competitiveness, *Global Competition: The New Reality,* vol. 1 (Washington, DC: U.S. Government Printing Office, 1985), p. 11.

2. Ibid., p. 7.

3. See, for example, Michael Porter, *The Competitive Advantage of Nations* (New York: Free Press, 1990). Paul Krugman would go further, dropping competitiveness as a worry to focus directly on productivity. See Paul Krugman, *Peddling Prosperity: Economic Sense and Nonsense in the Age of Diminished Expectations* (New York: Norton, 1994), pp. 268–80.

4. "Who's Sharper Now?" *The Economist,* January 15, 1994, p. 15. Productivity is another confusing term, since it can refer to the output of labor, of capital, or of a certain sector. It is important to identify what kind of productivity one is talking about, because the rates of change will differ.

5. Perhaps the most prominent (and sober) example is Paul Kennedy, *The Rise and Fall of the Great Powers* (New York: Random House, 1987). A particularly grim view of American prospects,

written from the left, is Samuel Bowles, David Gordon, and Thomas Weisskopf, *After the Waste Land* (Armonk, NY: M. E. Sharpe, 1990).

6. See Barry Bluestone and Bennett Harrison, *The Deindustrialization of America* (New York: Basic Books, 1982); and Stephen S. Cohen and John Zysman, *Manufacturing Matters* (New York: Basic Books, 1987).

7. Typical alarmist tracts are Harry E. Figgie, Jr., *Bankruptcy 1995: The Coming Collapse of America and How to Stop It* (Boston: Little, Brown, 1992); and James D. Davidson and William Rees-Moog, *The Great Reckoning,* rev. ed. (New York: Simon and Schuster, 1993).

8. Michael Prowse, "Is America in Decline?" *Harvard Business Review,* July–August 1992, p. 42.

9. See, for instance, Joel Kurtzman, *The Decline and Crash of the American Economy* (New York: Norton, 1988); and William S. Dietrich, *In the Shadow of the Rising Sun* (University Park: Pennsylvania State University Press, 1991).

10. George Friedman, *Coming War with Japan* (New York: St. Martin's, 1991).

11. Krugman, *Peddling Prosperity.*

12. Among the more enthused examples are Richard B. McKenzie, *What Went Right in the 1980s* (San Francisco: Pacific Research Institute for Public Policy, 1994); and Robert L. Bartley, *The Seven Fat Years* (New York: Free Press, 1992). More balanced but generally positive assessments include Richard Rosecrance, *America's Economic Resurgence* (New York: Harper and Row, 1990); and Henry R. Nau, *The Myth of America's Decline: Leading the World Economy into the 1990s* (New York: Oxford University Press, 1990).

13. Joseph S. Nye, Jr., *Bound to Lead: The Changing Nature of American Power* (New York: Basic Books, 1990).

14. See, for example, Brian Reading, *Japan: The Coming Collapse* (New York: HarperBusiness, 1992); Bill Emmott, *Japanophobia: The Myth of the Invincible Japanese* (New York: Times Books, 1993); Herbert Giersch, Karl-Heinz Paqué, and Holger Schmieding, *The Fading Miracle: Four Decades of Market Economy in Germany* (Cambridge: Cambridge University Press, 1992); and W. R. Smyser, *The Economy of*

United Germany: Colossus at the Crossroads* (New York: St. Martin's, 1992).

15. *OECD Indicators of Industrial Activity* (Paris: Organization of Economic Cooperation and Development, various issues).

16. "Ready to Take on the World," *The Economist,* January 15, 1994, p. 66.

17. George L. Church, "We're #1—and It Hurts," *Time,* October 24, 1994, pp. 50ff.

18. This obsession with rankings is reflected in the titles of such books as Ezra Vogel, *Japan as Number One* (Cambridge, MA: Harvard University Press, 1979), and Gail Schwartz and Pat Choate, *Being Number One: Rebuilding the U.S. Economy* (Lexington, MA: Lexington Books, 1980).

19. Adrian Wood, *North–South Trade, Employment and Inequality* (New York: Oxford University Press, 1994).

20. Louis A. Ferleger and Jay R. Mandle, *No Pain, No Gain: Taxes, Productivity, and Economic Growth* (New York: Twentieth Century Fund Press, 1992).

21. David Dollar and Edward N. Wolff, *Competitiveness, Convergence, and International Specialization* (Cambridge, MA: MIT Press, 1993).

22. Michael L. Dertouzos, Richard K. Lester, Robert M. Solow, and the MIT Commission on Industrial Productivity, *Made in America* (New York: Harper, 1990), Chapters 3, 7, and 9.

23. William J. Baumol and Kenneth McLennan, eds., *Productivity Growth and U.S. Competitiveness* (New York: Oxford University Press, 1985), p. viii.

24. Cuomo Commission on Trade and Competitiveness, *The Cuomo Commission Report* (New York: Simon and Schuster, 1988), p. 114; also see National Council on Public Works Improvement, *Fragile Foundations: A Report on America's Public Works* (Washington, DC: U.S. Government Printing Office, 1980).

25. Peter Gosselin, "Economists Question Infrastructure Plans," *Boston Sunday Globe,* October 18, 1992, p. 1.

26. The Educational Testing Service alleges these tests produce flawed comparisons. But even if the education gap is overstated, and the United States is not as far behind other countries as

thought, there is no doubt that many young people are not being well-prepared for competing in the global economy.

27. U.S. General Accounting Office, *Training Strategies: Preparing Noncollege Youth for Employment in the U.S. and Foreign Countries* (Washington, DC: U.S. Government Printing Office, 1990); U.S. Congress Office of Technology Assessment, *Worker Training:*

Competing in the New International Economy (Washington, DC: U.S. Government Printing Office, 1990).

28. "Smart Work," *The Economist*, August 22, 1992, pp. 21–22.

29. Lisa M. Lynch, ed., *Training and the Private Sector: International Comparisons* (Chicago: University of Chicago Press, 1994), p. 6.

absolutism The principle of absolute government, the governed having no share in administration.

adverse selection The market failure that happens when only buyers (or only sellers) know the quality of each unit under exchange.

affirmative action A government program to promote actively the employment of protected classes of people rather than merely forbidding discrimination against them.

antitrust law Public policy that prohibits monopolies and collusion among firms to inhibit competition.

applied research Research directed to a specific practical aim.

bankruptcy law Public policy to offer debtors a fresh start when they are burdened with debt beyond reasonable hope of recovery, and to allow creditors to recover as much of their losses as possible.

basic research Research undertaken for its own sake, without thought of commercial applications.

board of directors The body established to protect shareholders' interest in a corporation, and charged with developing broad policies and selecting top-level personnel.

bureaucracy An organization that carries out day-to-day policy, uses standardized procedures, has a hierarchy, and is based on specialized duties.

business environment The pattern of external factors that affect a business or other organization's performance.

business ethics Company practices and activities that are expected or looked on favorably by society, though they are not codified by law.

capital Produced goods that are used to produce other goods.

capital gain The excess over purchase value realized from the sale of a capital asset.

capitalism An economic system that depends mainly on private enterprise to invest in productive resources and to use them to make useful products at affordable cost.

cartel An association of firms to establish monopoly power through price fixing and other anticompetitive means.

CEO (chief executive officer) The most senior manager in a company, with authority over other employees.

Chapter 11 A section of the U.S. bankruptcy code that allows managers to reorganize a failing company while protected by a court from the people and organizations to whom it owes money.

civil law The body of law concerned with private rights of individuals such as a breach of contract or personal injury.

civil rights or liberties Legally secured immunities from state interference in certain spheres of action, such as conscience, speech, worship, publication, association, and assembly.

codetermination   Corporate governance in which employers and employees share in decision making.

command economy   A planned economy where crucial economic decisions are made to a large extent by government, not market forces.

common law   Law made by judges, as distinct from **statutory law.**

communism   The radical form of **socialism** used to describe an economic system where the government has a monopoly on power and runs a command economy.

conglomerate merger   A merger between firms operating in separate markets.

conservatism   An approach to economics and politics that views society as difficult to change arbitrarily, and that wants to limit the role of government to a few necessary spheres.

consumer sovereignty   The idea that consumers decide what items will be produced and how they will be distributed.

contract   An agreement, enforceable by law, between two or more parties to do or refrain from doing something.

cooperative   An organization of people who pool resources to buy or sell something, in which profits are distributed among members according to the business they do.

corporate governance   The structures and processes by which corporations are managed.

corporate social responsibility   The idea that, out of enlightened self-interest, companies should go beyond the minimum of the law to anticipate or head off future legal developments.

corporation   An organization given a legal personality for carrying on certain activities. It may be closely held or publicly traded.

corporatism   A theory of democracy where government represents and is answerable to officially recognized organizations that act for their members.

countervailing duty   A tax to offset the subsidies imports receive at home.

criminal law   The law on wrongs against society, such as tax evasion, false advertising, or reckless polluting.

customs duty   A tax on imports or exports.

deindustrialization   The loss of basic industries and industrial jobs in mature economies.

democracy   A system of government where citizens make political decisions through their representatives. Also called **liberal democracy** when the system has a constitution that protects individual rights.

deregulation   Efforts to end government regulation of economic activities and sectors, allowing firms to make more decisions alone.

direct foreign investment   Investment in overseas business operations over which the investor has control, as opposed to portfolio investment in bonds or small shares of stock.

discrimination   Treatment of someone less favorably than another because of a physical or cultural attribute.

distributive policy   Government activities such as tariffs and government contracts that give benefits to specific groups.

due process   A constitutional principle requiring that judicial and similar proceedings be done in a consistent and orderly way.

dumping   Predatory pricing practices in international trade, where goods are sold below cost in a foreign market, or at a cost lower than in the home market.

economic development   The process of material and social betterment resulting from increased economic production and productivity.

economic man   The idea that human beings behave rationally, making choices that will give them the best chance to obtain desired values.

economic rent   Excess payment to a factor of production (land, labor, or capital) beyond what is needed to keep it in its present use.

economic rights   Government services to meet the material needs of its citizens, provided as a social obligation. Also called *social rights.*

efficiency   The production of goods at minimum cost (productive efficiency) and their allocation according to people's desires, so there is no waste (allocative efficiency).

efficiency price   See **scarcity price.**

employer mandate   A requirement by government that employers spend money for certain purposes.

employment at will   The legal doctrine that permits

employers and employees to end their relationship at any time.

entitlement program   A program of individual benefits whose funds are automatically approved, such as government pensions and unemployment compensation.

entrepreneur   Proprietor of an enterprise who sees opportunities to introduce a new product, production process, or organizational setup.

ESOP (employee stock ownership plan)   A profit-sharing plan that allows employees to invest in the company for which they work.

E.U. (European Union)   Formerly the E.C. (European Community), this is Europe's Common Market, first established in 1957 and strengthened in 1986 and 1991.

excise   A tax on the sale or manufacture of a specific product.

excludability   The degree to which goods or services change hands only if both buyers and sellers agree on the terms.

externality   The partial cost or benefit of a transaction that is borne not by the producer or consumer of goods and services, but by other members of society, leading to a market failure.

factor of production   Economic resources that go into the production of goods.

fiduciary   A person having a legal duty to act primarily for another's benefit.

filibuster   The use of stalling tactics to keep debate alive and block final action on a bill in the U.S. Senate.

fiscal policy   The use of taxes and government spending to stabilize the economy.

free riding   The tendency of consumers to understate a preference for a **public good** and to consume the good without paying the full price for it.

free trade   The elimination of impediments to foreign trade so that goods, services, and capital can travel unchecked across international borders.

functional representation   Representation of society's functions (such as labor and management) through public institutions.

GATT (General Agreement on Tariffs and Trade)   An international code of trading rules, signed in 1947, that promotes freer trade.

GDP/GNP   The value of all goods and services produced for sale in a nation in a year. (GDP excludes investment income from abroad.)

general sales tax   A tax levied on retail sales.

globalization   The trend toward greater integration of the world's markets.

golden parachute   A contract by which a company agrees to make a payment to key officers should control of the company change hands.

government   The institutions that provide protection and justice to constituents by exercising monopoly power over the use of force. Also see **state.**

government failure   The inability of a government intervention in the economy to provide a socially desirable outcome.

greenmail   The repurchase of stock at a price above the market, used as a means to stop an investor who wants to take over a company.

horizontal merger   One company's acquisition of another company competing in the same product and geographic markets.

hostile takeover   An acquisition attempt by outsiders made over the objection of the management of the company being acquired.

human capital   The investment in the education and skills of a nation's population.

income tax   A tax levied on individual or corporate income.

independent regulatory commission   An autonomous unit of the U.S. government that deals with a specific industry or field of activity, often combining quasi legislative, judicial, and administrative functions.

industrial democracy   When workers participate in the management of companies. See also **co-determination.**

industrial policy   Selective government programs to create or revitalize particular industries or companies, usually so they can compete internationally.

Industrial Revolution   The time countries changed their manufacturing methods from individual production by hand to factory production using machines. Also see **industrialization.**

industrialization   The development of modern manufacturing industries, usually as a conscious government plan. Also see **economic development.**

infrastructure   The physical foundation on which a community's economy is built and public services delivered, and that weaves it together with other economies. Also called *social overhead capital.*

initiative   The mechanism by which citizens can petition to present a measure directly to the voters or to the legislature.

insider trading   The illegal practice of buying and selling shares based on information that is not available to the public.

interest groups   Private organizations, united by common goals, that organize to lobby and influence public policy.

International Monetary Fund (IMF)   An international organization established in 1944 that provides funds needed for balance of payments to stabilize currencies.

investment   Expenditure devoted to increasing or maintaining the economy's stock of **capital.**

invisible hand   The idea that the pursuit of profit in a free market leads to the material advantage of society as a whole.

iron triangle   A name for the steady, helpful relationships that often grow among a congressional committee or subcommittee, an administrative agency, and concerned interest groups.

joint venture   An association of firms assembled to carry out a specific business project.

junk bonds   High-risk bonds often used to raise funds for corporate buyouts and takeovers.

Keynesian economics   Analysis of the cause and consequence of aggregate spending and income, in which government compensates for deficiencies with deficit spending.

laissez-faire   The doctrine that the commercial affairs of society are best guided by the decisions of individuals, to the exclusion of government.

LBO (leveraged buyout)   A group of investors led by management buys the stock of a publicly traded company and takes the company private, financed by loans in which the company's assets are pledged as collateral.

LDC   A less developed country, with low average income and little industry.

liberal democracy   See **democracy.**

liberalism   Originally, and in most of the world, the political theory of limited government and the supreme value of human or civil rights. For the economy, the theory thus implies restricting government's functions and trusting individuals to make most decisions. In the United States, however, liberalism has come to mean advocacy of government intervention in the economy, which in part is the opposite of its original meaning.

licensing   Permission from government to do something that is otherwise against the law.

limited liability   The legal separation of a corporation from its shareholders, which protects shareholders from being held fully personally responsible for the corporation's liabilities.

loan guarantee   The practice of government promising to repay, in case of default, a private loan made for purposes deemed in the public interest.

lobbying   An effort to pass, defeat, or change the contents of legislative bills and other government decisions.

logrolling   Mutual aid among politicians with reciprocal support for each other's bills.

market   A system of voluntary exchange that generates prices to decide how to allocate scarce resources.

market failure   The inability of private transactions to provide certain goods or to operate with mutually satisfactory results.

mercantilism   The economic philosophy of merchants and kings during the 16th and 17th centuries to regulate trade, to promote an excess of exports over imports.

merit good   Something whose consumption is deemed intrinsically desirable.

meritocracy   A social and economic system that is open to all and where the rewards are given out according to talent and hard work.

methodological individualism   A theory of explanation in social science that says the reason for social processes and events can be deduced from principles governing the behavior of the participating individuals.

mixed economy   An economy where private and state-owned enterprises exist side by side.

MNC (multinational corporation)   An enterprise

that produces goods or services in more than one country.

monetary policy   Management of the money supply, and thus the availability of credit, to support price stability and full employment.

monopoly   When a firm or individual is the only seller of a given commodity.

moral hazard   The action of economic agents to maximize their utility to the detriment of others by hiding their actions.

nation   A people who consciously identify with some common cultural experience.

national competitiveness   The ability of a country's companies to win in international markets.

nationalize   For government to take over ownership and control of an industry that produces output for sale in the market.

NIC   A **newly industrialized country,** such as Taiwan or South Korea.

nonmarket failure   See **government failure.**

nonprofit sector   The sector of a mixed economy made of private organizations in which no stockholder shares in profits or losses. Also called the independent or voluntary sector.

nontariff barriers   Government measures other than tariffs to inhibit international commerce.

OECD (Organization for Economic Cooperation and Development)   An international organization (established in 1961) to promote economic growth and development. The 25 members are mostly economically advanced, capitalist nations.

opportunity cost   The alternative cost if a choice had been made differently.

PAC (political action committee)   An organization formed under U.S. law to funnel funds to selected candidates or to promote favored causes.

parliamentary democracy   A form of government in which the legislature is the supreme governing body and from which the executive is drawn.

peak association   An all-embracing organization that represents the interests of a large number of firms in different economic sectors.

pluralism   A type of political representation where power is distributed through many private organizations that can limit one another's action.

poison pill   A shareholder rights plan aimed at discouraging **hostile takeovers.**

policy-making system   A small and stable group that effectively controls decisions in a narrow policy area.

political economy   The study of the interaction of political, economic, and other factors in society.

political rights   Rights to join in the management of government and to influence public policy.

pollution   Industrial byproducts that are discharged into the physical environment and that have social cost.

pollution permit   A right to pollute that can be bought, sold, traded, or saved.

pollution tax   A tax that is theoretically equal to the external cost of pollution, so that prices reflect the full cost to the environment of making things.

pork barrel policy   Extra funding added to bills for local projects to please a legislator's constituents.

postindustrial society   Societies whose people predominantly work in services and where manufacturing provides a minority of jobs and national income.

principal–agent problem   A situation where the interests of a principal (e.g., a shareholder) and an agent (e.g., a professional manager) differ, and the principal cannot fully control what the agent does.

prisoner's dilemma   Situations where rational behavior at the micro level leads to irrational collective outcomes.

private goods   Items that one person can consume and preclude others from using.

privatize   To substitute private entities for government agencies to provide services. Also can mean to sell public enterprises to private investors or to allow citizens to choose among public service providers.

product liability   A firm's or person's legal responsibility for harm stemming from the use of a product that it made, sold, managed, or used.

productivity   The value of output produced by a unit of labor or capital.

progressive movement   A campaign for reform in the United States directed against Big Business and political machines, from around 1890 to 1920.

property rights   The permissible use of resources, goods, and services.

property tax   A payment levied by government based on the amount of property a taxpayer owns.

protectionism   A public policy of excluding imports to a country.

public choice   The economic analysis of politics that assumes voters, politicians, and bureaucrats are mainly self-interested and not primarily motivated by the public welfare.

public goods   Items that are simultaneously available to many people.

public interest group   Organizations that claim to seek to advance causes that will benefit society as a whole.

public policy   A government law or rule that expresses government's goals and provides rewards and punishment to promote their attainment.

quality circles   Groups of employees who meet to brainstorm ways to boost a firm's output.

R&D   **Research and development** to find and apply new technology.

rationality   The assumption in political economy that people make consistent, ordered decisions.

Reaganomics   See **supply-side economics.**

redistributive policy   Policies such as progressive taxation and welfare programs that redistribute income from one group to another.

referendum   The procedure by which citizens vote on a piece of legislation.

regulatory policy   Government action to control firms' price, sale, and production in the public interest.

rent seeking   Efforts to get government to create **economic rents** that can then be captured for private gain.

resource depletion   The using up of nonrenewable resources.

restraint of trade   An attempt by a company or companies to stifle or eliminate competition.

rights   Advantages that can be legitimately claimed according to law or tradition.

savings   All income not spent for current consumption.

scarcity price   A payment given in a transaction that is set by the forces of supply and demand.

scientific management   The management of organizations based on careful study of plant layout, work schedules, and job content, and on the use of wage incentives.

self-interest   The idea that individuals are motivated mainly to seek their own advantage.

separation of powers   The division of state power across several institutions that must cooperate in policy making.

sexual harassment   Unwanted offers of or requests for sex at the workplace, prohibited under U.S. federal law.

social democrat   An advocate of a gradual passage to state economic planning and state ownership. Also see **socialism.**

social insurance   Government programs that provide protection against financial losses associated with work.

social market economy   Germany's distinctive system of seeking consensus among workers, management, and government.

social regulation   Government control of the activities of firms and other organizations to promote a better quality of life, as opposed to narrow economic concerns.

socialism   A political doctrine emphasizing collective ownership of the means of production, ascribing a large role to the government in running the economy.

stakeholders   An organization's constituencies, who can affect its actions in significant ways.

state   An organization that claims a monopoly of legitimate use of force within a given territory. Also see **government.**

state-owned enterprise   A nationalized company that sells goods or services.

statutory law   Law created by legislative bodies.

strict liability   A no-fault theory of **product liability,** when neither care nor good faith can absolve the manufacturer of a defective product.

subsidy   An explicit cash payment or implicit assistance from government to business or other organizations and individuals.

subtractability   The degree to which goods or services may be used simultaneously by many consumers without being diminished in quality or quantity.

sunk cost   A cost that has been incurred and cannot be reversed.

supply-side economics   A body of thought that emphasizes tax cuts and deregulation to promote efficient use of labor and capital. Also known as Reaganomics.

tariff   A tax on imports.

tax expenditure   An allowance by government to reduce tax liability for certain activities.

technology   Skills, knowledge, and hardware for practical tasks, acquired through applied science or systematic thought.

technology policy   Government action to promote the discovery and use of better technology.

Third World   A loose term for all less developed countries.

tort   An intentional or negligent wrong against an individual.

total liability   A legal principle that holds producers liable for *any* injury associated with a product.

trade association   A nonprofit organization of companies in a common trade or industry that purports to serve the common interest of its members.

tragedy of the commons   The degradation that occurs when many individuals use a scarce resource in common.

transaction cost   The cost, often substantial, that arises from transferring the ownership of goods and services.

transfer payment   Government payments to individuals and firms *not* in exchange for goods and services.

user fee   A payment made by those who use a specified good or service provided by government.

utilitarianism   A system of ethics based on the maxim that people should act in a way that results in the greatest net social good.

utility maximizer   The idea that people act so that, if faced with the same item at different prices, they will buy the lower priced one.

VAT (value added tax)   A tax that accumulates on goods as they move from raw material through the production and distribution process.

vertical merger   A merger between two companies in the vertical chain of production or distribution.

warranty   A promise of quality or performance for a good or service.

welfare state   A nation in which government plays a positive role to promote the social welfare.

workers' compensation   No-fault insurance providing recovery for workers who sustain illness or injury on the job.

World Bank   Officially the International Bank for Reconstruction and Development, the World Bank was founded in 1944 to make loans to finance productive investment in member countries.

World Trade Organization (WTO)   The successor organization to the **GATT,** created in 1995, with stronger power to resolve trade disputes.

HARLEY-DAVIDSON INC.

Introduction

The name's Johnny. Johnny Callatino. You might've heard of me. I run a little business down off of 38th and Main. It's an investments business. You ain't heard of it? Oh well. Hey, you got a light? Thanks, man. Hey, while you're up, can you grab me a cold one? Thanks. Aaaah. That's more like it. Grab some wood, pal. I've got one hell of a story for you.

It all started a few months ago. I had just stalled the landlady for another week. So I'm sitting in my office, sipping a Jack and Coke, minding my own business, when this incredible blonde walks in.

"Johnny," she says, "I need a loan."

"Well, beautiful, you came to the right guy."

So, for the next few hours, I listened to her story. Great girl. Really smart. Her name was Connie. Maybe you know her. But anyway, turns out she had this hot tip on Harley-Davidson. A sure thing, she said. But she needed my money to play the market. So we'd be partners, or something like that.

At first, I thought to myself, this can't miss. Harley's like apple pie. I used to ride around on my Hog back in the 60s. Damn, those were some good times. Then my little voice went off inside my head. Only this time my voice ain't whispering; he's shouting.

"Hey, yo, Johnny! You snapperhead! What're you thinking, huh? Look at the economy. We're heading for a friggin' recession and you want to put your wad in Harley? Geez. And what about Holiday Rambler? Yeah, you forgot about them, you dunce! They're the RV sub that keeps sucking all of Harley's profits! Come on, Johnny, pull your head out before it's too late!"

Whew. My little voice never spouted off like that before. So, I figured I'd better listen to him. So, I told the dame that before I shelled out my coin, I was gonna have to check out Harley for myself. She gave me a week. And here's what I found out. So light 'em if you've got 'em . . .

Company History

In the Beginning . . . The year was 1903. Henry Ford introduced the first Model A, the Wright brothers flew over Kitty Hawk, and, in a shack near Milwaukee, Wisconsin, a machine called the Silent Grey Fellow was born.[1] Three brothers, William, Walter, and Arthur Davidson, had invented a machine which would exemplify "the American desire for power, speed and personal freedom"[2]—the Harley-Davidson motorcycle.

The Davidson's first crude machines found a ready market among both individuals and law enforcement agencies,[3] and by 1907, production had reached 150 motorcycles per year.[4] Two years later, a new engine, the V-twin, was introduced that enabled motorcycles to attain top speeds of 60 m.p.h.[5] Motorcycles were fast becoming the primary source of transportation in the United States.

The Harley-Davidson Motorcycle Company took pride in America, and, when the U.S. joined Europe in World War I, Harley-Davidson motorcycles helped the U.S. Army chase the Kaiser across Germany.[6] After World War I, however, it was the automobile, not the motorcycle, which gained popularity as America's principal means of transportation. Harley's annual production plunged from 28,000 to 10,000 units immediately after the war.[7] After a decade of struggle, Harley-Davidson again reached pre-war production levels, only to be ravaged by the Great Depression. By 1933, only 3,700 motorcycles were produced by Harley-Davidson.[8]

The economic boost provided by World War II and the military's high demand for motorcycles enabled Harley-Davidson to again match their 1920 production level.[9] But after World War II, the motorcycle industry crashed. As America's heroes returned, their focus was on housing and family necessities, not motorcycles.[10] At one time, Harley-Davidson was one of 150 U.S. motorcycle manufacturers, but by 1953, the weak motorcycle market had eliminated their final U.S. competitor,

Source: This case was prepared by Scott Draper, A. Scott Dundon, Allen North, and Ron Smith under the supervision of Professor Sexton Adams, University of North Texas, and Professor Adelaide Griffin, Texas Woman's University. Copyright © 1990 by Sexton Adams and Adelaide Griffin.

[1]Mark Marvel, "The Gentrified Hog," *Esquire,* July 1989, pp. 25–26.

[2]Ibid., p. 25.

[3]Robert L. Rose, "Vrooming Back," *The Wall Street Journal* (Southwestern Edition), August 31, 1990, p. 1.

[4]Peter C. Reid, *Well Made in America—Lessons from Harley-Davidson on Being the Best* (1988), p. 9.

[5]Marvel, "Gentrified," p. 25.

[6]Ibid., p. 25.

[7]Reid, *Well Made,* p. 9.

[8]Ibid.

[9]Ibid.

[10]Ibid.

Indian Motorcycle Company. Harley-Davidson stood alone as the sole manufacturer of motorcycles in the United States.[11]

The AMF Reign.   Harley-Davidson made its first public stock offering in 1965, and, shortly thereafter, the struggle for control of Harley-Davidson began. In 1968, Bangor Punta, an Asian company with roots in the railroad industry, began acquiring large amounts of Harley-Davidson stock. At the same time, AMF, an international leader in the recreational goods market, announced its interest in Harley-Davidson, citing a strong fit between Harley-Davidson's product lines and AMF's leisure lines. Bangor Punta and AMF then entered a bidding war over Harley-Davidson. Harley's stockholders chose AMF's bid of $22 per share over Bangor Punta's bid of $23 per share, because of Bangor Punta's reputation for acquiring a company, squeezing it dry, and then scrapping it for salvage. AMF's plans were initially perceived as being more favorable for Harley-Davidson's long-term existence by touting plans for expansion of Harley.[12]

AMF's plans did not, however, correspond with Harley-Davidson's ability to expand. Much of Harley-Davidson's equipment was antiquated and could not keep up with the increase in production. One company official noted that "quality was going down just as fast as production was going up."[13] These events occurred at a time when Japanese motorcycle manufacturers began flooding the U.S. market with high-quality motorcycles that offered many innovative features and cost less.

Many of Harley's employees felt that if AMF had worked with the experienced Harley personnel instead of dictating orders for production quotas, many of the problems could have been properly addressed. One Harley senior executive stated that "the bottom line was that quality went to hell because AMF expanded Harley production at the same time that Harleys were getting out of date, and the Japanese were coming to town with new designs and reliable products at a low price."[14] Unlike their Japanese competitors whose motorcycles failed to pass inspection an average 5 percent of the time, Harley's motorcycles failed to pass the end-of-the-assembly-line inspection at an alarming 50 percent to 60 percent rate.[15]

After a $4.8 million annual operating loss[16] and 11 years under AMF control, Harley-Davidson was put up for sale in 1981. A management team, led by Vaughn Beals, Vice-President of Motorcycle Sales, used $81.5 million in financing from Citicorp to complete a leveraged buyout. All ties with AMF were severed and Harley-Davidson Inc. was created.[17]

The Tariff Barrier.   While Harley-Davidson had managed to obliterate its U.S. competition during the 50s and 60s, the company took a beating from the Japanese in the 70s. Japanese competition and the recession presiding over the nation's economy had taken nearly all of Harley-Davidson's business. The company's meager 3 percent share of total motorcycle sales led experts to speculate whether or not Harley-Davidson would be able to celebrate its 80th birthday. Tariff protection appeared to be Harley-Davidson's only hope. Fortunately, massive lobbying efforts finally paid off in 1983, when Congress passed a huge tariff increase on Japanese motorcycles. Instead of a 4 percent tariff, Japanese motorcycles would now be subject to a 45 percent tariff. The protection was to last for five years.[18]

Slowly, Harley-Davidson began to recover market share as the tariff impacted competitors. Management was able to relinquish their ownership with a public stock offering in 1986.[19] Brimming with confidence, Harley-Davidson asked Congress to remove the tariff barrier in December 1986, more than a year earlier than originally planned. It was time to strap on the helmet and race with the Japanese head-to-head.[20]

Acquisition and Diversification.   Holiday Rambler was purchased in 1986 by Harley-Davidson, a move that nearly doubled the size of the firm. As a wholly owned subsidiary, the manufacturer of recreational and commercial vehicles provided Harley-Davidson with another business unit that could diversify the risks associated with the seasonal motorcycle market.[21] That move gave Harley-Davidson two distinct business segments, Holiday Rambler Corporation and Harley-Davidson Motorcycle Division. In addition, during the late 1980s, Harley-Davidson attempted to capitalize on

[11]Rose, "Vrooming," p. 1.
[12]Reid, *Well Made*, p. 9.
[13]Ibid., p. 25.
[14]Ibid., p. 27.
[15]Ibid.
[16]Harley-Davidson Annual Report—1989, p. 4.
[17]Rod Willis, "Harley-Davidson Comes Roaring Back," *Management Review*, March 1986, pp. 20–27.
[18]Rose, "Vrooming," p. 1.
[19]Ibid., p. 6.
[20]Harley Back in High Gear," *Forbes*, April 20, 1987, p. 8.
[21]Harley-Davidson Annual Report—1989, p. 4.

its manufacturing expertise by competing for both government and contract manufacturing opportunities in an attempt to further increase the proportion of revenues derived from nonmotorcycle sources.

Holiday Rambler Corporation

Harley-Davidson implemented many new management techniques at Holiday Rambler. The Yadiloh (Holiday spelled backwards) program was created in 1989. Yadiloh was an acronym for "Yes Attitude, Deliver, Involvement, Leadership, Opportunity, Harmony." The goal of Yadiloh was to address cost and productivity problems facing Holiday Rambler.[22] The employees of Holiday Rambler seemed to favor the program. "This program will help us solve a lot of problems in the long run. So I think it's a really big step, a positive step," said Raud Estep, a quality control inspector for Holiday Rambler. Another employee, Vickie Hutsell, agreed. "I think that most of the people who've gone through the Yadiloh training session are 'pumped up' about it."[23]

But Holiday Rambler did more than get employees excited. They built a new, centralized facility, scheduled to be completed in late 1990 to handle all of the company's manufacturing needs.[24] They also installed more computer-aided design (CAD) equipment to support the research and development staff, which led to a $1.9 million increase in operating expenses.[25]

Observers, however, felt that the success of Holiday Rambler had been mixed at best. Several strong competitors had entered the RV market in 1988. Holiday Rambler responded by discontinuing its "Trail Seeker" line of recreational vehicles after the unit experienced a $30 million sales decline in 1988.[26] Holiday Rambler continued to trim poor performing areas. In October 1989, Parkway Distribution, a recreational vehicle parts and accessories distributor, was sold. A $2.8 million decline in revenues from the business units of Creative Dimensions, Nappanee Wood Products, and B & B Molders was recorded in 1989.[27] Holiday Rambler enacted competitive pricing measures and a lower margin sales mix in 1989. The result was a decrease in gross margin percentage, from 19.0 percent to 18.2 percent.[28]

Some industry experts recognized a possible recovery for the sluggish RV market in 1990.[29] However, the message of H. Wayne Dahl, Holiday Rambler president, was unclear. "Whether our business is RVs, commercial vehicles or a related enterprise, we intend to keep it strong and growing by keeping in close touch with its customers."[30]

The Recreational Vehicle Market. In 1986, Harley executives claimed that the acquisition of Holiday Rambler would help to diversify the risks associated with the seasonal motorcycle market.[31] However, some industry experts questioned whether such an acquisition was a wise move for Harley. They pointed out that although the acquisition smoothed seasonal fluctuations in demand, cyclical fluctuations caused by the economy were unaffected. One expert asserted, "Because both items (motorcycles and recreational vehicles) are luxury goods, they are dependent on such key economic factors as interest rates, disposable income, and gasoline prices."[32]

In addition to the economy, demographics of the RV market presented a challenge to Harley. The main consumer of recreational vehicles in the 70s was the blue-collar worker who worked a steady 40 hours per week. However, economic trends led to a switch from manufacturing to a more service-oriented economy. The trends left most consumers with little time on their hands for recreational activities. Statistics revealed in 1989 that the typical owner of RVs was between 35 and 54-years-old with an average income of $39,800. Census projections also indicated that the American population was growing older at the end of the 1980s. The high incomes and older ages gave RV manufacturers the opportunity to include extra features that allowed them to raise total vehicle cash prices by $20,000 and more.

The RV industry had support from nonconsumer groups that existed specifically to accommodate the RV owner. The Escapees, for instance, offered insurance and cash handling services to members driving RVs. The Good Sam's Club provided road service to RVs in need of repair. RV owners were even treated to their own television program to watch while on the road—"Wish You Were Here." The show, broadcast via satellite by

[22]Ibid., p. 3.
[23]Ibid., p. 13.
[24]Ibid., p. 15.
[25]Ibid., p. 21.
[26]Ibid., p. 14.
[27]Ibid., p. 18.
[28]Ibid., p. 19.

[29]Ibid., p. 18.
[30]Ibid., p. 14.
[31]Ibid.
[32]Raymond Serafin, "RV Market Puzzled," *Advertising Age,* July 1988, p. 52.

the Nashville channel, highlighted RV lifestyles through interviews with owners across the country.[33]

Management

Vaughn Beals's outward appearance was far removed from the burly image that many might have expected of a "Harley" chief executive. The middle-aged Ivy Leaguer graduated from MIT's Aeronautical Engineering School and was known in manufacturing circles as a productivity guru.[34] But, on the inside, Vaughn Beals was a "H.O.G." (a Harley fanatic) in the truest sense of the word. He began working with Harley-Davidson as Vice-President of Motorcycle Sales with AMF.[35] Disgruntled with AMF's declining attention to quality, Beals led a team of 12 others which successfully completed a leveraged buyout from AMF.

But Beals had a difficult mission ahead. Even after receiving tariff protection, Harley-Davidson had to find a way to restore confidence in its products. So Beals decided to hit the high road—literally. He drove Harley-Davidson motorcycles to rallies where he met Harley owners. In doing so, Beals was able to learn about product defects and needed improvements directly from the consumer. Industry experts believed that these efforts were vital to the resurgence of the company.

Willie G. Davidson, grandson of the company's founder, rode along with Vaughn Beals on Harley's road to recovery. "Willie G." provided a sharp contrast to Beals. If Vaughn Beals looked more at home in a courtroom, Willie G. might have looked more at home behind the bars of a jail cell. Davidson's appearance was that of a middle-aged man who was a remnant of the 60s era. A Viking helmet covered his long, stringy hair, and his beard hid the hard features of a wind-parched face. He wore a leather jacket that, like his face, showed the cracks of wear and tear that the miles of passage over U.S. highways had caused. Nonetheless, Willie G. was named the new Vice-President of Design for Harley in 1981. Industry observers believed that he had been instrumental in instigating much needed improvements in the Harley Hog.

Beals stepped down as CEO in 1989, passing the reins to Richard Teerlink, who was then serving as chief

[33]Joe Schwartz, "No Fixed Address," *American Demographics,* August 1986, pp. 50–51.
[34]Willis, "Harley-Davidson," pp. 20–27.
[35]John Madock Roberts, "Harley's Hog's," *Forbes,* December 7, 1985, p. 14.

EXHIBIT 1

Harley-Davidson organizational chart

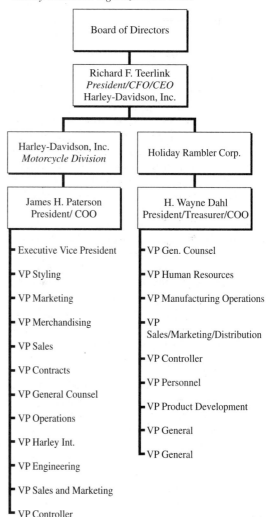

Source: Harley-Davidson, Inc.

operating officer for Harley-Davidson Motorcycle Division. Beals, however, retained his position as chairman of the board.[36] After the transition, Harley-Davidson retained a long list of experienced executives. The organizational chart (Exhibit 1) highlights the depth of the Harley-Davidson management team.

[36]Harley-Davidson Annual Report—1989, p. 2.

In a somewhat ironic turn of events, Beals and other executives of Harley-Davidson had traveled to Japan in 1981 to visit the factories of their competition in an attempt to uncover any secrets. What they found was surprising. The Japanese did not run a low-cost production facility due to sophisticated machinery; instead, they simply used effective management techniques to maximize productivity.[37] Armed with a new management perspective from the Japanese, Harley-Davidson began implementing quality circles, statistical operations controls, and just-in-time (JIT) inventory.[38]

The first dramatic change implemented by Harley management was to divide each plant into four to seven profit centers. The managers of each profit center were assigned total responsibility within their particular area. The increase in responsibility gave plant managers more authority and allowed Harley-Davidson to greatly reduce the staff functions previously needed to assist production.[39] Harley-Davidson was able to reduce its employee workforce by 40 percent after implementing these changes.[40] In 1982, the company adopted a just-in-time (JIT) system for control of "in-plant" manufacturing and a materials-as-needed (MAN) system which dealt with control of *all* inventories both inside and outside of the plants.

Next, Harley-Davidson attempted to increase employee involvement through the formation of quality circles (QCs). Thomas Gelb, Harley's executive vice-president of operations, noted that even though QCs were only a small part of employee involvement programs, they played a significant role in helping to break down the communication barriers between line workers and supervisors. Line workers who were previously given quotas from high-level management became involved, through the use of QCs, in setting more realistic quotas based on actual production capacity and needs.[41] Employee involvement gave workers a real sense of ownership in meeting these goals, according to Gelb.[42] Employees were viewed as links in a chain, and through employee involvement programs they could drive quality throughout the organization. Employees were involved, by direct participation, in discussions and decisions on changes which affected them in the perfor-

mance of their own work. Also, management trained employees on ways to recognize and eliminate waste in the production process.[43] According to 1986 figures, Harley's tab for warranty repairs, scrap, and reworking of parts had decreased by 60 percent since 1981.[44]

Employee involvement was further increased through a program called Statistical Operator Control (SOC). SOC gave employees the responsibility for checking the quality of their own work within a predetermined range. Employee quality checks took place on the production floor, and, on many occasions, the workers themselves were given the responsibility to make the proper correcting adjustments. SOC helped identify errors in the production process on a timely basis and gave line workers more responsibility through making quality checks and correcting adjustments in the production process.[45]

Although employees became more involved at Harley, labor relations remained strained. To correct the problem, management implemented an open-door policy to improve labor relations[46] and increased stock options to include a broader base of employees.[47] Management took a more sensitive stance toward the opinions of all employees.[48] Union relations also improved when management voluntarily agreed to put the "Union" label on all motorcycles produced and by sharing financial information with union leaders.[49] Harley attempted to deal with all employees, even those affected by layoffs, in a humane way. Several employee assistance programs were put into place. Among these were: outplacement assistance to cushion the blow of layoffs; early retirement (age 55) or voluntary layoffs; and drug abuse programs administered by the Milwaukee Council on Drug Abuse.[50]

In order for the above changes to work, Harley developed several overall goals. As stated in their annual report, Harley's 1989 management goals included: improvement of quality, employee satisfaction, customer satisfaction, and shareholder return. Their long-term

---

[37]Willis, "Harley-Davidson," pp. 22–23.
[38]Ibid.
[39]Ibid.
[40]Ibid., p. 26.
[41]Ibid., pp 22–23.
[42]Ibid.

[43]John A. Saathoff, "Workshop Report: Maintain Excellence through Change," *Target,* Spring 1989, p. 2.
[44]Dexter Hutchins, "Having a Hard Time with Just-In-Time," *Fortune,* June 9, 1986, p. 66.
[45]Saathoff, "Workshop," p. 4.
[46]Willis, "Harley-Davidson," p. 20.
[47]Harley-Davidson Annual Report—1989, p. 1.
[48]Ibid., p. 3.
[49]Willis, "Harley-Davidson," p. 25.
[50]Ibid., p. 27.

focus would address four major areas of concern for the 1990s: (1) quality, (2) productivity, (3) participation, and (4) flexibility.[51]

1. Quality—Management efforts in the late 1980s attempted to overcome their reputation for poor quality. Because most of Harley's upper management believed that quality improvement was an ongoing process, they made a commitment to a long-term goal.

2. and 3. Participation and productivity—These two areas were overlapping objectives, according to Harley executives. Because of this, the company emphasized employee involvement programs throughout the firm.

4. Flexibility—The diminishing domestic marketplace and the slowing U.S. economy created the need for flexibility. Harley-Davidson management hoped to explore other options for the firm.[52]

Management hoped to lead rather than follow the competition. In 1990, Harley cultivated a catch phrase of "Do the right thing and do that thing right."[53]

Production and Operations

After the leveraged buyout, manufacturing was still a major problem. According to one Harley executive, less than 70 percent of their motorcycles were complete when they reached the end of the assembly line.[54] Motorcycle production schedules were often based on the parts which were available instead of the planned master schedule. According to industry experts, "Japanese manufacturing techniques were yielding operating costs 30 percent lower than Harley's."[55] How did the Japanese do it? Though Beals and other managers had visited Japanese plants in 1981, it was not until they got a chance to tour Honda's assembly plant in Marysville, Ohio, after the buyout that they began to understand Japanese competition. Beals said, "We were being wiped out by the Japanese because they were better *managers.* It wasn't robotics, or culture, or morning calisthenics and company songs—it was professional managers who understood their business and paid attention to detail."[56] Harley managers attributed most of the difference to three specific Japanese practices: quality cir-

cles, the use of statistical process controls to ensure consistently high quality, and just-in-time manufacturing. The company quickly began to initiate the Japanese techniques.[57]

The Just-in-Time (JIT) Inventory Method. A pilot just-in-time (JIT) manufacturing program was quickly introduced in the Milwaukee engine plant. Tom Gelb, senior vice-president of operations, called a series of meetings with employees, telling them bluntly, "We have to play the game the way the Japanese play or we're dead."[58]

Gelb was met with extreme skepticism. The York, Pennsylvania, plant, for instance, was already equipped with a computer-based control system that utilized overhead conveyors and high-rise parts storage. In a meeting with the workforce of the York facility, Gelb announced that the JIT system would replace these effects with push carts. The production floor erupted with laughter. Surely, this was a joke. Plant managers mumbled that Harley-Davidson was returning to 1930.[59]

Observers noted that the overriding principle of the just-in-time method was that "parts and raw materials should arrive at the factory just as they are needed in the manufacturing process. This lets the manufacturer eliminate inventories and the costs of carrying them."[60] Anne Thundercloud, the York plant quality circle facilitator, stated that "it is the Harley employees who make JIT work, by having an investment in seeing it work." The same men and women who laughed out loud over the implementation of JIT began to believe in JIT's "exacting discipline."[61] Their belief was justified. Nearly 60,000 square feet of warehouse space were freed.[62] Costs of production plummeted. In 1986, Harley was able to lower its break-even point to 35,000 units—down from 53,000 in 1981.[63]

Supplier cooperation was also critical to JIT success, but Harley-Davidson had a poor track record with their vendors. As one industry observer noted, "Harley was notorious for juggling production schedules and was one of the worst customers when it came to last-minute panic calls for parts." Furthermore, suppliers were wary

[51]Harley-Davidson Annual Report—1989, p. 3.
[52]Ibid., p. 2.
[53]Ibid., p. 3.
[54]Ibid.
[55]Saathoff, "Workshop," p. 3.
[56]Hutchins, "Having a Hard Time," p. 65.

[57]*Fortune,* September 25, 1989, p. 161.
[58]Hutchins, "Having a Hard Time," p. 64.
[59]*Fortune,* September 25, 1989, p. 161.
[60]Ibid.
[61]Hutchins, "Having a Hard Time," p. 64.
[62]Ibid.
[63]Willis, "Harley-Davidson," p. 14.

of their role in the just-in-time picture. Edward J. Hay of Rath & Strong, a Lexington, Massachusetts, management consulting firm, stated, "The big problem is that companies treat just-in-time as a way of getting the suppliers to hold the inventories."[64] One expert noted that Harley had to "abandon the security blanket that inventory often represented for them and learn to trust their suppliers . . ."[65]

Critics believed that Harley erred initially by taking a legalistic approach in trying to sign up suppliers for a JIT system. The company insisted on contracts that were 35 pages long, devoted largely to spelling out suppliers' obligations to Harley.[66] This strategy was ambitious and too pretentious. Early results did not meet management's expectations, and the animosity was growing between Harley and their suppliers. One Harley supplier contended, "They're constantly renegotiating contracts, and tinkering with the layout of the plant."[67]

Finally, the company took positive steps to improve vendor relations. Contracts were reduced to two pages. According to one Harley executive, "We need to get out of the office and meet face-to-face." Experts noted, "Teams of its buyers and engineers fanned out to visit suppliers: they began simplifying and improving designs and helping suppliers reduce setup time between jobs by modifying equipment to permit quick changes of dies. To improve the quality of the parts, Harley gave suppliers courses in statistics to teach workers how to chart small changes in the performance of their equipment. The practice provides early tip-offs when machines are drifting out of tolerance."[68]

Materials-as-Needed (MAN). Harley's MAN system was tailored after that of Toyota Production's system, and was driven by "Kanban" technology—a control system that used circulating cards and standard containers for parts. The system provided real-time production needs information without the use of costly and complex resources which were typically needed for planning and support.[69] Tom Schwarz, general manager of Harley-Davidson Transportation Company, developed a strategically controlled inbound system for dealing with suppliers. As one executive noted, "Harley's ultimate goal is to control all inbound and outbound shipments themselves. They prefer to keep a minimum (number) of carriers involved. That reduces the chance of delays."[70] Harley-Davidson used its own leased fleet of 26 tractors and 46 trailers for the bulk of its road miles, using contract carriers only to supplement direct point service to its 700 dealers.

Harley-Davidson then began to evaluate its present suppliers based on manufacturing excellence and ability to provide small and frequent deliveries instead of evaluating suppliers strictly on price alone. Harley's trucks made daily, timed pickups from five to six suppliers on a predetermined route. Over the course of a week, the truck brought in all inbound shipments from 26–30 important vendors within a 200-mile radius of the plant.[71] This type of system also allowed for frequent, small deliveries while helping to reduce freight costs.[72] From 1981 to 1986, MAN cut York's inbound freight costs (mostly from vendor billing) by $50,000 since its inception.[73]

An important element in keeping freight costs down was the elimination of nonproductive travel and Harley's new purchase order system. The company reported in 1986 that only 4 percent of the two-million miles that their fleet traveled in the past year were empty.[74] Harley changed its purchase order system in 1986 so that the only prices it would acknowledge were F.O.B. vendors' shipping docks. This prevented suppliers from including freight in their prices and, in turn, discouraged them from using their own carriers for shipments to the motorcycle maker's plants.[75]

In 1986 Harley-Davidson began pressing some of its suppliers to start passing up the line more of the cost savings that just-in-time afforded.[76] "It's time," said Patrick T. Keane, project engineer at Harley's York, Pennsylvania, plant, "to enter an era of negotiated price decreases. And right now we are holding meetings to accomplish that."[77]

After five years of using just-in-time, reviews poured in. Between 1981 and 1988, the following results were achieved:

[64]Roberts, "Harley's Hog's," p. 14.
[65]Hutchins, "Having a Hard Time," p. 64.
[66]Ibid.
[67]Ibid.
[68]Ibid.
[69]Ibid., p. 65.

[70]Saathoff, "Workshop," pp. 3–4.
[71]"At Harley-Davidson JIT Is a Fine Tuned Cycle," *Purchasing,* April 24, 1986, pp. 46–48.
[72]Hutchins, "Having a Hard Time," p. 64.
[73]Saathoff, "Workshop," p. 5.
[74]"At Harley-Davidson," p. 46.
[75]Ibid., p. 48.
[76]Ibid.
[77]Hutchins, "Having a Hard Time," p. 66.

1. Inventory had been reduced by 67 percent.
2. Productivity climbed by 50 percent.
3. Scrap and rework were down two-thirds.
4. Defects per unit were down 70 percent.[78]

Some industry experts believed that "the results for Harley and its suppliers have been good, although the company still has not achieved all its goals."[79] "We are very inefficient," said Keane, "but the comparison of where we were five years ago is phenomenal."[80]

Quality.   In the 1970s, the running joke among industry experts was, "if you're buying a Harley, you'd better buy two—one for spare parts."[81] After the buyout from AMF, Harley-Davidson strove to restore consumer confidence by raising the quality of its motorcycles. Harley-Davidson's quality improvements did not go unnoticed. John Davis, a Harley dealer mechanic, stated, "I've been wrenching on Harley-Davidson motorcycles for 26 years. I think the main key to their success is quality. And since '84 they have been very good."[82] Teerlink boasted in his 1990 letter to shareholders that Harley-Davidson would be competing for the Malcolm Baldrige National Quality Award in 1991. "We will follow the example established by the 1990 winner (Cadillac)."[83]

Harley's commitment to quality may have led them to opt not to carry any product liability insurance since 1987. One Harley executive commented, "We do not believe that carrying product liability insurance is financially prudent."[84] Instead, Harley created a form of self-insurance through reserves to cover potential liabilities.[85]

Other Production.   In 1988, Teerlink proudly stated, "Capitalizing on its reputation as a world class manufacturer, Harley-Davidson is developing a strong contract manufacturing business. In April of 1988, the company became the first Army Munitions and Chemical Command (AMCCOM) contractor to be certified under the U.S. Army's Contractor Performance Certification Program. The company achieved the certification for its application of advanced manufacturing techniques in the production of 500-pound casings for the U.S. Army. Additionally, the company is the sole supplier of high-altitude rocket motors for target drones built by Beech Aircraft."[86]

Harley-Davidson formed an agreement with Acustar, Inc., a subsidiary of Chrysler Corporation, in early 1988, to produce machined components for its Marine and Industrial Division. Harley also manufactured small engines for Briggs & Stratton. The company planned to further broaden its contract manufacturing business by aggressively marketing its proven and innovative manufacturing efficiencies to the industrial community.[87] For 1990, management placed a goal of nonmotorcycle production to reach 25–30 percent.[88] Teerlink felt strongly that "this goal is actually quite conservative and can be easily accomplished."[89]

International Operations.   The international markets of England, Italy, and other European countries were hardly uncharted territory for Harley-Davidson. Since 1915, Harley-Davidson had been selling its products in these overseas markets.[90] Harley-Davidson's international efforts increased significantly during the mid-1980s. In 1984, they produced 5,000 motorcycles for export;[91] projections for 1990 called for production in the 20,000-unit range.[92]

Several international markets exploded for Harley-Davidson in the late 80s. In 1989, they expanded their motorcycle sales in France by 92 percent, England by 91 percent, and Australia by 32 percent.[93] Europeans also bought other Harley products, such as T-shirts and leather jackets.[94] Clyde Fessler, director of trademark licensing for Harley-Davidson, said, "In Europe we're considered Americana."[95]

[78]Ibid.
[79]Harley-Davidson News, 1988, p. 1.
[80]Hutchins, "Having a Hard Time," p. 66.
[81]Ibid.
[82]Marvel, "Gentrified," p. 25.
[83]Harley-Davidson Annual Report—1989, p. 8.
[84]Ibid., p. 4.
[85]Ibid., p. 34.

[86]Ibid.
[87]Harley-Davidson News, 1988, p. 2.
[88]Ibid.
[89]Willis, "Harley-Davidson," p. 27.
[90]Harley-Davidson Annual Report—1989, p. 10.
[91]Ibid., p. 9.
[92]Roberts, "Harley's Hog's," p. 14.
[93]Harley-Davidson Annual Report—1989, p. 9.
[94]Ibid.
[95]"The Harley Priority," *Popular Mechanics,* June 9, 1989, p. 24.

Marketing

> When it comes to pleasuring the major senses, no motorcycle on earth can compare to a Harley. That's why I've tattooed my Harley's name on the inside of my mouth.
>
> Lou Reed[96]

Probably not every Harley-Davidson owner had Lou Reed's loyalty. Nonetheless, loyalty to Harley-Davidson had almost always been virtually unparalleled. According to the company's research, 92 percent of their customers remain with Harley.[97] Even with strong brand loyalty, however, Harley's marketing division had not reduced its advertising. Harley-Davidson limited its advertising focus to print media, opting not to explore a radio or television campaign. The company used print ads in a variety of magazines, including trade magazines and the company's own trade publication, the *Enthusiast.* The advertising department, headed by Carmichael Lynch, had the benefit of a very well-known company name.[98] Unfortunately, the company's name also carried serious image problems.

One major problem which plagued Harley's marketing efforts was that bootleggers were ruining the Harley-Davidson name by placing it on unlicensed, unauthorized goods. This condition might not have been a problem, except that the goods were of poor quality. Furthermore, society was turning away from the attitudes of the 60s. With antidrug messages becoming a prevalent theme in American society, Harley-Davidson found itself linked to an image of the pot-smoking, beer-drinking, women-chasing, tattoo-covered, leather-clad biker. One industry expert observed, "When your company's logo is the number one request in tattoo parlors, it's time to get a licensing program that will return your reputation to the ranks of baseball, hot dogs, and apple pie."[99] This fact was not lost on management. Kathleen Demitros, who became director of marketing in 1983, stated, "One of our problems was that we had such a hard-core image out there that it was basically turning off a lot of people."[100] Demitros was speaking from experience. The Milwaukee native had been with the com-

pany since 1971. Furthermore, like many of the company executives, she owned a Harley. By her own admission, Demitros chose not to ride her "Hog" to work. She saved it for the weekends.[101]

Harley-Davidson took a proactive approach to solving the image problem. They created a licensing division responsible for eliminating the bootlegged products. This new division was led by John Heiman, who was formerly a mechanical accessories products manager.[102] Goods with the Harley-Davidson logo would have to be sold by licensed dealers to be legal. Using warrants and federal marshals, Heiman went to conventions of motorcycle enthusiasts and began to put an end to the bootleggers.[103]

After accomplishing this, Harley-Davidson was able to sell its own goods. They began to concentrate their efforts on a wide variety of products, ranging from leather jackets to cologne to jewelry to supplement motorcycle sales.[104] The concept was not new to Harley-Davidson. As far back as the 1920s, Harley had designed and sold leather jackets.[105] The hope was that consumers would buy the other products in order to get comfortable with the Harley name, and then consider purchasing Harley motorcycles. One company executive said, "It helped pull us through the lean years." In 1988, he continued, "we sold 35,000 bikes and over 3 million fashion tops."[106] For Harley-Davidson, these sales were crucial in offsetting the seasonal market of the motorcycle industry. Industry observers applauded Harley on this marketing ploy. "Historically, the winter months are tough on sales for the motorcycle industry. Harley-Davidson has been successful at selling fashion items." A Harley marketing executive went one step further. "If we can't sell someone a bike in the winter, we'll sell them a leather jacket instead."[107]

Essentially, the licensing division had become an extension of marketing. Heiman said, "If you've got a 6-year-old boy wearing Harley pajamas, sleeping on Harley sheets, and bathing with Harley towels, the old man's not going to be bringing home a Suzuki."[108] Additionally, retailers found that the licensed goods were

[96]Robert Parola, "High on the Hog," *Daily News Record,* January 23, 1989, p. 74.

[97]Marvel, "Gentrified," p. 25.

[98]Harley-Davidson Annual Report—1989, p. 8.

[99]"Thunder Road," *Forbes,* July 18, 1983, p. 32.

[100]Marie Spadoni, "Harley-Davidson Revs Up to Improve Image," *Advertising Age,* August 5, 1985, p. 30.

[101]"Thunder Road," p. 32.

[102]Ibid.

[103]Spadoni, "Harley-Davidson Revs," p. 30.

[104]Ibid.

[105]Harley-Davidson Annual Report—1988, p. 9.

[106]Parola, "High," p. 24.

[107]Ibid.

[108]Marvel, "Gentrified," p. 25.

popular. Major retail chains began selling Harley-Davidson products. The logic behind the selection of Harley goods was simple. "Harley is the only motorcycle made in the United States today, and I thought with pride in America high, the time was right for the licensed goods," explained one major retailer.[109] However, the hard-core biker image of Harley-Davidson was still a strong influence. For example, when Fifth Avenue Cards, Inc., decided to sell Harley items, they did so in a satirical manner. According to Ethel Sloan, the card store chain's vice-president of merchandising, "we were definitely shooting for tongue-in-cheek, selling this macho, all-black coloration merchandise to bankers in three-piece suits—it was a real hoot!"[110] It may have been this cynical and virtually unexpected market that Vaughn Beals hoped to exploit. Beals predicted the emergence of a new breed of Harley customer. "We're on the road to prosperity in this country, and we'll get there on a Harley."[111]

The customers he spoke of began to buy Harleys in record numbers. The new Harley consumers were a collection of bankers, doctors, lawyers, and entertainers who developed an affection for "Hogs."[112] They became known as Rubbies—the rich urban bikers. The Rubbies were not frightened by the high price tags associated with the Harley-Davidson product line. The Sportster 883, which was Harley's trademark motorcycle, and the Nova, which was specifically designed to capture the college student market, sold in a price range of $4,000–15,000 in 1987.[113] Harley continued to expand their product line in 1988 with the addition of the Springer Softail, the Ultra Classic Electra Glide, and the Ultra Classic Tour Glide. James Paterson, president and chief operating officer of the Motorcycle Division, commented, "The Springer goes to the heart of Harley-Davidson, the custom-cruiser type of motorcycle. The Ultra Classics . . . are aimed at the touring market, . . . a market we couldn't reach previously."[114] Product line expansion continued in 1989 with a move that several industry observers thought to be a questionable marketing decision. Harley-Davidson introduced the Fat Boy,

their largest motorcycle with 80 cubic inches of V-twin engine.[115]

The Rubbies had brought Harley back into the forefront. By 1989, Harley-Davidson was again the leader in the U.S. super heavyweight motorcycle market, with a nearly 60 percent market share (see Exhibit 2). One consequence of the Rubbie market was their impact on the demographics of the Harley-Davidson consumer. According to an August 1990 *Wall Street Journal* article, "One in three of today's Harley-Davidson buyers are professionals or managers. About 60 percent have attended college, up from only 45 percent in 1984. Their median age is 35, and their median household income has risen sharply to $45,000 from $36,000 five years earlier."[116]

Even with the growth of the Rubbie market, Harley-Davidson was careful not to lose touch with their grass-roots customers. In 1990, roughly 110,000 members belonged to the H.O.G., Harley Owners Group.[117] The fact that upper management continued to ride alongside of

EXHIBIT 2

1989 U.S. market share of super heavyweight motorcycles, in percent

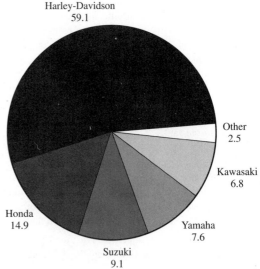

Source: R. L. Polk & Co.

[109]Spadoni, "Harley-Davidson Revs," p. 30.

[110]"Greeting Card Chain Scores Big with Macho 'Biker' Promotion," *Stores,* February 1986, p. 21.

[111]Ibid.

[112]Marvel, "Gentrified," p. 26.

[113]"Harley Priority," p. 24.

[114]Willis, "Harley-Davidson," p. 14.

[115]Harley-Davidson Annual Report—1988, p. 9.

[116]Harley-Davidson Annual Report—1989, p. 10.

[117]Rose, "Vrooming," p. 1.

their loyal throng was an important marketing tool. Paterson asserted, "Going to rallies and mixing with our customers has more value than you might initially expect. You begin to understand how important the motorcycle is and how important the Harley-Davidson way of life is to them . . . At a motorcycle rally, everyone's part of the same family—sharing their love for motorcycling and life in general."[118] Paterson's beliefs were shared by Harley owner Pat Soracino. "It's a family affair. My bike rides better with (wife) Vicki riding next to me. And our daughter has grown up with Harleys. It's more than a motorcycle to us. It's our lives."[119]

H.O.G. and Harley-Davidson combined their efforts often in 1989. One such venture was a series of national forest improvement projects. The First Annual National Poker Run motorcycle rally received the support of almost 160 Harley dealers nationwide. This rally and others raised about $1.7 million for the Muscular Dystrophy Association, a charity for whom Harley-Davidson collected over $6.5 million in the decade of the 80s.[120]

Although high performance was not a strong selling point for Harley-Davidson motorcycles, the company did enhance its reputation on the racing circuit in 1988 and 1989. In both years, Harley's factory-sponsored rider, Scotty Parker, captured the Grand National and Manufacturer's Championship in the American Motorcyclist Association's Class C racing season.[121]

Competition

Motorcycle Competition. Harley faced stiff competition from Japan's big four motorcycle manufacturers—Honda, Yamaha, Suzuki, and Kawasaki (see Exhibit 3). Industry analysts claimed that the Japanese manufacturers held a commanding lead in the world market with 80 percent of total motorcycle production.

In 1990, Honda was the world's largest motorcycle manufacturer.[122] The president of the company, Shoichiro Irimaziri, attributed their success to his company's philosophy of producing products of the highest efficiency at a reasonable price. In every aspect of the design of both its cars and motorcycles, the company's engineers endeavored to achieve a reasonable level of efficiency and obtain the last increment of performance. The president also placed a high value on the early involvement of production and engineering. His vision was one where the marketing and production departments are part of engineering; production departments are part of a bigger unit aimed at achieving quality and efficiency.[123]

Yamaha grossed $3 billion in sales in 1989 as the second largest producer of motorcycles in the world. For decades, Yamaha remained extremely diversified as the leading producer of outboard motors, sailboats, snowmobiles, and golf carts. At Yamaha Motor, many of the products were developed almost exclusively for overseas markets. Why so much diversification? First, Yamaha executives believed that the motorcycle business in the late 1980s was a shrinking one. Secondly, as voiced by the president of the company, "Diversification is a hobby of my father's. He gets bored with old businesses."[124]

Suzuki made its name selling motorcycles, but in 1987 they almost doubled their sales with the introduction of a jeep, the Suzuki Samurai. When first introduced, critics thought it would be a modern-day Edsel. "When these oddball vehicles first came out, nobody gave them a nickel's chance of success," says Maryann N. Keller, a vice-president and automotive analyst with Furman Selz Mager Dietz & Birney.[125] But the critics were wrong. Suzuki had a record 48,000 sales in 1986—the best model launch in history of any Japanese auto manufacturer.[126] Despite its success, however, the Samurai was hit with negative publicity in 1988. Specifically, the Consumers Union, a consumer protection organization, gave the Samurai a "not acceptable" rating and pleaded for the recall of 150,000 Samurai and for full refunds to all owners. The union claimed that the vehicle was unsafe because it rolled over easily when turning corners. Although the negative publicity caused a temporary decline in sales, Suzuki rebounded in the second half of 1988 through utilization of dealer and customer incentives.[127]

In 1988, Kawasaki's motorcycle sales increased 5

---

[118]Harley-Davidson Annual Report—1989, p. 10.

[119]Ibid., p. 5.

[120]Ibid., p. 11.

[121]Ibid.

[122]Ibid., p. 9.

[123]Andrew Tanzer, "Create or Die," *Forbes,* April 6, 1987, pp. 55–59.

[124]Shoichiro Irimaziri, "The Winning Difference," *Vital Speeches,* pp. 650–51.

[125]Tanzer, "Create," pp. 55–59.

[126]Rebecca Fannin, "Against All Odds," *Marketing and Media,* March 1988, pp. 45–47.

[127]Ibid.

EXHIBIT **3**

Harley-Davidson's share of the U.S. super heavyweight motorcycle market

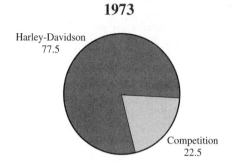

1973

Harley-Davidson
77.5

Competition
22.5

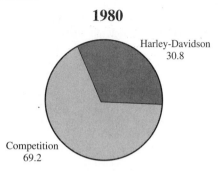

1980

Harley-Davidson
30.8

Competition
69.2

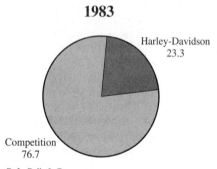

1983

Harley-Davidson
23.3

Competition
76.7

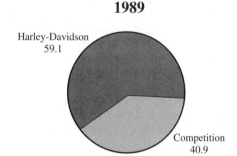

1989

Harley-Davidson
59.1

Competition
40.9

Source: R. L. Polk & Co.

percent, while the overall motorcycle market shrank 20 percent. Kawasaki's management attributed much of their success to a new service in which dealers could make sales with no-money-down financing. A computer network, Household Finance Corporation, allowed dealers to get nearly instantaneous responses on credit applications. Kawasaki also focused efforts to accommodate their dealers. The K-share program was developed in 1986 to act as a sales support system for dealers. K-share allowed dealers to make payments electronically; as a result, interest expense was reduced and keying errors made by Kawasaki were virtually eliminated because the manual input of checks was no longer necessary.[128]

Recreational Vehicle Competition.   With its acquisition of Holiday Rambler, Harley nearly doubled its revenues.[129] However, experts indicated that it also bought into a very troubled industry with declining demand. They further claimed that greater competition in the industry would lead to increasing marketing costs and decreasing profit margins.[130] Harley faced three top competitors in the RV industry—Fleetwood, Winnebago, and Airstream.

Fleetwood Enterprises, Inc., was the nation's leading manufacturer of recreational vehicles in 1989. Its operations included 21 factories in 17 states and Canada.

[128]Jack Bernstein, "Crisis Communications," *Advertising Age,* September 5, 1988, p. 29.

[129]David Ludlum, "Good Times Roll," *Computer World,* August 7, 1989, p. 51.
[130]Steve Kichen, "More Than Motorcycles," *Forbes,* October 3, 1989, p. 193.

For 1989, its sales totaled approximately $719 million.[131]

Winnebago was number one in sales with $420 million in 1988. The company experienced financing problems in early 1990 when Norwest Bank canceled a $50 million revolving credit line. This situation caused Winnebago to fall to number two in industry sales in 1990.[132]

Airstream ranked third among the RV manufacturers with sales of approximately $389 million for 1989.[133] Thor Industries bought the failing RV manufacturer from Beatrice Foods in 1980. They made assembly-line improvements and upgraded components to cut warranty costs and help the RV's image. In 1990, thousands of Airstream owners were members of the Wally Bran Caravan Club International. The club was started by Airstream and held regional rallies and caravans throughout the year. This cultlike following provided a loyal customer base, accounting for 60 percent of all Airstreams sold.[134]

The Impact of the Economy

Historically, the success of Harley-Davidson hinged significantly on the performance of the U.S. economy. The company suffered along with everyone else during the Great Depression, while the boom periods of both world wars represented times of prosperity for Harley-Davidson. Changing demands of consumers during the post-war years in the 40s and 50s had an adverse effect on the motorcycle industry, and, just when Harley was on the road to recovery in the early 1980s, the economy fell into a recession.[135]

Harley-Davidson proved time and time again that it was a survivor, having restored peak production levels after each economic downturn. The company had reached its highest levels of output in 1989. But, once again, the threat of recession was looming on the horizon. Standard & Poor's *Industry Surveys* warned that "leading indicators have been roughly flat and pointing to little growth, . . . recent financial market activity alternates between fears of recession and inflation.

Presently, inflation is a bigger worry for the markets, though recession is the larger worry for the moment."[136]

As the summer of 1990 was reaching its peak, a major international crisis unfolded. On August 2, Iraq invaded Kuwait, unleashing a series of events that seriously impacted the U.S. economy. In their August 16, 1990, *Trends & Projections,* Standard & Poor's discussed some of the effects of the anxiety in the Middle East. "The economy looks a lot more vulnerable than it did only a month ago. That was true before the Iraqi invasion; it is even truer with oil prices climbing . . . A very slow, sluggish economy is predicted for the second half of 1990."[137]

Valueline offered some further insight into the risks of the Middle East situation to Harley-Davidson. "The chief cause for concern would be curtailment of fuel supply in case of a shooting war. In any event, higher oil prices mean more inflation, which increases the risk of recession and with that, a slump in spending for big-ticket recreational goods."[138] Harley-Davidson's products traditionally carried a reputation of producing less fuel-efficient bikes than their Japanese counterparts. "This is no touring bike . . . that will take you nonstop from Tucson to Atlantic City."[139]

Other analysts predicted continued pessimism in the recovery of the recreational vehicle market. "Consumers are getting nervous about the economy; recent consumer sentiment reports show deteriorating trends . . . In the consumer durables category, weak auto sales are not likely to be reversed soon . . . the prospect of higher oil prices means more pressure on consumer spending. Because it is difficult to reduce energy consumption in the short run, many consumers react to higher oil prices by reducing their spending on other items."[140]

Legal and Safety Issues

As of 1988, 21 states had laws that required motorcycles to operate with their headlights turned on during the daytime as well as nighttime hours. In addition, 20 states required motorcycle riders to wear helmets. Motorcyclists argued that such laws were a violation of their constitutional rights and that helmets actually prevented

[131]Serafin, "RV Market Puzzled," p. 52.

[132]Fleetwood Annual Report—1989, p. 18.

[133]David Greising, "Unhappy Campers at Winnebago," *Business Week,* May 28, 1990, p. 28.

[134]Airstream Annual Report, 1989, p. 17.

[135]David Carey, "Road Runner," *Financial World,* November 1986, pp. 16–17.

[136]Reid, *Well Made,* p. 9.

[137]Standard & Poor's *Trends & Projections,* August 16, 1990, p. 3.

[138]Ibid., pp. 1–2.

[139]*Valueline,* p. 1751.

[140]Marvel, "Gentrified," p. 26.

them from hearing sirens and other important road noises. But such legislation was not without justification. The number of deaths on motorcycles reached 4,500 in 1987—a rate approximately 16 times higher than that for automobiles. Cycle enthusiasts had a tendency to push the blame on unobservant car drivers. However, statistics from the Insurance Institute for Highway Safety (IIHS) showed that 45 percent of these accidents involved only one vehicle. Of particular concern to the IIHS were the high-speed superbikes that became available to the general public. These bikes accounted for almost twice the number of fatalities as other cycles. Moreover, the IIHS blamed the motorcycle industry for marketing these bikes for their high speed and power. They claimed that this encouraged the reckless use of an already dangerous product.[141] The president of IIHS stated,

> The fact is motorcycles as a group have much higher death and injury rates than cars, so the last thing we need is this new breed of cycle with even higher injury rates.[142]

But what did all this mean to Harley? With the high revs of the traditional Hog and the production of lighter-weight race-style cycles like the NOVA, industry experts claimed that they were sure to be hit with the same adverse publicity and criticisms as their Japanese counterparts.

The Rubbie (Rich Urban Biker) Influence.

> I love riding the motorcycle. What a shame it nearly throws you into the jaws of death.
>
> Billy Idol[143]

> Every motorcycle rider thinks about the possibility of an accident. But I figured I was sharp enough in my reactions not to have one . . . But the fact is, on Sunday, December 4, 1988, there I was, sprawled at the feet of a policeman with paramedics on the way.
>
> Gary Busey[144]

Both Idol, the international rock star, and Busey, the Academy Award–nominated actor, suffered near-fatal accidents while riding Harley-Davidson motorcycles. Neither Idol nor Busey were wearing helmets at the time of their accidents. An apparent disdain for the

safety aspect of motorcycle riding was condoned by these role models. Busey, in fact, continued to be an opponent of helmet laws even after his ordeal. His stance remained among the throng of enthusiasts that felt "the decision to wear a helmet is a matter of personal freedom."[145]

The Rubbies that helped revive Harley-Davidson were a double-edged sword. Well-known personalities such as comedian Jay Leno, actors Sylvester Stallone, Mickey Rourke, Lorenzo Lamas, Kurt Russell, Daniel Day-Lewis, John Schneider, and Michael Hutchence of the rock group INXS were members of the Rubbie "fraternity."[146] Their high-profile status drew attention to the helmet laws. Many of these celebrities were often seen in paparazzi, mounted on their Harleys, without wearing helmets. Peter DeLuise, star of television's *21 Jumpstreet,* explained, "Biking is like sliding through the air. When you put a helmet on, it takes away part of the feeling."[147] Ironically, DeLuise's show, which was catered towards an adolescent audience, often depicted teenagers cruising streets and highways without helmets.[148]

Statistics showed that "142,000 Americans are injured in motorcycle accidents each year."[149] In the early 1970s, Congress used its power over the states to enact legislation that required all motorcycle riders to wear helmets. U.S. highway funds were cut in those states that did not pass the laws. Forty-seven states complied with the demand, but in the bicentennial year, aggressive lobbying efforts by biking groups succeeded in influencing Congress to revoke the sanctions. By 1980, 25 of the states had removed or weakened their helmet laws. Federal figures reported an increase in motorcycle fatalities of over 40 percent during this three-year period.[150] General Motors did a study in 1986 that revealed that one-quarter of the 4,505 motorcyclists killed that year would have lived had they worn helmets.

With models that can reach top speeds of 150 mph,[151] Harley-Davidsons continued to satisfy "the American

---

[141]Standard & Poor's *Industry Surveys,* August 16, 1990, p. 4.
[142]Fannin, "Against," pp. 45–46.
[143]Ibid., p. 47.
[144]"Billy Idol," *Rolling Stone,* July 1990, p. 174.

[145]Gary Busey, "A Near-Fatal Motorcycle Crash Changes an Actor's Life, but Not His Refusal to Wear a Helmet," *People,* May 15, 1990, p. 65.
[146]Ibid.
[147]Ibid.
[148]Ibid., p. 66.
[149]Ibid.
[150]Ibid., p. 65.
[151]"High Gear," *Time,* December 19, 1988, p. 65.

EXHIBIT 4

Harley-Davidson, Inc., net income comparison

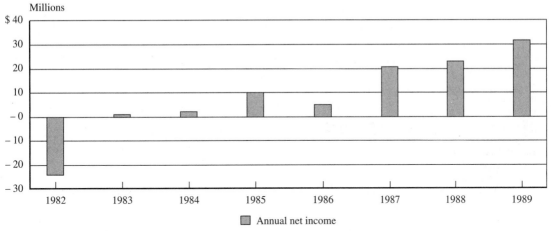

Source: Harley-Davidson, Inc.

desire for power, speed, and personal freedom."[152] The company was never in the business of manufacturing helmets, nor did they take a stance on the helmet issue,[153] but while the contention of pro-choice enthusiasts was that the decision was personal, statistics showed that society was absorbing the cost. According to *Time,* a 1985 survey in Seattle found that 105 motorcycle accident victims hospitalized incurred $2.7 million in medical bills, of which 63 percent was paid for from public funds.[154]

Financial Highlights

Harley-Davidson's financial position had improved greatly from 1986–1989 (see Exhibit 4). Even after the public stock offering in 1986, insiders continued to maintain some ownership of the company. *Valueline* reported in September of 1990 that insiders owned 11.6 percent of Harley-Davidson's stock. Other major shareholders included FMR Corporation (7.2 percent) and Harris Association (6.7 percent).[155] In June of 1990, Malcolm Glazer reduced his ownership in Harley-

Davidson from 7.29 percent to less than 1 percent, earning a $10 million profit in the process.[156]

Management's concern for employee satisfaction impacted their financial statements, when in April 1989, Harley paid a $1.3 million signing bonus to the Wisconsin labor unions.[157] Harley lowered its debt–equity ratio considerably in 1989, with the repurchase of $37.1 million of debt during the year. This created a decrease in their debt–equity ratio from 55 percent to 40 percent.[158] In 1990, Harley-Davidson's stock was pounded—from a high of $34, to a low of $13, before recovering to $18 as 1990 drew to a close.[159]

Epilogue

So, at the end of the week, I thought I'd go for it. I told Connie that I'd just need a few more days to raise some capital. So I'm hanging out at Bernie's Bank, flipping through a *Wall Street Journal,* when I come across this ad (see page 464).

---

[152]Busey, "Near-Fatal," p. 25.
[153]Marvel, "Gentrified," p. 25.
[154]Harley-Davidson Annual Report—1989, p. 30.
[155]"High Gear," p. 65.

[156]*Valueline,* p. 1761.
[157]Rose, "Vrooming," p. 6.
[158]Harley-Davidson Annual Report—1989, p. 20.
[159]Ibid.

Eᴄʜɪʙɪᴛ 5   **Consolidated Financial Statements**

---

a. Consolidated Balance Sheets (in thousands, except share amounts)

	December 31	
	1989	*1988*
Assets		
Current assets:		
Cash and cash equivalents	$ 39,076	$ 52,360
Accounts receivable, net of allowance for doubtful accounts	45,565	42,857
Inventories	87,540	89,947
Deferred income taxes	9,682	8,844
Prepaid expenses	5,811	4,795
Assets of discontinued operation	—	12,488
Total current assets	$ 187,674	$ 211,291
Property, plant, and equipment, net	115,700	107,838
Goodwill	66,190	68,782
Deferred financing costs	2,356	4,495
Other assets	7,009	4,307
Noncurrent assets of discontinued operation	—	4,401
	$ 378,929	$ 401,114
Liabilities and Stockholders' Equity		
Current liabilities:		
Notes payable	$ 22,789	$ 21,041
Current maturities of long-term debt	4,143	12,188
Accounts payable	40,095	36,939
Accrued expenses and other liabilities	69,334	63,047
Liabilities of discontinued operation	—	3,172
Total current liabilities	$ 136,361	$ 136,387
Long-term debt	$ 74,795	$ 135,176
Accrued employee benefits	5,273	3,309
Deferred income taxes	6,253	4,594
Commitments and contingencies (Notes 4, 7, and 9)		
Stockholders' equity:		
Series A Junior Participating preferred stock, 1,000,000 shares authorized, none issued	—	—
Common stock, 9,155,000 shares issued	92	92
Additional paid-in capital	79,681	76,902
Retained earnings	77,352	44,410
Cumulative foreign currency translation adjustment	508	374
	$ 157,633	$ 121,778
Less:		
Treasury stock (447,091 and 520,000 shares in 1989 and 1988, respectively), at cost	(112)	(130)
Unearned compensation	(1,274)	—
Total stockholders' equity		
	$ 156,247	$ 121,648
	$ 378,929	$ 401,114

The accompanying notes are an integral part of the consolidated financial statements.

EXHIBIT 5 **(continued)**

b. Consolidated Statements of Income (in thousands, except per share amounts)

	Years Ended December 31		
	1989	*1988*	*1987*
Net sales:	$ 790,967	$ 709,360	$ 645,966
Operating costs and expenses:			
Cost of goods sold	596,940	533,448	487,205
Selling, administrative, and engineering	127,606	111,582	104,672
	$ 724,546	$ 645,030	$ 591,877
Income from operations	$ 66,421	$ 64,330	$ 54,089
Interest income	3,634	4,149	2,658
Interest expense	(17,956)	(22,612)	(23,750)
Other—net	910	165	(2,143)
Income from continuing operations before provision			
for income taxes and extraordinary items	$ 53,009	$ 46,032	$ 30,854
Provision for income taxes	20,399	18,863	13,181
Income from continuing operations before			
extraordinary items	$ 32,610	$ 27,169	$ 17,673
Discontinued operation, net of tax:			
Income (loss) from discontinued operation	154	(13)	—
Gain on disposal of discontinued operation	3,436	—	—
Income before extraordinary items	$ 36,200	$ 27,156	$ 17,673
Extraordinary items:			
Loss on refinancing/debt repurchase, net of taxes	(1,434)	(1,468)	—
Additional cost of 1983 AMF settlement, net of taxes	(1,824)	(1,776)	—
Benefit from utilization of loss carryforward	—	—	3,542
Net income	$ 32,942	$ 23,912	$ 21,215
Per common share:			
Income from continuing operations	$ 3.78	$ 3.41	$ 2.72
Discontinued operation	.41	—	—
Extraordinary items	(.38)	(.41)	.55
Net income	$ 3.81	$ 3.00	$ 3.27

The accompanying notes are an integral part of the consolidated financial statements.

EXHIBIT 5   **(continued)**

c. Consolidated Statements of Cash Flows (in thousands)

	Years Ended December 31		
	1989	*1988*	*1987*
Cash flows from operating activities:			
Net income	$ 32,942	$ 23,912	$ 21,215
Adjustments to reconcile net income to net cash provided by operating activities:			
Depreciation and amortization	20,007	17,958	15,643
Deferred income taxes	821	(1,375)	(2,875)
Long-term employee benefits	2,741	1,037	(439)
Gain on sale of discontinued operation	(5,513)	—	—
Loss on disposal of long-term assets	28	1,451	1,505
Net changes in current assets and current liabilities	10,051	(30,346)	12,205
Total adjustments	$ 28,135	$ (11,275)	$ 26,039
Net cash provided by operating activities	$ 61,077	$ 12,637	$ 47,254
Cash flows from investing activities:			
Capital expenditures	$ (24,438)	$ (23,786)	$ (17,027)
Less amounts capitalized under financing leases	819	2,877	—
Net capital expenditures	$ (23,619)	$ (20,909)	$ (17,027)
Proceeds on sale of discontinued operation and other assets	19,475	—	—
Other—net	(2,720)	(1,204)	901
Net cash used in investing activities	$ (6,864)	$ (22,113)	$ (16,126)
Cash flows from financing activities:			
Net increase in notes payable	$ 1,748	$ 1,083	$ 5,891
Reductions in debt	(69,245)	(42,652)	(78,478)
Proceeds from issuance of common stock	—	35,179	18,690
Proceeds from additional borrowings	—	—	70,000
Repurchase of warrants	—	—	(3,594)
Deferred financing costs	—	—	(3,265)
Net cash provided by (used in) financing activities	$ (67,497)	$ (6,390)	$ 9,244
Net increase (decrease) in cash and cash equivalents	$ (13,284)	$ (15,866)	$ 40,372
Cash and cash equivalents:			
At beginning of year	52,360	68,226	27,854
At end of year	$ 39,076	$ 52,360	$ 68,226

The accompanying notes are an integral part of the consolidated financial statements.

Exhibit 5 **(concluded)**

d. Consolidated Statements of Changes in Stockholders' Equity—Years Ended December 31, 1989, 1988, and 1987 (in thousands, except share amounts)

	Common Stock		*Additional Paid-in Capital*	*Retained Earnings (deficit)*	*Cumulative Foreign Currency Translation Adjustment*	*Treasury Stock*	*Unearned Compensation*
	Outstanding Shares	*Balance*					
Balance, January 1, 1987	6,200,000	$62	$26,657	$ (717)	$287	$ (130)	—
Net income	—	—	—	21,215	—	—	—
Net proceeds from common stock offering	1,230,000	12	18,678	—	—	—	—
Repurchase of 230,000 warrants in connection with public debt and common stock offering	—	—	(3,594)	—	—	—	—
Cumulative foreign currency translation adjustment	—	—	—	—	443	—	—
Balance, December 31, 1987	$7,430,000	$74	$41,741	$20,498	$730	$ (130)	—
Net income	—	—	—	23,912	—	—	—
Net proceeds from common stock offering	1,725,000	18	35,161	—	—	—	—
Cumulative foreign currency translation adjustment	—	—	—	—	(356)	—	—
Balance, December 31, 1988	$9,155,000	$92	$76,902	$44,410	$374	$ (130)	—
Net income	—	—	—	32,942	—	—	—
Issuance of 72,909 treasury shares of restricted stock	—	—	2,779	—	—	18	$(1,274)
Cumulative foreign currency translation adjustment	—	—	—	—	134	—	—
Balance, December 31, 1989	$9,155,000	$92	$79,681	$77,352	$508	$ (112)	$(1,274)

The accompanying notes are an integral part of the consolidated financial statements.

Source: Harley-Davidson, Inc.

I couldn't believe it myself. Another American-made motorcycle. My little voice had some words of wisdom, but I already knew I was gonna have to break off the deal with Connie. It wasn't easy, but hey—that's why I'm Johnny Callatino. So there you have it. I don't know about you, but I could sure use another cold one.

TEKTRONIX, INC.

Ethics Program (A)

Earl Wantland, president and CEO of Tektronix, Inc. (Tek), a Beaverton, Oregon–based electronic instrument manufacturing company, sat at his desk looking at the September 14, 1987, *Wall Street Journal* article reporting improprieties and possible fraud in the company's West German subsidiary, Tektronix GmbH. This was just the latest problem facing the company, which had grown from an eight-person operation to a world leader in oscilloscope manufacturing in just over 30 years. In the 1980s Tek faced a recession in high-technology industries, intensified global competition, and shortened product life cycles, all of which put severe profit pressures on the company (see Exhibit 1).

The company's financial difficulties resulted in several expense reduction decisions which tended to change the atmosphere within the company. Tek's management tried to avoid workforce size reduction by implementing shortened work schedules, unpaid shutdowns, mandatory vacation usage, voluntary leaves of absence, hiring and pay freezes, upper management pay cuts, and the

Source: This case was prepared by Professor Steven N. Brenner and Research Assistants Patricia Bishop and Colleen Mullery as a basis for class discussion rather than to illustrate either effective or ineffective handling of an administrative decision. The help of present and former Tektronix employees is acknowledged. This research was supported in part through a grant from the Chiles Foundation, Portland, Oregon. Copyright 1988 by Steven N. Brenner.

EXHIBIT 1 Tektronix Consolidated Financial Performance ($000 except per-share amounts)

	1979	1980	1981	1982	1983	1984	1985	1986	1987
Net sales	$786,936	$971,306	$1,061,834	$1,195,748	$1,191,485	$1,332,958	$1,438,082	$1,352,212	$1,395,885
Earnings	77,151	85,072	80,167	79,290	46,807	112,054	90,181	39,327	51,188
Gross margin	54.3%	52.8%	51.7%	49.6%	47.6%	48.8%	50.9%	50.9%	54.2%
Operating margin	15.4%	15.2%	13.0%	12.2%	9.4%	9.8%	8.9%	5.1%	7.3%
Return on equity	21.3%	19.4%	15.5%	13.4%	7.2%	16.1%	11.1%	4.7%	5.9%
Return on capital	18.7%	15.8%	12.3%	11.0%	6.4%	13.5%	10.2%	4.7%	5.7%
EPS	2.14	2.33	2.17	2.12	1.22	2.87	2.20	0.98	1.33
Total assets	$642,907	$841,693	$ 953,753	$1,044,188	$1,092,446	$1,222,168	$1,224,372	$1,196,947	$1,159,413
Inventory turns	4.19×	4.02×	3.66×	4.04×	3.91×	4.60×	5.97×	6.94×	8.68×
Asset turns	1.44×	1.34×	1.19×	1.20×	1.12×	1.18×	1.22×	1.15×	1.16×
Debt/total assets	18.5%	27.4%	26.1%	23.9%	21.9%	20.3%	11.5%	10.3%	6.0%
Employees	21,291	23,890	24,028	23,241	21,121	20,816	20,525	19,251	17,099
Share price (year-end)	$24.63	$24.88	$30.38	$26.32	$37.00	$28.25	$29.00	$30.75	$34.88

Returns, ratios, and turnover are based on average assets and capital.

combining of redundant functions. Unfortunately, revenue growth slowed and the company undertook three major layoffs which trimmed its size from 24,000 to 17,000 employees.

Employees at all levels questioned the cutback decision, believing that management had violated the values and morality inherent in the Tek culture. Tek's corporate strategist felt so strongly that the personnel level reductions should have been avoided that he resigned from his position noting, "I'm not sure that because business conditions change, the ethics on which you operate a business has to change."

Historically, ethical issues had not been a concern for Tektronix. The company's founders, Jack Murdock and Howard Vollum, had a strong belief in the honesty and integrity of the individual employee. When the company was small there were open cash drawers, free coffee, and a tacit no-layoff policy. As the company grew larger and more divisionalized, it became more difficult to continue these policies. With growth there also came a diminution of commitment to the company. Examples of a change in atmosphere were numerous, including employees working for their divisions at the expense of the entire company, defections to competitors or to new startup companies, and moonlighting ventures (some of which were carried out on Tek premises).

In partial response to these issues, the electronic industry's ethical standards, and the overall climate at Tektronix in 1987, Earl Wantland decided to hold a business ethics seminar for upper-level managers. The intent of the seminar was to identify corporate values and the pressures which make it hard to live up to those values and to develop an action plan for managing ethical issues. The German subsidiary fraud disclosure coming only a few weeks after the initial ethics seminar made Wantland wonder if his decision to initiate an ethics program had come too late or had been too limited in scope. Was this the best method of reinforcing the Tek culture and values given the problems and pressures of the past decade? Should Tek pursue further ethics-related steps and, if so, what should be the actions' focus?

Tek History

The principal founders, Jack Murdock and Howard Vollum, started Tektronix in 1946. Their goal was to manufacture the finest oscilloscope in the world. (The function of an oscilloscope is to visually display the electrical signals of electronic devices.)

The 1950s were a time of dramatic innovation in the electronics industry. Tek introduced numerous innovations in its products and began to develop a reputation for producing the highest-quality, most technologically advanced oscilloscopes in the world. To assure that its customers were well-served, Tek established its own sales force of technically knowledgeable "field engineers" rather than depending on independent electronics distributors (which was the normal industry marketing approach). This sales technique was consistent with the founders' view of Tek's responsibility to its customers. Tek continued to grow and in 1956 purchased 313 acres in Beaverton, Oregon, for a new Tektronix "campus" (a term purposefully used to denote the collegiality and intellectual rigor of the work environment).

A new executive vice president was appointed in 1959 to deal with the management problems which followed the company's rapid growth. At the same time both Murdock and Vollum sought to reduce their responsibilities for day-to-day operations. The early years of the 1960s were among the most technologically challenging yet faced, and Tek funded virtually any research and development project which might meet the new marketplace demands. While such scientific freedom was important at Tek, it was a relatively expensive, duplicative approach to product development. Concerns about lack of direction and unsatisfactory financial results caused Vollum to resume direct leadership of Tek in 1962. In the next nine years Tek increased international sales, restructured into a functional organization, had its first public stock offering, and formed a joint venture with Sony Corporation.

Tektronix suffered its first downturn in 1971. Net sales dropped 11.6 percent to $146 million from the 1970 high of $162 million, while earnings fell from $14.3 million to $9.3 million in the same period. Tek's problems at this time were not just caused by the general economic climate. Explosive expansion, high profits, and inattention to management processes during the initial growth years had resulted in a poorly coordinated, complex organization. Informal communications channels that were effective in the old days were no longer adequate. As a result of the downturn Tek was forced to have its first layoff (350 manufacturing employees). A significant proportion of these workers were rehired within 90 days, but for many old timers the level of trust in management never returned.

While Tek had expanded its product line during its early years, it still concentrated on oscilloscope manufacturing. In an effort to increase revenue, R&D efforts were expanded and by the end of 1971 Tek had introduced over 100 new products. In December 1971 sales, orders, and earnings were at a record rate. Real diversification came as Tek moved into the information display business, which became 20 percent of company sales by 1987.

In 1972 Howard Vollum stepped down as president. The new president, Earl Wantland, retained the Boston Consulting Group and Stanford Research Institute to help Tek deal with its organizational problems. An insider described the company at that time as "a strong vertical organization centered around the oscilloscope." The informal leadership styles of both Jack Murdock and Howard Vollum had fostered an intensely competitive atmosphere within Tek. Efforts to diversify suffered from this situation. Ideas which were brought up within one part of Tek would not get support from the others. The organizational challenge was to improve efficiency and control without stifling creativity and innovation while preserving major managers' influence and status. The proposed solution was a divisionalized structure composed of two business groups and eight divisions.

The 1980s were marked by a recession in high-technology industries and increased competition. By 1984 Tek's core business (oscilloscopes) was under pressure from competitors both at home and abroad. Tek missed the emerging market for color display terminals (even though it was a leader in all aspects of the technology required to produce the devices) and it was slow to move into the new generation of digital test equipment known as computer-aided workstations. As a result, Tek experienced flat sales and declining profits and responded with a series of layoffs which reduced the workforce from 24,000 to 17,000 (see Exhibit 1). The layoffs further reduced the morale and loyalty of many long-term employees, who still believed in the unwritten no-layoff policy.

Between 1985 and 1987 Tek repurchased over 10 million shares of its stock at a cost of over $400 million. The company indicated that the goal of this use of funds was to increase shareholder return and to reduce the company's cost of capital. Observers questioned whether share repurchase was the best use of these resources given the competitive trends and conditions existing in the industry during these years.

Despite its recent economic problems Tektronix finished the 1987 fiscal year as Oregon's largest private employer and was ranked 249th on the Fortune 500.

Within the United States there were six manufacturing facilities, eight manufacturing subsidiaries, and 44 field offices. International operations included manufacturing in Japan (joint venture with Sony), the Channel Islands, the Netherlands, and the United Kingdom and 62 field offices in 23 countries. (For a more complete chronology, see Exhibit 2.)

The Tek Culture

The Tek culture is, in many ways, a direct reflection of the personalities, motivations, and values of Tek's two founders: Jack Murdock and Howard Vollum. The corporate motto, "Tektronix: Committed to Excellence," expressed their belief that customer service and quality products were the key ingredients to a successful enterprise. Success was not defined as acquiring great wealth, but rather as occupying honorably a financially secure market niche. An equally important guiding principle was the founders' innate respect for, and belief in, the dignity of the individual. They believed that the goals of the enterprise and of the employee should be complementary, not contradictory.

In the early days of the company there was no organization chart and no specific personnel policies. The founders wanted a small, friendly, family atmosphere. Early management practices and values such as open cash drawers, free coffee, use of first names, company-sponsored Friday afternoon birthday parties, and no reserved parking evolved out of the founders' personal views about the integrity of people and the climate in which they felt creativity and excellence could be fostered.

A Tektronix *Annual Report* put into words the elements which seemed to make up this culture:

Respect for the individual human being.
Profit sharing as part of the pay system.
Open communications.
Trust as evidenced by the honor system.
Informal atmosphere.
Little built-in awe of management.
High tolerance of criticism.
Absence of formal organization charts.
Preference for nonauthoritarian behavior.
Promotion from within the company.
Respect for technical expertise.
Absence of labor unions.
Passion for quality.

Exhibit 2 **Tektronix Chronological History**

Date	Operations	Technology
1946	Tektronix, Inc, an Oregon corporation, certified 2/2/46	
1947	Move to new location on Hawthorne Blvd., Portland, Oregon	511 series: first triggered scope
1948	Production sharing bonus instituted	
1949	Profit-sharing introduced (25 percent of pretax income)	Transformers and inductors produced in-house
1950	Tek's own sales force created	
1951	Move to Sunset Hwy, location, Beaverton, Oregon	Cathode ray tubes (CRTs) produced in-house
1952	Tektronix Foundation established	
1953	Profit Sharing Retirement Trust established	530 series: first plug-in scope
1954	Stock split (2,000 for 1) creating 266,000 shares with $1.00 par value	315D series: first portable scope
1955	10th Anniversary Bonus (15 percent of pretax income)	540 series: fast-rising, plug-in scope with vertical amplifier
1956	Purchase of 313 acres in Beaverton for Tek campus	
1957	Completion of first building on Beaverton campus	First transistor curve tracer
1958	Foreign operation established on island of Guernsey; first TEKEM shares issued in June; TEKEY program instituted for rewarding employees	
1959	Davis replaced Murdock as EVP	525 series: first vectorscope
1960	Profit share revised to 35 percent of pretax income; expansion into the Common Market	321 series: first solid scope
1961		Ceramic CRT envelope developed; 661 series: first sampling scope
1962	Vollum replaces Davis; retains presidency and assumes EVP duties	
1963	First public stock offering (54,000 shares)	
1964	Listed on New York Stock Exchange; acquires Pentrix Corp. (manufacturer of spectrum analyzers)	547 series: first all-transistorized scope
1965	Sony/Tektronix established	
1966	Employee Share Purchase Plan instituted	
1968		Decision to produce information display products (IDP)
1969	Corporate Group created	7000 series
1970	Began reorganization into functional groups	Development of Gilbert gain cell
1971	Death of Jack Murdock, May 16, 1971; first employee layoff; 110 new products announced or introduced	
1972	Wantland replaced Vollum as president; Stanford Research Institute and Boston Consulting Group create formal planning system for Tek	326 series: dual-trace miniaturized scope
1973	Operational planning leads to formation of business units; first dividend paid—$0.20/share	
1974	Statement of Corporate Intent developed; pension plan established; Grass Valley Group, Inc., acquired	200 series: ultraminiaturized scope
1975	Formation of business units leads to divisionalization	
1976	Formal corporate objectives published	
1977	Walker Road plant opened; 100 percent stock dividend paid	
1978	First executive incentive plan begun	
1979		7104 series: first gigahertz scope (fastest-writing scope in world)
1981	Functional division structure in place: 　Instruments Division 　Communications Division 　Design Automation Division 　Information Display Division	

Date	Operations	Technology
1983	Downsizing begins (early retirement package offered)	2400 series: state-of-the-art, small, portable scope
1984	Employee layoffs (severance pay provided)	Entered computer-aided engineering market
1986	Death of Howard Vollum	
1987	Fraud discovered in West German subsidiary	

While actual practices and procedures did not always follow the ideal (e.g., organization charts did exist and open communications were not always present), there were many examples of these values in action. An early expression of Tek's commitment to quality and service was its policy of providing replacement parts virtually at cost. Management assumed that the need to replace a component was caused by a design error and therefore the resulting costs should not be borne by the customer.

The founders believed that a successful enterprise could only be built through the close cooperation of all employees. Sharing a substantial portion (targeted at 35 percent) of the company's pretax earnings with employees was instituted as a method of instilling pride, creating a sense of ownership, and providing above-average compensation. This profit-sharing system was an enlightened management concept at its inception in 1949.

The egalitarian attitude of the Tek founder led to other innovative management and employee relations programs, including:

- A retirement trust fund was established in 1953 and two employee stock plans, TEKEM and TEKEY, were set up to enable employee ownership in the company prior to the stock being issued to the public.

    Workers were regarded as individuals with lifelong tenure; consequently, extreme care was taken in hiring.

    Some employees were kept on the payroll even when their performance was not up to Tek's standards.

    Direct effort was exerted, long before it became fashionable, to hire minorities and handicapped persons.

    Employees had access to an in-house counseling staff of psychologists and the company retained the Menningers, nationally known industrial psychologists.

    Employee participation in management was encouraged and formalized through the Advisory Group in the 1950s.

    The plant was designed to be bright and airy with the physical surroundings as natural as possible. Corporate signs were understated.

The Founders' Management Style and Leadership

Howard Vollum's and Jack Murdock's talents complemented one another as if they had been preordained to start a company together. Murdock, general manager and personnel director until 1958, represented the company in the business community and was influential in the development of many of Tek's innovative personnel policies and practices. In the early years at Tek he personally knew every employee and assumed the role of corporate father figure. As the company grew he was intimately involved in instituting humanistic policies aimed at imparting self-worth to every employee. He was particularly identified with maintaining the informal atmosphere throughout the company, encouraging participative management, and promoting company-sponsored social and recreational activities. These practices are credited by many in the company with creating high morale and increasing productivity.

Under Murdock's leadership Tek implemented a carefully designed profit-share program. Recognizing the cyclical nature of the electronics industry, Murdock sought a way to provide a soft landing to profits when volume declined and to share profits with employees when times were good. The program ultimately combined a salary (which averaged about 90 percent of the industry norm) and a profit-share payment (which generally ranged from 10 to 15 percent of the individual's salary). In most years the total of salary and profit share resulted in a rate of pay above industry average. When demand diminished, the profit-share percentage was reduced, thus trimming expenses.

Vollum, the engineer, pioneered the development of the oscilloscope and guided product development until 1971 when he resigned as president of Tek. His first love was the engineering lab and technical world. His leadership was marked by an "active interest in many aspects of the company: The design of the buildings, the landscaping, the tone and wording of ads . . . and the annual report to shareholders. Howard," someone said, "added value to everything."

The 1986 Tektronix *Annual Report* quoted Vollum as saying that he "disagreed with the concept of 'managing' and believed that a company should develop leaders rather than managers." To encourage creativity in product development, he promoted an unstructured work environment. Neither Murdock nor Vollum was comfortable with confrontation. Their management style, and thus the style of the company, was one of consensus and careful decision making.

Generosity was the hallmark of both founders and this was mirrored in the large-scale philanthropic actions of the company. The Tektronix Foundation was established in 1952 with 5 percent of the company's net profits. Since Tek was a closely held company at that time, a substantial share of these monies came directly out of Vollum's and Murdock's pockets, as did the profit share, which routinely exceeded 50 percent of pretax profits in the 1950s. Social responsibility and corporate generosity were values practiced by Tektronix as it became one of Oregon's major philanthropic donors.

Both founders believed in leadership by example and the provision of unconditional support to their employees. A Tek executive described Murdock and Vollum as having an "impeccable personal code of conduct." Honesty, humility, egalitarianism, and straight-forward dealings with people characterized their management style. Their belief that human nature was basically good was expressed in Vollum's words, "Every individual wants to do the best job he or she can." This attitude permeated the company. One former employee indicated that for many years there were no strong controls to ensure honesty—it was expected.

Ethical Problems, the German Subsidiary and Tek's Ethics Program

Ethical values have a special place at Tektronix. The founders' basic beliefs about the inherent integrity of the individual employee and the importance of an open and trusting environment set a clear behavioral tone for the organization.

Conversations with current and former employees indicate that Tektronix management believed its policies and controls were sufficient to eliminate significant unethical behavior. While this may have been true during the early years when the organization was small and top

management knew each worker by name, some observers have questioned the ethical correctness of a number of employee actions, including:

> Going to work for a competitor.
>
> Conducting an outside small business on Tek premises.
>
> Killing a project proposed by another division even though it would be good for the company as a whole.
>
> Circumventing the resource allocation approval system by acquiring capital equipment in component parts.
>
> Laying off workers during downturns (even though the benefits provided were considered generous) without seeking to take other possible steps, including living with reduced profits.

Beyond these activities, the most significant ethical problem in Tektronix history came to light on September 14, 1987. On that day *The Wall Street Journal* reported that:

> Tektronix, Inc. said "improprieties and possible fraud" in its West German unit forced it to take a charge of $3.4 million, or 10 cents a share for its fiscal quarter. . . .
>
> For the quarter, ended Aug. 22, the maker of scientific instruments posted an 88 percent drop in net income to $1.8 million, or 5 cents a share, from $14.6 million or 38 cents a share, in the year earlier period. . . . Sales fell 1.8 percent to $299.5 million from $304.9 million. . . .
>
> A Tektronix spokesman said the company's finance manager in West Germany and his assistant loaned money, without the company's knowledge, to Rhein Neckar, a West German leasing concern. The leasing concern went into bankruptcy-law proceedings in August, he said. . . . The finance manager and his assistant have been fired . . . no legal action had been taken against the pair so far, but [the spokesman] declined to say whether any would be pursued.

A few days later at Tek's annual stockholders' meeting, Larry Choruby, senior vice president and chief financial officer, reported that the fraud was not just a singular type of action, but instead involved a number of different "scams." While Tektronix indicated, in public documents, that its review of the matter showed that all prudent precautions had been taken to prevent criminal conduct, some observers felt that pressures for results and lack of attention to the accuracy of reports may have contributed to the problem.

The announcement of the German subsidiary problem came more than six months after Tek took the first steps toward implementing a more formal ethics program. Larry Choruby directed a memo on January 13, 1987, to Earl Wantland indicating that more than five years had passed since the senior management group had reviewed the company's written statements of business ethics. The memo further proposed that Tek's policy council meet to review existing ethics policies, discuss and document proposed changes, and verify the process of communicating these policies throughout the company.

The idea of reviewing Tektronix ethics-related policies and taking steps to refine and renew them seemed very appropriate to Earl Wantland, especially at a time when the entire corporation was looking to him for direction and leadership. After some thought he recalled that Kirk Hanson of Stanford Graduate School of Business had presented some interesting ethics materials to Tek's Manager of Managers internal management education program. He contacted Professor Hanson to explore the development of an ethics-focused corporate values workshop for Tek's senior management. At the conclusion of the discussions Earl was convinced that Hanson's approach would result in greater ethical awareness at Tek.

After some initial discussion between Tektronix and Professor Hanson, it was decided to modify and use a one-day business ethics seminar which Kirk Hanson had previously developed. After senior managers had gone through the seminar, a decision would be made about extending it to lower levels of management. The seminar was aimed at an "examination of the operating principles and values of the firm, the strains on those values, and techniques for managing the risks when those values are under pressure." The initial seminar was held for the policy council on June 9, 1987, and it was repeated for one Tek divisional management team on September 16, 1987.

The workshop's morning session explained the importance of the role that values and ethics play in an organization and used two case studies to involve participants and to communicate concepts. The afternoon session focused on identifying Tektronix stakeholders; the organization's values; pressures on these values; and an action plan to deal with these pressures.

Earl Wantland decided to initiate a more active ethical program at this time because he perceived a need to raise consciousness on ethical issues and bring ethics discussions to the table. He explained, "it's important that ethics is a legitimate thing to talk about with your subordinates, especially due to the number of unresolvable dilemmas present in the business world today."

Responses to the ethics workshop were mixed. Some

people were quite positive, indicating that it was taken very seriously and was found to be useful. One participant said that "it raised a lot of issues which is good . . . it made it an OK thing to talk about." Another attendee said that some participants were disappointed with the lack of concrete guidelines, "we were hoping to have some very clear-cut guidelines that you could pull out of your pocket and use to know what to do in any circumstance. . . . I'm not sure what we really got out of it . . . but it made people aware that there were shades of gray and there were behaviors that some thought acceptable and others unacceptable." Some insiders expressed frustration over the timing of the seminars and felt it was a "diversion from working on the things that we really needed to make decisions on. . . . [T]here were too many other pressing, critical business priorities and tremendous business pressures at that time."

At the same time the ethics workshops were being developed and presented, two other components of Tek's ethics program were moving forward. Alan Leedy, vice president, secretary, and general counsel of Tektronix, was given the task of updating the company's code of conduct. During summer 1987 a number of meetings were held and redrafts of the code of conduct written. The version, current at the time of the case, is shown in Exhibit 3. Tek's corporate controller and director of internal auditing were working on an internal controls seminar which was tentatively scheduled for early November 1987.

Earl Wantland's Dilemma

Earl Wantland realized that he was expected to improve Tektronix's profitability and to deal with the German subsidiary situation. Wantland was concerned whether recent external competitive and internal organizational pressures had simply overwhelmed both the company's traditional ethical values and its newly implemented ethics program.

Earl realized that his personal situation was a factor which had to be taken into consideration. It was common knowledge that Tek's board of directors was in the process of searching for a new president for the company. In fact, Earl, himself, had been quietly encouraging the board to find a successor so that he could move out of direct, day-to-day responsibility for operations.

As he sat and considered his alternatives, he was aware that there was a certain tension between increasing company profitability and improving the ethical behavior of its employees. By putting more emphasis on an ethics program, time and money which might be devoted to improved results would be allocated instead to assuring more proper behavior. For example, steps taken to assure product quality would be consistent with the Tek values, but such actions were likely to increase operating expenses and unlikely to increase revenues in the near term.

Some Tek employees and stockholders were urging Earl Wantland to expand its ethical programs. Suggestions for additional steps came from many differing sources. Earl hoped that he could gather information about the ethics programs of other firms and thereby not have to reinvent the wheel. (In February 1988 the Business Roundtable, a Washington, D.C.–based group of major United States companies, published a study of the corporate ethics programs of 10 major United States firms.[1] See Exhibit 4 for a selected look at corporate ethics program components.) As he thought about his situation, his eyes glanced across the room at the plaque containing Tektronix's Statement of Corporate Intent which served as a reminder of what Tek stood for:

---

[1]*Corporate Ethics: A Prime Business Asset* (New York: Business Roundtable, 1988).

EXHIBIT 3   Tektronix Code of Conduct

Business conduct that meets the highest ethical standards is fundamental to our success as a company. These standards were not acquired by accident at Tektronix. They grew out of the basic beliefs and values on which our company was founded and has operated since 1946. Today, Tektronix is a large and complex organization, operating in an increasingly complex world. Our traditional management and communication practices, based on individual initiative, judgment, and responsibility, are the "active ingredients." Preserving the advantages of this traditional Tek environment requires that we periodically revisit and reacquaint ourselves with the values on which it is based. That is what this brief statement is designed to do.

The basic standards of ethics and conduct that apply to Tektronix are simply stated. They are:

1. *Respect for the Individual*

   To base our business actions on a fundamental respect for the dignity and rights of each individual—including both those within our company and those outside it.

   Examples include the way we deal with our fellow employees and with our suppliers', customers', and competitors' representatives, and what we say about people, wherever they may work.

2. *Loyalty to Tektronix*

   To bring to Tektronix our undivided business loyalty.

   Examples include avoiding both actual and apparent conflicts of interest. (A conflict of interest exists when someone at Tektronix has an advantage from a position, or has a duty to take a position, that is opposed to the position of Tektronix.) Further examples include avoiding situations involving favors offered, given, or received, or any appearance of favoritism.

3. *Compliance with the Law*

   To know, and conform our action to, the requirements of all applicable laws.

4. *Observance of Other Ethical Standards*

   To conduct the company's business in accordance with the highest standards of ethics and integrity.

   Examples of those ethical standards, in addition to those listed above, include honesty, candor, and integrity, which are the essential bases for our relationships with customers, suppliers, fellow employees, shareholders, and the communities of which we are a part.

There is one further guidepost that belongs on this list: our primary, fundamental, and continuing commitment to give unmatched value to our customer. Customers keep us in business. They pay for our facilities and raw materials, our labor, our research and development efforts, our taxes, and the profits that go to our employees as profit share and to our shareholders as dividends and capital appreciation.

Much of what is included here is also reflected in our Statement of Corporate Intent, which underscores the importance to us as a company of these basic values. Whenever we depart from the basic standards set out in this brief list, we only diminish our ability to keep this central promise to our customers.

October 11, 1988

Exhibit 4   Corporate Ethics Program Components

In February 1988 the Business Roundtable of Washington, D.C., published *Corporate Ethics: A Prime Business Asset.* It contains descriptions of the ethics programs in 10 major international corporations: The Boeing Company, Champion International Corporation, Chemical Bank, General Mills, GTE Corporation, Hewlett-Packard Company, Johnson & Johnson, The McDonnell Douglas Corporation, The Norton Company, and Xerox. Six of these companies' ethics programs are summarized below.

The Boeing Company

1. All Boeing ethics policies are printed in one booklet entitled, *Business Conduct Guidelines.*
2. Operating divisions conduct ethics training programs which are presented by divisional top management and roll down to lower levels in each division.
3. An Ethics Advisor is designated for the entire company. The advisor's role is to interpret ethics policies and provide advice and clarification.
4. Some of Boeing's subsidiary companies organize Ethics Focal Points which serve as ethics advisors.
5. An Office of Business Practices handles employee calls relating to misuse of funds.
6. The Ethics and Business Conduct Committee, composed of Boeing's vice chairman and the senior corporate executives from the legal, controller, and human resources functions, oversees all company ethics programs.

Chemical Bank

1. The Code of Ethics is the keystone of the bank's standards of conduct. It is revised approximately every 18 months.
2. Specific functional areas have drafted behavioral guidelines and standards of conduct (e.g., the purchasing department has its Standards and Ethics of Buying).
3. The chairman reinforces the code and guidelines in speeches, meetings, articles, and letters to employees.
4. Employee ethics education begins with new-employee orientation. A video features the bank's chairman discussing corporate values and employees agree in writing to abide by the Code of Ethics.
5. Outside consultants conduct a two-day, off-site management seminar (Decision Making and Corporate Values). This seminar uses 12 case studies of actual ethical dilemmas faced by Chemical Bank managers.
6. A variety of special programs and procedures are used to head off unethical conduct (e.g., the reporting and compliance department and a hot line for employees with personal financial problems).
7. Various committees and units monitor enforcement of bank standards (e.g., the board of directors audit committee does ethics reviews).
8. Chemical Bank maintains a long-standing reputation for corporate responsibility through a variety of community outreach programs.

General Mills

1. A strong, continuous, clearly communicated ethics leadership stance is taken by the company's CEO.
2. The company tradition of ethical behavior is based on actual management action.
3. Explicit statements of belief and policy were developed, including a Statement of Corporate Values and Business Ethics and Conduct.
4. Compensation and performance evaluation is closely linked to individual social responsibility objectives.
5. High value is placed on open decision making and honesty.
6. A strong internal control network is maintained to supplement trust with awareness of actual behavior.
7. Violations of law or policy are punished.
8. The General Mills Foundation's gifts show support for community needs.

Hewlett-Packard Company

1. Three documents summarize HP values and ethics: "The HP Way" describes how employees are expected to act; "The Corporate Objectives" outlines the objectives and principles which govern behavior of managers and employees at HP;

EXHIBIT 4   **(concluded)**

and "Standards of Business Conduct" spells out an employee's ethical obligations to HP, to customers, to competitors, and to suppliers.

2. The core HP values include: confidence in and respect for people, open communications, honesty, integrity, concern for the individual, and the sharing of benefits and responsibilities.

3. The Internal Audit Department reviews compliance with the standards (e.g., the auditing team interviews the top managers of each entity asking a series of detailed questions related to ethical behavior and training of subordinates).

4. HP educational programs dedicate a major portion of their time to ethics.

5. A bimonthly magazine and video tape featuring company news items communicate HP values directly to all employees.

Johnson & Johnson

1. Our Credo is the ethical framework for all business decisions of the 150 J&J companies. It describes J&J's relationships with customers, employees, communities, and stockholders. The credo is revised every 3 years.

2. The Credo Survey provides employee feedback on company performance in relation to credo principles.

3. Management willingness to take stands on ethical matters reflects its commitment to the credo.

4. Compliance procedures include:

   a. The executive committee meets twice a year and goes over consumer complaints, surveys, audits, and safety records.

   b. Internal audits include safety, quality, and financial areas.

   c. Manager performance assessments cover credo-related factors.

Xerox

1. An Understanding states the basic code of ethics in straightforward, informal, understandable language.

2. The Xerox Policy on Business Ethics outlines how managers should deal with customers, government officials, political contributions, and conflicts of interest.

3. The manager's handbook, *Managing in Xerox,* discusses traditions, beliefs, values, policies, and practices in employee relations.

4. A large number of policy statements focus on specific issues or functional areas (e.g., Statements of Corporate Policy deals with antitrust laws, ethics of selling, and the ethics of buying).

5. An annual letter from the chairman and periodic letters from the president emphasize ethics and compliance.

6. Articles about ethics often appear in corporate publications like the *Agenda* or *Xerox World.*

7. Numerous training, development, and education programs focus on values and standards of conduct.

8. Strong internal control systems and an active audit committee of the board of directors monitor and enforce ethics.

9. Corporate responsibility is manifested in a number of company actions (e.g., the Xerox Foundation disburses over $10 million annually).

To provide unmatched value in the product and service we offer customers.

To recognize the one limitless resource: the individual and collective potential of the human being.

To provide employees with maximum opportunity to exceed their own expectations.

To achieve continued improvement in the use of company resources.

To grow as a means of maintaining and renewing vitality.

To ensure that corporate objectives, wherever possible, enhance the goals of the immediate and larger communities of which we are a part.

Earl wondered whether this document, which he had helped develop in the early 1970s, would help him sort out just what to do about Tek's ethics program.

Ethics Program (B)

The Oregonian newspaper reported on October 24, 1987:

> Tektronix, Inc. announced Friday that Earl Wantland will step down as president and chief executive officer of the Beaverton based electronics company on November 1. He will be succeeded by David P. Friedley, vice president and general manager of Tektronix communications group, one of the company's four operating divisions.

Although it was no secret at Tek that the board of directors had been interviewing possible successors for Earl Wantland, Friedley was not in the rumor mill as a possible choice and he experienced the same surprise expressed by other Tek insiders, "We're all sort of reeling over here. . . . This really came out of left field."[2] In their unanimous choice of Dave Friedley, the board had bypassed three senior vice presidents and an executive vice president.

The board's choice drew support from a number of Tek insiders. One manager explained, "Of all the dark horses, Dave's the best in my mind, partly because it is such a shock and partly because he does come with such a fresh attitude." Another manager described him as "very independent, strong minded, self-confident, and a bit of a maverick." Friedley describes his own leadership style as "relatively informal and direct." He does not like meetings or memos. Instead he prefers to talk with people as soon as a problem or issue surfaces. He wants a simple, lean organization where communication is fast and actions are taken rapidly.

Friedley, a marketing-oriented engineer, joined Tektronix in 1974 and spent his first four years in various marketing, engineering, and general management jobs. He then served a five-year stint as executive vice president and general manager of Tek's wholly owned subsidiary, The Grass Valley Group Inc. in Grass Valley, California. Friedley moved to the Beaverton campus when he was promoted to vice president in charge of Tek's communications group and proceeded to distinguish himself as the leader of the most successful and fastest-growing of Tek's primary business groups. Friedley explained, "I haven't been assimilated into the Tektronix culture for that long, and even when I was, I think I was somewhat of a rebel."

Friedley was well-aware of the problems he faced as the new president and CEO of Tektronix. The 1980s had

challenged the high-tech industry with a sluggish world economy, intensified competition, and a rapidly changing marketplace. This was a crucial time for the company given the past few years of flat sales and declining earnings. Analysts claimed that Tektronix must become faster on its feet and more customer driven. Increased competition had eroded some of Tek's markets and human resource problems provided additional complications. In recent years Tektronix had suffered from the loss of a large pool of talent as a number of key middle managers, engineers, and marketers departed. Employee morale was battered by several rounds of layoffs in the past six years.

Friedley knew that Tektronix's board of directors expected him to turn the company around and to regain the profitability and market position it enjoyed in previous years. He knew that among the key decisions he would make were the leadership style he would assume and the actions he would take to reach the board's goals. He was concerned about how the qualities which had earned him the job as president (a hard-driving, bottom-line, market orientation) would fit with Tek's traditional values and culture. He asked himself whether it would be more desirable to maintain the old culture or to forge a new culture which would be more compatible with today's competitive world? Along with these issues was the question of whether he should continue the ethics seminars initiated by Earl Wantland or make a clean break with past leadership? As Friedley mulled over these questions, he realized that soon he would be called upon to announce his strategic plan to Tek's employees, management, and board of directors.

Ethics Program (C)

In a memo dated June 6, 1988, Dave Friedley make it perfectly clear that the business ethics seminars conducted by Kirk Hanson were being put on the back burner: ". . . Because of the urgent profitability issues on our plate today, I do not plan to conduct follow-up sessions at this time." (See Exhibit 5.) While not commented on directly in the memo, work on a code of conduct and the internal controls seminar continued.

Friedley explained his decision this way,

> The reason is that Tek has such a strong culture related to ethics. Ethics is one of the things we're noted for in the industry. Our reputation on the outside world is based upon quality, honesty in business practices, and conservatism. . . .
>
> The electronics industry is not fraught with unsavory

---

[2]*The Business Journal,* November 2, 1987, p. 1.

Exhibit 5

Tek interoffice communication and subsequent ethics summary report

---

TO: DISTRIBUTION   DATE: June 6, 1988
FROM: Dave Friedley
SUBJECT: Ethics Sessions

At the time the Business Ethics sessions with Kirk Hanson were conducted, feedback was promised regarding the issues that surfaced and recommendations for next steps. Attached is a brief description of participant reaction to the sessions and a summary of the lists generated regarding guiding principles and pressures to violate those principles. Please make this available to the appropriate people in your organization, especially those who attended a session.

One of the things that attracted me to Tektronix originally was the high sense of ethics of its people. I continue to believe in that today and indeed to expect it of us all. Because of the urgent profitability issues on our plate today, I do not play to conduct followup sessions at this time. However, I'm counting on you to continue communicating to your organizations the importance of maintaining high ethical standards in all facets of our operations.

If you would like additional information regarding the sessions or the resulting roll downs that have been designed and delivered in various parts of Tek, call Pat Willard.

DISTRIBUTION

Larry Choruby
Fred Hanson
Larry Kaplan
Dick Knight
Stan Kouba
Pat Kunkle
John Landis
Allan Leedy
Tom Long
Phil Robinson
Wim Velsink
Dan Wright

Evaluation Summary

In fall 1987 ten sessions on business ethics were conducted with vice presidents and their direct reports. One additional session was held for corporate staff. Kirk Hanson, from Stanford University, facilitated these sessions.

Overall, the sessions were well-received. A number of people attending said the sessions brought out important and needed conversation about Tek's values and ethical standards. Some participants said the sessions reaffirmed their values as Tek employees. Participants' most frequently mentioned concern was the desire for greater clarity on Tek's values and ethical guidelines—they would have liked more guidance on specific tough calls and more dialogue about how Tek's historical values (as espoused by Jack and Howard) apply in today's competitive environment. Participants also commented that the purpose and outcomes of the ethics sessions should have been better defined.

**Summary of Principles and
Pressures Identified**

During the sessions, participants identified the principles which should guide their behavior in working with various stakeholder groups. They also identified the pressures that push on managers to violate those guidelines.
    The seven stakeholder groups considered were:

Customers
Vendors/suppliers

EXHIBIT 5 (continued)

Employees
Divisions
Shareholders/the corporation
Government
Community

The following is a summary of the principles and pressures identified in each stakeholder group, listed by major categories in order of frequency mentioned. You may obtain a complete list from each session by calling Pat Willard.

1. Customers (8 groups responding)
Principles

Serve customers with honesty and integrity. This principle included the need to be fair, honest, provide equitable treatment, respect, and confidentiality; take no kickbacks; comply with legal requirements; and advertise what can be provided in fact.
Provide quality, value-added products and services that meet customer needs.
Work in partnership with the customer.
Meet commitments; deliver what you promise when you promise it.

Pressures

Although the pressures identified vary depending on the group, they fall into three major categories:

Pressures to meet budget objectives.
Pressures to make the sale/keep the order.
Competitive pressures.

Also mentioned were pressures created by pay/incentive plans, pressure from bosses to act in ways that violate principles, and pressures resulting from limited resources.

2. Vendors/Suppliers (6 groups)
Principles

Establish long-term partnerships based on mutual commitments and goals.
Provide fair, equitable qualifying criteria.
Pay vendors within agreed upon times and not accept favors or gifts.
Vendor/supplier relationships should value confidentiality, teamwork, and competitive performance.

Pressures

Personal relationships that foster decisions based on friendship.
Personal gain.
Pressures from timelines.

3. Employees (8 groups)
Principles

Respect the individual and his/her contribution; treat individuals with honesty and dignity.
Provide an opportunity for employees to grow and develop to their full potential.
Maintain open communication channels with employees: employees need to be provided with information about business, corporate values, and feedback on their performance; the corporation must be willing to listen to their ideas.
Provide a fair, clearly communicated reward system for employee contributions.
Provide equal opportunity.
Maintain long-term relationships.

Pressures

Budget and profitability issues (e.g., lack of adequate resources, tradeoffs between profitability and commitment to employees).

EXHIBIT 5   (concluded)

Unclear standards for evaluating performance and current pay practices. (Some mention was made of discomfort and biases in dealing with employee performance.)

4. **Divisions (4 groups)**
   Principles

Build partnerships characterized by trust, openness, cooperation, shared strategies.
Share accurate, relevant information.

Pressures

Budget and financial performance issues.
Timelines.
Conflicts between meeting division needs and meeting customer needs, personal needs, business goals.

5. **Shareholders/Corporate Management (4 groups)**
   Principles

Manage assets and resources for the growth and success of the company.
Open and honest disclosure of information.
Implement corporate goals and values and let management know when you disagree with them.

Pressures

Meeting financial plans, including APIP, as a pressure related to a number of violations.
Demands for short-term results.
Little reward for "wearing the corporate hat."
The desire to look good.

6. **Government (2 groups)**
   Principles

Compliance with the spirit and letter of local laws.
Challenge and/or participate in the formation of legislation.
Cooperate with law enforcement.

Pressures

Financial targets.
Lack of information and resources.
Misguided loyalty.
Desire to maintain face.

7. **Community (4 groups)**
   Principles

Be environmentally responsible.
Support education efforts.
Support employee involvement in community activities.
Maintain a company image based on stability, consistency, honesty, and openness.

practices . . . both the internal and external environment we're operating in is just not that tempting . . . I don't think our business lends itself that much to unethical behavior as a way of improving performance. The nature of the busi-ness, the controls we have, and the historical values and culture, are strong enough to limit unethical behavior.[3]

_____
[3]Interview with David Friedley, August 3, 1988.

Friedley further indicated that his primary goals for his first year as CEO were increased profitability and a revised corporate mission statement.

Friedley moved rapidly and aggressively in pursuit of his increased profitability goal. He implemented dramatic management and strategic changes including the replacement of three of Tek's top four executives and the reassignment of its chief marketing officer. The workforce was reduced by 1,000 (which impacted largely middle management); a $24-million third-quarter write-off was taken to restructure or close unprofitable businesses; a CAE (computer-aided engineering) business was sold to rival Mentor Graphics Corporation for $5 million after Tek had invested some $150 million in it.[4] "I think Friedley is doing exactly what people thought he would do and that's shake up the troops," remarked a Tek marketing director.[5]

Increased pressures for profitability and the direction taken by Friedley called into question the viability of the traditional Tek culture and value system. A Tek executive remarked, "We have an old, reasonably defined culture that is in transition." Another manager stated, "In some ways we've gotten away from our values and we're just not living them like we have in the past."

In his first interview after being named CEO, Friedley affirmed his intention to have Tek become a faster-moving, more responsive, more competitive company. He commented, "A 41-year-old culture can get in the way. It can turn into a form of inertia which makes it difficult to change and be responsive."[6]

Friedley felt that certain cultural changes were nec-

---

[4]*The Business Journal,* April 18, 1988. (Note: the company would not confirm these numbers.)
[5]*The Business Journal,* February 25, 1988.
[6]*The Business Journal,* November 2, 1987.

essary. These included increased expectations of accountability and productivity for employees. "We will not provide on-the-job retirement," and, "we will be tougher in terminating nonperforming employees," Friedley asserted. Tek would move away from being technology/engineering-driven toward being more market/customer-driven. He believed that "in striving for elegance in engineering we have taken too long to get products to market and the competition has outperformed us."

Friedley's refocusing of the Tek culture and delayed follow-up on the business ethics seminars drew mixed support from Tek insiders. One executive commented, "I wouldn't encourage him to do more ethics seminars right now because they come across as airy, fairy, and fuzzy and we've got to make money." Former CEO, Earl Wantland, saw a need to have ethics discussions "at reasonable intervals" because "unless there is a pretty strong code of ethics driving what you're doing you can get into some pretty wrong behavior."[7]

While Friedley acknowledged that ethics are important, he indicated that he was not sure if a seminar or some other mechanism was the best way to remind employees of the necessity for ethical behavior. Friedley, true to his action-oriented management style, fired three employees who violated company policy even though their behavior did not result in personal gain.

A number of questions linger in the minds of Tek employees and observers: Is Dave Friedley making a wise management decision in putting Tek's ethics seminar on the back burner? Does increased emphasis on profitability necessitate or abrogate the need for focus on ethical issues? What will be the immediate and long-range effects of this decision?

---

[7]Interview with Earl Wantland, July 28, 1988.

Grassroots Public Affairs and the Campaign to Ban Drift Nets from Trinidad and Tobago

Martha D. Saunders, Ph.D

For the past two decades, coastal nations have been alarmed to witness the systematic decimation of fish stocks off their shores as a result of highly mobile, technologically advanced, modern fishing fleets. Both commercial as well as recreational fishing interests have looked for ways to protect their marine resources, only to find the problem far more advanced, and the damage far more serious, than previously thought.

In 1990, the center of this concern surrounded the use of huge, super-efficient drift nets. Often called "walls of death" and stretching up to 40 miles in length, these devices trapped and indiscriminately killed every living thing caught in them with horrifying efficiency, including marine mammals who were then unable to get air. The use of these nets ignited such a storm of international protest in the Pacific Ocean that the fishermen who used them were forced to either change their methods of fishing in the Pacific or move to other areas.

Sid Johnson

In mid-May 1990, Sidney Johnson, a member of the Trinidad and Tobago Game Fishing Association, was horrified to see a fleet of Taiwanese fishing vessels tied up in port to offload their catch. Several of the vessels were equipped with drift nets—the first to be sighted in the Atlantic, near the Caribbean Sea.

Johnson returned the next day with his camera, documented on film the drift-net equipment on some of the ships, and launched a vigorous campaign to ban the devices from his region. Johnson was able to arouse such vigorous protest as a result of his discovery that in September 1990, Trinidad's prime minister spoke to the United Nations in support of a total ban on drift-net operations.

Background

The introduction of drift nets in this part of the Atlantic threatened efforts of the United States and Caribbean countries to manage populations of migratory fish in Atlantic, Gulf, and Caribbean waters. Big, ocean-roaming species that swim the entire Atlantic, like swordfish, tuna, marlin and sailfish, were said to be vulnerable because drift net fishermen could intercept the fish on the high seas and reduce their numbers as they migrate between South and North American waters.[1]

Swordfish were especially vulnerable, as that species was on the verge of collapse. In addition, the numbers of bluefin tuna, which spawns in the Caribbean, had already been reduced to hazardously low levels.[2]

Trinidadian fishermen had previously reported hearing Taiwanese drift netters talking on their radios saying they were working waters off South America where nu-

trients from the Amazon River attract fish, but none had been directly observed at work in the western Atlantic until Johnson made his discovery.

Johnson's Response

When Johnson returned to the docks on May 16, 1990, the day after his discovery of the Taiwanese drift netters, he took his camera with him and took approximately 15 photographs. He noted in his diary that four of the vessels he had seen the day before had left and two others had arrived, causing him to suspect a 16–20 boat fleet.[3]

Johnson's next move was to alert the International Game Fish Association (IGFA), an influential conservation organization. The response was immediate. IGFA executive director Michael Leech, upon receiving Johnson's photographs, reported the finding to Carl Safina of the National Audubon Society, who called Johnson the next day for more information. Safina alerted the appropriate editors of *The New York Times,* who assigned the story to a staff reporter.[4]

Within two weeks, Johnson was contacted by Ken Hinman of the National Coalition of Marine Conservation, and Bill Stevens, reporter for *The New York Times* who requested photographs and information. The result of this exchange was an article in *The New York Times* (three months later) featuring Johnson's discovery of drift netters in the Atlantic.[5]

The day after *The New York Times* article appeared, Johnson and a colleague from the Game Fishing Association, Winfield Aleong, met with the editor of the *Trinidad Guardian* who wanted to do a news item on the issue. Later the pair were interviewed by Marlon Miller, of the Express newspapers. On August 15, the *Guardian* ran a front page article and the *Trinidad Express* covered the issue on page three. In addition, the Guardian ran an editorial critical of drift nets.

Official Resistance

Johnson's efforts met with some official resistance when the chief executive officer of Trinidad's National Fisheries Co. called a press conference and made allegations that Johnson was involved with a U.S. company making

---

[1]William K. Stevens, "Large Drift Nets Move to Atlantic," *The New York Times,* p. C1.
[2]Ibid, p. C4.

[3]Sid Johnson, Letter to All Concerned Parties, August 16, 1990, p. 1.
[4]Ibid.
[5]Stevens, "Large Drift Nets."

a bid for the National Fisheries Co. Johnson flatly denied any such connection.[6]

It is important to note that Trinidad's National Fisheries Co. was established a number of years ago by one of the first governments following that country's independence. The agency was organized to service the shrimping industry. The country bought approximately 15 shrimp boats to be used to bring up shrimp from Brazil. The National Fisheries Co. contracted out the boats and subsidized the fuel needed to operate the shrimping effort. When the agreement with Brazil was lost (after alleged mismanagement of funds), the already heavy Taiwanese presence in Trinidad seemed (to some) to take over the company, although this was never made official.

The result of this activity was a debt-ridden government-subsidized agency surrounded by a cloud of suspicion. Media reports reflect frequent bitter conflict between that agency and local commercial fishermen over docking privileges when the Taiwanese boats were in port.

Turning Point

Johnson's efforts, albeit dedicated, were not successful in moving the government to act until a serendipitous combination of events occurred in July. At that time, a number of international organizations—from Trinidad's Information Division, to Earth Trust Foundation of Hawaii—had begun to take notice of the situation and ask for more information and copies of Johnson's photos. Earth Trust sent Johnson a copy of a video titled "Stripmining of the Seas," which showed the working of drift-net equipment and the destruction it causes.

Coincidentally, on July 28, a small Muslim military group attempted to overthrow the government. A curfew had been imposed and most people were confined to their homes in the evenings. Realizing that people were probably watching television in record numbers, Johnson obtained a prime-time slot, directly after the news, to run the Earth Trust video. With a virtually captive audience, the conservationist's cause was rapidly advanced and the response from an outraged public was

immense. The broadcast was sponsored by the Hi-Lo Food Chain, the country's biggest foodstore chain. As a result of powerful public response, the food chain sponsored a second showing two weeks later.

Johnson and his colleagues from Trinidad and Tobago's Game Fishing Association gathered additional support from Greenpeace, Earth Island, and South Africa's Save the Dolphin Association. More published accounts of the Trinidad incident appeared in *Time Magazine, Wildlife Conservation,* and *Saltwater Sportsman.* Still, Johnson felt he was getting nowhere with his own government until August 21, when Brian Siler from the U.S. embassy requested information on the vessels. After that, Eddie Tung from the Taiwanese embassy in New York asked for a copy of the photographs so that they could identify the boats involved. Not long after that, on a visit to the United Nations (of which Taiwan is not a member), Johnson visited with Tung, who told him the offending vessels had been punished.

The next month, Johnson noted in the local newspaper that Trinidad and Tobago's prime minister was planning a visit to the United Nations. Johnson wrote him urging that, in keeping with U.N. resolution 44/225 (calling for a worldwide moratorium on high seas use of drift nets after June 30, 1992), it would look good if his country were to be the first country on the Atlantic side to make a positive ban on drift-net vessels. To the relief of Johnson and his conservationist associates, the prime minister took the arguments to heart and read, almost word for word, Johnson's letter to the United Nations.

Since that time, the government of Trinidad and Tobago has established The National Monitoring Committee on Foreign Fishing and Related Matters. The committee is charged with monitoring the operations of all foreign fishing vessels in the waters under the jurisdiction of Trinidad and Tobago to "ensure compliance with the resolutions of international organizations, the regulations of national entities that have influence on Trinidad and Tobago's fishing industry."[7] Sidney Johnson serves as a member of that committee, representing the Council of Presidents of Environmental Groups (COPE).

---

[6]Johnson, Letter.

[7]From "Terms of Reference of the National Monitoring Committee on Foreign Fishing and Related Matters," issued by the Government of Trinidad and Tobago, November 1991.

Exhibit 1   **Politics, Economy, and Outlook for Trinidad and Tobago**

Prime Minister: Mr. Patrick Manning
Inflation: 11.0 percent (1990)
Import Cover: 6.2 months (1990)

Politics

Mr. Patrick Manning, head of the People's National Movement (PNM), won 21 out of the 36 seats contested for the House of Representatives. This represented a turnaround for the National Alliance for Reconstruction (NAR), which had led the government since 1986.

The Economy

Petroleum accounted for approximately 57 percent of total exports (1990), but production has fallen steadily since 1978.

The gas fields have proven reserves sufficient to last 45 years.

Continued efforts have been made to promote the nonoil sector.

After years of economic contraction, the economy seems to be growing. Real GDPPP expanded from 0.7 percent in 1990 to 2.7 percent in 1991 and inflation fell to an estimated 5 percent in 1991.

Unemployment is a problem, with an estimated 20 percent of the total workforce unemployed.

Outlook

Barclay's ABECOR Country Report indicates moderate economic prospects, depending on the success of government in developing its nonoil activities and restrained public spending.

Source: Barclay's ABECOR Country Reports, 1992–94.

Exhibit 2   **Sidney Johnson**
                 Biographical Information

Name:	Sidney Alexander Johnson
Birthplace:	England
Education:	Secondary education to UK School Certificate Level.
	Apprenticeship with Ford Motor Company—Certificates in diesel hydraulics and mechanized farming.
Current employment:	Managing Director
	Mitco Water Laboratories Ltd.
	P.O. Box 482
	Port of Spain, Trinidad
Other activities:	President, Coalition for Conservation/Caribbean Sea

---

BASF's Proposed Paint Plant

A Community's Reaction

Max Douglas
Indiana State University

Introduction

In early 1988, BASF Corporation, a member of the international German-based BASF Group, released plans for a five-year, $2 billion capital expansion program. BASF Corporation is one of the largest chemical companies in North America. In 1988, net sales equaled $5 billion while net income amounted to $149 million. Nearly 22,000 people are employed by the four divisions of BASF Corporation. Its diversified product mix includes the following: basic, intermediate, and specialty chemicals, colorants, dispersions, fiber raw materials, fibers, automotive coatings, printing inks, urethane specialties and chemicals, plastics, advanced composite materials, antifreeze, crop protection products, pharmaceuticals, vitamins, fragrances, and audio, video, and computer recording media.

On March 10, 1988, BASF officials announced that the company intended to build a manufacturing facility somewhere in the American Midwest. Three cities were selected as finalists: Terre Haute, Indiana (located in Vigo County), Evansville, Indiana, and Portsmouth, Ohio. Terre Haute's drawing card was an undeveloped 1,476 acre county industrial park. Terre Haute has a population of roughly 57,480 and is located in the west central part of Indiana. As a community, Terre Haute was in dire need of expanded employment opportunities since several major companies had exited the area over the past decade. Statistics published by the local chamber of commerce showed that between 1979 and 1987, the community suffered a net loss of 6,062 jobs. However, data published by the local Democratic party reported that 4,125 new jobs had been created in the community between 1986 and 1991. During this same time span, new capital investment amounted to $729.5 million.

On March 28, 1988, the Vigo County commissioners signed a licensing agreement with BASF allowing the company to inspect and conduct soil tests at the county's 1,506-acre industrial park located south of Terre Haute. Approximately a month later, BASF released more precise information regarding the nature of the plant facility. Tentative plans called for a $150 million automotive paint plant that would employ approximately 500 local people. This projected economic infusion encouraged city and county government officials to court BASF Corporation. In mid-June an entourage of local government officials and business leaders visited a BASF plant in Gainsville, Ohio. On July 6, 1988, BASF announced that the soil tests at the industrial park were positive and that the company was initiating procedures to "option" land at the Vigo County industrial part. Further discussion between company and county government officials revealed that a small 30-acre parcel of land within the industrial park was still owned by the federal government. BASF stressed that the company would need this 30 acres to develop its plant operations. The Vigo County commissioners eventually purchased this acreage from the General Services Administration in order to accommodate BASF.

Controversy Develops

On August 10, 1988, Jack Wehman, Midwest Venture Director for BASF, announced that the company planned to build a hazardous waste incinerator and establish a landfill in addition to building its paint manufacturing plant. The proposed incinerator and landfill would handle on-site wastes and imported wastes trucked to the site from other BASF plants. Following this news release, the Evansville mayor, Frank McDonald, indicated that his city would no longer pursue the BASF plant. The mayors of Terre Haute and of Portsmouth, Ohio, Pete Chalos and Roger Bussey, indicated that their communities were still positive about the BASF plant regardless of the implications of the incinerator and landfill.

In contrast to the favorable reception of the August

10th BASF announcement by Terre Haute's mayor and other BASF supporters, a local community action group, Citizens for a Clean County (CCC), organized to begin an anti-BASF campaign. The initial purpose of the CCC was to stop BASF from building the waste treatment facility on the site and from importing waste to the incinerator/landfill. The CCC eventually became the primary opponent to BASF, although other BASF adversaries expressed their opposition regarding the importation of toxic wastes. For example, one local entrepreneur, Jim Shanks, mailed out 8,000 letters and petitions to Vigo County residents living in the southern and eastern parts of the county enlisting their opposition to BASF. Table 1 summarizes Shanks's concerns regarding the environmental impact of BASF's incinerator/landfill proposal.

In reaction to the growing anti-BASF sentiment, BASF Corporation hired Fleishman Hilliard, a St. Louis opinion research firm, to conduct community focus groups to solicit views regarding the proposed automotive paint plant, hazardous waste incinerator, and landfill. In addition, BASF launched a letter-writing campaign to reach local citizens, intended to help defuse controversy over the proposed paint plant and waste management facility. In these letters, BASF officials stressed the economic benefits of the plant to the community and outlined the steps that BASF would take to ensure that the environment would not be adversely affected. A summary of the points made by BASF is provided in Table 2.

Economic Development Plan Stirs Public Debate

While this controversy was dominating the community news, local government officials continued to pursue a plan for economic development of the industrial park. The Vigo County Council created the Vigo County Redevelopment Commission to oversee development of the industrial park. The County Redevelopment Commission hired the Terre Haute Department of Redevelopment to draw up a detailed Economic Development Plan for the industrial park. The existence of an Economic Development Plan for the park was a prerequisite for federal funds to underwrite the development of infrastructure such as sewer and water lines. The final Economic Development Plan proposal called for $6 million in improvements to the property in order to make it suitable for industrial development. On November 28, 1988, despite opposition from area residents, the Vigo County Redevelopment Commission declared that the industrial park was an economic development and tax allocation area. Following this official declaration, the Redevelopment Commission submitted the proposed Economic Development Plan to the Vigo County Area Planning Commission. The Area Planning Commission was charged with determining whether the proposed Economic Development Plan conformed with the comprehensive land usage plan for the entire county. On December 7, 1988, a public meeting at a local high school

---

TABLE 1   **Summary of Jim Shank's Concerns Regarding Environmental Impact of BASF's Incinerator/Landfill Proposal**

1. BASF would be exempt from local property taxes on their waste disposal operations; hence, Vigo County taxpayers would, in effect, be subsidizing the BASF toxic waste operation.
2. Vigo County would be importing, processing, and storing toxic wastes from other BASF plants whose host communities are allowed to enjoy the economic benefits of higher payroll and corporate property tax contributions while suffering none of the dangers associated with BASF effluents.
3. Initially it is projected that BASF would process 36 million pounds of hazardous waste annually. Transportation of these toxic wastes into Vigo County by truck or railroad will create a great risk because of the deadly danger of accidental spills.
4. Independent environmental experts seemingly agree that toxic waste incineration can be a health hazard particularly since the county's prevailing wind direction would carry emissions over large and unpredictable parts of the community.
5. Infusion of toxic substances into the underground water supply is also a probability because the clay and plastic barriers used in the dump site will eventually leak.
6. BASF's toxic waste operation would adversely affect the county's attractiveness to other industry. Environmental disasters associated with toxic waste disposal such as Hooker Chemical's Love Canal, Valsicol Chemical's Marshall, Illinois, plant, and Union Carbide's Bhophal, India, factory have left some communities environmentally crippled.

Source: Personal letter received by the author, November 10, 1988.

TABLE 2 Summary of Benefits to Vigo County Accruing from the Proposed Location of BASF's Paint Plant Facility

---

Economic Advantages

1. Immediate capital investment of $150 million in community compounded by future plant construction.
2. Five hundred skilled jobs with at least 400 hired locally; these assignments will be quality jobs with competitive wages. BASF will offer a comprehensive employee benefits program.
3. Building of paint facility will create 3,500 new on-site/off-site construction jobs.
4. One thousand new jobs will be created in the community to service the on-going operation of the initial plant and operations.
5. Estimated spillover of tens of millions of dollars into all sectors of the economy.
6. A significantly expanded tax base that will benefit all public-supported institutions such as schools, libraries, etc.
7. Infrastructure of community will be enhanced by improved road systems, utilities, and airport expansion.

Environmental Advantages and/or Protections

1. About 200 acres in the southwest corner of the site would be maintained as a wildlife preserve in concert with BASF's positive attitude towards environmental quality.
2. Less than 25 acres will be required for permanent storage of BASF wastes over the next 25 years. Based on projected new technology, BASF estimates that a maximum of 50 acres will be used for waste storage over the next century.
3. BASF will treat and dispose *only* BASF wastes. BASF is not a commercial waste treatment company and will not become one.
4. BASF will build a high-tech incinerator system to treat certain waste materials. Gases from incineration process will be cleaned in a five-step purification process before discharge. Incineration process produces *no* odors and poses *no* health hazards.
5. Incineration system has *no* liquid discharges, only clean gases and disposable ash. Volume of waste is reduced by 90 percent and the toxic nature of the waste is destroyed.
6. BASF will *not* burn or dispose of PCBs or radioactive wastes; no dioxin will be handled.
7. BASF plans to construct and monitor an *aboveground* hazardous waste landfill for disposal of certain solid waste including ash.
8. No liquids will be placed in the landfill. The active use area will be shielded by a portable roof preventing rain and snow from entering the storage cells.
9. Contamination of groundwater will be prevented by the use of natural and synthetic barriers.
10. BASF will temporarily import wastes from other BASF plants until the plant site is totally developed. As more plants come on line, the processing of outside BASF wastes will diminish.
11. BASF estimates that twenty truckloads of raw materials, finished products, and waste materials will move along Indiana Route 41. Proper training and modern equipment will ensure safe transportation.

Sources: Personal letters received by the author on November 21, 1988; December 7, 1988; and December 28, 1988.

---

was conducted by the Area Planning Commission. Despite much opposition from the audience, the Area Planning Commission approved the Economic Development Plan by a vote of 11–3.

Following this vote of approval, the Redevelopment Commission scheduled public hearings regarding the industrial park economic development plan. Some 30 hours of testimony were heard over 3 days. Spearheading the anti-BASF forces was the Citizens for a Clean County. Members of the CCC hired outside consultants to speak at the hearings.

One spokesperson, Hugh Kaufman, an employee of the Environmental Protection Agency, expressed concerns about the incineration and hazardous waste landfill components of the BASF proposal. According to Kaufman, hazardous waste facilities inhibit industrial and economic growth rather than promote it. Costs and burdens fall on local governments, which may have additional liabilities if waste from incinerators enters public water and sewage systems. Kaufman further stressed that increased industrial traffic and repairs, chemical spills, and the expanded need for continued training of emergency response teams add additional concerns and costs for taxpayers.*

Another environmentalist, John Blair, gave testimony during the marathon hearings. Blair was being paid $125 per diem by the Oil, Chemical, and Atomic Workers local in Giesmar, Louisiana, to help promote opposition to the BASF plant. OCAW had been engaged in a bitter four-year lockout with BASF at the Geismar plant. Blair said evidence suggests that BASF often acts in an immoral fashion. He claimed that BASF's real intentions were to locate a hazardous treatment plant using the paint plant as a carrot. Blair further charged that the economic development plan under consideration had no enforcement provisions. Blair claimed that Terre Haute would become a "national sacrifice zone" if it began accepting hazardous waste from other areas.

In addition to the above "expert" testimony, several citizens presented personal position statements. One opponent, Eva Kor, a survivor of Nazi Germany's World War II Auschwitz concentration camp, claimed that BASF was one of three companies formed out of the ashes of the German company I. G. Farben. Kor claimed that Farben used slave labor from the Auschwitz camp until "they were used up." She opposed BASF's locating in Terre Haute and suggested that a referendum be held to resolve the issue, CCC member Harold Cox reported that more than one-half of the polled respondents in a local survey opposed a hazardous waste facility. Although in the minority, BASF supporters cited the tremendous economic boost that the company would provide for the community. In addition, BASF advocates labeled the CCC as a biased group, more interested in protecting their property values than in stopping the importation of toxic waste. Nevertheless, the majority of statements presented during the 30 hours of public hearings conducted by the Vigo County Redevelopment Commission articulated opposition to the establishment of an incinerator and landfill adjacent to the automotive paint plant as well as the importation of hazardous wastes from other BASF plants for disposal in Terre Haute.

After the hearings, the Redevelopment Commission reviewed all written testimony regarding the Economic Development Plan. On January 19, 1989, the Redevelopment Commission conducted its final session to determine the fate of the proposed plan for the industrial park. One of the commissioners, Linda Burger, expressed concern that this plan would allow the importation of several truckloads of hazardous wastes into the community. Ms. Burger indicated further concern about the high cancer rates that already existed in Vigo County. Burger proposed an amendment to the economic development plan that would ban importation of toxic wastes into Vigo County. The amendment was rejected 3–2. The Economic Development Plan was finally approved 4–1.

Legal Action Taken

Shortly following the approval of the Economic Development Plan by the Redevelopment Commission, the CCC and 16 other people living near the industrial park filed a legal petition for judicial review against the Redevelopment Commission, the Vigo County Commissioners, and Vigo County. The petition made the following charges:

1. The Economic Development Plan was adopted by using impermissible procedures alleged to be (a) inadequate notice of when the Redevelopment Commission would meet, (b) holding meetings in rooms too small to accommodate interested parties, and (c) curtailment of public comment.
2. The Redevelopment Commission was wrong to meet during regular business hours because that precluded some people from attending.
3. Four out of five Commission members had conflicts of interest.
4. The Economic Development Plan jeopardized the public health, safety, and welfare of the community.

Coinciding with the filing of the legal petition by the CCC et al. was the public introduction of a BASF visitation team. The team consisted of employees from various areas of the company such as human resources, operations, and plant safety. BASF provided biographical sketches of each member and indicated they were sent to

---

*Environmental issues raised by Hugh Kaufman have become a priority concern of the Chemical Manufacturers' Association (CMA). In 1985, CMA started a Community Awareness and Response Program to encourage chemical companies to reexamine their emergency response programs. As part of these programs, an emergency planning committee is formed to determine the roles of various community groups, evaluate risks, develop and test crisis management plans, and educate the public. These plans require that the targeted company share material safety data sheets to inform the citizenry about the chemicals the company uses. Community groups, physicians, and sundry emergency responders (fire departments, Red Cross) are normally key participants in this type of response program.

discuss the quality of work life at BASF and to share their experiences with the environmental safety of BASF plants at other locations. Jack Wehman, Midwest Venture Director for BASF, indicated that the presence of this team did not mean that BASF had decided on Terre Haute. That decision, according to Wehman, depended on the outcome of the litigation over the industrial park. Wehman stressed that the visitation team's purpose was to gather and disseminate information pertaining to the proposed paint plant.

Shortly following CCC's legal petition and the arrival of BASF's visitation team, Terre Haute Mayor Pete Chalos expressed displeasure that a legal petition had been filed to overturn the Economic Development Plan for the county industrial park. Mayor Chalos stated:

> I think that there are some people on the loose here that want to take us back 20 years and put Terre Haute in the position of being called an injunction city. I certainly hope cooler heads and wiser people take a leading role in making sure BASF comes here.

During March 1989, the litigation filed to stop the already approved Economic Development Plan intensified. On March 1, the coalition of the CCC and local property owners filed an amended court petition claiming that the adoption of the Economic Development Plan by the Redevelopment Commission on January 19, 1989, should be canceled because county commissioners had failed to adopt an ordinance establishing the Redevelopment Commission. Hugh Kaufman charged that the purchase of the 30-acre tract of land for the Vigo County Industrial Park from the GSA was fraudulent. Kaufman contended that the GSA should have determined the environmental impact of potential development before selling federal land. He further implied that a new impact study should have been conducted rather than relying on the original assessment covering the 1,476 acres sold to Vigo County in 1986. County government officials responded that they had followed appropriate legal advice in purchasing the additional 30 acres for $50,000 at a public auction held on August 19, 1988.

Economic Development Plan Declared Null and Void

By mid-March 1989, Judge Frank Nardi had conducted a pretrial conference in an attempt to resolve questions and issues raised by the plaintiffs. Judge Nardi indicated he would review all evidence about the way the Vigo

County Redevelopment Commission had been formed and the procedures used to reach its decision. Following federal court hearings, Judge Nardi gave the CCC and Vigo County adequate time to file written briefs. The core of the plaintiffs' position was as follows: the Economic Development Plan had been written especially for BASF, had been adopted in violation of certain aspects of state law, and had been approved by government officials without giving proper consideration to all factors, including environmental impact issues. The defendants (county officials) testified that plaintiffs were given full rein during public hearings and that the plan was a reasonable one, designed with BASF in mind but seeking economic development by attracting not only BASF but other industry as well to the industrial park. Defendants also contended that monitoring the environment was a state and federal responsibility and that the incineration of waste from other BASF plants was permissible as part of the industrial park. On July 1, 1989, Judge Nardi ruled that the Economic Development Plan approved by the Redevelopment Commission was null and void. Nardi cited the following reasons:

1. Question of propriety regarding payments and alliances that suggested possible conflicts of interest among the commissioners: Judge Nardi concluded that Commissioner Harlan had a conflict of interest because his son owned acreage that BASF would have to purchase for easement purposes at an estimated cost of between $350,000 and $400,000. Business diaries subpoenaed from BASF also supported Judge Nardi's conclusions regarding other possible improprieties.

2. Prejudgment of the decision before the Vigo County Redevelopment Commission was formed: County government officials allegedly "packed" the Redevelopment Commission with advocates of the BASF location project and formed an unethical alliance with the company to stifle public opposition. R. Marc Elliot, director of the Terre Haute Redevelopment Department and primary "author" of the Economic Development Plan, testified that meetings with BASF officials were held as the plan was taking shape.

As a result of these findings, the Economic Development Plan was remanded to the Vigo County Commissioners for further action.

Meanwhile, Back at the Ranch

While Judge Nardi was analyzing the data contesting the approval of the Economic Development Plan (approximately April 1 to July 1, 1989), another controversy was brewing. BASF opponents expressed concern that the company had not produced a complete list of chemicals that would be imported, burned, and/or buried at its selected midwestern facility. Company officials indicated that the amount of waste handled, if Vigo County were selected, would be strictly limited by the redevelopment plan. BASF stressed that it would act responsibly and show concern for the short-run and long-run impact on the environment. BASF officials reassured the community that no third-party wastes would be imported. It was also pointed out that BASF was following common corporate practice in that partial lists were seldom released. According to BASF management, most large companies do not release lists of chemicals until they apply for a state permit for incineration operations.

Unfortunately for BASF officials, their responses were rendered completely suspect by an analysis of data conducted by a local Indiana State University chemistry professor, Dr. John Corrigan, who had been asked by a reporter of the *Sullivan Daily Times* (a local community newspaper 30 miles south of Terre Haute) to analyze some unpublished BASF documents. Data revealed that BASF intended to incinerate up to 152 chemicals—waste residues from 33 plants in 14 states in 1991–1992. Corrigan reported that metals for incineration included cadmium, chromium, lead, and barium, among others; these chemicals cannot be destroyed or rendered harmless by incineration. BASF officials responded that the data were not current and were subject to revision. Jack Wehman, Midwest Venture Director for BASF, responded to the community concern by saying that following Judge Nardi's decision, BASF would begin the permitting process and make a full disclosure of chemicals to be disposed of at the Vigo County facility. The controversy over the chemical list at this point remained unresolved. A major factor contributing to the impasse was the ruling by U.S. District Court Judge Nardi declaring the Economic Development Plan null and void.

A Proposal to Sell Industrial Park Land

Subsequent to Judge Nardi's ruling declaring the Economic Development Plan for the industrial park null and void, controversy continued regarding the possible sale of industrial park land to BASF. A joint meeting of the Vigo County commissioners, seven county councilmen, and the five members of the Redevelopment Commission resulted in a consensus not to appeal Judge Nardi's disallowance of the Economic Development Plan. The

county commissioners expressed concern that deed restrictions might have to accompany the sale of industrial park acreage in order to protect the environment. Special concern about importation of hazardous waste was expressed. John Scott, president of the commission, indicated that he was worried that BASF had not yet published a list of what wastes would be imported.

On July 15, 1989, anti-BASF groups met with county commissioners to share their views about the future of the industrial park. Harold Cox, representative of the CCC, said that a new economic development plan should be written to attract a wider spectrum of potential buyers. It was stressed that Vigo County needed to market to industries that did not present environmental health risks. The commissioners responded that they welcomed ideas for marketing the land but emphasized that the industrial park was still for sale and no specific time frame had been established to offer the property for public bid. About a month after this meeting, the Vigo County commissioners sought legal advice regarding the disposal of the industrial park. The commissioners also stated that public hearings would be conducted. BASF opponents hoped that the new hearings would result in a plan that would restrict ecologically unsound activities while promoting safe economic development of the industrial park.

BASF Modifies Plans

On August 31, 1989, Jack Wehman announced that BASF was scaling down its plans for an industrial plant in Vigo County. He stated:

> Our new plan calls for the construction of a stand-alone automotive plant with the necessary waste-management facilities for only the paint plant. This means that the waste-management facility will handle only the waste from the site's paint plant. These are on-site generated wastes.

Wehman further explained that the waste management operations would include a wastewater treatment facility, an incinerator system, and a landfill for the incinerated ash, all of which would dispose of on-site wastes. These revisions would require only 200 to 300 acres of land and about 300 local employees at a cost of roughly $100 million. Wehman further projected that these 300 local employees would complement 100 "imported" workers, each earning about $10.15 per hour or about $8.4 million in annual wages. In addition, Wehman estimated that the 2,000 construction workers employed for the two-year project would generate about $40 million per year in payroll. Wehman concluded by stressing the need to negotiate sale of needed land in the park within the next six weeks so that the plant could be operational by the end of 1992.

The Vigo County commissioners reacted favorably to BASF's revised plan and indicated that selling appropriate acreage with a clear title within six weeks seemed feasible. At this point, the commissioners stated that public hearings regarding the sale of the land seemed unnecessary, especially since wastes would not be imported into the community.

Many community members, however, still questioned the integrity of BASF's proposed revision. A member of one anti-BASF coalition, Mothers Against Toxic Chemical Hazards, indicated that opposition to BASF would continue because the revision still proposed a toxic waste incinerator and landfill for the site. Harold Cox, president of the CCC, stated that the proposed landfill was not allowed according to Vigo County's comprehensive land-use plan. Other opponents voiced concern that the industrial park had not been appropriately marketed. BASF adversaries stressed the previous "bait and switch" tactics in which the company initially announced plans for a paint plant and later added the hazardous waste facilities to its agenda. Pete Chalos continued to be a staunch critic of BASF opponents. He criticized environmental groups that had previously said they would accept BASF if toxic waste was not imported. Mayor Chalos indicated he had studied BASF's new proposal and was optimistic that the county commissioners would accommodate BASF.

Two days after announcing their revised plan for the paint plant operations, BASF released two bound volumes of printed material explaining in detail the list of chemicals that could be treated and disposed of at its midwestern paint plant. BASF officials assured the community that all of the tested materials would be handled using procedures that protected the safety, health, and environmental welfare of the citizens.

BASF's Bid for Industrial Park Land Approved by County

On October 27, 1989, approximately six weeks following its announced plant revision, BASF submitted a bid of $500,000 for 296.7 acres of industrial park land. Jack Wehman expressed hope for a successful culmination of the sale and stated that his company would begin a skills

inventory of the local workforce. The skills inventory was quite successful; 1,836 people completed surveys. BASF officials emphasized that the survey wasn't a job application; it was a tool to give BASF an idea of what skills local people have and what training would be needed.

At first it appeared that BASF was on the road to Terre Haute. But on November 2, 1989, four local anti-BASF groups united to form the Terre Haute Environmental Rights Coalition (TERC). TERC's attorney, Mike Kendall, wrote a letter to county attorney Robert Wright advising him that the terms of the BASF bid for the 296 acres of industrial park were extremely biased in favor of the company. Kendall said the county should reject the conditions of the BASF offer; Kendall reinforced TERC's opposition by stating that they would take whatever legal steps were necessary to prevent the sale.

Controversy heightened when BASF filed an amendment to its original bid that had substantial changes regarding its property rights at the industrial park if the sale was consummated. TERC's legal counsel indicated that BASF's amended bid might be in violation of the public bid law and expressed concern that the substantive changes made by the amendment might constitute a de facto new bid. Kendall also pointed out that the original bid was the only one available to the public between October 30 and November 14.

On November 20, 1989, a public hearing on the BASF bid proposal sparked heated debate. Several BASF officials made presentations of the company plans and fielded questions from the public and from county officials. Mike Kendall gave the following summary position:

> We are not against having a facility such as the one described per se, but BASF's revised bid is not enough. We question the legality of negotiating a revised bid and the granting of easements which the BASF facility would require. County Commissioners do not have authority to accept an amended bid except one that raises the price and then only after certain other notice provisions have been complied with.

Other BASF adversaries continued to remind county officials that the industrial park had never been properly marketed and that no such plan existed. Advocates of BASF stressed that the Vigo County area was in desperate need of jobs.

Despite the threats of TERC and other sundry opponents, on November 22, 1989, the Vigo County Board of

Commissioners and Vigo County Council voted unanimously to accept BASF's bid for 296.7 acres of land in the industrial park. Selected parts of the sale order were as follows:

1. The Board of Commissioners finds that the county has no other need for the real estate; Vigo County has severe economic stagnation; the use of real estate for industrial development would help alleviate problems of unemployment and economic stagnation; the soil conditions of the real estate are appropriate for the manufacturing facility, incinerator and landfill.

2. The Commissioners are satisfied that the proposed facility will not threaten the health of local residents as long as the incinerator and landfill are operated in accordance with federal, state, and local laws, ordinances, regulations, and rulings.

A few days after Vigo County approved the sale of land to BASF, the company announced formation of a Community Awareness Panel to provide information to the Vigo County region about BASF's plans and actions. Jack Wehman reported that the panel would meet monthly to discuss topics such as plant facilities, environmental standards, safety and emergency procedures, employment training, and social commitments. Wehman claimed that the Awareness Panel was a balanced representation of the community, except that anti-BASF people declined to serve. Two prominent leaders of the CCC, Harold Cox and John Strecker, rebutted Wehman's comments, stating that they had not been asked to serve. Cox pointed out that the makeup of the Awareness Panel was skewed in favor of BASF.

TERC Files Lawsuit

On April 10, 1990, the Terre Haute Environmental Rights Coalition filed a lawsuit in U.S. District Court charging that the Government Services Administration had violated the National Environmental Policy Act by selling land to Vigo County without requiring an environmental impact study before each of two land sales to the county. TERC requested that the sales be declared null and void and that the title to the industrial park land revert back to the U.S. government. The suit also requested that GSA be required to conduct an environmental impact study in light of the intended use of the land—e.g., a hazardous waste landfill and incinerator.

TERC also filed a motion for an injunction stopping the county from selling the 296 acres to BASF until the lawsuit was resolved.

TERC attorney Kendall also stated that the lawsuits would be filed against county officials for failing to disclose the true use of the property to the GSA—a violation of the Racketeer Influenced and Corrupt Organizations Act. In response to the charge that GSA was negligent in failing to conduct an environmental impact study, Assistant U.S. Attorney Sue Bailey filed a motion to dismiss the TERC lawsuit based on the position that the action taken by the federal government was several years old and that the property no longer belonged to the federal government. Jack Wehman issued a position statement:

> The frivolous filing of two federal lawsuits against the county and federal government by the Environmental Rights Coalition brings into question whether this group is concerned about the health and economic welfare of the citizens of Vigo County. BASF is not a defendant in either of the two lawsuits but, as a partner in the economic development of the community, we are disappointed in these self-serving delaying tactics. BASF is steadfast in its interest to invest more than $100 million in an automotive plant facility which will bring new jobs to Vigo County. BASF remains confident that the county and federal attorneys will resolve this matter to the satisfaction of the great majority of Vigo County residents.

Continued debate followed TERC's legal action. A countersuit was eventually filed by the Vigo County commissioners charging that TERC's complaint was "frivolous, unreasonable, and groundless." The countersuit further claimed that members of TERC were negligently and maliciously interfering with a contractual relationship simply to fulfill a goal of stopping the sale of land to BASF.

TERC responded with the following position statement:

> Some local government officials put all the public's marbles in one basket with BASF for less than 300 jobs. Instead of going after BASF, the commissioners should have spent the last two years enticing good corporate citizens with sound environmental records that would have provided hundreds of additional jobs. Having evaded the requirement for an environmental impact study and faced with a fickle BASF, the Vigo County Commissioners are in danger of being left with an empty plot of land, legal fees, and no jobs for our people.

In response to this legal impasse, Jack Wehman stated in mid-June 1990, that if the federal lawsuit wasn't settled by September 1, 1990, BASF might locate elsewhere. Wehman stressed that BASF must get its plant on line by the end of 1992.

BASF Breaks Off Courtship

On September 4, 1990, Jack Wehman announced that BASF corporate officials in Germany had decided that the corporation would no longer consider land at the Vigo County industrial park as an option for its automotive plant. A big stumbling block to the marriage of BASF and Vigo County was the unresolved litigation filed by TERC claiming that the original sale of federal land by the GSA to Vigo County failed to comply with environmental regulations. Reactions in the community ranged from bitter disappointment to jubilation. City and county officials faced the dilemma of developing a new marketing plan for the industrial park in order to attract new companies and create jobs. BASF executives wondered what they could have done to avoid the confrontation and how their plant siting strategy should be changed in the future. TERC's legal counsel, Michael Kendall, stressed that BASF's decision was not an issue about a group of people who allegedly kept a company out of Vigo County, but about a victory for environmental integrity.

References

BASF Corporation. *Annual Report 1988,* 28 pages.

_____ . "A Company at Work." January 1, 1989, 35 pages.

_____ . "BASF Corporation: Proposed Midwest Facility for Terre Haute." 1988, 9 pages.

_____ . "BASF Corporation: Proposed Midwest Facility for Terre Haute." January 1989, 10 pages.

"BASF Pulls Out of Wabash Valley." *Terre Haute Tribune Star,* September 10, 1990, p. A1.

Cox, Harold, and Pat Duffy. "Court Rules against Plan." *CCC Newsletter* 1, no. 3 (1989), p. 1.

Greenpeace. "Hazard Waste Incinerators." 1987, 4 pages.

"GSA Disputes Kaufman's Claim." *Terre Haute Tribune Star,* March 14, 1989, p. A3.

Halladay, John. "Testimony Ends in BASF Lawsuit." *Terre Haute Tribune Star,* March 24, 1989, p. A1.

_____ . "Development-Environmental Tie Possible." *Terre Haute Tribune Star,* July 13, 1989, p. A1.

_____ . "Officials Schedule New Hearings on Industrial Park." *Terre Haute Tribune Star,* August 26, 1989, p. A1.

Igo, Becky. "Chalos Says BASF Loss Could Hurt." *Terre Haute Tribune Star,* June 20, 1990, p. A3.

_____ . "BASF Foes Call County's Legal Retaliation Intimidation." *Terre Haute Tribune Star,* June 26, 1990, p. A3.

LeBar, Gregg. "Chemical Industry: Regulatory Crunch Coming." *Occupational Hazards,* November 1988, pp. 36–39.

Loughlin, Sue, "Several Foes Remain Opposed to BASF's Plans." *Terre Haute Tribune Star,* August 31, 1989, p. A1.

"Mayor Restates He Wants Both Central Soya, BASF." *Terre Haute Tribune Star,* January 31, 1989, p. A3.

Porter, Kelley. "BASF's Chemicals List Still Not Complete." *Terre Haute Tribune Star,* April 7, 1989, p. A1.

_____ . "Prof More Worried Now after Studying Incineration Data." *Terre Haute Tribune Star,* June 26, 1989, p. A3.

_____ . "Judge Voids Economic Plan; Cites Conflicts." *Terre Haute Tribune Star,* July 1, 1989, p. A1.

_____ . "BASF Scales Back Its Plant Plans." *Terre Haute Tribune Star,* August 31, 1989, p. A1.

_____ . "BASF Releases Chemical List in Continued Spirit of Sharing Facts." *Terre Haute Tribune Star,* September 2, 1989, p. A1.

U.S. Environmental Protection Agency. "Hazardous Waste Incineration: Questions and Answers." April 5, 1988, 53 pages.

Vigo County Redevelopment Commission. "An Economic Development Plan for the Vigo County Industrial Park." November 1988, 21 pages.

Walters, Gordon. "BASF Submits $500,000 Bid for Industrial Land." *Terre Haute Tribune Star,* October 28, 1989, p. A1.

_____ . "Environmentalists Form Anti-BASF Coalition." *Terre Haute Tribune Star,* November 3, 1989, p. A1.

_____ . "Coalition Promises to Sue Commissioners." *Terre Haute Tribune Star,* November 21, 1989, p. A1.

_____ . "County Approves Offer to Sell Land to BASF." *Terre Haute Tribune Star,* November 23, 1989, p. A1.

UNION CARBIDE INDIA LIMITED: THE BHOPAL GAS INCIDENT

I can say that I have seen chemical warfare. Everything so quiet. Goats, cats, whole families—father, mother, children—all lying silent and still. And every structure totally intact. I hope never again to see it.—MAYOR OF BHOPAL

In reality, there is but one entity, the monolithic multinational, which is responsible for the design, development and dissemination of information and technology worldwide.—INDIAN GOVERNMENT LAWYER

A corporation is not liable for the acts or omissions of another corporation by reason of ownership of stock—UNION CARBIDE CORPORATION LAWYER

December 2, 1984, began as a typical day in the central Indian city of Bhopal. In the northern sector of town, shoppers moved about a bustling, open-air market. Here and there a customer haggled with a merchant. Beasts of burden, donkeys and oxen, pulled carts or carried ungainly bundles through the partly paved streets. Children played in the dirt. In the shadow of a Union Carbide India Limited (UCIL) pesticide factory, tens of thousands of India's poorest citizens milled about the shantytown they called home.

Inside the plant, several hundred Indian workers and managers went about their duties, maintaining and operating the systems that produced the mildly toxic pesticide Sevin. The plant was running far below capacity and most of it was shut down for maintenance. Poisonous methyl isocyanate (MIC) was used in making Sevin, but the system which produced MIC had been idle for six weeks. The Sevin unit was using MIC from a one-ton charge pot, which was periodically resupplied from either of two 15,000-gallon tanks (tanks 610 and 611). The tanks were half buried and covered with concrete. Tanks 610 and 611 respectively contained 41 and 20 metric tons of MIC at the time. A third storage tank (tank 619) was available for emergencies and for dumping off-specification MIC.

Source: Copyright Arthur Sharplin and the *Case Research Journal* (a publication of the North American Case Research Association).

Courtesy of Arthur Sharplin, McNeese State University. The assistance and support of the Center for Business Ethics, at Bentley College, of which the author is a Fellow, is gratefully acknowledged. Union Carbide Corporation reviewed early drafts and suggested that certain factual errors be corrected, adding, "The fact that we have not commented on other statements [in the case] should not be construed as our affirming that they are correct." Finally, the author is grateful to certain anonymous Indian nationals without whose assistance this project would not have been possible.

Sometime before midnight, several hundred gallons of water entered tank 610. News accounts would suggest the cause was improper maintenance procedures. But an Arthur D. Little consultant, hired by UCIL's U.S. parent, Union Carbide Corporation (UCC), would conclude the water probably entered through a hose which a "disgruntled operator" connected to the tank during a 10:45 PM shift change.[1]

Whatever the source of the water, it reacted with the MIC, producing heat and gas. A relief valve soon lifted and MIC vapor began flowing through vent headers and out a discharge stack. Several of the workers noticed that their eyes started to water and sting, a signal they knew indicated an MIC leak. They reported this to the MIC supervisor and began to search for the leak. At about midnight, they found what they believed was the source, more than 200 feet from the tanks. They set up a fire hose to spray water on the suspected leak. It was 12:15 AM then, time for tea. The supervisors retired to the company canteen. A "tea boy" came to serve tea to the workers who remained on watch. The gas fumes were getting stronger, though, and the tea boy later said some refused to stop for tea. There were apparently other signals the reaction in the tank was growing more violent, such as increasing pressure gauge readings.

Within a few minutes, an operator called the supervisors back from the canteen. About a ton of MIC was transferred to the Sevin unit in an attempt to relieve the pressure. But the tank pressure gauge was soon pegged. A worker later said the concrete above tank 610 was moving and cracking. Someone sounded the alarm siren and summoned the fire brigade. As the futility of their

[1]Ashok S. Kalelkar (Arthur D. Little, Inc.), "Investigation of Large-Magnitude Incidents: Bhopal as a Case Study" (paper for presentation at The Institution of Chemical Engineers Conference on Preventing Major Chemical Accidents, London, May 1988), p. 26.

efforts became apparent, many of the workers evacuated upwind, some scaling the chain-link and barbed-wire fence at the plant perimeter. At about 12:45 AM, the vapor could be seen escaping from an atmospheric vent line 120 feet in the air.

The cloud of deadly white gas was carried by a northwest wind toward the Jai Prakash Nagar shanties, on the south side of the plant. In the cold December night, the MIC settled toward the ground (in the daytime, or in the summer, convection currents probably would have raised and diluted it).

As the gaseous tentacles reached into the huts, there was a panic and confusion. Many of the weak and elderly died where they lay. "It was like breathing fire," one survivor said. As word of the gas leak spread, many of Bhopal's affluent were able to flee in their cars. But most of the poor were left behind. When the gas reached the nearby railroad station, supervisors who were not immediately disabled sent out word along the tracks and incoming trains were diverted. This diversion cut off a possible means of escape but may have saved hundreds of lives. The whole station was soon filled with gas. Arriving trains would have been death traps for passengers and crews.

By 1:00 AM, only a supervisor and the fire squad remained in the area of the MIC leak. The supervisor stayed upwind, donning his oxygen-breathing apparatus every few minutes to go check the various gauges and sensors. The fire squad sprayed water on the vent stack.

Of Bhopal's total population of about 700,000, tens of thousands fled that night, most on foot. An estimated 2,000 or more died and over 200,000 were injured.[2] An Indian appeals court later set the number of seriously injured at 30,000–40,000.[3] The surrounding towns were woefully unprepared to accept the gasping and dying masses. Confused crowds waited outside hospitals for medical care. There was no certainty about how to treat the gas victims, and general-purpose medical supplies were in hopelessly short supply. Inside the hospitals and out, screams and sobs filled the air. Food supplies were quickly exhausted. People were even afraid to drink the water, not knowing if it was contaminated.

The second day, relief measures were better organized. Several hundred doctors and nurses from nearby hospitals had been summoned to help medical personnel in Bhopal. Just disposing of the dead was a major problem. Mass cremation was necessary. Islamic victims, whose faith allows burial rather than cremation, were piled several deep in hurriedly dug graves. Bloating carcasses of cattle and dogs littered the city. There was fear of a cholera epidemic. Bhopal's mayor said later, "I can say that I have seen chemical warfare. Everything so quiet. Goats, cats, whole families—father, mother, children—all lying silent and still. And every structure totally intact. I hope never again to see it." A U.S. appeals court would later call Bhopal "the most devastating industrial disaster in history."[4]

By the third day, the city had begun to move toward stability, if not normalcy. The plant was closed and locked. A decision was made to consume the 20 tons of MIC in tank 611 by using it to make pesticide. Most of the dead bodies had been disposed of, however inappropriately. The injured were being treated as rapidly as the limited medical facilities would allow, although many people simply sat in silence, stricken by an enemy they had never known well enough to fear.[5]

Company Background

The Ever-Ready Company, Ltd. (of Great Britain), began manufacturing flashlight batteries in Calcutta in 1926. The division was incorporated as the Ever-Ready Company (India), Ltd., in 1934 and became a subsidiary of Union Carbide Corporation (UCC) of New York. The name of the Indian company was changed to National Carbon Company (India), Ltd., in 1941 and to Union Carbide India Limited in 1959. The 1926 capacity of 6 million dry-cell batteries per year had expanded to 767 million by the 1960s. In 1959, a factory was set up in India to manufacture flashlights.

By the 1980s, UCIL was involved in five product areas: batteries, carbon and metals, plastics, marine products, and agricultural chemicals. Exhibit 1 shows production statistics for UCIL products. Eventually, there were fifteen plants at eight locations, including the headquarters operation in Calcutta, that employed over 2,000. UCIL's petrochemical complex, established in Bombay in 1966, was India's first petrochemical plant.

[2]*In re Union Carbide Corp. Gas Plant Disaster,* 809 F.2d 195 (2nd Cir. 1987).

[3]*Union Carbide Corporation* v. *Union of India.* Regular Civil Suit No. 1113 (High Court of Madhya Pradesh, Bhopal, India, April 4, 1988), p. 2.

[4]*In re Union Carbide Corp. Gas Plant Diaster,* 809 F.2d 195 (2nd Cir. 1987).

[5]Except where noted, information in this section was obtained from anonymous sources in India and from dozens of news accounts which appeared in the months following the disaster.

EXHIBIT 1　**Production Statistics**

	1989 Cap.	1988– 1989	1987	1986	1985	1984	1983	1982	1981	1980
Batteries (000,000)	917	718	536	572	528	510	510	512	411	459
Flashlights (000,000)	8	10	7	8	6	7	7	7	7	7
Arc carbons (000,000)	9	10	8	8	8	7	8	7	7	7
Carb. electrodes (000,000)	3	1	1	1	1	1	1	1	1	0
Printing plates (metric tons)	1,200	450	358	416	393	376	412	478	431	399
Metal castings (metric tons)	150	31	22	18	19	17	18	13	16	15
Mn dioxide (metric tons)	4,500	4,186	3,620	4,023	3,670	3,069	3,335	3,085	3,000	2,803
Chemicals (000 metric tons)	14	—	—	3	6	6	7	6	7	8
Polyethylene (000 metric tons)	20	—	1	7	19	17	18	17	20	19
Pesticides (metric tons)	—	—	—	—	18	1,240	1,647	2,308	2,704	1,542
Marine prod. (metric tons)	—	—	—	—	—	272	424	649	642	601

The marine-products operation of UCIL was begun in 1971 with two shrimping ships. The business was completely export-oriented and employed 15 deep-sea trawlers. Processing facilities were located off the east and west coasts of India. The trawlers harvested deep-sea lobsters in addition to shrimp. This division was closed in 1984 and the facilities were sold in 1986.

In 1979, UCIL initiated a letter of intent to manufacture dry-cell batteries in Nepal. A 77.5 percent-owned subsidiary was set up in Nepal in 1982, and construction of a Rs. 18 million plant was begun. The Nepal operation was solidly profitable by 1986.

The agricultural products division of UCIL was started in 1966 with only an office in Bombay. A letter of intent was issued by the Indian government that year to allow UCIL to set up a pesticide formulation plant at Bhopal. Land was rented to UCIL for about $40 per acre per year.

The initial investment was small, only $1 million, and the process was simple. Concentrated Sevin powder was imported from the United States, diluted with non-toxic powder, packaged, and sold. While UCC had no explicit technology-transfer agreement with the Indian government, there was continuing pressure under the Foreign Exchange Regulation Act to limit imports. This translated into demands by the government for UCIL to manufacture Sevin and its components, including MIC, in India. A UCC executive said later, "The last thing we or UCIL wanted to do was build a pesticide plant in India." Another UCC executive later explained, "UCC did not wish to incur the substantial capital investment of building a pesticide manufacturing plant in India because it was far less expensive to import finished pesticide from the U.S. and formulate it in India."[6] Eventually the investment at Bhopal exceeded $25 million, and the constituents of Sevin were made there. Another Union Carbide insecticide, called Temik, was made in small quantities at Bhopal. Exhibit 2 is a map of the Bhopal plant as it existed in 1984. Exhibit 3 is a flow diagram of the MIC production process.

---

[6]Robert A. Butler to author, July 17, 1989, p. 5.

The assets of UCIL grew from Rs. 558 million in 1974 to Rs. 1,234 million in 1983. (The conversion rate stayed near 9 rupees to the dollar during this period, moving to about 12 as the dollar strengthened worldwide in 1984 and 1985, then staying near 12 until 1989). The *Economic Times* of India ranked UCIL number 21 in terms of sales among Indian companies in 1984.

Primarily as a condition attached to permission to construct the MIC project, UCIL had voluntarily diluted UCC's equity from 60 percent to 50.9 percent in 1977–78.[7] At the time of the Bhopal incident, UCC still held 50.9 percent, financial institutions owned by the Indian government held 25 percent, and the remaining 24 percent or so was in the hands of about 23,000 Indian

[7]"Amended Written Statement and Set Off and Counterclaim," *Union of India* v. *Union Carbide Corporation* and *Union Carbide Corporation* v. *Union of India,* Regular Civil Suit No. 1113 of 1986 (Court of the District Judge, Bhopal, India), p. 10.

citizens. The Indian Foreign Exchange Regulation Act (see Exhibit 4) generally limited nonresident interest in multinational corporations operating in India to 49 percent. However, UCC was exempted from this provision based on its being a high-technology company.

Starting in 1967 an Indian served as chairman of the 11 member UCIL board of directors. And foreign membership on the board was limited to four. In 1985, an expert on Indian industry affairs said, "Though the foreigners on the board are down to four from six in previous years, they continue to hold sway over the affairs of the company." However, UCC's chief litigation counsel, Robert A. Butler, wrote.

> None of Union Carbide Corporation's directors are on the Board of the Indian Company. All of the employees and officers of the Indian Company, including its Chairman and Managing Director, are Indian residents and citizens.

UCC said UCIL was not required to get its approval for even major capital investments, which were con-

EXHIBIT 2

The UCIL pesticide factory at Bhopal

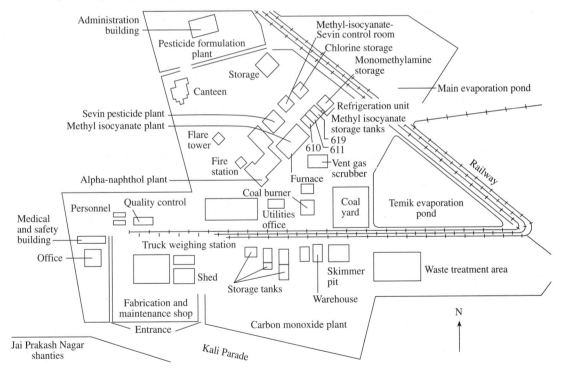

EXHIBIT 3

The methyl isocyanate manufacturing process

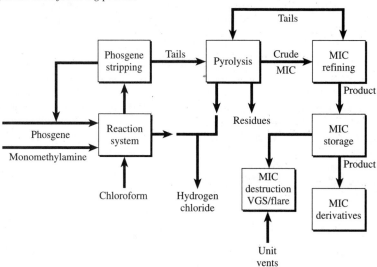

trolled by the UCIL board.[8] Monthly reports detailing operations and safety procedures were submitted by the Bhopal plant to UCIL headquarters in Bombay. UCC said these reports were not provided the U.S. parent, although certain periodic operating reports were submitted by UCIL to Union Carbide Eastern, a separate corporation charged with monitoring UCC investments in the Far East.[9]

UCC said it had conducted three safety audits at Bhopal at UCIL's request. The first two, in 1979 and 1980, were audits of personnel safety practices. The third was an evaluation of process safety in May of 1982. UCIL performed many safety audits itself.[10]

After the gas incident, UCC maintained it had never "had a presence in India"[11] and that UCIL was an essentially autonomous operation. A UCC executive said, "UCIL has been subject to less control by Union Carbide than any subsidiary I know of anywhere in the world."

---

[8]Robert A. Butler to author, July 17, 1989, pp. 5–6.
[9]Robert A. Butler to author, July 19, 1989, p. 6.
[10]Robert A. Butler to author, July 19, 1989, p. 6.
[11]Robert A. Butler to author, May 26, 1989, p. 9.

Operations at Bhopal

On the surface, the UCIL insecticide factory was a typical process plant. A wide diversity of storage tanks, hoppers, and reactors were connected by pipes. There were many pumps and valves and a number of tall vent lines and ducts. Ponds and pits were used for waste treatment, and several railway spur lines ran through the plant.

Sevin is made through a controlled chemical reaction involving alpha-naphthol and MIC. Alpha-naphthol is a brownish granular material, and MIC is a highly reactive liquid that boils and becomes a gas well above usual daytime temperatures. In 1971, when plans were first made to make alpha-naphthol at Bhopal, a pilot plant was set up. A full-size alpha-naphthol plant (in fact, the world's largest) was finished in 1977.

In the meantime, work had begun on the ill-fated MIC plant. UCC provided the process design for part of the plant. Twenty senior Indian engineers went to UCC's Institute, West Virginia, pesticide facility in 1978 to study that plant's design and operation. An engineering company headquartered in Bombay, Humphreys and Glasgow, Pvt. Ltd., was retained by UCIL to produce the detail drawings for the plant and serve as general contractor. All the subcontractors were Indian firms. In

1979–80, five Americans were sent to assist the 1,000 or so Indian employees of UCIL in starting up the plant. All except one of the Americans left in 1980. The other, with the title of "Works Manager," stayed on until December 1982, when he also left.

UCC was a world leader in MIC technology and provided much of the process design for the plant. But a UCC attorney later stated, "UCC was not involved with [the MIC plant's] construction and did not send engineers to supervise the construction."[12] A U.S. appeals court agreed, finding "The plant has been constructed and managed by Indians in India."[13] The attorney said UCC was uninvolved "both because UCIL was an autonomous company and because the Indian governmental regulations prohibited foreign involvement if Indians were capable of performing a given task."[14]

Even before 1980, when the MIC facility began operating, problems began to crop up with the alpha-naphthol unit. The latter system continued in various

---

[12]Robert A. Butler to author, May 26, 1989, p. 6.

[13]*In re Union Carbide Corp. Gas Plant Disaster,* 809 F.2d 195 (2nd Cir. 1987).

[14]Robert A. Butler to author, July 17, 1989, p. 7.

stages of shutdown and partial operation through 1984. V. P. Gokhale, managing director of UCIL, called the decision to make alpha-naphthol a "very large mistake." But he noted that the company was forced to do it to retain its operating license. The Bhopal factory was designed to produce 5,000 tons per year of Sevin but never operated near capacity; in the early 80s, UCIL was generally the third largest producer of pesticides in India, sometimes slipping to number four.

Annual profits of several million dollars from the Bhopal operation were originally predicted by 1984. But that was not to be, for several reasons. First, an economic recession made farmers more cost-conscious and caused them to search for less-expensive alternatives to Sevin. Second, a large number of small-scale producers were able to undersell the company, partly because they were exempt from excise and sales taxes. Seventeen of these firms bought MIC from UCIL and used it to make products virtually identical to Sevin and Temik. Finally, a new generation of low-cost pesticides was becoming available.

With sales collapsing, the Bhopal plant became a money loser in 1981. By late 1984, the yearly profit estimate had been adjusted downward to a $4 million loss based on 1,000 tons of output, one-fifth of capacity. To

---

EXHIBIT 4   **The Foreign Exchange Regulation Act**

The Act was originally enacted as a temporary measure in 1947. It was made permanent in 1957, then revised in 1973. The Act covers various aspects of foreign exchange transactions, including money changing, buying or selling foreign exchange in India or abroad, having an account in a bank outside India, and remitting money abroad.

The purpose of the Act is to restrict outflow of foreign exchange and to conserve hard-currency holdings in India. One provision requires that any company in which the nonresident interest is more than 40 percent "shall not carry on in India or establish in India any branch or office without the special permission of the Reserve Bank of India." But the Reserve Bank of India has authority to exempt a company from the provisions of the Act. The 40-percent requirement was changed to 49 percent by Rajiv Gandhi's government.

High-technology companies are frequently exempted from the equity-ownership provisions of the Act. Other companies that have operated in India for many years are sometimes exempted if they agree not to expand their Indian operations.

Policies in India regarding nationalization of foreign-owned companies have varied. A number of major oil companies have been nationalized. For example, Indian Oil Corporation, Bharat Petroleum and Hindustan Petroleum used to be, respectively, Burmah Shell, Mobil, and Stanvac (Standard Vacuum Oil Company, an Esso unit).

More typically, a multinational company is asked to reduce its holdings to 49 percent or less by offering shares to the Indian public and Indian financial institutions. Multinationals that have diluted equity to meet the 49 percent requirements include CIBA-GEIGY, Parke-Davis, Bayer (aspirin), Lever Brothers (which operates as Hindustan Lever in India), Lipton, and Brooke-Bond.

When Indira Gandhi was voted out of office in 1977, the Janata (Peoples') Party strengthened the Act. As a result, IBM and Coca-Cola pulled out of India. IBM's business in India was taken over by ICIM (International Computers Indian Manufacturers), a domestic firm. Another similar firm was set up to perform the maintenance services for the existing IBM computers.

EXHIBIT 5 Financial Statements (Rs. 000,000 except as noted)[1]

Balance Sheet

	1984	1985	1986	1987	1988–89[2]
Funds Employed					
Fixed assets	467	324	294	286	302
Investments	14	10	14	80	32
Net current assets	472	534	805	803	416
Deferred revenue expendenture					
Bhopal compn deposit					690
	953	868	805	803	1,448
Financed by					
Share capital and reserves	686	687	698	706	776
Loan funds	268	181	107	97	672
	953	868	805	803	1,448

Summary of Operations

	1979	1980	1981	1982	1983	1984	1985	1986	1987	1988–1989[2]
Income	1,465	1,720	1,881	2,092	2,122	2,245	2,444	2,175	2,010	2,578
Materials consumed	598	757	847	955	916	980	1,057	874	803	971
Operating expense employee related	188	199	218	246	272	283	337	325	347	438
Other operating expenses	228	265	315	364	395	391	382	385	315	390
Depreciation	32	37	41	42	48	50	56	39	22	24
Interest	20	32	28	53	58	47	31	24	19	33
Excise duty	261	270	258	287	286	340	431	420	431	623
PBT	138	161	175	147	148	153	65	90	73	100
Income tax	73	80	80	50	55	71	64	40	25	30
Net profit	65	81	95	97	93	82	13	50	48	70
Dividends	35	46	49	49	49	16	—	39	39	—

Note: Figures below in rupees

Share price:	High	30.9	36.0	31.7	28.1	28.3	29.8	37.0	43.0
	Low	25.5	22.0	24.9	23.3	21.5	18.5	17.1	20.0

[1]Column totals may not check and amounts less than 500,000 Rs. are shown as zero, due to rounding

[2]Financial data are for the period 12/26/87 to 3/31/89.

forestall what may have seemed inevitable economic failure, extensive cost-cutting was done. The staff at the MIC plant was cut from twelve operators on a shift to six. The maintenance team was reduced in size. In a number of instances, faulty safety devices remained unrepaired for weeks. Though instrumentation technology advanced at Union Carbide's other pesticide plants, the innovations were only partly adopted at Bhopal.

Upon reviewing the above paragraph, UCC's Chief Litigation Counsel, Robert A. Butler, wrote,

This . . . suggests that the incident was due to cost-cutting, faulty maintenance, and understaffing. The facts do not support that claim. In fact, at the time of the incident the plant was well overstaffed.[15]

[15]Robert A. Butler to author, May 26, 1989, p. 6.

However, UCC Chief Executive Warren Anderson and Director of Safety and Health Ron Van Mynen had expressed a different view shortly after the incident. Anderson said, "I feel badly about it now, that we could have an operation within the Union Carbide complex that was running the way it [the Bhopal facility] was running—in total disregard for operating procedures." Van Mynen remarked.

I had never been to Bhopal earlier, but some members of my team had been there. And I must admit that they were shocked at what they saw. When they had been there earlier the [safety] equipment was running according to s.o.p., and when we did get there in '84, after the event, it was not running, and it had not been running. And it was a surprise to those gentleman who had worked so hard in the startup of the plant.[16]

On the night of the disaster, several safety systems failed to work adequately or were at least suspect. For example, the flare tower, used for burning carbon monoxide, had been taken out of service to repair corroded piping a few days earlier. UCC recommended maintaining MIC at temperatures below 5 degrees Celsius (41 degrees Fahrenheit) because it was an unstable

---

[16]Kenneth Brooks, "Carbide's Report: How Bhopal Happened," *Chemical Week,* March 27, 1985, p. 9.

liquid that reacted unpredictably to changes in temperature. But the refrigeration unit cooling the three MIC storage tanks had repeatedly malfunctioned and had been shut down since June.

The UCIL directors, like the UCC parent, disclaimed fault for the incident. The "Report of Directors," included in UCIL's 1984 annual report, stated:

At no time had any significant fault been found with the working or safety precautions taken by your Company. Your Company had taken all safety precautions to avoid any accident in the Plant, which had been operated all along with trained and qualified operators.

In early 1985, the government of India canceled the operating license of the Bhopal plant, clearing the way for the plant's dismantlement. The likelihood that this would happen provoked a Bhopal political leader to remark, "We've lost 2,000 lives; now must we lose 2,000 jobs?"

Finance

Exhibit 5 provides financial summaries for UCIL. Exhibit 6 gives selected comparative financial statistics for the U.S. and India. During the months before the Bhopal disaster, UCIL's common shares, listed on the Bombay

---

EXHIBIT 6   **Comparative Financial Statistics for the U.S. and India**

Year	U.S. Producer Price Index[1]	India Wholesale Price Index[2]	Conversion Rate[3]
1974	161.1	169.2	8.111
1975	175.1	175.8	8.914
1976	183.6	172.4	8.985
1977	195.8	185.4	8.703
1978	197.1	185.0	8.189
1979	215.8	206.5	8.108
1980	244.5	248.1	7.872
1981	269.8	278.4	8.728
1982	280.7	288.7	9.492
1983	285.2	316.0	10.129
1984	291.1	338.4	11.402
1985	293.7	357.8	12.352
1986	289.7	376.8	12.680

[1]Wholesale Price Index before 1978. Arithmetic average of monthly figures. Base year, 1967.
[2]Arithmetic average of April–March monthly figures. Base year, 1970 (April 1970–March 1971).
[3]Arithmetic average of monthly figures (rupees per dollar).

and Calcutta stock exchanges, hovered around Rs. 30. They dropped to a low of Rs 15.8 on December 11, recovering only slightly in succeeding months. The shares reached a high of Rs. 43 in January 1986 but then fell steadily to the mid-teens by late 1987, rising again to the mid-twenties in July 1989. The exchange rate was Rs. 16.38 per U.S. dollar on July 16.

In 1975, the United States Export-Import bank, in cooperation with First National Citibank of New York, approved loans of $2.5 million to UCIL for the MIC project. Also, the Industrial Credit and Investment Corporation of India (ICICI), a government agency, authorized a Rs. 21.5 million loan, part of which was drawn in 1980. Finally, long-term loans were provided by several other Indian financial institutions and insurance companies. Some of these loans were guaranteed by the State Bank of India. UCC guaranteed none of the loans of UCIL.

UCC stock was listed on the New York Stock Exchange. It traded near $50 in the months before December 1984, down from its historical high of $74, reached in 1983. When news of Bhopal reached the U.S., the stock fell to near $30, to remain there until takeover rumors would propel it upward six months later. The rumors would soon subside, though, and the stock would trade near $30 throughout most of 1989.

The GAF Raid

GAF Corporation increased its holdings of UCC stock in 1985 and announced a takeover effort. The two companies had markedly different corporate cultures. GAF had a reputation for legal toughness, if not ruthlessness, having been successfully involved in massive toxic tort litigation (related to asbestos) for decades. GAF Chairman Samuel J. Heyman, an attorney, had muscled his way into control of the company in a bitter proxy fight in 1983. *The Wall Street Journal* reported a widespread belief that Heyman was likely to fire all the top managers of UCC if he ever gained control.

In contrast to what might have been expected from GAF, UCC Chairman Warren Anderson had expressed extreme sympathy for the victims of Bhopal and had even gone there to try to help. Though most of his attempts at providing financial and medical aid were rebuffed, he continued to assume major responsibility for the incident, saying it would be his main concern for the rest of his working life. Anderson also admitted the MIC plant should not have been operating in its condition at the time, one of several statements he made which later complicated his company's legal defenses. Anderson

said, "Right from the beginning . . . we said that we'd accept moral responsibility," but from a legal standpoint, he noted "It's their company, their plant, their people."[17]

Union Carbide managers rushed to erect takeover barriers and took actions to make the company less desirable as a merger candidate. Golden parachutes worth at least $8.8 million were adopted for 42 of the executives. Two operating divisions were set up, one for chemicals and plastics and the other for everything else. Various assets were written down by nearly $1 billion. The employee retirement plan was amended to free the $500 million "surplus" in the pension fund "for general corporate purposes." Union Carbide repurchased 56 percent of its outstanding common stock, issuing $2.52 billion in high-interest (avg. 14.2 percent) debt in the transaction.

The Wall Street Journal later reported 3.2 million of the shares were purchased by UCC in a private deal with Ivan Boesky. Boesky's UCC machinations figured prominently in his subsequent conviction for various securities violations. GAF, too, was later charged with stock manipulation and other offenses growing out of its efforts to take over UCC and, having failed in that, to profit from the adventure. Boyd Jeffries, also later convicted of stock manipulation, was involved in the alleged GAF crimes. There was never any suggestion UCC was involved in these alleged offenses.

After the takeover attempt was thwarted, much of the UCC debt was repaid. Money for the repayment came from three major sources. First, the sale of Union Carbide's agricultural products and electrical carbon units and the sale and leaseback of the Danbury, Connecticut, headquarters building provided $875 million. Second, 30 million new common shares brought $651 million. Third, the divestiture of UCC's Consumer Products Division provided substantial funds. Within months, Union Carbide stock recovered to predisaster levels. After a three-for-one split in 1986 the shares continued to climb, reaching the low thirties (high eighties corrected for the split) by early 1989.

Personnel

In 1984, all of UCIL's approximately 9,000 employees were Indians, according to UCC.[18] The Bhopal plant

[17]Ibid., p. 10.

[18]Amended Written Statement and Set Off and Counterclaim," *Union of India* v. *Union Carbide Corporation* and *Union Carbide Corporation* v. *Union of India,* Regular Civil Suit No. 1113 of 1986 (Court of the District Judge, Bhopal, India), p. 11.

accounted for 10 percent of these. In general, the engineers at Bhopal were among India's elite—better educated, according to a UCC official, than the average American engineer. Most new engineers were recruited from the prestigious India Institutes of Technology and were paid wages comparable with the best offered in Indian industry. Successful applicants were given two years of training before being certified for unsupervised duty.

Until the late 1970s only first-class science graduates or persons with diplomas in engineering were hired as operators at Bhopal. New employees were given six months of theoretical instruction, followed by on-the-job training. As cost-cutting efforts proceeded in the 1980s, standards were lowered significantly. Some persons with only high school diplomas were hired, and training was said to be less rigorous than before. In addition, the number of operators on a shift was reduced, and many supervisory positions were eliminated. UCC officials have said that there is no evidence that lowered educational standards had any impact on the incident.[19]

The Indian managers at UCIL developed strong ties with the local political establishment. A former police chief became the plant's security contractor. A local political party boss, who was also president of the Bhopal Bar Association, got the job as company lawyer. *Newsw*eek reported that a luxurious guest house was maintained by UCIL, and "lavish" parties were thrown there for local dignitaries.

In general, wages at the Bhopal factory were well above those in domestic firms. Still, as prospects continued downward after 1981, a number of senior managers and junior executives began to abandon ship. The total workforce at the plant dropped from a high of about 1,500 to about 900. This reduction was accomplished through voluntary departures rather than layoffs. An Indian familiar with operations at Bhopal said,

> The really competent and well-trained employees, especially managers and supervisors, got sick of the falling standards and indifferent management and many of them quit despite high salaries at UCIL. Replacements were made on an ad hoc basis. Even guys from the consumer-products division, who only knew how to make batteries, were drafted to run the pesticide plant.

A UCC attorney disputed this, writing,

> This is wholly inaccurate. Any individuals who left were replaced by competent, well-trained and experienced individuals. In addition, the reduction in the workforce resulted

primarily from the shut down of the alpha-naphthol unit rather than any alleged disillusionment on the part of the employees.[20]

In May 1982, a team from UCC headquarters audited the safety status of the MIC plant. The team listed as many as 10 major deficiencies in the safety procedures that the plant followed. The high turnover in plant personnel was noted and commented upon. (A UCC official later commented, "The plant addressed all of these deficiencies well before the incident. None had anything to do with the incident."[21]) The team declared it had been impressed with the operating and maintenance procedures at Bhopal.

Marketing and Demographics

The population of India was over 700 million persons in the 1980s, although its land area was only about one-third that of the United States. Three-fourths of India's people depended on agriculture for a livelihood. Only about one-third of the population was literate. Modern communications and transportation systems connected the major cities, but the hundreds of villages were largely untouched by twentieth-century technology.

English was at least a second tongue for most Indian professionals, but not for ordinary Indians. There were 16 officially recognized languages in the country. The national language was Hindi, which was dominant in 5 of India's 25 states. The working classes spoke hundreds of dialects, often unintelligible to neighbors just miles away.

India's farmers offered at best a challenging target market. They generally eked out livings from small tracts of land. Most had little more than subsistence incomes and were reluctant to invest what they had in such modern innovations as pesticides. They were generally ignorant of the right methods of application and, given their linguistic diversity and technological isolation, were quite hard to educate. To advertise its pesticides, UCIL used billboards and wall posters as well as newspaper and radio advertisements.

Radio was the most widely used advertising medium in India. The state-owned radio system included broadcasts in local languages as well as in Hindi. Companies could buy advertising time on the stations, but it was costly to produce commercials in so many dialects.

---

[19]Robert A. Butler to author, July 19, 1989, p. 9.

[20]Robert A. Butler to author, July 19, 1989, p. 10.
[21]Robert A. Butler to author, May 26, 1989, p. 9.

Much of the state-sponsored programming, especially in rural areas, was devoted to promoting agriculture and instructing farmers about new techniques. Often the narrators mentioned products such as Sevin and Temik by name.

Movies provided another popular promotional tool. Most small towns had one or more cinema houses, and rural people often traveled to town to watch the shows. Advertisements appeared before and after main features and were usually produced in regional languages though not in local dialects.

Until the 80s, television was available only in the cities. During 1984, a government program spread TV relay stations at the rate of more than one each day, with the result that 80 percent of the population was within the range of a television transmitter by the end of the year. Still, few rural citizens had ready access to television receivers.

Pesticide sales were highly dependent on agricultural activity from year to year. In times of drought, like 1980 and 1982, UCIL's pesticide sales suffered severe setbacks. In 1981, abundant rains helped spur sales.

India had a very extensive network of railways; the total track mileage was second only to that of the U.S.S.R. The road and highways system crisscrossed the areas in between the railway lines. The railway system was especially significant to UCIL's pesticide operation because Bhopal lay near the junction of the main east-west and north-south tracks in India. An Indian familiar with the agricultural economy remarked, "Overall, physical distribution of pesticides is not too monumental a task. Getting farmers to use them and teaching them how are the real problems."

The marketing division for agricultural products was headquartered in Hyderabad, in southern India. Eight branch offices were scattered all over the country. Sales were made through a network of distributors, wholesalers, and retailers. Representatives from the branch offices booked orders from the distributors and wholesalers. Retailers got their requirements from wholesalers, who, in turn, were supplied by distributors. The distributors got their stocks from the branch offices. The branch office "godowns" (warehouses) were supplied directly from the Bhopal plant. The retailers' margin was 15 percent. Wholesalers and distributors each received about 5 percent. Most of the retailers were family or individually owned concerns, although some of UCIL's pesticides were sold at retail through government agricultural sales offices.

The Legal Battle

After the Bhopal tragedy UCC and UCIL executives were charged with manslaughter and other crimes. UCC Chairman Anderson, along with the head of UCIL, was arrested and briefly detained by Indian officials when he went to India shortly after the incident. Seven UCIL employees were also arrested.[22] UCC investigators were barred from the plant at first, given only limited access to records and reports, and, for over a year, prohibited from interviewing employees.[23]

Anderson said, "The name of the game is not to nail me to the wall but to provide for the victims of the disaster." He volunteered UCC to help provide funding for a hospital to treat the Bhopal victims. The company contributed $1 million to a victim's relief fund. It and UCIL set aside $20 million for relief payments. Though Anderson said the offer was unconditional, the Indian government spurned it.

UCIL offered to build a new plant, one that would use nontoxic inputs, on the Bhopal site. One proposal was for a nonhazardous formulation plant to be constructed by UCIL and operated by the state government. Alternatively, UCIL suggested a battery factory it would own and operate. Both ideas were turned down by the Indian government.

A number of U.S. and Indian lawyers rushed to sign up gas victims and their relatives as clients. On December 7, 1984, the first of some 145 "class action" lawsuits was filed in the U.S. on behalf of the victims of the disaster. For example, famed attorney Melvin Belli brought suit for $15 billion. In March 1985, India enacted the Bhopal Gas Leak Disaster Act, giving the Indian government the exclusive right to represent the victims. The Attorney General of India was authorized to sue Union Carbide in an American court. A Minneapolis law firm that specialized in product liability cases was retained to represent India. In February 1985, a judicial panel in the U.S. ordered all the lawsuits related to Bhopal consoli-

---

[22]Ashok S. Kalelkar (Arthur D. Little, Inc.), "Investigation of Large-Magnitude Incidents: Bhopal as a Case Study" (paper for presentation at The Institution of Chemical Engineers Conference on Preventing Major Chemical Accidents, London, May 1988), p. 7.

[23]Ashok S. Kalelkar (Arthur D. Little, Inc.), "Investigation of Large-Magnitude Incidents: Bhopal as a Case Study" (paper for presentation at The Institution of Chemical Engineers Conference on Preventing Major Chemical Accidents, London, May 1988), pp. 3, 7.

dated in a single court—that of Judge John F. Keenan in Manhattan. The Attorney General of India asserted that compensation had to be in accordance with American standards and continued to press the lawsuit while engaging in out-of-court negotiations with Union Carbide.

In his statement before Judge Keenan, he argued,

Key management personnel of multinationals exercise a closely held power which is neither restricted by national boundaries nor efficiently controlled by international law. The complex corporate structure of the multinational, with networks of subsidiaries and divisions, makes it exceedingly difficult or even impossible to pinpoint responsibility for the damage caused by the enterprise to discrete corporate units or individuals. Persons harmed by the acts of a multinational corporation are not in a position to isolate which unit of the enterprise caused the harm, yet it is evident that the multinational enterprise that caused the harm is liable for such harm.

A UCC attorney later remarked, "The government's multinational enterprise theory has never been sustained by any court in the world, and it lacks any legal basis."[24]

The primary focus of the U.S. case was UCC's plea of *forum non-conveniens*—that India, not the United States, was the appropriate place for any trial because most of the documents, litigants, evidence, and witnesses were in India. UCC had reasons in addition to convenience and cost to prefer the Indian forum. Although both the Indian and the U.S. legal systems were based on English common law, punitive damages were almost unheard of in Indian courts and compensatory damage awards were generally much lower than in the United States. For example, an appeals court in India was soon to estimate the following scale of compensation for Bhopal victims should the matter go to final judgment there:

Death or total permanent disability	Rs 200,000
Partial permanent disability	Rs 100,000
Temporary partial disability	Rs 50,000[25]

As UCC struggled to recover from the disaster and restore its public image, two events thrust the company back to the forefront of international news coverage. First, in June 1985 hundreds of persons were affected by California watermelons grown on soil to which the Union Carbide pesticide Temik had been applied (improperly applied, according to the company). Second, in August a leak of the chemical intermediate aldecarb oxime at the company's Institute, West Virginia, plant, the only U.S. facility to make MIC, sent 135 people to hospitals. West Virginia governor Arch Moore publicly criticized Union Carbide's handling of the incident and Anderson admitted the company had waited too long to warn residents.

In May 1986 Judge Keenan ruled the Bhopal case should be tried in India.[26] The decision would be affirmed by an appeals court in early 1987.[27] In September 1986 consideration of the suit resumed in the Court of the District Judge in Bhopal. UCC attorneys denounced the central and state governments in India for their alleged liability for the disaster. The company's answer denied every charge leveled against UCC. It claimed the factory was run by UCIL and pointed out that no U.S. citizen had been employed there for two years before the disaster. UCC also stated that sabotage was responsible for the disaster and alleged that there was a conspiracy among UCIL employees and a separate conspiracy among government investigators to conceal evidence after the incident.[28] The Indian government expressed outrage at Union Carbide's position and set its damage claim at $3.1 billion.

The hearings continued concurrently with out-of-court negotiations. As 1987 drew to an end, there were rumors of a settlement. Union Carbide offered $500 million in payments over time (then present value, about $350 million). Each dependent of the 2,600 people Union Carbide said were killed in the incident was to receive $2,000 a year for 10 years. The chronically ill would get $1,000 annually for the same period. And those slightly injured would be given a single payment of $500. The Indian government offered to settle for $615 million in cash. When news of a possible settlement leaked out, there was a furious public outcry in India. Former Indian Supreme Court Chief Justice P. N. Bhagwati demanded that any settlement include an admission of guilt by Union Carbide.

As the settlement talks appeared to break down in December 1987, Judge M. V. Deo ordered UCC to pay

---

[24]Robert A. Butler to author, May 26, 1989, p. 10.

[25]*Union Carbide Corporation* v. *Union of India,* Order in Gas Claim No. 1113/86, Civil Revision 26/88 (High Court of Madhya Pradesh, April 4, 1989), p. 98.

[26]In Re Union Carbide Corp. Gas Plant Disaster, 634 F. Supp. 842 (S.D.N.Y. 1986, as amended June 10, 1986).

[27]In Re Union Carbide Corp. Gas Plant Disaster, 809 F.2d 195 (2nd Cir. 1987).

[28]Robert A. Butler to author, July 19, 1989, p. 10.

$270 million in interim compensation to the gas victims.[29] Union Carbide filed an appeal of the order, calling the idea of interim damages—before a defendant was found to owe anything at all—"unprecedented." The company continued to assert that it was confident of proving that the disaster was the result of sabotage and that it could not be held accountable in any case for the acts or omissions of UCIL, in which it claimed to only own stock. Judge Deo's decision was upheld by the High Court of Madhya Pradesh on 4 April 1988, although the interim award was reduced to about $190 million.[30] Both India and UCC appealed to the Supreme Court of India.

The Settlement

On Tuesday, February 14, 1989, company lawyers were presenting arguments before the Supreme Court, when Chief Justice R. S. Pathak interrupted the proceeding. He then issued an order that UCC pay $470 million by March 31 "in full and final settlement of all claims, rights and liabilities related to and arising out of the Bhopal gas disaster." Acceptance of the order had reportedly been unanimously approved by the UCC directors in a telephone poll hours earlier. The order applied to all "criminal and civil proceedings" related to the Bhopal tragedy and thus purported to be a complete settlement of the case. UCC and UCIL paid their agreed-upon shares of the settlement—$425 million and $45 million, respectively—on February 14, 1989. The Indian Supreme Court was to oversee distribution of the funds.

UCC had previously set aside $250 million for damages and the company's insurance coverage was estimated at another $200 million. So paying the settlement would only result in an estimated $0.50 per share charge against 1988 earnings of $1.59 per share. UCC stock rose $2 a share on Tuesday and another $1.38 Wednesday, to close at $32.50, more than double the price (corrected for the three-for-one split) before the Bhopal tragedy. UCC was immediately touted as a prime takeover candidate, with an expected purchase price of about $50 a share, or $7 billion.

There was evidence some knew of the approaching settlement. A week before it was ordered, UCC stock jumped $2 a share on volume totaling over 8 percent of all outstanding shares. That was the highest volume of any NYSE stock in five months. UCC said it had no knowledge of any purported leak.

It was uncertain how and when the settlement money would be distributed to victims—or even how much of it would be. Bruce A. Finzen, one of the Indian government's U.S. lawyers, said, "Even at the rate of one hour per claim, you are talking about years of court time." The Indian government had already paid some survivors $800 or so for each immediate family member who perished. Medical care and certain other benefits had also been furnished by the government. But there were about 500,000 claims for relief, and only about 100,000 persons had been in the disaster area.[31]

There were immediate objections in India to the amount of damages and the nature of the settlement. But an editorial in *The Times of India* took a self-critical view:

> The government has been caught in a trap of its own making. It wanted as many applications for relief as possible to support its case for a bigger settlement. . . . I feel that many decent citizens were suddenly overcome by avarice. . . . It will be a very difficult task now to eliminate wrong claims. . . . In the first few days of the tragedy the whole world sympathized with us. Carbide was prepared to do anything. . . . Aid was offered by several countries. . . . But at that time we thought it would hurt our national pride to take the help. (The Armenian earthquake has, however, set a new pattern of international help now). . . . We preferred to arrest the Carbide chairman. . . . The terrible suffering of the victims and their families has been subordinated, even made to appear irrelevant, by all the begging and brow-beating. All the bravery shown by those who struggled with the cloud's effect on the first day has been forgotten. . . . Now all that remains is to stand like vultures at the kill. The effect of all the propaganda war against Union Carbide will be apparent in the coming years when we find that all foreigners, even the Russians, will look at any contract with India with suspicion, and press for safeguards so that liability of subsidiaries is not transferred to them.[32]

UCC chief Kennedy called the settlement "a fair resolution of all issues." And UCC attorney Bud Holman

---

[29]*Union of India* v. *Union Carbide Corporation*, Gas Claim Case No. 1113 of 1986 (Court of the District Judge, Bhopal, India, December 17, 1987).

[30]*Union Carbide Corporation* v. *Union of India,* Regular Civil Suit No. 1113 (High Court of Madhya Pradesh, Bhopal, India, April 4, 1988).

[31]K. F. Rustamji, "Coming to Terms with Bhopal," *The Times of India,* March 8, 1989.

[32]K. F. Rustamji, "Coming to Terms with Bhopal," *The Times of India,* March 8, 1989.

said the negotiations were like "walking up a winding staircase in total darkness," adding, "It's nice to be in the light." In its 1989 proxy statement, UCC reported it was continuing to spend $7–$8 million a year on "Bhopal-related litigation."

EXHIBIT 7   Excerpts from Interviews

Gas victims and government officials in the Bhopal area were questioned in early 1987 concerning the gas incident. Upon reading excerpts from the questions and interviewee comments, a UCC attorney wrote they "are designed to inflame emotions, not inform the mind, and are of questionable value in an educational forum." He continued,

> Such inflammatory rhetoric simply permits the participants to facilely blame companies such as Union Carbide without evidence and without a trial, rather than forcing the participants to confront the fundamental ethical issues facing host countries and companies which, of necessity, use toxic substances in their manufacturing processes.[33]

The abbreviated questions and responses are presented below.

Description of the incident?

> A very thick layer of smoke caused uncontrollable tears, copious coughing, sneezing, vomiting. We ran to save our lives. We saw people in large numbers running here and there in great confusion, crushing each other, not bothering about anyone else.

> I felt chilled and soon could not see.

> I felt my eyes burning, like smoke coming from burning chilies. I was gasping for a breath of fresh air. I saw my neighbors in the same condition. A thin smoky layer was visible but its source was not known. Soon I was coughing and water was coming from my eyes and I fell unconscious.

> At first I did not know what was happening because all my systems were affected. I was vomiting. My stomach was dislocated. My muscles were loose. Everyone was gasping for breath, running without any direction to find a safe place. Some of them demanded death as if was readily available at a grocery shop.

Aftereffects?

> I still do not know how bad it will get. It has become difficult to tolerate anything that is going wrong. I cannot remember like before.

> I have become weak in body and mind. My memory has been affected badly. Carrying even small loads and fast walking has become a dream to me. I feel like an asthmatic patient.

> The effect has subsided. But the resistance of the body is still down. My body has become allergic to muddy areas. The cough remains permanent and breathlessness occurs sometime.

> Asthmatic, decreased vision, awfully unpredictable and irritable temper—future unknown, uncertain.

> Loss in appetite, loss in weight, breathing trouble, uneasiness, poor eyesight, and weak memory power.

> I cannot walk quickly and cannot run.

Assistance provided?

> A mere Rs. 1500 has been provided as compensation and that is only to those whose income is below Rs. 500 a year. So we have not got any assistance so far from anyone.

> Symptomatic treatment is being given without knowing the cause and the disease. This should stop.

> None.

> After three days I was treated at the hospital with antibiotics. But there was no definite diagnosis or treatment.

> So far, nil. The policies made by the local government are unbelievable. They pay by economic and social status.

> For us railway officers and our families nobody has done anything.

---

[33]Robert A. Butler to author, July 19, 1989, p. 11.

EXHIBIT 7   (concluded)

What should be done?

The M. P. [Madhya Pradesh, the state where Bhopal is located] government with the cooperation of the government of India and aided by Union Carbide or the American government should start a fully-equipped hospital basically concerned with lungs and eyes. Provision of work, housing, and education should be made.

Government should give proper treatment to the gas affected. They should rehabilitate those who lost their earner. They should stop a recurrence.

Next of kin of the deceased should be given sufficient money by UCIL. All affected people should be given suitable jobs by government. Proper treatment should be given by government out of fines imposed on Union Carbide because they have failed to give a safe design of the project and neglected all safety measures in the factory.

The affected people should be provided with good food to recoup their body. All over the world the Madhya Pradesh government has received donations for this so it must be utilized properly.

Nothing can be done now since everything is over.

Government should arrange to shift the factory to somewhere away from the town area.

The society at large, the government, and above all UCIL itself should have honorably taken to itself to soothe the sufferers. Their needs for the balance of their life span should be given gratis to them.

The government of India should pay compensation as applicable throughout the world. We are Indian nationals and all our interests are to be protected by the elected government.

What is likely to be done?

I am quite in the dark and disappointed.

I[t] appears no one is serious to do much.

Considering the indifferent attitude of the Indian government, we are forced to compromise with our miserable lives. If anything concrete is done, it will be done only by UCIL.

Well, I wonder if anything is in store, the way it has fallen out.

Victims will be compensated and plants like this will be moved to remote places by government.

I am confident the government of India will pay compensation to all real sufferers.

Nothing.

Mostly non-affected persons and unemployed illiterate people, who chase the surveyors, get compensated.

Message for U.S. Business School Students?

Press your government not to allow multinationals like Union Carbide to operate anywhere in the world since they play with the life of people to enrich themselves.

More was expected and much better from the advanced elite in the community of nations. There is nothing but delay, tossing it from one door to another and from one country to another. It is a disgrace of the basest order to have left it to an indefinite body to compensate the sufferers, even if it was an additional burden. How can the most advanced society tolerate it?

The advanced nation like America while making any investment in developing countries should themselves ensure that all safety precautions are taken—before installing their factories. When they have already made this mistake at Bhopal, they should pressure their government and the management of Union Carbide to pay compensation without hesitation.

There is no question of talking to any other country. There is nothing to say but to blame the local administration for not arranging in a proper, methodic way in this modern world.

Multinational companies are playing with the lives of people and their property for the self interest of earning money at any cost and by any means.

Note: All statements excerpted in this exhibit were made by gas victims and government officials in the Bhopal area.

TDK DE MEXICO

Manab Thakur

California State University—Fresno

"I want to be the main supplier base of magnets for South and North America," proclaimed Fumio Inouye, general manager of TDK de Mexico, located in Cd. Juarez, a border city of millions close to El Paso, Texas. He continued:

> To help gain this status, our operating targets need to be met, and that might include expansion of present plant facilities and more automation. Increasingly I feel, though, that people here don't want to see expansion. . . . They seem to enjoy excuses! Whether you call it Japanese or American management, I cannot accept delays, wastes, and excuses! Culture to me is important only when the process of production and the importance of work are clearly understood. Make no mistake, my parent company (TDK of Japan) wouldn't stand for anything other than making acceptable margins. I am having difficulty in putting reasons for all the problems on culture. . . . I refuse to take it as a dumping ground.

Production Methods and Technology

TDK de Mexico produced ceramic ferrite magnets of various shapes and sizes that were used for speakers, generators, and motors. It was one of the few plants in its area that produced a final product from the raw material. Production was based on job orders—in other words, production was scheduled as TDK de Mexico received orders for a given number of a given type of magnet. Exhibit 1 shows TDK's plant layout and production process. The raw material used to make the final product was a black powder called ferrite powder. The ferrite powder, a critical raw material, was imported, although it was available in the Mexican market. But to ensure quality, TDK of Japan insisted on using ferrite powder from Japan. The manufacturing process started by wetting and mixing the powder in large containers. The mixture was dried and then was fed into the press machines that gave the shape to the magnets. The shape was determined by the mold inserted into the press machine (Exhibit 2). All of the molds used also came from Japan. The various molds for the different shapes and sizes were stored at the plant and used as needed.

Two distinct methods were used during the press stage of the production process, the dry method and the wet method. The basic difference between the two was that the wet method, installed at TDK de Mexico in 1983 after Fumio Inouye took charge, utilized water during the pressing of the raw material. It made stronger magnets, but it took more time. With the wet method, the worker collected the magnets just pressed and placed them in a temporary drying area before they were baked in the ovens. With the dry method, the worker collected the magnets just pressed, and they were sent straight to the ovens for baking. While collecting the magnets, the worker visually checked each magnet for cracks or other defects. Defective ones were thrown out for scrap. It was important to spot defective magnets at this stage because it was much harder to convert them into scrap after they were baked. All scrap materials were broken down and used again in the raw material mixture.

After pressing, the magnets were mechanically moved through a series of ovens (Exhibit 3). One set of pressed magnets was placed in the oven every 12 hours. The magnets were baked at progressively higher temperatures from entrance to exit. After their exit from the ovens, the magnets continued moving to a temporary storage area to cool. The ovens presently in use were electrically powered, but there was a plan to convert them to gas ovens to take advantage of the lower cost of gas. Once cooled, each magnet was subject to process inspection by workers. This was one of two main quality control checkpoints in the production process.

Cooled magnets were taken to the scraper machine. The scraper machine smoothed the rough edges and surface of the magnets. The scrapings were collected and used again in the raw material mixture. From the scraper machine, the workers placed the magnets in water to be cleaned. After cleaning, the magnets were sent through the drying machine. At the exit point of the drying machine, the magnets were collected by workers and placed in boxes. The boxes of magnets were taken to the final process department where each magnet was given a final check. This stage was called the shipping inspection, and it represented the second main quality control checkpoint. Quality control and specification requirements adhered to at this stage included measurement of weight, length, and appearance of magnets.

EXHIBIT 1

Plant layout and production process

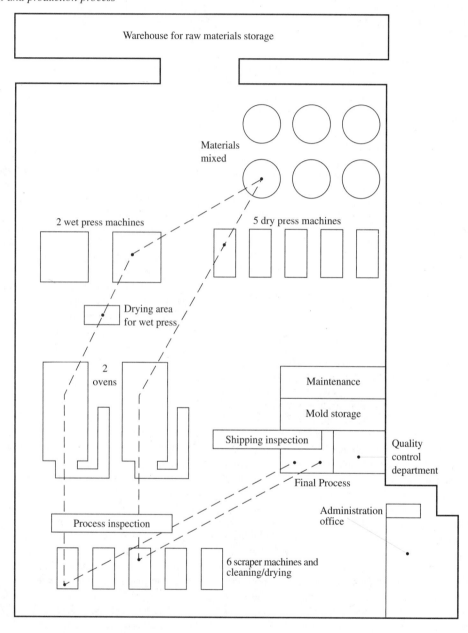

About 85 percent of production was exported to the United States—to TDK of America facilities in Chicago, Los Angeles, New York, and Indiana. The remaining 15 percent was exported to Hong Kong. The sales offices and warehouse facilities in these cities were in charge of all selling, shipping, and billing functions. TDK of

America sold most of its products to Briggs and Stratton of Milwaukee, Wisconsin, and to Buehler Products of Kingston, North Carolina.

TDK de Mexico had encountered no bureaucratic delays or customs problems in shipping out final products, even though other companies in the area were having dif-

ficulties arranging for timely shipment of their merchandise out of Mexico. Inouye was proud that he had been able to secure the necessary clearances and paperwork for getting the product out of the country without much hassle. His explanation was, "You don't create systems when you simply need some people who can do things

EXHIBIT 2

Production technology

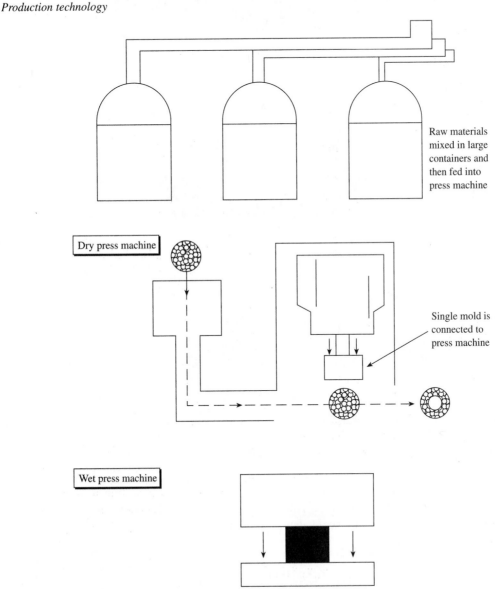

Raw materials mixed in large containers and then fed into press machine

Dry press machine

Single mold is connected to press machine

Wet press machine

EXHIBIT 3

Production technology and magnets made

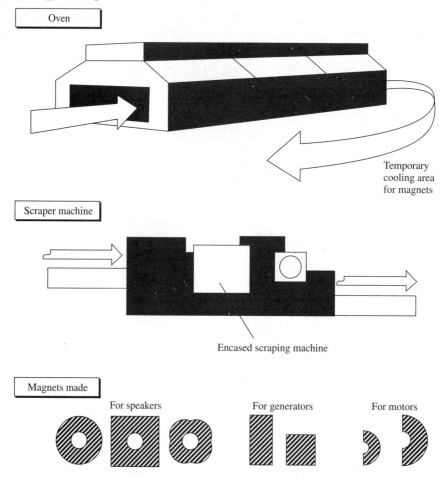

Oven

Temporary
cooling area
for magnets

Scraper machine

Encased scraping machine

Magnets made

For speakers   For generators   For motors

for you. You need to get out and find them. You create systems where systems are accepted. . . . It is not here!"

Hiratzuka, TDK's production manager, commented: "We hear that the Mexican government may change the rules of the game. There are rumors that we may have to buy 20 to 25 percent of our raw materials from Mexican suppliers." He went on, "Other than what the government will and will not do, I think you also need to understand that our primary concern is to attract quality labor, since our production process demands it. . . .We can't just hire anyone who walks in."

TDK de Mexico had not looked into possible changes in the Mexican government's local procurement rules to any extent, but had expressed its apprehension to Mexican officials if the firm was forced to buy ferrite powder locally. On another issue, Hiratzuka stated, "As you know, border plants in Mexico like ours have a 'no sale' rule where all goods produced must be exported. But the government is considering a compulsory selling rule whereby 20 percent of a border plant's goods must be sold locally." Such a rule was potentially more troublesome to TDK de Mexico because it was not clear that there was much of a market in Mexico for TDK's products.

The Mexican Maquiladoras

In 1965 the United States, working in conjunction with the Mexican government, set up the *maquiladora* program to create jobs for unemployed and underemployed Mexican workers. The idea was to get U.S. companies to open light assembly plants just across the Mexican border and to use cheap Mexican labor to assemble American-made parts into finished goods. In many cases, the components were manufactured in plants located on the U.S. side of the border; this allowed the components to be easily and quickly transported to the Mexican side for final assembly. The effect was to create twin plants a few miles apart—the U.S. plant being used for capital-intensive/skilled-labor operations and the Mexican plant being used for labor-intensive assembly operations.

When the finished products were shipped back into the United States, U.S. companies were taxed only on the value added in Mexico (mostly labor costs) rather than on the total value of the goods being imported. When the Mexican government experienced a debt crisis in 1982 and the value of the Mexican peso collapsed against the dollar, cheap Mexican wages triggered a *maquiladora* explosion. By early 1987, there were over 630 plants employing over 178,000 people along the Mexican side of the U.S. border. These plants, known as *maquiladora* (or "in-bond" or twin plants), were all engaged in assembling components in Mexico for reexport in the United States and elsewhere and had become an important economic force along the U.S.–Mexican border. Juarez, where TDK de Mexico's plant was located, had a big concentration of *maquiladoras*. Exhibit 4 presents some of the features of the *maquiladora* program.

Maquiladoras operated within a highly volatile political environment, one that affected every aspect of their existence. They were dependent upon the Mexican government continuing to permit raw materials and components to enter duty free and the U.S. government simultaneously permitting finished products to return with duty paid only on the value added in Mexico. Any major change in these policies by either country could shut down most *maquiladoras* overnight by making assembly operations on the Mexican side of the border uneconomical. Both countries had strong political groups opposed to the *maquiladora* concept. Opponents labeled such operations as sweatshops and claimed that workers were being exploited by capitalistic interests.

The average age of the *maquiladora* workers was 24,

with a relative dearth of workers over 30. Seventy percent were young women and teenage girls. Workers lived under crowded conditions—the mean household size of *maquiladora* workers was 7.8 persons. Their wages averaged about 50.80 per hour, barely more than half the 1987 Mexican manufacturing wage of $1.57 an hour (including benefits). The low wages made it very attractive for mass-assembly operations requiring low-skill labor to be located on the Mexican side of the U.S. border. Managers of the *maquiladoras* expressed a preference for hiring "fresh or unspoiled" workers that had not acquired "bad habits" in other organizations. The work was so low-skilled that workers received very little training. The turnover rate ran 50 percent to 100 percent a year in many plants.

However, many of the large multinational companies with *maquiladoras* paid more than the wage minimums, and their overall compensation package was more attractive than the lowest-paying operations. Some of the multinationals also spent substantial amounts in training and employee development.

The location of twin (or *maquiladora*) plants along the northern border of Mexico was increasing at a phenomenal speed, and unemployed Mexicans were flocking to northern border towns to fill the rapidly expanding number of job openings. By the end of 1988, it was predicted that *maquiladoras* would employ 350,000 workers, one tenth of Mexico's industrial workforce, and that the plants would import $8 billion in U.S. components, add $2 billion in value (mostly labor), and ship $10 billion in finished goods back to the United States for sale in the United States and other world markets. A number of Japanese-based companies had begun to set up *maquila* operations to handle the production and sale of their products in U.S. markets—TDK de Mexico was one of these companies.

Despite concerns over the *maquiladoras,* the program was central to the Mexican government's economic revival plans. Mexican leaders were most enthusiastic about a new kind of *maquiladora.* These were plants built in the interior of Mexico that were geared to exports, like the border plants, but unlike the border operations, they undertook in-house manufacture of many of the components used in the final assembly process. These plants used higher-skilled employees and paid wages much closer to the average manufacturing wage in Mexico, and they did not rely so heavily on the use of female labor. They also relied more heavily on Mexican companies for raw material supplies and services.

Exhibit 4   The Maquiladora Program: Legal and Regulatory Requirements Imposed by the Mexican Government

A. Foreign Investment

As a rule, a foreign company may subscribe and own only up to 49 percent of the stock in Mexican corporations with the exception of *maquilas,* which may be totally owned by foreigners. Except wearing apparel, all items may be produced by in-bound assembly enterprises. Wearing apparel, due to the restriction of textile imports into the United States, is subject to a quota.

B. Import Duties

In-bond plants are not required to pay import duties, but the product assembled or manufactured may not be sold in Mexico. Bonds are generally posted by bonding companies and are renewed yearly.

C. Taxes

The maximum income tax on corporate profits is 42 percent on taxable income of P$$500,000 or more in a fiscal year, and employees' share in profits before taxes is at the rate of 8 percent. There are other taxes such as the Social Security tax based on salaries earned and state taxes.

D. Maquiladora versus Joint Venture

A comparison of the different rules and practices for joint ventures between Mexican and foreign companies is summarized below:

Concept	Maquiladora	Joint Venture
Doing business in Mexico	To operate in Mexico under a *maquila* program, a company must be incorporated under Mexican laws.	To carry out industrial or commercial activities for the Mexican market, a corporation or other recognized corporate entity must be organized.
Equity ownership	100% foreign ownership is allowed.	The general rule is that foreigners may not hold more than 49% of the stock of a corporation doing business in the Mexican market. Exceptions to allow higher percentages of foreign ownership, up to 100%, may be authorized by the Mexican government under special circumstances.
Special operating authorizations	To operate under *maquila* (in-bond) status, the Ministry of Commerce must authorize a *maquila* program, setting forth the products or activities the company may manufacture/assemble or carry out. Certain commitments must be made, the compliance with which shall be reviewed periodically.	Unless the company intends to work within a branch of regulated industry, a joint-venture company may freely operate without the need to obtain any special operating permits.
Importation of equipment	All production equipment may be imported free of duties, under bond, subject to it being exported once the company ceases to operate under the *maquila* program.	The importation of equipment for the production of items that are to be sold in the Mexican market requires an import permit to be obtained and normal duties to be paid thereon.
Importation of raw materials	All raw materials and supplies may be imported free of duties under bond, subject to it being exported within an extendable six-month period, shrinkage and wastage excepted. Under special circumstances, *maquiladoras* may be authorized to sell up to 20% of a specific product within the Mexican market.	The importation of raw materials and supplies for the production of items that are to be sold in the Mexican market requires an import permit to be obtained and normal duties to be paid thereon. In all cases, import permits are granted on an absolutely discretionary basis. Currently such permits are quite restricted. Under certain conditions, the negotiation of a manufacturing or integration program with the government may be required.

EXHIBIT 4 (concluded)

Concept	Maquiladora	Joint Venture
Currency exchange controls	Any operating expense, including rent, payroll, taxes, etc., must be paid in Mexican pesos that must be obtained from a Mexican bank by selling dollars thereto at the controlled rate of exchange. Fixed assets may be paid for in dollars at the free rate of exchange.	There are no specific exchange controls on domestic transactions. If the company exports, it will, in general, be required to sell foreign currencies received to a Mexican bank at the controlled rate of exchange.
Labor law requirements	Subject to the Federal Labor Law.	Equally subject to the Federal Labor Law.
Acquisition of real estate	Real estate to establish a production facility may be freely bought in the interior of the country. In the border areas or coasts, it may be acquired through a trust.	Same as a *maquiladora.*
Leasing of real estate	Real estate may be leased under freely negotiated terms, up to a maximum of 10 years.	Same as a *maquiladora,* although the term may be longer.
Immigration requirements	Foreign technical or management personnel are readily granted work visas, subject to very lenient requirements.	Work visas for foreign technical or management personnel are granted on a very limited basis. Requirements for the obtainment thereof are significantly more stringent.
Transfer of technology	For tax purposes it is advisable that a Technical and/or Management Assistance Agreement be executed between the *maquiladora* and its parent. Such agreement would need to be registered with the National Transfer of Technology Registry (NTTR).	If technical or management assistance is granted to a domestic company from a foreign source and royalties or fees are to be paid therefor, an agreement must be registered with the NTTR. To obtain such registration the agreement must meet certain criteria and the amounts which may be charged are limited.
Taxes	A *maquiladora* is in principle subject to the payment of all Mexican taxes. However, since such operations are intended to be cost centers rather than profit centers, the income taxes to be paid are limited. Also, any value added tax paid by the *maquiladora* shall be refunded to it upon its request.	A domestic company is subject to all normal taxes such as income tax and value added tax (maximum corporate income tax rate = 42%).

TDK's Internal Management

TDK de Mexico had 183 employees (158 women and 25 men). Inouye, before he came to TDK de Mexico, operated machines in a Taiwan plant to help gain a better understanding of workers at that level. After his move to Mexico in 1983, Inouye organized the workforce into teams consisting of workers, subleaders, and leaders. Leaders were not entrusted with the job of supervision: all supervisory responsibilities remained with individuals having a title of supervisor. It took an average of two years for a worker to become a subleader. All subleaders at TDK de Mexico were Mexican; they had a median age of 28.2 years. Only three were women.

There were 11 leaders. The specifics of their job were dependent upon their department. Generally, they oversaw workers and machines in their respective departments but were given little authority and were not accountable for achieving set objectives. They were also in charge of training new workers. The leaders at TDK de Mexico had been at the company for an average of 6.4 years. The average time it took to become a leader

EXHIBIT 5

TDK de Mexico organization chart

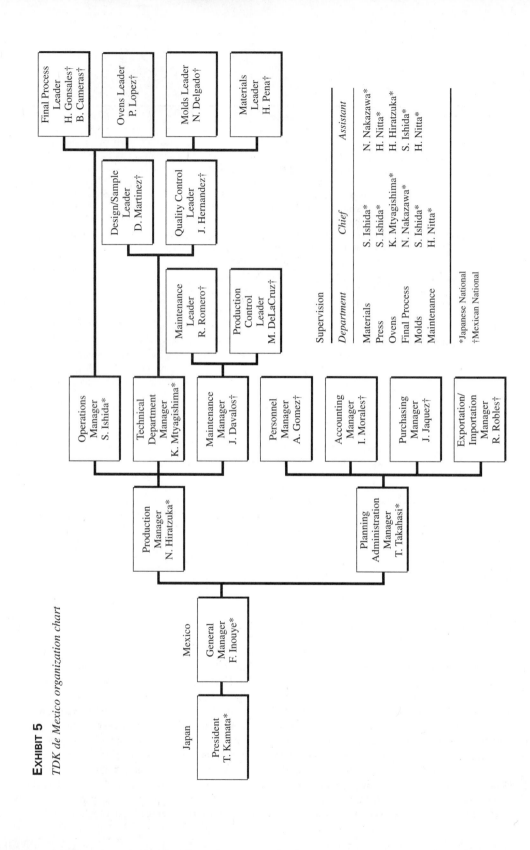

Japan

President
T. Kamata*

Mexico

General
Manager
F. Inouye*

Production
Manager
N. Hiratzuka*

Planning
Administration
Manager
T. Takahasi*

Operations
Manager
S. Ishida*

Technical
Department
Manager
K. Mtyagishima*

Maintenance
Manager
J. Davalos†

Personnel
Manager
A. Gomez†

Accounting
Manager
I. Morales†

Purchasing
Manager
J. Jaquez†

Exportation/
Importation
Manager
R. Robles†

Design/Sample
Leader
D. Martinez†

Quality Control
Leader
J. Hernandez†

Maintenance
Leader
R. Romero†

Production
Control
Leader
M. DeLaCruz†

Final Process
Leader
H. Gonsales†
B. Cameras†

Ovens Leader
P. Lopez†

Molds Leader
N. Delgado†

Materials
Leader
H. Pena†

Supervision

Department	Chief	Assistant
Materials	S. Ishida*	N. Nakazawa*
Press	S. Ishida*	H. Nitta*
Ovens	K. Mtyagishima*	H. Hiratzuka*
Final Process	N. Nakazawa*	S. Ishida*
Molds	S. Ishida*	H. Nitta*
Maintenance	H. Nitta*	

*Japanese National
†Mexican National

was about three years. All of the leaders at TDK de Mexico were Mexican. Very few had ever been promoted to the supervisory level.

Five Japanese filled the 12 positions of supervisors and assistant supervisors (Exhibit 5). Like the leaders, their jobs varied based on the department they supervised. Primarily their duties included supervision of the leaders as well as the teams under the leaders. They determined production plans for their respective departments. Although there were Mexican nationals in higher positions, all Japanese employees, irrespective of their job titles, reported directly to Inouye. Because most of the Japanese could not speak Spanish, Inouye thought it was wise to have this direct reporting relationship. However, some of the managers of Mexican origin did not accept this line of reasoning (one manager called it "clannish behavior"); their protests to Inouye had not met with much success.

Wage Policies

TDK de Mexico paid higher wages than most other companies located in the Juarez industrial park plants. TDK de Mexico had several pay incentives available to the workers. They received a bonus after 30 days on the job. There was extra pay for overtime, night shifts, weekend work, and also generous incentives for atten-dance. Yet, Alfred Gomez, personnel manager of TDK de Mexico, stated, "Absenteeism and lateness are becoming problems. In some cases, when a worker decides to leave her job, she just stops coming to work without any notice. One reason for this problem is that Juarez public health hospital gives out medical excuses to workers to miss work for the slightest illness . . . There is very little we can do about it."

Training

TDK had invested a lot of resources in training its employees; most of its training, however, had been confined to leaders and subleaders. Gomez, the head of personnel, did not go through any systematic training need analysis but professed to know "who needed training and who did not by sight." Inouye's position was, "We will spend money on training, of course, but only with those who show promise." Asked how did he see promise, he replied, "I have been working for 25 years . . . I know!" A leader who had just finished an in-house training program on motivation commented, "Whenever we face a major crisis, the six Japanese managers get together with Mr. Inouye and decide what course of action to take. It seems like the only decisions I am allowed to participate in are of routine nature that are easily solved. What do I do with what I learned from the training sessions?"

EXHIBIT 6 **Statistics of TDK de Mexico, 1984–87**

	1984	1985	1986	1987
Total sales (U.S. dollars)	$4,168,000	$3,774,000	$3,837,000	$3,168,000*
Employees	112	128	140	183
Sales per person	$ 29,000	$ 22,000	$ 20,000	$ 23,000
Efficiency rate	82%	81%	80%	80%
Labor turnover rate	16%	47%	46%	39%†
Selling/administrative expenses	$1,623,000	$1,529,000	$1,698,000	$1,878,000
Cost of raw materials	$1,052,000	$1,071,000	$1,099,000	$1,181,000

Shipping cost = .01¢ per gram or 2–10% of total costs.
Price of magnets = .05¢ per gram.
Average production for a year = 5,100,000 grams.
Production figure for 1987 = 6,900,000 grams.
Plant is presently at full capacity.

---

*Based on the then exchange rate.

†*Maquilas* in the park ranged from 35 to 170 percent per year.

Fumio Inouye's Concerns

In March 1988, Inouye met with all the managers (Mexican and Japanese) and presented the plant's most recent operating statistics (Exhibit 6). He was clearly unhappy with the data. A senior manager from Japanese headquarters also attended the meeting along with two other managers from TDK of America. Inouye laid out several options that could be pursued:

1. Downsize the labor force, to correct for the decline in sales and the increase in expenses.

2. Try to avoid downsizing and try to reduce operating costs by buying ferrite powder locally. Since it was not known where and how ferrite powder could be obtained from Mexican sources, Inouye suggested that immediate consideration be given to making the material locally or acquiring a native company.

3. Send some senior managers (Inouye emphasized Mexican nationals) to Japan for further training.

The Mexican managers thought the concerns expressed in the meeting were addressed specifically to them. One Mexican manager said after the meeting, "If these people would live in Mexico and not run to their comfortable homes on the other side of the border after 5:00 o'clock, maybe they would understand us a little better!"

Several Mexican managers again suggested to Inouye that the Japanese managers learn the language and work closely with the workers. Inouye was sympathetic to the suggestion but questioned whether learning the language was essential. He advised them to examine "the pockets of inefficiency" and lectured them about the value of hard work.

The manager from TDK Japan left with a stern warning for imminent improvement or else. He explained to the casewriter:

> You see, I came over here in late 1983, after spending years in Singapore, Taiwan, and Hong Kong. I don't know how useful it is to have a grand strategy or any plan per se for an operation like this. . . . What it boils down to is shooten (focus), shitsu (quality), and bunai (distribution). . . . I'm not about to give up because of cultural differences here; you do what you have to do to earn more money! And if the answer is anything but work harder, I have problem!

Inouye began to contemplate what actions he should take.

GENERAL ELECTRIC FIRES ED RUSSELL

Joseph Wolfe

Joann Babiak
Management and Marketing Department
College of Business Administration
University of Tulsa

Looking back, Ed Russell remembers how quickly and quietly it was done. He was summoned from his headquarters in Worthington, Ohio, by his boss and GE Plastics Senior Vice President Glen Hiner on November 11, 1991, ostensibly to attend a budget revision meeting at division headquarters in Pittsfield, Massachusetts. After being ushered into Hiner's office and exchanging a few obligatory pleasantries, Hiner handed over a letter telling Ed he was being discharged immediately as vice president and general manager of General Electric Superabrasives (GES). To soften the blow and extend executive courtesies, his $190,000 salary, an $85,000 incentive compensation award, the company's life insurance policy worth more than $750,000, and company health benefits and privileges, which included a 1990 XJS Jaguar costing GE $1,168.57 per month, would continue for one year unless he found another job beforehand. He was then put on a company jet and told to return immediately to Worthington and clear out his office. As Ed Russell recalled, "The whole thing took 15 minutes."

Thus ended a once-brilliant 18-year career at General Electric built on many successes as well as the eye and approval of Jack Welch, GE's often-feared but greatly respected CEO. Although in a state of shock, Ed did not believe he was fired for the reasons given by Glen Hiner, which were poor performance, incompetence, and possessing the "wrong values." Instead he felt he was fired for not going along with an industrial diamond price-fixing scheme hatched between his boss and the giant diamond firm of DeBeers or helping to cover up fraudulent behavior and malfeasance by executives forced into his division by Hiner. In an attempt to get back his job and to salvage his reputation, he filed a civil action suit on April 21, 1992, claiming wrongful termination in violation of Ohio's whistleblower statute, Ohio Rev. Ann. Code §4113.52, as well as contacting the Federal Bureau of Investigation and aiding in a Justice Department investigation of price fixing and collusion between GE and DeBeers.

Russell's lawsuit opened a Pandora's box of alleged corporate wrongdoing. These wrongs were brought to light through his use of the media and included reports of a long line of unsavory, illegal, and sensational activities conducted in the industrial diamond industry. One activity was a "stock parking" scheme conducted between General Electric and the Mitsui Company to falsely inflate the earnings of GE Plastics (GEP). Another included Operation Tailhook-like activities perpetrated by various executives at sales conventions and business trips. One final revelation was collusion between GE and DeBeers to destroy a South Korean entrant in the industrial diamond industry. In this effort, Henry Kissinger's political influence was also brought to bear.

For its part, General Electric felt Russell's charges were "pure nonsense." John Beatty, a lawyer representing GE, said Ed Russell "never blew any whistles at all, and we think we can prove it. Even if he did, that's not why he was fired. He was fired for very, very poor performance. We look forward to the trial and are confident it will show that Mr. Russell was discharged due to significant performance issues." Even though GE felt it was blameless in the matters revealed by Russell, it began to spend about $1.0 million a month to defend itself and its executives. GE responded to his allegations by claiming that Russell himself, through various actions during and after his employment, was guilty of a number of transgressions. These were identified as

1. Breach of fiduciary duty.
2. Breach of employee duty of loyalty.
3. Breach of an Employee Innovation and Proprietary Information Agreement.
4. Violation of Ohio Revised Code §133.51(c) and §1333.81 and misappropriation of confidential information.
5. Unjust enrichment.

As Russell's February 21, 1994, trial date neared, GE faced an ongoing Justice Department investigation, three shareholder suits, and three class-action suits related to his disclosures. GE also had to absorb the ill-will created by the large volume of stories appearing in both the popular and business press as well as an hour-long PBS *Frontline* documentary on collusion in the diamond industry featuring a segment on Russell himself. Additionally, the "turnaround" skills and management methods of Jack Welch as GE's CEO, as well as the morals and honesty of many of Russell's former business associates, were questioned. To many people, it is a David and Goliath story with Russell being a lone and courageous individual who was treated unfairly and has taken his story public. Others believe, however, this lawsuit is merely a ploy to improve his severance package. Because Ed's final termination is effective a few months before his 55th birthday, he does not receive those superior pension and insurance benefits attached to that retirement age. GE's Cincinnati-based lawyers are even more direct by stating Russell was using his lawsuit "to leak selected documents to the press or others in an effort to extort a settlement."

Natural and Man-Made Diamonds

Natural diamonds are lumps of carbon transformed by intense heat and pressure into the world's hardest (10 on the Mohs hardness scale) and oldest material, formed as long as 3.3 million years ago. These diamonds, sometimes known as "boart" or black diamonds, are forged from carbon deep in the earth's magma. At that depth, which can reach 300 miles, the heat is extreme. The material's heat causes it to expand and the resulting pressure drives it through fissures and cracks to the earth's surface. In the process, it produces a very long volcanic shaft often called a pipe. On its travels, the shaft's diameter is relatively narrow and varies in its thickness from less than one mile to as little as a few yards. This varying diameter creates an additional pressure source on the carbon material as it rises.

While the public's perception is that diamonds are rare and difficult to find, more than 3,000 pipes, of which only 50 or 60 have ever been worked, exist in South Africa, the world's greatest diamond-producing area. Moreover, diamonds are found throughout the world. Most recently, they have been discovered in Canada's Northwest Territories south of the Arctic Circle. Prospecting in this area in the early 1980s, Charles

Fiopke followed such telltale indicator minerals as garnet, pyrope, and chromium dioxide and began staking claims nine years later. Since 1991, more than 200 companies have laid claims over nearly 75,000 square miles. Tom McCanless, a geochemist at the University of Arizona, believes the Canadian Northwest "will be the next major diamond-producing area on the planet," although he adds "diamond exploration is probably the hardest exploration to do in the mineral industry." Exhibit 1 summarizes various estimates of the world's supply of diamonds for the year 2000 by country.

Since the early 1980s, the world's natural diamond output has doubled and is now about 100.0 million carats (one carat equals $\frac{1}{142}$ ounce avoirdupois or 200mg) a year. Of this production, more than half are not gem quality. Gemstones have few flaws or inclusions such as tiny bubbles, hairline cracks, feathers, clouds, or specks of uncrystallized carbon. They possess a clear, white, or near-white color on a 23-grade color scale of D (colorless) to Z (yellow) and are large enough in their boart state to yield a product that can be sold profitably after grinding and polishing. A stone with many inclusions, or one that possesses a yellowish color or a size that is too small to profitably cut and polish, is termed "industrial grade." While this diamond grade is inferior as an ornament or object of beauty, it possesses great utilitarian value as a grinding, sanding, or boring material. In this application, industrial diamonds minimize tool wear, allow precision cutting, and reduce production downtime needed for tool replacement. These diamonds are also used in machine tools as boring bits, grinding wheels, and cutting tools as well as for stone cutting and in cement construction for cutting and finishing poured concrete. Exhibit 2 shows the current applications for industrial diamonds with about 90.0 percent of all industrial diamond material being used for grinding wheels and saw blades.

The importance of industrial diamonds has increased dramatically over the years as manufacturing processes have become faster and more precise. In the 1930s, about 25,000 carats of industrial diamonds were consumed, while by the late 1960s this consumption had increased one thousandfold. With this rapid increase, the demand for industrial diamonds outstripped nature's supply, which accelerated research into the production of man-made diamonds. In the 1800s, scientists had tried to produce synthetic diamonds, and these efforts were intensified after World War II as advanced technologies were brought into play. In 1951, GE began its research into the development of synthetic diamonds, but several problems had to be solved. GE had to design an apparatus that could produce both extremely high heat and pressure without destroying the apparatus itself during the production process. They also had to identify the chemical reaction that transformed carbon into diamonds.

Their early processes used a metal solvent as a catalyst while time, temperatures, and pressures were varied to produce synthetic stones. On December 9, 1954, Herbert Strong grew the first industrial grade diamond from graphite in GE's laboratories. The process basically entailed the recrystallization of graphite to diamond while the carbon was in contact with a molten ferrous metal or alloy solvent catalyst at a pressure (48–60 kbar or 4.8–6.0 GPascal) and temperature (1200°–1500° centigrade) where diamond is in the stable phase. Under these conditions, numerous diamonds nucleate and grow larger under a thin skin of molten metal to sizes ranging

EXHIBIT 1 **Estimated Natural Diamond Production by Major Producing Nations for the Year 2000**

	Estimate in Carats		
Country	*Low*	*Best*	*High*
Angola	700	2,500	5,000
Australia	35,000	37,000	41,000
Botswana	11,000	17,000	20,000
Brazil	300	700	2,500
Central African Republic	400	500	600
CIS	11,000	16,000	19,000
Ghana	300	350	600
Guinea	250	450	700
Indonesia	100	400	500
Ivory Coast	200	250	300
Liberia	100	200	400
Namibia	500	900	1,200
Peoples Republic of China	500	1,000	2,000
Tanzania	50	125	200
Sierra Leone	250	400	650
South Africa	6,550	9,750	12,000
Venezuela	350	500	600
Zaire	16,000	24,000	27,000
Other and illicit	450	575	1,550
Total	84,000	112,600	136,000

Source: Cited in Peter Harben and Richard Nötstaller, "Diamonds—Scintillating Performance in Growth and Prices," *Industrial Minerals,* March 1991, p. 43.

Exhibit 2 Industrial Diamond Applications

Toolstones
Die stones
Drilling bits
Grinding wheels
Saw Blades
Electronics
Chemical processing
Medical and military technology

from 0.05 to 1.0 millimeters. In the original design, the reaction mixture was contained in an insulating cylinder of pyrophyllite and compressed and heated in the "belt" high-pressure apparatus of H. T. Hall. The process was able to create 60 to 70 tons of industrial diamonds per year. GE began to market its synthetic diamonds shortly thereafter and, by 1957, large quantities were available. They were also superior to natural diamonds as they were easily cut and shaped due to their uniform size, quality, and friability.

In the late 1970s, GE's patents for its high-temperature-high-pressure technology expired, but this fact did not open the industry to new competitors. Beginning in the late 1950s, GE and DeBeers had entered into a series of patent cross-licensing agreements that made it extremely difficult for other companies to enter the synthetic diamond business. During this time, GE had also made DeBeers the sole licensee of its patented technology. Today, the industrial diamond market consumes about 250.0 million carats a year, of which over 80.0 percent of these carats are synthetic or manmade and, in 1992, worldwide sales were about $600.0 million, with GE and DeBeers sharing about 80.0 percent of those sales.

DeBeers, Anglo American, and the Diamond Cartel

The DeBeers diamond cartel and the myriad operations and cross-ownerships that support the combine have a rich and varied history. In 1871, a South African farmer named DeBeers sold his rich diamond mine, the Kimberly claim, to Cecil John Rhodes and the Rhodes family. Nine years later, the Rhodes amalgamated their numerous mine claims to form DeBeers Consolidated Mines (SIC 1499, 3915, 5085, 5099) with financial backing by the English Rothschilds and a charter granted by the British Colonial Office in London. This new entity soon formed a trust to control the supply of diamonds and ultimately their prices. This was done by acquiring each and every start-up mining company upon its formation. At that time, these companies were constantly forming because of the great availability of diamond lodes in South Africa, the site of the world's most numerous kimberlite pipes and alluvial diamond fields.

Cecil John Rhodes died in 1901 and was eventually succeeded by Ernest Oppenheimer of Friedberg, Germany, who had a major interest in the Premier Diamond Mining Company of South Africa. Oppenheimer then bought control of Consolidated Mines Selection and used Consolidated to purchase some of the country's richest gold fields and to persuade other German landowners to merge with him. In 1917, the Oppenheimers formed the Anglo American Company (SIC 6719) to obtain money from J. P. Morgan and other American bankers and mining companies. Because of the rampant anti-German sentiment found in the United States during World War I, the name Anglo American was chosen to disguise the company's true German background.

Ernest Oppenheimer, through the Anglo American company, acquired highly productive diamond fields in German Southwest Africa (now Namibia) in 1920. This new supply of diamonds allowed Anglo American to break the monopoly over the supply of diamonds held by DeBeers. Anglo American subsequently took control of DeBeers and restored monopoly conditions in 1929. The company's penchant for control can be illustrated by its actions during World War II. During the war, DeBeers was the Allies' major supplier of the industrial diamonds necessary for the manufacture and machining of metal and metal parts such as aircraft engines, cannon barrels, and steel finishing. Rather than allowing the United States, the Allies' largest and most productive manufacturer of armaments, to build its own industrial diamond stockpile, State Department-level coercion was needed to allow America to obtain its DeBeers diamonds and then only through Canadian sources. After the war, questions regarding war profiteering were also raised regarding *Germany's* source of industrial diamonds. DeBeers ultimately quashed a British Secret Service investigation as it was believed South Africa's industrial diamonds were smuggled to Switzerland where they were shipped to Holland, which was German-occupied for much of the war.

When the war ended in 1945, Anglo American and DeBeers extended its controls to gold mining and, by 1958, it became South Africa's largest producer. The company is also one of the world's largest producers of coal, uranium, and copper, and it expanded its interests into industrial diamonds and finance in the 1960s and 1970s. Anglo American's holdings have also been shifted as it adjusts to new sources in the world's supply of diamonds and other mineral wealth. When knowledge of diamond discoveries in the USSR arrived in the West in the 1950s, DeBeers approached its government officials. DeBeers now has exclusive sales rights to all uncut gems found in Russia's Siberian mines.

Botswana is also a major producer of diamonds in terms of value. Diamond production in this country is in the hands of the DeBeers Botswana Mining Co. (Debswana), which is a 50/50 partnership between DeBeers Consolidated Mines Ltd. and the Botswana government. Debswana also owns 5.0 percent of DeBeers and, accordingly, is represented on its board of directors. In Tanzania, diamonds are obtained from the Williamson mine, which has received a capital infusion of $6.3 million by its joint owners, the Tanzanian State Mining Corporation and DeBeers. In 1989, Anglo American sold its interest in Consolidated Gold Fields through its 39.0 percent ownership of the Luxembourg-based holding company Minorco for $645.0 million and bought the American-based Freeport-McMoRan Gold Company. This latter company was renamed the Independence Mining Company in 1990. In addition to this ownership interest, Minorco has stakes in other American companies—Minorco has a 56.0 percent interest in the Inspiration Resources Company and a 49.0 percent ownership of Adobe Resources. In mid-1991, Minorco purchased the Hudson Bay Mining & Smelting Company of Winnipeg, Manitoba, Canada, for $87.0 million. Exhibit 3 summarizes Anglo American's major holdings and affiliations, of which there are more than 1,300 in total. In its largest companies—DeBeers Centenary, Minorco, and Rustenburg Platinum—the top positions, as well as those of the Anglo American Corporation, are held by Julian Ogilvie Thompson, age 58, and Nicholas F.

EXHIBIT 3   **Selected Anglo American Affiliates and Operations**

Affiliate/Operation	*Activity*
Amic	Holding company for Anglo American's manufacturing, forestry, and timber products interests
Amquip Ltd.	Manufacturer of construction mining and material-handling equipment
Anglo American Coal Corp. Ltd.	Coal mining and export
Anglo American Farms Ltd.	Grain, produce, meat, and wine production
Anglo American Industrial Corp. Ltd.	Steel, automobiles, paper, and chemicals
Anglo American Gold Investment Co. Ltd.	Investments in diamond and metals mining
Anglo American Property Services Ltd.	Real estate property management
Anamint	Diamond trading
Boart International Ltd.	Suppliers of drilling equipment and services
DeBeers Centenary AG	Gem and diamond brokers
DeBeers Central Selling Organization	Marketing of gem and industrial diamonds
DeBeers Consolidated Mines Ltd.	Diamond mining and marketing
Johannesburg Consolidated Investment Co. Ltd.	Holding company for mining finances
Minorco	A Luxembourg-based holding company that owns 100.0% of Minorco U.S.A.
Rustenburg Platinum Holdings Ltd.	Platinum mining
South American Investments Ltd.	Mining and other investments in South America
Vaal Reefs Exploration and Mining Co. Ltd.	Gold and uranium mining in South Africa
Western Deep Levels Ltd.	Gold and uranium mining in South Africa

Sources: A. Chai, A. Campbell, and P. Spain, eds., *Hoover's Handbook of World Business* (Austin, TX: Reference Press, 1993), pp. 132–133; and *1994 Directory of Corporate Affiliations,* Vol. VI (New Providence, NJ: Reed Reference Publishing Co., 1994), pp. 72–73.

Exhibit 4

EXHIBIT 4 Central Selling Organization's Supply Share of Rough Industrial Diamonds

Year	Percent share
1970	57.0%
1980	61.0
2000*	63.0

*Best estimate for this year.

Source: Peter Harben and Richard Nötstaller, "Diamonds—Scintillating Performance in Growth and Prices," *Industrial Minerals*, March 1991, p. 44.

Oppenheimer, age 47, in the respective offices of chairman and deputy chairman.

While these entities mainly control the supply of diamonds, Anglo American also controls their demand through various marketing and distribution operations. The sale of gemstones is directed through various selling organizations, and those who are dependent upon them—the Central Selling Organization, The Diamond Corporation, The Diamond Purchasing and Trading Company (Purtra), and the Diamond Trading Company; its three "sights" found in London, Kimberley, and Lucerne, Switzerland; and about 150 "sightholders" who place their orders for diamonds through the brokers I. Hennig & Co. Ltd., W. Nagel, Bonas & Company Ltd., H. Goldie & Co., and J. P. Morgan. Industrial grade diamonds are sold by the Central Selling Organization through either Industrial Distributors (Sales) Ltd. or Diamond Product (Sales) Ltd. Industrial stones are sold directly to tool manufacturers, but grits and powders are sold via authorized distributors with The Industrial Diamond Division handling the sales of DeBeers' natural and synthetic industrial diamonds. Exhibit 4 indicates the supply share of industrial diamonds held by DeBeers currently and in the near future.

Jack Welch, General Electric, and General Electric Superabrasives

General Electric (SIC 3724, 3630, 3511, 3641, 3812, 3845, 2821) is American's fifth largest company with 1993 sales amounting to $60.6 billion and profits of $4.3 billion and 274 manufacturing plants in 26 countries. Although it operates as a vast conglomerate dealing in the businesses of aircraft engines, household appliances, turbines and turbine generator sets, electric lamps, search and navigation equipment, electromedical equipment, plastics materials and resins, and finance, its roots lie in Thomas Edison's invention of the light bulb in 1879. GE was established as a New York State corporation in 1892 from the merger of the Edison General Electric Company and the Thomson-Houston Company. Even though Edison left the company in 1894, his emphasis on research remained. By combining its strength with J. P. Morgan's backing, GE created one of the nation's first corporate research laboratories in 1900. A series of successful inventions and applications in the elevator, trolley car, and home appliance industries followed, and sales grew to $456.0 million in 1940, $2.6 billion in 1952, and $25.0 billion in 1980. Despite this phenomenal sales growth, however, GE's earnings had flattened in the late 1970s and it was considered an unwieldy and underachieving giant.

Into the picture stepped John (Jack) F. Welch, Jr., who had worked his way through GE via chemicals, components, and consumer products. Given a need for change, Welch acted quickly and was soon labeled "Neutron Jack" for the speed, impatience, and abrasive methods he used to change the company. He jettisoned GE's air conditioning business in 1982, housewares and mining in 1984, and semiconductors in 1988 concentrating on medical equipment, financial services, and high-performance plastics and ceramics. In shedding these operations, he had two guiding principles: fix, close, or sell all poorly performing operations and make the remaining ones first or second in their industries. Additionally, Welch felt GE's culture had to change. In a letter to GE's stockholders in 1990, Welch stated the 1990s-style leader must learn to delegate, facilitate, listen, and trust. This leader must also cast aside those personal insecurities that support the walls of parochialism, status-seeking, and the "functionalitis" found in rigid bureaucracies. To impress these ideas on GE's management team, to ensure flexible, creative responses to business opportunities, and to create a boundaryless organization, the company created the management values statement found in Exhibit 5 after conducting many "think sessions" throughout all management levels.

Although Welch sold off many of GE's operations, he also acquired a number of high-performance ventures. In 1986, the Employers Reinsurance Company was acquired for $1.1 billion and the National Broadcasting Company (NBC) was obtained for $6.4 billion. One year later, GE swapped its consumer electronics di-

G.E. Management Values

G.E. leaders, always
with unyielding integrity:

•

Create a clear, simple, reality-based, customer-focused vision
and are able to communicate it straightforwardly to all
constituencies.

•

Set aggressive targets, understanding accountability and
commitment, and are decisive.

•

Have a passion for excellence, hating bureaucracy and all the
nonsense that comes with it.

•

Have the self-confidence to empower others and behave
in a boundaryless fashion. They believe in and are
committed to Work-Out as a means of empowerment
and are open to ideas from anywhere.

•

Have, or have the capacity to develop,
global brains and global sensitivity and are comfortable
building diverse global teams.

•

Stimulate and relish change and are not frightened or
paralyzed by it, seeing change as opportunity, not threat.

•

Have enormous energy and the ability to energize and
invigorate others. They understand speed as a competitive
advantage and see the total organizational benefits that can be
derived from a focus on speed.

Source: Reprint from "Turning Soft Values into Hard Results," *Leaders Magazine* 16, no. 4 (October, November, December 1993), p. 4.

vision for Thomson of France's CGR Medical Equipment unit. GE's most recent acquisition, the investment banking firm of Kidder, Peabody, was completed in 1990.

Today's GE is a much different company from the one Jack Welch came to head in 1981. Since becoming CEO, he has sold $12.0 billion in GE businesses and bought $26.0 billion more. At the beginning of his tenure, GE's only market leaders were lighting, motors, and power systems, and only aircraft engines and plastics were truly global. Today, 11 of its 12 business groups are first or second in their markets with the 12th one, NBC, the subject of much divestment discussion.

When Welch took over, business units typically had 9 to 11 management levels between the CEO and the line worker. Now there are four to six levels and it has 229,000 employees, of which about 45.0 percent have come aboard since 1981, compared to 412,000 in 1981.

Because of GE's dramatic changes and the energy and creativity Jack Welch brought to the situation, he has often drawn great admiration from the business press and fellow executives. Jack Welch was *Chief Executive* magazine's CEO of the year in 1993. This was a dramatic turnaround from his role as the most infamous SOB of the 1980s and the person *Fortune* magazine once labeled America's toughest boss. Now that some of GE's major changes have been accomplished, Welch talks of "soft" values such as nurturing, openness, and caring. He also believes, however, the only appropriate answer to bad leadership is to "take them out [and] clear the forest" so the company's real team players can excel.

Jack Welch started his GE career in plastics, and he naturally takes a special interest in this business and the people it employs. Its current top executives are

GE Plastics

Gary L. Rogers
President and Chief Executive Officer

Maura J. Abeln-Touhey
Vice President and General Counsel

Robert H. Brust
Vice President, Finance

John B. Blystone
Vice President, GE Superabrasives

GE Plastics (GEP) currently manufactures high-performance engineered plastics used in automobiles, computer housings and other business equipment, ABS resins, silicones, man-made diamonds, and laminates. Its 1992 sales were $4.9 billion and 1993 sales were $5.0 billion, with respective operating profits of $740.0 and $834.0 million. Future expansions are planned in Mexico through the purchase of a commercial resin business as well as engaging in a joint venture. GEP is also completing the construction of a compounding facility in India and will shortly begin constructing another compounding facility in Singapore. Exhibits 6 and 7 respectively present simplified income statements for GE Plastics and the General Electric Corporation.

While obtaining these financial results, GE has been a leader as a corporate citizen and it has received many

Exhibit 6 GE Plastics and Superabrasives Income and Operating Profits
(In millions of dollars)

	1990	1991
Revenue:		
GE Superabrasives	$ 268.8	$ 281.4
Other materials	4,871.2	4,662.6
Total revenue	$5,140.0	$4,944.0
Cost of goods sold:		
GE Superabrasives	211.8	213.6
Other materials	3,918.2	3,675.4
Total COGS	$4,130.0	$3,889.0
Operating profit:		
GE Superabrasives	57.0	67.8
Other materials	953.0	987.2
Total profit	$1,010.0	$1,055.0

Sources: General Electric 1993 Annual Report, p. 35, and court depositions.

awards for its accomplishments as a socially responsible company. Among its many recognition awards, GE earned Harvard University's George S. Dively Award for Corporate Public Initiative in 1990 for the involvement of GE volunteers in nationwide education programs. The National Science Foundation presented its first National Corporate Achievement Award to the GE Foundation in 1992 for its support of minority students, faculty, and professionals in science, engineering, and mathematics. In 1993, GE, the GE Foundations, and GE employees contributed almost $68.0 million to support education, the arts, the environment, and human services organizations worldwide. Additional support for many other community projects came from volunteer help given by GE employees. These efforts entailed hundreds of thousands of labor hours. Last, based on the "College Bound" program GE created in 1989, the company was awarded the President's Volunteer Action Award in 1994. This is a program that has doubled the number of college students coming from selected poor and inner-city schools in 12 cities where GE has major facilities.

Ed Russell's Fall from Grace

Ed Russell joined GE in April 1974 after graduating at the top of his MBA class at Columbia University's Graduate School of Business Administration. Earlier, he had received a Bachelor of Science degree in chemical engineering from Worchester Polytechnic Institute. His first GE assignment was as manager of its Group Strategic Planning and Review Operation at corporate headquarters in Fairfield, Connecticut. In this capacity, he managed the strategic planning process for the company's $1.4 billion Consumer Products Group. Two years later, Russell became vice president and general manager of GE's Gesamex Lamp division and was responsible for the manufacture and sale of lighting products in Mexico. In 1978 he became manager of GE International Lighting. In this position, Ed headed a 5,000-person operation with manufacturing sites in Brazil, Chile, Philippines, Turkey, Venezuela, and Canada. GE International Lighting was also in charge of exporting all lighting products produced by GE's American factories. Under Russell's supervision, the division's sales increased 47.4 percent while earnings rebounded from a $3.0 million loss to a $20.0 million profit.

On April 1, 1986, Ed became general manager of GE Superabrasives and was later made a vice president and corporate officer of the same unit in early 1990, one of

Exhibit 7 General Electric Financial Highlights
(In millions of dollars)

	1993	1992	1991
Revenues	$60,562.0	$57,073.0	$54,629.0
Earnings before accounting changes	5,177.0	4,725.0	4,435.0
Net earnings	$ 4,315.0	$ 4,725.0	$ 2,636.0
Dividends declared	$ 2,229.0	$ 1,985.0	$ 1,808.0

Source: General Electric 1993 Annual Report, p. i.

only 127 such officers in GE. In addition to the promotion, he also received a personal note from Jack Welch saying, "Congratulations on the wonderful job you are doing. I am so pleased for—and proud of—you. This is a hard-earned, well-deserved promotion." When Russell joined GES, it had 2,000 employees with manufacturing facilities in Worthington, Ohio, and Dublin, Ireland. Under his command, sales rose to $70.0 million in 1989 from only $16.5 million in 1986 and its actual return-on-sales consistently exceeded budgeted returns, as shown in Exhibit 8.

Unfortunately for Russell's long-term career aspirations, GES was placed within the GE Plastics Group under the direction of Glen H. Hiner in September 1986. Over time, Hiner proceeded to place his own people in key GES positions, and a culture and value clash erupted almost immediately. Russell would later write a memo stating Hiner's people lacked "mid-America values and work ethics and for the most part are heavy drinking womanizers, expense-account cheats [and are] the pond scum of American industry." Those individuals and their positions were

Pieter Rens, GES International Sales Manager

Jay Ferguson, GES Finance Manager

Peter Foss, GES Marketing Manager

Steve Palovchik, GES International Sales Manager

Hiner also made a number of decisions with which Russell disagreed. Some decisions adversely affected the costs and profitability of Russell's operation, other

---

EXHIBIT 8   GES Actual versus Budgeted Return-on-sales

| Year | Return-on-Sales ($000,000) | |
	Budgeted	Actual
1986	$10.0	$16.5
1987	20.0	30.5
1988	30.0	50.0
1989	50.0	70.0
1990*	54.0	57.0
1991	43.0	n.a.

*In this year, the GE Plastics Group switched from annual budgets to periodically revised operating plans. This planning system was later discarded.

Source: Civil Case filing C-1-92-343, April 21, 1992, Vol. 1, pp. 9–10.

decisions frustrated Ed's product development ambitions, and other decisions and actions supported Ed's feelings that Hiner possessed an improper tolerance for moral improprieties or condoned and rewarded outright illegal activities.

In 1988, Glen Hiner installed a new overhead allocation system in GEP. Under this system, the entire division's costs became intermingled. Russell quickly found the system favored those with high costs by shifting some of their expenses to the more profitable divisions, such as GES, which had either controlled or cut their costs. Especially irksome to Ed as a cost item was a $3.0 million annual charge allocated to GES to pay "maintenance" fees for a questionable "stock parking" scheme created by Hiner to inflate GEP's profits. In this plan, which was not approved by GE's accountants, GE Plastics sold the stock it had acquired in the Asahi Diamond Industrial Co. to Mitsui & Company, one of Japan's largest trading houses, for $80.0 million and an approximate $41.0 million paper profit in 1989. By doing this, GEP's earnings were artificially inflated to offset a $115.0 million third-quarter deficit. As part of the arrangement, GE agreed to repurchase the stock at its original price while paying Mitsui an annual carrying charge fee of $3.0 million. Mitsui's letter of agreement acknowledged GE's corporate accountants opposed putting the buy-back arrangement in writing:

> Mitsui's basic stance is to keep shares of Asahi Diamond on our side at your strong request until when you will be in a position to buy back shares from us. . . . Under any circumstances, our extra costs for this transaction should be fully borne by GE.

In defending its actions, GE contended Russell never objected to parking stock until his operation's results started to deteriorate. Jack Welch said he did not know of the affair until meeting with Ed to discuss Superabrasive's performance. "The way it came up, as I recall, is that Mr. Russell was describing why he was having these numbers problems and one of the elements of his numbers problems was a charge to carry this stock." Supposedly surprised by this revelation, Welch got mad but denies he was mad at Russell himself or sought revenge. "I was angry with our naïveté, in my view, in being hooked into the 'courtesy' with the Japanese." Russell also alleged that Welch offered Mitsui a China distributorship rather than having to buy back the Asahi stock, which had fallen in value over the interim period. GE corporate spokesperson Joyce Hergenhan says the charge about Welch's offer was "absolutely, categorically untrue. During the course of a general business meeting in Fall 1991, Jack Welch told Mitsui that they owned the Asahi stock and would have to live with its market fluctuations."

In another matter, Russell claimed Hiner suppressed his plan to get GE into the gemstone business for fear of upsetting DeBeers and endangering other agreements made between them. This indicated to Ed that collusive activities or agreements existed between Hiner and De-Beers executives. Since May 1970, GE had possessed the technology for making gemstone-quality artificial diamonds. The technology, however, was too expensive to operate and produced gemstones that were not price-competitive with DeBeers's natural diamonds. Throughout 1988 and 1989, General Electric R&D teams under Russell's management worked on process improvements. These efforts were successful in mid-1990 and produced uniform artificial gemstones that could be cut and polished easily and cheaply. This process improvement, as stated by Russell, produced diamonds for "several hundred dollars per carat as opposed to current prices of several thousands of dollars per carat for natural gemstone diamonds." To merchandise these diamonds, Ed met with the Swarovski family, owners of a number of Austrian jewelry stores, to sell 2–3 carat-sized, blue-colored, man-made diamonds. Hiner vetoed Russell's plan in January 1991, and all negotiations ceased with the Swarovskis. When asked for confirmation about Russell's story, the Swarovski family refused to comment.

Hiner's actions on another occasion further indicated to Russell that collusion existed between GE and De-Beers. In the early 1990s, the Iljin Corporation of South Korea was attempting to enter the industrial diamond industry. To accelerate its entry, it hired away from GE Chien-Min Sung, one of its key laboratory scientists who had deep knowledge of the artificial-diamond-growing process. While GE was suing Iljin in Boston's federal court for unfair trade practices, Russell contended it was also working with DeBeers to undermine Iljin's efforts by other methods. He says he warned Glen Hiner in August 1990 not to ask for DeBeers's cooperation "in restricting supplies of critical diamond equipment," namely tungsten carbide dies and anvils, to the Iljin Corporation. It appears GE took Iljin very seriously. Patricia A. Sherman, a top GE lawyer, said it was imperative the Iljin problem be solved as it had received "news this week that Iljin [had] captured three of GE's

major customers in Korea, with estimated lost sales of up to $100,000 per month." GE's general counsel, Benjamin W. Heineman, characterized the company's battles with Iljin was "trench warfare." For additional troops in his war, Heineman allegedly asked Henry Kissinger, who had been a GE consultant for many years and was about to visit South Korea, to "sound very threatening about how this use of stolen information threatens" Seoul's relations with the United States and General Electric. Henry Kissinger, through his consulting firm, denied he pressured the Korean government and that he (1) merely advised GE on strategy with Iljin and (2) met with only a mid-level Korean official on GE's behalf.

Ed Russell also felt he was constantly stymied in his attempts to correct the illegal or questionable activities perpetrated by Hiner or various executives installed by him. In November 1987, he brought knowledge of a kickback scheme to Hiner's attention. This scheme involved European customers, GE's Pieter Rens, and Sergio Sinigaglia, GES's Swiss distributor. Sinigaglia first added a "processing charge" to the price of the industrial diamonds. The European customer then paid the inflated price to Sinigaglia with half the processing charge going to him and the other half deposited in the customer's secret Swiss bank account. Under this scheme, the customer's industrial diamond expenses were greater, thereby reducing the firm's tax liability. The customer would also have a tax-free source of personal income. A GE internal investigation of the scheme concluded it violated company policy No. 20.4, but Hiner did not take disciplinary action and instead promoted the sales manager and continued using the GE distributor. Hiner denies he promoted him and said he had "absolutely no knowledge" of a Swiss bank account scheme.

Also in November 1987, Russell discovered Pieter Rens had met with the managing director of Diamant Boart, S.A., a Luxembourg industrial diamond company controlled by DeBeers, in an action he believed was to fix industrial diamond prices. He reported this meeting to Hiner, and the matter was investigated internally as a violation of Section 20.5 of GE's policies regarding antitrust activities as well as violating GE's antiapartheid policy No. 20.12, which prohibited all business with South African companies. In April 1988, Russell believed Rens again attempted to fix industrial diamonds in the United States through European companies and reported the activity to Hiner for disciplinary action. Instead of disciplining Rens, Hiner promoted him away from Russell's supervision and made him managing director of GE Plastics for France.

Russell was also extremely troubled by the immoral or wasteful and expensive behavior exhibited by various GE executives within GE Plastics. Although he did not complain about these activities, he noted the following episodes perpetrated by various GE executives:

1. The violation of German currency laws and company policy no. 20.4. This entailed the creation of a Swiss bank scheme through a GE Swiss distributor.

2. The sexual harassment of a female secretary. This harassment ceased only when Glen Hiner transferred the male offender to Europe and only after it was feared the secretary's husband might get involved.

3. An executive with an on-the-job alcohol problem who drank continuously during his trip in Japan. When the executive returned from Japan, he was drunk in the office and accused Russell and his wife of a 20.4 violation for trying to help the son of a Chinese employee. The charges against them were proven false, but Russell considered this "the worst type of personal harassment." At the company's 1990 Florida sales meeting, the same executive punched holes in the hotel's walls, threw beer bottles, and sexually harassed female associates. Damage amounting to $5,000 caused by him was covered up by falsifying company expense records. When this executive was in Russia, he was drunk again and vomited outside a government ministry while on a business call. Later, while sitting in a Russian hotel, he smashed a beer bottle as he threw it across its lobby.

4. An executive who on his trips to the Orient always stopped off in Bangkok to spend extended weekends with prostitutes at the best hotels. When he later left GE, he handed over an expense bill that was almost $70,000. Other executives laughed it off as a good experience for him.

5. One executive took a $20,000 transfer allowance to move to Worthington but never moved and never repaid the allowance. This same executive was out all night and arrived at the office so drunk he was unable to prepare the exhibits for Russell's September 4, 1991, presentation to Jack Welch.

6. A salesman charged several hundred dollars' worth of golf balls to his expense account. This person also obtained a temporary $20,000 loan from GE to join a local country club and only repaid $6,000 of the loan. This subordinate rolled over his expense account for amounts ranging from $6,000 to $7,000 to pay the mortgage on his house. By doing so, he avoided the IRS rule that prohibited keeping loans out for more than six months.

7. A subordinate who uses the company's station wagon for personal use and has the company pay for its gasoline.

8. A senior vice president whose "lifestyle is one of incredible disgust. He conducts restructuring meetings at resorts such as Troutbeck. He keeps on the payroll a valet and 'companion.'" While attending GES's 1989 sales meeting in Hawaii, $200,000 was spent on various amenities. A "daily delivery of Tulips was flown in from Holland for his room, along with a specific type of pillow for his bed."

Ed's problems increased in late 1990 when his unit's profits dropped to $57.0 million, and he was sometimes chided for his puritanical views and failure to recognize the importance of male bonding. The unit's climate seemed to deteriorate, and, in early 1991, Steve Palovchik went over Russell's head to complain about problems in GES. Hiner recalls, "We had a private meeting in Pittsfield at which time Mr. Palovichik described to me a business in disarray and in what I would describe as a palace revolt that was underway in GE Superabrasives." Hiner immediately telephoned Jack O. Peiffer, GE Senior Vice President for Human Resources, who enlisted Dr. Bradford D. Smart's aid. Smart is a well-known Chicago industrial psychologist and president of Smart & Associates, Inc. Peiffer told Dr. Smart that Russell was "in deep trouble job-wise. Some of his subordinates have gone above his head and have complained about his leadership style."

Brad Smart met with Russell in Chicago and provided him a report on April 29, 1991, listing a number of his strengths. Russell was characterized by such phrases as "very conscientious," "responsible," "very hard worker," "excellent analytic abilities," "accessible," "warm, supportive, and caring," "takes responsibility for problems," and that he had "greatly improved the organization climate," had "particularly good relationships with hourly workforce," and had "successfully implemented" GE programs. Smart, however, had previously issued a preliminary report on April 16, 1991, showing Russell in a different light based on interviews conducted with various GES staff members. Pieter Rens, Peter Foss, Jay Ferguson, and Steve Palovchik told him Russell was "totally lacking in strategic vision or leadership capabilities." They "also expressed deep concern about Mr. Russell's sometimes violent temper, viewing him as a 'loaded cannon.'" On a leadership scale of 1 to 10 with "10" being the highest rating, Russell's subordinates rated him a "3." Based on his assessment of the situation, Smart thought Russell "could be fired at any moment."

While problems within GES were slowly leaking out, two unimpressive and troublesome strategy analysis briefings Russell made to Jack Welch and his group of senior executives appeared to seal his fate. Ed's first damaging presentation was in early April 1991 at GE's Pittsfield headquarters, attended by Welch, Dennis Dammerman, GE's Senior Vice President for Finance, and other GE officials.

During the meeting, Dammerman questioned Russell at length about problems with metal-bonding saw (MBS) diamonds. Ed tried to reassure them by saying everything was "fine" and that events were "under control." However, after Ed left the meeting, Dammerman told Welch, "That son of a gun lied to us. He sat here and lied about what's happening out there." Dammerman told Welch things were not fine at all. Uncertain about Russell or GES's situation, Welch sent Robert Nelson, GE Vice President for Financial Analysis, to Worthington to make an on-site evaluation. Nelson remembers Welch saying his investigation should be "along the lines of, 'Can we get a handle on what the numbers look like out there? What's happening in inventories? Sniff around and see what's going on.'" He also had the impression Welch believed Russell had been untruthful during his strategy session.

Ed's second and final top management presentation was held on September 4, 1991. After that meeting, during his helicopter ride back to headquarters, Jack Welch faxed a note to Hiner saying he had until the end of the year to fire Ed. In a follow-up memo written to Glen Hiner, Welch said in part, ". . . Russell has to go. He made a fool of himself in July (sic), and yesterday, he appeared totally out of it. Imagine a presentation to you and I, and [Russell] had no numbers and more importantly knew none." Russell also appeared unable to answer Welch's questions. "I was probing him, questioning him, questioning him, and he wasn't giving me anything but air." Welch also said Russell's responses were vague "50,000 feet, high altitude" answers and that he brushed over the problems in MBS diamonds. In total, Russell "didn't get to the heart of the problem, which was DeBeers, DeBeers's quality, DeBeers's yields [of MBS diamonds] . . . He didn't understand the seriousness and the magnitude of the issues we were trying to deal with."

By October 1991, rumors where swirling through GES's offices that Ed was going to be fired. The rumors

obtained greater credence for Ed when his secretary, Denise Maurer, told him Peter Foss was telling people that Russell would be replaced by Gene Nesbeda, a GE Plastics man. Nesbeda had accompanied Hiner on his last trip to London to meet with DeBeers representatives and was known to be house-hunting in nearby Columbus, Ohio.

With this news on his mind, Ed dictated a "Fellow GE Associates" letter on his Lanier dictating machine in the late afternoon of October 30, 1991. In that letter, Ed outlined his feelings about the situation while cataloging some of the problems he saw with the personnel with whom he had to work in recent years. After summarizing GES's accomplishments, Ed cited events involving sexual harassment, expense account fraud, price-fixing schemes with DeBeers, and anticompetitive actions. Of his relations with Glen Hiner, Ed wrote:

> The problem has been, is, and will always be fundamental cultural differences with Glen Hiner and GE Plastics. In Glen's own words, we have always had a "chemistry" problem. GE Plastics' management team lacks the mid-America values and work ethics, and for the most part, are heavy drinking womanizers; expense account cheats, who disregard property, etc. They are the pond scum of American industry. They are not honest. Integrity at GE Plastics is an oxymoron, and Jack Welch has looked the other way.

Later, when Mrs. Maurer transcribed the Lanier cassette, she was shocked over its contents and discussed them off the record with Christopher Kearney, a GES lawyer and personal friend. "I told him that Ed had written a document that was very damaging and that he was just in a state of mind that I was afraid that he was going to do something with it and I was very concerned about the people that were being attacked in this letter." Although Kearney asked to see the letter, Maurer said no but instead discussed "Ed's state of mind at the time and just how he had been acting and just the chaos that was going on in our office." The letter was never circulated, although Russell sent a copy of it for safekeeping to his brother-in-law in Seattle.

On November 11, 1991, Ed Russell was fired by GE and Glen Hiner, thus beginning Ed's next battle. He was not replaced by Gene Nesbeda, however, but instead by John Blystone, another GE Plastics man.

The Whistleblower Lawsuit

After considering his situation and how he was treated, Ed contacted James B. Helmer Jr., a Cincinnati lawyer who had previously represented a number of other GE whistleblowers. One of his better-known plaintiffs was Chester Walsh, whose fraud allegations in the sale of jet engines to Israel led GE to admit to four criminal charges and the payment of $69.0 million in fines and penalties in 1992. Russell's trial was scheduled for February 21, 1994, in Cincinnati before U.S. District Judge Herman Weber. GE's lead attorney was Chicago lawyer Daniel Webb, who, when he was a Justice Department lawyer, prosecuted Lt. Col. Oliver North. In his lawsuit, which sought either reinstatement in his job or reimbursement for lost pay and undetermined damages, Ed alleged that a conspiracy existed between Glen Hiner, various GE executives, and DeBeers officials to fix high-grade industrial diamond prices and that he was wrongfully terminated for protesting these illegal activities.

To substantiate his allegations, Russell disclosed that on July 23, 1991, Glen Hiner asked him to prepare a briefing paper for an upcoming London meeting, only one of a series of meetings Hiner had already had with DeBeers since 1989. Although Hiner instructed Ed to prepare a paper dealing with possible technological exchanges, Russell believed the meeting's real purpose was to discuss fixing prices on industrial diamonds. Hiner also told Russell to make only one copy of the paper and to have as few people as possible involved in its creation.

Although the document went through a number of drafts written by a team headed by Dr. Mark Sneeringer, GE Superabrasives Manager of Research and Development, Russell delivered it on September 3, 1991, to Glen Hiner as a one-page paper. In that briefing paper, Russell claimed he had written a strong warning about the meeting's antitrust implications and recommended the meeting not be held. Despite Russell's admonition, Hiner and others from GE met with DeBeers officials on September 19, 1991. As proof that a price-fixing scheme emerged from the meeting, Ed observed that, after he was fired, GES announced list-price increases of 12.0–15.0 percent on January 20, 1992. DeBeers followed with similar increases in February.

Many in the industry found the price hikes inexplicable and unjustified. Industrial diamond prices had fallen steadily since the mid-1950s and the demand for them was weak due to low demand for mining, automobile manufacturing, and road cutting and oil drilling equipment. Elsewhere it was noted by Peter Bell, Vice President for Technology at Norton Inc., that industrial

diamond prices should be falling, not rising. "Generally, industrial prices follow gem prices, although not in a one-to-one manner. Gem prices are fairly low [now] because of the recession and the low inflation rate." In response to Russell's allegations and the industry's observations, Brian Cullingworth, Director of Public Affairs at DeBeers's Industrial Diamond Division Pty, said, "Fierce competition characterizes the relationship between GE and DeBeers and any suggestion of price fixing or other violations is absurd."

Under the requirements of the Ohio whistleblower statutes, an employee who claims he was wrongfully terminated because of his whistle-blowing activity must file "a written report that provides sufficient detail to identify and describe" a violation of state or federal criminal statutes. See Appendix A for the relevant text of Ohio's whistleblower statute. This requirement was created so the employer can respond to the employee's complaint by either (1) explaining why the employer feels its actions did not violate any relevant laws or (2) rectifying the situation if the employee was correct and a crime had been committed or was about to be committed. The statute was also written this way to protect the employer from retaliatory lawsuits initiated by hostile exemployees, or from fabricated claims of corporate wrongdoing for the litigant's personal gain, and to guard against the plaintiff's selective recall. Accordingly, the existence and contents of Ed Russell's briefing paper was a cornerstone to his whistleblower suit, although he said the action warned against in the paper was only one of a long series of illegal actions perpetrated by GE executives.

Because Russell complied with Hiner's request to produce only one copy of the briefing paper, this document could not be appended to his brief as evidence of prior notification. Therefore, as part of the lawsuit's discovery process, he subpoenaed the paper from GE. In a sworn deposition, Hiner confirmed a copy of the paper existed and that it was in his trip folder at GE Plastics' headquarters. Unfortunately, it could not be found by either Hiner, his secretary Louise E. Koval, or GE Executive Audit Manager Robert H. Swan, who conducted a companywide search from April to July 1992. In this search, more than 20 GE auditors and lawyers were involved and more than 10,000 labor hours were expended. The search also covered several locations in the United States as well as foreign offices in Europe, the Far East, and Saudia Arabia. As had been the case from the litigation's very beginning, GE pledged complete cooperation. other evidence of its cooperative attitude can be seen from the following excerpt of an April 22, 1992, letter addressed to all GE employees from Maura Abeln-Touhey, GE Plastics General Counsel.

> The United States Department of Justice, in conjunction with the Federal Bureau of Investigation, is currently conducting an investigation into the Company's pricing practices in the superabrasives business and its sale of securities of the Asahi Diamond Industrial Company Ltd.
>
> The Company intends to cooperate fully with the government in this investigation by providing information requested by the government. Yesterday, the Company received a subpoena for documents from a Federal grand jury investigating this matter. The subpoena calls for, among other things, documents relating to the production and sale of industrial diamonds in the United States and abroad, travel and expense records of Company executives, correspondence and memoranda relating to contacts with competitors and internal electronic mail dealing with these and related topics. Accordingly, it is essential that all documents, including electronic files, bearing on this matter be preserved, whether or not called for by the subpoena. Nothing that is conceivably relevant to this investigation should be destroyed, altered or removed.

The judge hearing the case was very concerned about this important paper's disappearance, although the state's whistleblower law does not require the parties to preserve evidence of a written report describing the alleged violations.

When asked whether the briefing paper contained any warnings about antitrust implications, Hiner could not recall whether the warning did or did not exist. He *did* recall that when Russell delivered the final briefing paper, he did not mention any antitrust concerns he had about the DeBeers meeting.

In late May 1992, a preliminary, three-page draft version of the briefing paper was discovered in Steve Palovchik's files. A facsimile of the briefing paper is presented in Appendix B. In commenting on the similarities between this draft and its final version, Russell said, "we took [the] first two pages, and we made them the last two pages of the memo . . . because page 1 and 2 are really just an appendix. The final briefing paper was three pages. It had a main page, which I called— was the one-page mail. It had these two things attached to it, which were perceived assets and DeBeers and GE." Because Mark Sneeringer was the person most involved in writing both versions of the paper, his opinions and ideas about its creation and contents were solicited. As for why so few people should be involve in

its drafting, Sneeringer said, "The knowledge that De-Beers and GE were considering this meeting was thought to be potentially harmful from the standpoint that customers, if they heard about it, may have a misperception as to the meaning of the meeting." Sneeringer also felt Russell "did not like the idea of the meeting as laid out [and was] planning to annunciate some of those risks in the briefing paper." Sneeringer acknowledged, however, that Russell did not tell him to state warnings or cautions in the briefing paper about antitrust risks or concerns or of GE's violation of its policy regarding apartheid in South Africa.

In pre-trial proceedings, Russell's lawyers suggested this document could also constitute a complaint and therefore fulfilled the Ohio whistle-blower statute's requirements of prior notice. GE's lawyers immediately challenged the value of the draft paper on a number of grounds. Russell first said the final paper was three pages in length but later stated it contained one page with a two-page appendix to bring it into line with the only proof he had that he had warned GE in advance. Additionally, Mark Sneeringer swore the early draft's antitrust language was deleted from the final version delivered to Hiner. According to him, the last version did not use the term antitrust and did not suggest a violation of the law. Given these ambiguities about the briefing paper's form and content and its importance to the whistleblowing case, GE contended Russell "surely would either produce this mysterious briefing paper or be more specific about its contents if he could. His failure to do so amply demonstrates that he cannot honestly allege that he ever provided GE with a written report describing a violation of law before he was given a notice of termination."

GE Defends Itself

Despite the plaintiff's allegations about price fixing and corporate wrongdoing, GE steadfastly maintained it fired Russell for poor performance. As Jack Welch said in summarizing why he was fired, "In two words, poor performance." Welch became concerned about GES's operations and particularly Ed's management style. The CEO saw that inventory levels were rising although the end-user market was in a recession, the division's products were losing their technological edge to DeBeers, and reports of a "palace revolt" had come to his attention through Jack Peiffer. Earlier, in April 1991, Peter Foss reported that a technology gap existed in MBS diamonds, the highest quality and most profitable synthetic diamond application with net profits of about 30.0 percent in 1989. "That's where DeBeers had taken the leadership position away from us. Our customers told us when I joined in 1990 that we had not been listening to them when they told us in the '80s that we needed to get our technology in shape and to improve our product line." In the high-quality MBS market segment, Foss stated DeBeers had obtained more than 50.0 percent of the market while GE's share had fallen to less than one-third.

Word also came to Jack Welch that Russell's new wife, Shirley Costantino, a former GES marketing executive whom he married in 1988, was masterminding the office and influencing business decisions. The situation was discussed by Welch and others during a performance review, and Welch made a note to himself, "Make sure his wife is out of the business equation." Commenting on this particular notation, Welch commented, "That's a pretty strong statement. I don't recall ever seeing this in an evaluation of any GE officer, to keep a family member out of the running of the business, in my 25 years in the business." Denise Maurer said the office staff called Russell's wife "Nancy Reagan," although Ed says statements about his wife's role are "gross exaggerations."

Even though Ed had been a rising star for many years at GE, the company contended his performance began to fall shortly after his promotion to vice president. It also maintained his firing should not have been a surprise as he had received many warnings his performance was below expectations. His incentive pay was reduced for 1990, and Russell recognized that a deficiency existed when he wrote to Hiner, "I fully realize the bad miss we had in 1990." See Appendix C for a facsimile of Russell's performance review for that year. Hiner said he warned Ed as early as February 1991 that his performance was becoming even more unsatisfactory, although he received a $15,000 raise five months later. In a meeting held on October, 23, 1991, Hiner told Russell he was "evaluating whether [he] could continue being [GES's] leader" and would soon let him know whether he was going to be replaced. Ed was also told at this time he had no support from his staff, his peers, or his customers. The interviews by Brad Smart were also cited as evidence of failures on Ed's part. Jack Peiffer said those interviews found "Mr. Russell was viewed by his subordinates as being untrustworthy, insecure, paranoid, indecisive, inconsistent, a poor communicator, and

unproductive." Russell claimed, however, the negative comments came from three individuals forced on him by Hiner. These were also the people whose activities had troubled Russell regarding improper practices.

Ed's credibility as a whistleblower was challenged by GE's contention that it had received no prior warning from Russell that its meeting with DeBeers was perceived by him to be unlawful. No copy of Russell's briefing memo was available to support his contention that he had emphatically warned Hiner about illegal activities. Russell also did not mention his antitrust concerns to Hiner after the memo had been delivered, and its draft version made only a passing mention of problems associated with the London meeting. Moreover, Russell certified in February 1990 he was unaware of any violations of GE's policy requiring compliance with antitrust laws. Jack Peiffer, who conducted Russell's exit interview, also noted he did not mention any unethical or illegal practices or violations of company policies at that time other than a complaint over expense reports. Ed claims, however, he reported violations of GE's policies Nos. 20.4, 20.5, and 20.12, as well as those of No. 30.3, during this interview. Additionally, on the evening Russell was fired, Brad Smart spoke to him when he was back at his Worthington office. Although Smart did most of the talking and offered Russell his condolences, at no time during this call, or in any of his counseling sessions or other telephone conversations with Smart, did Russell express the fear he might be fired for protesting or reporting criminal misconduct by GE employees.

GE's Legal Battles and Court Experiences

General Electric is no stranger to the world's courts. In this regard, it is well-armed to defend itself. The corporation has a 435-lawyer in-house law department and also has at its disposal the lawyers from such law firms as Weil, Gotshal & Manges (500 lawyers in New York); Sidley & Austin (647 lawyers in Chicago); Davis, Polk & Wardwell (397 lawyers in New York); and Mayer, Brown & Platt (496 lawyers in Chicago). The law firms of Arnold & Porter (310 lawyers in Washington, D.C.) and Dinsmore & Shohl (125 lawyers in Cincinnati) worked exclusively on the Edward Russell case. GE's legal department, under the guidance of Benjamin W. Heineman Jr., has developed over the past six years the reputation for being one of the most formidable legal teams available. To obtain this repute, he has hired lawyers away from some of the country's most prestigious law firms and they have been paid law-firm market rates or better. Heineman, whose vita includes a Rhodes scholarship, a Supreme Court clerkship, government posts, and a private law partnership, earns $1.2 million a year from GE, which makes him America's second-highest-paid corporate general counsel.

This legal team has had to defend GE quite often. In a case directly related to industrial diamond price fixing, the Kidder Concrete Cutting Co. and Kidder Building & Wrecking Co. filed a class-action suit against both GE and DeBeers, charging they have established artificially high prices for their industrial diamond products. Other cases have been international in scope. Herbert Steindler, a GE international sales manager, pleaded guilty to four felony counts involving a scheme to divert funds from defense contracts between GE and the Israeli government. The parties received seven-year prison terms and a $1.7 million forfeiture judgment. GE itself pleaded guilty and paid $69.0 million in fines and penalties to settle charges of conspiracy, money laundering, and failing to make and keep accurate books and records. Through its own internal investigation, GE fired a top executive and disciplined about 20 of the unit's high-level managers.

In another international military-related matter, a shareholder suit filed in January 1994 before the New York State Supreme Court is pending. This action entails charges of fraud and violations of the Foreign Corrupt Practices Act in connection with U.S. government-funded sales of military equipment to Egypt by GE's Aerospace unit. GE had sold the unit to the Martin Marietta Corporation in 1993, and the plaintiffs charge the sale's proceeds to GE were depressed due to the ongoing criminal investigation.

Judgment Day Arrives

Amid the vast number of claims and counterclaims and the assertions and denials made by all parties, truth must be determined and injustices rectified. To some great degree, Russell has tried his case in the popular and business press, but now the legal system must decide the legitimacy of his claims. Was Ed treated unfairly by GE, and is he being punished by this huge conglomerate for standing up to criminal behavior? Does guilt lie within other parties at GE and the industrial diamond industry, and what forces led to the collapse of Ed Russell's career?

Appendix A: Abstract of the State of Ohio Whistleblower Law

4113.52 Employees to report violations of state or federal law; retaliatory conduct prohibited

(A) (1) (a) If an employee becomes aware in the course of his employment of a violation of any state or federal statute or any ordinance or regulation of a political subdivision that his employer has authority to correct, and the employee reasonably believes that the violation either is a criminal offense that is likely to cause an imminent risk of physical harm to persons or a hazard to public health or safety or is a felony, the employee orally shall notify his supervisor or other responsible officer of his employer of the violation and subsequently shall file with that supervisor or officer a written report that provides sufficient detail to identify and describe the violation. If the employer does not correct the violation or make a reasonable and good faith effort to correct the violation within twenty-four hours after the oral notification or the receipt of the report, whichever is earlier, the employee may file a written report that provides sufficient detail to identify and describe the violation with the prosecuting authority of the county or municipal corporation where the violation occurred, with a peace officer, with the inspector general if the violation is within his jurisdiction, or with any other appropriate public official or agency that has regulatory authority over the employer and the industry, trade, or business in which he is engaged.

(b) If an employee makes a report under division (A) (1) (a) of this section, the employer, within twenty-four hours after the oral notification was made or the report was received or by the close of business on the next regular business day following the day on which the oral notification was made or the report was received, whichever is later, shall notify the employee, in writing, of any effort of the employer to correct the alleged violation or hazard or of the absence of the alleged violation or hazard.
***

(3) If an employee becomes aware in the course of his employment of a violation by a fellow employee of any state or federal statute, any ordinance or regulation of a political subdivision, or any work rule or company policy of his employer and the employee reasonably believes that the violation either is a criminal offense that is likely to cause an imminent risk of physical harm to persons or a hazard to public health or safety or is a felony, the employee orally shall notify his supervisor or other responsible officer of his employer of the violation and subsequently shall file with that supervisor or officer a written report that provides sufficient detail to identify and describe the violation.
***

(D) If any employer takes any disciplinary or retaliatory action against an employee as a result of the employee's having filed a report under division (A) of this section, the employee may bring a civil action or appropriate injunctive relief or for the remedies set forth in division (D) of this section, or both, within one hundred eighty days after the date the disciplinary or retaliatory action was taken, in a court of common pleas in accordance with the Rules of Civil Procedure.

(E) The court, in rendering a judgment for the employee in an action brought pursuant to division (D) of this section, may order, as it determines appropriate, reinstatement of the employee to the same position he held at the time of the disciplinary or retaliatory action and at the same site of employment or to a comparable position at that site, the payment of back wages, full reinstatement of fringe benefits

and seniority rights, or any combination of these remedies. The court also may award the prevailing party all or a portion of the costs of litigation, and if the employee who brought the action prevails in the action, may award the prevailing employee reasonable attorney's fees, witness fees, and fees for experts who testify at trial, in an amount the court determines appropriate.[1]

---

[1]Ohio Rev. Code Ann. §4113.52 (Banks-Baldwin Law Publishing Co., 1990). Title 41, Labor and Industry, Ohio Revised Code Annotated Complete to November 1, 1990 (USA: Banks-Baldwin Law Publishing Co., 1990) pp. 163–64.

Appendix B: Preliminary Draft of Russell Briefing Paper

TECHNOLOGY EXCHANGE-ASSESSMENT
DeBeers
9/4/91

Perceived Assets

DeBeers

Large apparatus capabilities
- Die/punch design
- Large carbide piece production facility
- Die support design (belt set)

Large cell capabilities
- Assumed better P,T distribution
- Raw materials
    Co/Fe catalyst
    Graphite
    "Powdered" reaction constituents

Single crystal growth
- Large press/multiple seed process
- Assumed better cost position
- Finishing technology

Drill blank technology
- Syndrill SP considered more robust in customer bit fabrication
- Broader performance range?
- Long integral stud product and process

Patents
- Coatings
- Refractory metal layer between diamond and carbide in compacts
- Incomplete but more later

CVD Diamond
- Diamond finishing and metallization technology
- High quality thick film product

Environmental/Safety in-house developments?

GE

- Saw diamond P,T,t profiling
- Highest grade on market
- Control of particle size mean, if not distribution

Cubic boron nitride process
- Industry standard products
- Very good cost position
- Highest market share

Gasketing technology (GT)
- Powder preparation methods
- Product consistency

Commitment to Quality (CTQ)
- Program definition and philosophy well established and proven
- Teaching methods and materials

Patents
- GEOSET* Drill Diamond
- BORAZON* CBN 550 and related
- Coatings for compacts

ISOPURE* Diamond
- Process patent likely
- Composition of matter patent possible

Coating capabilities
- Electroless coating considered to be industry standard
- Low Pressure CVD for compacts
- Spiked coatings
- CRD work, not yet commercialized

CVD Diamond
- Cost effective thick film process
- Access to electronics markets

2 lines long

Perceived Assets (continued)

DeBeers	*GE*
	Recovery technology/equipment
	• Bromination
	• Electrochemical cleaning/waste recovery
	(CRD initial work under way)
	• Equipment design
	Environmental
	• No_x suppression via peroxide
	• Solid waste recycling
	• Electrochemical cleaning/waste recovery
	Safety
	• Carbide handling equipment and procedures
	• In-situ die monitor technology
	Carbide apparatus failure analysis
	• Cause of failure investigative techniques/expertise

Benefits from Technical Interchange

Reduce effort and time required to achieve large apparatus capability.

Apparatus design sourced from DeBeers.

Large carbide dies sourced from DeBeers and/or their vendor.

Share environmental and safety best practices.

Reduce time to development of long integral stud drill blank.

Increase technology gap between two market leaders and the rest of competitors.

Leverage CVDD assets to gain competitive edge over multiple small, recent entries in this technology.

Risks in Establishing Technical Interchange

DeBeers and customers' perception of GE products and capabilities may be higher than actual fact. Recalibration may provoke damaging competitive response based on recognition of technical weaknesses.

Capitalize on assumed cost advantage to gain dominant share.

Loosely controlled distributors using GE capability (and approach to DeBeers) as a sales tool.

No standardized product testing leading to erroneous claims that cannot be disproved.

Anti-trust actions by government(s).

DeBeers already restrained from direct presence in US due to gem trade monopolistic activities.

More plentiful DeBeers resources used to leverage GE provided technology faster and more completely.

Shift in market share more than anticipated.

History of relationship.

Only significant contact as adversaries in patent battles.

Large number of trade secrets, hard to segregate from technologies subject to discussion.

Contact never considered before, requiring radical change in mind set.

Proposed Plan of Action

Initiate discussions at senior management level to cover "non-threatening" technologies only.

Environmental

Safety (if can be separated from apparatus design).

Commitment to Quality, ISO 9000 registration/continuing requirements.

New technologies (CVDD, ISOPURE)

Establish contact between key technologists on topics above.

Assess willingness to share information.

Assess probability of damaging commercial response.

Gauge leakage/reaction in marketplace.

Monitor key DeBeers distributors (Eskanazi, DAC).

Monitor DeBeers connected customers (e.g. Diamant Boart, Boart International, CITCO)

Initiate large apparatus discussions.

Begin at technical level to establish technologies to trade.

Develop plan of action, outlining exact nature of exchange.

Validate plan with upper management of both companies.

Mark Sneeringer

2 lines long

Appendix C: Facsimile of Edward Russell's Performance Review

ANNUAL ACCOMPLISHMENT SUMMARY AND DEVELOPMENT REVIEW

This side to be completed by immediate manager   Strictly private

NAME _____ Russell _____ Edward _____ J. _____
   (last)   (first)   (initial)

PERFORMANCE SUMMARY AND TREND   (Summarize your view of employee's accomplishment vs. goals in the past year.)

The GE Superabrasives business had a difficult and disappointing year in 1990. 1991 is off to a better start. In 1990, sales of $268MM were down 5% while earnings of $57MM were off 19%. There were both competitive product deficiency issues and pricing issues which needed an earlier response. Cost control was effective, once identified as an issue, and good progress was made in productivity improvement. As usual, Ed has excellent workforce strategies through CTQ and Work-Out. The commercial restructuring was on target and the Excellence in Manufacturing Award was especially gratifying to the business.

Trend: Recovering, looking to a good 1991

STRENGTHS/GROWTH   (Describe the employee's strengths and how they have changed in the past year.)

Ed is both good as a business planner and in the execution of those plans. His extremely high energy level allows him to globalize his presence and represent the business worldwide. He is a good listener and accepts advice and has a willingness to try new managerial processes.

IMPROVEMENTS/DEVELOPMENT NEEDS AND PLANS   (Identify most critical needs and responsive action plans, including job expansion if appropriate.)

Ed has a tendency to be stubborn, to go it alone which prevents him from maximizing the opportunities of a boundaryless organization. This has also created a break in his business team which he needs to repair. Ed needs to reach further out in time to better position his business to take advantage of cycle changes.

JOB/CAREER RECOMMENDATIONS   (If a job change is appropriate, identify alternatives and timing. Discuss your views of employee's potential and career path.)

Ed needs to remain on his current position, rebuild his team, fix his product line problems and then consider other potential options.

26 June 1991

_____   _____   _____
Immediate Manager/Date Prepared   Date Discussed   Reviewing Manager
                                        with Employee

EMS 2 Rev. 10/89

ANNUAL ACCOMPLISHMENT SUMMARY AND DEVELOPMENT REVIEW
This side to be completed by employee

NAME ___Russell___ ___Edward___ ___J.___ SOCIAL SECURITY NO. _____

(last) (first) (initial)

ACCOMPLISHMENT SUMMARY (Summarize your accomplishments vs. goals in the past year.)

Financial Objectives:			
	Sales	$268MM	(5) %V
	Income	57MM	(19) %V
	ROS	21.3%	
	Cont. Base Costs	64.7MM	(6) %V
	Var. Cost. Prod		6%
	Salary Headcount	489	(7) %

- In a flat physical volume year, maintained high quality (ROS) earnings through tight cost control, P&E cuts, associate reductions, and continued productivity.
- Reorganized marketing and sales into a more effective customer responsive organization by moving more associates into the field, flattening the structure, implementing more customer alliances to leverage technology, and creating business teams to promote a boundaryless organization.
- Reorganized marketing and sales into a more effective customer responsive organization by moving associates into the field, flattening the structure, implementing more customer alliances to leverage technology, and creating business teams to promote a boundaryless organization.
- Workout/quality strategies continue to be effectively driven in Superabrasives, with major advances in empowerment and self direction. Significant internal and external recognition of progress, including State of Ohio's Governor's Award for Excellence in Manufacturing.
- Foreign countries trade. China (BIBM) finishing alliance, USSR sales development successes.
- Significant advances in safety awareness with LTA's and OSHA recordables down 38% in 1990.
- Maintained Union free status through more communications. Union organization attempt soundly defeated.
- PULSE audit conducted with no serious issues or deficiencies identified. Significant progress made in environmental abatement, e.g. visible NOx emissions eliminated.
- Plansee selected as European carbide die source.
- Continued push to resolve trade secret theft case resulting in guilty plea by Sung. Legal actions against Iljin started.
- Quickly transferred new C12 isotopically pure diamond from CR&D into production. Redirected GENASYSTEMS™ along with the C12 diamond, into thermal management market.

STRENGTHS/GROWTH (Describe your strengths. How have they changed in the past year?)

- Broad multifunctional business experience
- Good technical/analytical abilities
- Dedicated to succeed
- Good interpersonal skills
- High personal energy level
- Good presentation skills

IMPROVEMENTS/DEVELOPMENT NEEDS AND PLANS (Identify most critical needs and responsive action plans. Describe opportunities to broaden/expand current job.)

- Build an integrated business team that openly shows its harmony and integration.
- More management team development to assure focus and functional integration on critical business issues (most notably— MBS product leadership and inventory control) to eliminate organizational and hierarchical boundaries.
- Optimize continuous improvement and Workout successes to next generation of involvement and participation to accelerate thrusts in productivity, environment and cultural diversity.

JOB/CAREER INTERESTS (If interested in a job change, list preferences including position title, type business, location, desired timing, etc. Also, describe longer-term interests.)

- Short term, return GES to growth performance level and regain MBS product leadership position in the market.
- Longer term, I'm always willing to accept additional challenges.

Signed _____ Date ___13 March 91___

BMS 3 Rev. 10/89

Appendix D: Whistleblowing Law and the Whistleblower

Traditional American Employment relationships stipulate that either party may terminate the relationship at any time or "at will." This at-will relationship, however, exposes both the employee and the employer to risk regarding the terms and conditions of ongoing employment. It is easy to see that the large corporation, with its vast economic resources, could use the at-will doctrine maliciously or to stifle dissent when employees complain about such matters as fairness, favoritism, workplace safety, undue performance pressure, sexual harassment, and rights and discrimination. Through collective bargaining, unions have been able to protect their members from many of these abuses, but this protection is afforded only to those who are unionized. More than two-thirds of the American labor force is not unionized and, accordingly, collective bargaining does not help them. Many industries are not unionized, and those in the professions or executive ranks can be subjected to employer reprisals.

More recently, a special group of laws has been created to protect workers from an employer's abuse of the at-will doctrine when those workers seek to expose unsafe or illegal activities engaged in by the employer. These so-called whistleblower laws have been created at both the state and federal levels and basically protect the employee from retaliatory acts by the employer for blowing the whistle on them.

Three broad types of whistleblowing cases are commonly seen in court.

1. The employee refuses to participate in an illegal act that the company says must be performed. If the firm threatens to fire the employee under these conditions, the courts have found in most cases the company's behavior to be wrongful and damages must be paid to the wronged employee.

2. The employee reports the employer's illegal acts to internal or external sources and is subsequently terminated, harassed, or otherwise wronged by the company. Some courts have upheld the whistleblower's rights in these circumstances, but in some states the whistleblower's rights have been protected only when the employee must choose between breaking the law or losing his/her job.

3. The most difficult problem for the courts occurs when an employee criticizes company acts that are legal but that can also cause public harm. In most instances, employees cannot complain about legitimate activities, and no legal duty exists to support the whistleblower's claims.

Based on the observations of whistleblowers by Billie Garde and Bruce Fisher, four basic types can be drawn—the Visionary, Deep Throats, Nitpickers, and Bad Faith whistleblowers.[2] The Visionary is an idealistic individual who sees a bigger picture and attempts to correct perceived injustices. In this struggle, he seems to be a heroic figure embarking on a solitary crusade to correct corporate wrongs. Deep Throats are pragmatists who are torn between the fear of personal reprisals if they report company wrongs while simultaneously fearing injuries to the public good if they maintain their silence. This type tends to operate behind the scenes and sends or telephones anonymous clues and tips to corporate executives and the media. The Nitpicker holds all people accountable for even the smallest infraction. This type abhors waste in any form as well as the abuse of corporate resources. In the public's eye, the Nitpicker often seems petty and is unflatteringly portrayed as a childish "tattle tale." The fourth type is the Bad Faith whistleblower. This person's intentions are to make a preemptive strike prior to experiencing adverse action by the employer. This type uses as ammunition information about alleged corporate improprieties to counter justifiable attempts by the employer to terminate, demote, or transfer the employee. Bad Faith whistleblowers use their claims of company wrongdoing as bargaining chips to secure desired personal outcomes.

---

[2]Billie Pirner Garde, "Representing the Whistleblower—A Case or a Cause?" *Trial,* July 1992, pp. 32–36; and Bruce D. Fisher, "The Whistleblower Protection Act of 1989: A False Hope for Whistleblowers," *Rutgers Law Review,* Winter 1991, pp. 355–416.

PHILIP MORRIS

The Export Warning Labels Issue

W. Kent Moore

Phyllis G. Holland
Valdosta State University

In 1992, the management of Philip Morris Companies faced a potentially major problem. One of Philip Morris's shareholders, the Midwest Province of the Capuchin Order, planned to present a resolution at the next annual shareholders' meeting. The resolution would require that the company print warnings about the dangers of cigarette smoking on every package of cigarettes produced, including exported cigarettes.

While a similar measure had been defeated by stockholders at the 1991 annual meeting, the introduction and discussion of the resolution by the religious order would provide antismoking activists with a highly visible forum for airing their views. The negative publicity could be damaging to the company. Publicity on this issue was particularly unwelcome because there were indications that Congress was turning its attention to warning labels for exported cigarettes.

There were several alternatives for dealing with the situation. The company could take a proactive stance by placing the warning labels on all cigarettes before the motion could be made. Other possible responses included seeking procedural methods to inhibit the motion, distributing a position paper describing the views of the company, or simply doing nothing. In any case, a decision was needed prior to the upcoming meeting.

Background

Philip Morris Companies, Inc., is a diversified, multinational firm that obtains revenues from the manufacture and distribution of tobacco, food, and beer products, from financial services, and from real estate operations. In 1991 Philip Morris had net earnings of $3.9 billion on revenues of $56.4 billion. The company's operating revenues from international tobacco operations ($12.2 billion) had topped operating revenues from U.S. opera-

tions ($11.5 billion) for the second consecutive year. Earnings for domestic tobacco operations were $4.7 billion compared to earnings of $1.6 billion for international tobacco. Philip Morris International, Inc. (PMI), is the subsidiary which manufactures and exports cigarettes to a growing number of countries worldwide. During 1991, PMI increased export volume nearly 10 percent over 1990 and contributed $3.6 billion to the U.S. balance of payments.

From 1987 to 1991 unit sales of cigarettes in the United States declined while world sales increased. Differences in performance in the domestic and international cigarette businesses may be attributed to a number of factors, not the least of which is antismoking activism. The U.S. Surgeon General, American Cancer Society, and the Heart Association are just a few of the individuals and groups who have sought to reduce, if not ban, smoking from American life. A measure of their effectiveness is found in the diminishing percentage of Americans who smoke. Antismoking groups have begun to turn their attention to the export of cigarettes. Former Surgeon General C. Everett Koop has stated:

> At a time when we are pleading with foreign governments to stop the export of cocaine, it is the height of hypocrisy for the United States to export tobacco. Consider these figures. Last year in the United States, 2000 people died from cocaine. In that same year, cigarettes killed 390,000.[1]

Antismoking activism was not limited to the United States. The Asian Pacific Association for Control of Tobacco was formed in 1989 with a goal of a smokeless Asia by the year 2000. Another group, the Asian Consultancy on Tobacco Control, representing 14 nations met in Hong Kong in January 1991 to devise a 4-year plan to combat smoking in the region. The essence of their plan was to train antismoking activists and persuade Asian countries to adopt uniform tobacco control regulations. In 1990, Philip Morris shareholders voted down a shareholder proposal which would have required exported cigarettes to carry the same labels in the appropriate language as those marketed domestically.

The U.S. Cigarette Industry

With sales in excess of $35 billion in 1990, the U.S. cigarette industry continues to be a huge enterprise. According to a 1990 survey, 32 percent of American

[1]Alexander Cockburn, "Getting Opium to the Masses: The Political Economy of Addiction," *The Nation*, October 30, 1989, p. 482.

men and 27 percent of American women were smokers. In 1989, U.S. cigarette production was 685 billion, and worldwide, sales of cigarettes ran into the trillions. This sales volume has been achieved with a product which has been linked to cancer and heart disease since the landmark Surgeon General's report in 1964, which has carried health warnings on packs since 1966, and which has been banned from television and radio advertising since 1971. Although Americans have typically started smoking before age 21, by industry agreement, advertisements have not appeared in youth-oriented media or used illustrations or themes aimed at young people.

Smoking Trends in the United States

Trends in domestic consumption of cigarettes and percentages of smokers have been of great concern to tobacco companies. Figure 1 shows domestic consumption of cigarettes in the 1980s; Figures 2 and 3 show percentages of smokers by gender and educational level. If these trends continue, the Centers for Disease Control

estimated that by the year 2000, only 22 percent of the adult population in the United States will be smokers. The percentage of female smokers (23 percent) was projected to be slightly higher than the percentage of male smokers (20 percent). By 1987, there were more teenage girl smokers than teenage boy smokers. Also, smoking in the United States is more and more becoming primarily a behavior of the less educated and the socioeconomically disadvantaged.

Almost half of all the adults who ever smoked have quit. Each year, about 2 million American cigarette customers have been lost, either through death or quitting smoking. A 1991 Gallup poll revealed that 70 percent of smokers would like to quit and 80 percent wished they had never started smoking. For 16 consecutive years, the per capita consumption of cigarettes has decreased, and during the last 5 years, the total national consumption has decreased also.

Table 1 shows the impact of these trends on the major U.S. tobacco companies. From the peak in 1981, cigarette production for the domestic market had dropped by almost 15 percent in 1989. Annual profits were still in-

FIGURE 1

Domestic consumption of cigarettes

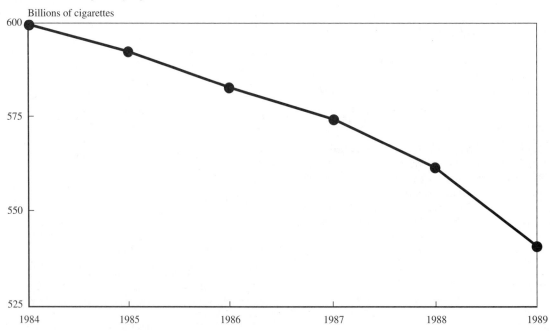

Source: *Farmline,* March 1990, p. 20.

FIGURE 2

Smoking prevalences for men and women with projections to year 2000

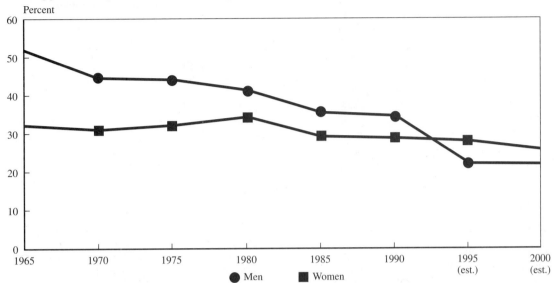

Sources: *Editorial Research Reports,* March 24, 1989, p. 153; *Statistical Abstract of the United States,* 1990, p. 123; *The Atlanta Journal and Constitution,* June 27, 1990; *Journal of the American Medical Association,* January 6, 1989, p. 63.

creasing in 1989, but at modest levels in the 10 percent range rather than at the dramatic rates of previous decades. The industry had been involved in an increasing number of legal and political battles and smoking had been banned from domestic airline flights, many public buildings, portions of restaurants, and some workplaces.

FIGURE 3

Smoking prevalences by education level with projections to the year 2000

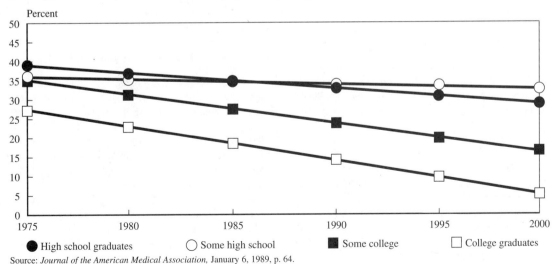

Source: *Journal of the American Medical Association,* January 6, 1989, p. 64.

TABLE 1   Rankings of Cigarette Manufacturers, 1985 to 1988

Company	Market Shares (%)				Sales, Billions of Cigarettes			
	1988	*1987*	*1986*	*1985*	*1988*	*1987*	*1986*	*1985*
Philip Morris	39.38	37.83	36.77	35.89	218.7	215.5	214.2	213.6
Reynolds	31.78	32.53	32.33	31.61	176.4	185.3	188.3	188.1
Brown and Williamson	10.95	10.97	11.67	11.88	60.9	62.5	68.0	70.7
Lorillard	8.26	8.23	8.15	8.12	45.9	46.9	47.5	48.3
American Brands	6.85	6.88	7.18	7.53	38.1	39.2	41.8	44.8
Liggett	2.88	3.56	3.90	4.97	16.0	20.3	22.7	29.6
Total	100.0	100.0	100.0	100.0	556.0	569.7	582.5	595.1

Sources: *Business Week,* January 23, 1989, p. 59, *Business Week,* January 18, 1988, p. 89.

International Markets

To offset declining sales at home, American cigarette manufacturers, led by Philip Morris, had begun to devote more attention to international markets, with special focus on the Pacific Rim. Figure 4 shows the percentages of men and women in various countries in 1990 who smoked and the total population of those countries at the time. Until the mid-1980s, most Asian countries protected their state-run tobacco monopolies either by banning foreign cigarettes or by imposing high tariffs on imports. For example, quotas and protective tariffs in Taiwan and Korea almost tripled the price of imported tobacco. In 1985, the U.S. Cigarette Export Association, under Section 301 of the 1974 Trade Act, threatened trade sanctions against Asian countries which restricted tobacco imports. The first target was Japan, which was seen as an entry point for the rest of the Pacific Rim. In 1986, the Reagan administration drew up a list of possible retaliatory tariffs on Japanese products, including supercomputers, textiles, and automobile parts. Soon, Japan lifted its tariff on foreign cigarettes, and U.S. cigarette exports to Japan quadrupled.

Taiwan's cigarette markets were opened next. Again, Section 301 was used, and lobbying was intense. In 1987, Taiwan agreed to drop its restrictions on foreign cigarettes, including its ban on advertising. Within a year, Philip Morris's Marlboro brand had captured 30 percent of the sales in its price category. The South Korean and Thailand markets were opened in 1988 and 1990, respectively, but unlike the other countries, Thailand continued its ban on advertising.

The U.S. government played a crucial role in opening these markets, largely because of its desire to reduce balance of trade deficits. Figure 5 shows U.S. merchandise trade balances for 1973 to 1991. Tobacco was one of only four major categories of goods which produced a positive trade balance.

The response of Asian markets is reflected in the export data shown in Table 2. U.S. cigarette exports to Japan increased by 56 percent in 1987 and exports to Asia increased by 75 percent in 1988. Total U.S. cigarette exports increased by 17 percent in 1989 and 7 percent in 1990. In 1990, cigarette consumption increased by 5.5 percent in Asia, and the smoking rate in these countries was increasing by 2 percent annually while the smoking rate was decreasing by 1.5 percent annually in industrialized countries.

Marketing Cigarettes in the Pacific Rim

The presence of U.S. firms in the Asian market has been manifested in both an increase in the number of cigarette ads and a change in the type of ads and promotion used by all cigarette manufacturers. In Japan from 1986 to 1988, advertising time devoted to cigarettes on primetime television rose from a rank of fortieth to a rank of second. Before the entry of American firms, Japan had planned to ban cigarette ads on television.

With the assistance of the U.S. government, tobacco companies used sophisticated advertisements that included techniques not allowed in the United States. Voluntary agreements not to advertise heavily in ways that target young people or women were dropped. Since 90

FIGURE 4

Percentages of smokers in selected countries (1980–1985)

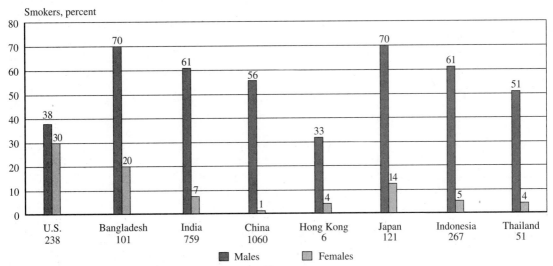

Note: The numbers below the country names refer to population, in millions.

Source: *Journal of the American Medical Association,* June 27, 1990, pp. 3315–16.

FIGURE 5

Merchandise trade balances

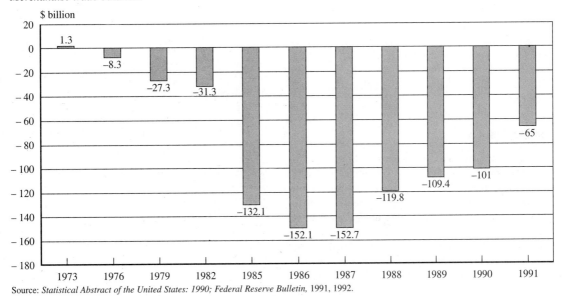

Source: *Statistical Abstract of the United States: 1990; Federal Reserve Bulletin,* 1991, 1992.

TABLE 2 **Domestic Exports of Tobacco, 1970 to 1988**

	Total Tobacco and Manufacturers	Leaf Tobacco	Cigarettes
1970	679	481	159
1980	2,426	1,334	1,055
1981	2,723	1,457	1,229
1982	2,845	1,547	1,235
1983	2,647	1,462	1,126
1984	2,704	1,511	1,120
1985	2,789	1,521	1,180
1986	2,732	1,209	1,298
1987	3,400	1,090	2,047
1988	4,153	1,252	2,645

Source: *Statistical Abstract of the United States: 1990*, p 811.

percent of smokers began before the age of 21 and a low percentage of Asian women were smokers, promotion to these groups was considered very important. Television commercials were aired during sports events and youth-oriented movies, and American companies sponsored motorcycle races and rock concerts. Young women gave away cigarette samples on Tokyo street corners, and, in Taiwan, free samples were handed out at discos. Domestic tobacco companies responded by intensifying their promotional efforts at the same targets. For example, Japan Tobacco introduced a new brand, Dean, capitalizing upon the young, rebellious image of actor James Dean.

In countries less affluent than Japan, American cigarettes were promoted as symbols of success, sophistication, and wealth. This was reflected in the practice of disguising cheap local brands in Marlboro or Camel wrappers.

Health Issues

The primary concerns about smoking, and consequently about cigarette exports, have been health-related. The Advisory Committee to the Surgeon General of the United States concluded that there are causal relationships between smoking and many diseases, including emphysema, cancer of the esophagus, and lung cancer. Exposure to smoke in the environment has been related to lung cancer in nonsmokers. Women who smoke while pregnant are more likely to deliver low-birth-weight babies. Deaths attributable to smoking include 30 percent of cancer deaths, 21 percent of coronary heart disease deaths, 18 percent of stroke deaths, and 82 percent of deaths from chronic obstructive pulmonary disease. Each year in industrialized countries, 1.8 million deaths are linked to smoking; this number exceeds "the combined total of all deaths due to any form of violence, be it accident, homicide, or suicide."[2] Smoking two or more packs of cigarettes a day decreases life expectancy more than 8 years, and one pack a day shortens life expectancy 6 years. Smoking has been costing an estimated $23 billion annually in the United States for medical expenses, and another $30 billion has been lost to society each year because of illness and premature death.

On the basis of health issues, various spokespersons within the United States have strongly and persistently criticized cigarette sales overseas. A U.S. congressman said, "For the past 100 years, America has been the world's foremost exporter of public health . . . Now the U.S. Trade Representative wants to add a new chapter to that legacy . . . a chapter entitled: America the world's greatest exporter of lung cancer, heart disease, emphysema, and death."[3] Koop stated:

> It's reprehensible for industrial nations to export disease, death, and disability in the way of cigarette smoke to developing countries, putting on their backs a health burden that they will never be able to pay for 20 to 30 years from now.[4]

One observer described U.S. policy as "trading the lungs of people who wear ties for those who wear kimonos."[5]

In recent years, foreign groups have also become vocal about the perceived evils of cigarettes from the United States. The Asia-Pacific Association for the Control of Tobacco sent a letter to President George Bush in 1989 stating:

> The cigarette issue is not an issue of trade or trade imbalances. It is an issue of human health, and Asian health is as

[2] Jan Gehorsam and Rebecca Perl, "Smoking Is the No. 1 Killer, World Health Survey Shows," *Atlanta Journal and Constitution*, April 26, 1991, p. E3.
[3] Ted T. L. Chen and Alvin E. Winder, "The Opium Wars Revisited as U.S. Forces Tobacco Exports in Asia," *The American Journal of Public Health* 80, no. 6 (June 1990), p. 661.
[4] Ibid., p. 659.
[5] Sarah Glazer, "Who Smokes, Who Starts—And Why," *Editorial Research Reports* 1, no. 11 (1989), pp. 150–63.

Tobacco and the Economy

Tobacco, the sixth largest cash crop, is one of the most profitable crops a farmer can grow. It is an important source of cash income for America's family farmers.

Tobacco grown on the nation's farms is dried and sold at auction, then transported to manufacturers who make all different types of tobacco products.

Finally, the finished tobacco products are delivered to American consumers by wholesalers and retailers.

All of these businesses which make up the tobacco industry create jobs for over 414,000 people. These same businesses pay their employees more than $6,72 billion.

These jobs and wages are not limited to tobacco growing states. Although industry employment averages 100,000 people in the major tobacco growing states—Kentucky, North Carolina, Tennessee, South Carolina, Virginia, and Georgia—more than 314,000 additional workers are employed by the industry elsewhere around the nation.

At a time when the United States is buying more goods from overseas than it is selling, it is important to note that the world loves America's tobacco and tobacco products. In 1987, the tobacco industry exported $3.4 billion worth of products and only imported $730 million. The result? A $2.7 billion trade surplus in tobacco products.

Jobs, wages, and a positive trade surplus are only a part of the contribution the tobacco industry makes to our economy. (See Table 3.)

Tobacco Supplier Industries

The tobacco industry buys many goods and services from other industries which can be referred to as tobacco supplier industries.

Tobacco farmers purchase farm machinery and fertilizer. Tobacco manufacturers buy equipment and paper. Tobacco retailers buy vending machines and advertising. Examples of the goods and services provided by the tobacco supplier industries could go on and on.

The main point is clear: Tobacco supplier industries produce more than $35 billion worth of goods and services to meet the requirements of the tobacco industry. These same supplier industries employ 296,000 workers and pay out almost $7.4 billion in compensation.

Add the tobacco industry and tobacco supplier industries together and what do you get? Jobs for 710,000 people

and a $31.5 billion contribution to the Gross National Product (the value of all goods and services) of the United States.

But the story doesn't end here.

The Full Impact

Workers in the tobacco industry and in the tobacco supplier industries are also consumers. They take vacations and buy houses, cars, groceries, appliances, gas and so on. They also buy services, such as day care, legal help, medical care and insurance.

When you add up all the money these employees spend on goods and services, the total is surprising. The value of all these goods and services totals $50.6 billion, which is a tremendous contribution to this country's Gross National Product. To meet the demand for goods and services generated by tobacco industry and tobacco supplier industry employees, more than 1.59 million people are employed by all sorts of companies.

The Tobacco Industry and Taxes

The big spenders in government who oppose the tobacco industry are biting the hand that feeds them. Why? Because tobacco excise taxes and sales taxes by federal, state, and local governments added up to more than $10 billion in 1987.

The industry's tax liability doesn't end there, however. If you add individual and corporate income taxes paid by the tobacco industry to the more than $10 billion already mentioned, the total tax payment exceeds $13 billion. In fact, tobacco companies are among the largest taxpayers in the world.

In short, government red ink would be a lot redder without the tobacco industry.

Millions of jobs, billions of dollars spent on products and services, a boost to America's family farmers, a trade surplus, and billions of tax dollars—these are the contributions of the tobacco industry to our economy. Keep these contributions in mind as you read the rest of *The Great American Smoker's Manual.*

Source: Philip Morris, *The Great American Smoker's Manual,* pp. 1–3.

TABLE 3   The tobacco industry—employment and compensation

Sector	Average Annual Employment	Annual Compensation ($ millions)
Tobacco growing	100,000	$ 610,700
Auctions	9,240	90,800
Manufacturing	76,900	2,837,000
Wholesale trade	35,357	883,900
Retail trade	192,720	2,303,100
Total	414,217	$6,725,500

important as American health. Asians want to purchase good American products, not harmful ones.[6]

The Executive Director of the Hong Kong Council on Smoking and Health has noted that smoking-related illnesses, like cancer and heart disease, have overtaken communicable diseases as the leading cause of death in parts of Asia. Health warnings have not been required and have not appeared on cigarette advertisements in Asian countries, and the general level of awareness of the health hazards of smoking has been much lower than in the United States. In the mid-1980s, 95 percent of developed nations had laws pertaining to cigarette marketing and health warnings, but only 24 percent of underdeveloped nations had such regulations. This disparity has continued to exist.

Other Concerns about Exports

Beyond the health issue has been the concern that the Office of the U.S. Trade Representative's "full-throttle pursuit of profit is fueling an anti-American backlash that could translate into hostility towards other American exports."[7] Many people feel that exporting cigarettes puts the United States in the position of pushing drugs. In 1989 one critic of the industry said: "In a government purportedly concerned with drug abuse, this [exportation and aggressive marketing of American cigarettes] is hypocrisy of the first order."[8]

Still another concern has arisen in countries where per capita income is low. There has been some evidence that cigarettes divert spending from food purchases.

---

[6]Chen and Winder, "The Opium Wars Revisited," p. 661.
[7]Peter Schmeisser, "Pushing Cigarettes Overseas," *The New York Times Magazine,* July 10, 1988, p. 20.
[8]Kenneth E. Warner, "Smoking and Health: A 25-Year Perspective," *The American Journal of Public Health* 79, no. 2 (1989), p. 143.

In Bangladesh, studies revealed that higher cigarette consumption by adults resulted in reduced caloric intake among children and decreased survival among children.

The Effect of Tobacco Products upon the Economy

Philip Morris's view is quite different from the view of the antismoking activists. The box on page 543, "Tobacco and the Economy," is taken from the Philip Morris publication *The Great American Smoker's Manual.*

A Brief History of Cigarette Warning Labels

In 1957, 20 years after the first study of smoking and lung cancer appeared, Senator Wallace Bennett (R—Utah) introduced a bill which would require the following warning label on cigarettes: "Warning: Prolonged use of this product may result in cancer, in lung, heart, and circulatory ailments and in other diseases."

When the first warning labels appeared, in 1966, they read: "Warning: The Surgeon General has determined that cigarette smoking is hazardous to your health." In 1971 the label was changed to read "Warning: The Surgeon General has determined that cigarette smoking is dangerous to your health."

Beginning in 1986 a new labeling system was mandated. Four labels were required to appear an equal number of times annually on each brand. The labels read:

Surgeon General's Warning: Cigarette Smoke Contains Carbon Monoxide

> Surgeon General's Warning: Smoking by Pregnant Women May Result in Fetal Injury, Premature Birth, and Low Birthweight

> Surgeon General's Warning: Quitting Smoking Now Greatly Reduces Serious Risks to Your Health

> Surgeon General's Warning: Smoking Causes Lung Cancer, Heart Disease, Emphysema and May Complicate Pregnancy

Although the tobacco industry resisted these labeling requirements, it has been suggested that the industry also benefited. Specifically, agreeing to label cigarettes in 1966 was part of a deal which won the industry exemption from the normal federal, state, and local regulatory processes and also made the consumer responsible for the legal risk of cigarette usage. When cigarette ads were banned from radio and television as part of the anti-smoking campaign in 1971, free air time for anti-smoking ads also ended. Subsequently, the print media was saturated with cigarette ads, and anti-tobacco stories began to appear less frequently in magazines, which were the recipient of the advertising revenue bonanza. Finally, the original version of the new warnings in 1986 contained the words "death" and "addiction." Neither appears in the final version of the warnings.

While the United States and Scandinavian countries had the harshest cigarette warnings in 1992, some type of warning labels was mandated in about 100 countries. Philip Morris estimated that only 10 percent of its exported cigarettes were not labeled for health risks. Countries not requiring labels included Thailand, the Philippines, the Dominican Republic, Morocco, and the former Yugoslavia.

The competitive situation for Philip Morris was clouded by the presence of former government tobacco monopolies in many of their overseas markets. Members of Asian Consultancy on Tobacco Control admitted that a strong anti-American sentiment fueled antismoking efforts. Richard L. Snyder, executive vice president of PMI, was more blunt: "It's just covert protectionism."[9] American tobacco interests pointed out that most

Asian governments controlled tobacco monopolies and stood to lose from American competition. China's revenues from the state-owned monopoly were approximately $5.2 billion annually, 10 percent of the Korean government's revenues came from the sale of tobacco products, and Japan's government monopoly had an 84 percent share of a market in which 60 percent of all males were smokers. The cigarette warning label mandated by the Japanese government may be translated "For your health, don't smoke too much."

It was difficult for Philip Morris to assess the effects of a unilateral labeling of export cigarettes. The effect could be to hurt Philip Morris's market share but not necessarily reduce overall smoking. That is, Asian customers might conclude that Marlboro (a Philip Morris brand) was hazardous to their health but that other American or domestic brands were not dangerous. In some countries, such an unmandated warning label was actually misleading. In Taiwan, for example, the brand with 90 percent market share was the government brand, Long Life. This cigarette had 24 milligrams of tar compared to Marlboro's 16 milligrams. Similarly, Thailand's top brand, marketed by the government, had 25 milligrams of tar, while the Thai government also sold a filterless brand for about 16 cents a pack.

Those familiar with the process of marketing cigarettes in underdeveloped countries questioned whether the cigarette warnings would do the good hoped by the antismoking activists or simply cause the competitive problems feared by PMI. Where illiteracy was high, a warning label would have little impact. In some areas, cigarettes were sold individually by street vendors, and the smoker never saw the warning-labeled package. Others pointed out that where per capita cigarette consumption was low, there was less likelihood that the majority of smokers would smoke enough to develop smoking-related health problems.[10]

A decision to change the warning label policy for exported cigarettes had a number of implications. Politically, a change might be preferable to a policy and wording mandated by Congress. In the United States, 30 members of the House of Representatives sponsored a bill which would require exported cigarettes to meet all domestic standards including warning labels and

---

[9]"Asia: A New Front in the War on Smoking," *Business Week,* February 1991, p. 66.

[10]"Should the Activities of the Tobacco Industry in Third World Countries Be Restricted?" In *Taking Sides: Clashing Views on Controversial Issues in Business Ethics and Society,* ed. Lisa H. Newton and Maureen M. Ford (Guilford, CT: The Dushkin Publishing Group, Inc., 1990), p. 310.

nicotine and tar labels. This legislation also would make cigarette ads abroad subject to the same restrictions as the United States. Competitively, a change might put Philip Morris at a disadvantage in foreign markets. Philip Morris has been in the forefront of the attacks on studies linking smoking and health. To add a warning label without being required to do so might be viewed as an admission of the health hazards of smoking. On the other hand, a full-blown discussion of the ethics of exporting unlabeled cigarettes was not an attractive agenda item for a stockholders' meeting either.